THIRD EDITION

WRITING WORTH READING
The Critical Process

Nancy Huddleston Packer
STANFORD UNIVERSITY

John Timpane
LAFAYETTE COLLEGE

BEDFORD/ST. MARTIN'S
Boston ◆ New York

For Bedford/St. Martin's
President and Publisher: Charles H. Christensen
General Manager and Associate Publisher: Joan E. Feinberg
Managing Editor: Elizabeth M. Schaaf
Developmental Editor: Michelle McSweeney
Editorial Assistant: Joanne Diaz
Production Editor: Heidi L. Hood
Production Assistant: Ellen C. Thibault
Copyeditor: Jane M. Zanichkowsky
Text Design: Anna George
Cover Design: Snider Design

Library of Congress Catalog Card Number: 96–86778

For information, write: Bedford/St. Martin's, 75 Arlington Street, Boston, MA 02116 (617–426–7440)

ISBN: 0–312–06101-3

Acknowledgments

Isaac Babel, "My First Goose," from *The Collected Stories of Isaac Babel.* Copyright © 1955 by S. G. Phillips, Inc. Reprinted by permission of S. G. Phillips, Inc.
Glenn Blackburn, "Why Did Communism Collapse?" from *The West and the World Since 1945,* Fourth Edition, by Glenn Blackburn, pages 38–41. Copyright © 1995. Reprinted by permission of St. Martin's Press, Inc.
Paul Butler, "Black Jurors: Right to Acquit?" from *Harper's Magazine,* December 1995. Originally appeared as "Racially Based Jury Nullification: Black Power in the Criminal Justice System" in *The Yale Law Journal,* vol. 105. Copyright © 1995 by Paul Butler, The Yale Law Journal and Fred B. Rothman & Company. Reprinted by permission.
J. V. Cunningham, "Dr. Drink" from *Collected Poems and Epigrams of J. V. Cunningham.* Reprinted by permission of Ohio University Press/Swallow Press, Athens, Ohio.

Preface for Instructors

This book is based on the belief that writing does not exist in a vacuum but is part of a continuum of thinking-reading-writing. To write effectively, students must learn to think critically about significant matters. A giant step toward this goal is reading critically. When students engage and challenge difficult texts, their thinking and their writing will improve. As writing instructors know, good writing gives rise to better thinking and better reading. The best way to improve one part of the process is to work on all parts.

So goes the credo on which we based the first and second editions of *Writing Worth Reading*. This third edition reflects that belief even more strongly while it improves on earlier editions with new and updated materials throughout. In this edition, we have included expanded coverage of researching and writing online, computer tips for every stage of the writing process, updated MLA and APA documentation styles, and five new professional essays.

Precept and example are perhaps the oldest of all teaching tools. We have both in this book, as we did in earlier editions. We offer advice on specifics of writing and careful analysis of examples. We analyze writing by students and professionals, problematic writing, and writing that works. When a passage has a problem, we discuss it and suggest possible solutions. Understanding why a passage succeeds or fails can be informative and encouraging. Such evaluation may furnish a model for the kind of close reading we advocate.

Because we believe that good habits of mind are crucial for any writer of expository prose, we begin our book with "Steps to Good Thinking: The Critical Process." The first two chapters offer suggestions on how to achieve an open mind and prepare to think. We discuss the distinction between logical and faulty thinking, acceptable and unacceptable rhetoric, cogent and sloppy argumentation, and the proper and improper uses of induction or deduction. We offer advice on how to maintain a skeptical attitude toward the thinking of others and how to evaluate one's own thinking.

The steps to good reading are retained in this edition, as are the eight practical questions a reader can ask to get the most from reading. We have added a section on how to interrogate your own writing and a brief new case study in which a student maps and annotates a short history text.

Part Two is "From Start to Finish: The Writing Process." We offer suggestions for inventing, organizing, drafting, and revising. New material on keeping a journal appears throughout this section. The section also includes two case studies. The first one follows a student from assignment to completion of a personal essay. The second shows a student developing an essay in response to a reading. We read along with the student and watch him take notes, make an outline, and draft and revise.

Persuasion comes next. As with all writers, students think more clearly and argue more effectively when they understand why evidence is important. We therefore begin Part Three with a chapter on the use and evaluation of evidence. This chapter concludes with a new case study in which we show how a professional writer successfully uses many types of evidence in his persuasive essay. The next chapter, "Making the Argument," offers some thinking tools students will find useful in constructing a strong argument. A case study at the end of the chapter shows a college writer putting these tools to work.

"The Art of the Writer: Paragraphs, Sentences, Words, Style" is the title of Part Four. "The Structure and Strategies of the Paragraph" chapter treats the paragraph as a concrete unit and as the product of strategies of development, such as description and definition. "From Paragraph to Essay: The Strategies at Work" provides new material on choosing the appropriate strategy, linking one paragraph to the next, and using strategies as throughlines of an essay. It offers advice on the beginning and concluding paragraphs and on titling. This chapter contains two new case studies of professional essays, the first demonstrating how transitions connect paragraphs, the second showing how different strategies are combined in an essay.

Chapter Ten discusses sentences. It includes the rules governing the grammar of sentences, their various constructions, and some ways to make them livelier and richer. Chapter Eleven offers advice on diction and suggests what kinds of words are appropriate in various situations.

Next comes style, in which the arts of the writer come together. A stylistic choice is a crucial moment of critical thinking. It involves the writer's understanding of self, purpose, audience, and tools. After pointing out some stylistic pitfalls, we go on to describe a style appropriate for college writing and suggest how students can achieve it. We have also added a new section on revising for style.

The fifth section of the book, entitled "Putting It All Together: College Writing," treats the four most common college writing tasks: the research project, the report, the essay on literature, and the in-class examination. Our account of the research project, spanning two chapters, is much enlarged and updated from the second edition. We survey the resources and tools available on the Internet, and we discuss how to find the best sources, how to evaluate them, and how to use them in research papers.

As before, "Doing Research" gives advice on how to avoid plagiarism and when to summarize, paraphrase, and quote, and how to integrate sources into a paper. "Writing Research" carries the story from documenting sources to revising and presenting the final draft. The chapter includes a thoroughly annotated case study of a student research paper.

The non-argumentative report is perhaps the most common form of college writing assigned outside the humanities. In Chapter Fifteen, we discuss ways of organizing material and writing a report. Especially important is the organizational thesis, used when the primary purpose of the project is not to argue a thesis but to present information. Common organizational strategies, including the ready-made format for scientific reports, appears here as well.

Our discussion of the literary paper in Chapter Sixteen is much expanded. It covers topics important to all literature as well as those specific to poetry and to fiction. We offer methods and levels for interpretation. This chapter includes two case studies: in one we follow a student brainstorming about a poem and in the other, a student reading, taking notes, and writing an essay on a story.

The in-class essay examination is covered in Chapter Seventeen. In it, we offer advice on preparing for such an exam as well as on actually taking it. The chapter concludes with one of the best in-class student essays we have ever read.

Because most of our students will travel and write far from the discipline of English, we have included as appendixes discussions of APA reference format and the MLA footnotes and bibliography system as well as a list of style manuals and handbooks students may find useful in other disciplines and in their careers. We have also added a new bibliography of Internet research books, listing some of the best guides to working on the Net that we have found.

At the end of each chapter or section, we summarize our general advice in "Tips" boxes, a popular feature from previous editions. We would not want to have these tips misunderstood. We see no quick and easy—and certainly no mechanical—way to write well. The tips only represent pieces of advice students can use as a checklist. Throughout we also provide computer tips enclosed in boxes.

The *Resources for Teaching* contains sample syllabuses, overviews of each chapter (including "demonstration points" in the text that deserve classroom discussion), analyses of exercises, and suggestions for teaching strategies in each section.

Acknowledgments

We have learned from many other composition teachers and writers. We have also learned from our students. We wish particularly to thank those at Stanford University, Rider University, Rutgers University, and Lafayette College, who were, perhaps without knowing it, the guinea pigs on whom we tried out many of our ideas and exercises. Most of all we would like to acknowledge the help of Hal Bialeck, Larry Boyd, Cornelia Condry, Kimberly Corsaro, Ines Echevarria, Christina Gerke, Terese A. Heidenwolf, Courtney Hough, Stephanie Klein, Lia Kudless, Tracy Logan, Allen Parker, Lorene Russo, Tom Russo, Matt Samuelson, Jeri Shikuma, Jeff Sloan, Erin Strasser, and Tripti Thomas. We thank them for letting us use their work and for being such good writers.

We also want to thank all those who helped us lay the groundwork for the first edition: David Bartholomae, Helen Brooks, Mary Butler, Robert DiYanni, Howard Dobin, Kevin Dungey, Irv Hashimoto, Maria-Christina Keller, Barbara King, George Lee, Robert Levine, Dagmar Logie, Dennis Matthies, John McClure, Tom Miller, Geoffrey Moore, Shirley Morahan, Joseph O'Mealy, Mike Rose, Martin Schwartz, Haskell Springer, and Ann Swidler. We would also like to thank Christopher Wells of Brandeis University, who did a wonderful job updating the instructor's manual for this third edition.

We owe a debt of thanks to the many teachers who used earlier editions and commented on them, especially Abe Bernstein, Paul S. Burdett, Jr., Mary Cross, Patricia Donahue, Kenneth Fields, Ed Fryzel, Dona Hickey, Julia Hornbostel, Linda Karell, Stephen Mantale, Anne Matthews, Ozzie Mayers, Katherine Meeker, Harriet Naperbowski, Gary D. Pratt, David Riggs, Agatha Taormina, Susan B. Taylor, Eleanor Vardetti, Charles Vogel, Wendy Weiner, and Ellen Wolff.

The staff at Bedford Books has been wonderful. Every contact with the Bedford people has increased our admiration and gratitude. They have saved us from horrendous gaffes, solved problems that caused us to throw up our hands, and ignored our occasional churlishness. We thank everyone at Bedford, particularly Charles Christensen and Joan Feinberg for their guidance and general help, John Sullivan for his work on the book and the instructor's manual, Joanne Diaz for clearing permissions and for attending to many details, and Heidi Hood and her able assistants Ellen Thibault and Deborah Baker for efficiently taking our manuscript through the production process. Above all we want to thank our exemplary editor, Michelle McSweeney, for her many helpful suggestions, her unfailing good humor and patience, and her canny ability to balance flexibility and firmness.

    The book, finally, is ours, and we take responsibility for it. We hope you find it writing worth reading.

Introduction for Students

The only thing we have to fear is fear itself.
—FRANKLIN D. ROOSEVELT (1882-1945)
PRESIDENT OF THE UNITED STATES

No one is born knowing how to write. Unlike breathing, walking, even talking, writing has to be learned. Most of us don't think or talk in concise, well-rounded sentences and neat paragraphs. In conversation, we don't start out with our main point firmly in mind and our proof all lined up—often we don't know what our main point is until halfway through the conversation. Listeners make allowances, readers don't.

Learning to write well takes effort. So, too, does learning to program a computer, to play tennis or chess, to clone a cell, or set a bone. Like these activities, writing can be very rewarding. You can communicate with your readers, inform them, maybe change their minds, and show them how the world looks to you. Getting it right is worth the effort. All the best writers—whether novelists, journalists, academics, or letter writers—work and work to get it right. Their writing may seem effortless, but then so does Michelangelo's *David,* and that was once just a hunk of rock.

At this point you may be asking yourself why, in an age of instant communication, you should struggle to write better. We think there are two very good reasons, one professional, one personal.

First the professional. All through our working life most of us are called on to put our ideas in orderly form. Police officers take evidence and describe crimes and accidents. Engineers write abstracts of projects they hope to undertake. Executives write reports to the boss and directives to the staff. Lawyers present briefs and judges hand down written opinions. And with every rung of the ladder, people rely more and more on clear, forceful writing. Even the most spontaneous and informal e-mail needs to be written so it can be understood.

Second the personal. We think this reason is even more important. Writing is the road to knowledge both of the subject and of the self who writes. We write and we understand better. We write and we think better. Above all, we write and we learn what we really think. As the South African writer Nadine Gordimer says, "Writing makes sense of life."

Many people are afraid of writing. That blank piece of paper or computer screen can look as resistant as any rock. Many times as we approached a new chapter of this book, we were a good deal less than eager. But because both of us have done a fair amount of writing, we believed we could do it, and we went ahead. Our experience as teachers and writers tells us that fear is the most pervasive reason people cannot write well. It paralyzes, it stultifies. If you suffer from fear of writing, your first task is to get over it. You can write, if you will. It will require work, yes, but armed with knowledge and seasoned by practice, you can get beyond the fear to the confidence.

For writing is not a mystery. It is, as the English novelist Laurence Sterne observed over two hundred years ago, "when properly managed . . . but a different name for conversation." When you write, you must of course be a little more careful than when you speak, but with the proper management your meaning can be just as powerful.

This book is about proper management. It is about finding something to say that is worth saying. It is about reading more productively and thinking more forcefully in order to write more persuasively. It is about identifying your audience and shaping your language, though not your opinion, accordingly. If you want to improve your organizational skills, you should find some useful tips here. If you are embarking on a research project, you can find help in these pages. If you want to make certain once and for all that you know the proper use of the colon and the semicolon, that is here, too. Our aim in writing this book was to provide help with whatever you write, be it an essay, a business letter, a report, a law brief, or an exam.

We don't expect you to come up with a *David:* Michelangelo, Mozart, Austen, and Einstein had a rare brilliance no one can teach or learn. We do, however, expect you to learn to write what you mean— and with a touch of style.

Brief Contents

Contents

PART THREE
WRITING TO PERSUADE: THE ARGUMENTATIVE ESSAY   133

PART ONE

Steps to Good Thinking
The Critical Process

1

The Critical Sense

The critical sense is so far from frequent that it
is absolutely rare, and the possession of the
cluster of qualities that minister to it is one of
the highest distinctions.
> — HENRY JAMES (1843-1916)
> AMERICAN NOVELIST AND ESSAYIST

THINKING, READING, WRITING:
A BRAIDED CHAIN

We've based our book on critical thinking, which we believe is the key
to good reading and good writing. In college work — and for many of us
afterward — thinking and reading and writing are so interwoven that we
should think of them as a single entity: thinking/reading/writing. For us,
thinking (and by that we mean good college-level thinking on a worthwhile topic) is the strand that twists the other strands of reading and
writing tightly together.

When we read well, we place what we read into the context of our
ideas and experiences and knowledge. We recall what an instructor or a
classmate or another book said. We puzzle out difficulties and assemble

3

scraps of understanding. Many of us imagine an inner voice speaking the words. Some of us are constantly arguing with the reading—much the way people argue with television—proposing counterarguments, thinking of examples pro and con, comparing one thought with another, evaluating assertions, determining significances. Reading is, in short, thinking.

In college work, our writing very often responds to what we've read, a poem, a report, an argument, a piece of research. As we read, our thoughts begin to take shape, and we begin to summarize, analyze, interpret. Even before we put pen to paper or finger to keyboard, we think about how to go about the writing, make mental notes, organize and clarify thoughts, try out possible responses—all the brainwork that surrounds the actual deed of putting words on paper or inputting them at the computer.

During the act of writing, we will probably pause along the way and read what we have written. Our ideas will very likely begin to develop, perhaps even to change. We may decide to start all over again, return to the book, essay, story, or poem for another look. We explore, clarify, and expand our thinking. Just as thought creates writing, so writing creates thought. The better the thinking, the better the writing; the better the writing, the better the thinking.

We can make mistakes in thinking—base our ideas on poorly defined terms, make up our minds too early, refuse to let go of prejudices. We may have preconceived notions about a subject, an author, an instructor, or an assignment. Those and other errors in thinking show up in our response to reading and most glaringly in what we write. Thinking/reading/writing starts best and goes best when the writer takes a critical stance.

Good consumers of ideas are always critical. By *critical* we don't mean having disrespect for others, faultfinding, or carping over details. We mean a healthy skepticism, an unwillingness to accept something at someone else's evaluation, a willingness to postpone agreement or disagreement until after thorough analysis.

We are all skeptical in some areas of life. As soon as an elected official opens his or her mouth, "Oh yeah?" "Who says?" and "So what?" ready themselves for the asking. Each time we see an automobile commercial featuring a sleek cheetah, a brilliant desert landscape, a beautiful woman clad in flowing chiffon, and a virile-looking, handsome man, we feel a scoff coming on. And we should. We know that politics and commercials are notorious for humbug. Perhaps less obvious, humbug and sleights of hand exist throughout the world of ideas. A healthy skepticism uncovers less obvious humbug.

Remember, too, that we manufacture ideas as well as consume them. That means we must try to be skeptical about our own thinking as well as that of others. We should watch ourselves as we think—be aware of our assumptions—watch as we reason from A to Z. In this chapter, we offer some observations and suggestions we hope will help you become a better consumer and manufacturer of ideas.

OPENING THE MIND:
CLEARING OUT THE UNDERBRUSH

The thinker about whom few of us are skeptical enough is our very own self. When we believe something, we assume we have it right. If we weren't right, we would believe something different that *was* right, wouldn't we? We certainly don't need to listen to conflicting views. We lock the doors of our mind.

Yet all of us have been wrong and have had to change our minds. A candidate we vehemently supported turns out to be morally flawed. A policy or rule we opposed suddenly makes good sense. A behavior we once abhorred now seems harmless. We have either learned more or listened to someone else who persuaded us otherwise. When we open our minds to new ideas and fresh insights, we gain a better understanding of the world.

In this section we suggest ways of opening the mind and clearing out bad thinking habits and attitudes that stunt intellectual growth.

Shedding Stereotypes

To *stereotype* means to judge another person according to some preconceived ideas about a group that person belongs to—a race, religion, gender, nationality, physical type, occupation, and so on. Stereotyping assumes that all members of the group share the same set of fairly simple characteristics, frequently unpleasant and sometimes immoral. Too often, the more ignorant we are, the more certain. We don't have to think: our judgments come to us precast.

> Fraternity men drink.
>
> Surely you aren't consulting a woman lawyer (women lack reasoning power).
>
> Kinnard was elected only because he's black (blacks aren't really qualified).

To bring the injustice of this kind of judgment close to home, think of a stereotype an outsider might have of a large group to which you belong. Are you Italian? left-handed? a midwesterner? a woman? a "rich kid" or a "poor kid"? How do you feel about that stereotype? Compare yourself with the other people like you. When we've seen one, have we seen 'em all? Are the differences trivial or significant? Would you be willing to be judged solely on the basis of your membership in this group?

Sometimes we come to our writing already harboring prejudices. We don't mean only notions about race, class, gender, and so forth, but also preconceived ideas about many topics. Many of us, for instance, dislike the thought of engaging in intellectual work. "Intellectual work is for _____" (fill in the blank with the current stereotypical slur). Some of us won't willingly read on a particular subject, like poetry, because "poetry is only for _____" (fill in the blank again).

We may have preconceived notions about a book or a writer. We decide in advance that *Pilgrim's Progress* is irrelevant, T. S. Eliot is not politically correct, biology is only for pre-meds. And we haven't even mentioned strong feelings about issues we may be asked to write about: abortion, gun control, drug use/abuse, and so on. We open textbooks, poetry books, law books already bearing hosts of unhelpful notions.

Such prejudices, besides being unfair, waste time and effort. When you open an book, make sure your mind is open, too.

To stereotype others hurts us as well as those we have prejudged. It encourages us to shut ourselves off from enlarging experiences and limits the range of our understanding. And so we misinterpret signals and act inappropriately. If, for instance, we assumed that all politicians were corrupt and we heard a politician make an important proposal, we might ignore it—and thereby close ourselves off from the debate.

Writing can help us recognize our stereotypes and ill-founded assumptions. As we read our own writing before the second draft, a still, small voice will often ask, Is that fair? Are you so convinced? Listen to the voice and think again. Many good writers keep journals in which they constantly explore their thoughts and their ways of thinking. This practice provides an advance critique for their more public writing. Whether or not you use a journal in this way, be sure you check your writing for prejudices and preconceptions.

Questioning Authority

No one can study every subject, and all of us rely on authorities for information and ideas. (See the first section of Chapter 6 for a discussion of using expert testimony as evidence.) What were the causes of the Second World War? Read what historians have to say. Is cholesterol bad for me? Just ask nutritionists. How can I collect the money my ex-brother-in-law owes me? Get a lawyer.

But we need to remember two things about authorities. First, most issues worth discussing usually have at least two sides, supported by authorities. One economist wants to raise taxes to decrease the deficit; another wants to lower taxes to increase the gross national product. Their debate helps us to clarify the issues. As nonexperts, we listen carefully, analyze the evidence and the reasoning, challenge with further questions—and then take responsibility for our own thinking.

Second, expertise in one field rarely extends into another. As a coach or a television commentator, John Madden speaks as an authority on football and could give an expert analysis on the choice for most valuable player. But his background and experience do not qualify him as an authority on beer, cameras, or even philanthropic organizations. Scientists and artists often express their opinions on political matters, and they certainly have that right. But their opinions are no more authoritative than any citizen's and should never be accepted without a thorough analysis. (When we appeal to unqualified "experts," we commit the logical fallacy called *ipse dixit,* a Latin phrase meaning "He himself has spoken.")

In your everyday life, you confront important decisions: what career to choose, how to invest, what to believe about U.S. policy in the Middle East. Listen to the experts in their own fields, but remember that no human being has cornered the market on truth. Learn what others think—and then do your own thinking.

Slowing Down Judgment

We are constantly making generalizations. Indeed, we couldn't do without them. We generalize almost daily about the weather: when we see dark clouds, we decide to wear a raincoat. We base our generalizations on past experience and use them to anticipate the future.

A problem emerges, however, when we make a *hasty generalization,* that is, when we rush to an unwarranted conclusion from insufficient evidence:

> That banana I bought was soft inside. The fruit in that grocery store is rotten.
>
> I can't do calculus. College is not for me.
>
> Officer Fuhrman lied on the witness stand in the Simpson trial. You can't believe anything cops say.

One tiny fact—a soft banana, difficulty with a subject, a bad cop—is hardly a sound basis for rushing to a conclusion. Don't judge on one piece of the picture, but look at the whole thing. Don't generalize too hastily.

> Neither Senator X nor Senator Y went back home after leaving the Senate. Senators would rather live in Washington.

But Senator X and Senator Y may not be typical. We need a broader base of evidence, and even then, unless we know what happened to every single senator, the claim cannot be absolute—we must qualify it accordingly:

> If the experience of twenty-five senators is typical, then many senators remain in Washington after they leave the Senate.

Qualifying a generalization to fit the evidence is an important thinking skill. (We discuss qualification in "Considering the Opposition" in Chapter 7.)

Acknowledging Complexities

Almost any idea worth thinking about is complicated. If it weren't, we wouldn't have to think about it. Unfortunately, most of us try to fly over the complications. We seek a simple explanation, we ignore contrary evidence, we settle for the obvious. In short, we indulge in the logical fallacy *oversimplification.*

Oversimplification takes many forms. Sometimes we claim that a problem has only one solution:

> If we want to improve education, we have no choice but to eliminate electives from the curriculum.

Slow down. This issue is too important to treat it superficially. Mightn't reducing extracurricular activities or raising teacher salaries have some good effect?

Similarly, we often justify a belief or a course of action on the basis of one single reason:

> We would never have had a drug problem had it not been for rock and roll.

Even if rock and roll is *one* reason for the drug problem (a very debatable claim), it is certainly not the only reason, and may not even be a main reason.

Occasionally we consider only the positive side of a proposition, ignoring the negative or harmful effects:

> Let's disband the CIA in order to improve the reputation of the United States.

For all its problems, the CIA helps the United States in many ways, and if we disbanded it, we could lose those benefits. Few proposals have only good effects. We need to analyze carefully and weigh the alternatives.

When a certain goal is desirable, we may believe that it does not matter how we achieve it. We say the end justifies the means.

> We should remove restraints on police behavior because they interfere with apprehending criminals.

It's not that simple. Apprehending criminals is certainly desirable, but removing restraints could lead to excessive force and lack of accountability by the police. We have to examine the means of attaining a proposed end at least as closely as we examine the end itself.

Putting issues into their simplest form is natural. It saves time in the short run and allows us to get on with something else. It makes us feel good about ourselves and confident that we have a grasp of the world. But it doesn't lead to good thinking. When we oversimplify, we distort reality and kid ourselves into thinking we have accurately pictured the world, when in fact we have only drawn a cartoon.

Where is the best place to check out our thinking? Our writing. That is where our thinking stands still.

When rereading early drafts or journal entries, and especially when preparing new work, turn a cold eye on your thinking. Ask, "Do I hold any unfair stereotypes? Do I just follow what the experts and authorities say, or do I think for myself? Am I a patient thinker or a leaper to conclusions? Do I oversimplify matters or work with them in their full complexity?" Hard questions—but essential to the growth of any writer.

Tips for Opening the Mind

- Unlock your mind and let in new ideas.
- Don't let stereotypes shut you off from real people.
- Listen to the experts but decide for yourself.
- Don't base generalizations on insufficient evidence.
- Avoid oversimplified analyses and solutions.

EXERCISE FOR OPENING THE MIND

Read the following statements and identify the "underbrush" that needs clearing out (there may be several specimens in each):

a. I don't like broccoli or spinach. I won't like asparagus.

b. Vietnamese are gifted in math. Three of them got A's in our calculus class.

c. What a glorious tenor—he could only be Italian.

d. Only believe people who have firm, incontrovertible evidence for their opinions.

e. Everybody knows children should be seen and not heard.

f. I don't know anything about art, but I know what I like.

g. Right after Carl started using Odoroff Deodorant, Wanda agreed to go dancing with him. Odoroff does it again!

h. The president should have the right to make national security decisions without media criticism.

i. The threat of inflation caused the 1987 stock market crash.

j. Drug abusers are mentally ill. My mother is a lawyer and has defended a lot of them, and she says so.

k. Priests make lousy marriage counselors.

EVALUATING RHETORIC:
SEEING BEHIND THE WORDS

Whether they are advertisers, politicians, or friends, people are always trying to get us to think or behave in a particular way. To persuade us, they use *rhetoric*. Aristotle defined rhetoric as "the art of discovering the available means of persuasion in a given case." The available means include anecdotes, statistics, expert opinion, humor. Rhetoric can appeal to reason and to emotion.

"Sticks and stones may break my bones but words can never hurt me" is a patently untrue saying. Rhetoric can be quite as powerful as sticks and stones. The rhetoric of poetry can bring great joy and help us articulate our experience; the rhetoric of politics can make a population docile or even cruel or can inspire people to a great cause. Rhetoric can fog an issue or it can lead us to greater understanding.

In this section we analyze some of the most important issues in evaluating rhetoric. In Chapter 2, The Logic of Argument, we discuss in greater detail the part of rhetoric called *argument*.

Weighing Emotional Appeals

Sincere and honest emotion has a legitimate and significant place in our thought. Used with care and scruple, it can be an effective ally of reason. In many situations, it would be foolish to pretend that reason performed alone and that we didn't *care* one way or the other. To discuss without emotion a famine in Ethiopia or a hostage crisis in Egypt would be perverse. In virtually everything we read or hear, the appeal to emotion is part of the message. We think (perhaps unfairly) of science and medicine as realms of emotionless objectivity, but even new medical procedures can hardly be described by doctors without expressions of joy and pride. As the philosopher Ludwig Wittgenstein pointed out, being convinced is an emotional condition, even if reason leads us to it.

Writers and speakers often arouse our emotions by appealing to our *values*. When a biochemist speaks of the promise of gene therapy, he or she appeals to our hope for progress and the betterment of humanity. Values, of course, vary from culture to culture. An Iranian writing for Iranians would perhaps appeal to the audience's reverence for Islam. A Japanese writer might appeal to tradition or respect for elders. Appealing to the values the audience shares is an important technique of the rhetorician.

What values do contemporary Americans share? Two communications experts examined this question and came up with the following list:

value of the individual
achievement and success
change and progress
ethical equality
equality of opportunity
effort and optimism
efficiency, practicality, and pragmatism
rejection of authority
science and secular rationality
sociality
material comfort
quantification
external conformity
humor
generosity and "considerateness"
patriotism
(E. D. Steele and W. Charles Redding, "The American Value System:
    Premises for Persuasion")

Not all Americans share all these values, and some of the values even seem contradictory: for example, "external conformity" and "rejection of authority." But speakers and writers appeal to one or many of them—often with conscious intent.

The director of communications of a major university suggested as a marketing device that the faculty and staff use certain key words—such as *challenging, pioneering, vibrant*—to describe the university. The words all packed an emotional wallop that presumably would appeal to donors, prospective students, the media, and the general public. (This marketing plan was subsequently withdrawn because, as one professor put it, it was "anti-intellectual, vapid, embarrassing, insulting, and crying out to be jettisoned"—words that similarly pack an emotional wallop.)

Effective use of emotion need not be as direct as a marketing plan. In her coolly rational and factual dissection of the rise of Nazism, Hannah Arendt makes an emotional appeal in the middle of an analysis:

> Many Germans and many Nazis, probably an overwhelming majority of them, must have been tempted *not* to murder, *not* to rob, *not* to let their neighbors go off to their doom (for that the Jews were transported to their doom they knew, of course, even though many of them may not have known the gruesome details), and not to become accomplices in all these crimes by benefiting from them. But, God knows, they had learned how to resist temptation. (*Eichmann in Jerusalem*)

The emotion of this paragraph is carried by the italicized *nots*, by heavily freighted words such as *doom* and *temptation*, and by potent words such as *murder* and *neighbors* and that final cry from the heart, "God knows." Take away those words and the facts may remain but the persuasive power of this passage is lost, and with it, perhaps, the reader's assent.

We need to bear in mind that emotion is a powerful ingredient, volatile and sometimes overwhelming. With clever manipulation of language, the unscrupulous can mask their real message by arousing our emotions. Too often appeals attempt to arouse not our best emotions, such as sympathy and generosity, but emotions that are morally debilitating and destructive:

> Federal efforts to control what goes out over the Internet will have such a chilling effect that you might as well kiss the First Amendment goodbye.
>
> Unless we want more and more citizens to become slaves to sloth and dependence, we should limit welfare payments to one year.
>
> Gun control would undermine the very fiber of this nation and destroy what makes us great.
>
> Try some of this stuff—everybody is doing it.
>
> Any intelligent person would agree that we need a proctoring system at this school because only a small fraction of the student body has the inner strength to resist cheating.

Each of these appeals goes right to the heart of a human emotion: fear, prejudice, pride, conformism, greed, vanity.

Awareness of language can protect us against unwanted or dishonest appeals to emotion. We can become more sensitive to vocabulary. Certain words come ready-made to excite our emotions: *brutal, vicious, stealthy, innocent, baby, soft, gentle,* and *honorable* are a few that spring to mind. Notice the difference between these two sentences:

> The dog attacked the man.
>
> The vicious dog brutally attacked the man.

The first is fact; the second is an outrage. But how about

> The dog attacked the stealthy intruder.

Pin a medal on that dog.

A second way to become more sensitive is to be aware of the emotive impact of images. Notice the marked difference between these two sentences:

> Yeats spent seven hours a day carefully crafting his poems.
>
> Yeats was a slave to the grinding process of creating poems.

In the first we have an image of a serious artist; in the second he's a drudge. (We have more to say on the power of words, especially on connotation and imagery, in Chapter 11, Working with Words.)

Advertising often incorporates an especially insidious form of emotional appeal. Whether photograph, film, or audio, the image makes a direct, immediate appeal to the senses and can sometimes overwhelm reason. Pictures of handsome youths drinking beer after a game of tag football suggest that if you prize good fellowship you had better buy this beer. A kiss follows when a man changes his toothpaste; true romance awaits you on the drugstore shelf. A grinning man in an automobile is seen first taking curves at high speeds and then driving sedately through traffic with his wife and two perfect children, meaning this car will bring back youth without sacrificing the pleasures of family: you can have it both ways. In a world inundated with graphic images and plangent sound, we must be ever more vigilant.

Appeals to our values and our emotions are legitimate—and inevitable. To think clearly, however, we need to recognize the appeals and stay out of their grasp, at least until we have evaluated them.

Separating Fact from Opinion

Some statements are facts, some are opinions. Nothing is more essential to good thinking than being able to tell the difference. A fact is a certainty, a piece of information agreed on by all those in a position to investigate the matter. Some facts are obvious or known to everyone:

> Round objects roll downhill.

Other facts are known to experts:

> Pellagra is caused by an inadequate amount of niacin in the diet.

When experts agree that something is a fact, the rest of us generally accept it. (See "Expert Testimony" in Chapter 6 for more on this point.)

An opinion is a belief based not on certainty or consensus by those who investigate, but on personal judgment that something is true or false, good or bad.

> Once soccer catches on, people will prefer it to baseball.

An opinion may turn out to be a fact: in twenty years we may find that soccer *is* more popular than baseball. That the earth revolves around the sun was once an opinion but is now a fact.

Some opinions cannot become facts because they express personal preference:

> Chocolate ice cream tastes better than strawberry.
>
> Ballet is more enjoyable that opera.

If we recognize the unstated "in my opinion," we don't bother to argue.

We may confuse fact and opinion when we read or listen carelessly. Someone may say,

> Baseball is called the favorite national pastime

and we disagree. Disagree with what? The statement does not say that baseball *is* the favorite national pastime (an opinion in the absence of evidence), only that it is *called* so (a fact). We need to pay close attention to what is actually being said.

Sometimes an opinion claims to be a fact:

> Left-handed people are smarter than right-handed people.

This is not a certainty, nor is it a widely held belief. In fact, there is no evidence for it. Opinion (and possibly prejudice) is pretending to be fact. The sound of certainty is no substitute for the real thing.

Sometimes an opinion subtly claims the status of fact:

> Because the Palestinians lack confidence in Arafat's government, we should support the Hamas guerillas.

We all recognize that the last part of the sentence is opinion, but the writer apparently wants us to assume that the first part is an established fact, when it isn't. It begs the question: Are the Palestinians without confidence in Arafat?

Often received opinion masquerades as incontrovertible wisdom:

> Male children are better at math than female children but not as good at language.

Maybe, maybe not. The jury is still out.

We all have opinions. We eat, buy, vote, marry, all on the basis of our opinions. It is our right to express them. We need to recognize, however, that not all opinions are equally valuable or equally useful to others. An opinion is only as good as the facts and reasoning on which it is based.

> Don't bother studying Chinese: it's the most difficult language to learn

could be based on knowledge of only one other language, in which case the listener should not act on this advice. We might be impressed by the statement

> Plato's *Republic* is irrelevant to our society

until we discover the speaker has never read any Plato. It is idle chatter for me to say

> Candidate J is the most qualified of all the candidates

if I know nothing about the other candidates. If, however, I have studied the background and proposals of all the other candidates, perhaps my opinion is worth listening to.

Our opinions aren't sacrosanct. Learning is the process of gathering information, rethinking, and then reformulating our opinion. Even a personal preference can be more or less valuable. Our liking for chocolate ice cream becomes more interesting when we've sampled other flavors.

Uncovering Assumptions

An assumption is a belief that we take for granted as a basis for an assertion. All kinds of statements rely on assumptions—questions, commands, promises, assertions. The simple command *Pass the salt* is based on several assumptions, including that the salt can be passed, that you can pass it, and that I have the right to ask you to pass it. Some assumptions are unexpressed. We would be the joke of the neighborhood if we went around articulating our assumptions every time we asked someone to pass the salt.

We get into thinking trouble, however, when we fail to recognize important assumptions that subtly guide our thoughts. Sophocles said,

> Reason is God's crowning gift to man.

A statement like this seems innocent enough. When we think about it, we easily recognize that he was basing his statement on two major assumptions: (1) that man has a mind, and (2) that God exists.

Hidden in the statement, however, are some subtle assumptions that we may or may not support. Here are some of the more obvious: (1) God is a personal force capable of making a gift; (2) reason is a more important gift than heart, soul, or body; and maybe (3) woman's mind is not a gift of God. Once we articulate these assumptions, we might disagree.

Or suppose we read the following statement:

> To alleviate overcrowding in prisons, we should convert prison terms to time doing community service. The inmates then could expiate their sins through retribution to society and at the same time discover that doing something useful can be quite satisfying.

Sounds pretty good, but concealed in all the high-minded words are some dubious assumptions:

1. Converting a prison term to time doing community service is allowed by the law.
2. Retribution and rehabilitation, rather than keeping criminals off the streets, are the main purposes of prison sentences.
3. Community service would serve more or less the same purpose as a prison term.
4. Requiring prisoners to perform community service will not have a destructive effect on the community.

5. Experience can change character.
6. "We" have the right to change matters.
7. Performing community service is a worthy endeavor.

There are other assumptions, but this list should be enough to warn us against jumping on that bandwagon before thoroughly examining the assumptions pulling it.

Hidden assumptions are not necessarily dishonest: the salt can be passed and the prisons are overcrowded. Nevertheless, we can avoid many thinking problems by becoming more sensitive to the assumptions of others and more critical of our own.

Finding the Argument

When we use the word *argument* in the following pages, we don't mean a violent disagreement. We mean a statement supported by reasons. Arguments answer questions all of us have: Why should I believe this? Why is this true? Why should I do this? Why is it worthwhile?

Not all statement are arguments. Notice the difference between these two (possibly familiar) sentences:

You must pick up your room.

and

You must pick up your room or no television tonight.

The first is an *assertion,* for which no reasons are provided. The speaker gives us nothing to think about. That's not an argument. The second makes the same statement but also provides a reason. This *is* an argument. Now we have to think about whether or not the reason is persuasive. Is the privilege of watching television worth picking up the room?

When an assertion lacks reasons, all we can do is vote it up or down:

When volatized, bromine is irritating to mucous membranes.

Deforestation will affect world peace more than terrorism will.

These statements offer no justification for our agreeing with them. When we ask Why? they are silent. When people make statements like these, they may have reasons in mind, but we can't evaluate them because they aren't stated.

Of course, not every statement needs its supporting reasons to be articulated right out loud. We do share certain values and beliefs.

The rule of law is essential to a democracy.

This may be a platitude and not worth saying, but for most of us it needs no support.

Drive carefully

is a command we are always making, but we seldom provide reasons for it. Some statements based on common knowledge need no justification:

Paul was converted on the road to Damascus.

A statement like that can stand as the basis for what will be an argument:

When Paul was converted on the road to Damascus, Western civilization was changed.

Because we accept the first part of the assertion, the writer can spend his or her time and energy arguing the second part. If we had to provide reasons for everything, we would never get to the crux of the matter.

Some statements that are phrased as simple assertions contain hidden arguments:

The great biologist Camille Fox believes vitamin K can cure insomnia. (If a great scientist believes it, it must be true.)

Don't put that greasy stuff on your pretty hair. (You hair won't be as pretty if you do.)

The advertising industry employs hidden arguments all the time. A four-color photograph in a magazine shows a beautiful young woman in a low-cut dress lounging in an elegant apartment. In the forefront is a large bottle of perfume. The hidden argument is

If you use this perfume, you will be as glamorous as this woman.

Ha!

If we aren't aware of the hidden arguments, they can have a very insidious effect: we may find ourselves with a carload of vitamin K and unruly hair but smelling like a rose.

We have done only part of the job if we evaluate rhetoric only in other people's writing. Think for a moment of what you've said over the past two hours. Now think of instances where you phrased an idea, changed your tone of voice, or used a hand gesture to make your words more persuasive. What techniques did you use, and why? Look over your writing in the same way. Get to know your own rhetoric. Note the techniques you like to use and those you need to improve or master. Above all, recognize your motives for using rhetoric. Becoming a better rhetorician is not only a matter of technique—it's also a moral activity.

Tips for Evaluating Rhetoric

- In everything you read or write, be aware of the important role of rhetoric.
- Avoid being trapped by an emotional appeal you don't share.
- Think about the values that underlie what you read and what you write.
- Distinguish between fact and opinion.
- In everything you read and write, articulate obvious assumptions and uncover hidden ones.
- Remember that an opinion is only as valuable as the knowledge and experience on which it is based.
- Differentiate between flat assertions and arguments (assertions backed up by reasons).
- Be aware of hidden arguments, particularly in advertisements and politics.

EXERCISES FOR EVALUATING RHETORIC

1. Automobile bumper stickers are public appeals to (presumably) shared values. To which values do the following bumper stickers appeal?
   a. Touch Dis Truck and I'll Rip Yer Face Off!
   b. Overworked Mother on Board
   c. Easy Does It
   d. Teachers Do It with More Class
   e. If You Can Read This Sign You're Following Too Closely

2. Referring to the list of values on page 11, read the following passages and determine what values are appealed to in each one. These writers are attempting to establish common ground with the reader. What is that common ground?
   a. I believe that American people expect sex-ed courses to teach their children the relevant physiology, what used to be called "the facts of life," but they also expect that those facts will be placed in a moral context. In a recent national poll, 77 percent of the adults surveyed said they thought sex-education programs should teach moral values, and about the same percentage believe the programs should urge students not to have sexual intercourse. And believe it or not, teens agree. According to a recent survey, seventh- and eighth-graders who have chosen not to engage in intercourse say that the greatest influence on their decision is the fact that "It is against my values for me to have sex while I am a teenager." (William J. Bennett, "Why Johnny Can't Abstain")
   b. The proper question, I believe, is not, How good a document is or was the Constitution but, What effect does it have on the quality of our lives? And the answer to that, it seems to me, is, Very little. The Constitution

makes promises it cannot by itself keep, and therefore deludes us into complacency about the rights we have. It is conspicuously silent on certain other rights that all human beings deserve. And it pretends to set limits on governmental powers, when in fact those limits are easily ignored. (Howard Zinn, "Some Truths Are Not Self-Evident")

    c. Nothing in the world can take the place of persistence.

Talent will not; nothing is more common than unsuccessful men with talent.

Genius will not; unrewarded genius is almost a proverb.

Education will not; the world is full of educated derelicts.

Persistence and determination alone are omnipotent. ("Press On," motto of McDonald's Corporation)

3. The following sentences raise issues in their use of rhetoric. Identify the issues in each.
   a. You are either part of the solution or part of the problem. ([Leroy] Eldridge Cleaver)
   b. Prisons teach inmates to be better criminals.
   c. Because the English have government drug clinics, they have fewer addicts than we do.
   d. People are no damn good.
   e. Get an engineering degree if you want to get a good job.
   f. Be aware of hidden arguments in advertisements.
   g. Wheaties—the breakfast of champions.
   h. You wouldn't want anyone to see you crying, would you?

4. Every writer has an aim and manipulates words, thoughts, and feelings to achieve that aim. Read each of the following passages. What is the writer trying to achieve? What aspects of the writing are meant to achieve that aim? What is meant to be persuasive in each one?
   a. Hundreds of white women swarmed along Hill Street—our route and the university's fraternity row. They huddled in packs, hugging and squealing and sometimes singing, defiantly stopping traffic. The crowd reeked of money: pearl necklaces and the effects of orthodontia were everywhere in evidence. (M. G. Lord, "Frats and Fraternities: The Greek Rites of Exclusion")
   b. The majority of homeless single individuals have not spent time in mental institutions. Even among the 22 percent of men in emergency centers who once were institutionalized, almost half had been discharged at least five years before they became homeless. And two-thirds of the homeless in families are children who have no history of institutionalization. (Peter Marcuse, "Why Are They Homeless?")
   c. Therefore to our best mercy give yourselves,
   Or like to men proud of destruction,
   Defy us to our worst; for as I am a soldier,
   A name that in my thoughts becomes me best,
   If I begin the battery once again,
   I will not leave the half-achieved Harflew
   Till in her ashes she lies buried.
   The gates of mercy shall be all shut up,

And the fleshed soldier, rough and hard of heart,
In liberty of bloody hand, shall range
With conscience wide as hell, mowing like grass
Your fresh fair virgins and your flowering infants.
(King Henry V to the surrounded town of Harflew, in William Shake-
speare, *Henry V*)

5. Each of the following passages contains an argument. Determine what that argument is and whether it is reasonable.

   a. I don't know where Hoboken is. Pull into this gas station and let's ask the attendant.

   b. Well, if he's rich and has a nice car, he'll probably be fun on a date. Call him back.

   c. I called you Friday, and you said you were sick. I called you Saturday, and you said you had homework. I called you Sunday, and you said you had church all day long. Don't you like me or something?

   d. Scientists are calling AIDS fatal because AIDS patients generally die within five years of diagnosis of the disease.

   e. Let's go to Asbury Park. That's the place Bruce Springsteen is always singing about.

   f. So I looked again at all the acts of oppression which were being done under the sun. And behold, I saw the tears of the oppressed and that they had no one to comfort them; and on the side of their oppressors was power, but still the oppressed had no one to comfort them. So I congratulated the dead who are already dead more than the living who are still living. (Ecclesiastes 4:1–2)

   g. If God hadn't wanted there to be poor people, He would have made us rich people more generous. (Caption of a *New Yorker* drawing by Dana Fradon)

   h. Dear Miss Lonelyheart: Between you and me, the people who write to your column are either scoundrels or idiots.

6. Read some of your own writing, looking for your characteristic uses of rhetoric. What values are important to you? What facts and opinions stand behind your arguments? What do you do to make your words more persuasive? Write a short essay in which you report on your own use of rhetoric.

2

The Logic of Argument

But there must be some use for reason. There *is* a
real world of people, things, and events.
— F. G. BAILEY (b. 1924)
ENGLISH ANTHROPOLOGIST

In Chapter 1, we focused on some of the difficulties we face in analyzing ideas. We discussed various impediments to clear thinking, of our
own creation or buried in what we hear and read. Now we turn to a discussion of logic, our intellectual tool for understanding a reasoning
process, our own and others'. By means of logic we evaluate the connection between evidence and the conclusion we draw from it. We answer the question, Am I justified in thinking this is true?

PREMISES AND INFERENCES:
THE PATH TO CONCLUSIONS

The terms *premise* and *inference* are not as difficult as they may sound.
The first refers to the point from which an argument begins, and the second refers to the process of arriving at the conclusion.

Premises

When we reason, we start with some idea or fact or belief. That starting point is called a premise. A premise is the idea we don't try to prove. We assume it is true. A premise is our reason for concluding something. When we reason, we combine two or more premises and draw a conclusion based on their connection:

PREMISE 1	Arsenic can be deadly.
PREMISE 2	My dog ate arsenic.
CONCLUSION	It may die.
PREMISE 1	Any thirty-five-year-old or older nonfelon born in the United States is eligible for the presidency.
PREMISE 2	James is a thirty-eight-year-old nonfelon born in the United States.
CONCLUSION	James is eligible for the presidency.

Not all premises are stated. Some may be implicit or hidden.

PREMISE	All living things require water.
CONCLUSION	A cactus requires water.

The unstated premise is "A cactus is a living thing." That's right: a premise is the same thing as an assumption. (For discussion of hidden premises, see "Uncovering Assumptions" in Chapter 1 and "What's Behind All This?" in Chapter 3.)

The premises must be true to justify the conclusion. If, for instance, James is a felon, we are not justified in concluding that he is eligible for the presidency. Basing an argument on an untrue premise makes for faulty reasoning.

Even true premises may not justify a conclusion. Good reasoning requires that the premises include *all* relevant considerations. If James had relinquished his U.S. citizenship or served in a foreign army, he would not be eligible for the presidency. Had the premises included these facts, we would surely have drawn a different conclusion.

In reasoning, especially about values, we may disagree vociferously about what constitutes an acceptable premise. And if you disagree with the premises, you won't think the conclusion is justified. Here is a familiar argument:

> Controlling crime and criminals is the most important problem in our society. If the police violate due process once in a while, well, that's just too bad.

If you don't accept the premise that controlling crime is the most important problem in our society, you might conclude that it is worse than "too bad" to violate due process.

Inferences

The process of moving from the premises, or reasons, to the conclusion is called inference. Based on what we know or believe, we infer ideas about what we don't know:

> Where there's smoke there's fire.
>
> Look over there—a cloud of smoke.
>
> There must be a fire.

When we analyze inferences, we are evaluating not the truth or adequacy of the premises but whether the reasoning from them to the conclusion is justified. When we make an inference, we consider the premises and then derive a conclusion that follows from them.

> People are standing in line in front of that movie theater.
>
> They will attend the movie.

The strength or weakness of an inference depends on the extent to which the premises compel us to the conclusion. In any argument, we need to evaluate how compelling those premises are.

Each of the following statements contains a premise and an inference. How compelling are the premises and how strong are the inferences?

> I wrote her twelve letters but she never answered.
> She does not want to correspond with me.
>
> Although we have been in two classes together, David has never invited me to go mountain climbing.
> David hates me.
>
> A course in Western civilization provides understanding and appreciation of our institutions, and that is desirable.
> It should be required for all our students.

In the first statement, the premise is so compelling that no one would quarrel with the inference, although we might be amused that a person bothered to draw such an obvious conclusion.

In the second, David's failure to extend an invitation to climb a mountain hardly justifies the conclusion "David hates me." The inference is weak to ridiculous.

The third statement is trickier. Even granting the truth of the explicit premises—that such a course gives students understanding and appreciation of our institutions, which is desirable—is the inference strong or weak? Can we confidently take the next step to the conclusion?

Three steps can help us evaluate inferences. First, we should articulate both the stated and the unstated premises to make sure we understand what is being claimed. For the first example, an unstated premise is

> If she had wanted to correspond with me, she would have answered at least one of my letters.

Reasonable enough, though it hardly needed saying. But for the Western civilization argument, we have some fairly important and subtle unstated premises to analyze. In laying out the argument, we might come up with something like this:

> A course in Western civilization provides understanding and appreciation of our institutions, and that is desirable. We should require students to take whatever is desirable. Its being required will not undermine the teaching of the course.

We have identified just two of the many unstated premises here, but they give us a better idea of whether the inference is strong or weak.

Second, we should state the argument in its baldest terms by adding a *therefore* before the conclusion.

> A course in Western civilization provides students understanding and appreciation of our institutions, and that is desirable. Therefore, it should be required for all our students.

Put in that way, the conclusion appears in its most absolute form, and you might decide you don't agree. Often poor reasoning is concealed because it is worded in moderate terms. When reasons are put baldly, you can decide whether the conclusion is justified, as, for instance, it is in the cactus argument:

> Therefore, a cactus requires water.

Finally, we should reframe the conclusion to test its limits. First, reframe to make the inference less of a jump:

> A course in Western civilization provides students understanding and appreciation of our institutions, and that is desirable. Therefore, we should encourage it as an elective.

How does that strike you? Now make the inference more of a jump:

> A course in Western civilization provides understanding, and that is desirable. It should be required of all citizens.

Given this range, you can better determine what inference is justified, and you can decide whether to accept or reject the original conclusion. Even with these helps, you are really on your own when it comes to evaluating inferences. It is often a matter of *feeling*, of gauging how strongly the premises compel you to the conclusion.

INDUCTION AND DEDUCTION:
HOW WE REASON

Through induction and deduction we reason from what we know or believe to draw conclusions about what we don't know. Although they follow more or less the same form—from premise by means of inference to conclusion—they differ in the kinds of premises we start with and in the degree of certainty we end with.

Induction

Induction is the process of reasoning from premises that constitute good, but not absolutely certain, reasons to a conclusion that is *probably* correct. We do this kind of reasoning all the time—choosing a college or even buying sneakers:

> It's time to buy new sneakers. I've had five pairs of Nikes and never had any foot problems. Reeboks gave me blisters, and L. A. Gears made my ankles ache. Therefore, I probably ought to buy Nikes.

The conclusion to buy Nikes is based on experience with Nikes, Reeboks, and L. A. Gears, good premises from which to reason. We cannot be absolutely certain, however, that this conclusion is the correct one. Perhaps the problem was with only a particular pair of L. A. Gears, and all the others are fine, or perhaps the machinery on which the Nikes were made has been replaced, and the sneakers will never be the same. The possibilities are endless. Nonetheless, the inference is strong, the conclusion justifiable. Go with the Nikes.

Scientists and doctors often use the inductive process. They start with particular facts, analyze their connections, and reason to conclusions. A doctor sees many patients suffering from swollen tongues, loose teeth, and watery eyes. By asking questions, the doctor discovers that all these patients have the same kind of diet. Reasoning from these two premises—the symptoms and the diet—the doctor tentatively concludes that the problem is a deficiency in a particular vitamin. She tests this hypothesis by depriving laboratory rats of the vitamin. When rat after rat develops the symptoms, the doctor firms up her conclusion.

Judges and juries also reason inductively. They bring together all the pieces of evidence (the premises) presented by the lawyers and come up with a verdict (the conclusion). Here is a lawyer summarizing the evidence in a custody case before a judge:

> Mrs. Wiggs sometimes left the seven-year-old to look after the two younger children. Therefore, Your Honor, custody should be denied Mrs. Wiggs and given to my client, Mr. Wiggs.

Hardly an adequate premise for inferring such a momentous conclusion. Did Mrs. Wiggs just go next door, or was she out all night? The lawyer provides other premises:

> The neighbors have testified that Mrs. Wiggs drinks and leaves the children alone at night. Because she did not pay her bill, her electricity was shut off for a week during the winter. Therefore, Your Honor, custody should be denied Mrs. Wiggs and given to my client, Mr. Wiggs.

The judge is beginning to find this lawyer's reasons compelling and the inference strong.

Mrs. Wiggs's lawyer, of course, offers a compelling reason not to give custody to Mr. Wiggs:

> Mr. Wiggs watches pornographic movies on his VCR.

The judge decides to investigate on his own.

Even months of investigating, however, could not uncover every relevant fact: Will one or both parents cease their vices? Which is worse for these particular children, the booze or the movies? With less than complete knowledge, the judge must decide what is *probably* in the best interest of the children.

The best inductive arguments are only "highly probable"—probable enough to justify the movement from the premises through the inference to the conclusion.

Deduction

When we reason deductively, we move from general statements we accept as true to an inevitable conclusion. When the general statements are indeed true and the reasoning valid, then the conclusion is *certainly* true. The most famous example of deduction is

> All men are mortal.
>
> Socrates is a man.
>
> Therefore, Socrates is mortal.

Logicians refer to this form of argument as a *syllogism*. It contains two statements and a conclusion. The first statement makes a general assertion, called the *major premise*. This assertion is the foundation of the argument. For the argument to proceed, we have to accept that all men are mortal. The second statement, called a *minor premise,* provides a specific instance of the major premise. Without the minor premise, we would have

> All men are mortal.
>
> Therefore Socrates is mortal.

But we don't know about this thing called Socrates. Is it a city?

> Socrates is a man.

The minor premise links the major premise to the conclusion. It indicates the way in which the conclusion fits into the major premise. Reasoning from the two premises, the conclusion is inevitable. If all men are mortal and Socrates is a man, then he is mortal.

Scientists and physicians sometimes think deductively:

> White blood cells multiply to combat infection. This blood sample indicates a rapid rise in the white blood cell count. There must be an infection.

So do plumbers, electricians, secretaries, and automobile mechanics:

> The car's electrical system is not operating. The battery is the source of electricity. I'll check the battery.

We frequently use this form of reasoning in everyday life too, as in this statement:

> All movies starring Jim Carrey are enjoyable. He's in a new movie. This new movie will be enjoyable.

Usually our deductive reasoning is so casual and fast we hardly know we're doing it:

> I like Russian novels and haven't read this one by Dostoevsky. I think I'll buy it.

To agree with the conclusion of a deductive argument, we must agree with the premises. Both premises. Here is an argument based on a dubious major premise:

> All my friends are brilliant.
>
> Conrad is my friend.
>
> Therefore, Conrad is brilliant.

We have to wonder about the truth of the major premise. Surely everyone has at least one friend who isn't brilliant.

Even when we accept the major premise, we need to look carefully at the minor premise. Here are the bases for two deductive arguments regarding test-tube fertilization. They are based on the same major premise but arrive at opposite conclusions.

> Major premise: Any practice that detracts from the dignity of human life should be illegal.

The minor premise of one side of the argument is

> Test-tube fertilization detracts from the dignity of human life.

The minor premise of the other side is

> Anything that denies infertile couples the right to have children detracts from the dignity of human life.

Never the twain shall meet. We need to analyze the minor premise as closely as we do the major.

We often think in syllogisms when we try to anticipate the consequences of a course of action. We set up a hypothesis and see how things work out. The major premise projects a condition that *if* something is the case, *then* something else will be or will happen:

> *If* I see someone cheating, *then* I am honor bound to report it.

The minor premise states that the condition of the *if* clause does exist in a particular case:

> I saw that student cheating.

The conclusion states that the *then* clause obtains in the particular case:

> *Then* I am honor bound to report him.

We use forms of hypothetical reasoning every day in subtle ways:

> If a highway patrolman observes me speeding, he will give me a ticket. A highway patrolman is hiding behind that billboard. I will slow down.

> If I eat any more pizza, I will gain weight. I love pizza, but I won't have any more.

Very few arguments in real life are completely deductive. Most are based on some prior induction. In the argument about white blood cells, for example, the major premise—that white cells multiply to combat infection—is the product of an inductive process. And of course we wouldn't know that all men are mortal if we hadn't known about particular people who had died. When you come across a deductive argument, look closely at the inductive argument on which it probably rests. That is the best way to test it.

Enthymemes

An argument in which one part—either of the premises or the conclusion—is missing is called an *enthymeme,* a term based on a Greek word meaning "to hold in mind."

> The leaves of my camellias are yellowing. I should put on some nitrogen.

What we have to hold in mind is the second premise, necessary to justify the conclusion:

> Yellow leaves usually indicate that a plant needs nitrogen.

A nongardener would probably have needed that second premise to understand the conclusion. Often, however, the missing premise is just too obvious to require stating:

> He just committed a murder. Arrest him.

No one would bother to say,

> Anyone who commits a murder should be arrested.

Or the conclusion may not need stating:

> If you don't mail your taxes in by April 15, you're going to get hit with a huge penalty. Tomorrow is April 15.

It would actually be less effective to state the conclusion outright:

> So you should send in your taxes by tomorrow.

Although enthymemes can be quite innocent, as these examples suggest, sometimes they create problems in reasoning because they can be used to deceive:

> Milovic is a Serb. Therefore, he hates Croatians.

Missing from this deductive argument is the major premise:

> All Serbs hate Croatians.

We know this statement to be false, and if it were stated we would challenge it. When it is unstated, however, we may be misled into accepting the argument.

Asserting two premises and leaving the conclusion unstated can be even more insidious:

> Serbs hate Croatians. Milovic is a Serb.

We're supposed to fill in the blank:

> Milovic hates Croatians.

Stated, this could be grounds for a libel suit. We should insist that people who make sly insinuations make their conclusions explicit.

Sometimes unintentional enthymemes confuse the reader, as did this one from a student essay:

> Ernest Hemingway loved big-game hunting and contests of strength and skill. He often had fights with friends and competitors, and he especially loved boxing and bullfighting. His stories are often about men trying to prove their masculinity. It seems as though he was very much afraid that he wasn't much of a man.

The missing part of the argument is

> Any writer so concerned with masculinity must be insecure.

We would want to examine that premise before we agreed with the conclusion.

Sometimes a good argument seems absurd because an important part is missing:

> You should exercise daily because blood lactates are responsible for mental dullness and lethargy.

Huh? Missing premise, please:

> Exercise lowers the quantity of blood lactates.

Oh.

Although enthymemes can be dangerous, they can also enrich prose. They can have a strength and elegance that every writer should try to master. Enthymemes involve the audience in the argument by inviting them to supply the missing part of the syllogism. They work best when the part to be supplied is reasonably apparent and is something the reader will either agree with or find interesting. Supplying that missing part can be a great source of reader satisfaction.

We see this use of enthymemes every day. Here is the same movie review put into three different enthymemes. Can you supply the missing part?

> *Dark Passions* does not have good acting, brisk direction, or especially good cinematography. That's why it won't be getting many Academy Award nominations.

> A movie needs good acting, brisk direction, and especially good cinematography to earn Academy Award nominations. That's why you won't be seeing *Dark Passions* among the nominees this year.

> A movie needs good acting, brisk direction, and especially good cinematography to earn an Academy Award nomination. *Dark Passions* has none of these.

Write out the complete syllogism, and you'll be able to see why each enthymeme has an unmistakable—and completely different—impact.

As a reader, be aware of enthymemes. Supply missing elements in reasoning. Say them aloud to yourself, or just make a mental note. By doing so you will learn more about both the writer's intention and your own reasoning process. As a writer, experiment with enthymemes. They invite the reader to join you in the process of reasoning.

FACTS OR VALUES:
TELLING *IS* FROM *OUGHT*

In deciding whether a reasoning process is valid and whether we agree with its conclusion, we need to recognize exactly what kind of argument is being made, whether of fact or of value.

In an argument of fact, the conclusion establishes what was, is, or will be:

> John von Neumann was largely responsible for inventing the computer.
>
> If we let people use water indiscriminately, we will deplete our water supplies.

These conclusions rest on factual premises shared by anyone in a position to investigate. The premises behind "John von Neumann was largely responsible for inventing the computer" might be various expert studies on the history of the computer, testimony of contemporary witnesses, and the influence of von Neumann's ideas on contemporary computer design—all facts. Environmentalists arguing that indiscriminate use of water will deplete the water supply would base their argument on, among other facts, documented examples of such occurrences elsewhere and an examination of current water tables.

Don't let the phrase "argument of fact" mislead you. People disagree over arguments of fact all the time. That's because different people can and do draw different conclusions from the same facts. Keep in mind that such arguments at least start from facts.

> Lower taxes will lead to greater federal revenues.

Because the conclusion anticipates future events, economists on both sides of this debate would base their argument on mathematical models.

Sometimes arguments of fact are not valid, as we suggested earlier in this section. Perhaps the facts are not true or not adequate, or the inference is weak. Nonetheless, the argument rests on fact, however precariously.

In an argument of value, the conclusion establishes whether an idea or an object is or is not worthwhile, whether a person should or should not do something, whether an action is good or bad. Conclusions of value rest not on established facts but on norms, a sense of what is right or wrong, good or bad. The writer seeks to persuade us not of what is, was, or will be but of what ought to be. Because the premises rest on values, no investigation, no experimentation, no mathematical model could prove these conclusions.

> Capital punishment should be outlawed.
>
> *Star Wars* is the greatest movie ever made.
>
> The state should institute term limits for officeholders.

Sometimes arguments of value are premised on a fact. In arguing against capital punishment, for instance, a writer might claim as one premise the fact that innocent people have been executed. But the importance or weight of that fact rests upon an unstated premise of value: more important than punishment is the sanctity of the innocent.

Arguments of value cannot be directly proved, for finally they rest on personal interests and considerations and emotionally charged beliefs. This does not mean that we should dismiss such arguments—they involve the most important issues of our lives. But it does mean that we should be clear about what kind of argument is being made. For an argument of fact, when we muster sufficient evidence, we will probably persuade our audience. But it is extremely difficult to persuade another person that our values are superior to his or hers. No amount of haranguing will help. The best we can do is express our own values clearly and hope that in some way we touch the reader.

PROBLEMS IN LOGIC: IDENTIFYING LOGICAL FALLACIES

The validity of an argument, whether inductive or deductive, depends on both the premises and the reasoning to the conclusion. Errors in either premises or inferences can lead to logical fallacies. Logical fallacies are patterns of reasoning that are at worst invalid and at best weaker than they appear to the unwary. Human beings have invented so many logical fallacies that we could never name, let alone discuss, all of them. In Chapter 1, The Critical Sense, we discussed several, including hasty generalization and oversimplification. Here we discuss other fallacies you will often encounter.

The Undistributed Middle

Logicians point out that a syllogism won't work unless the assertion found in the major premise is true of all members of the group. In the Socrates syllogism, "mortality" is true of "all men." But look at this syllogism:

> Many border patrol officers take bribes.
>
> Tim is a border patrol officer.
>
> Therefore, Tim takes bribes.

The major premise does not claim that all border patrol officers take bribes: although Tim is a border patrol officer, he may not be one of the bribe-takers. The syllogism is faulty because what is true of "most" may not be true of a specific individual. Logicians call this the fallacy of the undistributed middle, meaning that the middle term (takes bribes) is not necessarily true of, or "distributed to," all members of the group (border patrol officers). Carefully check the wording to be sure you know exactly what is being asserted.

Affirming the Consequent

Although its name may be a bit daunting, the fallacy called "affirming the consequent" is important and frequent enough to merit study.

> The state punishes embezzlers.
>
> The state punished Lester.
>
> Therefore, Lester is an embezzler.

The facts here may be correct, but the reasoning is faulty because the major premise does not specifically exclude punishing criminals other than embezzlers. The state may be punishing people for other crimes. Lester may have robbed a bank for all the two premises tell us. If the major premise had stated

> The state punishes embezzlers only.

the reasoning would have been valid, and we would know Lester to be an embezzler. Make certain the major premise specifically includes the minor premise.

Circular Reasoning

Occasionally people will argue in a circle, using as a premise what in fact they are setting out to prove.

> Freud's investigations were truly scientific because they were based on Freud's own clinical research.

In this argument we end up where we started out. Some logicians call this *begging the question* because the careful thinker would ask something like, Why are Freud's clinical studies scientific?

Another form of circular reasoning is the *tautology,* that is, an argument that only repeats the same idea in different words:

> This car doesn't work because something is wrong with it.

And slightly more subtly:

> We must preserve the American way of life because without it, we won't be able to live the way Americans should.

This is a tautology because it is a tautology.

Non Sequitur

The Latin phrase *non sequitur* means "it does not follow." It applies to any argument whose conclusion simply has nothing to do with its premises:

> Warfield will make an excellent governor because he was a fine captain of his football team.

Football experience has little relevance to political skill and tells us nothing about political goals. The premise may be correct, but the conclusion does not follow.

As we suggested in the discussion of assumptions in Chapter 1, television commercials specialize in non sequiturs. Just because we see a sleek cheetah, a handsome man, a beautiful woman, a desert landscape, and a car, it does not follow that we should buy that car.

As we suggested earlier, sometimes what seems to be a non sequitur is really an enthymeme.

> Although human beings did not eat barley in the sixteenth century, barley was necessary for war.

This apparent non sequitur is really an enthymeme lacking a part:

> War-making depended on horses, and horses ate barley.

Be sure you fill in all the necessary parts of an argument.

Post Hoc, Ergo Propter Hoc

Also from the Latin, *post hoc, ergo propter hoc* means "after this, therefore because of this." We commit this fallacy when we argue, without other reasons, that because X occurred before Y, X caused Y.

> Herbert Hoover was inaugurated as president in the spring of 1929, and that autumn the stock market crashed. Hoover must have caused the crash.

The causes of the stock market crash go much further back than the spring of 1929 and involve much more than the actions of a single individual.

A variant of the post hoc fallacy is the argument that because A was one of the conditions for bringing B about, we can eliminate B by eliminating A.

> Neville Chamberlain's negotiation with Adolf Hitler allowed Germany time to rearm and increased its ability to wage war. To avoid war, we should never negotiate.

It may not have been wise to negotiate with Hitler, but this does not mean that negotiation is always unwise. Be sure to examine the connection between things that are claimed as causes and their effects.

Ad Hominem

Still another Latin phrase, *ad hominem* means an argument "to the man," that is, to the person making the statement. Someone guilty of this fallacy argues by making irrelevant assertions—usually character slurs—about the opponent, rather than attacking the opponent's reasoning.

> I don't believe anything Gingrich says about the economy. He's power hungry and self-righteous.

Maybe he is, but his *opinion* is the point, not his character; he may still have important and informed ideas about the economy.

Ridicule is a particularly insidious ad hominem technique because it is based on humor. Once, when he saw Stafford Cripps, an old opponent with a reputation for arrogance, Winston Churchill said, "There but for the grace of God goes God," Nevertheless, Churchill had finally to debate the merits of Cripp's arguments.

Following the line of our own logic is sometimes difficult. We have to disassemble the purring Rolls Royce of our own prose and get down to the drive shaft, the chassis, the struts. But all of us use logic, and all of us need to examine it and criticize it, rods and rivets.

Because paragraphs are mini-arguments, containing a main point and supporting points, they are a good place to take our own logic apart. Do they keep a steady direction? Does each sentence emerge from the previous one and lead logically to the next? Is there something extraneous rattling around in the engine, probably doing serious damage? The point is to recognize that we do use logic, to understand how to use it, and to improve.

Tips for the Logic of Argument

- Check all premises to be sure you agree with them. Remember premises must be true and adequate for an argument based on them to be true.
- Articulate stated and unstated premises to be sure you understand the argument.
- To evaluate an inference, state the argument in its baldest terms.
- Test an inference by reframing the conclusion less drastically and then more drastically.
- Remember that even in the best case, a conclusion from induction is only highly probable.
- Check both premises and reasoning to evaluate a deductive argument.
- Remember that most deductive arguments rest on prior induction.
- Check enthymemes to be sure the missing part — whether premise or conclusion — doesn't change the argument.
- Carefully distinguish between arguments of fact and arguments of value.
- Be aware of logical fallacies: for instance, the undistributed middle; affirming the consequent; circular reasoning; non sequitur; post hoc, ergo propter hoc; and ad hominem.

EXERCISES FOR THE LOGIC OF ARGUMENT

1. In the following passage, identify the premises, stated and implied:

   It is outrageous for GoodHealth Insurance Company to cancel insurance for 8,000 people on the ground that the policies did not pay for themselves. What further proof do we need that the health-care industry cares only about money? The state should provide coverage for all people at a cost proportionate to their income.

2. What inferences are you expected to make in the following examples? Are the inferences strong or weak?
   a. At a grocery store checkout counter: "She's eighty-five and she has six shopping bags to carry to her car."
   b. Only drink when you're alone or with somebody else. (Meredith Wilson, "Belly up to the Bar, Boys")
   c. Persons attempting to find a motive in this narrative will be prosecuted; persons attempting to find a moral in it will be banished; persons attempting to find a plot in it will be shot. (Mark Twain, *Adventures of Huckleberry Finn*)

3. Determine whether each of these arguments is inductive or deductive, and then evaluate the reasoning.
   a. There has never been a female president. There has never been a female vice president. There has never been a female secretary of state or of the treasury. Women have no chance in politics in this country.
   b. Cats are vicious creatures. They disturb the dogs in the neighborhood and sometimes kill birds. If their owners let them out of the house, the neighbors ought to have a right to shoot them.
   c. The law says that you are liable for taxes on your share of the taxable income of any partnership in which you are a partner. Your share of the income of our partnership was $500. Therefore, you must pay taxes on $500.

4. Rewrite any questionable arguments in Exercise 3 to make them more acceptable. Change the premises or the conclusion as necessary.

5. Here are a series of enthymemes. Which part of each argument is missing? Restore the missing part, and then determine whether the argument is valid. Identify the arguments that do not really need the missing part.
   a. Used-car salesman: "So you're a student. Well, here's a 1978 Lemon. It's sort of beat up, but, heck, it runs, and it's cheap."
   b. On a sports talk show: "What you need to win the Super Bowl is great passing, superb defense, and good special teams. That's why Denver is a lock on the Bowl this year."
   c. You know as much about embroidery as a pig does about rocket science.
   d. A truly desirable home is hard to find. So are the homes at Hidden Hollow Estates.
   e. Homosexual acts between consenting adults are victimless acts and therefore should not be considered criminal.
   f. Water pollution is everybody's fault. That means it is your duty to help clean it up.

6. Which of the following conclusions should be based on fact and which on value? Explain your identifications.
   a. If you see a situation in which something is wrong and you could rectify it yet do nothing, then you are also responsible for that situation.
   b. Meat eaters have a much higher chance of developing cancer of the digestive system than do vegetarians.
   c. Watching television makes a child less sensitive to violence and an adult more indifferent to actual violence in the world.
   d. I prefer Kobe's peach ice cream because it contains real fruit.
   e. Writing well is the sign of an educated person.

7. Evaluate the use of logic in this letter written to the editor of a newspaper. Do you find any fallacies or questionable assumptions?

   The United States had to invade Iraq in 1991. Iraq was an Islamic state and therefore was working against our interests. Its leader, Saddam Hussein, was a dictator, and, like most dictators, he wouldn't have stopped until he was completely destroyed. By invading Kuwait, he set himself up to take over Saudi Arabia, which would have given him control of over 40 percent of the world's oil. From there, it's a short step to Israel. We simply had to confront Hussein for the sake of freedom everywhere. Anyone who thinks we did it out of self-interest is a moron.

8. Evaluate the use of logic in a piece of your own writing. Try your hand at spotting inductive and deductive arguments. Identify your premises and your conclusions. Check the strength of your inferences. Look for enthymemes (you do use them) and evaluate them. Weigh your arguments of fact and value. Are there any errors in logic? Write a brief essay reporting on your use of logic. Analyze at least three examples of your logic in depth.

3

Critical Reading

Do not dictate to your author; try to become him. Be
his fellow worker and accomplice. . . . If you open
your mind as widely as possible, then signs and hints
of almost imperceptible fineness, from the twists
and turns of the first sentence, will bring you into
the presence of a human being unlike any other.
— VIRGINIA WOOLF (1882-1941)
ENGLISH AUTHOR

Understanding a text is not an automatic consequence of running our eyes over the print. To read well takes more than eyesight: it takes full engagement of the mind. Some writing is, of course, not difficult—just look at the sports page or popular novels. We can usually understand this easy-access reading on the first try and without effort. But college reading is by its very nature different. Its purpose is not to divert but to inform and stimulate thought. It almost always requires a second and often a third try, for the meaning accumulates from page to page. College reading requires, then, that we put our minds in gear and feel the traction as our thought moves over the writer's thought.

We call this process *critical reading.* By *critical* we do not mean fault-finding or carping over details. We mean a healthy skepticism—respectful but inquisitive—and a willingness to analyze a text step by step. Critical reading helps us to remember. When we read casually, uncritically, we don't nail the text into our memory. When we read critically, however, the ideas and facts stay in place. Being more engaged, we pay closer attention. We relate one idea to another and notice similarities. As we read, our knowledge accumulates and our understanding grows.

We do not naturally adopt a critical stance when we read. We tend to accept what we see in print, forgetting that no matter how well qualified writers may be, they are nonetheless fallible. We cannot assume that mistakes, deceptions, and illogicalities just won't appear in what we read. They will.

A CRITICAL ATTITUDE: ENGAGING THE TEXT

This chapter covers certain habits of mind appropriate to reading. Some of its terms will be familiar from other chapters. Here we discuss ways of sifting out the good in what you read and throwing away the bad.

Critical readers perform three main activities:

They participate. They do not sit back and read passively. Before starting to read, they map the whole terrain they will cover. They look ahead and know what to expect. They make notes, put concepts into their own words, group important topics, relate main ideas. They summarize or paraphrase, the better to capture the essence of a thought or a text.

They analyze. Developing analytical skills is a—perhaps *the*—major purpose of a college education. To analyze is to break large items or ideas into smaller units or complex items into simpler components. Critical readers look at each major idea separately and examine its subordinate parts. They study how major ideas connect to make up the whole.

They interrogate the text. Critical readers know that almost all writers—whether of textbooks, essays, editorials, or advertisements—are trying to impose their opinions and thoughts on their readers. Although they appreciate the effective, smart, honest essay, they are on the lookout for hidden assumptions, missed steps, "fast ones," and sloppy reasoning. They take nothing for granted and judge for themselves.

AN OVERVIEW: MAPPING THE TEXT

You have a piece of writing before you. It could be a textbook, a newspaper editorial, a magazine article, your latest journal entry, or a roommate's essay that you have just been asked to look at. In each case, you have a good reason to read critically: you want to learn, you want to understand, or you want to help. The following four tactics will give you an effective way to map the text:

1. Think about your purpose for reading. Do you need to accumulate facts or to understand the development of an idea? Are you studying the text to prepare for an examination? Will you be writing a paper on it?

2. Take a quick tour of the ground to be covered. First, note the title and the author's name and read any information given about the author. Next, scan the table of contents. Page through and note any headnotes, subdivisions, or illustrations. Note repeated terms and names. Finally, scan the questions, if any, at the end of the chapter or article to determine what the author thinks is important. At this point, although you have not started your actual reading, you are already familiar with the whole piece.

3. Check the length of the piece and estimate how long it will take to read. Don't always try to finish in one sitting. Your brain likes to store information gradually rather than to have everything rammed in at once. We recommend that when reading textbooks, you read in a fifteen- to twenty-minute chunk, take a short break, and continue.

4. Get as much background as possible on this text and on the author. Who wrote it? What makes the author an expert? What else has the author written? What have others said about the author's ideas? Your library's literary reference section is a good starting place.

⌨ Computer Tip

To go along with the standard books there are many new reference tools. Look at CD-ROM databases such as First Search, CD-ROM encyclopedias such as *The New Grolier Multimedia Encyclopedia,* and CD-ROM versions of important reference works such as *The Reader's Guide to the Humanities and Social Sciences.* The Internet is not yet adequate for author searches, but if you are a well-versed cybertraveler, comb through subject trees such as the Virtual Library and Yahoo as well as search engines such as Lycos and Alta Vista. In the Appendix we list many reference books to help you navigate on the Internet.

---

5. Respond. This may be the most important phase of critical reading. You cannot expect to understand and retain important material if you just turn pages. Some people underline or use marking pens to highlight significant passages. This process has drawbacks, how-

ever: it allows the reader to register passively that a word or phrase is important but not *how* it is important. We once saw a copy of *Othello* that was almost entirely highlighted, because almost every line has something good. You could sit there highlighting all day.

We strongly urge you to take notes, putting what you have read in your own words. Taking notes forces you to discriminate constantly, reducing and reorganizing the ideas as your understanding grows. Some people prefer to write their notes in the margins of the text, but then the notes remain scattered and are difficult to use. We recommend jotting your notes in a notebook or on notecards. This method forces you to organize the notes apart from the text—a good way to get a handle on the material—and provides quick access for review. And if you are writing a paper on the reading, your notes will put you one step closer to the finished product.

🖳 **Computer Tip**

The laptop computer is especially useful for taking notes because it can be taken to study hall, library, or beach. Because computer-generated notes are so easy to make, however, they are likewise easy to forget. Read and reread your notes soon after taking them. Edit them to make them tidier and more accessible. To make notes discrete and to avoid word-cramming the screen, separate each note by hitting **Enter** twice.

The following are suggestions for note taking:

1. Summarize the major sections in the text, writing down the primary ideas and most significant evidence. You can go back to fill in details.
2. Write down page numbers or paragraph numbers so that you can easily find specific material.
3. Include in your notes your agreement, or disagreement, and any reservations you have—but be sure to keep these comments separate from the summary.
4. After completing your reading, make an outline of the main points and supporting ideas so that you can see how the text was organized, how the parts were related, and how the argument developed. (For a discussion of outlining, see "Organizing" in Chapter 5.)

Yes, all this is trouble, and yes, it is worth it. Reading critically will vastly enhance both your retention and your understanding. (See Chapter 13 for a fuller discussion of note taking.)

EIGHT QUESTIONS: EVALUATING READING

In the following section, we discuss eight questions a critical reader can use to interrogate difficult texts as an aid to understanding and retention. Thinking through—or even better, writing down—the answers to these questions can help you know what is really in the text and develop an informed opinion about it. Also keep these questions in mind when reviewing your own writing.

1. What Are They Talking About? The Subject

You cannot enjoy a game unless you know the point of it, and you cannot start understanding your reading until you know what it is about. Your first task is to articulate the subject.

The title will sometimes, but not always, indicate it. "Politics and the English Language" does—"Boring from Within" does not. When a title does not communicate the subject, try the first two or three paragraphs and then the last two or three. Page through to see whether subheadings disclose the subject. Don't go any further with your reading until you know what the subject is. Don't assume you know it. Say it aloud or write it out just to be sure. Or put the subject in the form of a question the whole text will answer: for example, "What is the function of the mitochondrion within the cell?" At the head of your notes, write down your idea of the subject. Now you have made it yours.

2. Why Are They Talking About It? The Purpose

Writers have different purposes for writing. Aristotle broke down these purposes into three motives: to report, to explain, or to persuade. (See Chapter 4, "Getting Ready to Write.") Sometimes the purpose is concealed and sometimes it is right out front. Some writers—journalists, for instance—have a clear purpose: to report an event or describe a situation or scene. Remember, though, that some writing purporting to be pure reportage has a concealed motive. Here is an interesting headline from a newspaper:

> Mayor Scolds Cry-baby Cops

Even allowing for the distortions of brevity, such "reportage" is hard to accept. One scolds a child; "cry-baby" suggests unjustified complaints and whining. The headline implies that the police are behaving like little children. Consciously or unconsciously, the writer of that headline meant not merely to report but to persuade. Bias has a way of slipping in, and a good reader will be on the lookout for it. When you find evidence of bias in a piece that pretends only to report, be wary.

Much of what you read in college will be not reporting but explaining: *The Rise of the Novel,* "Letter to a Young Surgeon," "Kant and Hegel: The Emergence of History." As these titles suggest, the writers of these works are explaining how something came about, how it works, what its consequences are. What the writing will explain is usually made explicit fairly early. In "Letter to a Young Surgeon," Richard Selzer's first sentence is "At this, the start of your surgical internship, it is well that you be told how to behave in an operating room." The purpose is clear.

Frequently you will read works whose purpose is to persuade the reader that a particular view or course of action is the right one. We can usually discern that persuasive purpose in an early sentence. In his "Letter from Birmingham Jail," Martin Luther King, Jr., begins,

> While confined here in the Birmingham city jail, I came across your recent statement calling my present activities "unwise and untimely." Seldom do I pause to answer criticism of my work and ideas. If I sought to answer all the criticisms that cross my desk, my secretaries would have little time for anything other than such correspondence in the course of the day, and I would have no time for constructive work. But since I feel that you are men of genuine good will and that your criticisms are sincerely set forth, I want to try to answer your statement in what I hope will be patient and reasonable terms.

His purpose—to persuade "men of genuine good will" to join his crusade for justice—is clear.

3. What's the Big Idea? The Thesis

The Explicit Thesis.   The single most important sentence in most essays is the thesis statement, that is, the articulation of the author's main idea. The thesis is not the subject but *what the writer has to say* about the subject. Recognizing the thesis is important for understanding the rest of the essay. The first paragraphs may not contain the thesis. There may be anecdotes, accounts of recent controversies, disclaimers, all manner of greetings and promises before the writer hones in on the thesis. Even so, as you read you will probably feel the subject area narrowing until the author's major point becomes clear.

Most frequently, however, an introductory paragraph establishes the subject, narrows it, and then presents the thesis:

> *Flesh and Stone* is a history of the city told through people's bodily experience: how women and men moved, what they saw and heard, the smells that assailed their noses, where they ate, how they dressed, when they bathed, how they made love in cities from ancient Athens to modern New York. Though this book takes people's bodies as a way to understand the past, it is more than an historical catalogue of physical sensations in urban space. Western civilization has had

> persistent trouble in honoring the dignity of the body and diversity of
> human bodies; I have sought to understand how these body-troubles
> have been expressed in architecture, in urban design, and in planning
> practice. (Richard Sennett, *Flesh and Stone*)

Sennett gives the broad historical background of his book, then sharp-
ens the focus to his overarching thesis: that attitudes toward the body
determine the shape of the living spaces we construct.

Occasionally a writer comes right out and identifies the essay's point
or argument: "My thesis in this section will be . . ." "It is, however, more
likely that . . ." or "The answer is . . ." Watch for words that indicate either the assertion of a differing opinion (*on the contrary, nevertheless,
although*) or a conclusion (*therefore, because, for*)—frequently words
like these introduce the thesis statement.

The Implicit Thesis.   Sometimes the writer will try to make the main
point obvious without actually expressing it. We then say the thesis is
"implicit." Identifying implicit theses can be a tricky business, because
we could always be wrong about what the author means us to infer.
Still, at times the thesis will shine as clear as day:

> The McDonnell-Douglas Outplacement Center occupies a storefront in
> what was once a mini-mall retail strip—a strip that bustled back when
> it seemed the defense dollars would rain on this region south of Los
> Angeles forever. Now it's almost empty. The strip's only other lessee is
> the state's unemployment office. There's no sign over the McDonnell-
> Douglas office, no lettering to advertise the fact that McDonnell-
> Douglas layoffs in Long Beach, California—nearly 30,000 since 1990—
> are on such a grand scale that the city, with the company's and state's
> assistance, had to set up a satellite office just to handle the army of
> castoffs from the nation's master builder of military aircraft. A specimen
> of one of the few "industries" still thriving in southern California has
> gone up right in front of the center, obscuring it from the road: a red-
> enameled fast-food chalet named the Wienerschnitzel. (Susan Faludi,
> "Grounded," from *DoubleTake*)

The writer relies on her manipulation of language to make her thesis
clear. Note "army of castoffs," "master builder," the "strip" (absent any
sign identifying the place), and then the hard fact of 30,000 layoffs. The
final touch, reference to the fast-food restaurant, completes the picture.
From such hints we can begin to identify the thesis: efforts to help the
laid-off workers have been woefully inadequate.

When you have identified the thesis, check for vague or ambiguous
terms, and then be sure they are defined later and used consistently. If
not, be wary. And look for qualifying words or phrases, such as *sometimes, may, perhaps, to some extent*. Careful writers use words like these
to limit exactly what they intend to argue, and readers have to evaluate
the argument accordingly.

The Organizational Thesis. Many of the texts you read will simply report or explain, and thus have an organizational, not an argumentative, thesis. A political science textbook, for example, could purport to "discuss various forms of contemporary political organization." All the information in the book would be viewed from that perspective and fulfill that purpose. For a book describing the approaches to literary criticism, the author might indicate in a thesis statement that the material is organized around a few important themes. A cookbook writer points out that fresh ingredients are available, according to the season, and he subsequently organizes his recipes by season. An anthropologist writes a history of a dying community based on systematic interviews with the people. The organizing idea of a manual for assembling an amplifier would no doubt be chronology. Identifying the organizational thesis can help organize the way we read a text. Once we understand the organizational thesis, we can more easily follow the text. (See Chapter 15, Writing in All Disciplines: The Report, for a full discussion of the organizational thesis.)

4. How Do You Figure? Main Supporting Points

Now the real analysis starts. Pay attention to the main supporting points under the thesis. You can often spot these ideas in the topic sentence or main statement of each paragraph. Write out the main supporting points, especially if the reading is difficult, and note how they tie into the thesis.

In his essay "Were Dinosaurs Dumb?" Stephen Jay Gould puts forth the thesis that dinosaurs were as smart as one ought to expect. He provides three main supporting points that could be summarized this way:

1. Dinosaurs had the right size brain for reptiles of their body size.
2. Dinosaurs exhibited intelligence in their behavior.
3. As a species, dinosaurs survived for a relatively long period of time.

Arranging the main points in clear relation to the thesis or purpose lets us see the argument develop and opens a clear path into real critical analysis.

Once you've done your analysis, ask the following questions:

1. Do the main points directly support the thesis? If not, what is their purpose?
2. Are they logical and relevant divisions of the thesis? Were you confused or surprised by any of them? If so, was your reaction the result of careless reading or careless writing?
3. How much space is devoted to each point? The greater the emphasis, probably the more important the point.

4. Does the author seem equally confident of all the points? If one point is significantly more hedged with *maybes* and *possiblys,* perhaps it is the weak link.

5. Are there any big jumps from one main point to another? If so, how badly does the jump damage the argument?

5. What's Behind All This? Assumptions

An assumption is anything taken for granted. (In Chapter 1, The Critical Sense, we discussed assumptions, particularly in our own thinking.) Everyone makes assumptions. You have to in order to say *anything.* Some wonderful jokes depend on a fairly obvious but unspoken assumption. Will Rogers said, for instance,

> I don't belong to any organized political party. I'm a Democrat.

Sometimes assumptions, however, are not merely unspoken but hidden:

> Rock stars become folk heroes to young men precisely because of the strings that are obviously not attached. Lead singers can attract as many women as they want and jettison them in full view of the public. They flit from flower to flower, virile, cheerful, and irresponsible—and they get away with it.

The hidden assumption here is "And that's what men want—right?" You as critical reader are the one to say "right" or "wrong." When you become aware of hidden assumptions you don't agree with, your attitude toward the argument will change. If you think men can be sensitive people, you won't appreciate the crude stereotype of male desire hidden in this passage.

Careful, honest writers know what their assumptions are and lay the most important ones out for all to judge. Hidden assumptions may be all right for humor or fairly harmless in topical journalism, but they can be dangerous in serious written argument. Important assumptions should be explicit and detailed, for then the reader can judge their validity. If we do not agree with a writer's assumptions, we will never agree with his or her arguments.

In the following four examples, for the purpose of illustration, we present the same assertion supported by four different bits of hypothetical evidence. In each case, there is a hidden assumption. Before reading the analysis, try to put the assumption into your own words. Determine whether the assumption is valid and whether the writer should make it explicit.

> Soviet behavior around the world was hostile to the United States. Soviet troops planned to blow up the Washington Monument.

The hidden assumption is that any foreign power that plans to blow up the Washington Monument is hostile to the United States. This assumption is obvious, and the author need not make it explicit.

> Soviet behavior around the world was hostile to the United States. In 1962 missiles were sighted in Cuba.

The hidden assumptions are that these missiles were threatening to the United States and that anything Cuba did the Soviets instigated. Most, though not all, readers would find such assumptions acceptable. Cuba is ninety miles from the United States, and sighting missiles there was cause for thinking the Soviets were involved. Many people would agree without further explication.

> Soviet behavior around the world was hostile to the United States. The Soviet Union invaded Afghanistan in 1979.

The hidden assumptions are that America had important interests in or near Afghanistan and that this invasion intentionally threatened those interests. Their validity is shaky. The Washington Monument is right at home and Cuba only ninety miles from our shores, but Afghanistan is half a world away. Perhaps the author thinks that the USSR planned to cut the United States off from the oil fields of the Middle East and that the invasion was one more step toward this goal. If so, these are exactly the kinds of assumptions that the author must write out.

> Soviet behavior around the world was hostile to the United States. The Soviets persecuted Russian citizens who practiced their religion.

One hidden assumption is that because the United States allows freedom of religion, religious persecution in the Soviet Union struck directly at our values. Many readers will find this assumption to be the least acceptable of all. The Communist system always inhibited religious practice, even in times of friendship between the two countries before the Cold War. Once we make this assumption explicit, we reveal a hole in the argument. Now the author must either find evidence to provide the connection between Soviet policy on religion and hostility toward the United States or give up this line of argument.

Most evidence is neither as self-evident as the first example nor as questionable as the last. The middle two examples represent the middle ground where you must be particularly careful and on guard.

Careful, honest writers will take pains to make sure their important assumptions are out on the page, in full view for the reader to inspect. Writers who do this gain our trust. Writers who don't make us suspicious: are they lazy? sloppy? shifty?

Where are we likely to find assumptions we ought to analyze? At almost any point, but particularly in the following:

introductory paragraphs
definitions
pivotal or impassioned moments.

Introductory Paragraphs.   At the very beginning of their essays writers often feel the need to justify or defend what they are about to do. They cart out their assumptions for all to see. To establish the common ground with the reader, they state the facts and values in which they believe. In beginning an argument to limit immigration into the United States, the sociologist Garrett Hardin identifies several assumptions:

> Though insisting on their commitment to democracy, most Americans conveniently close their eyes to two facts. First, ours is not a democracy in the original Greek sense but a representative government in which the many vote for a few and then the few make the laws that govern all. The consequences of this arrangement have never been fully worked out in political theory. Particularly—and this brings us to the second aspect of our willful blindness—it should be noted that very frequently the will of the majority can be thwarted for a long time by the normal working of the machinery of representation. The fact deserves the closest study by those who want the will of the majority to prevail. ("Smokescreens and Evasions"; our underlining)

Are these stated assumptions self-evidently true, or are there some hidden assumptions behind *them* that need stating and support?

Definitions.   When writers define their central terms, they can't help bringing important assumptions to light. In his famous essay "The Art of Motion Pictures," Bruno Bettelheim, a Freudian scholar and interpreter of modern culture, selects some movies he finds especially valuable for modern viewers. He tells us that he has picked these particular movies because they offer "an affirmation of man." Immediately he attempts to clarify what he means and reveals some assumptions that we have underlined:

> When I speak of an affirmation of man, I do not mean the presentation of fake images of life as wonderfully pleasant. Life is best celebrated in the form of a battle against its inequities, of struggles, of dignity in defeat, of the greatness of discovering oneself and the other.

Not only has Bettelheim defined the kind of "affirmation" he seeks in pictures, but also he has given us a very important assumption about how life is "best celebrated." This assumption runs forward and backward throughout his essay.

Pivotal or Impassioned Moments.   When an argument heats up at controversial or emotional moments, writers often reveal important beliefs and opinions—again bringing assumptions to light. In the following example, Richard C. Cowan argues that the government itself has been one of the main causes of the current drug crisis—a controversial point indeed. Note all the important assumptions that come to light at this heated moment in his argument:

> The American criminal-justice system, meanwhile, is on the verge of collapse because of drug prohibition. Even if expensive drug habits did not create criminals—and there is no doubt they sometimes do— the cost of illegal drugs certainly increases the number of crimes that criminal addicts must commit. Drugs are without a doubt the most powerful corrupters of the police and the court system. For those who have not been corrupted, the failure of the drug laws to have a positive impact on the drug problem has caused great frustration. This has led to calls for more power to be given to the police, and even for calls for suspending the Constitution. There is no prospect of this happening on a wholesale basis, but our liberties are being incrementally eroded at a rapid pace. The existing and proposed laws constitute the basic elements of a socialist police state. There are already controls on cash and capital transfers, calls for the canceling of hundred dollar bills, violations of the long-standing principle of lawyer-client confidentiality, and the authority to seize the accused's property *before* trial or even *after* acquittal. ("How the Narcs Created Crack"; our underlining)

Note that the author italicized certain words. When writers raise their voices like this, they direct us to important assumptions. Here, Cowan wants us to see the terrible breach of constitutional rights when authorities seize people's property in this way.

Anywhere a writer has something at stake, he or she may well bring assumptions to light. Look carefully at concluding paragraphs—where writers make a last effort to convince readers—and at all moments when the heat rises.

Here are some pieces of advice for dealing with assumptions, the trickiest part of reading:

1. Subject all arguments to intense scrutiny at the beginning to determine whether you share a starting point with the author. Think about a writer's stated assumptions. Are they what you would assume in the same instance? Or do you find them biased? naïve? unreasonable? If you disagree with the assumptions on which the argument is clearly based, you will probably not accept the rest of the argument. If, for instance, you believe desirable social change can come about peacefully, you no doubt will disagree with an essay based on the assumption that change will come only with revolution. But you need to be clear about that assumption.

2. Find and articulate the hidden assumptions. When the tone or angle of a piece strikes you as unusual or unexpected, look carefully to determine what is behind it. When you suddenly find yourself confused

about where an idea came from or why it appears where it does, trace the confusions to their source. Are there missing steps or strange twists? Once you isolate the hidden assumptions, ask yourself whether you share them. You may have spotted a dark corner where an unacceptable assumption lurks.

6. How Strong Is the Support? Evidence

Without some hard evidence, an argument is just talk. (Throughout this book, we have much to say about evidence, and we specifically refer you to Chapter 6 for a detailed discussion.) When you have ascertained the thesis and main supporting point and articulated all the assumptions of a work, you must delve even further and evaluate the evidence that backs up every step in the argument. Be especially tough on the evidence provided for crucial points. Ask each bit of proof the following five questions:

1. *Is it relevant?* Does it directly and unambiguously support the point? Or do you have to make a great leap to determine how the evidence actually supports the point? When the leap is too great, perhaps the evidence doesn't really fit.

2. *Is it accurate?* Three things can produce inaccurate evidence. The first is simple human error. The *Manchester Guardian* once quoted the U.S. secretary of the treasury as saying, "We will make certain that there will be calamities in the banking system." One tiny missing *not* invalidated the evidence. If you find errors in quotations or statistics, begin to wonder about the writer. The second cause of inaccuracy is ignorance. Some writers present obsolete research or peddle pop wisdom as fact. The third cause is plain human guile. Writers may disguise or distort the meaning or context of a piece of evidence, the better to fit it into their argument. You must make sure the evidence is accurate.

3. *Is it specific and detailed?* Vague allusions to "the thinking of Freud" or "the well-known development of South American dictatorships" will never be enough to prove a point. The closer the evidence is to facts, numbers, actual quotations from the text, the better. Demand a thorough analysis of such references as "Freud's notion of the Oedipal complex" or "the strife between the press and the dictatorship of Chile in 1983."

When an author paraphrases rather than quotes another author, be alert. A paraphrase poses tricky questions, since you must trust that it fairly represents the original. Don't just accept it; analyze it. Does the paraphrase sound accurate? Is it enough to make the point believable?

4. *Are the sources for the evidence clear?* You have the right to know the source of all evidence, and the writer has the responsibility to pro-

vide it. We are not suggesting that you look up every reference or follow every footnote. When you hit a surprising or unclear bit of proof, however, pursue it further. If the source is suppressed or vaguely presented, you may begin to doubt the author.

5. *Is there enough support?* Only you can decide whether the author has presented enough proof to persuade you. Withhold your assent until you feel ready to give it. Sheer quantity is not the criterion, however. Sometimes you will find that good arguments are based on quite scanty evidence; sometimes a flood of facts will not suffice. Look for the intelligent commentary that makes the evidence relevant.

7. So What? The Conclusion

The conclusion is the payoff to the argument. Locate it—it is usually in the last few paragraphs or the last chapter of a book, but some writers offer it in a next-to-last section and then discuss its implications in the final section. Some studies in the social and natural sciences offer conclusions in the beginning and then show how the authors reached those conclusions. Track the conclusion down and compare it with the thesis. How has the thesis changed in the conclusion? Does the conclusion surprise you? Can you think of alternative conclusions?

Notice we said "Compare the conclusion with the thesis." Often they are similar; just as often, however, the author has argued the thesis in order to point out a larger significance for his or her piece of writing. The last sentence of Gould's essay on the dinosaur makes an unexpected point:

> Do you know anyone who would wager a substantial sum, even at favorable odds, on the proposition that *Homo sapiens* will last longer than Brontosaurus?

Hardly a person would read that ending without feeling a sudden chill.

Frequently an argument develops from the thesis to the conclusion. Comparing the two is a useful way to keep track of where an argument has led. Here is a very simplified version of the thesis and conclusion of Sigmund Freud's *Civilization and Its Discontents:*

> Thesis: The individual's instincts of aggression and self-destruction inevitably conflict with the prescriptions of civilized life.
>
> Conclusion: Whether instinct will finally triumph over culture is the fateful question facing the human species.

The thesis and the conclusion are similar, but they harbor a crucial difference. The conclusion suggests that unless controlled, the conflict could lead to great problems. It makes no sense to accept the conclusion unless you understand the thesis and believe that the argument has adequately supported it.

If you think creatively, you can sometimes come up with a different conclusion from the one the author has drawn. Here is a hypothetical argument:

> For five years, five rats were forced to breathe in the smoke of sixty cigarettes a day. Of the five rats, four died of lung cancer. For experimental purposes the physiology of rats is close to that of human beings.
> Therefore:

Before reading further, imagine some possible conclusions. The results can be enlightening. Here are just a few:

> You shouldn't do things like that to rats.
>
> Any human being who smokes sixty cigarettes a day for five years has a 20 percent chance of survival.
>
> One out of every five rats has a constitution stronger than that of human beings.
>
> Eighty percent of the rat population will not last five years.
>
> Cigarette smoking may cause cancer in human beings.

All these conclusions follow, more or less validly, from some or all of the evidence. The point of imagining alternatives is that *no conclusions are inevitable.* Your acceptance or rejection of a conclusion will depend on your acceptance or rejection of the author's analysis of the evidence.

8. Was It All Worth It? The Whole Work

When you have finished reading, sit back and take stock of the book or essay and decide what you think of it. Page back through your notes and pause at important points. Carefully examine the evidence. Think about the definitions. Think about the overall argument: was it closely and persuasively reasoned, or were you forced to make some pretty strenuous leaps across the gaps? Was the conclusion justified? When you read critically and actively, you will be in a good position to evaluate even the most illustrious authors.

Evaluating Your Own Writing

These are not questions to ask only of other writers. We need to turn this critical battery on our own writing as well. Ask the same questions of any piece of writing you do. "Do I have a well-defined subject? Do I have a clear purpose for writing the paper? What do I want to accomplish in this essay? Do I have an effective thesis? In fact, do I have a thesis at all? Are my main supporting points appropriate and strong? Do I know what my major assumptions are—and have I clearly set forth these assumptions for the reader to judge? (Check your beginning and concluding paragraphs, your definitions, your impassioned moments.) Is my evidence relevant? accurate? detailed? traceable? adequate? clearly tied to the points I'm trying to prove? Do I have an effective, worthwhile conclusion that follows clearly from the discussion?"

CASE STUDY: CRITICAL READING

This short essay appeared in a textbook, *The West and the World Since 1945*, 4th edition, by Glenn Blackburn. Tom Russo took notes and answered the eight questions as a way of understanding and remembering the points the essay makes.

Why Did Communism Collapse?
Glenn Blackburn

Will explain

The collapse of the Communist system in the Soviet Union and the 1
Eastern European countries was one of the most dramatic, most influential developments of the twentieth century. <u>The collapse was caused</u>

Failure of leadership and quiet rebellion

<u>in part by a failure of leadership and in part by a quiet rebellion in</u> <u>which ordinary people in the Communist countries gradually stopped</u> <u>supporting the Communist governments.</u>

The fundamental cause of the failure of leadership was the Stalin- 2

Main point: rigid bureaucracy

ist system itself, a system so bureaucratically rigid that it did not allow for peaceful change. The system encouraged people to follow orders

Led to economic stagnation and massive environmental degradation

and not take any initiatives. One result was economic stagnation, which gradually led to a decline in the quality of material life. For example, by the late 1960s the Soviet health care system was so ineffective that infant mortality rates began to rise and life expectancy rates to

Examples

decline. Another result was massive environmental degradation, as the Soviet system stressed industrial production and paid little attention to environmental problems. (For details, see the section "The Environ-

Examples cross-referenced in another chapter

mental Problem" in Chapter 2). By the 1980s it was increasingly obvious to many ordinary citizens in the Communist countries that the Communist system was not working very well. Gorbachev believed that the system could be reformed, but he did not realize that the system had already lost much public support. When Communism began

When Gorbachev lost confidence

to collapse in the late 1980s, Gorbachev was unwilling to resort to force to maintain himself in power, so in a sense he also repudiated the Stalinist system, based as it was on coercion and violence.

The quiet rebellion by ordinary people was a gradual process that 3

Main point: began with dissidents

began with the dissident movement—a small collection of artists, intellectuals, environmentalists, and some religious groups—that maintained a moral opposition to the tyranny and brutality of the Commu-

Look up

nist regimes. (Détente) encouraged dissidence, and small human rights groups appeared in the 1970s. Gradually, growing numbers of people

Examples tied to pre-
vious statement by
strong assumptions

found ways to escape the control of Communist authorities. For example, art institutes in Czechoslovakia began to hold competitions in which prizes were awarded by teachers and artists rather than by Communist officials. Another example was books. Communist governments in some Eastern European countries allowed publication of such American novels as John Steinbeck's *Grapes of Wrath* and J. D. Salinger's *Catcher in the Rye,* on the assumption that the books revealed the decadence of American life; but ordinary readers often found such books to be expressions of freedom and creativity. By the

People disaffected

1980s many people had escaped spiritually and morally from the Communist system, in the sense that they no longer took Communist ideology seriously. The spiritual and moral escape was the foundation of the political escape—that is, the actual overthrow of the Communist system.

Other causes
(disclaimer)

There were, of course, many other causes of the collapse of   4 Communism. The costs of maintaining the arms race with the United States helped undermine the Soviet economy. The rebellions of various nationalities helped cause the disintegration of the Soviet econ-

Conclusion repeats
thesis

omy. In the final analysis, however, the most fundamental causes were the failure of leadership and the quiet rebellion by ordinary people.

Response by Tom Russo

1. Subject: the collapse of Communism.
2. Purpose: to explain why the collapse came about.
3. Thesis: that in part failure of leadership and in part loss of citizen support brought about the collapse.
4. Main support: rigid bureaucracy led to stagnation and inefficiency; the "quiet rebellion" allowed "ordinary people" gradually to free themselves from Communist ideology.
5. Assumptions: that the stability of Russia was the major force keeping the Soviet system together; that the same explanation applies to all Communist countries in Eastern Europe; that problems in Communist countries are different from those in other nations.
6. Evidence: health care, industrial and environmental decline, Gorbachev, more open artistic life.
7. Conclusion: basically a repeat of thesis; could have emphasized other aspects, like Cold War expense; ignores worldwide environmental problems and health care problems in the U.S.
8. Worth it? Yes, though maybe the essay oversimplified the situation. But it got across a lot in a few words.

Once Russo had answered these questions, he knew what the essay said and what he thought about it, and he was now ready to write his response.

> **Tips for Critical Reading**
> - Read critically; that is, participate, analyze, interrogate the text.
> - Before starting to read, leaf through the text to get some clues about its most important ideas.
> - To help both understanding and retention, take notes on what you read.
> - Summarize the main ideas and the most important supporting ideas.
> - Use the eight questions to analyze the text.
> - Consider the entire argument when you have finished reading.

EXERCISES FOR CRITICAL READING

1. In a large general encyclopedia, follow all the steps under "Mapping the Text" for one of these entries: Rabindranath Tagore, Omar Khayyám, Lao-tzu. What is the writer's purpose? What is the article's thesis or organizing principle? Are there hidden assumptions that should have been explicit? What is your overall evaluation of the article? Write a short essay on your reading of this text.

2. In the library you will probably find copies of *Dissent, Policy Review, New Criterion, The Nation,* or *National Review.* Using the eight questions, analyze an article from one of these periodicals. Was the article persuasive? Should the author have added anything or made the assumptions more explicit? Write an essay evaluating the article.

3. Using the *Readers' Guide to Periodical Literature,* the *Humanities Index,* the *Social Sciences Index,* or the index to a major newspaper, locate an article or column concerning one of the following controversies:

   changes in search and seizure laws to make it easier for law enforcement officials to discover evidence of a crime
   a constitutional amendment to ensure a balanced budget
   the quality of large cultural awards such as the Pulitzer Prize or the Nobel Prize in literature
   government dispensing to addicts such drugs as cocaine and heroin

   Analyze the article. Would you have preferred a clearer thesis? Was the support adequate? Do you think it should have made its underlying assumptions more explicit? Your answers to these questions could take the form of either a short essay or an in-class report.

4. Here are some definitions. What assumptions underlie them? Do you agree or disagree with any of the definitions? Where you disagree, can you come up with your own definition?

   Graft: The main element in any smoothly running government
   Immorality: What you do that I wish I could do but cannot
   Free enterprise: The same thing as greed

Liberalism: The guilty conscience of people who are well off
Conservatism: The defense of old ideas in the absence of new ones

5. *Time, Newsweek, U.S. News and World Report,* and the *New York Times* "Week in Review" cover some of the same topics. Choose a topic prominent in last week's news and analyze how it was treated in these four publications. Write an essay on the different treatments.

6. Here is another essay by Glenn Blackburn from *The West and the World Since 1945.* Analyze it according to the eight questions.

An Evaluation of the Cold War
Glenn Blackburn

The Cold War lasted from 1945 until 1991. Several times during   1
that period, the United States and the Soviet Union appeared to be close to a military confrontation, notable examples being the Berlin blockade crisis of 1948 and the Cuban missile crisis of 1962. However, fear of nuclear war always impelled the two superpowers to find a way to avoid direct military conflict. In the final analysis, the Cold War was a period of sometimes frightening crises and of a very dangerous arms race, but it never became World War III. American historian John Lewis Gaddis argues that we should refer to 1945–1991 as the "long peace." He notes in particular that, in terms of relationships among the most powerful nations, the years after 1945 were much more stable and peaceful than were the three decades before 1945.

However, the fact that the superpowers did not fight World War   2
III does not mean that the world has been at peace since 1945. According to one count, since 1945 there have been at least eighty wars in the world, killing between fifteen million and thirty million people. Some of those wars, such as the Korean War and the Vietnam War, were a part of the Cold War conflict. Others, such as the Iran-Iraq War of the 1980s, were basically unconnected to the Cold War but were more destructive because of the weapons proliferation engendered by the Cold War. Both the United States and the Soviet Union (and other nations as well) sold or gave increasingly sophisticated weaponry to their allies, and the result was a continued expansion of the amount of military firepower in the world. A recent example of such expansion is the attempt of North Korea to produce an atomic bomb in 1993–1994.

The Cold War also played a part in another deadly phenomenon   3
of the twentieth century, the genocides in which states and/or armies murdered large numbers of people. One estimate is that between 1900 and the late 1980s over 150 million people were killed in mass murder campaigns in various countries. Some mass murders were designed to kill alleged racial or ethnic enemies, examples being the destruction of Jews in Nazi Germany and the killing of Bosnians by Serbs in 1992–1994 (in the former Yugoslavia). Other murder campaigns were aimed at those who opposed, or were thought to oppose, the ruling ideology of a state, the most famous example being the murder of as many as twenty million people directed by Joseph Stalin in the Soviet Union of the 1930s. Still others were wartime atrocities in which victo-

rious soldiers killed the weak and defenseless. Such atrocities occurred in World War II and in the Vietnam War, to give just two examples.

It may be years before historians develop a thorough evaluation of the Cold War years. At this point, the preceding paragraphs would indicate a mixed judgment. The Cold War years of 1945–1991 were more peaceful than the World War years of 1914–1945. Furthermore, the Cold War ended quietly with the collapse of an often-brutal totalitarian empire. On the other hand, the Cold War contributed to a continued increase in the amount of weaponry and military firepower in the world, and that legacy will be with us for some time.

PART TWO

From Start to Finish
The Writing Process

4

Getting Ready to Write

What we need to learn to do we learn by doing.
— ARISTOTLE (384–322 B.C.)
GREEK PHILOSOPHER

Writing is both a thing we read and an action we perform, a product and a process. As readers, we look at the product. We want to know what is being said and how well. As writers, however, we must look at the process. We want to be sure that we are getting across what we want to say and that what we want to say is worth reading.

The writing process is a continuing development, a growing through time, one stage shaped by the preceding stage and shaping the following. No two writers go through the process in exactly the same manner. One may have a rich fund of ideas but may need to make several drafts and revisions. Another may find that ideas come slowly but once they arrive the rest is easy. And the process may vary according to subject and occasion. If, for instance, an instructor assigns an explicit topic, you will not need to find your own. If you are required to hand in a first draft, you will not revise.

But in most cases the writing process occurs in four stages:

generating ideas

settling on a subject and thesis

getting the ideas written

getting the writing right

Writers do not always follow this order: sometimes in drafting an essay the writer discovers a better subject; sometimes the most effective ideas are generated during revision. But almost all writing goes through these stages in one way or another.

Before discussing the four stages, we want to discuss two concerns all writers must bear in mind: purpose and audience. No matter what kind of writing we do, we write with a purpose and for an audience. These concerns provide the context for the whole process and govern what we say and how we say it.

Lord, let me shake with purpose.
—JAMES DICKEY (B. 1923)
AMERICAN POET AND NOVELIST

PURPOSE: THE AIMS OF WRITING

Behind all good writing is a writer with a purpose. The purpose is like the destination of a journey. Where do we want to end up? with what effect? And how can we best get there?

Our overall purpose in all kinds of writing is to learn what we think and to communicate it. This means we have to get the facts clear, distinguish the important from the trivial, recognize relationships and hierarchies, and write correct and interesting prose. Sometimes our true purpose will emerge in the process of writing. We may need a few paragraphs or even a full draft before we know our destination, as when on a journey we take a wrong turn. But when we hold our destination in mind, we find the whole process easier. What Aristotle said about speech making holds for writing: our purpose will usually be to report, to explain, or to persuade.

Almost all the writing you will do in school—and most of your writing after you graduate—will have one of these purposes. You may be asked to *report* on the contents of a book or on the performance and results of an experiment. You may be asked to *explain* the causes of war or rust or inflation. You may want to *persuade* someone that the sound of the clarinet is more beautiful than the sound of the oboe or that careerism is destroying education.

Often you will have several purposes to bear in mind within a single piece of writing. In an essay on inflation, for instance, you may need one section to *report* a particular example of inflation—say, the last twenty years in Israel—one section to *explain* how inflation generally works, and one section to *persuade* your reader to undertake a specific course of action to stop inflation.

To Report

Good reporting is a faithful, detailed account of something. By *faithful,* we mean presenting the facts as truthfully as we can. Just as though we were witnesses in a court of law, we swear to tell the truth, the whole truth, and nothing but the truth. We do not repress the unpleasant or the contradictory. We do not distort in order to support a point of view.

By *detailed,* we mean presenting specific and concrete facts. When statistics are relevant, we cite them. When the story is at issue, we narrate. When how something looked is important, we describe it as exactly and vividly as we can. We try to bring the reader close to the subject.

Sometimes we will base a report on firsthand information, as we might if we were documenting a psychological experiment, describing a sporting event, or narrating an episode from our lives. Sometimes we will base a report on information gleaned from books or articles, as we would if we were relating a marriage ceremony in Ghana or describing the devastation in Sarajevo. However we obtain our information, we must bear our purpose in mind: to tell the facts. (For more on reporting, see Chapter 15, Writing in All Disciplines: The Report.)

To Explain

Explaining goes beyond simply presenting facts to include interpreting, accounting for, and making sense of them. If we were only reporting on the Black Death, which historians say killed 20 million people beginning in 1347, we might write,

> Sufferers from the plague exhibited swellings the size of an orange in their groin or armpit. Sometimes victims lasted five days; sometimes they were dead within twenty-four hours.

Something concrete and physical, like the appearance of the victims, can be reported, that is, described and narrated in a straightforward manner. But if something is obscure or complex, the reader will probably need more information, placing the event or idea in a larger context or showing how it functions and why it happened. In discussing the Black Death, for instance, we might want to explain where it came from and how it affected victims, and so we might write,

> The disease was brought to Italy by infected rats from Eastern ports. Fleas carried by these rats infected other rats and people. The plague affected three areas of the body: the lymph glands, the lungs, and the blood.

Now we show what caused the plague and what it caused. We indicate the process and the principles by which it worked. We show the relation of the parts to the whole and to each other. Within the word *explain* lies the idea of making obscure or complex things *plain*.

Explanation is a large part of most college papers. In a chemistry class, you might explain how the nonmetallic element bromine works on metals and on skin or what other elements it combines with to do what. In an American history class you might explain Lyndon Johnson's decision to withdraw from the presidential campaign in 1968. In a communications class, you could explain how Microsoft's marketing strategies changed with Windows 95. Virtually every paper requires some form of explanation.

To Persuade

Persuasion builds on both accurate reporting and clear explanation. In addition, it requires the ability to identify the crucial issues, muster the supporting evidence, and present the whole so that it appeals to both reason and emotion. Only then will we achieve our purpose: to convince the reader that our view of a controversial issue is a reasonable one.

Many college papers will require you to take a position on a debatable subject and defend it. Suppose you were to write about Russian politics and to identify responsibility for Russia's troubles. You would first report the facts and then explain the country's political history, the legacy of the Communist dictatorship, the role of the military, and the effect of U.S. policy as well as that of other nations. Then you would reason carefully to show how the facts lead to your assessment of the responsibility.

You would also need to discuss these controversial issues in the right tone, using the words appropriate to your own feeling and conviction. Part of the purpose of a persuasive essay is to get the reader to feel the emotion the writer feels—joy, anger, indignation. Emotion can be a helpful tool in constructing an essay. It can also be dangerous. It cannot be ignored. (We have more to say on this issue in Chapter 1, The Critical Sense, and Chapter 7, Making the Argument.)

Tips for Purpose
- As you write, keep your purpose in mind.
- When reporting, concentrate on accuracy.
- When explaining, concentrate on clarity.

> • When persuading, remember that you must appeal to both reason and emotion.

EXERCISES FOR PURPOSE

1. Think of an intense experience you had within the past year and report it as factually as possible. Who was there? Exactly what happened? In your last paragraph, evaluate your ability to be objective in recounting the experience. Would another observer have reported it differently?

2. Write one paragraph *explaining* why you decided to attend your present school. Write a second paragraph *reporting* on your first week of classes. Now write a third paragraph *persuading* the reader your decision was correct.

3. Read the following three opening paragraphs and identify the purpose of each—whether to report, to explain, or to persuade. What elements point specifically and clearly to each passage's purpose? In passages that strike you as attempting to be persuasive, identify the specific sentences and words that express emotion. Write a paragraph in which you justify your assessment of one of the paragraphs.

The environmental crisis tells us that there is something seriously wrong with the way in which human beings have occupied their habitat, the earth. The fault must lie not with nature, but with man. For no one has argued, to my knowledge, that the recent advent of pollutants on the earth is the result of some natural change independent of man. Indeed, the few remaining areas of the world that are relatively untouched by the powerful hand of man are, to that degree, free of smog, foul water, and deteriorating soil. Environmental deterioration must be due to some fault in the human activities on the earth. (Barry Commoner, *The Closing Circle: Nature, Man, and Technology*)

Niagara Falls is a city of unmatched natural beauty; it is also a tired industrial workhorse, beaten often and with a hard hand. A magnificent river—a strait, really—connecting Lake Erie to Lake Ontario flows hurriedly north, at a pace of a half-million tons a minute, widening into a smooth expanse near the city before breaking into whitecaps and taking its famous 186-foot plunge. Then it cascades through the gorge of overhung shale and limestone to rapids higher and swifter than anywhere else on the continent. (Michael Brown, *Laying Waste: The Poisoning of America by Toxic Chemicals*)

Sagebrush and lizards rattle and whisper behind me. I stand in the moonlight, the hot desert at my back. It's tomato harvest time, 3 A.M. The moon is almost full and near to setting. Before me stretches the first lush tomato field to be taken this morning. The field is farmed by a company called Tejo Agricultural Partners, and lies three hours northeast of Los Angeles in the middle of the bleak, silver drylands of California's San Joaquin Valley. Seven hundred sixty-six acres, more than a mile square of tomatoes—a shaggy vegetable-green rug dappled with murky red dots, 105,708,000 ripe tomatoes lurking in the night. The field is large and absolutely level. It would take an hour and a half to walk around it. Yet, when I raise my eyes past the field to the much vaster valley floor, and to the mountains that loom farther out, the enormous crop is lost in a big flat world. (Mark Kramer, *Making Milk, Meat, and Money*)

I shot an arrow into the air,
It fell to earth, I knew not where.
> — HENRY WADSWORTH LONGFELLOW
>   (1807–1882)
>   AMERICAN POET

AUDIENCE:
IS ANYONE OUT THERE LISTENING?

Although writing and talking are similar, there is one enormous difference: when we talk, we have that other person sitting there asking questions, interrupting, responding with body language as well as with words. We probably know something about that person, including prejudices and cherished values. As we speak, we naturally adjust what we say to fit the listener.

Similarly, when writing we must adjust to the reader. In writing a personal letter, we have an image of the recipient and gauge the most effective way to reach him or her. A student visiting in Italy might want to express the glories of the trip. To her close friend, she might send a postcard of the Tuscany countryside, describing a bicycle ride down the mountain in the rain. The student might send her mother a postcard of Giotto's *Madonna and Child,* saying she had been to the Uffizi Gallery twice and this was her favorite painting. Both true, both wonderful examples, but different—because the readers are different.

Most people find writing an essay more perilous than talking or sending postcards. We may not have a clear idea of the purpose or know what the reader needs to be told. We may not even know who the reader is. Too often, we don't think of our writing as communicating with a reader. When we have to write, we just start in. No wonder writing frequently seems scattered, unfocused, far from any target.

Sometimes an instructor will set up the target. One instructor we know tells students, "Think of the reader as an intelligent person, familiar with the subject but not expert, and eager to know what you think most important or misunderstood about it." Another says, "I want you to prove to me you understand the basic concepts." A third says, "Write for your classmates. Give them what they need in order to understand your position." More likely, however, the instructor will say something like "Write a five- to seven-page paper on some aspect of the subject that catches your fancy." And you start shooting arrows.

Stop. Lay down your quiver and bow until you have set up your target.

You may not have a *specific* reader in mind when you write, but imagining an audience is still important for focus. When you are not sure for whom you are writing, try to imagine the following all-purpose audience. Write for readers who are

between your age and 120

as familiar as you are with your topic

interested in your topic

respectful but skeptical—that is, they are open to your viewpoint but remain to be convinced

liable to be disconcerted by errors in fact, grammar, or usage.

Writing for such a specific audience allows you to write sincerely and straightforwardly. It frees you from having to explain absolutely everything from the beginning, so that you can focus on the essential. Finally, it obligates you to work, to prove your points, and to write well, correctly, and persuasively.

With your target reader in mind, think about these questions:

What do my readers know, and what do they need to know?

What ideas and information do my readers and I share?

Will I need to argue about values?

What level of detail will be necessary?

What response do I want, and what can I expect from my readers? respect? amusement? agreement? action? feeling?

What kind of language will elicit the response I desire?

Are technical items appropriate?

What illustrations and examples will achieve the desired effect?

These questions boil down to two very important ones: How much and what kind of information must I supply to this audience? And what kind of writing will be most appealing?

Suppose you were writing a persuasive essay calling for more nuclear power plants. If you were writing for a professor of physics, you could assume a good deal of scientific knowledge and a familiarity with the technical terms as well as the background of the debate. You would not, for instance, need to define the difference between fusion and fission unless showing your knowledge was a purpose of the assignment, but you would need to treat the economics of the various forms of energy, a subject in which your professor may not have expertise. And because you were writing for a scientific audience, you probably would attempt to sound objective and judicious.

If, however, you were writing the same essay for a wider, less specialized audience, you would take a different tack. You would probably define in simple terms the difference between the two kinds of nuclear energy. Furthermore, you would make a major effort to examine the safety of nuclear power plants. And you might mention how savings from using nuclear energy could be used for other programs, such as highway construction, child care, and so on. At appropriate points, you would probably make an effort to write with feeling.

We are not suggesting that you shape your opinions and values to please your audience. Your writing would be worthless if it only reinforced someone else's ideas. It becomes worthwhile when it carries your conviction about a significant subject. What is important to you is exactly what your reader wants to know. The goal is to persuade your audience to *your* way of looking at something or *your* plan for doing something. To reach that goal, you must bear your audience in mind throughout the writing process.

Tips for Audience

- Visualize your reader before you start writing.
- When you are not sure who your audience is, write for someone informed, interested, respectful, skeptical, and liable to be disconcerted by errors.
- Ask yourself how much background your reader needs.
- Decide what details will appeal to that particular audience.
- As you write, stop occasionally to think about your reader.

EXERCISES FOR AUDIENCE

1. Select one of the topics below. Decide whether you will argue for or against it. Now consider Reader 1. Compile a list of the points that would best make your case with Reader 1, and then write a paragraph arguing that case for that audience. Now repeat the process for Reader 2 and Reader 3, maintaining your pro or con stance.
   a. Topic: a more stringent grading policy for college papers
      Reader 1: president of your institution
      Reader 2: an instructor you now have
      Reader 3: a fellow student
   b. Topic: a proposal to allow oil drilling in Yellowstone National Park
      Reader 1: president of the United States
      Reader 2: head of the Union of Oil Workers
      Reader 3: a member of the Friends of the Earth conservation group
   c. Topic: a proposal to allow marijuana to be used as pain relief for terminally ill cancer patients
      Reader 1: president of the American Medical Association
      Reader 2: director of the FBI
      Reader 3: a local pastor

2. Imagine that last night, while kidding around, your friend balanced your typewriter or word processor on the windowsill and it fell two floors to a

cement driveway. Write letters explaining this event to your mother or father, the dean of the school, and your best friend at another institution. To each, tell the truth, the whole truth, and nothing but the truth. Write up a brief analysis of the differences.

Most of the basic material a writer works with is acquired before the age of fifteen.
— WILLA CATHER (1873-1947)
AMERICAN NOVELIST

INVENTION: GENERATING IDEAS

As soon as we are required to write on a particular topic, many of us find writing the last thing in the world we want to do and our topic the least interesting. And, of course, the more we resent or fear the task, the more difficult, going on impossible, it is to get started.

A first step to getting started is to find a way to care about the subject. If the writer does not care, the reader will not care either. And caring is almost impossible to fake. Yes, we can be sure all the commas are screwed into place and the topic sentences all present and accounted for. But mechanical or surface correctness, though necessary, is not sufficient for good writing. Unless we write about something that engages our imagination and intelligence, our writing will be sluggish, dough-like, dull.

No matter what the subject, there is apt to be something to engage us. "Nothing human is alien to me," said the Roman dramatist Terrence. And nothing need be inaccessible to any of us. Some would probably groan audibly if asked to write on the Spanish-American War, the fight against malaria, or *Moby-Dick*. But we could probably find in the recesses of our imagination a way in which each of those subjects could interest us: the dissolution of the Spanish Empire or the beginnings of American imperialism; the selfless desire to eradicate disease or the economic costs of poor health; the destructive power of obsession or the courage of seamanship.

Almost every subject is multifaceted. When we enter the writing task with sincerity and an open mind, we can discover something that will stimulate our imagination and generate energy. Our ideas find roots in the real world. We begin to see enriching connections. We enjoy writing much more.

In the following pages, we describe six invention techniques that may help you discover your way into a subject:

> brainstorming
>
> free writing
>
> clustering
>
> designing a topic tree
>
> directed questioning
>
> using a journal

You can use these techniques at almost any point in the writing process. They can help you get ideas, see connections, discover evidence, even organize an essay. Not every one will work for all writers or under all circumstances. Tried seriously, one of them may help you break up a mental logjam.

We end this section by discussing journals, which many writers have used as workshops in which to mine and refine ideas.

Brainstorming

The word *brainstorming* usually refers to the way a group of people—movie writers, advertising agents, political advisers—throw ideas and questions at one another, banging out the shape of a project or generating ideas to solve a problem. Writers, too, can brainstorm, alone or with friends. Brainstorming requires an open mind, a fearless attack on a subject, and a tolerance for some temporarily disordered searching.

Although brainstorming follows no set pattern, you might try this four-step process. First, think about the general subject: to the best of your ability, rid your mind of extraneous ideas. Second, jot down as many questions about the subject as you can think of, whether you know the answers or not. Third, narrow in on the questions that spark your imagination, and make brief notes on the answers, if any. Don't bother with full sentences or attempt perfect mechanics. Just try to generate a mass of questions and ideas, however outrageous and remote. Fourth, now that you have narrowed your focus, go through the process again in the area you find most interesting. This process may lead you to an idea you want to pursue in an essay.

The following is an example of some brainstorming Allen Parker did on the subject of high-school education. Since brainstorming often takes the form of scratch lists, Parker's first effort looked like this:

> boring as a whole
>
> pace of instruction too slow
>
> science classes slightly better—still too slow
>
> a few of us wanted to go faster
>
> frustrating
>
> AP Calculus best
>
> we could move as fast as we wanted

teacher humorous

Chemistry fun

Mrs. Carcione: excellent teacher: funny: good examples

examples very important

English worst

After a rather desultory start, he warmed to the process and began to get closer to something interesting. Why, he began to wonder, had English been the "worst"? More brainstorming:

English worst

being a science and math person, I'm not as interested

I'm not much for grammar and classic literature

English is a Catch-22

you need it, but it's frustrating

people like me want answers that are generally constant

Unsystematic as this brainstorming was, it brought out unexpected ideas or points and perspectives the brainstormer might otherwise have missed. Once Parker brainstormed "you need it, but it's frustrating," the point he found most interesting, he was much closer to beginning to write a paper on his experience as a scientist in English class.

 Computer Tip

On the computer, brainstorming can easily turn into directed free writing (see below). Start with a list of brainstormed items. Put a few inches of space between each item and use each as a heading for further brainstorming. Use italics, **boldface**, underlining, or different fonts to emphasize promising new ideas.

Freewriting

If brainstorming leaves you with questions but no clear direction, try freewriting. It is similar to brainstorming, but it can offer a steadier vision of your subject.

Free writing, as developed by Peter Elbow, is based on the notion that writing is a process and that you may need to be in the process, writing and rewriting, to find out what you think and know. This notion has much in common with the saying "How do I know what I think until I hear what I've said?"

The method is called freewriting because you write for a designated period completely free of censorship or editing. You do not stop writing for any reason. You do not think about what you are writing; you just write. Evaluating your ideas or your sentences before or during the writing may abruptly halt the flow of words. Just let yourself go—no one else will read or judge what you write. Try to get as much out as you can, regardless of form. Editing will come later, after you recognize what you really want to say.

You can freewrite as long as you like, but of course you should make sure you stick to the designated task and the time you establish. Here is a freewriting procedure that we think works very well:

With the overall subject firmly in mind, write for ten consecutive minutes without lifting your pen. Put down anything that pops into your head, relevant or irrelevant, sense or nonsense. In fact, don't even think about relevance and sense at this stage. Don't judge; keep writing. If your mind goes blank, write "My mind is a blank on subject X, my mind is a blank on subject X . . ." and keep on writing it until your mind begins to function. Don't let your hand stop writing.

Instead of brainstorming on the subject of secondary education, Erin Samuelson tried freewriting and came up with this after the first ten-minute period:

> Overall I really enjoyed my high school education my fa-
> vorite English teacher was Mrs. Obermiller and I had her
> for two years a caring and interesting person my favorite
> subject became Math: I liked the teacher and did well in
> the class but then in Senior year I had a bad teacher.
> That's when I began to hate Math and now am not sure what
> my favorite subject is. Also I liked Criminal Justice,
> again, a really down to earth teacher who could relate
> with us well, and I did well in the class. As Freshman,
> my class got picked on and when we came to be seniors for
> some reason the principal took away our privileges, so
> now we couldn't do the same to the new freshmen. Some of
> the teachers needed to retire. You can tell this because
> they no longer show care or interest in their students,
> who show no care or interest in their class. I was really
> upset when we graduated. Well, excited for a change but
> there were so many good things already it was hard to say
> goodbye I don't regret a thing.

We recommend taking a five-minute break after the first ten-minute nonstop effort. Then read what you have written. Some of it may sound like gibberish. But you will very often find something worth thinking about. Underline that passage or idea and begin again, again writing freely without stopping or editing. Erin Samuelson was attracted to what made her math teacher so good:

```
I just remembered the name of my good math teacher: Mrs.
Potter. For some strange reason I had her for my first 3
years. Her class was serious but also laid-back and she
didn't seem to have to work to earn students respect.
That was when I decided to be a mathematics major, or did
until the next year at least. The reason I think I did as
well as I did was her pushing hard and supporting me at
the same time. That gave me the idea that I could do it.
That I had the brains. Sometimes you look at something
hard and just figure I can't do it and it is such a sur-
prise when you find out you can. You learn about the sub-
ject and about yourself.
```

After the second writing, again do something else for five minutes. Then read what you have written, think about it, and repeat the ten-minute exercise.

By the end of the third step, you will probably be honing in on a subject. In our example, Erin Samuelson was ready to concentrate on the elements that make for an effective mathematics teacher. After going through the process yet again, she was ready to state a thesis, the specific point her essay would make:

```
The key to teaching a technical subject like math is main-
taining a balance between being serious and being informal,
and a balance between being demanding and being supportive.
```

Keep repeating the exercise until your ideas have crystallized and you have developed a line of thought or at least recognized what material you need. You may need to go through the process four or five times. At the end, flesh out your ideas with the necessary support, arrange them appropriately, revise, and polish.

🖥 Computer Tip

When freewriting on a computer, try turning off the monitor and simply writing as the ideas come to you for ten minutes. When done, turn on your screen and see what you have written. Repeat the process as you would when writing longhand.

Another computer freewriting technique is to use split screens or multiple windows to display two documents at once. Put your notes in one window and start freewriting in the second. If you are responding to a short text, type the text into one window and respond in the other.

Freewriting doesn't work equally well for all writers. It seems most helpful to those who cannot decide on a thesis and who find themselves blocked when faced with a blank page.

Clustering

Clustering is somewhere between freewriting and the more systematic forms of invention. It works best when you have a topic—perhaps one assigned by an instructor—but no clear ideas about it. Suppose you are asked to write on high-school education. If the ideas are not exactly flowing, take a sheet of paper and somewhere near the middle write "high-school education." Circle the words. Now think about your own high-school education. As other ideas emerge—topics, memories, images, names—jot them down anywhere on the paper (see Figure 4.1).

After you have a number of ideas, circle the ones you find most in-

Figure 4.1   Clustering

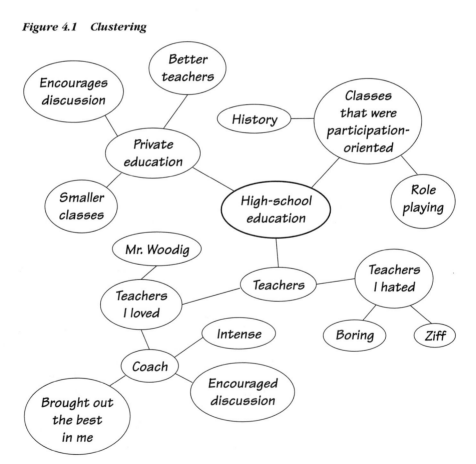

triguing and begin to make clusters around them. In his cluster, Hal Bialeck started with "high-school education" and branched off to "teachers" and then to "teachers I loved," where he formed a new cluster of names. One of these, "Coach," led to "intense," "encouraged discussion," and "brought out the best in me." Make clusters around each of your subordinate ideas. Now you can do one of two things: note which ideas are connected and cluster around the connection, or choose a phrase, image, or idea that appeals to you, write it on another sheet of paper, and do the clustering process all over again.

As you cluster and connect, you will find your ideas getting more and more specific and insightful. Hal Bialeck has promising clusters around "private education" and "teachers I loved." Either of these might become a paper topic.

🖳 Computer Tip

Unless you have an interfaced drawing pad on your computer, cluster the old fashioned way, with pen and paper. Don't waste valuable time trying to perform this task electronically. This same advice applies to designing topic trees (see below).

Designing a Topic Tree

The topic tree combines elements of brainstorming, clustering, and directed questioning (see the next section). To make a topic tree, draw a diagram of your topic that resembles a tree. First, draw the "trunk," which is your general subject. Now draw the tree's main "branches"— that is, general aspects of your topic. You'll have to brainstorm these. Keep the number of main branches small, or your tree will turn into a tangled mess. In the case of education, four main branches might be the aims, benefits, drawbacks, and illusions of education. From these main branches, draw examples of the main divisions. The only rule is that a branch must be directly related to the subject from which it branches. At any time, you can "break off a branch" and use it as a "slip" from which to start a new tree. Figure 4.2 shows what a topic tree for education might look like. Topic trees help you see your topic grow before your eyes. They can be useful ways to elaborate on a subject.

Directed Questioning

When you aren't sure how to approach a subject, try directed questioning. Instead of encouraging your mind to go where it will, with this

Figure 4.2   Topic Tree

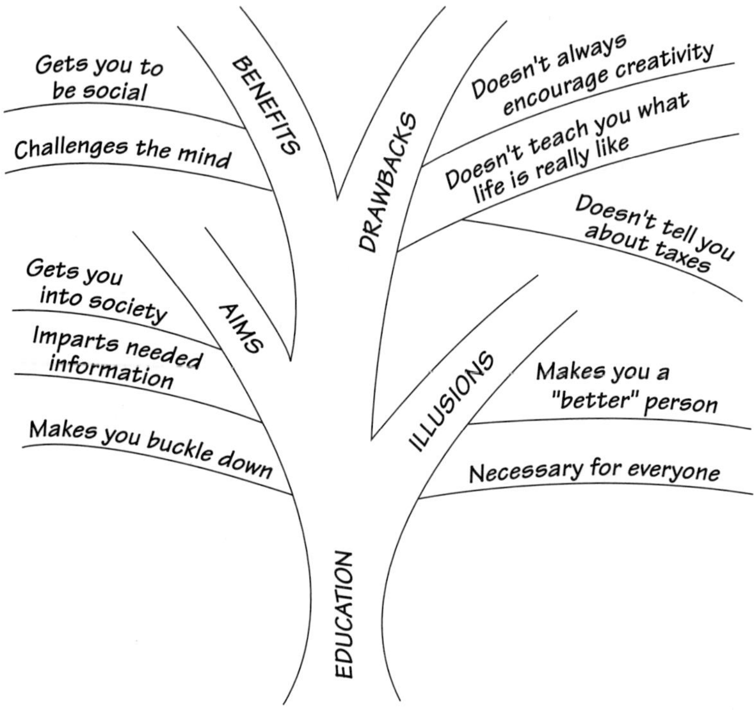

Gets you to
be social

BENEFITS

DRAWBACKS

Doesn't always
encourage creativity

Challenges the mind

Doesn't teach you what
life is really like

Doesn't tell you
about taxes

Gets you
into society

AIMS

Imparts needed
information

ILLUSIONS

Makes you a
"better" person

Makes you buckle down

Necessary for everyone

EDUCATION

method you close in on the major points. For when you have your basic
ideas in mind, you want to limit and focus, not search and expand. Two
directed questioning techniques are the journalistic method and the classical method.

The Journalistic Method.   The journalistic method simply answers six
questions: who? what? when? where? why? how? Asking these questions
may help to narrow your focus and order your thoughts. The questions
will prove particularly useful when you narrate or describe human
events. (We discuss this important method fully in Chapter 15, Writing in
All Disciplines: The Report.)

The Classical Method.   Many teachers suggest that rhetorical devices
used by the ancient Greeks and Romans can help today's writers. These
devices were, not surprisingly, forms of critical thinking. The ancients
analyzed a topic by using definition, comparison, relationship, and testimony. You will get to know some of these devices later as "strategies"
you can use to construct a paragraph. Using them to analyze a subject
can help you develop ideas about it. If the student who wrote on sec-

ondary education had used the classical method for invention, his questions and answers might have followed this pattern:

Definition—What is it? What isn't it? What are its characteristics? What are its parts? Are there concealed implications or values? Are all the terms sufficiently clear?

He might have started with the dictionary definition: "The process of being trained or gaining knowledge through a formal or informal course of instruction." Then he might have gone on to think about that definition:

> Suppose I learned how to shoplift—is that education? How can you tell the difference between a good education and a bad one? I think it's what you know. How well adjusted you are to society. Whether or not you have skills so you can support yourself afterward. Some people would not agree. Definitions vary from person to person.

Comparison—How does your subject resemble something else and how does it differ? Are the differences trivial or significant? Is the comparison compelling enough for an entire essay?

> Education is like other ways of socializing people to participate in society, like joining the army or becoming a member of a club. Going to school is not the only way to get an education. You could listen to informed people, read books and magazines, get some on-the-job training. But school is different. Maybe because so much of what goes on is brain training, which you may get occasionally in these other activities but only incidentally.

Relationship—What preceded and what followed the subject? What were its causes and what were its consequences? What events happened at the same time, and how did they relate to the subject?

> What precedes education is not being educated. What happens at the same time? Well: life. While learning one kind of thing in school you learn other things outside. Everything from how to play the xylophone to how to fly a plane. But inside and outside often connect. What follows education is what the debate is all about: happiness? maturity? success? or being a cog in the economic machine?

Testimony—What has previously been said and written on this issue? Have opinions changed over time? How does your view differ from "received" or conventional opinion? Why?

> Plenty has been said and written, including "A little learning is a dangerous thing." Ideas about education are always changing. Once teachers would try anything in class, but they are getting conservative. Seems to be a pendulum, from conservative to liberal and back. And that is good. When new ideas are being tried, even when they are really old ideas, students get more interested.

The student would have covered vast territory. Depending on his interests and impulses, he could select any of his answers as a starting point.

He could compare the structured learning in school with the unstructured learning out of school, or he could trace the various changes in schoolroom tactics. The advantage of the classical method is that it puts ideas into categories and directs that all-important fund of ideas, daydreaming.

Using a Journal

Many writers use journals as part of their personal writing process. A journal can be many things: diary, notebook, drawing board. We direct you, however, to the root word *jour* in *journal*. French for *day,* this word reminds us that a journal is a place for daily writing. To keep a journal is to commit yourself to writing frequently and regularly.

One excellent use of a writing journal is as an invention workshop. Here is where you can brainstorm, freewrite, cluster, grow topic trees, outline, or use the journalistic or classical questions. Journals are fine places for writing without a thesis. Often the best way to start thinking about something is to start writing about it. In your journal, you can identify potential in your unfinished ideas. No one will see what you write without your permission. So why not speculate? wonder aloud? explore?

Your journal is a good place to revisit and solidify what you learn in class. Here is where you can summarize class meetings; note where you started and ended; identify the main question or discovery of that day's meeting; note high points and questions to ask next time; write down what you think.

Your journal can be useful even after you have received a grade on your paper. You can meditate on your instructor's response, rewrite passages, speculate on new directions, plan and draft a revision. One journal-keeper we know routinely treats her concluding paragraph as the *introduction* to a new paper.

Here are some other related techniques:

Writing Diary.   Record times and places of activities related to assigned writing: when you did research, when you read, when you began to write. Note difficulties, holes in your research, questions. Note your responses as you write. How do you think it's going? What do you wish you were doing better? What interests you most? Where do you feel most and least confident? Write out a paragraph and then evaluate it. Many writers like to do so with their introductory paragraphs. ("Not a bad first try, but I need a better opening line and some more examples.")

Reading Workshop.   Before you read, recall preparatory notes from class; note your expectations, your goals in reading, and, if any, your anxieties. While reading, note surprises, interesting issues, striking quotations, obscure or confusing points, things you want to ask classmates or instructors about. Free-write in response to passages with which you strongly agree or disagree. After reading, summarize or outline what you have read. When reading literature, try interpreting on the spot. Speculate on the meaning of metaphors, allusions, unfamiliar turns of phrase.

Collaborative Journals.   With a classmate, write a journal in which you share ideas, argue over interpretations, speculate together on confusions and perplexities, plan questions or research strategies, or show each other drafts.

⌨ Computer Tip

You may elect to keep your journal on a computer, particularly if you are a good typist. Here are some common ways to keep an electronic journal:

- **Electronic notebook.** This method works best if you have a laptop, which can go just about anywhere. Build this electronic journal just as you would a longhand one, but exploit its capabilities. Build your list of works cited as you read, for example, and store your notes in organized files for easy reference. Just remember: always keep a backup of your electronic notebook on disk — not on your hard drive.
- **E-mail.** Many classmates keep running collaborative journals, sending their entries back and forth on a daily basis.
- **Chat groups and bulletin boards.** Sometimes whole classes will create chat groups in which all members of the group keep up a running conversation on the major topics of the class. Some classes have even created home pages at which other interested parties (experts, students, instructors) can join in.

All of these practices can lead to promising ideas. All of them qualify as invention. Using a journal may seem like "just more work." Indeed it is more work, but helpful work. Journals can be veritable smithies of thinking/reading/writing.

Tips for Invention

- There is nothing about which you have nothing to say; you only need to find a way to care about a subject.
- Keep an open mind about all the techniques of invention: brainstorming, freewriting, clustering, designing a topic tree, directed questioning, and using a journal.
- Remember that one technique may be effective for one kind of task, another for another kind.

■■■■■■■ **EXERCISES FOR INVENTION** ■■■■■■■■■■■■■■■■■

1. From the following topics, choose one that interests you and free-write on it
    for ten minutes. Read what you have written, and select the idea you find
    most interesting. Using it as your starting point, free-write on it for another
    ten minutes. Stop again and select the most appealing sentence. Free-write
    on it for a final ten minutes.

    heroes
    temptations to lie or steal
    being a foreigner
    how parenting has changed
    why biology, or any academic subject, is fascinating

2. Write a paragraph in which you describe doing Exercise 1. Was it easier or
    harder to free-write the second and third times? Did you develop un-
    expected ideas? Look at your first free writing. What ideas might you
    have pursued instead of the one you did? Why did you choose the one you
    did?

3. This exercise takes a partner. Agree on one of the following topics, and
    then brainstorm separately for ten minutes. Compare your notes. List the
    ideas and images that appear on both sheets. Which seem most promising
    as writing topics? Choose one of these items and repeat the process. Now
    each of you write an essay on an item from the second brainstorming list.
    Compare the two essays and account for the differences. What choices did
    each of you make? Why?

    entering a party full of strangers
    the hazards of exercising
    taking responsibility for your actions
    the value of intramural sports

4. Take notes on a particular topic and store them in your computer. A day
    later use your notes for twenty minutes of free writing. Using the split
    screen or multiple windows feature, transfer the most important passage to
    the second document and free-write again. Repeat the process. Now write a
    short essay based on your free writing.

5. Cluster ideas around one of these general topics. From this first cluster, pick
    an idea and cluster another set of ideas around it. Choose one of the ideas
    in this second cluster and cluster ideas around it. Write an essay on an idea
    in your third cluster. Explain your choice. (You may substitute the topic tree
    for this exercise.)

    foreign policy
    intercollegiate athletics
    imports from Asia
    studying philosophy

6. The classical method was originally used to generate ideas from general
    topics. Try it on one of the following: civil disobedience, faithfulness in
    marriage, racial diversity, the Third World, social welfare programs. Now
    write an essay on one of these topics. At the end of the essay, discuss
    which strategy—definition, comparison, and so on—was most fruitful.
    Which led you to your topic? Why?

7. Using a journal as a writing diary, track your progress on your next writing assignment from the time you receive the assignment until the time you turn in your paper. Then write an essay in which you discuss whether or not journal keeping helped you write the paper, and why.

5

Putting Words on Paper

Any writer overwhelmingly honest about pleasing
himself is almost sure to please others.
— MARIANNE MOORE (1887–1972)
AMERICAN POET

SUBJECT AND THESIS:
SAYING SOMETHING

Generating ideas is a first step toward writing, but once you have a fund
of possibilities, you need to decide which idea or ideas are worth writing about.

If there is nothing to say, there is no point writing. All of us know
people—and some of us have dear friends—who chatter on about
nearly nothing. We put up with it because we love the person or the
voice is soothing or the sound serves as a cover for our thoughts. But
imagine finding that same chatter in print. We would not read it.

Writing worth reading must have both a worthwhile subject and a
thesis. The invention methods we discussed in Chapter 4 may help a
writer settle on a subject and an approach before he or she actually begins to write. Frequently, however, something worth saying does not
precede the writing. In the act of writing, you may come upon the subject meant just for you. Putting sentences or paragraphs onto the paper
may continue the invention process.

The Subject

The subject of an essay is often the "given" of a writing assignment. It may be as broad as the title of a course: "United States Foreign Policy after the Cold War," "Abnormal Psychology," "Classical Greece." Just think of the possible ramifications of those topics. Classical Greece could include anything from structures of daily life or political organizations to philosophy or literature. And any one of these would be enormous. Greek philosophy, for instance, covers hundreds of years and dozens of important thinkers. You would have to narrow the subject to a size commensurate with your knowledge, your interests, the time you can allot, and the instructor's expectations.

Sometimes instructors provide a narrow subject with built-in limits that tell you where you can and cannot go. These limits, implicit and explicit, help you focus in on the subject. Even then, you have to do some narrowing of your own. Suppose you receive this assignment in the Classical Greece course:

> Compare the preoccupations and methods of Socrates with those of the pre-Socratic philosophers. Six to eight pages.

This is a huge topic. Books have been written on it and barely scratched the surface. A whole army of important Greek philosophers lived before Socrates, and, of course, Socrates alone is an immense subject. Your instructor would expect you to *select* one or perhaps two pre-Socratics for consideration. You might decide that Pythagoras is representative and interesting (besides, you have known his name ever since high-school geometry).

You would now have set up the two sides of the comparison: Socrates and Pythagoras. But you would still need to narrow the focus: "preoccupations and methods" covers just about everything. You would limit the number of headings under which to compare Pythagoras and Socrates. You might brainstorm a list of the preoccupations the two philosophers had in common:

> the irrational
>
> problems in perception
>
> the physical universe

and many more. Which of these topics do you want to analyze? The same constraints operate: your knowledge, your interests, your sources, and the time and space allotted.

You may be drawn to "the irrational," just as Pythagoras was. You may "feel" a distinct difference between Pythagoras and Socrates on this subject, but you may not know exactly what the difference is.

At this stage, let the problem percolate. Review all you have read by and about the two philosophers. Compare representative passages from their writings. Review your class notes. When something strikes you, jot it down. But also let your mind wander (Hey, didn't Pythagoras believe in reincarnation?). Follow your thoughts wherever they lead. Take the brakes off your imagination. Speculate.

When a central concern begins to firm up in your mind, concentrate on it. Write it down so you will be sure not to forget: "What the two philosophers thought about the limits of reason." Having narrowed your subject and thereby set up a manageable comparison, you are well on your way to developing your thesis.

The Thesis

The idea around which your essay is organized and to which all the parts contribute is called a thesis. It is the point of the essay. In the following sections we discuss two kinds of thesis: the argumentative thesis, which argues a point, and the organizational thesis, which organizes information.

The Argumentative Thesis.   When assigning an essay, most instructors call for an *expository* essay, that is, an interpretation of a topic. They expect students to develop an idea about a subject and then argue to prove it. This process demonstrates how students think, how they handle concepts, and how much they understand.

The argumentative thesis represents your opinion on the subject, your conviction, your evaluation, your discovery, your approach, your point of view. Note the word *your*. The subject belongs to the world; the thesis is your stamp on it.

You must, of course, get to the narrowed subject before you arrive at your thesis. The following examples show the narrowing process:

Assignment: A three-page essay on a difficult social issue

Broad subject: Marijuana

Narrowed subject: Marijuana and its use in medical treatment

Thesis: Because of its capacity to relieve pain, marijuana should be treated as a prescription drug for the very ill.

Assignment: A six-page essay on a novel read in this course

Broad subject: Charles Dickens's *Great Expectations*

Narrowed subject: The protagonist Pip (still too broad)

More narrowed subject: Important places in Pip's life

Thesis: Three important places—the forge, Satis House, and the graveyard—shape Pip's fate.

Notice that the subjects are sentence fragments, but the theses are complete sentences. They make a completed thought about each subject.

You may not know what your thesis is when you start writing—it may result from putting ideas and impressions down on paper (yet another good use for free writing and journal keeping). But when you set about writing your final draft, you will certainly need to know your thesis. An essay without a thesis is like a ship without a rudder. It moves in circles.

Although a thesis need not be stated in a sentence or two, such an explicit statement can help you and your reader. Like a lodestar, it can help you stay on course and enable your reader to determine whether you are actually traveling where you said you would. Usually this explicit statement will occur in the first or second paragraph. From then on, you and your reader can check whether the essay is on course.

More often than not, you will state your thesis in a single sentence. There may be times, however, when your idea would burst out of a single sentence because it requires immediate explanation or qualification. You may then need two or more sentences. But remember that the longer the thesis, the more difficult for the reader to grasp. Try to make your thesis statement hard, tight, unmistakable.

A thesis is not a litany of cold facts. Facts say nothing about themselves. They simply are. When we write, we must show how facts connect and what they mean. In short, we must interpret. In a class on twentieth-century European history, the assignment was "In a four- to six-page paper, discuss the Aisne-Marne offensive." One student wrote this as his thesis:

> On July 18, 1918, a quarter of a million American troops began the month-long Aisne-Marne offensive. This offensive forced the Germans to retreat to the Vesle River. It was followed by the Meuse-Argonne drive. The armistice was signed on November 11, 1918.

This paragraph consists entirely of facts you could find in any encyclopedia. The writer did not say why the facts are important. The rest of the essay was a simple chronology. This happened and then this and then this. The facts are cold indeed.

The writer warmed the facts up in his revision:

> On July 18, 1918, a quarter of a million American troops began the month-long Aisne-Marne offensive. This offensive halted what had seemed to be an irresistible German attack, fortified the sagging Allied defenses, served notice of the American presence, and—perhaps most significant—caused widespread dissatisfaction and political unrest in Germany. It was the turning point of the war.

With that last sentence as his thesis, he now had the start of a very meaty six-page essay.

A thesis is not a gusher of feeling. We are not against feeling. On the contrary, we are all for expressing it in essays. But feeling alone will not help the cause. Readers will not be stampeded—they *can* be persuaded. "Computers are fantastic and fun" is not very arguable or scintillating. Neither is "Enrico Caruso and Maria Callas had the most beautiful voices ever" or "Abortion is a horrible sin." These explosions of feeling hardly promise an essay worth reading, one that is reasoned and supported.

In a second effort, the computer fancier tried to modulate her tone:

> Computers are the most fantastic innovation ever to revolutionize human life.

Imagine trying to prove that a piece of hardware is "the most fantastic innovation." What about the internal combustion machine, the lever, and the wheel? This thesis is still too large and too emotional for an essay. The writer made a final try:

> Computers have revolutionized human life by drastically shortening the time it takes to perform previously difficult and lengthy intellectual operations.

The writer still has her work cut out for her, but now it is doable.

The thesis is not a grandiose generality. It is an assertion you can support in the time and space allotted. In a six- to eight-page paper, you can neither prove nor disprove the superiority of jazz over classical music or vice versa. You can neither prove nor disprove that the novel is dead. These assertions are too far-reaching for an essay. Don't claim more than you can support. Be modest:

> The very form of jazz has stimulated great creativity from musicians otherwise thwarted.

The thesis is not a recitation of the obvious. No one wants to read that "senators are subject to pressure from special-interest groups." We know that already. We know that slavery is evil, that defense costs money, that science is challenging. Conventional opinions do not a lively essay make. If something is not worth arguing about, it is unlikely to be worth writing about. A good thesis is controversial. Although it should not be wild or crazy, it ought to have a sharp edge.

Sometimes you can turn blank statements of received wisdom—like those in the previous paragraph—into sharp statements with an argumentative edge:

> Because special-interest groups—such as lobbies, religious groups, and corporations—have become so powerful, balancing their demands is at the heart of the American political system.

> Slavery helped to bring about the development of democracy in Greece by providing philosophers leisure from onerous work.

> Our Pacific fleet may be worth what it costs if it keeps China from attacking Taiwan.
>
> An obsessive desire for scientific knowledge can be dangerous because, as the Frankenstein story suggests, we may lose control of our experiments.

We do not necessarily agree with these assertions, but they do have an argumentative edge, and we want to read what the writers have to say about them.

A thesis is not just the bald assertion of an opinion. The best theses do not make bald statements of opinion, however reasonable. A reader wants to know right away whether the issue is worth discussing and whether the writer will pursue an interesting idea. The following flat-footed assertions offer little for a reader to anticipate:

> Live theater is a declining entertainment.
>
> We should turn the churches into grain bins or art museums.
>
> I prefer men who know they are chauvinists but don't care to men who are chauvinists but don't know it.

Why? why? and why again? Answering *why?* would limit the thesis, direct the discussion, sharpen the argumentative edge, and promise a more interesting essay. Look at the difference between

> We should not allow the president to wage covert wars.

and

> We should not allow the president to wage covert wars because such a right would upset the balance of powers mandated by the Constitution.

Another writer on waging covert wars might frame the thesis this way:

> If we let the executive branch wage covert wars, we sacrifice the very basis of our Constitution.

Many theses will answer not *why?* but *how?* This question becomes particularly important when we make a proposal. Here is a proposal that could use a dose of *how?* to lift it above the platitudinous:

> High-school students can become more sensitive to the needs of the elderly.

Sure, but ho-hum. Add the *how?* and the idea becomes more interesting:

> If the high schools hired retired people as teachers' aides, high-school students would become more sensitive to the needs of the elderly.

Suppose we keep the *how?* and add a *why?*

> From such contact, students would learn how the elderly view the world and why they see it that way.

Now the writer promises a thoughtful essay.

Sometimes answering the question *under what circumstances?* can make a drab thesis more compelling:

> Experimentation on animals should not be allowed.

can become

> Unless laboratory scientists place the highest priority on minimizing pain, experimentation on animals should not be allowed.

Although and *when* clauses can suggest the circumstances under which the thesis assertion is true:

> When voters suffer economically, they blame the party in control of the White House rather than Congress.
>
> Although some individuals manage to climb the social ladder, social class is largely predetermined on the basis of inherited wealth and privilege.

A thesis that answers a question predicts the shape and even the content of the essay. It tells the writer what kind of support is needed, and it tells the reader that the journey won't be shrouded in fog but will be sharp and clear.

The most effective theses are succinct and their terms clear. The following thesis may well contain an idea worth pursuing, but the language in which it is expressed is so vague and scattered that we don't know what it really means:

> The United States government concealed the whole question of CIA involvement in the Haitian military dictatorship because of what it thought Americans would tolerate, and Aristide and his supporters, once they were reestablished in power, weren't straight about it, and I think that explains these problems.

What involvement? What does *straight* mean? What *problems?* This thesis is so wordy and imprecise that the reader can have little idea what is coming. The student redesigned the thesis:

> Because the United States government refused to admit that the CIA helped to finance the Haitian military dictatorship, Aristide and his democratic supporters remained suspicious of U.S. intentions and refused to accept American advice.

The difficulty between the two nations has now been focused. The subsequent sentences or paragraphs can give background for the U.S. position, the Haitian position, and the history of relations between the two countries, including Aristide's return to Haiti.

Notice that in the revision, the student dropped "I think." Because readers assume that the ideas expressed belong to the writer, phrases such as "I think" or "I feel" are redundant. When you clutter up your prose with them, you sound unsure of yourself. The thesis is your special twist on the subject; *you* are the expert on what you think.

The Organizational Thesis.   Thus far we have been discussing the expository essay, in which the writer makes an arguable assertion and then sets out to prove it. You may often be asked, in school and out, to do other kinds of writing—book reports, personal essays, explications, surveys of writings about a subject. You may be asked to narrate or describe, summarize or analyze. For these kinds of assignments, you will need to determine the most effective way to present the information. Accumulating and throwing facts at the reader higgledy-piggledy would lead to chaos. You need an *organizational thesis.*

Unlike the argumentative thesis, the organizational thesis does not primarily represent a point of view or an opinion. Rather, it prepares the reader for the information to come. It suggests the form and the focus of that information. It is as essential to the report and summary as the argumentative thesis is to the expository essay. Even a straight newspaper article has an organizational thesis, as in this opening paragraph:

> Should home windows or shutters be required to withstand a direct hit from an eight-foot-long two-by-four shot from a cannon at thirty-five miles an hour, without creating a hole big enough to let in a three-inch sphere? That is the central question between home builders and insurance companies over new standards for windows designed to stand up to the high winds and flying debris of hurricanes. (Michael Quint, "A Storm Over Housing Codes," *New York Times,* December 1, 1995, p. C1.)

Now we know what kind of information to expect: a description of two positions regarding changes in building codes.

(For a full discussion of various kinds of organizational theses, see Chapter 15, Writing in All Disciplines: The Report.)

Tips for Subject and Thesis

- Narrow your subject to a manageable size.
- In papers that support an opinion, devise a sharp and clear argumentative thesis.
- Ask yourself, Is my thesis too factual? too emotional? grandiose? trite?
- Have you made your thesis interesting by answering *how?* or *why?* or *under what circumstances?*
- Are the terms of your thesis succinct and clear?
- In your thesis, avoid phrases such as *I think* or *I feel.*
- For reports or summaries, be sure you have a good organizational thesis.

EXERCISES FOR SUBJECT AND THESIS

1. The following subjects are too broad for an essay of 750–1,000 words. Reduce four of them to an appropriate size. You need not construct a thesis: this is an exercise in narrowing the subject. Be prepared to explain how and why you narrowed as you did.

newspapers	American children	DNA
violence	women in literature	missionaries
Rwanda	building bridges	rodents

2. Sometimes it is a good idea to narrow step by step. Choose two of your subjects from Exercise 1 and narrow them a step at a time four times.

3. With a partner, select three of the following overly broad assertions and separately write thesis statements appropriate for an essay of 750–1,000 words. Assert the negative if you prefer. Test the statements by the standards discussed in this chapter. Compare your thesis statements with your partner's. What kinds of differences do you find?

   James Joyce was the greatest writer of this century.
   The quality of life ought to be improved.
   Affirmative action is essential.
   Taxes should be reduced.
   Genetic engineering is dangerous.
   Movies are more entertaining than television.

4. Rewrite the following statements to give them an argumentative edge.
   a. Beethoven was a musician.
   b. Waterskiing is exciting.
   c. In time of war, traitors should be punished.
   d. Police should be nice.

5. Evaluate the effectiveness of the following statements as theses for essays of 750–1,000 words. Rewrite the ineffective ones to make them workable. Bear in mind *why? how?* and *under what circumstances?* Note: you may not know what the writer had in mind—a major flaw in some thesis statements. If this is the case, construct a sound thesis for the indicated subject.
   a. Fraternity initiations are like animal aggression.
   b. The feminist movement threatens the institution of marriage.
   c. Wood stoves obviate the internal redistribution of thermal energies.
   d. Violence on television is a complex topic, but in this paper I will attempt to deal with it.
   e. Private ownership of handguns poses a serious problem.

A man may write at any time, if he will set himself doggedly to it.

> —SAMUEL JOHNSON (1709-1784)
> ENGLISH WRITER AND CRITIC

DEVELOPING, ORGANIZING, DRAFTING: GETTING THE IDEAS WRITTEN

To get a workable and interesting thesis may take several tries, and you may even change your thesis after you finish your first draft. But when you feel you have a pretty good idea of what you are going to write, it is time to begin to get those thoughts clear and to put them on paper.

Writing involves our psychological state and our physical state, so much so that the ease of it depends on how good we feel, what response we hope for or fear, even our regard for the audience. No wonder it can sometimes not be free-form fun. As Samuel Johnson suggests, we must sometimes just be dogged about it.

Getting Ready

Before you start, plan your attack on the project. Think through your best way of getting down your thoughts. This part of the process will vary from person to person. Some will want to be tightly organized; others will just start writing. Save time and energy by proceeding in the way best for you.

The following advice should help with any writing task. It contains no big secrets or surefire tricks, only some points that will make your writing more enjoyable during the process and more effective with your reader.

First of all, make it easy on yourself. Don't wait until the last minute. Starting early provides a margin for error as well as ample time to perform the task.

Schedule a block of time for writing, and do nothing else during that time. When you write in tidbits, you are constantly starting up. This is as hard on writing as stop-and-go traffic is on cars.

Put yourself out of temptation's way. Find a quiet, well-lighted, nonsocial place where you won't be disturbed. Take the phone off the hook. Have a snack or soda nearby.

Keep supplies handy. When you have a head of steam, going off to the store for a new pencil or eraser will undoubtedly dissipate it.

Be sure your references and source materials are easily accessible. Your dictionary should always be nearby. Keep *Writing Worth Reading* around for questions about writing. If you are using research, check to see that your major sources are with you. Be sure your notes are together, legible, and in order.

 Computer Tip

Keep all word-processing supplies close at hand and plentiful. This includes at least one box of unused disks, one ream of printer paper, and at least one extra printer ribbon, ink cartridge, or toner cartridge.

Developing

Once you have settled on a subject and formulated a thesis, however tentative, start jotting down major supporting ideas. A good source of supporting ideas is what you generated from brainstorming, directed questioning, or one of the other invention techniques. Identify the ideas that relate directly to the thesis you are working on. Try the invention techniques again, this time with your thesis in mind.

Your major supporting ideas will probably be somewhat general or abstract, and you will need to develop evidence for them. *Evidence* is whatever the reader will accept without further explanation. It includes numbers, quotations, examples, the word of someone you and your reader both trust, the values you know you share. It is the common ground you and your reader can stand on. (For more on evidence, see Chapter 6, Using Evidence.)

Evidence lies also in your sources. If you are, for instance, writing an essay on a novel, refer to notes you took while reading, and page through the novel itself for apt quotations or examples. If you are writing about history, look in your textbook and other readings for facts you can use. If you are discussing a problem in sociology, develop your ideas by working up a chart or graph based on statistics you have collected. Always take careful notes.

You might find the *reasons chain* helpful in developing support. This is a chain of *becauses*. Write down your thesis, and then write down *because*. Fill in the answer, and again write *because*. Keep going along that chain until the answer is self-evident. Then go back to the beginning and see whether you can develop another chain of *becauses*.

Here is the reasons chain in action:

Thesis: The college curriculum should include a two-semester history requirement.

> Because: It is the best way to ensure a knowledge of where we came from and how our values developed.
>
> Because: Only with the knowledge of history can we fully understand contemporary society.
>
> Because: Only when we fully understand our society will we know how to protect democracy.
>
> Because: History teaches us that forces hostile to democracy lurk just below the surface of society and can break out at any time.
>
> Because: The frequent reorganization of the Ku Klux Klan is an example.

We have probably hit the self-evident wall here, and so we try another chain based on the same thesis:

> Because: Without a requirement, many students would not take the history course.
>
> Because: The drive toward professionalism is so great in our schools.

That may or may not be self-evident. If not, the *because* might require some statistical evidence or a quotation from an expert.

Now we should look back at all the *becauses* to be sure we have followed them. We can see, for instance, that the first *because* mentions cultural values, but we did not build a chain on that. It might be fruitful to forge that chain of reasons.

> Because: Only if we understand how our values developed will we be able to protect them.

By means of the reasons chain, you can extend your understanding of your thesis and be far along the way to organizing. But always make certain that your evidence connects directly with your major point.

Organizing

When you organize, you systematically arrange the ideas and evidence that you intend to use in your essay. If you're not certain about your thesis, you may need to draft first, organize later. But if you have a good idea of what your thesis is, then arranging your ideas before you begin to write provides a sense of direction through the morass of facts and helps you find connections between important points.

As a first step, identify your major supporting ideas, making sure they are neither repetitious nor irrelevant. Under each, jot down the supporting evidence. If a piece of evidence won't fit, don't force it. If you have not generated enough evidence, try one of the invention techniques—they can work for small as well as for large points. Invention techniques can also help you get started organizing because they can help you see connections and group similar ideas.

Computer Tip

List your major points on your computer screen and check to be sure they are in the appropriate order. If not, move them around and test a different order. Likewise, you can reorder your supporting points.

With split screens and multiple windows, put your note file in one window and your major points in another. Scroll through your notes, find the ones you want, and lift them across to the appropriate major point.

Summary Paragraph.   At this stage try writing a paragraph that begins with your thesis and continues with each major point expressed in a complete sentence. Such a summary paragraph could help you determine your general direction and focus. Here is a paragraph encompassing the thesis and all the major ideas for an essay on the Electoral College:

> Because the Electoral College is unnecessary and potentially dangerous, we should support efforts to change the system. It once worked. The "winner-take-all" principle for each state's delegates is unfair to minority political groups. It violates the "one-person, one-vote" principle. It threatens the federalist system. There is also the problem of small states having inordinate influence. The victory could go to a candidate the majority of people don't want. Many have suggested changes. The best would be direct election.

Although it will not appear in the final essay, this paragraph—the whole essay boiled down—will help the writer see forward.

 Computer Tip

Put several inches of space between each sentence of your summary paragraph. Developing each of those sentences into a paragraph will form a preliminary sketch of your essay.

Outlining.   Whether you are writing a personal essay or a lengthy research paper, outlining can help you organize and develop your material. When you outline, you first divide your thesis into major components or headings and then arrange your ideas under those headings. This process can help you in several ways:

It forces you to get that thesis down on paper.

It identifies the main points.

It indicates at least a tentative organizational plan.

Outlines come in both informal and formal varieties.

Informal outlines or scratch lists: Making an informal outline, or scratch list, sometime during the writing process can help you figure out where you're going and how to get there. To write an informal outline, divide your thesis into its major parts and use each part as a heading under which you place your supporting ideas.

Suppose your thesis is "Although profit margins have improved, downsizing of various corporations has resulted in economic decline for all but the highest economic classes." Within that sentence lie several major ideas that you can jot down in a word or short phase:

> profit margins
> downsizing
> economic decline
> the highest economic classes

You can then place your supporting ideas under the relevant heading. Under *profit margins,* for instance, you might jot down reminders to define the term, check the annual reports of a few typical corporations, and compare those with earlier reports. Under *downsizing,* again remind yourself to define the term and compare the number of employees now working at your selected corporations with, say, the number of employees ten years ago. After treating all the key terms with similar care, you should pretty well know the shape of your essay and the information you need. Of course, the more detailed your outline, the closer you are to a completed essay.

Formal outlines: Formal outlines break down, group, and arrange your ideas more thoroughly than informal outlines or scratch lists. We call this type of outline *formal* because it is a detailed, methodical effort to set forth the ultimate shape and even the content of your paper.

As with the informal outline, you start by dividing your thesis into major elements. Now, just as you carefully divided your thesis, you divide your major elements into their component ideas, and, where feasible, continue to subdivide until you have all your evidence clearly identified. In this way, you preserve your major divisions and establish the relative importance of your minor ideas.

In devising a formal outline, follow the conventional system of numbered or lettered headings. In the following example, we outline an essay on the gun control controversy:

> Thesis: The two sides of the gun control controversy line up over the issue of individual rights versus society's needs.
> I. Background
>   A. Description of issue
>   B. Evidence of controversy
>   1. News media
>   2. Legislative action

        a. Federal
        b. State and local
  II. Individual rights
      A. Constitutional rights
          1. Right to bear arms
             a. Legislative history
             b. Supreme Court interpretations
          2. Right to self-defense
      B. Tradition of vigilantism or citizen policing
      C. Need to exercise rights
          1. Increase in crime
          2. Inadequacy of police
  III. Society's needs
      A. Need to oversee access to firearms
          1. Easy to purchase
          2. Hard to control
      B. Need to limit consequences of both illegal and legal use of guns
          1. Crimes
             a. Comparison of United States and Great Britain
             b. Domestic violence and violence against strangers
          2. Accidents
             a. Children
             b. Adults
      C. Changes in society since Constitution
          1. Intention of Founders
          2. Growth of police forces

This outline is called a *topic outline* because it sets forth the paper's main topics in words and phrases. If you want more detail, try a *sentence outline*. Write a complete sentence for each item. Number III.A.2. above might read

> States that try to control traffic in firearms fail because different states have different laws and purchasers in stringent states can simply go into adjacent states where firearm laws are more relaxed.

You can add more detail if you wish. You could, for instance, subdivide III.A.1. into a. and b. and write:

> a. Sporting goods stores often provide handguns without identification.

> b. Many people order handguns from mail-order businesses, as did Lee Harvey Oswald, accused of killing John F. Kennedy.

How much you subdivide depends on how near the completed essay you want to get by means of an outline. A complete formal outline appears on pages 405–07.

Three general rules apply to making outlines. First, items on the same level should be of the same general importance: that is, I. should be of equal importance to II., A. to B., and so on. After all, the point of the outline is to understand the relative importance of topics.

Second, whenever you divide a level, you need at least two parts beneath it: you can't cut a cake into one piece. Under I., if you have A., you need B., and so on. Each level in the preceding outline follows this rule.

 Computer Tip

Many word-processing programs offer convenient outlining tools that will automatically keep track of your numbering as you add and delete entries and subentries. If you haven't done so already, explore your word-processing software's capabilities for outlining.

Third, items at each level should be grammatically parallel. If A. is a complete sentence, B. should be also. If (1) is a phrase, (2) should be a phrase. Otherwise, you may find it difficult to grasp which ideas belong together and in what way.

Even if your outline is less formal than our example, be sure you

connect all points in intelligible order

distinguish major points from minor ones and emphasize them accordingly

gather evidence adequate to support each point.

 Computer Tip

When outlining, leave extra space between each item. As you read over the outline, assess the smoothness of the logical progression. If you can't get across the spaces easily, you need to rethink your outline.

Organic Progression.   Organization is not only form, but also order. How do we decide what order our ideas should follow? The best organization is, not surprisingly, organic: one idea grows out of another, and the essay proceeds according to inherent connections. To see these connections, do as much reading as you think you should—in fact, do more. Be as comfortable with the subject as possible. And then, after reviewing your notes, free-write, brainstorm, talk it out with a friend, or just think about it. Work it over in your journal. The more familiar you are with the subject, the more likely you are to see connections that appear natural, even inevitable. Here is the summary of one essay that grew organically:

> Because of the inevitable depletion of fossil fuel sources, we must immediately seek new sources of energy.
>
> Coal is becoming scarce and more hazardous.
>
> People have therefore turned to nuclear energy.
>
> Fission has great problems, including safety.
>
> Fusion is safer but costly.
>
> Wind and waves produce energy but can't be major sources.
>
> A major source has been hydroelectric power, but its capacity is limited.
>
> Although expensive, unlimited solar energy promises to be our best source of energy.

This "organic" progression is actually quite logical. The first idea (depletion of resources) leads to an example (coal) and a cause-and-effect argument (because coal is scarce, people have turned to nuclear energy) and so on: the seed idea of depletion grows into the final thought.

The least interesting essays are those in which one idea is placed next to another without thought to connection, like stacking logs: "First, second, third, and so on." To test whether your essay is a stack of logs, reverse the order of its ideas. If you find that the order doesn't matter, you have a stack of logs.

Drafting

Drafting should be the least pressured stage of writing. You should let your ideas flow—no one is going to read your first efforts. Drafting can be free-form fun, a snap compared with the other stages.

Well, that is a bit of an exaggeration. It does not work that way every time. Sometimes getting that first draft on paper is painfully slow. Perhaps the subject is genuinely difficult, and it takes time to cobble together all the bits of information or fill out each step in a closely reasoned argument. Sometimes those very first inkblots are paralyzing and sometimes you may spend hours at a midparagraph sentence. Even James Joyce, a great writer, would stare out the window for hours on end seeking the right word.

Although no method is right for everyone, here are some suggestions for the drafting stage:

1. Keep three basic elements of your paper always in view: your purpose, your reader, and the big picture. Think about your goal. Can you get there from here? Have new ideas opened up new routes? Con-

sider whether you should revise your plan. Think about your reader. Imagine how the essay will sound, how it will look, and how it will be received.

2. Don't try to write and edit at the same time. Writing a sentence, crossing it out, rewriting it, and worrying over the grammar or the wording can slow you down and endanger your mental health. When you hit on a new twist, you don't need to go back right away to adjust the beginning—you can do that on the next draft. If a start-and-go-back method is the best way for you, however, then follow it. But most of us find it easier and more effective to write now, edit later.

By all means, when those blinding flashes of insight tell you, "Hold on! That sentence on page 3 should have read . . ." or "Use that juicy Smith quotation on page 5," obey them. Fix up the suddenly offending passage, or at least make a note of it. And if you have an idea you know will work beautifully at the end of the essay, be sure to make a note of that. But what writers usually need most at this stage is a natural rhythm in writing, not an agonizing halt-and-about-face process. Try to press on.

3. Do not, however, force sections that just will not come. Many writers cannot begin with the introduction; they think it demands too much formality and precision all at once. Yet some cannot get started until that first paragraph is right.

Don't fret: if you feel happiest writing middle paragraphs, go straight to one. Use any invention technique at any point in drafting. The satisfaction you derive from the easier writing will often speed the harder writing.

🖳 Computer Tip

Try "triple priming"—a word-processing technique that helps you when you just can't get started. First, force yourself to draft one version of a passage and save it. Wait twenty minutes and then, without consulting the first effort, write another version of the same passage and save it. After another twenty minutes, write a third version. You may be pleased with one version in its entirety or with parts of all three, or you may have to start all over again. But at least you have started to think your way through the passage.

---

4. Read aloud to yourself. When you come to a natural pause—for instance, the end of a section—give voice to your silent words. Reading aloud is a good way to stay in close touch with your writing. It will tell

you whether you are moving at an appropriate pace and whether the writing flows smoothly. Of course, you will revise later, but reading aloud can help you to anticipate your next moves. It may give you some new ideas, reveal rough spots, or encourage you.

5. Recognize signs of tension. This may sound more like therapy than writing advice, but it concerns every writer. Frustration tends to grow slowly for a while and then hit a point at which it sends you through the roof. If you feel frustration building, stop before you explode. Take a break. Take a walk. Take a nap.

Like frustration, fatigue is an enemy of good writing. If you begin to get very tired, rest your eyes and your mind. Stop writing. Of course, if your paper is due in two hours, not writing may be hard to do—a good reason to make sure you are never in that position.

6. Regard the first draft as provisional. Few if any writers ever get it right the first time. A first draft is almost bound to be changed and improved. Be ready—perhaps even eager—to revise.

 Computer Tip

As you draft, you can make comments to yourself, using capitals, different fonts, or different type sizes. If a paragraph seems underdeveloped, write **Need more.** If you haven't quite proved your point, write PROVE IT. With this method you preserve your train of thought and you can return later to respond to your comments.

Tips for Developing, Organizing, Drafting

- Look in your background material and your invention notes for evidence and ideas that need developing.
- Identify your main ideas and place supporting ideas under them.
- Select a congenial method of organization: a summary paragraph, an informal outline, or a formal outline.
- Think about the organic progression of your major ideas; avoid stacking ideas.
- While drafting, bear in mind your purpose, your audience, and the big picture.
- Use the invention techniques to develop points.
- Remember that few writers can write and edit at the same time.
- Treat your first draft as temporary, subject to drastic change.

EXERCISES FOR DEVELOPING, ORGANIZING, DRAFTING

1. Choose two ideas from a recent invention exercise you've done—brainstorming, free writing, clustering, using a journal—and develop each one with three pieces of evidence. Draft a paragraph for each.

2. Imagine that you have been asked to write your autobiography, including your life-to-be. Free-write or brainstorm your life, and then plan how you would go about writing it. Divide the subject into major periods, themes, events, people, or however you want to organize it. Turn in your organizational plan.

3. With a partner, identify the major supporting ideas for or against one of the following theses. Now each of you choose a form of organization from this list: summary paragraph, informal outline, formal outline. Compare what you have done. What differences do you find? Which organization seems better and why?

   Because of hazards to health, football should be prohibited in high school.
   Medicaid encourages fraudulence on the part of doctors and hospitals and sloth and dependence on recipients and should cease.
   To control the spread of drug abuse, federal employees should be subject to random testing.

4. From the following list, choose the topic that most appeals to you. Construct a thesis, develop support, organize your ideas, and draft an essay—in that order.

   anything that makes you particularly angry
   the virtues and foibles of your mother's family
   allergies you have known
   the value of wearing, or not wearing, a wristwatch
   the pitfalls of borrowing and lending

I'm goin' to change my way of livin'
   and if that ain't enough,
Then I'll change the way I strut my stuff.
   —BILLY HIGGINS AND W. BENTON OVERSTREET
   AMERICAN POPULAR-SONG WRITERS

REVISING: GETTING THE WRITING RIGHT

Novelist Vladimir Nabokov once said, "I have rewritten—often several times—every word I have ever published. My pencils outlast their erasures." Professional writers like Nabokov do not treat a first draft as sacred, engraved in stone. They know that words rarely march onto the page in perfect order, thoughts clear, sentences elegant, phrases vigorous, punctuation accurate. They know that to be a good writer is to be a good rewriter.

Although with most people revision is about as popular as house-breaking puppies, it is the most important stage of writing. We need the spontaneity of the first draft, yes, but the first draft is only *a first draft*. If we are honest with ourselves, we know we will need a second go, and probably a third.

Revising brings into play everything this book covers, from thinking large thoughts to selecting the proper dot or dash. Like writing, revising is a process. When we revise, we make a series of decisions and we try out alternative ideas and words. We reorganize, perhaps even find a better thesis. We experiment with sentence shapes and with emphasis. We keep on changing things until we are satisfied—or have run out of time.

Some people write a first draft and then in the name of revision gussy it up with a few minor changes before presenting it to their bosses or instructors. Here it is, folks: the first-and-a-half draft. That is not revision. Revision follows a slow and objective reexamination of that first draft. It allows us to react to our first thoughts and to refine and expand them.

The Critical Distance

A brand-new piece of writing is like a brand-new baby: it looks perfect. We can no more read our recent writing objectively than we could list the baby's flaws. We need critical distance. We need to separate ourselves from our creation. Professional writers are very good at achieving critical distance. One newspaper writer once said, "I know my readers are going to be hard on what I write—so I beat them to the punch and really tear into my first drafts, *assuming* that they have problems."

Before trying to revise, you should put your essay away for a while. The Roman poet Horace recommended nine years. If you don't have that sort of time, try a few hours. Take a walk, see a movie, practice the flügelhorn—anything that will give your objectivity a chance to grow.

If you would like to know what critical distance feels like, find a letter or essay you wrote two years ago, or five. If you have the sensation of reading someone else's writing, you are feeling critical distance. The perfect writer would treat his or her first draft like another person's writing—that would guarantee that the distance would be critical. Because most of us are not virtuous enough to attain such a state, we take a long break between drafts.

Once you have achieved some critical distance, return to your first draft. Read it. Read it aloud. Have a friend read it to you. Hearing your written words is almost always surprising. You may even want to interrupt with an occasional "Well, that isn't exactly what I meant." Feel the critical distance grow.

Blowing the Essay to Pieces

If you start revising line by line straight through, you risk seeing the essay the way you first saw it. Good revisers try to break the pattern in order to get a clearer look. They have various ways of blowing the essay to pieces.

Some writers start at the end and work backward. They check the conclusion against their purpose. They compare the ending and the opening to see whether they can get to one from the other. Going backward, they note the transitions between paragraphs. They read sentences out of context—and perhaps wonder what they meant.

> 💻 **Computer Tip**
>
> Separate paragraphs into discrete sentences, thus nakedly displaying their individual weaknesses and faults. You can more easily judge whether you need different examples, more extensive discussions, or smoother transitions. With the sentences lined up one under another, you can also tell whether they are all more or less the same length and too often follow the same form.

A few actually take scissors—either a real pair or a command from a computer tool bar—to their first effort. They cut it up into sections and arrange them in different combinations. Wrenched from their context, passages lose that "finished" look.

Anything that disrupts the way you are used to seeing or thinking about your writing helps you lose the pride of ownership that makes objectivity so difficult. It allows you to read with fresh eyes.

Once you have established the distance needed for a rigorous examination, you are ready to revise. You will probably want to cross out repetitions, underline good points, write questions to yourself, circle ideas, draw boxes and arrows. Gather some pens or sharp pencils and erasers. If you cut and paste with your hard copy, you will need scissors and tape or staples. And you will need plenty of time. This process cannot be rushed.

Computer Tip

Print out your hard copy, do large-scale revision by hand, then enter the changes. Some of our students print out two or three drafts and lay them next to one another on the table or the floor. That way they can see how their essays evolve.

The Levels of Revision

Revision takes place on several levels, with a number of discrete tasks on each. As you revise, you'll find that you naturally move between levels. Changing a single word will sometimes mean changing your whole organization—just as changing a single note changes the whole tune. And changes in thought usually compel changes in commas and periods. Our advice is work first on the biggest elements (we call this *macrorevision*) and then the smaller (*microrevision*), but don't be rigid: let yourself move freely between levels.

Macrorevision.   The most important level of revision is what could be called macrorevision. On this level you rethink your big ideas. You must be ruthless with yourself, perhaps eliminating what cost you anguish to create.

First, think about your thesis. Are the terms clear and succinct enough for your reader? Perhaps you should try to sharpen the wording for the next draft. If any of the terms seem vague or too abstract, define them—and then be sure you include that definition in the next draft. Is the thesis strong enough? A weighty essay cannot stand on a weak thesis. Having gone through all the writing, do you think that thesis is what you now want to say? And is it worth writing about? If not, find another.

Look separately at each major supporting idea. Does it support the thesis, or have you let a digression slip in? If you find a digression, get rid of it. Are any of the ideas, though expressed differently, really the same? Combine them. If forgotten good ideas come back to you now, try to work them in if they fit. If you feel your essay is skimpy, look back at your earlier notes or try an invention technique to generate more material.

Check your evidence. Do you provide the common ground for you and your reader? Is there enough support for your major ideas? If a weak thesis provides a poor foundation for your thought, scanty evidence makes for a shaky scaffolding. If you need more evidence, do the necessary research or go through another invention process. Be sure to adjust your thesis and your major ideas accordingly. Don't try to prop up a rickety argument.

> 💻 **Computer Tip**
>
> Computers make revision both easier and riskier. It's easier because you can change anything at any point and you can save drafts at each stage for comparison. It's riskier because you can be tempted to change too much too often and because on screen you can see only a small section of your work at a time, making large-scale revision difficult. Most important, the ease and speed of word processing tempts you to start too late and not do any real revision.

Step back a bit and look at your organization. Try a paragraph-by-paragraph outline of the first draft. Jot down in a sentence the topic discussed in each paragraph. (You can find an example of such an outline on page 94.) This technique will help even if you used an outline initially. The sentences ought to read like a tightly focused (although general) paragraph similar to the summary paragraph described on page 94.

> 💻 **Computer Tip**
>
> For macrorevision:
>
> 1. Save your draft under an appropriate title ("draft1").
> 2. Save it again under a different title ("draft2").
> 3. Close draft1 and open draft2.
> 4. **Boldface** and <u>underline</u> your thesis statement.
> 5. **Boldface** the topic sentences of your paragraphs. If a topic sentence is implied, write an explicit statement of the topic in boldface.
> 6. Write your conclusion in one sentence, also boldfaced.
> 7. Delete everything that is not boldfaced.
>
> You now have a sentence outline and still have a copy of your original essay.

Having such an outline allows you to see how your essay developed. If there are no missing links, then you know you have not omitted a major idea in the chain of argument. If one of the sentences seems to stand out, examine it closely to be sure it isn't a digression. Ask yourself whether the ideas flow smoothly toward the conclusion or whether they are just logs stacked one on another. It isn't too late to write new paragraphs.

Microrevision.   On the second level of revision, microrevision, you look at your writing phrase by phrase, sentence by sentence, paragraph by paragraph. And you ask hard questions. Is the topic of each paragraph clear, whether stated or implicit? Do all the points relate to the topic? Are the sentences in the right order? Is the meaning of each sentence clear? Is there ample variety in the writing? And what about word choice: is the writing concise, concrete, and vivid?

Reading an essay aloud is particularly helpful for microrevision. Be sure you have a pencil handy to mark those places where you question the shape or sound of your prose. If your first draft is too simple or too complicated, you can change it in the second draft.

The last task at this level is pencil editing, correcting grammar, punctuation, spelling, and mechanics. For specific information about these sentence-level concerns, be sure to consult Part Six, The Nuts and Bolts: A Handbook of Grammar, Punctuation, and Usage (pp. 487–545).

🖥 Computer Tip

Most word processing programs offer wonderful tools to make revision easier. Word search programs can help you avoid repetition. Other programs can assist you with grammar and punctuation. Spell checkers make good proofreaders, but they will not pick up errors that are also words — for example "form" when you meant "from." There is still no substitute, in other words, for traditional proofreading and copyediting on a hard copy.

Often, microrevising for style turns into rethinking. If, for instance, you find your illustrations inadequate or uninteresting, you may try to think up additional ones, and that could lead you to conclude that a point you made really was not justified. You would then go back and rethink the point and its relation to your whole argument. If excess verbosity or pomposity has made your prose fat, the slimming process may make your point more visible. Searching for a better word may lead to a better idea.

(For appropriate manuscript form, see pp. 400–03.)

CASE STUDY:
A STUDENT'S PERSONAL ESSAY

Here is the story of how a writer made her way from a first draft that embarrassed her to a final draft that was much better. Her task, set by the instructor, was to write an essay discussing one of the following subjects: *creativity, prejudice, mental health,* or *mental illness.*

Inventing

The student, Kimberly Corsaro, first spent a few minutes thinking about the terms. *Prejudice* did not appeal to her, and she knew she would not do a good job if she did not like the subject. Although *mental illness* was interesting, she knew so little about it that she would have to do research, and that was not the point of the assignment. The point was to think. *Mental health* seemed to her a very broad term—too broad for a short paper. In the end, nothing attracted her as much as *creativity.*

She had always enjoyed freewriting, and so she chose that as the way to get deeper into the subject.

> Creativity. Poets, dancers, painters, musicians. But
> don't all of us have some somewhere? My pictures look
> like baby scrawls. Can't carry a tune. But funny--
> Mother's friend laughed when I sang that song. Still, I
> tried. Nobody quite like you in the whole human race or
> something. No two pictures alike. Twins even but each has
> thoughts nobody else has. I can't do it but I can think
> it. Where do I fit? Creative? Not just artists. Would
> anyone agree with that? My ideas may be different.

Developing, Organizing, Drafting

When Corsaro read over her paragraph of freewriting, she identified three major ideas:

My approach differs from most people's.

Everybody is distinctive in some way.

Creativity is not limited to artists.

The second idea seemed vague, and she decided that the best way to sharpen it was to use artists themselves as the model for distinctiveness. That would help tie the paper together. She still believed in the third idea, but she had to admit that too often she felt quite uncreative. At the bottom of her page of free writing, she wrote, "More creative if less time in groups? Do I lose my indiv. or not?" After a moment, she added, "Not."

She thought she was probably interpreting the assignment in a way her instructor had not intended, but that was all right because the instructor—her audience—liked students to take chances with their writing.

Here is her first draft:

> Most people think of something physical or tangible   1
> when they think of creativity. However, the most creative
> thing that I am capable of doing is neither visible nor
> concrete. It is my ability to think as an individual.
>
> There are many people who may be artificially tal-   2
> ented, but it is through their imagination that we see
> their creativity. Without thought and imagination from
> individuals, creativity would be nonexistent and con-
> sequently this would be a rather dull and boring place
> to live.
>
> This is not to say that I or other people do every-   3
> thing differently from others, because that would be
> an exaggeration. It is very common for people to do
> things in large groups because they enjoy company and I
> am no exception. However, you can be yourself and part
> of a group at the same time. Nobody is you, and you are
> nobody else. You can see this most clearly if you think
> about artists. If a group of artists were asked to draw a
> picture of a house, all the pictures would be different.
> The theme of the pictures is all the same, but yet all
> the houses vary. This is because each artist has his or
> her own ideas; each perceives a house differently. This
> is where uniqueness and originality enter into a person.
>
> Everyone has the potential to be creative. It is   4
> dependent upon the person to develop his or her own tal-
> ents. In the cases of some people, such as artists or
> musicians, the creativeness is somewhat obvious, whereas
> others' talents are less apparent.
>
> Creativeness is the ability to be inventive or to   5
> transform original thoughts into something others can
> enjoy. To most people a creative work is a painting or
> great music. While these are good examples of creativity,
> it can also be expressed in various other ways, such as a
> poet or a writer.
>
> But as I said above, I cannot paint or sing. When I   6
> draw it looks terrible, and when I sing everybody asks me
> to stop. But I do think for myself, and that is creative.

```
If it was not, I would be thinking everyone else's
thoughts. It can be very difficult to think for yourself,
because there are many pressures to conform to other
people's ways of thinking. I try not to do that, though
I catch myself doing or thinking somebody else's way.
Sometimes I am glad I have other role models. If we did
not have other people telling us how to think when we
were younger, how would we know how to think at all? But
I still think I put my thoughts together in my own way.
That is my creativity.
```

Corsaro put the essay in a drawer.

Revising

When Corsaro returned five hours later to take a fresh look, she blew the essay to pieces. She looked first at the conclusion. It seemed jumbled. She didn't know how she had arrived there. She checked it against the opening. That opening, she saw, was thin. She began to read the essay aloud. *She* wrote *that?* The essay started and stopped. Some paragraphs seemed to lack a topic. She wasn't sure what she meant by certain phrases, and the writing was awkward. The critical distance became so great she almost ran out of the room. She was ready to revise.

Macrorevising.   Corsaro was concerned about her thesis. She didn't want her own creativity to be the central idea. She tried again: imagination, not works of art, is the important part of creativity. Although it needed work, the idea was worth arguing.

She turned to the evidence. Her first evidence had been "Most people think of something physical or tangible when they think of creativity." To make that less vague, she needed an example, and she found one in the fifth paragraph: "To most people a creative work is a painting or great music." She thought it ought to be even more specific, and so she added, "like the Sistine Chapel or Beethoven's Fifth Symphony."

She realized she had not fully established the difference between her idea and the conventional one, which was a main idea. After a trip to the dictionary, she wrote: "Dictionaries often define the word as the ability to be inventive, or to transform one's original thought into a form others can enjoy." Then she saw that both the dictionary and "most people" defined the word according to the *results* of creativity—what it creates. In contrast, she was concerned with imagination itself, a quality possessed by all people, not just artists.

Now she stated her thesis more clearly: "Creativity exists in each person's particular thoughts and imagination." She wrote a new second paragraph to focus this idea and then systematically checked the thinking in all the paragraphs.

In the old second paragraph, the phrase *artificially talented* no longer made sense. She looked up *artificial* in the dictionary: "of a human, as opposed to natural, agency." So what was human? Hard work, training, performance. People like Marie Curie, Leontyne Price, Gregory Hines. And what was *natural?* Imagination was natural because we all have it. Eureka: she had clarified her own half-articulated distinction. She was ready to write a new third paragraph, one related to her thesis and illustrated concretely.

The central idea of the old third paragraph seemed to be that "you can be yourself and part of a group." Or was it that "each artist has his or her own ideas"? Whichever, she couldn't see how it related to her thesis. She put it aside. That decision was extremely important: Corsaro had resisted the temptation to preserve at all costs her original organization.

Her main point was that everyone has imagination and so is potentially creative. Come to think of it, maybe she should define *imagination*. Her original fourth paragraph—three diffident and unsuccessful sentences—had pawed at that idea. How to improve it? Give the example of "everybody." Well, although her own creativity was not the central issue, it could serve as an example. By thinking for herself, she demonstrated her own imaginativeness. She had said this in the old sixth paragraph. Polished and refined, that paragraph could become the new fourth.

And then she saw the old third paragraph had a place after all. In her new third paragraph she could combine the material about the distinctiveness of artists with the idea of how hard artists work. She could put the material about everybody's distinctiveness in a strong new fourth paragraph.

She looked at the old fourth and fifth paragraphs and realized they were floating loose. The fourth was simply a summary of the whole essay she was better off without. As for the old fifth paragraph, she had already transplanted its heart—the example about painting and music—to the new first paragraph. All she needed was a strong concluding paragraph. She decided to finish with creativity and society.

Now she made an outline of her essay:

```
Paragraph 1--Most people think of great works of art when
     they think of creativity.
Paragraph 2--All people share imagination, the most im-
     portant and least understood part of creativity.
```

```
Paragraph 3--Artists differ from other people in their
    dedication to work and training, not in possessing
    imagination.
Paragraph 4--Having one's own distinctive thought is a
    creative act.
Paragraph 5--We can be ourselves and part of a group.
```

Microrevising. Now it was time to examine the details and how the different parts fit. Her second paragraph was a problem:

```
    I fit the first part of the definition (I have orig-
inal thoughts) but not the second (I can't transform them
into creations other people can enjoy). A person's unique
thoughts and imagination are the most important part of
creativeness, and that is the part most people know the
least about.
```

The connection between the two sentences was not clear—hadn't she heard someplace that two-sentence paragraphs are dangerous because often the connecting link is missing? She put in the link:

```
    I fit the first part of the definition (I have orig-
inal thoughts) but not the second (I can't transform them
into creations other people can enjoy). I and people like
me nonetheless qualify as creative. That is because a
person's unique thoughts and imagination are the most im-
portant part of creativity, and that is the part most
people know the least about.
```

The last sentence looked limp. "That is because" was wordy and imprecise, and the word *unique* was overused. Worse yet, the elongated ending dragged down the thought. She revised: "A person's thoughts and imagination are the most important, though least understood, part of creativity." By reducing an eleven-word clause to three, and incorporating it in the middle, she had improved her clarity.

Corsaro went through the same kind of analysis for all the other paragraphs. She put in connecting links, cut back verbiage, added examples, moved always toward the clearer support of her thesis. She was shocked by how often she had used *creative* and *creativity, because* and *people*. These repetitions were nothing compared with many clumps of the lazy verb *to be*.

As she deleted *to be*s and *people*s, she discovered that her language became more vivid. She noticed that she had concluded the third paragraph with "Without thought and imagination from individuals, creativity would be nonexistent and consequently the world would be a rather dull and boring place to live"—a dull and boring sentence. She now had a second chance at that statement, and she wrote, "Creativity begins when individuals think and imagine. Their actions light up the world." Then she extended the metaphor: "but their imaginations provide the current."

This image created a transition problem. She was no doubt delighted when she came up with "Like most of the human race, I have the current but not the light," as a new first sentence of the next paragraph. She went back over the manuscript to sharpen all her transitions. She did not find another quite as brilliant as that, but she locked her paragraphs tightly together.

As the last task in revising, she went to work on her grammar, punctuation, spelling, and mechanics. She used her handbook and her dictionary.

Was this essay perfect? Far from it. Professional writers revise twelve, twenty, thirty times. One of the authors of this book revised a short story over twenty times—the story was published and won a prize. It could have been better. Corsaro's essay still has awkward moments and almost-but-not-quites. She knew her last sentence was not strong—perhaps she would revise it again. But with revision her essay had become fuller and more interesting. For us, the essay provides the most exciting reward of reading: the sense of a mind moving.

New Meaning for an Old Word

When most people think of creativity, they think of   1
something tangible--Michelangelo's Sistine Chapel or
Beethoven's Fifth Symphony. Dictionaries often define the
word as the ability to be inventive, or to transform
one's original thoughts into a form others can enjoy.
Since dictionary definitions often reflect widespread
attitudes, it is not surprising that even Webster's
stresses the results of creativity rather than the thing
itself.

I have a problem with such definitions--namely that   2
I fit the first half (I have original thoughts) but not
the second (I cannot transform them so other people can
enjoy them). I and people like me nonetheless qualify as
creative. A person's thoughts and imagination are the most
important, though least understood, part of creativity.

We share this gift of imagination with stars and   3
geniuses--Marie Curie, Leontyne Price, Gregory Hines--

whose creativity shines through in performance, the product of many hours of training and hard work. What sets them apart is not their natural talent, for many people have an aptitude for science, a fine voice, or a sense of melody or rhythm. The true difference began even before they held a test tube, sang a note, or danced a step. It was their outlook, their approach to what they do, and their personal sense of style. Creativity begins when individuals think and imagine. Their actions light up the world, but their imaginations provide the current.

Like most of the human race, I have the current but   4
not the light. When I draw, my pictures resemble nothing in the real world, and when I sing, everybody asks me to stop. I do think for myself, though. My thoughts are my own and no one else's--quite an achievement, just as difficult as many other creative acts. Just think of all the pressures to conform to other ways of thinking, to accept what others believe. Parents, teachers, and friends all have their own influences to exert. Just having a thought of my own is a creative act.

I do not mean to say I am totally original. Nobody   5
is. If we did not like to do things in groups, we would hardly be human. We also owe a great deal to the parents, teachers, and friends who teach us how to think in the first place. But what we learn from them is a sort of creative conformity: we learn to be ourselves and part of a group at the same time.

Tips for Revising

- Set aside time to revise your first drafts.
- Develop critical distance: separate yourself from your work.
- Read your first draft aloud or ask someone else to read it to you.
- Don't edit in a straight line; blow your essay to pieces.
- Start by revising large elements; move to small elements later.
- Stay flexible: be ready to change anything at any time for any good reason.

EXERCISES FOR REVISING

1. With a partner, select a topic from the following list and separately write a first draft of an essay on that topic.

   an actor you think is bad
   your preference for either dogs or cats
   a crowd activity you did or did not participate in
   student politics on campus
   respecting other cultures

   Make an extra copy. Exchange drafts and revise each other's essay. Be respectful but pitiless.

2. Compare your first draft for Exercise 1 with your partner's revision of it. Evaluate the changes. Write a paragraph on your comparison and evaluation. Give the paragraph to your partner. Be honest but kind.

3. On your computer, open a file of past writing and make a sentence outline of an old essay. Now, on a second screen, revise the writing.

CASE STUDY:
GETTING WRITING FROM READING

Not all your assignments will be as personal and open-ended as the one Corsaro responded to in the previous case study. In political science, history, literature, or sociology courses, for instance, you will undoubtedly be asked to read and evaluate a substantial piece of writing. This task will draw on all your thinking, reading, and writing skills. Going from reading to writing includes nine steps:

    mapping the text
    reading and taking notes
    rereading and taking more notes
    asking—and answering—the eight questions
    forming a thesis as the basis of the evaluation
    planning the essay
    selecting evidence
    drafting
    revising

Mapping the Text

In a seminar on twentieth-century American society, Larry Boyd received this assignment from the instructor:

> Read Michael Levin's essay "Feminism, Stage Three." How fair is his portrayal of feminism's impact on American society? Is his argument convincing to you? Why or why not? Make sure you back up your points with detailed analysis of the essay.

Boyd took careful note of what the instructor was asking him to do: evaluate the fairness and persuasiveness of Levin's analysis of this important social concern.

Boyd learned that the essay came from the August 1986 issue of *Commentary* and was reprinted in Levin's book *Feminism and Freedom,* published in the same year. Surfing the Internet, Boyd discovered that Levin was a professor at City College of New York and the author of an essay titled "Comparable Worth: The Feminist Road to Socialism." That title suggested Levin's viewpoint.

The essay was about five pages long. Although it had no internal headings, it was divided into five sections, marked by space breaks. Boyd made a mental note of that: it might help him see the shape of Levin's whole argument. As he turned the pages, Boyd picked up information for mapping ahead: the words *women, work,* and *working* appeared frequently, as did *children* and *day care.*

Boyd thought he could do a first reading and take notes in about forty minutes. He turned on his laptop and was ready to start.

Feminism, Stage Three
Michael Levin

To judge by the recent eruption of books, articles, and editorials   1
with titles like *The Crisis of the Working Mother, The Divorce Revolution, Not as Far as You Think, Smart Women/Foolish Choices,* "The Birth Dearth," and "A Mother's Choice,"[1] confusion and distress have overtaken much of American womanhood. Ruth Sidel's *Women and Children Last* and Sylvia Hewlett's *A Lesser Life,*[2] in particular, have received a great deal of attention for the grim picture they paint of the "women's movement," and are widely perceived to mark a historic turn in that movement's concerns—away from the goal of transforming women into pseudomen and toward a new appreciation of motherhood and children.

It is easy to see what has brought on this talk of crisis and less-   2
ened lives. Twenty years ago women were assured that psychological fulfillment and a previously unsuspected need for independence from men could be met by paid employment, or, as it was usually called, pursuing a career. Being "only" a housewife and mother was said to be a sure path to catatonia. More strident voices urged women not to have children at all, or, if it was too late for that, to place self-realization above the demands and the illusory satisfactions of family.

The contrast between those brave promises and current reality   3
could hardly be more stark. A major reward for the 5,375,000 women

---

[1]Barbara Berg, *The Crisis of the Working Mother,* Summit, 249 pp. $16.95; Lenore Weitzman, *The Divorce Revolution,* Free Press, 504 pp., $19.95; Lynda L. Moore, ed., *Not as Far as You Think,* Lexington, 201 pp., $15.95; Ben Wattenberg *et al.,* "The Birth Dearth," *Public Opinion,* December 1985/January 1986; "A Mother's Choice," cover story, *Newsweek,* March 31, 1986.

[2]*Women and Children Last,* Viking, 236 pp., $16.95; *A Lesser Life,* Morrow, 461 pp., $17.95.

with children under six who work full time has been strain and guilt at, in Barbara Berg's words, "the excoriating interface of our two roles." From what one may observe in any playground in any major American city, this is almost an understatement. At noon, babysitters far outnumber mothers. (Nine-and-a-half million children under six, or 60 percent of all American children under six, have mothers in the part-time or full-time labor force.) In the late afternoon the mothers retake possession of their offspring, or retrieve them from day-care centers, to spend a little "quality time" before a bedtime made excessively early by the mother's need to recuperate or excessively late by the mother's inability to discipline her emotionally demanding children. Working mothers are always tired and worried that their children will start to call the sitter "Mommy."

4   Then there are the single women who blazed a trail into "nontraditional" fields. Now approaching the end of their childbearing years without husbands or children or, in most cases, the career triumphs of men, many are beginning to wonder out loud if preparing legal briefs is all there is to life. This group is relatively small, but the extensive attention, not to say adulation, accorded it has ironically diminished the status of the motherhood its members now yearn for.

5   For their part, American men have responded to the message that they are no longer needed by giving women their independence in the form of unprecedented rates of divorce and abandonment: 1.6 million women now raise children under six with "no spouse present," in the language of the Bureau of Labor Statistics. Most of these women receive some form of public assistance (whose regulations, many economists believe, encourage men to stay away). Overall, the no-fault divorce laws now in force in most states, along with the Supreme Court's abolition of female-only alimony in *Orr v. Orr,* have proved financially catastrophic for women. As Lenore Weitzman has amply documented, after the average divorce the husband's standard of living rises while his ex-wife's standard of living falls dramatically.

6   Not only do a quarter of single mothers and their children end up below the poverty line; most of those who end up in poverty are single mothers and their children. A study prepared for the Census Bureau estimates that, had family composition remained constant throughout the 1970s, white median family income would have risen by 3 percent instead of the actual figure of .8 percent, and the black median family income would have risen by 5 percent instead of *falling* 11 percent. Had the rate of family break-up not increased, there would have been 4,200,000 families below the poverty line in 1980 instead of 6,217,000; of that 2,017,000 surplus, 1,377,000 are female-headed. At the margin, in other words, over 68 percent of those becoming poor are single mothers and their children.

7   Almost nothing is heard about "traditional" American women— still the majority, if barely—who raise children within a family supported by the husband's wage. Yet the fact remains that families of this sort experience far lower rates of divorce, poverty, and other forms of social pathology. In short, women do best when they raise children

with a hard-working man. By the test of experience, sexual egalitarians have lost the argument.

Not that anyone has stopped arguing, however. In fact, the major 8 participants are currently embroiled in a curious dispute about who should be blamed for a series of mistakes and in manufacturing new reasons for discredited proposals.

Sylvia Hewlett favorably contrasts the practical "social feminists" of 9 Europe who, she says, pressed for subsidized day care and maternity leave from the beginning, with American feminists, whom she accuses of being so preoccupied with the Equal Rights Amendment and with obliterating sex roles that they forgot to care about the real needs of women. Dr. Hewlett has been roundly attacked, apparently for daring to suggest that feminists might be wrong about *anything* (and, perhaps, for her candor about the lesbianism and man- and child-hating that permeate certain feminist circles); but the particular error, if error it be, of which she accuses American feminists is not one that they have committed.

When paid employment was supposed to be good for women, 10 and the question naturally arose of what to do with the children, American feminists proposed "the institutionalization of motherhood" (to use Jessie Bernard's phrase). In *Rethinking the Family* (1982), Barrie Thorne and Marilyn Yalom summarized what they took to be the orthodox feminist agenda:

> Maternity and paternity benefits and leaves as well as accessible and subsidized parent- and community-controlled day care, innovative worktime arrangements, shared parenting, and other nontraditional child-rearing and household arrangements.

It was this vision that propelled the Mondale-Brademas Comprehensive Child Development Act through Congress in 1971 (after which Richard Nixon vetoed it).

The issue is of far more than antiquarian interest. As it has become 11 apparent that paid employment is not living up to its billing as the road to female happiness, the argument now is that women *must* work. Divorced and abandoned women must support themselves somehow, and declining real wages have made it impossible for one income to support a family. According to a *Newsweek* poll, 56 percent of all women who work do so for the money; the figure is presumably much higher for mothers who work. Something must be done for the children, and if Americans really cared they would institute a "national family policy."

Thus, although eloquence about the glories of paid labor has 12 given way to eloquence about its miseries, the end remains the same— and so, for the most part, do the means. Betty Friedan, for example, announcing her willingness to "accept—rather than deny—the fact that 93 percent of American families fit patterns other than the traditional one," has called for "new responses to the conditions that are

cause and effect of such change." And what, putting aside the con-
trived statistic on the demise of the family, are these responses to be?

> [A]lternative forms of quality child care, both center and home
> based, and creative development (by business, labor, and
> government) of . . . flextime, flexible leave policies for both
> sexes, job-sharing programs, dependent-care options, and
> part-time jobs with pro-rated pay and benefits.

It is difficult to distinguish these proposals from Dr. Hewlett's list: "pay
equity," "federally-mandated partially-paid parental leave," public pre-
school for three-year-olds, "Public-Sector Initiatives" for child care,
private-sector day care, flexible work schedules, and federally-funded
health care for pregnant women and children. Ruth Sidel adds only
"collective action enabling women to enter male-dominated occupations" and a much less compromising insistence on "a national system
of day care and after-school care."

Now, it is generally agreed that a national day-care system should   13
be geared to serve at least nine million children. Even strong day-care
advocates urge that the ratio of children to adults not exceed 5 to 1,
which means that 1,800,000 "care-givers" will have to be recruited and
paid a living wage. Pegging that wage at a modest $20,000 a year
(about 85 percent of what the average teacher makes) already runs the
bill to $36 billion. Then there is the equipment for the hundreds of
thousands of individual facilities, the administrative salaries, licensing,
inspection, insurance, etc. With very moderate assumptions, total costs
quickly approach $90 billion.

Ruth Sidel is aware that "There will be those who say that we can-   14
not afford such a program. To them I say we cannot afford to continue
on our present course." (She, like Dr. Hewlett, raises the specter of
public disorder if three-year-olds are not properly socialized now.) Yet
even if day care and maternity leave were intrinsically unobjectionable,
the persistence of these recommendations is puzzling. One would
think that the goal of anyone who takes seriously the problems of the
mother who must work would be to make her working unnecessary,
and one way to help do so would be to increase the dependent deduction for minors on the federal income tax. This deduction is intended
to allow families to retain income sufficient to raise their children. In
1948 it was $600; it is now $1,080. Had it risen with inflation—and it
costs just as much today to raise a child as it did in 1948—the deduction would be about $4,500 more. As the average marginal tax rate is
25 percent, raising the deduction to match inflation would lower the
tax bill on the average family by $1,125 per child—*and* end up costing
the government less than national day care. Yet this is a proposal
which advocates of "national family policy" pass over in silence,
though it is surely more sensible to let people spend their own money
on the day-care facilities they need, or stay home with their children
and buy groceries with the money, than to spend it for them on the
same thing with all the overhead attendant on bureaucratic transfer.

Or consider the argument that women must work because a single   15
wage no longer suffices to support a family. It is true that average
weekly gross earnings fell from $189 in 1977 to $173 in 1984 (in constant 1977 dollars); no doubt, too, expectations are higher today, and
for many there are new expenses perceived as necessities (such as private school for parents who find the public schools unacceptable). But
wages are not doomed to fall; in 1955, let us remember, average gross
earnings were only $153. An increase in husbands' earnings is known
to lower the labor-force participation of women and increase marital
stability. Would not a curb on inflation and a rise in real wages solve a
big part of the "feminization of poverty"?

Dr. Hewlett is alone among family-policy advocates in even con-   16
sidering this topic:

> In May 1983 I interviewed Faith Whittlesey at the White
> House. At that time she was assistant to the President for pub-
> lic liaison and dealt with policies toward women and chil-
> dren. . . . She told me that Ronald Reagan was tremendously
> concerned about the care and nurturing of children and that
> he did in fact have a policy in this area. The policy was to lick
> inflation and encourage the economy to grow so that men
> could once more earn a family wage.

Dr. Hewlett, an economist by training, professes puzzlement at this
idea and sets forth the following objection to it:

> The odd thing is that Reagan himself grew up in the '20s and
> had a working mother; she worked in a dress shop for $14 a
> week in order to help out with the precarious family finances.
> You might imagine he would relate to the difficulties faced by
> contemporary working mothers. Instead, he clings to a vision
> of motherhood '50s-style which did not exist in the 1920s and
> does not exist today.

There follows a grotesque caricature of what the '50s supposedly represented motherhood to be. Such evasive maneuvers strongly suggest
that, like the radical egalitarians she is allegedly criticizing, Dr. Hewlett
does not *want* the problems of women to be solved except in ways
which facilitate their working.

The main argument by which family-policy advocates attempt to   17
reinforce the "need" for mothers to work, and to rebut the counter-
charge that subsidized day care is too expensive and/or may harm children, is to invoke the example of Sweden, where most mothers work,
most children spend most of their time in government-run crèches, and
90 percent-paid parental leave is mandatory. (The example of the Soviet Union, which has also socialized child care, is less frequently invoked. Israel, where the egalitarian experiment has failed, is not mentioned at all.)

One crucial difference between the American situation and Swe-   18
den, however, is that the Swedish government was not responding to
any prior need; the Swedish experiment was part of a conscious

decision made by the Labor party in the mid-1960s to implement the full feminist program of obliterating sex roles. It was to encourage women to work that crèches and maternity leave were established in the first place. The costliness of these and allied measures then raised taxes so high—the Swedish government currently consumes over 70 percent of the nation's GNP—that one income no longer sufficed to support a family. Sweden took advantage of the situation by abolishing the joint tax return in 1971, making the marginal tax rate on any extra income the husband might earn prohibitively high, and effectively forcing a non-working wife to seek employment, in a (relatively) lower tax bracket. Swedish women are thus working to finance the facilities that allow them to work. While nothing so drastic is likely to happen in the U.S., this tale does illustrate how governmental steps to create the "option" of work outside the home tend at the same time to create incentives to work, and are thus not neutral.

The Swedish experiment is too new for its full effect on the gener-   19
ation of Swedes currently growing up to have been measured longitudinally, but certain trends have already emerged. Marriage is becoming a thing of the past. The cohabitation rate has risen from 1 percent in 1960 to 30 percent. Almost as many conceptions result in abortions or illegitimate births as in live legitimate births. Most significantly, the Swedish birth rate, like that of other Scandinavian countries committed to sexual equality, has fallen far below replacement. The average pair of Swedes is producing only 1.5 new Swedes, about the same rate as in Germany; in Denmark, the rate is 1.4.

A birth rate this low—replacement is 2.1 offspring per woman—   20
is a consequence of biology and arithmetic. It takes a woman nine months to have a baby; she will normally wish to spend at least three years with her child before sending it off somewhere, and it is considered advisable to space pregnancies by no lesser an interval. Therefore, a woman who has three children will typically spend at least a decade of her most energetic years in maternal pursuits; conversely, the practical limit on the number of children that can be born to a woman pursuing a career has been found to be two. We need not think of a low birth rate as a symptom of some deeper malaise to see that a society which encourages its women to work away from home to anything like the extent men do will eventually disappear.[3]

The long-term effects of institutional child-rearing are unclear. Its   21
advocates have recently announced the discovery that day care actually benefits children by offering them "alternative role models" and that a child raised institutionally need not be emotionally deprived if he receives sufficient love and attention. That is the sort of thing known as a mighty big if. Clinicians are unanimous that a child needs the attention

---

[3]On these grounds alone it is hard to understand the appeal of a system of values which guarantees the end of any society that embraces it. Yet it certainly continues to exercise an appeal, even to those, like Ben Wattenberg, aware of and worried about the falling birth rate. Wattenberg wants there to be more children, but he also wants to preserve the triumphs of feminism. His solution to the birth dearth: parental leave and day care.

of his mother for at least his first year, and continuity in his personal caretaker for at least his first three years, if he is to have the best chance for satisfactory personal relations later in life. These inconvenient truths irritate Dr. Hewlett, since they "would rule out a job for most women. . . . What [working women with children under one] need is decent maternity leave and high-quality child care, not another guilt trip." Surely, however, since the large-scale rearing of children by strangers is new to human history, it would be prudent to place on its advocates the onus of proving that it does no harm. It is not enough to intone "day care, day care," and thereupon consign to it the most valuable things anyone will ever possess.

It is becoming an intellectual commonplace that social institutions   22 cannot be understood apart from the biological sources of human behavior. It is no more possible to explain what creates and sustains a society in terms of that society itself than it is to explain how a clock keeps time by positing another clock inside it. By the same token, social norms and government actions based on ignorance of human nature are doomed to be irrelevant or positively mischievous.

Those who take seriously the innateness of sex differences could   23 have predicted (and in many cases did predict) the woes besetting women liberated wholly or partly from motherhood and marriage. Women have not risen as high in business or government as they were supposed to do, not because of discrimination but because they have not wanted to rise as badly as men. It is generally the career woman with children, rather than her husband, who diverts energy toward the children—because she is the one with the more intense desire to do so. Those women who have reached the top experience abnormal rates of divorce, childlessness, and spinsterhood because, like other women, they are attracted to men of status higher than their own, and far up the ladder such men are rare (and these men can select mates from the much wider range of women of lower status). Children impair a divorced mother's earning ability not merely because having them interrupts the accumulation of working skills, but because, unlike a man who wins custody and is psychologically capable of hiring a nanny and getting on with his work, a mother cannot easily put her children out of her mind. These impulses, besides being self-evident, all make perfect sense from the point of view of evolutionary biology.

In following the family-policy literature, one is repeatedly struck   24 by the completeness with which it has absorbed the basic errors of the sexual egalitarianism it is said to have transcended. The first error is the assumption that the female traits which are causing all the trouble are learned by socialization, and can be unlearned. Ruth Sidel deplores "the continuing socialization of women to perceive themselves as dependent." For Barbara Berg, the guilt experienced by mothers who spend too little time with their children is not a response to a nurturant drive gone unheeded but to

> the decision to be different from our mothers, to choose a different lifestyle, to challenge her values, attitudes, child-rearing

practices—this appears to conflict with what we learned from
our mother, with her standards of mothering, which are also
ours.

Her solution is correspondingly superficial: "streamline the family
chores, . . . hire as much help as [you can] afford. . . . Exercise—biking,
dancing, jogging—are all good for stress management, and they have
the added advantage of keeping you in shape."

At a deeper level, while the family-policy literature catalogues   25
with bitter relish all the trials of motherhood-on-the-run, it expresses
little joy in motherhood itself, and has no praise whatever for the male
protective role, the natural complement of the mother's need for protection. Not only does family policy begin with the mother who must
be eased back into the workforce after her man has left her (the task of
keeping him at home in the first place being treated as mission impossible), but its call for teaching young girls "realism" about the unrelia-
bility of men often lapses into open hostility toward male protective
impulses. During the 1981 congressional hearings on "Sex Equity in
Vocational Education," Carol Jabonaski explained the problem:

> We are beginning to see that younger female students are rec-
> ognizing the fact that they do have to work and they are be-
> ginning to plan for those careers. . . . The young males, how-
> ever, are still seeing themselves as the sole breadwinner and
> that the females will be at home. That presents a conflict. . . .
> These conflicts are there and no one has helped to train them
> or to let them understand that it is OK to have an alternative
> lifestyle. All of that area still needs to be addressed.

"A wife is only a divorce away from welfare," goes the slogan, and
most family-policy advocates do not want anyone to forget it.

But the fundamental error retained from feminist egalitarianism is   26
the idea that the elements of a satisfying life are ultimately the same for
women and men. Despite the to-do accompanying the recent discovery that women have maternal impulses—which was never doubted
for a second by anyone but sexual egalitarians—it has yet to be
grasped that these impulses weaken the drive for extrafamilial achievement so evident in men.

The female as currently conceived is literally too good to be true,   27
possessed of female needs superimposed on male aspirations. Because, in Dr. Sidel's words, "The opportunity to work at a job that offers some measure of dignity, security, and respect—with rewardable
recompense—is a fundamental right of both women *and* men, as well
as the foundation of a meaningful family policy," the best female life is
taken to revolve around a fulfilling job, paid maternity leave, then back
to the 9-to-5 challenge. The wife is to be secure in the knowledge that
her child is being cared for by a licensed, federally-inspected caregiver,
just as men once went off to work secure in the knowledge that their
children were being well cared for by their wives. In the end, Dr.
Hewlett and others acknowledge the physical impossibility or difficulty

of returning to work only for the period immediately after giving birth. Motherhood remains an obstacle to be circumvented.

For two decades now, Western society has reserved its highest 28
praise for atypical women, indirectly encouraging all women to judge themselves by and pursue standards they are unlikely to meet, and to judge motherhood, which virtually all women can succeed at, as of little intrinsic worth. It was inevitable that the "status of women" should fall in a world of firepersons and affirmative-action astronauts. The conditions under which the typical male and female drives evolved may no longer be present, but our genes have yet to receive the message. Meanwhile, despite changes in the rhetoric of the women's movement in speaking of motherhood, the pressure for collectivized child-rearing continues.

Reading and Taking Notes

Boyd went through the entire text paragraph by paragraph. At the end of each paragraph, he wrote a brief summary. These are his summaries for the first five paragraphs:

```
Paragraph one: women are in confusion and distress.
Paragraph two: women have been told that being a wife and
     mother is not enough, that fulfillment comes only
     through work.
Paragraph three: actually, working women are tired, frus-
     trated, and worried about their kids.
Paragraph four: single women w/o children now wonder if
     "preparing legal briefs" has been worth it.
Paragraph five: men have responded to the new situation
     by divorcing and abandoning women.
```

When Boyd came to a space break, he summarized the entire preceding section. At the end of his reading, he saw that the section summaries did indicate the shape of the argument, as he had suspected they would. Here are his section summaries:

```
Section one: the harm to women and society emerge from
     idea that women should work outside the home
Section two: despite stress on women, feminists continue
     to push for day care and other "family policy" pro-
     grams
Section three: attacks family policy programs on economic
     grounds
Section four: warns of consequences of adopting measures
     such as those in Sweden, with its welfare state and
     attendant problems
```

```
Section five: explains ideas behind whole argument, that
          women and men have different biological drives and
          women are not meant to have both a career and a
          family
```

Rereading and Taking More Notes

Boyd went over the essay several times, adding to and revising his notes. He consulted his dictionary for words such as *catatonia, egalitarians,* and *antiquarian.* He noted the disparaging references to feminist positions and asked himself whether he agreed with Levin about biological drives. Boyd agreed that expectations for and of women were certainly high and could lead to unhappiness. He was unsure about the wisdom of instituting national day-care programs.

He was ready to answer the eight questions.

Asking and Answering the Eight Questions

```
1. Subject: women and working; family policy programs
2. Purpose: to persuade readers "toward a new apprecia-
   tion of motherhood and children" (paragraph 1)
3. Thesis: Contrary to feminist propaganda, day care and
   similar programs are harmful to women and society
   (Sections two and three), and "Women do best when they
   raise children with a hard-working man" (paragraph 7)
4. Main supporting points:
   working women are experiencing strain and guilt
   high rates of divorce and abandonment and low birth
        rates have followed
   national family policy programs are too costly and
        will lead to further social disintegration
   the new expectations of women pull against their ge-
        netically ingrained impulses
   unrealistic expectations will continue to make women
        unhappy and lead to foolish and dangerous ideas
```

There were other interesting ideas—increasing the tax deduction for minors, for example—but Boyd thought these five underlay all the others.

```
5. Assumptions:
   feminist propaganda has forced women to seek careers
```

```
women inherently are driven to nurture more than to
    succeed in business
women have not risen in business and the professions
    because of their own limitations, not society's
many feminists are really hostile to men and some to
    children
our social ills are directly attributable to a too-
    open and liberal society
government programs are less good at solving problems
    than is individual initiative
American economic problems are solvable
women would be content to retire to the home and chil-
    dren--if the feminists would just leave them alone
biology is destiny, and women are destined to a sub-
    ordinate role
6. Evidence: recent history, statistics, quotations,
    economic analysis, common knowledge, reasoning
```

Boyd checked the evidence he could, such as statistics on the growth of real wages, quotations from Hewlett, Sidel, and other writers, how the dependent child deduction works. Other evidence, such as that concerning the Swedish national-welfare system, he couldn't check. He noted that Levin didn't always document his ideas. Levin didn't, for instance, name the economists he refers to (paragraph 5) or offer expert opinion from biologists and psychologists to support his idea of innate drives. These lapses weren't enough, Boyd thought, to trash Levin's argument, but they hurt it.

```
7. Conclusion: Our society is forcing male aspirations
    to be superimposed on female needs. This can only
    lead to continued strain and guilt for individual
    women and continued harm to family and society.
8. The whole work: provocative, informative, and at
    times disturbing.
```

Boyd agreed with some but not all of what Levin had to say. He was bothered by the idea of innate drives, which suggested the biological inferiority of women, and he thought the real issue—our social ills—had not been addressed very well. Although he had many strong feelings about the essay, Boyd knew he would make his points better through carefully reasoned analysis than through emotional outbursts.

After his analysis, Boyd was ready to respond to Levin's essay. He freewrote on the topic several times until he had clarified his thesis enough to write it down:

```
     While Levin shows that it is hard for women to have
both family and career, he does not really demonstrate
that feminist thinking has produced our social evils. He
bases his claim on some very questionable assumptions
about male and female biology--and an even more question-
able portrayal of feminist thinkers.
```

Planning the Essay and Selecting Evidence

Boyd turned to his notes. Although extremely useful when we turn reading into writing, raw notes—that is, those taken while reading—are not a good basis for organizing an essay. They follow the shape of the reading, and adhering closely to them usually makes for a poorly constructed essay. Successful essays seize on a significant point and organize the writer's thinking around that. An argument's shape must take priority over the shape of the text.

An outline can help at this point. It allows the writer to devise a general structure and then to place the ideas where they belong. It provides a plan to work by. Boyd found that his thesis statement actually suggested the shape of his essay (often the case with a good thesis statement).

Notes are the relay station between reading and writing. From our notes we identify our major support, select examples, distill what we need from the text, and remind ourselves of our thoughts. After establishing his outline, Boyd went over his notes and decided what to put where. He decided, for instance, that in paragraph 23 Levin had made some dubious assertions about social ills that would fit in nicely under item V. A. of the outline. Thus he created what is called a *working outline*—that is, an outline with major evidence and references underneath the points they support. When our notes are organized according to the plan for the essay, the writing becomes simpler, almost a matter of filling in the blanks. When Boyd plugged in his evidence, his outline looked like this:

```
     While Levin shows that it is hard for women to have
both family and career, he does not really demonstrate
that feminist thinking has produced our social evils. He
bases this claim on some very questionable assumptions
about male and female biology--and an even more question-
able portrayal of feminist thinkers.
```

I. Argues women and society are suffering because of the expectation that women will find fulfillment in work
   A. Women (paragraphs 3, 23, 27)
   B. Society (5, 6, 7, 20, 23)

II. Government-run programs too expensive and inefficient to support working women (paragraphs 13, 14, 15)

III. Much truth in Levin's argument
   A. "Superwoman" syndrome really does exist (Mom)
   B. So do the ideas he dislikes (paragraphs 24, 25, 26)

IV. But he doesn't convincingly show that feminism is behind all these social ills
   A. No real evidence (paragraph 5)
   B. His picture of the feminist movement a little unfair
   C. Feminism by itself not enough to cause these social ills
   D. Levin never addresses other possible causes

V. Least convincing are his ideas about biological differences
   A. Pretty questionable (paragraphs 7, 23)
   B. Differences not established or inevitable
   C. Bad basis for social policy

VI. Levin ignores the fact that many women want to work (e.g., Mom) and has no real answers for social ills

Drafting and Revising

After he had reorganized his notes according to his outline, Boyd went back over his overall plan. Because he was writing an analysis of a difficult work, he knew his writing had to be especially clear and precise. He had to do justice both to Levin's thinking and to his own. He created a two-paragraph introduction that established the background and general topic and allowed him to work more leisurely toward his thesis.

Several drafts later, he was ready to turn in this version:

Does Superwoman Want to Fly?

My mother, who works as a marketing consultant, is [1]
Superwoman. She tries to be everything to everybody, and
I know she's worrying all the time. If family life is
good, she worries about the office. If the office is

fine, she worries about her husband. If he's fine, what
about the children? She is always tired, and she
sometimes wonders if it is worth it.

In his essay "Feminism: Stage Three," Michael Levin   2
definitely has a point: our expectations make it harder,
not easier, for women to be happy. However, he is arguing
more than this. Feminist ideas--especially the idea that
women should seek fulfillment in their work--are hurting
women and society in general. He says it is hard for
women to have both a family and a career. I begin to
question him when he starts to blame feminist ideas for
divorce, abandonment, and poverty. He doesn't really
prove that feminist thinking has produced all these
social ills. He bases his claim on some very questionable assumptions about male and female biology, and his
portrayal of feminist thinkers isn't really fair.

Levin's portrayal of the working woman is pretty   3
sad. She has to live up to an ideal that is "too good to
be true" (paragraph 27). She follows a crazy schedule
that leaves no time for family or home life, and she is
worried that the children "will start to call the sitter
'Mommy'" (paragraph 3). Despite all her work, she, like
most working women, has not risen as high as she expected
(paragraph 23). According to Levin, work has led to "abnormal rates of divorce, childlessness, and spinsterhood" (paragraph 23).

Society has suffered, too. Levin links feminism with   4
many social ills, including the rising rates of divorce
and abandonment (paragraphs 5 and 23), poverty (paragraphs 6 and 7), and low birth rates (paragraph 20). As
I will discuss later, many of these issues and trends
really do exist. The question is whether they add up as
Levin says they do.

With the plight of women, Levin ridicules feminists   5
who call for a national family policy. His best point
is that the bill for national day care would "quickly
approach $90 billion" (paragraph 13). He says government-
run programs are too expensive and inefficient to do the
job. I'd add that taxpayers wouldn't support such a

program, even if it cost half that much. So how do we
help women who want to work? Levin thinks that higher
deductions for children (paragraph 14) and a healthier
economy (paragraph 15) will do the trick.

There is a lot of truth in Levin's argument. Some   6
of the "errors" he dislikes the most are definitely out
there. The Superwoman Syndrome is something real. Some
people do talk as though innate biological female traits
are "learned by socialization" (paragraph 24), but I
agree with Levin that you shouldn't deny differences:
they're there. If feminists are really putting down
motherhood and the male role, as Levin says they are
(paragraph 25), that's the wrong way to go. Hostility
won't get anything accomplished. Neither will treating
women "the same" as men, as the "sexual egalitarians"
(paragraph 26) want to. Nobody is the same as anyone
else.

Levin makes a sort of side-argument against fem-   7
inists, however. He says they have persuaded women that
fulfillment comes from "paid employment" (paragraph 2)
and have told men that "they are no longer needed"
(paragraph 5). They see motherhood not as praiseworthy
but as an obstacle to get around (paragraph 27).

If we add all Levin's portrayals together, we get a   8
picture of a foolish, dangerous bunch. You can probably
find all these ideas in some author or other, but that
does not prove that these are what all feminists stand
for. We learned in class that feminism includes many
diverse thinkers, including political conservatives and
middle-of-the-roaders. Some feminists just want equal
opportunity under the law. (That's the kind I agree with
most.) At the other end of the spectrum, others do
believe women must avoid marriage if they want fulfillment. They have gotten most of the big headlines, but
they are a minority. It is unfair to treat all feminists
as radicals.

Are feminist ideas the major cause of these prob-   9
lems, as he claims? I can't get excited about the low
birth rate, but the other things like the increase in the

divorce rate and the fact that most of the poor are women and children (paragraph 6), those are important. So did feminism cause them? I can't find much evidence really linking the two. Levin blames feminist ideas for the no-fault divorce laws and the abolition of female-only alimony that has been "financially catastrophic for women" (paragraph 5). But were these things caused by feminist ideas? Lots of people want no-fault divorce laws. For one thing, they alleviate the legal and material hassles around divorce. And suppose there was a really rich woman divorcing a poor man--shouldn't she pay alimony? So I can't agree with Levin here.

Maybe there's no one, or no one thing, to blame for 10 our social ills. Even if all the feminists are man-hating lesbian radicals, they still wouldn't be enough to cause such huge changes. Other causes are there, too. Attitudes toward sex have changed, probably a result of the Pill. And Levin never bothers to address the gap between rich and poor and the big changes in the world economy, which contribute a lot to family problems and poverty.

Least convincing of all is what Levin says about the 11 biological differences between men and women. He claims women can't concentrate on their careers because they have "the more intense desire" (paragraph 23) to stay home and raise the kids. Men want to work, protect, be the breadwinners. Families based on these differences "experience far lower rates of divorce, poverty, and other forms of social pathology" (paragraph 7). His conclusion is that "women do best when they raise children with a hard-working man" (paragraph 7).

That would come as news to my mother. She would not 12 like the idea that somehow women's economic lives should depend on a man's. She would get rather upset by Levin's closing section. He claims that some set of clear traits is somehow "self-evident" (paragraph 23) and inevitable, and that we should construct our social policy on those traits.

I don't think things are that clear. Where are the 13 biologists and psychologists to define these clear differences for us? I don't question that some differences exist--but I don't think they are etched in stone or that all people react in the same ways to them. I don't think you can base policy decisions on some idea of innate impulses.

Levin basically ignores the fact that many women   14
want to work. Many are being raised to expect a career, and they hit the job market ready to go. Maybe all that contradicts what they biologically want, but we're not trying to give women a life without problems (nobody can have that), just the chance to be both mothers and workers if they want. Levin says that's suicidal for both women and society as a whole. But there's evidence that women were unhappy the way it used to be. My mother really likes her job and wants to keep working. Levin implies that women like her don't know their own impulses--or that they're "atypical" (paragraph 28). If so, then there are millions of atypical women out there.

Again, he has a point. Work and family pull my   15
mother in opposite directions. No doubt about it. But we don't have much support for women who work. Tax breaks might help, but not enough. Neither will good times: the 1980s ended with more poor and a bigger gap between rich and poor than before. Levin doesn't discuss anything but returning to single-income families. In other words, solve the problems of working women by encouraging them not to work. That won't help the family finances, and it won't appeal to the woman who thinks she wants her own life, the Superwoman who wants to fly.

Tips for Getting Writing from Reading
- Follow the nine steps when writing about reading: map, read and take notes, reread and take more notes, ask the eight questions, form a thesis, plan your essay, select evidence from the text, draft, and revise.
- Let the organization of your argument take priority over that of the text.
- When writing an analytical essay, take special care to write clearly and precisely.

EXERCISES FOR GETTING WRITING FROM READING

1. For your next assignment, write a brief essay discussing your comfort level with each of the nine steps in the first tip above. Which were easiest? Which were least comfortable? Was the working outline helpful? Did you have to change the outline once you began to draft? Assess the usefulness of the nine-step program.

2. With a partner, make an outline for a paper on a work you have both read. One of you will then turn the outline into a working outline by reading through your sources and plugging evidence into the outline. The other will go directly from the bare outline to drafting, plugging in evidence as he or she goes. Once the two of you are done, compare your experiences in writing the essay. Was the working outline helpful? Were there any advantages from going straight from outline to drafting? Why or why not? Write a brief essay comparing your processes and the essays that resulted.

PART THREE

Writing to Persuade
The Argumentative Essay

6

Using Evidence

Some circumstantial evidence is very strong, as
when you find a trout in the milk.
— HENRY DAVID THOREAU (1817–1862)
AMERICAN WRITER AND NATURALIST

In much of your college writing, you will try to persuade your reader to
see things your way. In a political science class, you may want to persuade your instructor that voting patterns changed in the 1980s because
of the growing disparity between the rich and the poor. In an American
literature class, you may want to argue that the three major characters in
Melville's *Billy Budd* represent the three main American national character types. In a history class, you may want to claim that pollution is, or
is not, a major problem for southern California's ecology. Underlying
strong persuasion is valid evidence. Without good evidence to support
your ideas, you will hardly persuade anyone of anything. Although we
mention evidence throughout this book, we have three reasons for examining the subject in its own chapter. First, evidence usually takes up
the bulk of an argumentative essay. For a single assertion, you may
need to present two, three, perhaps four pieces of evidence. For the
Billy Budd essay, for example, you would probably need to refer to experts to establish a definition of national character, and you might well
want to incorporate your own experience with various American types.
You would then reason your way to your conclusion.

Second, handling evidence well is essential to a good essay. The process of gathering, evaluating, interpreting, and defending evidence is a major part of college work. If you were writing about voting patterns, you would need to be very careful in selecting the statistics on which you would base your assertion. Not all numbers would be relevant, or even true.

Third, evidence is extremely varied and complicated. The essay on California's ecology, for example, would certainly require expert testimony to analyze the situation and statistics to indicate the pollution rate. To make your case, you would probably need examples of the ecological damage or lack thereof.

In the pages that follow, we discuss seven kinds of evidence and how to use them.

EXPERT TESTIMONY: LEARNING FROM THOSE WHO KNOW

Learning to evaluate experts and what they have to say is one of the most important goals of education. All our lives, our opinions and even our values and actions are shaped by experts—the doctor, the lawyer, the engineer, the secretary of the treasury. These experts will not always agree with one another. One lawyer may advise suing, another negotiating. One foreign policy expert says we should send financial aid to Country Y, another says absolutely not. Most of us have not had legal training, and few will know much about Country Y. We have to rely on experts.

What is an expert? An expert is someone who has special skill and knowledge based on careful study and wide experience in a certain area. More than that, an expert has tested his or her skill and knowledge in a public forum—through books, articles, performances, lectures, debates—where other experts can challenge any idea or opinion. Expertise must be able to survive public scrutiny. The testimony of self-styled experts carries little weight. Albert Einstein did not achieve the status of an authority until other scientists found evidence for his theory of relativity in their own calculations and experiments. Gregory Bateson became an expert in anthropology by first doing fieldwork and then publishing his findings so that other anthropologists could examine them.

Many assignments in college will test your ability to use expert testimony. An economics instructor could ask you to write an essay on monetary theorists. An Asian history instructor could assign a study of the various interpretations of the 1899–1900 Boxer Rebellion in China. They will want you not merely to condense and repeat what the experts say but also to evaluate it and use it to help you form your own opinion.

Once your opinion is firm, you can use expert testimony to support it. To use expert testimony wisely, be both respectful and critical.

You will need to differentiate among three kinds of evidence that experts provide: facts, informed opinions, and speculations. First are *facts*. Facts are incontrovertible: anyone investigating a subject would come up with the same information.

> The United States has experienced inflation almost steadily since 1776.
>
> Until recently, bacteria were a genuine household threat.

If you use only recognized experts, you can have greater confidence in the validity of the factual evidence they supply.

Experts become experts not only by knowing facts but also by developing *informed opinions* about them; this is the second kind of evidence experts provide. Facts need the play of the human intellect to give them significance. Careful experts constantly bring facts together and interpret them. When a scholar or professional concludes that the facts justify a particular generalization, you can use that generalization as support for your claim. It is not quite a matter of "If Professor *X* thinks so, it must be so"—Professor *Z,* also an expert, may disagree. But if Professor *X* thinks so, then that does carry some weight. For instance, the historian A. J. P. Taylor's opinion that the major factor leading to the end of World War I was a revolution in Germany lends considerable, if controversial, strength to any argument advancing the same point.

The third kind of evidence experts offer can be dangerous for the unwary to use. It is *speculation,* neither contradicted nor adequately supported by the facts. As do the rest of us, experts like to project their ideas beyond provable limits. Often this imagining opens up new areas for research and study and may give rise to new knowledge. But speculation is only what one person, albeit an expert, thinks is plausible. It should be treated as merely a suggestion or a hypothesis, something that *could* be true.

When experts speculate, they usually qualify their hypotheses with words and phrases such as *perhaps, seems, may be, conceivable, possibly.* It is up to the reader to notice those qualifiers and to use the statement accordingly, that is, not as a claim or as an interpretation but as a conjecture.

Check the credentials of any authority you cite. Find out the background and the source of his or her expertise. Assess the range and breadth of any bibliographies provided at the end of articles or books. Check for possible bias—a scientist employed in industry may be slow to find harm in his or her company's products, and a scholar holding a government post may have lost some objectivity. Be aware, too, that their opponents could be equally biased. Be particularly careful with accounts in which the observer has a stake in what happened. For example, you should check the official Chinese account of the 1966–1976 Cultural Revolution in China against the descriptions by experts with other political and cultural viewpoints. The same goes for the State Department's account of its successes in foreign policy. Experts, yes. Unbiased? Maybe not.

🖳 **Computer Tip**

Evaluating online sources is particularly important and particularly difficult. Since much of the material on the Internet is hard to trace, it is often impossible to know whether your sources are reputable. For more information on using Internet sources, see Chapter 13, Doing Research.

STATISTICS AND SAMPLES: THE MAGIC OF NUMBERS

Whether they are raw data or translated into charts and figures, numbers are powerful evidence. Properly used, they can prove a claim rapidly and conclusively. Understanding numbers has become essential to a college education. It is basic to the sciences, the social sciences, and disciplines such as history.

Statistics are numerical data gathered and tabulated to yield information. Statistical data can be used in many ways. An investigator who had collected a mass of data on grades in a chemistry class, for instance, could construct from it a graph in the form of a curve. At one end of the curve would be the highest grade and at the other end the lowest. If the curve is a bell curve, a gradual increase of numbers would appear from the lowest grade to the middle grade and then a gradual decrease to the highest. Most students, that is, would fall in the middle, where the curve bulges. Or the investigator could compare each individual's performance with that of the rest of the class by examining his or her place on the curve.

An investigator could also determine the performance of the statistically average student. There are three ways to do this. To compute the *mean,* you add all the grades and divide the total by the number of students. To compute the *median,* you find the grade in the exact middle of the range from highest to lowest. Half the grades would be above the median, half would be below. To compute the *mode,* you determine what grade the greatest number of students achieved. When dealing with averages, pay close attention to which of these methods is used, for computing the mean, median, and mode will render different results.

Scientists often use the technique called *sampling* to discover the typical acts, beliefs, characteristics, or qualities of a very large population. Rather than trying to interview or test each individual, the investigator studies a representative number of individuals in a group. This is the technique used by Gallup polls. To discover what the American public thinks about an issue, Gallup poll-takers interview a small representative group of Americans.

The problem arises in selecting the individuals to be studied because they must truly represent the group as a whole. The findings of a study on what Americans think about pornography on the Internet, for example, would be distorted if the proportion of pornography watchers in the group studied was higher than that in the general population. The result would almost certainly indicate a higher percentage of approval than is the case. Be sure any sampling data you use comes from a representative group.

Numbers can mislead the unwary. Say you are going to write an essay on unemployment. In your research you find a graph in a reputable journal indicating that X million Americans are presently employed, the largest number of workers in America's history. You would perhaps conclude from this that unemployment is not a problem. But then you read in another reputable journal that Y percent of Americans are presently out of work, the largest percentage since 1940. Based on this evidence, you would perhaps conclude that unemployment is in fact a serious problem. Both journals may be correct. The problem is that different ways of calculating the numbers tell different stories.

Deep down most of us still believe in the magic of numbers. We trust them. But alas, nothing obscures the truth more effectively than numbers misused. Fifty million Frenchmen can't be wrong, says the song. If polls say Senator Smith will be defeated, why bother to vote? Our point is, fifty million people *can* be wrong, and even the best polls have been far off the mark. Cite numbers, yes, but handle with care.

EXAMPLES: BEING SPECIFIC

Every day of your life you use examples as evidence for your claims. You might say, "*Hamlet* has some very perplexing scenes. In one, Hamlet pretends to be pursuing a rat, but he actually kills Polonius, who is hiding in the draperies." Or you might write to your parents, "Sorry I haven't written much but I've been very busy. I spent last week in the library, bent over the books studying for two midterms." In each case, you establish your claim ("*Hamlet* has some perplexing scenes," "I've been very busy") and you back it up with a specific example.

Examples serve three purposes. First, they clarify meaning. Your parents may not know exactly what you mean by *busy* until you show them. Second, examples demonstrate why, at least in one instance, you are justified in making your claim. Studying for two midterms does sound like being busy. Third, examples make for entertaining reading. Abstractions are dry. Claiming that you are busy isn't very interesting. But the image of you bent intently over a book probably pleases your parents, who may now forgive you for not writing.

We wish we could offer a rule about how many examples you need to prove what, but of course the number varies. Trust your intuition. How many examples do you need to support your point? Err on the side of abundance, but don't exhaust your reader.

PERSONAL EXPERIENCE: WHAT YOU KNOW ON YOUR OWN

If we actually experience something directly, we don't need experts or statistics to back us up. We saw the robber running from the scene of the crime. Although we know that our experience is not totally reliable—the robber turned out to be a cocker spaniel—until proved wrong, we trust our senses and our ability to understand our personal experience.

In complex matters, however, beware of jumping to conclusions based on limited personal experience. One occurrence does not make an immutable law. Your experience may help to explain, but it cannot prove a more general thesis. Knowing someone who cheats on her income tax does not prove that the problem with income tax cheaters is pervasive. Even if you know five or ten or twenty cheaters, all that proves is that you are unlucky in your acquaintances. For such a complex subject, you need more than personal experience. You need statistics and expert interpretation.

Personal observation can be useful, nonetheless. At the beginning of an essay it may sharply focus your argument. In a conclusion it may sum up points more emphatically than further exposition. Throughout an essay it may powerfully illuminate facts and figures. Personal experience may not prove a proposition, but it enlivens reading.

ANALOGY: SHOWING HOW THINGS ARE SIMILAR

An analogy is a comparison of apparently dissimilar things, and its purpose is to illuminate one thing by showing how it is like and not like the other. To the extent that analogies make a point easy to see, they are evidence. But they don't prove the point—they can never be sufficient evidence for a complex idea. A student wrote an essay on World War II in which she wanted to suggest that General Eisenhower functioned as coordinator of the armies in the European theater rather than as strategist, tactician, or field commander. She constructed this analogy:

> Eisenhower served as the conductor of the invasion of Europe. He did not write the music or play an instrument, but he selected the music and the musicians, determined the interpretation, kept the beat, and then evaluated the whole performance.

Although this analogy does not prove that Eisenhower was only the coordinator, it clarifies what the student wanted to say. Because she had other powerful evidence, the analogy drove the point home.

Problems may arise, however, when writers either ignore or suppress differences that invalidate the analogy. Depending on how damaging the differences are, analogies can be weak, unclear, or false:

> We can view the African practice of sister trading to be exactly analogous to conversation, the trading of words.

This analogy is false: conversation is portable and repeatable in a way a sister is not, and it has no inherent right to be treated with dignity and consideration.

Sometimes a writer uses an analogy indirectly to argue a point the reader would not otherwise agree with, as here:

> Human beings in society are like the bees in a hive. Each person's identity is determined by his or her function and place in the overall system. Like drones, no one has any identity apart from the work he or she does. If people do not work or refuse to conform to the role the system has assigned them, they, like weak or unfit bees, should be thrown out of the system to live or die on their own.

Hey, wait a minute. Analogies are valid only when the two things compared are clearly similar, which beehives and human society are not. The difference between bees and human beings is too great. Think of dissimilarities, and keep your eye on where an analogy will lead you.

KNOWN FACTS AND SHARED BELIEFS: WHAT WE ALL HAVE IN COMMON

When writing, you can safely assume that you and your reader share a vast body of facts and beliefs. You do not need to point out that Columbus arrived in America in 1492, that Theodore Roosevelt was once president, that false arrest is wrong. No one wants to waste time and eyesight reading that sort of thing.

But generally known facts can be effective when used in a surprising context.

> Columbus brought Western civilization to the Western Hemisphere in 1492, but the Mayans knew mathematics and astronomy and practiced urban planning long before that.

Juxtaposing this generally known fact about Columbus with less familiar information about the Mayans can underscore our cultural bias. Or you might write,

> We all believe false arrest is wrong, but what do we believe about social programs that incarcerate unwilling bag ladies in overnight shelters?

Here, reference to the truism about false arrest aggressively questions some elements of our liberal, democratic tradition. When we appeal to known facts and shared beliefs, we strengthen our point.

REASONING AND LOGIC: THINKING IT THROUGH

Sometimes the only evidence you bring to bear is your ability to reason and employ logic. If, say, your instructor asked you to respond to Plato's *Apology* or John Stuart Mill's *On Liberty,* he or she would want to know what you think about these works. The only relevant evidence would be your reasoning. In Chapter 2, we discussed the basic ways of reasoning. Here, we just want to point out that in your arsenal of evidence, thinking itself is a very powerful weapon.

CRITERIA FOR GOOD EVIDENCE: MAKING SURE

Solid evidence of every variety exhibits the following five qualities: relevance, representativeness, accuracy, detail, and adequacy.

Relevance

Good evidence speaks directly and unequivocally to the point. You should select a particular piece of evidence because it supports the point, not because it is novel or comic or elegant. In discussing similarities between the foreign policies of Presidents Bush and Clinton, for instance, describe their attitudes toward Syria, for they are relevant. Don't present evidence on domestic policy, which is irrelevant. Be sure your evidence speaks to the topic.

Representativeness

Evidence should fairly represent its source or the situation it describes. Sometimes writers ignore large segments of relevant information in order to make a point, as this one did:

> The people of California enjoy an incredibly high standard of living. Malibu has one of the highest concentrations of wealth in the world.

The writer misrepresents the situation by ignoring cities with pockets of poverty, such as East Palo Alto, San Jose, and Fresno. Be sure you let your reader know the full context of any material you use.

Accuracy

You, the writer, are responsible for the accuracy of all the evidence you present. The first way to ensure accuracy is to cross-check. Even if evidence appears to be from a reputable, bias-free source, cross-check it against other sources.

Once you have good evidence, present it accurately in your writing. When you use statistics, check and double-check your numbers to make sure you have transferred them correctly. When you quote an expert, get every letter, space, and comma right. Verify both your source's and your own use of evidence.

***

 Computer Tip

> Online sources are often careless in their own presentation. Whenever possible, cross-check any online material you retrieve against a reputable print source.

***

Detail

The closer your evidence is to the concrete—facts, numbers, direct quotations—the more believable and acceptable it is. If you are writing a paper on global warming, you might write

> From New England to England, from Spain to New Orleans, global warming has become a major environmental calamity that cannot be ignored.

But how much more potent is what Ross Gelbspan did in "The Heat Is On":

> After my lawn had burned away to straw last summer, and the local papers announced that the season had been one of the driest in the recorded history of New England, I found myself wondering how long we can go on pretending that nothing is amiss with the world's weather. It wasn't just the fifty ducks near my house that died when the fallen water levels in a creek exposed them to botulism-infested mud, or the five hundred people dead in the Midwest from an unexpected heat wave that followed the season's second "one-hundred-year-flood" in three years. It was also the news from New Orleans (overrun by an extraordinary number of cockroaches and termites after a fifth consecutive winter without a killing frost), from Spain (suffering a fourth year of drought in a region that ordinarily enjoys a rainfall of 84 inches a year), and from London (Britain's meteorological office reporting the driest summer since 1727 and the hottest since 1659).

This level of detail is more effective than paraphrase or summary. Except where space dictates otherwise, provide the poet's own words, the pollster's charts, the Health Department's statistics. Then interpret them.

Adequacy

No one can state a general rule for the appropriate quantity of evidence. We think lavishness is preferable to stinginess. But choose your places to be lavish. Your main supporting points deserve the most detailed and concrete substantiation. Your second-level points (those that support your main supporting points) need evidence, too, but don't let them overshadow more important ideas. Your third-level points are lucky to be there at all. And don't be sentimental: if you can't make the evidence fit the idea, let the idea go. In the end, the best way to determine whether or not you have enough evidence is to ask a familiar question: Would a reasonable member of my intended audience be convinced?

CASE STUDY: EVIDENCE IN ACTION

The following essay was written by Paul Butler, a professor of law at George Washington University Law School. It has been adapted by *Harper's* magazine from a longer essay in the *Yale Law Journal*. In the margin we identify many, but not all, of the various kinds of evidence Butler uses. Although relying predominantly on reasoning, the writer bolsters his argument with evidence from many different sources and seamlessly mixes different kinds even in a single paragraph.

Pay particular attention to the way Butler develops his argument. He presents his personal experience before his major claim, thus establishing rapport with the reader before asserting his very challenging claim that the judgment of black jurors is more to be trusted than the rule of law. He backs this assertion with background on the plight of black communities and the long and honorable history of jury nullification, that is, the power of juries to acquit even when they know the defendant is guilty. He concedes that some limitations must be imposed, and he then lays out a detailed proposal for the fitting application of jury nullification. At the end of the essay, he qualifies his argument by saying he hopes it will "encourage African Americans to use responsibly the power" of jury nullification.

Black Jurors:
Right to Acquit?
Paul Butler

Personal experience

In 1990 I was a Special Assistant United States Attorney in the District of Columbia. I prosecuted people accused of misdemeanor crimes, mainly the drug and gun cases that overwhelm the local courts of most American cities. As a federal prosecutor, I represented the United States of America and used that power to put people, mainly African-American men, in prison. I am also an African-American man. During that time, I made two discoveries that profoundly changed the way I viewed my work as a prosecutor and my responsibilities as a black person.   1

Examples (explain change of viewpoint)

The first discovery occurred during a training session for new assistants conducted by experienced prosecutors. We rookies were informed that we would lose many of our cases, despite having persuaded a jury beyond a reasonable doubt that the defendant was guilty. We would lose because some black jurors would refuse to convict black defendants who they knew were guilty.   2

Examples

The second discovery was related to the first but was even more unsettling. It occurred during the trial of Marion Barry, then the second-term mayor of the District of Columbia. Barry was being prosecuted by my office for drug possession and perjury. I learned, to my surprise, that some of my fellow African-American prosecutors hoped that the mayor would be acquitted, despite the fact that he was obviously guilty of at least one of the charges—an FBI videotape plainly showed him smoking crack cocaine. These black prosecutors wanted their office to lose its case because they believed that the prosecution of Barry was racist.   3

Known facts (appeal to common knowledge)

There is an increasing perception that some African-American jurors vote to acquit black defendants for racial reasons, sometimes explained as the juror's desire not to send another black man to jail. There is considerable disagreement over whether it is appropriate for a black juror to do so. I now believe that, for pragmatic and political reasons, the black community is better off when some nonviolent law-   4 breakers remain in the community rather than go to prison. The decision as to what kind of conduct by African Americans ought to be punished is better made by African Americans, based on their understanding of the costs and benefits to their community, than by the traditional criminal justice process, which is controlled by white lawmakers and

Shared belief

white law enforcers. Legally, African-American jurors who sit in judgment of African-American accused persons have the power to make that decision. Considering the costs of law enforcement to the black community, and the failure of white lawmakers to come up with any solutions to black antisocial conduct other than incarceration, it is, in

Reasoning (sets forth argument)

fact, the moral responsibility of black jurors to emancipate some guilty black outlaws.

Why would a black juror vote to let a guilty person go free? Assuming the juror is a rational, self-interested actor, she must believe that she is better off with the defendant out of prison than in prison. But how could any rational person believe that about a criminal? 5

Analogy (draws instructive comparison)

Imagine a country in which a third of the young male citizens are under the supervision of the criminal justice system—either awaiting trial, in prison, or on probation or parole. Imagine a country in which two-thirds of the men can anticipate being arrested before they reach age thirty. Imagine a country in which there are more young men in prison than in college. 6

Reasoning

The country imagined above is a police state. When we think of a police state, we think of a society whose fundamental problem lies not with the citizens of the state but rather with the form of government and with the powerful elites in whose interest the state exists. Similarly, racial critics of American criminal justice locate the problem not with the black prisoners but with the state and its actors and beneficiaries. 7

Known facts

The black community also bears very real costs by having so many African Americans, particularly males, incarcerated or otherwise involved in the criminal justice system. These costs are both social and economic, and they include the large percentage of black children who

Examples

live in female-headed, single-parent households; a perceived dearth of men "eligible" for marriage; the lack of male role models for black children, especially boys; the absence of wealth in the black community; and the large unemployment rate among black men. 8

Statistics (support an essential part of the argument)

According to a recent *USA Today*/CNN/Gallup poll, 66 percent of blacks believe that the criminal justice system is racist and only 32 percent believe it is not racist. Interestingly, other polls suggest that blacks also tend to be more worried about crime than whites; this seems logical when one considers that blacks are more likely to be victims of crime. This enhanced concern, however, does not appear to translate 9

Example

to black support for tougher enforcement of criminal law. For example, substantially fewer blacks than whites support the death penalty, and many more blacks than whites were concerned with the potential racial consequences of the strict provisions of last year's crime bill. Along with significant evidence from popular culture, these polls suggest that a substantial portion of the African-American community sympathizes with racial critiques of the criminal justice system.

Known facts

Reasoning

African-American jurors who endorse these critiques are in a unique   10
position to act on their beliefs when they sit in judgment of a black defendant. As jurors, they have the power to convict the accused person or
to set him free. May the responsible exercise of that power include voting to free a black defendant who the juror believes is guilty? The answer is "yes," based on the legal doctrine known as jury nullification.

Known facts

Jury nullification occurs when a jury acquits a defendant who it   11
believes is guilty of the crime with which he is charged. In finding the
defendant not guilty, the jury ignores the facts of the case and/or the
judge's instructions regarding the law. Instead, the jury votes its conscience.

Known facts
Examples

The prerogative of juries to nullify has been part of English and   12
American law for centuries. There are well-known cases from the Revolutionary War era when American patriots were charged with political
crimes by the British crown and acquitted by American juries. Black
slaves who escaped to the North and were prosecuted for violation of
the Fugitive Slave Law were freed by Northern juries with abolitionist
sentiments. Some Southern juries refused to punish white violence
against African Americans, especially black men accused of crimes
against white women.

Expert opinion

Shared belief

The Supreme Court has officially disapproved of jury nullification   13
but has conceded that it has no power to prohibit jurors from engaging
in it; the Bill of Rights does not allow verdicts of acquittal to be re-
versed, regardless of the reason for the acquittal. Criticism of nullification has centered on its potential for abuse. The criticism suggests that
when twelve members of a jury vote their conscience instead of the
law, they corrupt the rule of law and undermine the democratic principles that made the law.

Known facts

Reasoning

There is no question that jury nullification is subversive of the rule   14
of law. Nonetheless, most legal historians agree that it was morally appropriate in the cases of the white American revolutionaries and the
runaway slaves. The issue, then, is whether African Americans today
have the moral right to engage in this same subversion.

Known facts

Examples

Reasoning

Most moral justifications of the obligation to obey the law are   15
based on theories of "fair play." Citizens benefit from the rule of law;
that is why it is just that they are burdened with the requirement to follow it. Yet most blacks are aware of countless historical examples in
which African Americans were not afforded the benefit of the rule of
law: think, for example, of the existence of slavery in a republic pur-
portedly dedicated to the proposition that all men are created equal, or
the law's support of state-sponsored segregation even after the Four-
teenth Amendment guaranteed blacks equal protection. That the rule
of law ultimately corrected some of the large holes in the American
fabric is evidence more of its malleability than its goodness; the rule of
law previously had justified the holes.

Reasoning

Analogy

If the rule of law is a myth, or at least not valid for African Ameri-   16
cans, the argument that jury nullification undermines it loses force. The
black juror is simply another actor in the system, using her power to
fashion a particular outcome. The juror's act of nullification—like the
act of the citizen who dials 911 to report Ricky but not Bob, or the po-

lice officer who arrests Lisa but not Mary, or the prosecutor who charges Kwame but not Brad, or the judge who finds that Nancy was illegally entrapped but Verna was not—exposes the indeterminacy of law but does not in itself create it.

Reasoning

A similar argument can be made regarding the criticism that jury   17
nullification is anti-democratic. This is precisely why many African Americans endorse it; it is perhaps the only legal power black people have to escape the tyranny of the majority. Black people have had to

Examples

beg white decision makers for most of the rights they have: the right not to be slaves, the right to vote, the right to attend an integrated

Known facts

school. Now black people are begging white people to preserve programs that help black children to eat and black businesses to survive.

Reasoning

Jury nullification affords African Americans the power to determine justice for themselves in individual cases, regardless of whether white people agree or even understand.

Reasoning

At this point, African Americans should ask themselves whether   18
the operation of the criminal law system in the United States advances the interests of black people. If it does not, the doctrine of jury nullification affords African-American jurors the opportunity to exercise the authority of the law over some African-American criminal defendants. In essence, black people can "opt out" of American criminal law.

Reasoning

How far should they go—completely to anarchy, or is there   19
someplace between here and there that is safer than both? I propose the following: African-American jurors should approach their work cognizant of its political nature and of their prerogative to exercise their power in the best interests of the black community. In every case,

Personal experience

the juror should be guided by her view of what is "just." (I have more faith, I should add, in the average black juror's idea of justice than I do in the idea that is embodied in the "rule of law.")

In cases involving violent *malum in se* (inherently bad) crimes,   20

Reasoning

such as murder, rape, and assault, jurors should consider the case strictly on the evidence presented, and if they believe the accused person is guilty, they should so vote. In cases involving non-violent, *malum prohibitum* (legally proscribed) offenses, including "victimless" crimes such as narcotics possession, there should be a presumption in favor of nullification. Finally, for nonviolent *malum in se* crimes, such as theft or perjury, there need be no presumption in favor of nullification, but it ought to be an option the juror considers. A juror might

Example

vote for acquittal, for example, when a poor woman steals from Tiffany's but not when the same woman steals from her next-door neighbor.

How would a juror decide individual cases under my proposal?   21

Example

Easy cases would include a defendant who has possessed crack cocaine and an abusive husband who kills his wife. The former should be acquitted and the latter should go to prison.

Example

Difficult scenarios would include the drug dealer who operates in   22
the ghetto and the thief who burglarizes the home of a rich white fam-

Shared belief

Example

ily. Under my proposal, nullification is presumed in the first case because drug distribution is a nonviolent *malum prohibitum* offense. Is nullification morally justifiable here? It depends. There is no question that encouraging people to engage in self-destructive behavior is evil; the question the juror should ask herself is whether the remedy is less evil. (The juror should also remember that the criminal law does not punish those ghetto drug dealers who cause the most injury: liquor store owners.)

Reasoning

As for the burglar who steals from the rich white family, the case   23
is troubling, first of all, because the conduct is so clearly "wrong." Since it is a nonviolent *malum in se* crime, there is no presumption in favor of nullification, but it is an option for consideration. Here again, the facts of the case are relevant. For example, if the offense was committed to support a drug habit, I think there is a moral case to be made for nullification, at least until such time as access to drug-rehabilitation services are available to all.

Known facts

Why would a juror be inclined to follow my proposal? There is no   24
guarantee that she would. But when we perceive that black jurors are already nullifying on the basis of racial critiques (i.e., refusing to send another black man to jail), we recognize that these jurors are willing to use their power in a politically conscious manner. Further, it appears that some black jurors now excuse some conduct—like murder—that they should not excuse. My proposal provides a principled structure for the exercise of the black juror's vote. I am not encouraging anarchy; rather I am reminding black jurors of their privilege to serve a calling higher than law: justice.

Reasoning

I concede that the justice my proposal achieves is rough. It is as   25
susceptible to human foibles as the jury system. But I am sufficiently optimistic that my proposal will be only an intermediate plan, a stopping point between the status quo and real justice. To get to that better, middle ground, I hope that this essay will encourage African Americans to use responsibly the power they already have.

Reasoning

Tips for Using Evidence

- When examining what experts say, distinguish facts from informed opinions and speculation.
- Be careful when using statistics: they can be dangerous.
- Use examples to clarify meaning, demonstrate a point, or entertain your reader.
- Use personal experience sparingly; it is most effective in introductions and conclusions and as support for points you have demonstrated already with other kinds of evidence.

- Remember that although they can clarify a point, analogies cannot prove anything by themselves.
- Use known facts and shared beliefs to highlight a point.
- Remember that reasoning can provide powerful evidence.
- Be sure the evidence you use exhibits relevance, representativeness, accuracy, detail, and adequacy.
- Present your evidence accurately.

EXERCISES FOR USING EVIDENCE

1. Write an essay in which you interpret the following examples and statistics concerning the crime rate in Bodie, California, a frontier town that boomed in the late 1870s and early 1880s.

   Fistfights and gunfights were regular events.

   Stagecoach holdups were not unusual.

   The old, the young, the weak, and the female were generally not harmed.

   In modern American cities, the old, the young, the weak, and the female are often the objects of crime.

   There were 11 stagecoach robberies in Bodie between 1878 and 1882, and in 2 instances passengers were robbed. Highway robbers usually took only the cashbox carried on the coach.

   There were 10 robberies and 3 attempted robberies of individuals in Bodie from 1878 to 1882.

   Bodie's total of 21 robberies over a five-year period converts to the rate of 84 robberies per 100,000 inhabitants per year.

   New York City's robbery rate in 1980 was 1,140 per 100,000 people; Miami's was 995; and Los Angeles's was 628.

   The rate for the United States as a whole in 1980 was 243 per 100,000 people.

   Between 1878 and 1882 there were 32 burglaries in Bodie; 17 were of homes and 15 were of businesses.

   At least 6 of these burglaries were thwarted by the presence of armed citizens.

   Bodie's burglary rate for those five years was 128 per 100,000 inhabitants.

   Miami's burglary rate in 1980 was 3,282 per 100,000 people; New York's was 2,661; Los Angeles's was 2,602.

   The burglary rate for the United States as a whole in 1980 was 1,668 per 100,000 people.

   In the relevant period in Bodie, only one woman, a prostitute, was robbed; there were no rapes.

   Thirty-one people in Bodie were shot, stabbed, or beaten to death from 1878 to 1882.

   The homicide rate was 116 per 100,000 inhabitants per year.

   In 1980, Miami led the nation with a homicide rate of 32.7 per 100,000 people; Las Vegas was second with 23.4.

The homicide rate for the United States in 1980 was 10.2 per 100,000 people.

The majority of Bodie's residents were young, single males.

Courage was the most admired characteristic.

Alcohol was heavily consumed.

Most of the young men carried guns.

Most of the shootings in Bodie between 1878 and 1882 involved willing combatants. (Based on Roger D. McGrath, "The Heritage of the Frontier")

2. What kinds of evidence are represented by the following?

   If the efficiency of the car had improved at the same rate as that of the computer over the last two decades, a Rolls-Royce would cost about three dollars, would get 3 million miles per gallon of gas, and would deliver enough power to propel an ocean liner.

   The notion that the best way to avoid war is to destroy nuclear weapons goes against common sense.

   A baby chimpanzee far outstrips a human infant in the rate of development of its motor ability, reflexes, and physical coordination.

   We once lived next door to some Somalis. Their house was, of course, always dirty.

   Evaluate the quality of the evidence. Write a statement that each item could be used to illustrate. Now decide whether you would need another illustration to make the point. If so, provide it (make it up if you must). Make the whole into a paragraph.

3. Find the answers to three of these questions:

   What is the dollar-and-cents value of the human body?

   What were the numbers and national origins of immigrants to America between 1900 and 1910?

   In which countries is French the official language, and how was it established in each?

   What area in the United States had the highest cost of living in 1990, and what area had the lowest? (Be sure to explain how the term *cost of living* is defined.)

   What professional basketball team's players received the highest average salaries in 1995, and how did their salaries compare with the average salaries of players on the best-paying teams in football and baseball?

   Describe how the statistics or facts in your answers were arrived at. Explain and define any statistical concepts you came across in your research.

4. Using as many different kinds of evidence as you can, write an essay narrating the history of your family. If you have the information, go back three generations. Include date and place of birth, age, sex, national origin, and occupation for each family member mentioned. Set your family's experience against the backdrop of major historical events of that time, using experts and statistics if you can. In your last two paragraphs, speculate on the future you see for the family as a whole. Base your speculation on the evidence presented in the essay.

7

Making the Argument

We reason deeply,
When we forcibly feel.
— MARY WOLLSTONECRAFT (1759-1797)
BRITISH WRITER

Throughout this book, we've discussed argument in several guises: the argumentative thesis, the logic of argument, and, in the previous chapter, evidence as the basis for successful argument. In this chapter, we discuss how to construct a persuasive argument. The skill of persuasion is essential in school, and you will continue to exercise it after you graduate. Lawyers try to persuade the jury that their clients are innocent. Engineers and architects, executives and developers try to persuade boards of directors to approve their projects. Parents try to persuade school boards, speeders try to persuade traffic officers, husbands try to persuade wives and vice versa. The stronger the skill, the more likely the desired outcome.

In *The Uses of Argument,* philosopher Stephen Toulmin describes a method for building a strong argument. Although he uses terms different from those you learned in Chapter 2, he discusses the same ideas: premises, inferences, enthymemes, and the like. In this chapter, we will use Toulmin's terms, but we will indicate when one of his terms has the same meaning as a term we've previously used.

THE BASIC MOVES:
CLAIM, EVIDENCE, WARRANT

Toulmin calls the three basic components of argument *claim, evidence,* and *warrant.* We can illustrate these ideas with an example found in Chapter 2.

> James is eligible for the presidency. He was born in Cincinnati, is thirty-eight, and has never been arrested, and any thirty-five-year-old or older nonfelon born in the United States is eligible for the presidency.

This is an argument with a claim (James is eligible for the presidency), evidence (he was born in Cincinnati, is thirty-eight years old, and has never been arrested), and a warrant (any thirty-five-year-old or older nonfelon born in the United States is eligible for the presidency). The claim makes an assertion; the evidence supports it; the warrant explains how the evidence supports the claim. This a sturdy three-legged stool on which you can rest an argument.

Claim

The claim is the assertion the argument will back up. It is the *conclusion* of the argument. Here are some claims:

> Cigarette vending machines should be outlawed.
>
> Cytochrome is important in cell respiration.
>
> All students should be required to take computer science.
>
> Arthur killed Daphne in self-defense.

Claims have two parts: the topic and what is asserted about the topic:

TOPIC	ASSERTION
Cigarette vending machines	should be outlawed
Cytochrome	is important in cell respiration
All students	should be required to take computer science
Arthur killed Daphne	in self-defense

An expository essay contains a large claim—the thesis—that the essay as a whole supports.

> All students should be required to take computer science.

In supporting a thesis, the writer makes smaller claims, generally supported in a paragraph.

> Understanding computers is essential to understanding the contemporary world.
>
> Learning to program is good mind training.
>
> Using a computer effectively will make college work easier.
>
> More and more jobs require familiarity with computers.

There may be several claims in a single paragraph:

> The school should prepare students for the job market, and more and more jobs require familiarity with computers.

A good claim tells the audience exactly what is being argued. Only when the claim is clear and unambiguous can the audience properly weigh the evidence.

Evidence

Evidence (discussed further in Chapter 6) is any support for your claim that your audience accepts without further proof: the specific example, the statistic, the fact, the next logical step, the quotation, the shared belief. It is a *premise* for the argument. If the evidence is adequate, you can logically infer the claim. Consider the lawyer's argument in Arthur's murder trial.

> Arthur does not deny that he killed Daphne. In fact, several witnesses say they saw the two of them struggling, saw Daphne fall, and saw the gun in Arthur's hand. But it was clearly self-defense. Daphne was out to kill Arthur, and he had to protect himself. Daphne's friend Louella testified that Daphne admitted hating Arthur and said he ought to be done away with. Louella quoted Daphne as saying, "If no one else will do it, I will." And Daphne was killed with her own gun.

Arthur's lawyer has built a good case for the claim of self-defense. Each piece of evidence supports the claim: the struggle, the killing, Daphne's statement of her motive, the ownership of the gun. The jury would probably begin to think that, yes, the claim of self-defense is upheld by the evidence.

Arthur's lawyer knows, however, that the prosecutor may claim the gun was not Daphne's, an assertion that might undermine the defense argument. So the lawyer constructs a subargument to support the subclaim that the gun was Daphne's.

> The gun, as I say, belonged to Daphne. It had been purchased by her two days before her death. The police found in her handbag a receipt indicating she had charged the gun on her American Express card.

If the prosecutor challenged the signature on the charge receipt, the defense lawyer would have to construct another subargument regarding the signature. Could this go on forever? It could, until the evidence had become so detailed that no further proof was necessary to convince the jurors.

Writing a college paper bears a close resemblance to arguing in a court of law, for it also requires a claim supported with evidence. Suppose we were writing an essay on the poet Robert Frost and we devised this thesis:

> Although his poems are direct and accessible, Robert Frost himself was a many-sided person, ambitious and so competitive that he was cruel, yet he could be kind and generous.

To set out to prove this large claim, we would divide it into subclaims, to be treated separately in a paragraph or two each.

1. Frost's poems are direct and accessible.
2. Frost was extremely ambitious for fame and admiration.
3. He was highly competitive and sometimes cruel to other poets of his time.
4. But he responded to kindness with kindness.
5. He was generous to students and loving to old friends.

We would now need to develop evidence for each subclaim, just as Arthur's lawyer developed evidence for each subclaim in Arthur's defense. We might, for instance, support the third point this way:

> He was highly competitive with other poets of his time. Edwin Arlington Robinson seemed to give him the most trouble. Even the poet Archibald MacLeish came in for a cruel attack. Frost did not hesitate to show disdain for Ezra Pound and Wallace Stevens. He seemed unable to accept the success of his peers.

After providing this series of what could be called "subsubclaims," we ask ourselves whether in doing so we have reached the common ground or need still more detailed evidence. We examine each piece of support. Standing alone, the sentence

> Edwin Arlington Robinson seemed to give him the most trouble

is too vague. What kind of trouble? Maybe Robinson beat Frost at poker or squash. We add some more evidence:

> for time and again Frost expressed a deep-seated jealousy of him.

But is it clear what kind of jealousy this was? Did they fight over a woman? We need to demonstrate what we mean by *jealousy:*

> Perhaps he thought Robinson's fame was greater than his.

When we provide similar evidence for the other points, we get this:

> He was highly competitive with other poets of his time. Edwin Arlington Robinson seemed to give him the most trouble, for time and

again Frost expressed a deep-seated jealousy of him. Perhaps he thought Robinson's fame was greater than his. Even the poet Archibald MacLeish, seldom considered as good as either Frost or Robinson, came in for cruel attack. At a testimonial dinner, Frost so upstaged MacLeish that the audience became hostile. Frost did not hesitate to show disdain even for those whom some consider the most important poets of the era, Ezra Pound and Wallace Stevens. According to a biographer of Frost, Frost made open fun of Pound and had several heated arguments with Stevens. He seemed unable to accept the success of his peers.

Now we have reached something closer to common ground. Most readers would be satisfied that they understood our subclaim and our reasons for making it.

Warrant

A warrant is the glue that holds an argument together. It links the evidence to the claim. It says something like "This evidence supports this claim because. . . ."

CLAIM	I think you should join my t'ai chi class.
EVIDENCE	T'ai chi clears the mind and brings peace to the soul.
WARRANT	As an airline pilot, you need a clear mind and a peaceful soul.

Although an argument can be presented in any order, most start with the claim, move straight to the evidence, and wrap things up with the warrant. You can see this pattern in many essays and even in paragraphs.

Because people sometimes have trouble with the word *warrant,* we want to clarify it right off. Its oldest meaning is "protector" or "defender." It also means "justification or reasonable grounds for an act or belief" as well as "an authorization or assurance or guarantee." In signing a warrant for someone's arrest, the judge authorizes that arrest. In sentencing a criminal, the judge indicates that the crime warranted the punishment. When Ford sells a truck, it warrants that the truck will operate properly.

These meanings are included in Toulmin's use of the term. A warrant in an argument authorizes or provides the justification for linking the evidence to the claim. It guarantees that the claim is supported by the evidence.

CLAIM	Forks were not used in France in the fifteenth century.
EVIDENCE	Paintings of banquets from that period show no forks on the tables or people eating with them.
WARRANT	Contemporary paintings are very good indications of the customs of an age.

Without a warrant to explain why the evidence or premises support the claim adequately, your audience may not understand the connection. The argument in the following example is impossible to follow:

> The most popular soap opera on American television is *Wild Wet Winds of Love*. We know that because fully 76 percent of the viewing public in Wadkins, Florida, watches this program.

What does that prove? the reader wants to know. Who cares about some little town in Florida? A warrant is needed:

> And the viewing public in Wadkins, Florida, is a cross section of viewers much like those in the rest of the United States. Thus, a show's popularity there indicates its popularity throughout the land.

Now we have the missing link in the chain of argument. We may or may not accept the warrant, but at least we know why the writer thought the evidence supported the claim.

Sometimes the connection between the claim and the evidence is so obvious that the writer does not need to state it in a warrant:

> Someone has been eating my porridge. It's eaten all up.

Perhaps you recognized that this argument is an enthymeme (Chapter 2). The missing warrant is

> When my porridge is gone and I didn't eat it, I can safely assume that someone else did.

Not even the bears needed to spell it out.

Let's go back to the murder trial, where Arthur's lawyer is constructing a subargument about Daphne's ownership of the gun.

> The police found in her handbag a receipt indicating she had charged the gun on her American Express card. The police verified that it was her signature on the receipt.

The lawyer pauses. Is the connection clear? Does he need a warrant? If stated, the warrant would be

> Charge receipts are reliable proof of purchase when the signatures on them have been verified.

But that is painfully self-evident. Deciding not to risk insulting the jurors' intelligence, the lawyer leaves the warrant unspoken and moves on to the next point. If you make every single warrant explicit, your audience may find you condescending.

More frequent than overdoing warrants, however, is underdoing them. People often leave out warrants essential to understanding the argument, as in this pair of conflicting arguments:

First Baseball Fan:

CLAIM	Ty Cobb is the best hitter in baseball history.
EVIDENCE	He had a lifetime batting average of .367, the highest of any player.

Second Baseball Fan:

CLAIM	Hank Aaron is the best hitter in baseball history.
EVIDENCE	He had more total homers, runs batted in, and extra base hits than any other player.

Both arguments are based on valid evidence, but the claims conflict. How can that be? What is wrong? To get at the problem, we need those warrants:

FIRST FAN'S WARRANT:	Lifetime average is the best measure of a hitter.
SECOND FAN'S WARRANT:	Power statistics are the best measure of a hitter.

If these two fans are to resolve their dispute, they will have to argue the validity of their warrants. The warrants would become subclaims, and the two fans would have to provide evidence for each of them. If the fans cannot resolve their differing criteria for the best hitter, they will have to agree to disagree. In the meantime, by presenting their warrants they at least identify the real argument.

When should warrants be stated, and when can they be implicit? When the evidence obviously illustrates the claim, you do not need a warrant. When, however, the connection is at all unclear or complicated, write out the warrant. This decision is, of course, a matter of judgment. In this as in all aspects of expository writing, err on the side of overclarification.

PUTTING THE COMPONENTS TOGETHER: BINDING THE ARGUMENT

So far we have looked at claim, evidence, and warrant as separate building blocks. In an argument, however, they form a unit of continuous thought. The following is a passage from an essay whose thesis is "Computer-aided instruction can be extremely valuable in teaching writing":

Computers have many advantages over human teachers when it comes to giving the repetitive drills needed to teach writing. Computers are more patient and can run the same drill over and over until the student masters it, something few teachers can endure. Computers can provide instant feedback, which busy teachers often cannot do. Where large classes make it difficult for teachers to gear their instruction to the needs of individual students, computer programs are entirely adaptable to each student's pace. Best of all, they cost almost nothing to operate.

A computer really is a video textbook. It presents information on screens rather than on sheets of paper. Students press buttons instead of turning pages or writing down answers. Quizzes appear every few screens to ensure that students are getting the point. If they pass these quizzes, students can go on; otherwise, they must go back, review the material, and take the quiz over. Video textbooks can do anything regular textbooks can do, from drills to the actual teaching of writing.

In sum, the computer can engage students' attention and guide their progress without involving a teacher. Thus, it is preferable to today's expensive and often ineffective methods of teaching writing.

The first paragraph consists of a claim, evidence, and warrants. The claim appears in the first sentence. The rest of the paragraph is composed of pieces of evidence and warrants connecting the evidence to the claim. Diagramed, the first paragraph would appear like this:

Claim: "Computers have many advantages over human teachers when it comes to giving the repetitive drills needed to teach writing."

First piece of evidence: "Computers are more patient and can run the same drill over and over until the student masters it,"

Warrant: "something few teachers can endure."

Second piece of evidence: "Computers can provide instant feedback,"

Warrant: "which busy teachers often cannot do."

Third piece of evidence: "Computer programs are entirely adaptable to each student's pace."

Warrant: "Large classes make it difficult for teachers to gear their instruction to the needs of individual students."

Fourth piece of evidence: "Best of all, they cost almost nothing to operate."

Warrant: not needed because the connection is obvious. It would insult the intelligence of the reader to say "and human teachers must be paid."

The same ingredients appear in the second paragraph, but in this example, the final sentence serves as an overall warrant that connects all the evidence to the claim.

Claim: "A computer really is a video textbook."

First piece of evidence: "It presents information on screens."

Second piece of evidence: "Students press buttons instead of turning pages."

Third piece of evidence: "Quizzes appear every few screens."

Fourth piece of evidence: "If they pass these quizzes, students can go on;"

Fifth piece of evidence: "Otherwise, they must go back, review the material, and take the quiz over."

Warrant: "Video textbooks can do anything regular textbooks can do, from drills to the actual teaching of writing."

In writing, we need not have one warrant for each piece of evidence, but we do need to be sure the evidence is securely attached to the claim.

The third paragraph of the computer example might be called a *reinforcing warrant*. It treats as a unit all the evidence and warrants in the first two paragraphs and connects that unit to the thesis of the essay. Stopping to combine paragraphs into summary units like this and then tying each unit to the thesis helps maintain clarity for both reader and writer.

The 1-2-3 Rule

If you want to think of claim, evidence, and warrant in more familiar terms, consider what many composition teachers call the "1-2-3 Rule." Good writers naturally obey this rule whenever they are about to discuss an important piece of evidence. Here is how it works:

Step 1. Establish the context and purpose of the evidence.

Step 2. Present the evidence.

Step 3. Show how the evidence fits into the argument.

The following paragraph is from an essay by Lia Kudless, a student, in which she discusses John Donne's poem "A Hymn to God the Father." Her thesis is this: "Although the speaker seems to be trying to make a clear statement on faith, the poem suggests that such faith is hard to achieve." Her fifth paragraph is a fine example of the 1-2-3 rule.

    In the third stanza, the speaker continues to hover
    between belief and disbelief, writing himself into cir-
    cles and ultimately ending up just as confused as when he
    began:

        I have a sin of fear, that when I have spun
            My last thread, I shall perish on the shore.
        Swear by thyself, that at my death thy Son
            Shall shine as he shines now and heretofore;
                And, having done that, thou has done,
                    I fear no more. (13-18)

> In this stanza, we see the speaker's confusion most
> clearly. It seems that he truly wants to be pious, but he
> simply cannot ignore the questions gnawing at his mind.
> He seems to believe in the Christian God because he calls
> his "fear" a "sin"--recognizing that his feelings are
> abhorrent to God. But he does have that fear of nonexis-
> tence, which, despite being a sin, is very real.

In Step 1, Kudless rightly tells us the evidence is from the third stanza and then sets up the context, the purpose for using it. In Step 2, she quotes the poem accurately. In Step 3 she comments on the quotation, showing us in detail how it bears out her idea about the speaker's "belief and disbelief."

This is the way our minds work and the way paragraphs are built. When you follow this rule with any piece of evidence—a bar graph, a sonnet, a spectrum—you are using claim, evidence, warrant, but it may well feel less inhibiting to think of the process as 1-2-3.

CONSIDERING THE OPPOSITION: BACKING, REBUTTAL, CONCESSION/QUALIFICATION

The claim-evidence-warrant model is fine if you think your audience is open to your line of argument. Careful writers, however, assume skeptical readers who wait to be convinced. Skeptical readers ask hard questions, demand more evidence if they are not satisfied, and attack weak places in the argument. Writing for a skeptical reader demands three further tools: backing, rebuttal, and concession/qualification.

Backing

Backing shores up a warrant. When you cannot assume your audience will accept your warrant, you need to prove it. To do this, you treat the warrant as a claim that needs evidence.

Suppose you were sick of living in a sloppy dormitory, so you made the following argument in a meeting with college administrators:

> The college should provide janitorial service for the dorms. The dorms are falling apart, and it is costing the college a great deal of money to maintain them. *This high cost of maintenance justifies hiring janitors.*

Skeptical administrators might ask, What have maintenance costs to do with the janitors?

You would need to respond by building an argument around the warrant, italicized in the following paragraph:

> *The high cost of maintenance justifies hiring janitors.* Because of yearlong neglect, dorm rooms are in such serious disrepair that they must be painted and refurbished at the end of each spring term, and this costs nearly $1 million a year. If the college had routine janitorial service, we would not need annual painting and refurbishing.

The administrators might also question the warrant of the argument found in the last sentence here. Why would routine janitorial service make annual painting and refurbishing unnecessary?

You would answer with still more backing:

> *Routine janitorial service would make annual painting and refurbishing unnecessary.* If walls were washed regularly, they would not need painting every year. If floors were swept and carpets vacuumed regularly, they would last much longer.

Backing clarifies and supports weak or unclear connections.

When you use backing, you are not assuming that your reader disagrees with you, only that he or she holds an understandable skepticism. Rebuttal and concession/qualification, however, assume a doubting or even antagonistic audience. Anyone who wants to convince such a reader—a very common kind—must address the reader's contrary beliefs or opinions.

Rebuttal

Rebuttal is the process of refuting the opposing view. In essence, it says, "People who say *X* are wrong because . . ." Rebuttal demands a great deal of tact because it is aggressive. You want to confront the differing opinion without alienating readers so that they refuse to hear what you say. If you imply that a reader is a fool or a knave, as in these openings, you will fail to persuade:

> Ignorant people would perhaps think . . .
>
> People with bad judgment or ulterior motives would claim . . .

Writers sometimes begin their rebuttals by attributing the erroneous view to some hypothetical group.

> Some people may think . . .
>
> There is a widely held but false view that . . .

More diplomatic writers might go even further.

> Many reasonable people do hold this opinion, even though it has turned out to be mistaken.

Once you have found the right tactful entry into your rebuttal, you face the real work. You must fairly present the opposing claim and then show why it is invalid.

Suppose that in the argument about janitors, the administration has asked you to put your proposal in writing for the board of trustees. In writing the report, you anticipate that the trustees will say something like

> College kids can clean up after themselves. They never had janitors at home—why should they have them in college?

You rebut this point by fairly paraphrasing the opposing claim and acknowledging the evidence on which it rests. If you distort the claim or ignore the evidence, your reader will lose confidence in you.

> The opposition thinks that students ought to just live in their dirt.

will persuade no one, but

> Many people may think that students can be made to care properly for their rooms themselves. Certainly, these people argue, the students never had a janitor at home.

will show your reader how fair and reasonable you are.

Merely saying "the opposition is wrong" won't accomplish anything. You must erect a counterclaim and give evidence for it.

> Our experience, however, indicates that students will not take care of their dorm rooms, no matter how they behaved at home. Three years ago, the college instituted a program of weekly inspections. After one semester, the administration abandoned the program as a failure. There was no good effect, and in fact students, their parents, and faculty complained. Last year the college tried again, providing housekeeping equipment and supplies to each wing of every dormitory. The students agreed to keep their particular wings clean. In one wing the original bottle of cleanser was three-quarters full at year's end. In another, students used the broom to prop open a window. Apparently, whatever action the college takes, the problem persists.

When the evidence is sufficient, the argument effectively refutes the opposition.

Concession/Qualification

At times all of us have to make concessions. When you cannot find a way to refute the opposition, there is nothing to do but admit it: "You have a good point—I'll give you that one." It would be counterproductive to deny a solid claim just because the opposition has made it. It would be equally useless to hold tenaciously to an untenable position. Just concede the good point and qualify your own claim accordingly:

that is, redefine it so that it no longer conflicts with the valid claim the opposition made.

Qualifications often appear at the beginning of arguments, where we define our terms, or at the end, where we admit the limitations of our position but reassert its strength. As for concession, a time-honored place is the next-to-last paragraph.

In response to the report about the need for janitors in the dorms, suppose the trustees say,

> Students are, after all, adults and should be fully capable of taking care of their living accommodations. They should be trained to do so.

Now that is a good point. Who would want to argue that students are not adults or are not capable of taking care of their rooms? You'll have to concede these opposing claims and then find a way around them.

> Of course, students ought to be more responsible than they have shown themselves in this matter, but that is a problem for society, not for the school. The issue here is whether janitorial service makes good economic sense.

You acknowledge that students should be responsible enough to take care of their rooms and then qualify your claim by limiting it to a point the trustees will accept: dollars and cents. See Figure 7.1 on page 165 for a full Toulmin model.

Using the Toulmin Model as a Revision Tool

Revision is where Stephen Toulmin's model—claim/evidence/warrant/backing/rebuttal/concession/qualification—becomes truly powerful. You can use it as a tool to test and sharpen your written argument. A good way to do this is to turn each element into a series of critical-thinking questions:

> ***Claim.*** Are my claims clear? specific? worth arguing? Apply these questions to your thesis, topic sentences, and subordinate claims.
>
> ***Evidence.*** Do my major points have adequate evidence? Is my evidence relevant, representative, accurate, and detailed? Do I need other kinds of evidence (statistics, personal experience, and so on)? Apply these questions to your entire essay and to every paragraph.
>
> ***Warrant.*** Are my warrants clear, careful, well defined? Where do I need to explain more fully the connection between claim and evidence? Is there any piece of evidence without a warrant, and if so is the point really self-evident? Apply these questions to every part of your essay but especially to major or crucial points.
>
> ***Backing.*** Where do I need to add explanations, analysis, or interpretation to shore up my warrants? In what manner can I best back up my warrants?

Rebuttal. Have I seriously considered opposing or alternative view-points? Have I found a tactful yet firm manner of addressing those points? Have I erected a convincing counterclaim and adequately supported it?

Concession/Qualification. Am I weakening my argument by pretending it is airtight? Which opposing points should I concede? How and where should I qualify my claim to acknowledge its limitations?

There are many questions, to be sure, but answering them—or at least considering them—cannot fail to improve your essay. Experienced writers ask these questions out of habit. Getting into that excellent habit can make your writing truly persuasive.

The Other Tools of Persuasion

Reason is only one of our many ways of understanding problems and finding solutions. We are feeling, desiring, wishing animals as well as

Figure 7.1   The Full Toulmin Model.   This model for a persuasive argument says, in effect, "I have evidence that warrants a claim. Because I anticipate skepticism from my audience, I will provide additional backing for warrants, rebut any conflicting arguments that I can, concede opposing arguments I cannot rebut, and qualify my original claim to account for the concession." Mastering this form can help you conduct a persuasive argument.

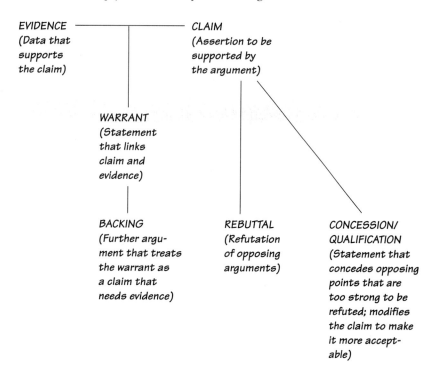

EVIDENCE
(Data that
supports
the claim)

CLAIM
(Assertion to be
supported by
the argument)

WARRANT
(Statement
that links
claim and
evidence)

BACKING
(Further argu-
ment that treats
the warrant as
a claim that
needs evidence)

REBUTTAL
(Refutation
of opposing
arguments)

CONCESSION/
QUALIFICATION
(Statement that
concedes opposing
points that are
too strong to be
refuted; modifies
the claim to make
it more accept-
able)

thinking ones. Appeals to values, emotions, and the senses are very powerful sources of persuasion, and we should not slight them. In writing "In Defense of the Harp Seal Hunt" (see below), Stephanie Klein takes into account both the emotional appeal of the opposing argument and the need for an appeal of her own. Her reference to "killing of lambs in an abattoir" is an example. The comparison of hunting for a livelihood and hunting for sport is another. Even the phrase "the protection of nature and our duty to other species" carries an emotional charge.

You should not hesitate to use this kind of appeal. True, some papers will demand a rigorous, dispassionate presentation. You may, however, find yourself writing about the most challenging and affecting issues of the day. How could we write about child abuse, AIDS, or poverty without an appeal to compassion? How could we write about Charlie Chaplin without an appeal to humor? How could we write about pathogens' growing resistance to antibiotics without a certain fearfulness? All these emotions are appropriate to their occasions, and no good writer will ignore them.

Because of their power, we need to use these appeals sparingly and with extreme care—but using them well is one of the true pleasures of writing persuasively.

CASE STUDY: ARGUMENT IN ACTION

In the following essay, Stephanie Klein bravely argues in defense of the harp seal hunt, a hunt that many people consider cruel and inhumane. Such a controversial and emotionally charged issue required the utmost in reasoning and tact. To prepare her backing, rebuttal, and concession/qualification, Klein brainstormed the concerns, objections, and contrary opinions of the opposing side. She came up with this list on her computer:

```
danger of extinction
immoral or unethical
ecological damage
```

She used the Toulmin model to help her construct her argument and to revise her essay. Here is her final revision.

In Defense of the Harp Seal Hunt

The yearly hunt for the baby harp seal has aroused   1

Background   the American public's indignation for over twenty years.

The controversy began after filmmakers distributed across

the United States some powerful film clips of the kill.
Seeing the killing of the seal pups triggered an immediate public outcry against the hunters. Supported by
celebrities like Brigitte Bardot, opponents organized a
nationwide campaign to ban the hunt. Although no doubt
well-intentioned, the opponents of the seal hunt have
been influenced more by emotion than by facts. If we look

Thesis (claim)   at the evidence, we see a different, and much more complex, picture.

Subclaim   The seal hunt is not a sport but a necessity. The   2
hunters do not kill for pleasure, as perhaps do hunters
Evidence   of fox and deer and doves. The seal hunt provides the
livelihood of a large population that has for many generations survived by hunting. "It is," explained one
hunter, "both a cherished tradition and a livelihood"
(Lavigne 139). These hunters are hardly growing rich from
hunting. The average sealer earns from all sources less
than $8,000 a year. To deprive the sealer of hunting
income would reduce this paltry sum by as much as 30
Warrant   percent. It would remove millions of dollars a year from
an "already depressed Atlantic economy" (Bryden 69).

Subclaim   Sealing provides not only employment but also essen-   3
Evidence   tial goods. Contrary to the propaganda, the hunters do
not leave the carcasses to rot on the ice. Although most
of the income to the sealer comes from selling the fur,
much more than the pelt is salvaged. Both the meat and
the oil are processed. The hides can be used for boats.
Warrant   As with the livestock industry, the by-products are
almost as important as the main product.

Subclaim   The fishing industry indirectly benefits from the   4
Evidence   seal hunt. The seals are a carnivorous species that con-
Warrant   sumes schools of fish. Without the hunt, the fishing in-
dustry in this poor area of the world would be damaged
(Lavigne 139).

Opposing argument   Despite the economic necessity of the seal hunt,   5
many people argue that it must be stopped, and they offer
several reasons. They argue that the hunt threatens the
Concession   harp seals with extinction. If true, this is a powerful
argument. As a nation, we are determined to protect other

Rebuttal

Evidence

Warrant

species from extinction. The efforts made to save the
condor are a good example. The fact is, however, that
the harp seal is not an endangered species. According to
studies made by the North Pacific Fur Seal Commission and
Convention, the seal population has actually increased
during the past seventy years and continues to grow at
the rate of 2 percent a year. In 1911, only 200,000 harp
seals had survived the uncontrolled commercial slaughter
at sea. In 1975, there were over 1.3 million harp seals
("Seals and Seal Fisheries" 483).

Rebuttal

Evidence

Warrant

The increase resulted from hunting regulations im-   6
posed by the Canadian government. Beginning in 1965, the
government established quotas limiting the number of
seals that can be taken each year. In his book An American Crusade for Wildlife, James Trefethen points out
that the Front population of seals--the herd that winters
in Labrador--is now fully protected against all hunting
(326). In the Gulf of St. Lawrence, sealing is closed
to aircraft and ships over 65 feet in length. Other re-
strictions also apply. Although sealing continues, the
Canadian government closely monitors it (Bryden 69).

Rebuttal

Evidence

Warrant

Even environmental organizations, quick to protect   7
nature, acknowledge that the seal is not on the verge of
extinction and that the population will remain stable
through regulation of hunting. According to Lewis Regenstein in The Politics of Extinction, many conservation
groups "have implicitly condoned this and other seal
'harvests' as long as they are done . . . as part of a
sound, rational management program" (87). The harp seal
"has not been classified as an endangered species"
(88).

Qualification

Whether the seals are endangered or not, the ques-   8
tion of the cruelty of the hunt remains. Opponents have
asserted that the pups suffer unduly, and indeed are even
skinned alive. Anyone who has seen pictures of these
little pups can hardly be unaffected by that argument.
But what is the evidence?

Rebuttal

The means and the manner of death are also regulated   9

Evidence

by the Canadian government. The pups are struck with
clubs, and death is almost invariably instantaneous.
The tales of skinning them alive are untrue. Government
agents have inspected hundreds of baby seal carcasses and

Warrant

found almost all the pups to be dead before skinning began ("Seal Hunt" 62). As for the clubbing, it does seem
cruel, but Victor Scheffer, author of A Voice for Wildlife, compares it to the slaughterhouse and says it is

Claim

"no worse than the killing of lambs in an abatoir" (67).

Evidence

We can't view the hunting of the seal in isolation   10
as a special case. It is part of the larger issue of the
protection of nature and our duty to other species. We
are naturally moved by film clips depicting cute little

Qualification

seal pups, as we would be by pictures of lambs and
calves. We should never allow any harmless species to

Rebuttal

suffer or die simply because we have technology and intelligence on our side. Yet surely our compassion must
extend in both directions: to the seal that is hunted and

Conclusion

to the human being whose livelihood depends on hunting.
Only when we examine these complex issues coolly--taking
into account all the economic, ethical, and cultural
ramifications--can we expect to arrive at an intelligent
understanding.

Works Cited

Bryden, Ronald. "They Impale Bleeding Hearts, Don't
     They?" Maclean's 20 Mar. 1978: 69.

Lavigne, David. "Life or Death for the Harp Seal." Na-
     tional Geographic Jan. 1976: 129-142.

Regenstein, Lewis. The Politics of Extinction. New York:
     Macmillan, 1975.

Scheffer, Victor. A Voice for Wildlife. New York: Scrib-
     ner's, 1974.

"Seal Hunt." Life 21 Mar. 1969: 61-63.

"Seals and Seal Fisheries." Encyclopedia Americana. 1985
     ed.

Trefethen, James. An American Crusade for Wildlife. New
     York: Winchester, 1975.

(In her notes and bibliography, Klein used the MLA parenthetical references and list of works cited format. For detailed information on this
system, see Chapter 14.)

Tips for Making the Argument

- Make your claims clear and unambiguous.
- Be sure you have sufficient evidence to support all parts of your claim.
- When the connection between the claim and the evidence is un-clear or complicated, provide the warrant.
- If a connection seems weak, supplement it with backing.
- Anticipate the opposing arguments and provide rebuttal.
- When an opposing idea is too strong to be denied, concede the point and qualify your argument accordingly.
- Use the elements of the Toulmin model as powerful revision tools.
- Don't forget that emotional appeals, when used appropriately, are potent, too.

EXERCISES FOR MAKING THE ARGUMENT

1. Choose either the affirmative or the negative of one of the following claims:

   Creationism should be taught in high school along with evolution.

   The Internet should be censored for child pornography.

   The government should decriminalize possession of marijuana.

   The state should help finance parochial schools.

   List points of evidence to support your position and all the opposing points you can think of. Now try to rebut each point on both lists. Write a para-graph accounting for any discrepancies or failures to rebut. With the oppos-ing points in mind, qualify your claim.

2. Here is a list of claims, each of which is paired with a piece of evidence:
   a. Dolphins should be considered equal to human beings. They have their own language.
   b. Shakespeare must not have been interested in women. His female char-acters are not drawn in detail.
   c. The Beatles were better musicians than Elvis Presley. They sold more records than Elvis did.
   d. We must all start learning Chinese. Otherwise we cannot hope to under-stand China.

   Provide the implied warrant for each argument. If the warrant needs back-ing, provide it.

3. Here is a claim followed by supporting statements. Which statements would a reader accept as evidence, and which require more proof? Explain. *Claim:* This institution should discontinue participation in intercollegiate football.

   Evidence:
   a. Played throughout the United States, football is a brutal sport.
   b. Our school should not give even tacit approval to anything brutal.
   c. Players often are injured during games.
   d. Few if any people like to see players injured.
   e. Only players benefit from whatever character building football provides.
   f. Studying history also can build character for all students.
   g. Basketball has become a dangerous contact sport.
   h. Playing in or watching football games may distract students from important intellectual pursuits.
   i. The school may be liable for injuries incurred during practice or games.

4. From the following list of topics, choose one that you and a partner disagree about.

   All students should be required to take computer science.

   All students should be required to take a foreign language.

   Playing radios and stereos should be forbidden every evening between seven and ten o'clock and after midnight.

   Motorcycles should be excluded from campus.

   Write an essay stating your belief and providing an argument. Try to anticipate what your partner will say. Exchange essays. Now revise your essay, backing, rebutting, and conceding or qualifying on the basis of what your partner wrote.

5. Write an essay in which you argue for or against one of the following controversies:

   A doctor should be allowed to help a terminally ill patient end his or her life.

   Taxpayers should be able to withhold part of their taxes when they are dissatisfied with government actions.

   Female reporters should be allowed access to male locker rooms following sports events.

   Provide three reasons why you think the way you do; give an example for each. These reasons will now become the main supporting points for your chosen thesis. Provide at least one claim of fact and one claim of value to support each reason. (See "Facts or Values" in Chapter 2.) Accompany these claims with one sentence each of further explanation.

6. Here are opposing arguments from interviews in the *New York Times* on the issue of police decoys, that is, disguising police officers in order to trap suspects in criminal acts. Analyze both arguments for effective persuasion, claim, evidence, warrant, backing, rebuttal, concession, and qualification. Also evaluate the use of emotion in the arguments. Write an essay taking the same general position as the side you support, but include a rebuttal of all the points the opposition made and, if necessary, concede points you cannot rebut.

I think decoy squads, even well trained and well supervised, eventually self-destruct. This is a result, in most cases, of the inevitable pressure to produce when there is this much investment in personnel and resources in what usually turns out to be not an extremely productive squad. You have four or five officers on a detail, spending one set of tours at least and probably more, five days a week, conducting operations which result in sometimes several but other times not so many arrests. And there is an inevitable, inexorable pressure to justify that expenditure.

Regrettably, the only way the police have traditionally attempted to justify that enormous expenditure is through arrests. Consequently decoy squads are under pressure, at the end of a week when there have been few arrests, to move toward entrapment, toward framing somebody, toward "flaking" [planting evidence on] somebody.

They usually think they can get away with it and they usually can get away with it, because it's four or five officers' words against one suspect, who's usually picked because he or she is vulnerable. But sooner or later that sort of scam catches up with the decoy squads, just as it did in the mid-1970s when the "dollar collars" scandal ended the last transit decoy squad. That's when kids were lured by dollars hanging out of decoys' pockets.

There's concern at this point over evidence of alleged flakes of suspects, where valuables are planted on arrestees by decoy officers, and robberies are staged between decoys to rope in an innocent bystander who's the target and has the goods dumped on him by one of the decoys posing as the mugger.

The tragedy of the decoy squad is that if improper arrests are made, it is extremely difficult to defend against them. Any defendant caught up in a decoy scam stands almost no chance at all. There's this large number of cops, and their testimony will be tailored, given their extensive training and understanding of the entrapment laws, to obtain a conviction, and the target will often be a person with a criminal record, even though he or she did not commit this particular offense.

There is also something just fundamentally offensive about cops creating crime. Obviously, targeting people who are predisposed to criminal conduct is a desirable law enforcement technique. It's efficient, and it protects the public. But creating temptations that are often questions of instantaneous judgment for the target, where it's extremely ambiguous as to what the target's intent really was at the time he or she was arrested, is a very, very troubling side of police work, and really walks on the precipice of a violation of due process.
(Richard D. Emery, former staff counsel to the New York Civil Liberties Union)

It's better that the crime victim be a trained officer with a backup team than an innocent citizen walking the streets or the platforms of the subways. That's why the decoys were put in there. They're put in where there have been a lot of reports of crime. I would expect that on a referendum it would get 99 percent of the vote.

It's also very strong from a legal standpoint. You've got a police officer who's trained. You've got an ironclad case, as opposed to a citizen who may not have seen the person, who may be afraid to follow through and make a complaint. So, with the police officer, it's the same as with a drug sale. If you sell to an undercover officer, you've got an ironclad legal case.

It's also a theory called proactive policing, as opposed to reactive policing. All progressive police administrators today try to be proactive. Instead of waiting around for things to happen, they go out where the numbers say there is a lot of crime. If the numbers say a lot of businesswomen are getting mugged, you might put a female officer out there with a briefcase.

It is dangerous, even with a backup team. The perpetrator can get in some pretty good licks. But you're doing something about preventing crime, rather than waiting and writing a report on it. My basic quarrel with the extreme civil liberties point of view is that most everything they've been criticizing is good, solid, sound police work. If it's done in the wrong way, the answer is not to say, "Let's abolish it."

The basic principle is that these things are not some weird idea that somebody thought up. They're based on standard police practices. And if you posit the idea that there are crime problems in the subways, and I think everyone would agree that there are, then the way you deal with it is with standard police practices.

A police force is created to maintain order and protect people against crime, and it isn't always going to come out neat and sweet. Most cases are not 100 percent clear-cut either way. A lot of them are judgment calls. Certainly there are ethical difficulties. The rule has always been that you're not supposed to flash money. The standard on entrapment is you're not supposed to persuade people to commit a crime who would not have committed a crime otherwise.

(Thomas Reppetto, president of New York City's Citizens' Crime Commission)

7. Choose a political cartoon from a newspaper and analyze it according to the 1-2-3 Rule.

PART FOUR

The Art of the Writer
Paragraphs, Sentences, Words, Style

8

The Structure and Strategies
of the Paragraph

Sentences are not emotional but paragraphs are. . . .
I found this out first in listening to Basket my dog
drinking.
> — GERTRUDE STEIN (1874-1946)
> AMERICAN WRITER

The paragraph is the laboratory of your thinking. In it, your mind says what it has to say on the major points of your argument. Within paragraphs, your thinking takes major steps, and the reader, if you manage your paragraphs well, can follow. Many are the ways of constructing a good paragraph—but all good paragraphs *get something accomplished.* They have shape, purpose, direction. Knowing how to shape a paragraph is essential to good writing.

Some people, however, write paragraphs by charging ahead in a straight line, one sentence after another, until they run out of words or their fingers get tired. Then they draw a deep breath, indent five spaces, and start up again. This may be fine for a first draft, when we are still sifting ideas and discovering what we want to say, but it won't do for a finished essay. No reader would be able to follow the thoughts, and few would be willing to try.

No matter how wonderful our ideas are, we still need to organize and package them carefully. Suppose you took a sackful of coins to the bank and demanded a twenty-dollar bill. Before any bank teller would give you the bill, you would have to sort the coins. That is what paragraphing is all about: sorting, combining, packaging ideas so that the reader can figure out how much each packet is worth and whether you get the twenty-dollar bill.

Successful paragraphs share three main qualities. They have *unity*, or a sense of togetherness; *development*, or a sense that the paragraph's topic has been discussed adequately; and *coherence*, or a sense of hanging together. Accordingly, the critical thinker/reader/writer will be a tough interrogator of his or her paragraphs.

UNITY: A SENSE OF TOGETHERNESS

As a roll of coins contains only one kind of coin, so the reader needs paragraphs organized around one idea, or main point. This main point is what the paragraph as a whole supports or proves. What does not support or prove the main point doesn't belong in the paragraph. In the following passage, Malcolm Cowley states the main point in the first sentence and supports it in the following sentences:

> The vanity of older people is an easier weakness to explain, and to condone. With less to look forward to, they yearn for recognition of what they have been: the reigning beauty, the athlete, the soldier, the scholar. It is the beauties who have the hardest time. A portrait of themselves at twenty hangs on the wall, and they try to resemble it by making an extravagant use of creams, powders, and dyes. Being young at heart, they think they are merely revealing their essential persons. The athletes find shelves for their silver trophies, which are polished once a year. Perhaps a letter sweater lies wrapped in a bureau drawer. I remember one evening when a no-longer athlete had guests for dinner and tried to find his sweater. "Oh, that old thing," his wife said. "The moths got into it and I threw it away." The athlete sulked and his guests went home early. ("The View from 80")

The first sentence identifies the main point. It is a statement of the idea that governs the paragraph. Cowley first turns to the ex-beauties and then to the ex-athletes. He demonstrates why it is easy "to explain, and to condone" the vanity of old people.

Sometimes no single sentence announces the main point, but all the sentences work so closely together that just to read them is to understand what main point they are making. The following paragraph contains one main point, but no single sentence conveys it:

> I don't find evidence, as some radical feminists do, for the claim that all men are rapists and murderers. If all men are, potentially, rapists and murderers, then they are so only as women, too, have a potential for destructive behavior. Women, however, have been tradition-

ally trained away from such behavior (how else would the two-year-olds of the world survive?), except as we can turn it on ourselves in madness and self-destruction. Why else would Sylvia Plath's suicide inspire myths rather than simple pity? Men are trained to kill in circumstances of war. Because for most men such behavior is abhorrent, it must continually be glorified to persuade them against their own moral sense to destroy rather than protect other members of their own species. (Jane Rule, "Pornography Is a Social Disease")

Every sentence contributes to make the main point, that both men and women are conditioned to behave in certain ways. That is the point that unifies the whole paragraph.

Staying with the Main Point

Every idea, every fact, every opinion in the paragraph must be part of the main point. No extraneous ideas should be dropped in, no matter how witty or arresting—no nickels among the pennies. A paragraph may have more than one sentence. It may include statistics, quotations, facts, observations, assertions of value. But they must all unite to form the main point.

Some associations are so beguiling that following them leads the writer right out of the paragraph. Imagine a paragraph with consecutive sentences on these subjects: paint, color, green, blue, blues, jazz, rock, stone, stoned. We have rarely seen paragraphs that aimless, but we have seen some in which the writer similarly drifts down the stream of consciousness. Here is a fairly tame example:

> When we think about animal experimentation, we should look at the animals used. Because so many are required, only abundant species are chosen. Scientists may test a drug on anything from a small mouse to a monkey. Testing is helpful to scientists because it enables them to study the effects of new chemicals. Limiting tests to cell and tissue cultures only is inadequate. Scientists can find out a good deal from tissue analysis, but drugs do not act the same way when other kinds of tissue are absent. Not even with the capabilities of computers can scientists discover enough about the effects of drugs. Tests on experimental animals are still our best means, short of human trials, of learning how drugs work in human bodies.

The paragraph's first sentence seems to promise a discussion of the lab animals, and for the next two sentences that is what we get. But the word *testing* in the fourth sentence diverts the writer from her point, and she drops the animals. If the student had checked each sentence against that initial promise, she would have seen right away that at her fourth sentence she had begun to go astray. In the fifth and sixth sentences, she discusses another kind of test, and in the seventh, quite far afield, she points out the inadequacy of computers. The closing sentence brings us back to animals but makes a point that seems to have little to do with the original topic.

In the revision, the writer refuses to be diverted and concentrates on supporting her main point.

> When we think about animal experimentation, we should look at the animals used. Because so many are required, only abundant species are chosen. Scientists may test a drug on anything from a small mouse to a monkey. They choose animals that share certain biological functions with human beings. By observing the effect of drugs on these animals, they can learn something about the effects of the drugs on human beings. This kind of testing is still our best means, short of human trials, of learning how drugs work in human bodies.

Not only will the reader understand better but also the writer will. Writing is a kind of thinking, after all.

Getting Help from the Topic Sentence

Often the main point of a paragraph is indicated in a single sentence, called the *topic sentence*. Usually it either expresses the main point outright or makes that point unmistakably clear. It says, "This is what this whole paragraph is all about." All the other sentences support the topic sentence.

Having such an explicit statement can help both the writer and the reader. It is a constant reminder of what kinds of evidence can be included. Bearing this statement in mind while revising, the writer can check the other sentences to gauge the unity of the whole paragraph.

"The vanity of older people is an easier weakness to explain, and to condone" (p. 178) is a topic sentence that informs the reader that the paragraph will be about the vanity of older people. This sentence is general enough to include all the evidence the writer provides, and thus holds the paragraph together.

Although a topic sentence can come anywhere in a paragraph, it is most commonly the first sentence. Placing it at the top alerts the reader to what will be coming up. Look at these initial topic sentences, and think about the expectations they create.

> Much of the public debate in recent years about the breakdown of the African American family has failed to acknowledge that the traditional nuclear family has never been the typical model of the black family. (Angela Davis, "Child Care or Workfare")

> The intellectual interest of a child in the riddle of sexual life, his desire for knowledge, finds expression at an earlier period of life than is usually suspected. (Sigmund Freud, *The Sexual Enlightenment of Children*)

> The modern business organization, or that part which has to do with guidance and direction, consists in numerous individuals who are engaged, at any given time, in obtaining, digesting or exchanging and testing information. (John Kenneth Galbraith, "The Technostructure")

Each of these sentences makes a promise to the reader: this is what the following evidence will support. We expect, for instance, that Galbraith will describe how exchange and testing go on, that Freud will give some examples of the child's desire for knowledge, that Davis will define the model of the black family.

Frequently a first sentence does not state the main point but provides a transition from the previous paragraph. The topic sentence may then appear later in the paragraph. Describing the way lawyers speak and write, David S. Levine refers to a decision in a court case, beginning with a transitional sentence and then stating the topic sentence:

> In the example given, the court embraced decisional authority ranging from 1891 to 1976. Because lawyers are constantly searching for the leading edge of the law, of necessity they face backward to cases already decided in order to determine where the edge came from and where it trails off into the ether. ("'My Client Has Discussed Your Proposal to Fill the Drainage Ditch with His Partners': Legal Language"; our underlining)

The transitional sentence summarizes the previous paragraph and how judges decide cases. The topic sentence shifts the subject to how lawyers respond.

Paragraphs sometimes conclude with a topic sentence. So placed, it seems to sum up the earlier sentences. In the following example, the writer—novelist and naturalist Wendell Berry—could have begun the paragraph with the last sentence, but note the impact of placing it at the end:

> In the early spring of 1965 I had planted a small orchard; the next spring we planted our first garden. Within the following six or seven years we reclaimed pastures, converted the garage into a henhouse, rebuilt the barn, greatly improved the garden soil, planted berry bushes, acquired a milk cow—and were producing, except for hay and grain for our animals, nearly everything that we ate: fruit, vegetables, eggs, meat, milk, cream, and butter. We built an outbuilding with a meat room and a food-storage cellar. Because we did not want to pollute our land and water with sewage, and in the process waste nutrients that should be returned to the soil, we built a compacting privy. And so we began to attempt a life that, in addition to whatever else it was, would be responsibly agricultural. We used no chemical fertilizers. Except for a little rotenone, we used no insecticides. As our land and our food became healthier, so did we. And our food was of better quality than any that we could have bought. ("The Making of a Marginal Farm"; our underlining)

Berry has carefully guided the reader through a narrative of his life on the farm. That last sentence is like putting the sum at the bottom of a column of figures. The reader says, Ah, now I know what all these ideas mean.

In the hands of a superb writer like Berry, the topic sentence can be very effective in the last position. But unless carefully tended, this arrangement has dangers. The reader, abruptly arriving at the final sum, may have to retrace the steps to be sure they were tallied correctly. Write paragraphs with topic sentences at the end, of course, but double-check them.

Sometimes a writer places the topic sentence deep in the paragraph, as in this passage describing the plight of some college students:

> The unhappiness and discontent of young people is nothing new, and problems of adolescence are always painfully intense. But while traveling around the country, speaking at colleges, and interviewing students at all kinds of schools—large and small, public and private— I was overwhelmed by the prevailing sadness. It was as visible on campuses in California as in Nebraska and Massachusetts. <u>Too many young people are in college reluctantly, because everyone told them they ought to go, and there didn't seem to be anything better to do.</u> Their elders sell them college because it's good for them. Some never learn to like it, and talk about their time in school as if it were a sentence to be served. (Caroline Bird, "The College Mystique"; our underlining)

The main idea, underlined in the fourth sentence, summarizes the description in the first three sentences and anticipates the explanations of the last two. It encompasses the whole paragraph.

Sometimes a paragraph reaches back to a previous paragraph to find its main idea. In "The View from 80," Cowley ends one paragraph with

> We start by growing old in other people's eyes, then slowly we come to share their judgment.

In the next paragraph, he provides the evidence for that main point.

> I remember a morning many years ago when I was backing out of the parking lot near the railroad station in Brewster, New York. There was a near collision. The driver of the other car jumped out and started to abuse me; he had his fists ready. Then he looked at me and said, "Why, you're an old man." He got back in the car, slammed the door, and drove away, while I stood there fuming. "I'm only 65," I thought. "He wasn't driving carefully. I can still take care of myself in a car, or in a fight, for that matter."

Likewise, writers will often continue a topic in a second or even a third paragraph without any additional topic sentence. In an essay comparing our fears with those of the Eskimo, Loren Eiseley begins one paragraph this way:

> For what is it that we do? We fear. We do not fear ghosts but we fear the ghost of ourselves. We have come now, in this time, to fear the water we drink. . . .

He finishes that paragraph with a series of things we fear and then goes to a new paragraph and continues listing our fears:

> We fear the awesome powers we have lifted out of nature and cannot return to her. We fear the weapons we have made, the hatreds we have engendered. We fear the crush of fanatic people to whom we readily sell these weapons. We fear for the value of the money in our pockets that stands symbolically for food and shelter. We fear the growing power of the state to take all these things from us. We fear to walk in our streets at evening. We have come to fear even our scientists and their gifts. ("The Winter of Man")

The topic sentence controls the development of both paragraphs.

Paragraphs containing only a topic sentence also occur occasionally; their main idea is so obvious that it needs no further support. Frequently these one-sentence paragraphs are rhetorical questions, as in this example from Eiseley's essay:

> Has the wintry bleakness in the troubled heart of humanity at least equally retreated?—that aspect of man referred to when the Eskimo, adorned with amulets to ward off evil, reiterated: "Most of all we fear the secret misdoings of the heedless ones among ourselves."

Almost always, however, you will need to flesh out the topic sentence with a series of supporting sentences.

Our examples of topic sentences so far have laid out the main point in fairly explicit terms. Some topic sentences are more subtly phrased yet express the main point. In an essay on criminal justice, the writer summarizes what he found wrong with indeterminate sentencing and expresses the topic sentence as a question:

> Then should we get rid of indeterminate sentencing?

He follows this question with reasons why we shouldn't. Another writer presents the opposition's view of animal experimentation in one paragraph and begins the next paragraph with

> But that is all wrong . . .

and proceeds to explain why. In neither instance does the topic sentence indicate exactly what opinion the paragraph will support. It nonetheless guides the reader into the subject.

The best writers use a variety of paragraph constructions, none of which is ever mechanical. Their topic sentence may be first, middle, last, or only implied. They are guided by the flow of ideas between and within paragraphs.

Inexperienced or uncertain writers, however, will find topic sentences very helpful, particularly when they come at the beginning of the paragraph. Starting a paragraph with the main point clearly stated can help to keep the writer on track.

One further suggestion: a bold and intriguing topic sentence up front can entice readers into the paragraph. Make your topic sentence interesting so that the reader will want to read on.

A Special Word about the Thesis and the Topic Sentence

Topic sentences not only tie all the sentences of a paragraph together but also tie the whole paragraph to the essay's thesis. The topic sentence says, This is what this paragraph has to do with the argument developing through the whole essay. When the topic sentences are clearly related to the thesis, they help keep the whole essay together.

Remember Stephanie Klein's essay on the harp seal hunt in Chapter 7? By analyzing it, we can see how the topic sentences relate to the thesis and promote the argument:

> Thesis: If we look at the evidence, we see a different, and much more complex, picture [rather than supporting the notion that the harp seal hunt should be banned].
>
> Topic sentence 1: The seal hunt is not a sport but a necessity.
>
> Topic sentence 2: Sealing provides not only employment but also essential goods.
>
> Topic sentence 3: The fishing industry indirectly benefits from the seal hunt.
>
> Topic sentence 4: Despite [assertions to the contrary] the harp seal is not an endangered species.
>
> Topic sentence 5: Although sealing continues, the Canadian government closely monitors it.
>
> Topic sentence 6: Even environmental organizations . . . acknowledge . . . that the [seal] population will remain stable through regulation of hunting.
>
> Topic sentence 7: The question of the cruelty of the hunt remains.
>
> Topic sentence 8: The means and the manner of death are also regulated by the Canadian government [and the cruelty has been exaggerated].
>
> Concluding topic sentence: Only when we examine these complex issues coolly—taking into account all the economic, ethical, and cultural ramifications—can we expect to arrive at an intelligent understanding.

Each topic sentence is both a logical development from and a support for the thesis. If you read them as though they formed a single paragraph, you will see how tight and clear the argument is. We suggest you do this sort of postwriting outline of your topic sentences to see how well your argument has turned out.

Reading and Revising for Unity

Read your essays from paragraph to paragraph. Ask yourself constantly: what is the topic of this paragraph? do I have a strong topic sentence, or at least a strongly implied topic? do the rest of the sentences support that topic?

Read your paragraphs in order. That will give you a sense of flow. You might also try reading your paragraphs from last to first. That will take your paragraphs out of context, forcing you to focus on their inner workings.

 Computer Tip

Blow up your paragraph by hitting ENTER after each sentence. With each sentence defenseless in the cold light of reason, you can ask some tough questions. Does this sentence have a role? Does it further the topic? Does it move the paragraph along? Once you have interrogated and, if necessary, revised each sentence, reassemble the paragraph and see it as a whole again.

Tips for Unity
- Be sure each of your paragraphs has a single main point.
- Remember that all ideas must relate to that main point.
- Delete any sentences not related to the main point, no matter how clever or intriguing.
- Think about using a topic sentence to express the main point.
- Putting the topic sentence at the beginning of the paragraph can help you stay on course.
- When you place the topic sentence in the middle, be sure it combines both ends of the paragraph into a single idea.
- When you place the topic sentence at the end, be sure all sentences lead to it.
- Remember that every main point, whether expressed in a topic sentence or implied, should relate to the essay's thesis.
- When revising for unity, read your paragraphs both in order and out of order.

EXERCISES FOR UNITY

1. The following two paragraphs lack unity because their authors have gone off on tangents:

> Popular fiction focuses on a few basic fantasies, continually readapting them to the latest fashions in the culture. In the 1950s, for example, the private eye was the basic adventure hero, in the 1960s it was the spy, and in the 1970s the ex-Vietnam veteran against organized crime. In the 1980s and 1990s it was the cop or undercover detective against the terrorists and drug runners. But each hero faces essentially the same challenges—rich and powerful supervillains—and has the same resources—hand-to-hand combat skills, inventive intelligence, and that most crucial of all ingredients, sex appeal. Indeed, whatever the decade of their flourishing, these heroes always succeed in seducing women. And this is what their readers want to experience vicariously. In airports, on trains, at bus stops, you see mild-mannered and well-groomed men, briefcases in hand, reading the latest stories. Who would suspect the brutal and lascivious fantasies exploding within their brains? As Gilbert and Sullivan once observed, "Things are seldom what they seem."

> There is great power not only in the denotative meanings of words but in their connotations as well. Consider, for example, this familiar phrase: "We hold these truths to be self-evident." Ask yourself, How is this different from "We hold these truths to be sacred and undeniable"? Thomas Jefferson himself actually wrote the second phrase. The Continental Congress, however, delegated the task of writing the Declaration of Independence to five men, including John Adams and Benjamin Franklin. Adams had suggested that Jefferson write the document by himself, in part because Jefferson was known to be a good writer, in part because he was a Virginian and Adams wanted to secure Virginia's support for the rebellion. Who actually changed the wording, though, we do not know.

   In each case, identify the point at which the paragraph gets off track and rewrite the paragraph from that point forward.

2. Here are three pairs of sentences, one a topic sentence for a paragraph and the other a piece of support. Identify the topic sentence in each pair.
   a. Perhaps the finest painting in the church is Lorenzo Lotto's *St. Anthony Giving Alms,* in which the warm colour scheme seems to have been derived from the soft Turkish carpets which play a prominent part in the composition. Although the church is not as rich in paintings as in sculpture, it contains several of note. (Hugh Honour, *The Companion Guide to Venice*)
   b. The Beatles could afford not to grow up because a certain childlike magic had always been central to their appeal. They were bound up with the decade in more ways than one, for the sixties were a period that believed in magic and innocence, that had a touching faith in the omnipotence of individual desire. (Morris Dickstein, *Gates of Eden: American Culture in the Sixties*)
   c. Early one morning the sub-inspector at a police station the other end of the town rang me up on the phone and said that an elephant was ravaging the bazaar. It was a tiny incident in itself, but it gave me a better glimpse than I had had before of the real nature of imperialism—the real motives for which despotic governments act. (George Orwell, "Shooting an Elephant")

3. Identify the topic sentence in each of the following paragraphs. Analyze how the other sentences support that topic. Do you get a sense of movement or direction?

> I used to cut vegetables in the kitchen. String beans had to be cut in one-inch pieces. The way you were supposed to do it was: You hold two beans in one hand, the knife in the other, and you press the knife against the beans and your thumb, almost cutting yourself. It was a slow process. So I put my mind to it, and I got a pretty good idea. I sat down at the wooden table outside the kitchen, put a bowl in my lap, and stuck a very sharp knife into the table at a forty-five-degree angle away from me. Then I put a pile of the string beans on each side, and I'd pick out a bean, one in each hand, and bring it towards me with enough speed that it would slice, and the pieces would slide into the bowl that was in my lap. (Richard P. Feynman, *"Surely You're Joking, Mr. Feynman!"*)

> The Hebrews craved to settle for good in the fertile plains. But characteristically they dreamed of lands overflowing with milk and honey, not lands of superabundant crops like those the Egyptians imagined for their hereafter. It seems that the desert as a metaphysical experience loomed very large for the Hebrews and coloured all their valuations. It is, perhaps, the tension between two valuations—between a desire and a contempt for what is desired—that may explain some of the paradoxes of ancient Hebrew beliefs. (H. and H. A. Frankfort, *Before Philosophy*)

4. Each of the following statements could serve as a thesis for an essay:
   a. Attempting suicide should/should not be a crime.
   b. The government should/should not provide funds for abortions for women on welfare.
   c. The United States should/should not send troops to keep peace in countries where our national interests are not directly involved.
   d. The traditional summer recess should/should not be cut from three months to one.

   For each, write four topic sentences suitable for supporting paragraphs. Exchange your sentences with a partner and discuss the differences.

5. Examine a recent essay of yours paragraph by paragraph. If you are working on a computer, "blow up" the paragraphs by hitting ENTER a few times after each sentence. Identify the topic sentences. Do all clearly relate to the thesis? Do any paragraphs fail to adhere to their topic sentence? Do any end far away from where they began? If you find examples of disunity, revise them.

DEVELOPMENT: STRATEGIES FOR EXPANDING YOUR THOUGHTS

At the end of a well-designed paragraph, we have a sense of completeness. But some paragraphs leave us hungry for more. This paragraph, for example, was written for an exam in a religion class in which the students were asked to describe in a paragraph the God of the Old Testament:

> The God of the Old Testament was uncompromising. Command-ing Abraham to sacrifice Isaac is a case in point. Another is Job. There is no reasoning with the All-Powerful.

That's it. Is it unified? Yes. Is there a topic sentence? Yes. Is there sup-port? Yes. The paragraph is promising, but it needs to be expanded so that we know how the details fit with the main idea. Remind us of Abra-ham, we want to say. How is his story a case in point? And how does the story of Job fit the topic? As for that fine last sentence, how did we get there? Who was trying to reason?

Whether such writing results from impatience, stinginess, or timidity we don't know. But we do know that no writer should expect the reader to fill in the blanks. When we provide an example, we should in-dicate exactly what is being exemplified and how it supports the main point. When we use a term, like *reasoning,* we need to back it up and show how it is used.

Given a second chance, the writer might have come up with some-thing like this:

> The God of the Old Testament is uncompromising in the demands He makes on humanity. In Genesis, He tests Abraham's faith by de-manding that Abraham sacrifice his son Isaac. Only at the last minute, after he is sure that Abraham will obey, does God relent. In the Book of Job, every calamity imaginable is visited on the once-proud Job. When Job argues with God that he does not deserve the ill treatment, worse is inflicted on him. Only after Job accepts his afflictions and God's power does God accept and bless Job. There is no reasoning with the All-Powerful.

Now the student has laid out the details, and the last sentence does what a last sentence ought to do: It provides us with a sense of *closure*— that is, the feel of completion as well as the fact of it.

That feeling of closure is important. Readers often take away from the paragraph the thought expressed in the last sentence. Although no degree of eloquence in the wrap-up will make a thin broth into a robust soup, a strong last sentence can contribute to the reader's sense of satis-faction.

How do you know when enough is enough and not too much? Readers will think a paragraph is too much when they find it difficult to retain the overall shape of the argument or their eyes and mind begin to tire. Try to anticipate both of these problems.

No hard-and-fast rules can govern how well-developed a paragraph should be, but our experience tells us that writing is one area in which fat is generally better than skinny. Where do you find the details, the ex-planations, and the examples that develop your thoughts? In your own mind, of course. In the following pages, we suggest eight strategies that can help you locate them:

description

narration

illustration

process analysis

cause and effect

division and classification

comparison and contrast

definition

You can use these strategies at any stage in the writing process. As invention strategies (see Chapter 4, Getting Ready to Write), they can help you discover ideas. They can also, of course, help develop those ideas once discovered. They can help organize your thoughts. And they can help you draft and revise for complete and effective paragraphs. They are natural ways of thinking.

Government is invading our lives. Take taxes, for example.

We've just used illustration, one of the most basic strategies.

If I dyed my hair, all my friends would laugh at me.

This sentence suggests cause and effect.

All you have to do is take hold of the handle and turn.

This is an example of process analysis.

Sometimes a paragraph will be developed according to a single strategy. You will see examples of such paragraphs throughout this chapter, paragraphs of description, process analysis, classification, and so on. More often, a paragraph will intermingle several strategies. Few essays go by without a paragraph or two of definition, illustration, and cause and effect, and almost certainly description or narration. Look at the following passage, in which Richard Rodriguez argues against bilingual education:

> Many years later there is something called bilingual education—a scheme proposed in the late 1960s by Hispanic-American social activists, later endorsed by a congressional vote. It is a program that seeks to permit non-English-speaking children, many from lower class homes, to use their family language as the language of school. (Such is the goal its supporters announce.) I hear them and am forced to say no: It is not possible for a child—any child—ever to use his family's language in school. Not to understand this is to misunderstand the public uses of schooling and to trivialize the nature of intimate life—a family's "language."
>
> Memory teaches me what I know of these matters; the boy reminds the adult. I was a bilingual child, a certain kind—socially disadvantaged—the son of working-class parents, both Mexican immigrants.
>
> In the early years of my boyhood . . . *(Hunger of Memory)*

After *defining* two terms *(bilingual education* and *socially disadvantaged),* Rodriguez offers himself as an *illustration* of his point and then begins to *narrate,* the major strategy of his essay. Within the narration will be description and more illustration.

The strategy you use at any particular point will depend on your purpose. You wouldn't use the same strategy to convey the impression of a Zulu war dance that you would use for placing surrealism in its historic context. The dance requires description, narration, and perhaps process analysis. Surrealism must be defined and illustrated and then analyzed for its historic causes and effects. With each task, you will have to decide what strategy or strategies to employ. And after the decision comes the performance.

Tips for Development
- Prefer well-developed paragraphs to skinny paragraphs.
- End your paragraphs with a sense of closure; don't leave it to the reader to fill in the blanks.
- Keep your purpose in mind when selecting a strategy; let your point drive your development.

EXERCISES FOR DEVELOPMENT

1. Here are three skinny paragraphs.

   America's many foods take their characters from their countries of origin. Spaghetti is a good example, as are tacos and burritos, which are both spicy and hot. And we must not forget the hamburger, one of America's most popular foods.

   Children learn language by imitating their parents. At first, all a newborn can do is cry, but then it can see better. It starts imitating its parents, and soon it can make sentences by itself. Now it is a member of society.

   Roads are becoming a real problem for modern cities. Many cities have grown too fast. They build new roads. As those fill up, soon they have no place to put more roads. Public transportation is the only solution.

   Study each one, determine where the gaps are, and fill them in, providing missing material and connections. Feel free to rewrite any of the sentences if that will help. After you finish revising, be prepared to discuss what you added and why.

2. Find a recent essay of yours and look for skinny paragraphs. Revise it, adding what is needed. What did you add and why? (You can do this with a partner, too: exchange recent papers and look for skinny paragraphs. Then take your own paper back and revise it. Or revise a skinny paragraph in your partner's essay.)

Description: Showing It

When we put into words what our senses tell us, we are describing. "Meet me by the broken copper fountain under the gnarled old tree that gives off a pungent, almost acrid smell." We frequently use description in our college work as well. In a film class, the instructor might assign the description of a scene from a movie; in a history class, a battle or a political event; in a law class, a court trial or an accident. Accurate and detailed description is one of the fundamental tasks of writing in the sciences.

Description is one of the primary strategies. We can use it by itself or to support other strategies. A narration almost always includes description. A definition frequently relies on describing.

The writer's task is, as Joseph Conrad said, "by the power of the written word, to make you hear, to make you feel—it is, before all, to make you *see*." The details we choose for a description must be vivid enough to call up images from the reader's store of remembered impressions. Good description demands the exact, the concrete, and the familiar. Abstract or imprecise words make for slower understanding and are generally less effective.

Describing is thinking; we describe things usually to support a claim we are making. Our details, images, and appeals to the senses must, therefore, have a point to support. If our claim is "Frank Lloyd Wright influenced the American urban scene," we might support our claim with a description of the Guggenheim Museum. Our point will determine the details we include and how we present them.

Those details must add up to something, however: an impression, an effect. Only when we select details with our idea in mind will the reader *see*.

The following passage describes a great painting:

> The *Mona Lisa* is a portrait by Leonardo da Vinci of an Italian woman about whom we know little. Her hands are folded in her lap. She is looking out of the painting, wearing her famous smile. She has on dark clothes and is poised at a window. Her hair is mostly straight. The surface of the painting has deteriorated so that closer examination is difficult.

This description is too vague. It doesn't tell us, for instance, whether the folded hands are tensely gripping each other or are relaxed. The phrase *her famous smile* could mean a death's-head grin for all we know. The condition of the painting's surface appears as an isolated fact. The details are too disorganized to make a point. Indeed, there was apparently no point, no idea the description supports. After some critical rethinking, the writer realized that the main impression the *Mona Lisa* made on him was of "serene repose." Now he had a main point around which to organize his description.

The revision is considerably better:

> Everything in the *Mona Lisa* communicates serene repose. Her hands, folded loosely, and her gaze, neither avoiding nor confronting the viewer, indicate a woman at peace with herself and the world. Her smile shows inner contentment. Da Vinci reinforces this mood of quiet by using muted hues—dark hair, dark clothing, the distant valley. Yet even here there are bits of brightness, in both the hair framing the subject's face and the river behind her. Time itself has supported da Vinci's theme, for the deteriorating surface of the painting prevents examination of its structure. One must instead absorb the *Mona Lisa* whole, and in this way, perhaps, come away a bit more serene oneself.

Now we understand that the mood of the painting is the point. We can see the kind of smile on the subject's face, her hands as part of the whole, the window as framing the river. All the details are relevant. We understand that the hues reinforce the meaning of the smile.

Tips for Description

- Use details that are vivid enough to call up an image in the reader's mind.
- Make sure there is a point to the description.

EXERCISES FOR DESCRIPTION

1. Choose an object that you think is a symbol of the American way of life, for example, a McDonald's, a dollar bill, or a football. Using either free writing or clustering, develop ideas about the object. Choose the most promising idea, and support that idea by describing your object. Emphasize details that strike you as important, and explain their significance in relation to your interpretation of American culture.

2. Go to the library and find a photograph of one of the following people:

Billie Holiday	Tina Modotti
Jim Thorpe	Robert E. Lee
Calvin Coolidge	Golda Meir
Jean Harlow	Charles Darwin

   Photocopy the photograph and describe it in a paragraph. Do not name the subject of the photograph in your paragraph. All the paragraphs will be reproduced and distributed in class, and the photocopied photographs will be passed around. Members of the class will try to match the descriptions to the photocopies.

Narration: Telling It

"Where did you go?"

"Out."

"What did you do?"

"Nothing."

When we tell what happened, even if it was "nothing," we narrate. A narration is an account of what happened. Short stories and novels are narrations, but so is a joke, an anecdote, or an autobiography. We narrate when we summarize the plot of a novel, tell what happened during a rebellion, or trace the course of a disease. We also narrate in a lab report or a summary of a research project.

Along with description, narration is a primary writing strategy. Frequently, we use it in conjunction with other strategies. When we write a descriptive piece, we almost always narrate part of it. The examples we give are often narrations. And we may use narration in process analysis, cause and effect, and definition.

The building blocks of good narration are the same as those of good description: a point to be made and concrete, relevant details. You must first determine the point you wish to make. To help the reader get the point, concentrate on the most illuminating events. Let the story unfold scene by scene. Using vivid detail—concrete nouns, active verbs, exact adjectives and adverbs—try to re-create the narrative in the reader's imagination. *Show* rather than *tell* the story, so that the reader has a sense of watching and listening. Arrange the scenes so that they rise to a climax.

The following passage attempts to narrate an important event in the life of the writer:

> When we came back from the store that Christmas Eve, I realized I had been given too much change from my final purchase. I showed the money to my brother and then to my father. My father didn't like it and he made me give back the money. My brothers and sisters all laughed at me. I should have returned the money myself, without father's having to tell me.

This narrative is an abstract and general summary of happenings, without dialogue, contrasts, or drama. If the writer has a point here (we sense one in the last sentence), she has not used it to direct and organize the narration. Telling everything but showing little, the writer ignores many important questions: we don't really know why the father took the narrator back to the store or why the siblings laughed. As for the point, at the end the writer tries to incorporate a neat—far too neat—little moral. But does the story only want to tell us to be honest? Do we really need to be reminded of that?

In the revision the writer reconsidered and revised her main point. Then she visualized the happenings and presented them as vividly as she could.

> When the salesclerk gave me back my change, I thought she had given me too much. At age six, I didn't count money very well, and so when we got home, I showed the coins to my brother. "I gave her fifty cents," I said, "and she gave me this."
>
> "That's sixty cents," he said in an admiring voice I seldom heard from him. "You're smarter than I thought." Beaming with pride, chortling over my new fortune, I went sailing in to my father to receive his praise.
>
> "The salesclerk gave me too much change," I said.
>
> With deliberation, he went over all my purchases with me. He examined my dog-eared Christmas list and the sales slips. "Get your coat," he said.
>
> The news flashed through the house, and, as my father and I prepared to leave, my brothers and sisters hid behind the banisters and silently mocked me.
>
> "Honor," my father said as he closed the front door. "Honesty," he said as we walked to the car. "Fairness," he said as he started the car. "These are virtues without which civilization cannot endure. Money," he went on as we backed away from the curb, "may threaten virtue but must never be allowed to defeat it. Let this be a lesson to you." And in truth it was, though I could not have said in what.

In her revision, the writer lets us watch the people act and hear them talk. The scenes now build to the climax. Perhaps the greatest improvement, however, is in the point of the story. Now it is left ambiguous, as it should be. Sibling rivalry, parental instruction, honesty, the joys of praise and of money—all are inextricably mixed in the narrator's mind. The whole narrative supports that point.

Tips for Narration

- Decide what point your narrative should have.
- Show, don't tell, developing your narrative scene by scene.

EXERCISES FOR NARRATION

1. Narrate a story having to do with one of the following feelings: pain, fear, hunger, affection, hope. Do not name the feeling. Let your choice of events and your words communicate it. Be sure the story has a climax and a point, but don't state the point. In a follow-up paragraph, describe how you selected the key events to make the episode climactic.

2. After developing ideas through the journalistic or classical method (see "Directed Questioning" in Chapter 4), write a page narrating one of the following events:

high-school commencement

your arrival at college

registration for classes

the first meeting of this class

the first social occasion at school

Now exchange your essay with a partner, each analyzing the other's essay. Based on your partner's critique and your own increased focus on narration, rewrite your essay.

Illustration: Making It Specific

When we see a questioning look on our listener's face, we instinctively provide an illustration, an example of what we mean. "Daniel Day Lewis is excellent at portraying diverse characters—he was a frontiersman in *The Last of the Mohicans,* for example, and an upper-class New Yorker in *The Age of Innocence.*" In much of your college writing, you will need to provide illustrations. When you make a point about a work of literature, you must go to the text to find illustrations for it. When you generalize about a historic event, illustrations clarify your meaning. They support your assertion about a work of art, a social phenomenon, a laboratory procedure.

Illustrations serve three purposes. First, they clarify your thought by bringing the general idea to a more easily understood specific level. Second, they help prove your idea by showing that, at least in this particular instance, your assertion is reasonable. Third, they make reading more entertaining. Nothing brings the reader and the writer together quite so quickly and effectively as the well-chosen illustration.

As with all strategies, writers must plan and arrange illustrations carefully. Critical thinking once again comes into play. Each illustration must support the point and be accessible to the reader.

In this paragraph, from an essay analyzing the distinctive qualities of various movie stars, the writer uses illustrations in his discussion of Humphrey Bogart:

> Humphrey Bogart occupies a unique and permanent place in the imagination of the American moviegoer. His success lies in his ability to portray a complex character, at once a ruthless, utterly self-seeking loner, and a tender, even sentimental, defender of the weak. In *The African Queen,* Bogart is a buffoon and Katharine Hepburn is the tough one. In *The Desperate Hours,* Bogart displays tenderness and toughness. When the character dies, we feel both relief and a touch of sorrow. Fredric March plays the father, who is loving and selfless. In *To Have and Have Not,* Bogart is again both hard and sensitive. Lauren

> Bacall is as usual honest and humorous. Moviegoers still value the qualities Bogart represented and look for them in today's actors. But we can no more imagine a new tender-tough Bogart than we can a new Garibaldi riding through the Italian countryside, unifying his country.

Did you feel this paragraph going awry? The writer has a great many details, but he has not selected them wisely or arranged them well. Keep his main point in mind here: Bogart's genius was in portraying characters who are both ruthless and tender. Notice that the writer reverses the description of Bogart from tough-tender to tender-tough and then back to tough-tender. Once we establish an order, we ought to stick to it. Otherwise the reader's eyes will be flying up and down the field, looking for home base.

Many of the details are irrelevant. The references to Katharine Hepburn and Fredric March distract the reader. The writer has an interesting point about Bogart as a buffoon; however, he introduces this idea far too early—before he has developed his main idea. The comparison in the last line is farfetched. Few readers would easily connect Garibaldi, the nineteenth-century Italian revolutionary leader, with Bogart, the twentieth-century actor. And *The Desperate Hours* is an obscure film. The writer should have told the reader more about this important but unfamiliar illustration.

Still a Bogart fan, the writer went back to the writing desk.

> Humphrey Bogart occupies a unique and permanent place in the imagination of the American moviegoer. His success lies in his ability to portray a complex character, at once a ruthless, utterly self-seeking loner and a tender, even sentimental, defender of the weak. A good example of this character is the protagonist of *The Desperate Hours.* In this movie, Bogart's willingness to destroy his fellow convict, to pistol-whip the innocent father of the family he holds hostage, and to jeopardize the lives of the family contrasts with his love for his brother and, finally, his unwillingness to harm the little boy in the family.
>
> In *To Have and Have Not,* Bogart again plays the tough-tender guy, but his toughness is softened by Lauren Bacall's irony and his sentimentality undercut by her honesty. Bogart did not always play the same role, of course—in *The African Queen* he is a weakling and a buffoon until near the end—but he was always most appealing in his tough-tender guise. Moviegoers still value the qualities Bogart represented and look for them in today's actors. But we can no more imagine another tough-tender Bogart than we can another ironic-honest Bacall.

Here the writer maintains the tough-tender order all the way. He sticks to his subjects, and where needed he elaborates with more detailed illustrations. He saves his point about Bogart-as-buffoon until he has completed his main point. At the end, he illustrates his point by a comparison with the well-known Lauren Bacall, who had already been characterized.

Tips for Illustration

When providing illustrations, follow the same pattern as the idea the illustrations support, and offer enough detail and explanation so your reader will find them easily understandable.

EXERCISES FOR ILLUSTRATION

1. Think up two illustrations for each of the following statements:

    Money is the root of all evil.

    Shyness can be an asset.

    Buying stocks can be hazardous to your financial health.

    Politics is the art of the possible.

    Exchange your illustrations with a partner. Choose one of the statements and write a paragraph analyzing the difference between your illustrations and those of your partner. Which are more accessible? Which need to be more specific? How would you make your partner's illustrations better?

2. Take your most recent essay and find points for which you need more illustrations. Rewrite the essay accordingly.

Process Analysis: Explaining How It Works

Process analysis is a special kind of narrative, one that shows *how* something happens. We often use process analysis to *instruct*. If we want to teach someone how to use a computer, how to dissect a frog, how to write an essay, how to play the flute, we focus on the process.

We use process analysis also to *explain*. Scientists use process analysis to explain how a strand of DNA replicates. Economists use it to explain how supply and demand work. If psychologists wish to explain the development of personality in the infant, they will probably call on this strategy. It is important in virtually every academic discipline and outside of school too, for instance, telling a stranger how to get there from here.

Writing Process Analysis.   Process analysis may seem easy because it is, like most writing, a written version of a natural way of thinking. We often wonder how things happen or work, and if we can figure them out, we think we should be able to explain them. As with most writing, however, a gap exists between understanding a process and effectively conveying it in writing. And sometimes in our headlong rush to get it down, we fall into that gap.

As with all strategies, the first step in writing process analysis is to articulate your purpose or ultimate goal and identify your reader. If you are telling someone how to put together a bicycle, say so right off. The purpose determines both the order of the presentation and the emphasis each part receives. And identifying the reader will determine how much background you need and how specific you should be.

The second step is to divide the process into major and minor elements. In explaining the assembly of a bicycle, for instance, you would divide the process into assembling the frame, fitting the gears, and attaching the wheels. You would then discuss the minor elements as subdivisions of the major elements. Without this division into major and minor, your reader would have a difficult time understanding how the process was developing. And of course the more important elements should receive more prominent placement and more thorough explanation. You will spend much more time on packing the bearings than on installing the seat.

Decide which details are essential to your analysis. You don't want your reader to get bogged down in excess, but you do want to provide an adequately concrete analysis. Because a process is a sequence of steps or operations, you need to show how one step is related to the previous and following steps. Clear transitions help to keep the order in focus. It is also important to stop every once in a while and recapitulate briefly where you are in the process.

The final step is to suit your language to your audience and purpose. You would not discuss circumference/velocity ratios on a bicycle with someone who merely wanted to get the thing on the road. But do not hesitate to use special terms when they are the best way to convey your meaning; just be sure to define them clearly the first time they come up.

When process analysis goes wrong, the writer usually has not articulated the overall purpose, emphasized major steps, or shown how the parts connect, as this passage demonstrates:

> To buy a house will probably take about three months. Look the place over to be sure it meets your family's needs. If you have young children, you may want a play yard; if the children are older, perhaps a family room. You will want to show the house to family members. Next draw up a contract. Then come the title search and the house inspection. This house inspection should include termite infestation, structural integrity including the roof and beams, and quality of water, sewer, gas, and electrical systems. Almost everyone needs a mortgage. And a lawyer. Once the bank makes the commitment, you can close and move in.

Too much important information is missing and too much irrelevant information is emphasized for this paragraph to work as a process analysis. What is the writer's overall purpose? What are the main elements of the process? How are the steps in the process related? What is a title search, and how can I inspect the house for termites? Why a lawyer? And why three months—will it take that long for all those family members to troop through?

In the revision, the writer addressed these problems.

> Buying a house is seldom either smooth or easy, but anticipating what lies ahead—from signing the contract through buying to taking actual possession—may lessen the difficulties. First, you and the seller draw up a contract establishing the purchase price and the date on which the sale will be completed. Before signing and making the down payment, you should get a lawyer's advice about the legality and adequacy of the contract. Your lawyer can also perform a title search, that is, make sure that no one other than the seller has a claim on the house. Your next step is to hire experts to inspect the house for problems that might not be visible to the naked eye, like insect infestation or inadequacies in the electrical system. If anything is amiss, you may have to renegotiate the contract. Unless you are a millionaire, your next step is to apply for a mortgage, the most trying aspect of the whole process. The lending institution will want to know everything about your financial condition, including your tax returns. No matter how quickly you comply, the bank can take up to three months to decide. When your mortgage is approved, you can "close"—that is, make the agreed-upon payment to the seller and get the house and the keys in return.

The writer starts with a clear statement of purpose, indicates the broad outlines of the process, and discusses the major steps in chronological order. She defines terms and relates each step to the whole. She does not dwell on unimportant details. And she left that extended family back home.

Tip for Process Analysis

Group elements into major components, include only essential details, and occasionally point out where you are in the process.

EXERCISES FOR PROCESS ANALYSIS

1. Choose something you do well—playing a musical instrument, operating a machine, waterskiing, playing tennis—and write an essay in which you explain to a novice the skills necessary for this activity.

2. Choose one of the following topics and, after you have done the necessary research, write a process analysis of it:

how an Individual Retirement Account works

the courting rituals of the praying mantis

how one becomes a minister

how continental drift works

how a "rite of passage" functions

Cause and Effect: Explaining Why It Happened

Cause and effect analysis answers the question *why?* Why did you ruin the peas? I left the burner on too long. Why is Joe in the hospital? He had a car accident. Why did he have the accident? He was driving too fast, the roads were wet, and there was a sharp curve. Breaking down a train of events into causes and effects can be a powerful analytical tool. It can help us to understand not only small, simple events, such as burning the peas, but also large, complicated ones. When illegal immigration increased, experts argued over the causes and the effects and the demographic changes. Futurologists attempt to analyze what life will be like when people shop and pay bills and even entertain via television and the Internet.

Cause and effect analysis helps answer two fundamental questions about an event. The first is, Why did something happen? To answer that, we look for causes. What factors, for example, brought about the increase in illegal immigration? Was it lack of border surveillance? economic problems in the home countries? need for low-cost labor in the United States? The second question is, What happened because of it? To answer this question, we look for effects. What changes resulted from the illegal immigration? Has the quality of life in the border states declined because of overcrowding? Is crime increasing?

Because this form of analysis is so important to understanding our world, instructors often assign cause and effect essays. A psychology instructor may assign a paper on the causes of neurosis. A history instructor may assign one on why the Weimar Republic collapsed. A physics instructor may ask for an analysis of the effects of ultraviolet radiation on the skin. Most research projects and most argumentative essays include cause and effect passages to support their theses because almost always we want to know why.

In constructing a cause and effect argument, you start with a situation and work your way forward to the effects or backward to the causes. This intellectual adventure may include both research and speculation. A good way to begin is to brainstorm. Once you have a group of possible causes and effects, you can organize them. This way you can distinguish essential elements from incidental ones, clarify relationships, establish a hierarchy of importance, and ensure that your analysis is comprehensive.

Beware of oversimplification. Sometimes we think we have discovered *the* cause or *the* effect when in fact we have only come upon one of several. Complex phenomena have more than one cause or result in more than one effect. Even a simple effect, such as "I ruined the peas," cannot be explained simply by saying "I left the burner on too long." Of course, if the focus was on only the agent—or the *precipitating cause*—of the ruin, "I left the burner on" would be enough. In most cases, however, we would need to explain why I left the burner on: the telephone rang and I answered it and it distracted me because it was long distance, there had been an accident, Joe was injured . . .

In constructing a cause and effect essay, you must also distinguish between *remote* causes and close or *proximate* causes. Proximate causes contribute directly and forcefully to the effect: "The telephone rang" is a proximate cause and must be included in any explanation of burning the peas. To say "The peas were ruined because Joe was in the hospital" would not make much sense: what has Joe's being in the hospital to do with burning the peas? You must include the proximate cause of each effect: "The telephone call informing me that Joe was in the hospital distracted me, and I left the burner on too long, ruining the peas."

Remember the old saying "For want of a nail the shoe was lost, for want of a shoe the horse was lost, for want of a horse the rider was lost"? Causes happen in chains, and every cause has causes, usually more than one. Yet we must limit our search for causes. In explaining the peas, we might trace the causal chain to Joe's reckless driving, and then we might conclude, "Joe's mother didn't discipline him when he was a child." Joe's recklessness may indeed go back to being overindulged by his mother, but if the question is why the peas were burnt, his upbringing will seem a rather remote cause.

How far back to go is a matter of judgment. Critical thinking is the key to making that judgment. If the purpose is to explain the ruined peas, we do not need to state that Joe's mother did not discipline him. If, however, the purpose is to explain Joe's recklessness, we probably do need to talk about his mother's overindulgence.

We cannot include everything that may have contributed—I may have burned those poor old peas in part because the range light was dim, I was tired, and I have always loathed peas. Maybe I simply wasn't paying attention. Even though these facts contributed marginally, we clutter up our argument by trying to be all-inclusive. We should mention only causes that contribute significantly.

Sometimes we mistake coincidence for cause. We think that because something happened either before or at the same time as the effect, then that something caused the effect. (This fallacy, *post hoc, ergo propter hoc,* is discussed in Chapter 2.) "Joe never had an accident until he got that convertible. Obviously, convertibles aren't safe." This is patently illogical. The convertible did not cause either the accident or Joe's recklessness. It certainly did not cause the peas to burn. You must limit your discussion to causes that have real agency.

When cause and effect analysis fails, it is usually because the writer has not sorted out the essential elements from the nonessential or has not thought critically about his or her purpose. Such is the case in the following paragraph from an essay on the changing status of women in American society:

> The main reason that women improved their position is that the media focused so much attention on the women's liberationists at the beginning of the 1970s. Sexual emancipation also contributed, as did fairer hiring policies in business and government. A liberal political climate and a succession of Democratic presidents and Congresses in the 1960s cleared the way for the climb, as did the invention of the Pill. Women in high places—like Golda Meir, Indira Gandhi, Margaret Thatcher, senators and representatives, business executives, university presidents—became role models. Rising divorce rates also contributed. Of course, many minorities of other sorts were seeking their rights at the same time. Many women were not interested any longer in the traditional roles of housekeeper, wife, and mother. Women had been a large part of the war effort during the Second World War, and afterward more women started going to school and earning higher degrees.

It is all in there somewhere—yet who could understand this mishmash? The writer does not evaluate his findings. Which causes does he think are important, and why? All receive the same treatment. Nor does he differentiate between causes and effects. In the first sentence, media attention is called "the main reason," but media attention was probably more an effect of the change than a cause. It was without doubt not the main cause.

The writer establishes no chain of causation and does not show how the elements he lists are related. Is there, for instance, a connection between women participating in the war effort and women not being interested in traditional roles? between the contraceptive pill and sexual emancipation? The writer does not say. By slapping the causes on the page without grouping them or analyzing the chain in which they figure, the writer fails to provide a clear explanation of how this enormous social change came about.

For the revision, he decided that the two most important causes were women's experience in industry and contraception. He clustered his other causes around these and showed how they were connected.

> The improvement of the position of women in American society resulted from many events occurring in the last half of the twentieth century. During World War II, the country and women themselves learned that women could perform well in an industrial society. This success led to a demand for greater opportunities in education and employment. With the advent of effective contraceptive devices, especially the Pill, women began to feel that they were not bound to motherhood. This sexual emancipation became a symbol for other kinds of

freedom: freedom to pursue education and a career, and freedom to reject the traditional roles of housekeeper, wife, and mother. When the civil rights movement focused national attention on the rights of minorities, people began to see more clearly that women, too, had been denied rights. The political climate of the 1960s and 1970s led to fairer hiring policies in business and government. And, as though they had been waiting in the wings, there emerged a group of prominent public women—Golda Meir, Indira Gandhi, Margaret Thatcher, senators and representatives, business executives, university presidents—ready to show younger women the path to the halls of power.

Improvement begins early with a very firm topic sentence that brings previously scattered points into order, sets forth a hierarchy of causes, and controls the rest of the paragraph. Notice that the writer maintains clarity by dealing first with the more remote causes—the experience during World War II—before turning to the recent chain of events. And he completes the analysis of causes before going on to the effect. By careful use of transitional devices—"This success," "this sexual emancipation," "women, too, had been denied rights"—he indicates relations between the various ideas. This is a good paragraph because it is a good piece of thinking.

Tips for Cause and Effect

- Distinguish between significant causes and incidental ones, and resist the temptation to look for an only cause or single effect.
- Differentiate between the remote causes and the proximate causes, and let purpose determine how far back to go in the causal chain.

EXERCISES FOR CAUSE AND EFFECT

1. Here is a list of possible causes for the increased suicide rate among Americans aged fifteen to twenty-four from 1960 to 1977:

   political and social decline in the United States since 1960

   trauma of the Vietnam War

   alienation from society

   decline of religion

   unemployment

   racial tensions

   sexual and love-related matters

   parents too permissive

   parents too strict

migration to big cities

lack of clear and consistent values

Which do you think are proximate causes? Which are remote? Which do you reject? Put them in ascending order of significance.

2. Find three causes of one of the following effects:

the rise in the number of American bison since 1911

the upward trend in sports salaries

the constant appeal, whatever the economic situation, of diamond rings

the near-disappearance of the California condor

the overthrow of the Somoza regime in Nicaragua

Determine the importance of each cause, and in a short essay argue for your interpretation.

Division and Classification: Putting It in Its Place

When we divide, we start with a single entity and break it into its parts. To say something useful about the practice of medicine, we might first divide it into its functional components: diagnosing, treating, curing, and preventing disease. We may need to subdivide: *diagnosing* includes use of sight to observe the patient, touch to determine abnormalities, hearing to examine functioning of lungs and heart, and microscopic, chemical, and bacteriological examination of blood and urine. And we could divide further.

Division is often the first step in the other strategies. When we write process analysis, cause and effect, or definition, we almost always begin by dividing the whole subject—the picture, the event, the world—into parts. Even when we compare and contrast, we divide items into their attributes. And division is at the heart of the strategy we call classification.

When we classify, we sort individual items into categories based on shared attributes or qualities. First we divide the whole into categories. For example, if we are classifying dogs, we might set up categories based on size: small, medium, large. Once we have set up the category, we can make general observations about all the items within it, describing the shared attributes or qualities. We can say small dogs eat less, bark more, learn quickly, or whatever we find to be true of small dogs.

By putting any phenomenon into a classification, we often understand it better. A new government takes over a country, and we immediately want to place it: is it democratic or authoritarian? Was it the result of an election or a coup? We hear music on the radio, and without even thinking we shuffle it into a known category: rock, rap, country and western, classical.

Often instructors ask students to apply what they have learned by classifying individual items into the proper categories. Why is this poem called lyric? Is this rock igneous, sedimentary, or metamorphic? What makes a rabbit a rodent like a rat? These categories are all ready-made. Occasionally, however, you must invent your own classifications.

Classifying people, places, ideas, and acts is natural, but doing it well requires care. First of all, articulate the point so that you will have it clearly in mind. Second, settle on the principle of classification, like color, size, personality type, religious beliefs, and so on. The principle should divide the whole subject in categories. In the Middle Ages, for example, human beings were classified as sanguine, choleric, melancholic, or phlegmatic, and to each of these categories specific characteristics of personality were attributed.

Effective classifications have several qualities. They are, first of all, based on a single consistent characteristic. For instance, the Middle Ages classification was based on the humors, that is, the fluids of the body. Second, this characteristic is significant to the subject and relevant to the point you are making. Someone who was choleric, for instance, was thought to have yellow bile. Third, all the individual items you wish to consider should fit into one and only one of the categories. A person of the Middle Ages would not be characterized as both sanguine and phlegmatic.

When a writer ignores these guidelines, a first draft may look like this:

> The men at this college fall into categories. First are the hackers, who are round-shouldered and bleary-eyed from all-night sessions with the computer. Next are the fraternity boys, many of whom come from well-off families. Next are the athletes, who are shaped like Vs and call women *babes*. Next are the men who wear jeans and sneakers. Next are the hard-working types, who will probably go to law or medical school. And finally there are the men who spend most of their waking hours drinking beer or smoking dope.

This classification is not a success. Its problems are twofold: lack of a clear purpose or unifying point and failure to hit upon a consistent characteristic for classifying the individuals. Some hackers may have money, some athletes may wear jeans and sneakers. Furthermore, the categories do not exhaust the subject: where are the foreign students, the married students, the commuters?

The writer went back for a second go. First, she came up with a point: from their clothing, an observer can tell a good deal about male students, how they view themselves, and what their aspirations are. Next, she *divided* the whole topic into categories that were mutually exclusive. Luckily, a natural division stood waiting: preppy, jock, brain. When she asked herself if the categories exhausted the whole group of male students, she decided she had to add one more: others.

With her point clear and categories established, she was ready to write.

We can learn a good deal about college men from their clothes. The preppy's uniform—a boat-neck sweater over a blue cotton button-down shirt above a pair of wrinkled chinos above Top Siders—says he comes from the best suburbs and the good prep schools. For him, college is a rehearsal for the good life. The giant V-shaped jock wears a shirt so tight you can see his tattoo and pants so form-fitting you can see the freckles on his knees. His shoes say Nike, Adidas, or Reebok. He, too, is rehearsing: for pro scouts, big bucks, adoring fans. Those who want to advertise that they are brains also do it through the choice, or lack of choice, of their clothes. Notice the row of pens or the calculator hooked to the pockets of white, probably polyester, shirts, wash-and-wear pants, hard-soled shoes and maybe mismatched socks. These men take their studies very seriously.

As extremes of fashion, these three stereotypes make clear what is also true for the others, whose nameless sneakers and nondescript jeans make them harder, but not impossible, to read. The way a college man dresses indicates an attitude—toward performance in school, toward social acceptance, toward the future beyond school.

In this draft each category is treated in the same manner: description, then interpretation of clothes. The last sentence makes the categorizing significant, for now we see that they have helped transcend the stereotypes and convey a meaningful point about students and clothing.

By using this method of analysis, you make an implicit argument: dividing and classifying experience in this fashion can yield worthwhile insights. Should we regard styles of dress as a useful principle by which to classify college males? The writer above says both yes and no in enlightening ways, thereby justifying the method. Be prepared to explain or defend your division and classification at some point in your argument.

Tip for Division and Classification

Choose a significant principle of classification and stick to it, making sure that your categories are mutually exclusive, all the categories are described in the same fashion, and all the individual items fit into your categories.

■■■■■■■ **EXERCISES FOR DIVISION AND CLASSIFICATION** ■■■■■■■

1. Create at least three categories under each of the topics below. Choose one of the topics and provide two examples for each category you created.

fast foods	religions
middle-class people	airliners
forms of government	sports played with a ball

2. Choose one of the following abstract terms:

    language   wars

    classification   beauty

    goodness   immorality

Find a way to divide it and classify its components.

Comparison and Contrast: Showing Likeness, Showing Difference

In deciding which college to attend, or whether to attend at all, most people consider as many possibilities as they can think of—cost, social life, sports, and, of course, academic challenge. They then compare and contrast them. Once they have evaluated differences and similarities, they can make a more informed, intelligent choice.

In college essays and examinations, students are often asked to compare or contrast two or more ideas or things: investment in equities, bonds, or real estate; reproduction in amoebas and paramecia; the treatment of Hell in Milton's *Paradise Lost* and Marlowe's *Doctor Faustus;* the views and actions of Presidents Reagan, Bush, and Clinton regarding Mexican immigration. Sometimes the point will be to show the depth of our knowledge, at other times to make a choice and back it up.

Although comparing and contrasting will support and clarify your ideas, it still must make a general point, not merely be a collection of specifics. If, for example, you compared the three major investment vehicles, you might say something like, "A comparison of equities, bonds, and real estate suggests that equities are preferable for the long-term investor." That kind of statement provides a structure for the comparison.

For the reader to understand and evaluate the comparison, you need to maintain a consistent pattern. There are two patterns that help to organize a comparison and contrast. Attribute by attribute is one pattern. In following this pattern, whatever attribute you identify in one of the items of comparison, you must identify in the other, and in the same order. If, for example, you discuss the profitability of equities, you then discuss the profitability of bonds and then of real estate. Then you go on to the next attribute, such as the safety of the investment.

Using the second pattern, you describe all the relevant attributes of one item before going on to describe the other items. If, for example, you discuss equities in terms of profitability, safety, and flexibility, you then discuss those same attributes, in the same order, for bonds and real estate.

Unfortunately, unless the writer remains alert, he or she may intermix the pattern and confuse the reader, as happened in the following paragraph:

> It is funny to think that both the *New York Times* and the *New York Daily News* are published in New York City. The *Times* doesn't have a long sports and entertainment section as does the *Daily News*.

> The *Daily News* will usually have a long section on deejays and soap operas. It runs huge headlines that scream out raw, sometimes profane headlines. The *Times* is written in a more objective, balanced way. It may have a long article on Mozambique's political situation. Many of its writers, like Thomas Friedman and Anthony Lewis, have written books about their subjects. The *Daily News* has huge photographs, often of partially clad young women. There's not much room for print. The *Times* devotes space to the legal profession to go along with its section on science. The *Daily News* has a lot about celebrities, though. The two papers are obviously imagining different audiences.

Though vigorously written, this comparison and contrast is rather a mess. First, the writer has not identified his thesis well enough. He presents many little facts without any context. The item-by-item pattern at the beginning gives way to attribute by attribute. Nor has he made clear the terms of comparison or grouped the facts so that they more directly make the comparisons. He also has violated the rule of parallelism: there is nothing to balance the mention of the foreign correspondents of the *Times*. The reader's head spins.

With a little rethinking, the writer made it work. He decided to establish the overall point, to stick to the attribute-by-attribute pattern, to group the facts, and to omit any extraneous references.

> The *New York Times* and the *Daily News* are like night and day in the news business. Even a quick glance indicates a major difference. The *Times* is famous for running long articles accompanied by very few pictures, while the *Daily News* runs huge photographs—often of a partially clad young woman—with only a little explanation. A closer look suggests an even more important difference: what is covered. The *Times* concentrates on presenting national and world affairs, spending whole columns, for instance, on the political situation in Mozambique; sports and entertainment have their own sections, but they are usually much shorter than the news sections. The *Daily News,* by contrast, obviously has other priorities: the entertainment and sports sections take up more than half the newsprint. The rest of the paper focuses on such things as deejays, soap operas, and celebrities. Even the tone in which all this is presented is different. The *Times* is written in an objective, balanced way, whereas the *Daily News* screams out raw, sometimes profane headlines and concentrates on the sensational aspects of the news. The two papers are obviously imagining different audiences. The *Times* assumes its readers want to know what is happening in the world and why; the *Daily News* assumes its readers have short attention spans and little interest in the outside world.

This revision is effective because it is consistent, clear, and parallel. The items are compared under three clearly defined attributes: balance between print and pictures, coverage, and tone. Best of all, the writer concludes with an observation that ties the comparison and contrast together.

> **Tip for Comparison and Contrast**
>
> Follow a consistent pattern throughout, either attribute by attribute or item by item, providing the same kind of information in the same order.

EXERCISES FOR COMPARISON AND CONTRAST

1. Write a brief consumer report comparing and contrasting three brands of a product you would like to buy, perhaps a car, a computer, a stereo, or even blue jeans, pizza, detergent, or shampoo. Justify buying one brand rather than the others.

2. Select one of the pairs below and write a brief essay comparing and contrasting them. Start by brainstorming similarities and differences, advantages and disadvantages. After organizing your brainstorming material, free-write to determine a thesis, then write an essay defending your thesis.

   allowing a friend to indulge in self-destructive behavior / stepping in and attempting to correct the friend's behavior

   selecting a career based on moral and ethical ideals / selecting a career based on financial considerations

   listening to music primarily for its entertainment value / listening to music primarily to understand it as artistic expression

Definition: Establishing What a Word Means

Whether you write about art or science, world affairs or personal affairs, you will probably need to define some term. What is it? What is it not? What are its uses? What are its characteristics? Can I recognize it on the street if I see it? Can I recognize it in this essay?

You need to define terms because arguments often rest on definitions. Do apes have language? That depends on what you mean by *language*. Is the death penalty cruel and unusual punishment? That depends on what you mean by *cruel* and *unusual*. If your readers accept your definitions, fine: now they will be able to follow your argument. If they do not accept your definitions, that is also fine: at least now they know where they differ with you.

Defining *Definition*.   Few things are more challenging than establishing meaning. Simple dictionary definitions are not always adequate for complex terms or terms used in special ways. The dictionary definition of *modernism,* for instance, is "modern practices, trends, and ideas, or showing sympathy with any of these." With that definition, we would not get a very deep understanding of the great cultural movement called modernism. An adequate definition would probably require paragraphs.

Even greater difficulty comes with words that have several meanings or meanings that are confusing or controversial. The writer must define these terms precisely. Suppose, for instance, that a writer says, "Nude sunbathing is normal." *Normal* has many meanings. it could mean "conforming, adhering to, or constituting a usual or typical pattern, level, or type" or "functioning or occurring in a natural way" or "average in intelligence, ability, and emotional traits or personality." Other definitions from mathematics and chemistry are also possible. We see a world of difference between "average," "natural," and "conforming to the usual." Which does this writer mean? Einstein was natural, and he conformed to a type, albeit the type called "genius," but he was far from average. Was he "normal" or not?

Terms such as *normal, average,* and *natural* are tough enough, but some words are dynamite and a lighted match. Words such as *fascism, patriot,* and *Christian* can arouse great passions. To use them well, you must define them with care. With loaded words, it is sometimes helpful simply to stipulate a definition: "By Christian, I mean any person who has been baptized into a community of Christian believers." You cannot now say, "Anyone who accepts abortion is not a real Christian" because you did not exclude believing in choice in your definition. When you shift your meaning or leave it vague, your reader won't be able to follow your argument. You have to stay within your stipulation.

Writing Definition.   Definition often involves the other strategies. To get at a term's essential meaning, you may need to compare and contrast it with similar words. Except for the most obvious definitions, you will almost certainly need to provide illustrations. Remember that in definition, as in all strategies, you are trying to bring your reader to the common ground, to establish a meaning that the reader will accept. Thus, even with abstract terms you need to be as specific and concrete as possible.

To deal with the different attitudes toward war of the World War II and Vietnam generations, a student defined *patriotism.*

> In evaluating the two generations, we should think about whether or not they were patriots. *Patriotism* is love of country and a willingness to sacrifice for it. During the Vietnam War, many young Americans refused to take up arms to fight for their country, some going so far as moving to another country, others serving time in jail. The generation of 1941 was more patriotic and willing to fight for the country.

Did you feel disappointed, as though you had been promised steak and been given white bread? What are "love of country" and "willingness to sacrifice"? This simple, and abstract, definition is inadequate for such a highly charged issue.

Once he had achieved some critical distance, the writer recognized that what he had written was platitudinous. He spent a few hours doing research and discovered that the meaning of *patriotism* has varied from place to place and time to time. During the American Revolution, the idea of *patriot* was purely affirmative. Writing about the Boston Tea Party, John Adams said, "There is a dignity, a majesty, a sublimity, in this last effort of the patriots that I greatly admire." Across the water, however, the word had a different meaning. In eighteenth-century England, it meant "a factious disturber of the government," and Samuel Johnson wrote, "Patriotism is the last refuge of a scoundrel." Were Johnson and Adams talking about the same thing? What *were* they talking about?

The writer looked carefully at the attitudes of World War II and Vietnam War veterans. He discovered that veterans of World War II had accused the anti-Vietnam demonstrators of not being "patriotic" because they did not support all the decisions of the president and the Congress. But many of the men who refused to fight in Vietnam claimed that a true patriot would not support a cause that destroys the values the country cherishes. They felt that they were the "true" patriots.

After absorbing all these ideas, the student tried again to define the word *patriotism:*

> In 1941, for most people patriotism meant an immediate response to the war effort; such a definition was understandable and reasonable in light of the clear threat posed to the nation by the belligerent forces of Japan and Germany. In 1965, the threat in Vietnam was neither as clear nor as present. Patriotism for many meant upholding certain values like questioning authority and refusing to serve in what they considered an unjust war. For our time, perhaps we should put these two experiences together and define the word anew. In a society like ours, patriotism cannot be blind, or we chance losing the very values that have established our country. At the same time, we cannot expect to enjoy the privilege of those values without being willing to sacrifice to maintain them. Patriots, then, will be critical of their country for the country's own good and yet be ready to sacrifice for it when reason, combined with the force of events, tells them they must.

This paragraph shows that the writer went far beyond the dictionary to gain his understanding of the concept. When it came to writing, he was explicit about the differing definitions, stating exactly how the experience of the two generations differed. Notice the careful comparison and contrast. The writer divided the concept into its two parts: the willingness to sacrifice and the necessity to uphold values. Thus he made a fairly complex definition clear to the reader.

Tips for Definition

- Use the dictionary, but go beyond it to examine crucial, debatable, or controversial terms.
- Use the other strategies to help you define.

EXERCISES FOR DEFINITION

1. Research and define one of the following words or phrases: *anima, balance of power, karma, law of supply and demand, Occam's razor, Planck's constant, surrealism, transubstantiation*. In a short essay, describe the process you went through in formulating your definition.

2. Define from your own experience one of the following words: *apathy, discipline, egotism, fantasy, insecurity, negotiation, nostalgia, power, success, wealth*. Try one of the invention methods to help you sharpen your ideas. Narrate an experience of yours that illustrates your definition. If you think your definition may be unusual, account for the difference.

COHERENCE: HANGING IDEAS TOGETHER

A good paragraph hangs together. One thought logically and naturally follows from the preceding thought and gives rise to the next. The sentences are locked one to the other like the cars of a train. Ideas receive the appropriate emphasis. There is a sense of closure, of coming to a natural stop. Few aspects of writing are as important as how you lock your ideas together.

In this paragraph from "Letter from Birmingham Jail," Martin Luther King, Jr., maintains coherence in a passage of rich detail, subtle thought, and moving argument:

> In your statement you assert that our actions, even though peaceful, must be condemned because they precipitate violence. But is this a logical assertion? Isn't this like condemning a robbed man because his possession of money precipitated the evil act of robbery? Isn't this like condemning Socrates because his unswerving commitment to truth and his philosophical inquiries precipitated the act by the misguided populace in which they made him drink hemlock? Isn't this like condemning Jesus because his unique God-consciousness and never-ceasing devotion to God's will precipitated the evil act of crucifixion? We must come to see that, as the federal courts have consistently affirmed, it is wrong to urge an individual to cease his efforts to gain his basic constitutional rights because the quest may precipitate violence. Society must protect the robbed and punish the robber.

This statement of conscience gains power with each sentence. Each idea builds upon the one before it and increases the intensity of the argument. All the questions point to that completely persuasive reference to the Crucifixion in the fifth sentence. At the end King wraps up his thought by referring back to the robbed and the robber. Every sentence illuminates the main idea. Important ideas are accentuated—the reference to Jesus is placed for maximum impact. In addition, each sentence seems to rise from the one before it and to reach out for the one after it. The ideas grow as if organic, and with each sentence the impact builds.

When a paragraph is coherent, thoughts and ideas develop continuously, and the relationships are clear. The current of thought flows. There are no jerks, no backing and filling, no long leaps from the period of one sentence to the capital letter of the next.

Paragraphs can fall apart for many reasons. Thoughts may appear out of logical order. One subject may give way to another, only to be picked up later. Connections between ideas may be fuzzy. Unimportant ideas may be stressed. We discuss ways to avoid all these disorienting problems in the pages that follow.

Grouping Related Ideas

Sometimes when we write, we stop one thought, go to the next, realize we have more to say on the first, and return to it. It is natural to write this way on a first draft, because ideas take a while to develop. But we must group all related ideas together by the final draft. If we don't, the reader's mind will be shifting back and forth, forth and back. It can be like watching a Ping-Pong match.

In an essay arguing that first-year college students should be required to live on campus, a student wrote this paragraph:

> Living in a dormitory can facilitate the difficult transition from dependence on parents to independence. For students who live near their parents, the change is not so dramatic. But for most students college is the first experience of living far from their parents. Without recognizing why, they may feel lonely and deserted. Students living near home can visit or call when they feel the need. Those who live far away may fear rejection. Discussing the problem with others similarly situated can ease the transition. For some students, the transition is not so difficult. There are those who have gone off to boarding schools and so have probably made something of an adjustment. Students who have never lived away before and who don't live near their parents now will find understanding and sympathy from others in the same situation. Other freshmen may not offer quite the acceptance of parents, but living with them beats living in a lonely apartment in town.

By the end of this paragraph, the reader's mental eyeballs are weary.

In the revision the student grouped similar ideas (the exceptions and the typical), finished each thought before going to the next, and thus did not need to return. Notice, too, that the grouping removes the awkward phrasing "Students who have never lived away before and who don't live near their parents now" and substitutes a pronoun. Reading this paragraph is no longer like watching the little white ball bouncing back and forth.

> Living in a dormitory can facilitate the transition from dependence on parents to independence. The transition is easier for some than for others. Students who go to college near their parents won't find the change so difficult. They can visit or call when they feel the need. And students who have attended boarding schools have probably made some adjustment already. But for most students college is the first experience of living away from their parents. Without recognizing why, they may feel lonely and deserted. In a dormitory, they can find sympathy from others in the same situation. Other freshmen may not offer quite the acceptance of parents, but living with them beats living in a lonely apartment in town.

Accentuating the Important

Good writers distinguish between important ideas and lesser ones. They decide who are the stars of the show, bring them front and center, and direct the spotlight accordingly. They give them the best lines and the most lines. The minor players stay back in the shadows. These decisions usually boil down to choices about the extent of the discussion and placement of the major points.

Extending the Discussion.   Some writers seem to know intuitively which points to play up and which to play down. But for most of us, this is a tricky business. We worry that if we don't hammer a point home the reader may miss it altogether. But at the same time we worry about overemphasizing a minor point and knocking our argument out of shape.

We don't need to emphasize what everybody knows and agrees to. We need not slave to prove that Microsoft is innovative. We can just say, "Always innovative, Microsoft . . ." and everyone will go on reading. If we start citing examples ("Microsoft, which developed DOS, Word, Windows, and . . ."), readers will see that we are wasting their time. We have to be wary of saying too much.

We must be wary, however, of saying too little. Controversial ideas dropped in a paragraph without elucidation can distort the balance of an argument. And the more controversial the point, the more we need to say. If we want to argue that Microsoft really has not been innovative but has merely built on the ideas of other companies, we will need much more than a paragraph, maybe more than an essay (if we seriously try to argue that point at all).

Sometimes writers lose sight of important points because they become enamored of minor points and spend too much time on them. In the following paragraph, the writer argues that our sense of time depends on how involved we are in what we are doing. The notion of "psychological time" is interesting, but the writer loses sight of the important points and offers too much evidence for tangential ideas.

> Our sense of how fast time passes indicates our involvement in what we are doing. In any activity—like studying at the library—we experience periods of absorption punctuated by periods of disengagement. Then we usually glance around, or perhaps actually get up for a drink of water, take a walk, or go to the bathroom. These breaks may hark back to the survival instinct, readily witnessed in films of animals in the wild pausing in the midst of feeding or drinking to take a look around and sniff the air. Even while dashing across the plains, the whole herd may stop as though to take its bearings. When we look around, we check the time. We compare the reading with what time we expect it to be. Intense involvement can distort our expectation. We can be so absorbed in an activity that we are not aware of time passing, and we expect that a normal interval has passed when it has been longer. We get the idea that time passed swiftly. But who ever heard of a clock going faster at one time and then slower at another?

Unity is not the problem here. Every sentence is about interrupted time. Nor is development the problem. The problem is emphasis. The paragraph bulges out of shape. The writer describes the lessons of the wildlife documentaries at such length that a reader may begin to think the subject is the sense of time of animals. He jams discussion of the real subject—the disparity between clock time and perceived time—into a few short sentences. At the end, he seems to be on a mad dash out of the paragraph.

The revision retains the virtues of the original but improves on its wandering ways:

> Our sense of how fast time passes indicates our involvement in what we are doing. In any activity—like studying at the library—we experience periods of absorption punctuated by periods of disengagement, in which our minds pull back from the immediate situation. We glance around at our surroundings, and we usually manage to check the time. When we do, we compare the reading with what we expect it to be, based on our normal span of involvement. For some this may be twenty minutes, for others forty; but however long, it tends to remain fairly constant. Intense involvement, however, can extend this time markedly: when we are intensely absorbed we have little sense of time passing. When we check the clock, we discover that it is much later than we expected. Thus, we get the idea, patently illogical, that time itself has passed swiftly.

In revising, the writer sorted out his main idea (that our perception of time depends on how involved we are) and added to the two major supports (the normal expectation of time passing and the effect of absorption). He de-emphasized everything else. Removing his reference to the animals was painful: this was the writer's favorite material. Nevertheless, out it went, and with it the improper emphasis.

Placing the Accent.   Placement also creates emphasis. Your major points—the ones you want the reader to carry out of the paragraph—should come at the beginning and the end. In writing, as in life, those are the places to make an emphatic statement.

Sometimes you can present your material so that the paragraph rises to a peak. If, for instance, you have three points, you can arrange them so that the paragraph moves from interesting point to more interesting point to most interesting point. Speech writers, novelists, moviemakers, and musical composers are well aware of the advantages of this order. They build toward a climax of increasing interest and tension.

Because the beginning and ending are the most important positions in a paragraph, writers work hard to make them right. With a strong beginning, they can entice the reader to read on. The interest aroused provides the energy for reading the rest. If, however, the opening sentence fizzles, the reader may not wish to struggle on to the end. The art of the opener—the grabber, the hook—is one to be mastered.

The following paragraph opens with a dull, unemphatic, and imprecise sentence:

> <u>Many of us spend hours every week watching television.</u> We are shown products guaranteed to automate and begadget the most mundane household tasks. If we tried all the beers we are invited to taste, we would float down the avenue—and get run over by all those fast cars our neighbors have been seduced into buying. To close the evening, Cutprice Music presents its Infinite Original Hits: Do you remember this? and that? It is not the commercials that interrupt the programs, but the programs that interrupt the commercials, ever more briefly.

The paragraph itself is not bad, for it moves toward a climax. But who would get to it after that dull start? And what is the paragraph going to be about? What major idea does the writer want us to carry forward? All this writer needed was a snappier and more informative opening:

> The barrage of commercials never ends.

The word *barrage* alerts us; the word *commercials* tells us exactly where we are going. An emphatic opening sentence acts like a magnet, drawing the other sentences toward it.

The other traditional place for emphasis is the end of a paragraph. In some ways this position is even more important. Leave 'em laughing, says the comedian. Just as the first sentence can provide momentum into the paragraph, the last sentence can provide momentum into the *next* paragraph. If the last sentence is a bore, the reader may be reluctant to push on.

The following paragraph comes from an essay on "wild" children, that is, those not raised in human communities.

> The wild children that horrified the anthropologists of the early 1900s were made into heroes by fiction writers. For anthropologists, the wild children were animalistic and repulsive and did not demonstrate human values and characteristics. The scientists described, for example, children eating live chickens and garbage. But fiction writers idealized wild children. Both Tarzan of the Apes and Mowgli were depicted as noble, representing the very best of the human species. The anthropologists didn't find that at all.

This paragraph has a point, but it is not pointed. It fizzles. No thought, no energy, concentrates at the end to carry the reader onward. In revising this interesting material, the student replaced the last uninspired sentence with an emphatic one:

> But the anthropologists looking for a noble savage looked in vain.

Just as the "barrage" sentence exerted an upward surge, this new ending exerts a strong forward pull. It properly focuses the reader's attention on the significance of the difference between the fiction writers and the anthropologists. Now the reader wants to know what resulted from this difference.

Thoughts Descending a Staircase

Movement between ideas should be gradual enough for the reader to stop from one idea to the next without feeling jolted. But some paragraphs—usually underdeveloped, "skinny" paragraphs—suffer from a dangerously steep staircase. The steps may all be there, but they are too far apart. Readers may feel as though they are dropping into space. Such is the case in reading this paragraph, in which a student discusses Carl Sagan's essay "The Abstractions of Beasts":

> Research indicates that certain kinds of monkeys have considerable language skills. Carl Sagan deals primarily with three chimpanzees—Lucy, Lana, and Washoe—who were taught Ameslan (American Sign Language) and developed vocabularies ranging from 100 to 200 words and eventually were capable of constructing phrases. James Dewson and colleagues found that chimpanzees have a language center in the neocortex of the left hemisphere of the brain, just as human beings do. Apes are thought to transmit extragenetic or cultural information. Differences in group behavior have been documented among chimpanzees and other related species.

Although all the sentences relate to the topic, something seems to be missing. How does the reader get from the three chimps to James Dewson? What is the connection between cultural information and differences in group behavior? The last four sentences are piled one on top of the other without relation to the first or to each other—like pancakes stacked on a plate. And one thing a paragraph should not be is a stack of sentences.

Recognizing the gaps between the ideas and the apparent discontinuity of his thoughts, the writer went back to work. He provided elaboration of some ideas and even additional sentences. These changes help us to descend through the paragraph.

> Research indicates that certain kinds of monkeys have considerable language skills. Carl Sagan deals primarily with three chimpanzees—Lucy, Lana, and Washoe—who showed considerable linguistic talent. When they were taught Ameslan (American Sign Language), they were able to develop vocabularies that ranged from 100 to 200 words and eventually to form phrases. Medical research provides further support for the idea that chimpanzees are capable of linguistic tasks. James Dewson and colleagues found, for example, that monkeys have a language center in the neocortex of the left hemisphere of the brain, just as human beings do. This center may explain why their language capacity is far beyond that of other lower mammals. In addition, investigators think apes transmit extragenetic, or cultural, information that differs from tribe to tribe depending on the environment and what is needed to survive. Differences in group behavior among chimpanzees and related species have been documented. Such differences could come about, some investigators claim, only through language skills.

In the revision the writer does more than merely list pieces of evidence about the monkeys and the neocortex. Recognizing that the steps between the main idea and some of the concrete evidence are too steep, he builds intermediate steps. The addition to the second sentence allows us to move gracefully from the main idea to the Sagan research. The fourth sentence makes a general statement about research on the issues and eases us from the Sagan research to the evidence on the neocortex. These two steps help us descend through the paragraph. The last sentence is not so much a new step as an elevator: it carries all the freight back up to the topic sentence. Without it, and without those intermediate steps, all that evidence would lie inert in the basement of the paragraph.

We can think of the paragraph as a staircase the reader can smoothly descend, one foot safely on a step before the other foot moves. If the steps are too steep, the reader must jump and may fall. We must build on the intermediate steps—those statements somewhat less general than the topic sentence, somewhat more general than the evidence, that make for continuity of thought.

Something Old, Something New

Even when our ideas are properly grouped and the staircase well constructed, we still must provide clear transitions between sentences. As the main idea descends the staircase, each sentence almost always refers to something in the previous sentence. This reference backward indicates the connection between one thought and another. It helps the reader feel secure and oriented.

To see how something old, something new works, look at the paragraph by Martin Luther King, Jr., on page 212. The second sentence asks a question about the first. The third repeats the question, in a more concrete form. The fourth and fifth continue the questioning in the same form. Each sentence seems to reach back for an idea from the previous sentence and then to add another step. The steps are continuous, the connections firm.

Here is a paragraph of seemingly unconnected ideas:

> Housing prisoners one to a room is a controversial proposition. Some citizens say our society is already too permissive with criminals. Army recruits live in barracks. Some people see real advantages. Hardened criminals would have less opportunity to corrupt first offenders. Violence would decrease. Prisoners would have a chance to reflect on their past actions. Everybody agrees that taxpaying citizens are in no mood to underwrite experimentation in any area of government service. It might have ended up saving money, not to mention lives.

All the ideas are there, but we didn't have any pleasure reading them. Every sentence contains something new, but the paragraph lacks flow. The steps lack apparent connection. The writer might as well have made a list headed by "Pro" and "Con."

A writer can provide something old, something new in three ways:

1. by repeating words or phrases
2. by carefully using pronouns and demonstrative adjectives
3. by repeating a grammatical construction

In revising, this writer used all three. Note the underlined words that refer backward and move forward.

> Housing prisoners one to a room is a controversial proposition. Some citizens oppose such housing as unwarranted luxury. They say our society is already too permissive with criminals. They say that army recruits live in barracks. Other citizens claim that there are real and practical advantages to the plan. They say it would offer less opportunity for prison violence. It would offer less opportunity for hardened criminals to corrupt first offenders. At the same time it would offer more opportunity for prisoners to reflect on their past actions. These citizens also recognize that, despite the advantages, taxpayers are in no mood to underwrite experimentation in any area of government

service. But they contend that it might end up saving money, not to mention lives.

Repetitions and Synonyms. When a writer repeats a word or uses its synonym from sentence to sentence, the reader obviously recognizes that the same subject is being discussed. That recognition ties the two sentences together. The revised paragraph on housing prisoners contains many examples of this kind of reinforcement. The synonym *criminal* takes the place of, and makes more emphatic, the word *prisoner.* Notice how *they say* is repeated, as are *opportunity, advantages,* and *citizens.* These words are like Velcro, binding the sentences together.

Sometimes repeating a word throughout a paragraph tightens the connections:

> Experience, intelligence, and personality would not be enough to elect a person president. There must be money. Money influences delegates. Money buys airtime. Money pays for television advertisements. Money pays hairstylists and speech coaches. Money pays for the campaign directors, whose main job is to find more money.

Pronouns and Demonstrative Adjectives. The revised passage on housing prisoners uses both pronouns (*they, it*) and demonstrative adjectives (*such, that*) to connect ideas. When readers see a pronoun standing for a noun, they expect that the writer will say more on the same subject and that the ideas will accumulate, as in this example:

> Your basic president is a man who combines the common and the uncommon. He is white, and he stands somewhere around six feet tall. He is always religious, or at least a member of a religious organization. He is almost always a millionaire.

What holds true for pronouns also applies to demonstrative adjectives such as *this, that, these, those,* and *such.* The paragraph on presidents goes on to say:

> These qualities do not prevent his being an astute politician with many supporters. Those supporters get him to the White House, and, if he is at all competent and lucky, keep him there.

Read these sentences substituting *the* for *these* and *those.* Although with those changes you can figure the passage out, your reaction time is just a little slower. Your eye climbs back through the sentences, seeking connections that the demonstrative adjectives make plain.

Parallel Construction. Later we will discuss parallel construction in regard to diction (see Chapter 11, Working with Words), but here we want to point out that repeating a grammatical form links sentences and helps to make a more coherent paragraph. Responding to the repeated pattern and the repeated rhythm, the reader can make connections more easily.

This passage from John F. Kennedy's inaugural address is an excellent example of the power of parallel construction:

> To those old allies whose cultural and spiritual origins we share, we pledge the loyalty of faithful friends. United, there is little we cannot do in a host of cooperative ventures. Divided, there is little we can do, for we dare not meet a powerful challenge at odds, and split asunder.
> To those new states whom we welcome to the ranks of the free . . .

And on he went, holding firmly both his paragraphs and his audience.

Transitional Words

No matter how hard we try, we sometimes cannot write a paragraph that holds together without outside help. Frequently we need to insert transitional words, such as *furthermore, however,* and *for instance.* These linchpins help to keep ideas logically connected. They explain to the reader whether the previous idea is being modified, qualified, amplified, or contradicted.

Before we discuss transitional words in depth, we want to make two important points. First, you will not need to insert such a word in absolutely every sentence. Whole paragraphs, in fact, can flow along without a single *however, this,* or *furthermore,* just on the strength of a strong topic sentence and implicit relationships among ideas. In fact, when overused, explicit transitions make writing wooden and mechanical. But carefully and sparingly employed, they make writing tight, emphatic, and clear. Second, transitional words carry a meaning and function of their own. They help determine the meaning of a sentence. Thus, you must be sure to choose a word that does exactly what you intend. Don't, for instance, use *therefore* when you mean *furthermore.*

Here are eight relations that transitional words can signal, with examples of each:

Number.   *First, second, third, finally.* If you have a series of complex ideas, you can give your reader a sense of order by treating the ideas as a list and numbering them. To show that you are closing the list—or to show that you are ending a narrative—you can use the word *finally.*

> In becoming a successful owner of securities, follow these four basic steps. First, learn to read Standard & Poor's monthly stock guide, which shows price/earnings ratio, long- and short-term debt, and so on, of many companies. Second . . . Third . . . Finally, be prepared to tolerate some wrong judgments.

Addition.   *And, furthermore, moreover, in addition, besides.* When you attach another idea to a point already made, use one of these words or phrases.

> And everything will be crystal clear. Moreover, your writing will be smoother.

Comparison.   *Similarly, likewise, in the same way.* One of these words or phrases will tell the reader to notice that two ideas are alike.

> Western explorers have always misunderstood the foreign cultures they "discover." In the same way, most American and European listeners fail to comprehend Indian music and think of it as a mixture of nasal caterwauling and groaning strings.

Contrast.   *Even so, still, nonetheless, but, yet, notwithstanding, nevertheless, however, on the other hand.* To signal the reader that a new idea differs from the previous idea, insert one of these words or phrases.

> Babe Ruth was overweight, bandy-legged, often drunk, and always slow. He became, nevertheless, one of baseball's greatest hitters.

Example.   *For instance, for example, to illustrate, in particular.* When you use an example to support a statement, you can flag the example.

> Earning a college degree in the sciences is only one of many ways to a promising future. You could inherit your father's oil well, for instance, or score 100 points a game for your high-school basketball team.

Concession.   *Of course, to be sure, granted, given that, no doubt.* Concessions are an important part of any argument. They demonstrate that you are aware of other ways of looking at questions.

> More wars have been fought in the name of money than in the name of religion. Granted, millions have suffered and died for their religious beliefs. But behind every religious purge we can usually find an economic motive.

Summary.   *Briefly, in short, in conclusion, in sum, to sum up.* These signals warn your reader that you have ended your argument and want to make it a bit plainer by summing it up.

> Templeton's writing style is full of dense sonorities, a polished perfection that serves to avoid the untidy, irrational moment. In short, it stinks.

Consequence or Conclusion.   *Thus, and so, as a result, consequently, therefore, hence, accordingly.* These words and phrases provide a sense of finality. We want to caution you, however, against using such words inaccurately. Be sure you don't claim a conclusion you haven't earned. For example, we could not in all conscience now write

> <u>Thus</u> have we exhausted the subject of transitions, and you <u>therefore</u> <u>know</u> all you ever need to know.

With this brief survey, we have not earned either the *thus* or the *therefore*.

As their name indicates, transitions assist the flow of your thought from one sentence or phrase or clause to the next. They are the bridges over which your thought moves. Rather than asking your reader to jump the gap between thoughts, provide a bridge.

Coherent writing conveys the reader smoothly and considerately from thought to thought. Much of your writing will do this naturally, but when rereading and revising your writing, watch for the gaps or missed connections that could cause your reader to stumble. Working for coherence will help your reader understand and will also help you chart the progress of your thought.

Tips for Coherence

- Remember that few considerations are as important as how you get from one idea to the next.
- Finish one idea before you take up another so that you won't have to double back.
- Check to be sure you have adequately emphasized important points and haven't over-emphasized unimportant ones.
- Sentences you want to emphasize should come at the beginning or the end of the paragraph.
- Be sure your reader doesn't have to jump too far between steps in the paragraph.
- Check your sentences for something old, something new.
- Be both sparing and accurate with transitional words; make sure you earn your *therefores* and *moreovers*.

EXERCISES FOR COHERENCE

1. Underline everything in this passage that aids coherence, including all transitional words.

   > Sport may be the toy department of life, but one of its abiding compensations is that, at least on the field, it is the real thing. Much has been done in recent years in the attempt to ruin sport—the ruthlessness of owners, the greed of players, the general exploitation of fans. But even all this cannot destroy it. On the court, down on the field, sport is fraud-free and fakeproof. With a full count, two men on, his team

down by one run in the last of the eighth, a batter (as well as a pitcher) is beyond the aid of public relations. At match point at Forest Hills a player's press clippings are of no help. Last year's earnings will not sink a twelve-foot putt on the eighteenth at Augusta. Alan Page, galloping up along the quarterback's blind side, figures to be neglectful of that quarterback's image as a swinger. In all these situations, and hundreds of others, a man either comes through or he doesn't. He is alone out there, naked but for his ability, which counts for everything. Something there is that is elemental about this, and something greatly satisfying. (Joseph Epstein, "Obsessed with Sport")

2. Go through a recent essay of yours and locate a passage near the middle. If you can, find a passage you recall writing with special ease. Now read that passage closely. How did you get from sentence to sentence? What is it about your sentences that made transitions possible? Look carefully for passages *without* either repeated words or transitional words.

3. Revise the following pairs of sentences so that something old and something new are in the second sentence of each pair.
    a. In the nineteenth century, being well padded with flesh was a sign of beauty. My friends like the slender look.
    b. Football games are not called on account of weather. Rain fell and they postponed the third game of the World Series.
    c. Pug dogs are fawn colored. Siamese cats are fawn colored.
    d. Genes are the elements that determine human inheritance. Some people believe we may eventually abuse our ability to change things that were not defects in the first place.

4. Revise the following passages to improve coherence.
    a. One writer suggests that solar power is the answer to our energy needs. Nuclear power should be our source of energy is what the other writer argues. Solar power is too expensive for many homes. No commercially viable power source has been devised on a scale large enough for private use. Nuclear power is used on a national scale.
    b. Antivivisectionists are opposed to any scientific experimentation on animals. The desire for new and safe cosmetics does not justify the pain and death necessary to test various products. Scientists want to learn the effects of chemicals and drugs on human beings.

5. The following paragraph has improper emphasis.

    Pulling a person out of quicksand is a delicate process. You must lie on the nearest solid piece of ground. The ground can be wet or even a little sandy, but you must test it to make sure it will hold when you start pulling. Wind your rope around one shoulder. Two-thousand-pound nylon test is the best, though conventional silk-wound or hempen rope will do. Some rescuers have used their own belts, but these must be of leather rather than the weaker synthetic materials. The whole question of exactly what material to use is sorely debated. Then throw the rope and pull the victim out.

    Revise this paragraph to correct its problem, deleting unnecessary elaboration, adding what is missing, or rearranging the text. Be prepared to answer the question What did you change and why?

9

From Paragraph to Essay:
The Strategies at Work

The contemporary essay is a house with many
rooms.
— DONALD HALL
AMERICAN WRITER (B. 1928)

In the previous chapter, we discussed single and discrete strategies for developing a paragraph and how to make a paragraph unified and coherent. But most writing tasks, whether in college or in later life, are too large and complex to be contained in a single paragraph or explored with a single strategy. Whether writing an essay, a report, or a proposal, you will use many skills and many strategies. In this section, we discuss ways of choosing the right strategies as well as ways of binding strong, tight paragraphs into a strong, tight essay. We conclude with advice on beginning, ending, and titling your essay.

CHOOSING STRATEGIES:
QUESTIONING YOUR MAIN POINT

Good tennis players don't rely on just one shot. Instead, they use the shot appropriate to the specific situation—crosscourt, drop shot, volley, lob—and combine them in a game for the greatest effect. The same is true of good writers. They develop skill in using all the strategies and then select the right one for the particular idea they want to get across.

Your choice of strategy will often emerge from the point you are making. If, for instance, the overall subject of your essay is the bassoon and you want to discuss the difficulty of playing it, you would naturally think of writing a process analysis. Almost as automatically, you might decide to compare and contrast playing the bassoon with playing another instrument, such as the oboe. Similarly, if you wanted to discuss your first experience with the bassoon, you would think of narration.

Even if choosing the appropriate strategy is not always this easy, as you think about your overall subject and your supporting points, a particular strategy may occur to you. Don't fight it—give it a try. Our instincts are often our best guides. See whether the strategy you've thought of gives rise to other ideas or illuminates the point of the paragraph.

If the appropriate strategy isn't obvious and you can't get started on your own, try questioning the particular idea you want your paragraph to support. Write your idea—perhaps your topic sentence—on a page and ask these questions, in no particular order:

> Will it give the reader a context for the subject of the paragraph? A straight narration or a cause and effect analysis might effectively place the idea.
>
> Will the reader find the point vague? Ground the idea in an example or describe its concrete features.
>
> Is the subject markedly like or unlike another subject the reader might be familiar with? Compare and contrast them.
>
> Would separating the point into its components make it clearer? Try dividing it. If it is part of a sequence of actions, perhaps process analysis would support it best.
>
> Does the reader need to know what you mean by the terms you use? Try a definition or an illustration.

Often a single strategy will not adequately support your point. You will need to combine strategies even in a single paragraph. If you were discussing your first experience with the bassoon, in addition to narrating you would probably need to describe this strange instrument as you first saw it. And for some readers you might even need to incorporate a definition.

Here are two examples of paragraphs using several strategies. Notice how smoothly the sentences in each are combined.

> I was in jail. I had been sentenced to six days in the Women's House of Detention, a fourteen-story prison right in the middle of Greenwich Village, my own neighborhood. This happened during the American War in Vietnam, I have forgotten which important year of the famous sixties. The civil disobedience for which I was paying a small

penalty probably consisted of sitting down to impede or slow some military parade. (Grace Paley, "Six Days: Some Rememberings")

In this paragraph, the author *narrates* a particular event while using *description* to bring details to life and even suggests a definition.

This next paragraph is largely, but not exclusively, one of *definition*.

> In the past hundred years, individualism and its ambiguities have been closely linked to middle-class status. As pointed out in chapter 5, the "middle class" that began to emerge in the later part of the nineteenth century differed from the old "middling condition." In the true sense of the term, the middle class is defined not merely by the desire for material betterment but by a conscious, calculating effort to move up the ladder of success. David Schneider and Raymond Smith usefully define the middle class as a "broad but not undifferentiated category which includes those who have certain attitudes, aspirations, and expectations toward status mobility, and who shape their actions accordingly." Status mobility has increasingly depended on advanced education and competence in managerial and professional occupations that require specialized knowledge. For middle-class Americans, a calculating attitude toward educational and occupational choice has been essential and has often spilled over into determining criteria for the choice of spouse, friends, and voluntary associations. From the point of view of lower-class Americans, these preoccupations do not necessarily seem natural. As one of Schneider and Smith's informants put it, "To be a square dude is hard work, man." (Robert N. Bellah et al., *Habits of the Heart*)

The writers *define* the term *middle class* by both what it is and what it is not. They then suggest a *process analysis* of how one attains middle-class status. They provide *examples* of how being middle class affects one's life and close with a *comparison* of middle-class and lower-class attitudes. All this they do seamlessly.

Tips for Choosing Strategies

- If a particular strategy occurs to you, go with it.
- Question your main points to decide on the appropriate strategy or strategies for developing those points.

EXERCISES FOR CHOOSING STRATEGIES

1. Here is a controversial thesis supported by four main points.

   Thesis: The United States government should be allowed to get information from terrorists by any means necessary, including torture.

    a. International and national terrorism is on the increase.

    b. The police and other law enforcement agencies are so limited in their methods that they fail to stop terrorism and bring terrorists to justice.

    c. One terrorist's civil rights are less important than those of the hundreds or thousands of citizens his or her actions threaten.

    d. Torture should be used only to prevent catastrophe, not to punish for past deeds.

    Question each main point to decide the most effective strategy for developing it, and write a paragraph on one of the main points. Now write a paragraph using a different strategy for the same point. Determine which strategy was more effective, and why.

2. Select a past paper that didn't work very well. Examine your thesis carefully, and identify your main points. Revise two of your interior paragraphs using altogether different strategies. If, for instance, you developed a paragraph largely by narration, try comparison and contrast or definition.

LINKING PARAGRAPHS: BONDING FORE AND AFT

Each paragraph usually presents a new major point in support of the thesis. These points are not isolated ideas but rather aspects of the overall thought and should be connected. We have read essays that seem little more than a bunch of ideas splattered on the page. One paragraph goes in one direction, the next in another. The writer seems to change the subject willy-nilly. There is no sustaining momentum, no sense of going somewhere. Such a haphazardly built essay can be incomprehensible and will be tedious.

A good essay reads smoothly, continuously. Each paragraph is bonded to the one before and the one after, like a series of connecting rods for transmitting power. The thought flows through the essay, gathering momentum and strength, and the reader flows with it.

As a critical thinker, take a step back to review your writing for its logical flow. With your thesis in mind, ask whether your paragraphs are truly consecutive. When one paragraph makes a statement that will be developed in the next few paragraphs, check to be sure each one bears out that controlling statement. Look at the natural sections into which your essay falls—do they move consecutively, projecting from your thesis? Your last step back is to see the essay as a whole. Is its flow unbroken? If not, remove the obstacles. Critical thinking can help you move even the biggest.

Consecutiveness—logical progression—from paragraph to paragraph is essential to a good essay. But just as there are ways to bind sentences in a paragraph, so there are ways to clarify and tighten the bond between paragraphs.

Observing Chronology

A clear chronology is essential to most narratives and will help to tighten paragraph connections in a general essay. In an essay on the writer Dawn Powell, Gore Vidal concludes with a description of an important event in the writer's life and begins the next paragraph with

> In later years Dawn reviewed books, shrewdly if somewhat wearily, in *Mademoiselle*.

Vidal goes on to discuss Powell's views on the literature of her day.

Repeating Words or Ideas

Frequently the first sentence of one paragraph will repeat a word from the last sentence of the previous paragraph or provide a synonym, thus showing that the thought is continuing:

> *Last sentence:* What I knew that those snobs didn't know was that their attitudes exposed their own insecurities.
>
> *First sentence of next paragraph:* Recognizing these insecurities should have gratified me, but I was unconsoled.

Now the writer is ready to tell us her own feelings.

Providing an Example

Sometimes the first sentence of one paragraph will provide an example of an idea in the last sentence of the previous paragraph:

> *Last sentence:* During his investigation of the shelters, the social worker sometimes felt afraid—an emotion that might occur in anyone.
>
> *First sentence of next paragraph:* He ducked into one shelter and came face-to-face with a very hostile ex-pimp looking for his girlfriend.

This paragraph goes on to show what caused the social worker's fear.

Summarizing the Preceding Paragraph

After describing both liberal and conservative attacks on the media, a follow-up paragraph begins:

> For both the left and the right, the media have become the scapegoats for America's ills.

The writer now explains why this is a distorted view.

Questioning the Previous Paragraph

After describing a position regarding affirmative action, a writer begins the next paragraph with a question:

But is this stance a matter of public policy or the preservation of private advantage?

This paragraph goes on to determine which characterization is more just.

Using Transitional Phrases

Terms such as *moreover, therefore, on the other hand,* and *for example* can help clarify the connections. After several paragraphs analyzing and describing the post-Vietnam histories of some soldiers, a follow-up paragraph began with

In addition, many brought back serious drug addiction problems.

This paragraph goes on to describe what has and hasn't been done about the drug problems of veterans.

Shifting to Personal Pronouns and Relative Pronouns

You can connect one paragraph to another by shifting to a pronoun or relative pronoun. In the opening paragraph of an essay on General Colin Powell, the writer describes the tremendous call for Powell to run for the presidency and then uses both a pronoun and a relative pronoun to tie in the next paragraph:

He was apparently pleased but unpersuaded by *these* clamorings.

This paragraph describes both Powell's pleasure and his decision not to run.

CASE STUDY:
ILLUSTRATING TRANSITIONS

In the following essay, Nancy Mairs passionately yet with humor conveys some of the experiences of the disabled. In the margins, we have noted the various paragraph transitions she uses to construct a very tight, swiftly developing essay. Note also how the strength of her argument pushes the entire essay along—that is really what holds all the paragraphs together.

Disability
Nancy Mairs

For months now I've been consciously searching for representations of myself in the media, especially television. I know I'd recognize this self because of certain distinctive, though not unique, features: I am a forty-three-year-old woman crippled by multiple sclerosis; al-

1

though I can still totter short distances with the aid of a brace and a cane, more and more of the time I ride in a wheelchair. Because of these appliances and my peculiar gait, I'm easy to spot even in a crowd. So when I tell you I haven't noticed any woman like me on television, you can believe me.

2

Actually, last summer I did see a woman with multiple sclerosis portrayed on one of those medical dramas that offer an illness-of-the-week like the daily special at your local diner. In fact, that was the whole point of the show: that this poor young woman had MS. She was terribly upset (understandably, I assure you) by the diagnosis, and her response was to plan a trip to Kenya while she was still physically capable of making it, against the advice of the young, fit, handsome doctor who had fallen in love with her. And she almost did make it. At least, she got as far as a taxi to the airport, hotly pursued by the doctor. But at the last she succumbed to his blandishments and fled the taxi into his manly protective embrace. No escape to Kenya for this cripple.

Capitulation into the arms of a man who uses his medical powers to strip one of even the urge toward independence is hardly the sort of representation I had in mind. But even if the situation had been sensitively handled, according the woman her right to her own adventures, it wouldn't have been what I'm looking for. Such a television show, as well as films like *Duet for One* and *Children of a Lesser God,* in taking disability as its major premise, excludes the complexities that round out a character and make her whole. It's not about a woman who happens to be physically disabled; it's about physical disability as the determining factor of a woman's existence.

Take it from me, physical disability looms pretty large in one's life. But it doesn't devour one wholly. I'm not, for instance, Ms. MS, a walking, talking embodiment of a chronic incurable degenerative disease. In most ways I'm just like every other woman of my age, nationality, and socioeconomic background. I menstruate, so I have to buy tampons. I worry about smoker's breath, so I buy mouthwash. I smear my wrinkling skin with lotions. I put bleach in the washer so my family's undies won't be dingy. I drive a car, talk on the telephone, get runs in my pantyhose, eat pizza. In most ways, that is, I'm the advertisers' dream: Ms. Great American Consumer. And yet the advertisers, who determine nowadays who will get represented publicly and who will not, deny the existence of me and my kind absolutely.

I once asked a local advertiser why he didn't include disabled people in his spots. His response seemed direct enough: "We don't want to give people the idea that our product is just for the handicapped." But tell me truly now: If you saw me pouring out puppy biscuits, would you think these kibbles were only for the puppies of cripples? If you saw my blind niece ordering a Coke, would you switch to Pepsi lest you be struck sightless? No, I think the advertiser's excuse masked a deeper and more anxious rationale: to depict disabled people in the ordinary activities of daily life is to admit that there is something ordinary about disability itself, that it may enter anybody's life. If it is effaced completely, or at least isolated as a separate "problem," so that it remains at a safe distance from other human issues, then the viewer won't feel threatened by her or his own physical vulnerability.

Starts with relative
pronoun, then re-
peats "effaced" and
"isolated"; transitional
word "however" sug-
gests contradiction of
previous ideas.

This kind of effacement or isolation has painful, even dangerous 6 consequences, however. For the disabled person, these include self-degradation and a subtle kind of self-alienation not unlike that experienced by other minorities. Socialized human beings love to conform, to study others and then to mold themselves to the contours of those whose images, for good reasons or bad, they come to love. Imagine a life in which feasible others—others you can hope to be like—don't exist. At the least you might conclude that there is something queer about you, something ugly or foolish or shameful. In the extreme, you might feel as though you don't exist, in any meaningful social sense, at all. Everyone else is "there," sucking breath mints and splashing on cologne and swigging wine coolers. You're "not there." And if not there, nowhere.

Starts with transitional
word "But"; "this de-
nial of disability" re-
peats idea of "not
there."

But this denial of disability imperils even you who are able-7 bodied, and not just by shrinking your insight into the physically and emotionally complex world you live in. Some disabled people call you TAPs, or Temporarily Abled Persons. The fact is that ours is the only minority you can join involuntarily, without warning, at any time. And if you live long enough, as you're increasingly likely to do, you may well join it. The transition will probably be difficult from a physical point of view no matter what. But it will be a good bit easier psychologically if you are accustomed to seeing disability as a normal characteristic, one that complicates but does not ruin human existence. Achieving this integration, for disabled and able-bodied people alike, requires that we insert disability daily into our field of vision: quietly, naturally, in the small and common scenes of our ordinary lives.

Tips for Linking Paragraphs
- Make sure each paragraph is bonded fore and aft.
- Remember that the best transition is a logical progression.
- Consider the following methods when linking paragraphs: chronology, repeating words or ideas, examples, summary, questioning the previous paragraph, transitional words, and personal and relative pronouns.

EXERCISES FOR LINKING PARAGRAPHS

1. Select a recent essay of yours and examine the transitions between the paragraphs. Tighten the transitions by using the methods discussed in this section.

2. Reread "In Defense of the Harp Seal Hunt" (pp. 166–69), and identify the transition methods. If you can devise better transitions, do so.

OVERARCHING STRATEGIES: THROUGHLINES

You have probably noticed how in some essays paragraphs come in groups within the sweep of an argument. An overarching sense of purpose seems to create a "throughline," that is, an idea running through several paragraphs and organizing them into a subunit of the essay.

These throughlines have in common a strong controlling statement at the beginning of the series of paragraphs—somewhere between a thesis statement and a topic sentence. This statement identifies the overall strategy used in this group of paragraphs. Throughline statements often are aspects of your thesis statement (see "Class Acts: America's Changing Middle Class," pp. 236–40). An essay may have several throughlines. The white space frequently found in professional essays usually indicates the end of one throughline and the beginning of another. (See Michael Levin's "Feminism: Stage Three" on pp. 115–23.) You can choose throughlines just as you choose individual strategies, that is, by questioning your main point.

In the pages that follow, we discuss some natural throughlines.

Extended Definition

An extended definition can serve as a throughline. The writer often will establish an overall definition as the thesis of an essay and then elucidate, using different strategies, over the next few paragraphs. An example is the definition of *patriotism* on page 211.

> Patriots, then, will be critical of their country for the country's own good and yet be ready to sacrifice for it when reason, combined with the force of events, tells them they must.

Can you predict how the rest of this section of the essay went? The writer used the definition as a throughline. He divided the definition into its three elements and wrote one or two paragraphs on each.

Critical of the country for the country's own good
   Defined *critical*
   Compared and contrasted being critical and not being critical
   Gave illustrations of "critical for country's own good"
Ready to sacrifice for it
   Defined *sacrifice*
   Illustrated with sacrifices
   Narrated a story of a particularly poignant sacrifice
When reason, combined with the force of events, tells them they must sacrifice
   Stipulated meaning of *reason*
   Used cause and effect to show force of events

Each of the main ideas served as a throughline for a part of the essay, employing different strategies to give substance and content along the way. Note that at several points the extended definition required definitions of other terms.

When writing an extended definition, be sure to do the following:

Establish clear boundaries for the extended definition, and then stay within them. Don't be distracted even by fascinating subtopics.

Finish one part of the definition before starting the next. If you let ideas stray back and forth, you will lose coherence.

Provide clear transitions between paragraphs. Repetition of the word being defined is one way of providing a transition. For the patriotism essay, the writer introduced the second part of the definition ("Ready to sacrifice for it") with "But patriotism is not only an attitude but also an action: sacrifice." With such a clear transition, the reader knows that the throughline is continuing.

Write with concrete details. This is a truism of writing, of course, but never more necessary than with an extended definition. Too often writers move toward the abstract, wrongly thinking that that way lies precision of thought. On the contrary: generally speaking, that way lies dullness and vagueness.

Extended Narrative

Because readers have listened to stories since childhood, time sequence is an excellent and natural throughline. Sometimes whole essays, and often several paragraphs, are organized chronologically. The reader easily follows the events. In this section of an essay arguing against gun control laws, consider how the following paragraph's strong topic sentence establishes chronology as the throughline.

> Gun control is not a new idea. The first government restrictions on handgun ownership in the United States were implemented in the post–Civil War South as part of the Black Codes—a body of laws designed to keep the blacks in legally mandated serfdom. (Bruce Powell Majors, "Gun Control: Historically Ineffective, Imprudent, and Coercive")

In the next paragraph, he takes the narrative through the late 1800s and early 1900s, in the next paragraph down to the 1920s, and so on to the present day. Once he has finished his historical survey, he moves on to another aspect of the subject.

Chronology provides excellent organizing throughlines when we write about history, narrate a story, explain a process, or examine a cause and effect relation. When using this method, remember two things:

Divide the time sequence into major periods, according to what is important. Don't get bogged down in too many small subdivisions about which you have little to say. Subordinate shorter or less important periods under the major ones.

Let your reader know when you have moved to the next period in the sequence. We do not suggest that you begin the discussion of each new period with the date, but we do think your reader has a right to know when you enter a new part of the sequence.

The term *chronological development* suggests that time brings significant changes. Thus, narrative throughlines often take the shape of a comparison and contrast between what was and what is. In such cases, follow the general procedures discussed under "Comparison and Contrast" in Chapter 8.

Assertion and Illustrations

When we argue a highly controversial main point, we probably will need to support the point with many examples, and if those examples are fairly complex, we will need to enlarge on each of them with more illustrations, definitions, narratives. The main point can serve as the throughline on which we string all the examples.

In the following passage, watch how the strong assertion in the lead paragraph binds the subsequent paragraphs.

Assertion

Privacy, as George Orwell pointed out, rests on some level on a bargain between people and their machines. Long before 1984, communications technology had the potential to become surveillance technology. Now it is. Not, as Orwell might have predicted, because Big Brother wants to keep his subjects in thrall but simply because most people want it to be. By giving up some protective anonymity, people get safety and service. A majority seem to think the bargain a very good one—which is why everybody should look very carefully at the fine print.

Illustration

Somewhat ironically for the nation that gave birth to Orwell, Britain is leading the way in creating the kind of society that he taught the world to fear. More than 300 British city streets are wired for twenty-four hour surveillance by closed-circuit television cameras. From control rooms, police and private security officers scan everything that moves, or doesn't, and dispatch police officers to investigate anything suspicious.

Illustration

More cities are getting wired all the time, often by popular demand. Whatever qualms Britons have about privacy, they are more concerned about crime. The cameras do seem to reduce crime—at least in the areas underneath the cameras. Academics point out that surveillance seems to have no impact whatsoever on the overall level of crime, which is rising, but people just don't seem to care about where the muggers go when they leave their neighborhood—particularly when their neighborhood wasn't too good to begin with. (John Browning, "Rights of Privacy")

The next paragraphs continue to illustrate the assertion. Note that the author starts the third paragraph right out with an interesting fact rather than something like "Another example of this point is . . ." When the throughline is strong, we can do without those clumsy crutches.

A variation of this technique occurs when the throughline is classification and the topic sentence in the lead paragraph establishes the class of objects or ideas to be discussed. In an essay arguing that propaganda is everywhere in commercials and advertisements, one writer uses this technique:

> What kind of propaganda techniques do advertisers use? There are seven basic types. (Ann McClintock, "Propaganda Techniques in Today's Advertising")

In subsequent paragraphs she identifies and discusses each type.

CASE STUDY:
FUSING MANY STRATEGIES

In the following essay, Ralph Whitehead, Jr., devises a new way of looking at class structure in the United States. The overall essay is based primarily on classification, but the writer uses many other strategies to get his point across. In the margins we have identified only the major strategies and throughlines.

Class Acts:
America's Changing Middle Class
Ralph Whitehead, Jr.

As we enter the 1990s, American society exhibits a vastly different social and economic makeup from the one that we grew accustomed to in the thirty years that followed World War II. The gap between the top and bottom is far greater now, of course, but the economic position of people in the middle is changing, too. This new social ladder is seen most vividly in the lives of our younger generations, the baby boom and the later baby bust. Because the new ladder is so much steeper than the old one, it's creating an alarming new degree of polarization in American life.   1

Illustration

As it held sway for roughly the first three decades after World War II, the old social ladder was shaped largely by the continuing expansion of the middle class. For the first time, many people could afford to buy a house, a car (or two), a washer and dryer, an outdoor grill, adequate health coverage, maybe a motor boat, and possibly college for the kids. And for the first time, a growing number of blacks and Hispanics could enter the middle class.   2

Definition throughline

Illustration

Within this expanding middle class, there were a couple of fairly well-defined ways of life: white-collar life and blue-collar life. White-   3

Classification

collar life was typified by TV characters like Ward and June Cleaver and later Mike and Carol Brady. Blue-collar life was typified by characters like Ralph and Alice Kramden and later Archie and Edith Bunker.

Classification At the top of the old social ladder stood a small number of rich 4 people. A larger but declining number of poor people stood at the bottom, and the rest of the ladder was taken up by the middle class. The old social ladder looked roughly like this:

THE RICH

THE EXPANDING MIDDLE CLASS:
White collar
Blue collar

THE POOR

Definition throughline The new social ladder is markedly different. Within the baby 5 boom and baby bust generations, the middle class is no longer expanding. Therefore the new social ladder is shaped by—and at the *Classification* same time is helping to shape—a new polarization between the haves and the have-nots. The social ladder of the 1990s looks roughly like this:

UPSCALE AMERICA:
The Rich
The Overclass

THE DIVERGING MIDDLE CLASS:
Bright collar
New collar
Blue collar

DOWNSCALE AMERICA:
The Poor
The Underclass

The rich are still on top, of course. But the new generation of rich people is typified by Donald Trump, the billionaire developer of luxury buildings for the newly rich, rather than by someone like his father, Fred Trump, a developer who made millions building modestly priced postwar homes and apartments for the expanding middle class—the kinds of homes in which the Kramdens and Bunkers lived.

The poor are still with us, of course, but they're no longer at the 6 bottom. It's not because they've risen to the middle class but rather because some of them have fallen into the underclass. Because defini-
Classification tions of the underclass vary, so do estimates of its size. However, it does include at least two million people who lead lives that aren't typified in America's popular culture. To belong to the underclass is to be without a face and without a voice.

Just as an underclass has emerged, so has an overclass, which oc- 7
Classification cupies the rung just below the rich. Located chiefly in a dozen metropolises and heavily concentrated in lucrative management and professional jobs, the overclass is roughly the same size as the underclass. Its significance lies not in its numbers, however, but in its immense power

throughout American society. The overclass holds the highest-level positions in the fields of entertainment, media, marketing, advertising, real estate, finance, and politics. It's pursued for its consumption dollars and cajoled for its investment dollars. It is crudely typified by the media stereotype of the yuppie.

Comparison/contrast

What clearly stood out on the old social ladder that shaped American society during the fifties and sixties was the dominant presence of an expanding middle class. What is noticeable about the new social ladder is the unmistakable emergence of distinct upper and lower rungs and the vast social, economic, and psychological distance between them. Together, the rich and the overclass form Upscale America. Together, the underclass and the poor form Downscale America.

Classification through-line

The expanding middle class, with its white and blue collars, has given way in the baby boom and baby bust generations to a diverging middle class. It consists largely of three kinds of workers:

Definition

Bright collars. Within the ranks of managerial and professional workers a new category of job has emerged. The white-collar worker is receding and the bright-collar worker is advancing. The bright collars are the 20 million knowledge workers born since 1945: lawyers and teachers, architects and social workers, accountants and budget analysts, engineers and consultants, rising executives and midlevel administrators. They earn their living by taking intellectual initiatives. They face the luxury and the necessity of making their own decisions on the job and in their personal lives.

Comparison/contrast

Bright-collar people lack the touchstones that guided white-collar workers like Ward Cleaver in the 1950s and 1960s. The white collars believed in institutions; bright collars are skeptical of them. The corporate chain of command, a strong force in white-collar life then, is far weaker for bright collars today. They place a premium on individuality, on standing out rather than fitting in. Although the older white collars knew the rules and played by them, bright collars can't be sure what the rules are and must think up their own. The white collars were organization men and women (mostly men); bright collars are entrepreneurs interested in building careers for themselves outside big corporations.

Description

Three quarters of the managers and professionals of the 1950s were men. Today half are women. Seven percent are black or Hispanic or Asian. Bright collars make up a third of the baby boom work force. They're typified by figures like *L.A. Law*'s attorneys.

Comparison/contrast

Blue collars. Within the manufacturing workplace, blue-collar work endures, but on a much smaller scale. Thirty years ago almost 40 percent of the adult work force did blue-collar work. Today, after the relative decline of American heavy industry, it's done by less than 25 percent of baby boom workers. During the fifties and sixties, blue-collar wages rose steadily, thus helping fuel the expansion of the middle class. In the past 15 years these wages have been relatively flat. Young blue collars often must live near the economic margins.

8

9

10

11

12

13

Description

The blue-collar world is still a man's world. Roughly three quarters   14
of today's younger blue collars are men—the same percentage as in
the 1950s. Twelve percent are black, Hispanic, or Asian. Within a
growing number of innovative manufacturing workplaces, new models
of blue-collar work have begun to emerge, but they haven't yet advanced enough to trigger a new category of American worker. In the
popular culture the new generation of blue collars finds a voice in
Bruce Springsteen, but it still hasn't found a face.

Definition

New collars. These people aren't managers and professionals, and   15
they don't do physical labor. Their jobs fall between those two worlds.
They're secretaries, clerks, telephone operators, key-punch operators,
inside salespeople, police officers. They often avoid the grime and reg-
imentation of blue-collar work. Two-thirds of the new collars are
women. More than 15 percent are black, Hispanic, or Asian. The new
collars make up at least 35 percent of the baby boom work force.

Illustration

Federal Express truck drivers are typical new-collar workers. They   16
design pickup and delivery routes, explain the company's services and
fees, provide mailing supplies, and handle relatively sophisticated information technology in their trucks. They aren't traditional truck drivers so much as sales clerks in offices on wheels.

Cause-and-effect
throughline

The rise of the new social ladder has helped to drive a number of   17
changes in American life, but one of them, already evident, should be
underscored: the dramatic shift of power within both the middle class
and the society as a whole.

Narration

As members of the expanding middle class of the postwar years,   18
blue collars once held considerable leverage. In the electorate, for
every vote cast by the white collars in 1960, the blue collars cast two.
In the workplace, they acted through powerful unions. In the market-
place, they were valued as consumers. As a result, blue collars dealt
with white collars as equals. In the fifties and sixties, whatever class
lines still divided the two groups seemed to be dissolving.

Comparison/contrast

Within the diverging middle class today, the balance of power is   19
much different. In the electorate, for every vote cast by younger blue
collars in 1988, bright collars cast two. In the workplace, younger blue-
collar workers are losing union power, while bright collars exert the
power of their knowledge and privilege of their status. In the market-
place, blue-collar consumers are written off as too downscale, while
the bright-collar consumer is courted as an aspiring member of the
overclass. Deep divisions have sprung up between bright collars and
blue collars. They look a lot like class lines.

Description

The rise of an overclass throws the decline of blue-collar life into   20
sharper relief, and vice versa. Upscale yuppie haunts spring up: the
health club, the gourmet takeout shop, the pricy boutique, the atrium
building. Downscale blue-collar haunts wither: the union hall, the lodge,
the beauty parlor, the mill. The guys with red suspenders began showing
up in the beer commercials right about the time the loggers and guys
with air hammers began to disappear. The overclass's stock portfolios

began to get fat just as blue-collar families were losing their pensions and health insurance. Condo prices were climbing in Atlanta just as bungalow prices fell in Buffalo. It seems that there's a battle here, a zero-sum game, whereby the rise of one comes at the expense of the other.

Illustration

The contrast between the rich and the underclass is sharper than   21
ever. If you look at the new social ladder in New York, you see Donald Trump in his penthouse and the homeless people in the subways.

Classification

This situation intensifies the shift of power in society as a whole.   22
With the middle class divided, the center cannot hold. The dominant forces in society become Upscale America and Downscale America—or, more precisely, Upscale America *versus* Downscale America. Upscale America uses its power to secure privileges such as proposed cuts in the capital gains tax. Downscale America strikes back blindly through rising rates of crime. Through the old social ladder, the expanding middle class acted as the nation's glue. With the new social ladder, the diverging middle class is merely caught in the crossfire.

Tips for Overarching Strategies

- Develop the body of your essay by means of throughlines that bind groups of paragraphs.
- Choose throughlines the same way you choose strategies.

EXERCISES FOR OVERARCHING STRATEGIES

1. Identify throughlines in the Levin essay and Larry Boyd's response in Chapter 5, Putting Words on Paper.

2. For your next paper, draft a first version in the usual way. Now go through your first draft and look for a paragraph that contains one of the following: narrative, cause and effect, division and classification, extended definition, or assertion and illustrations. Expand your chosen paragraph into three or more paragraphs. The first paragraph should have a very strong controlling statement; the rest need not have strong topic sentences but must follow the lead of the first paragraph. When you have finished, read your new passage over and assess how strong the throughline is. If it needs to be stronger, improve it.

3. The following statements establish possible throughlines:
   a. The years between fifteen and eighteen were the least productive/poorest/quickest-moving/laziest/most surprising years of my life. (Choose one—or make up another adjective that fits; but be specific.)
   b. Over and over in my life I have learned that it pays/does not pay to be kind to people in need. (Choose one.)
   c. A creative person has the ability to be inventive—that is, to transform his or her original thoughts into a form others can appreciate.

   Write a paragraph for each statement, and then write a series of new paragraphs that follow the statement's lead.

YOUR OPENING PARAGRAPH:
A BOLD BEGINNING

The first paragraph makes your essay's first and lasting impression. Some opening paragraphs sound like an ancient truck trying to warm up on a very cold day. Old trucks don't offer a very enticing ride, and neither do essays that start off with a grind or a groan. The reader wants a sense of movement and purpose.

An introductory paragraph should aim to do three things:

grab the reader's attention

identify the central issue or subject

create the tone of the essay

The way you start will determine how your reader responds to your essay. It is so crucial that many writers draft the first paragraph only after they have finished the essay and can put all their energy and artistry into it. And the good writers we know tune up their openings over and over again. They don't want the engine to die before the reader even turns the corner into the rest of the essay.

The Shape of the Opening Paragraph

The thesis statement can appear in the first sentence or in the last or even in the middle of the opening paragraph. In fact, it does not have to be in the very first paragraph at all (but it is a good idea to state it fairly early in the essay). Nor must you begin with a series of generalizations. You could start with something descriptive or narrative and then show how this description or narration gives rise to the thesis. Anything that works goes—if it grabs the reader's attention and leads right into your essay.

One especially effective shape for opening paragraphs is the *funnel,* so named by Sheridan Baker. The wide end of the funnel is the first sentence, a focused generalization that provides the necessary context and the subject. Each succeeding sentence narrows the subject. The last sentence is the thesis statement, the least general statement in the paragraph.

Lewis Thomas provides a clear model of this shape in the opening paragraph of an essay titled "Information."

> According to the linguistic school currently on top, human beings are all born with a genetic endowment for recognizing and formulating language. This must mean that we possess genes for all kinds of information, with strands of special, peculiarly human DNA for the discernment of meaning in syntax. We must imagine the morphogenesis of deep structures, built into our minds, for coding out, like proteins, the parts of speech. Correct grammar (correct in the logical, not fashionable, sense) is as much a biologic characteristic of our species as feathers on birds.

Here Thomas moves from the general idea of genetic endowment to the concept of DNA to the linguistic notion of "deep structures" to his thesis in the last sentence.

Not all essays open with a funnel. In Chapter 6, we quoted the opening paragraph of an essay by Ross Gelbspan that begins this way:

> After my lawn had burned away to straw last summer, and the local papers announced that the season had been one of the driest in the recorded history of New England, I found myself wondering how long we can go on pretending that nothing is amiss with the world's weather.

There's his thesis, bold, clear, and right up front. The rest of the paragraph explains what the first sentence means, and the rest of the essay supports it.

Another possible way to begin an essay is the multiparagraph opener, which unfolds in more leisurely fashion. The first paragraph may provide historical background, an extended definition, or a series of illustrations or facts that are then developed in the second paragraph. The following opening passage reaches its thesis statement at the beginning of the third paragraph:

> About 225 million years ago, at the end of the Permian period, fully half the families of marine organisms died out during the short span of a few million years—a prodigious amount of time by most standards, but merely minutes to a geologist. The victims of this mass extinction included all surviving trilobites, all ancient corals, all but one lineage of ammonites and most bryozoans, brachiopods, and crinoids.
>
> This great dying was the most profound of several mass extinctions that have punctuated the evolution of life during the past 600 million years. The late Cretaceous extinction, some 70 million years ago, takes second place. It destroyed 25 percent of all families, and cleared the earth of its dominant terrestrial animals, the dinosaurs and their kin—thus setting a stage for the dominance of mammals and the eventual evolution of man.
>
> No problem in paleontology has attracted more attention or led to more frustration than the search for causes of these extinctions. (Stephen Jay Gould, *Ever Since Darwin*)

The multiparagraph introduction can be graceful and appealing, as this one is. It slides the reader deep into the essay. Remember, though, that regardless of length or shape, the goal of the introduction is a clear indication of the thesis and an attractive invitation to the reader to join you in exploring it.

The First Sentence

Perhaps the most important single sentence in an essay is the first one. An excellent opening sentence is like the first bite of a superb dinner: it stimulates the taste buds and starts the digestive juices flowing. But if the first taste is badly seasoned or poorly cooked, no one will be eager for the next. Here are some ways to provide a good appetizer.

A Revealing Anecdote, Historical or Personal.   An essay by Roland Barthes analyzing the significance of the Eiffel Tower begins,

> Maupassant often lunched at the restaurant in the tower, though he didn't care much for the food: *It's the only place in Paris,* he used to say, *where I don't have to see it.* ("The Eiffel Tower")

The humor of this opening entices the reader.

An Interesting or Illuminating Fact.   An essay calling for drastic changes in our penal system might begin with a sobering fact: "Does society as a whole share in the blame when one-third of young black males are under the supervision of criminal law institutions, on trial, in jail, on probation, or on parole?"

An Arresting Image.   An essay on gambling in America might begin, "The Dixie Unlimited is a red, white, and blue neon-lighted paddleboat casino that plies the muddy reaches of the Mississippi, stopping only to take on fresh passengers and unload the losers and the loot."

A Provocative Opinion Asserted Provocatively.   Your position can either be supported or refuted: "American doctors have lost their halos, for very good reasons." Remember, though, it is one thing to be provocative and another to be outrageous. You need to arouse interest, not animosity that drives away the reader.

A Sharp Quotation.   A quotation such as Sir Isaac Newton's "Errors are not in the art but in the artificer" could introduce an argument favoring genetic engineering. When selecting a quotation, however, be sure you don't choose one that is overused.

Pitfalls to Avoid

We have made some suggestions for good beginnings, but we have hardly exhausted the subject. Indeed, the possibilities are almost limitless. Having said that, we now want to identify some openers that are to be avoided at almost any cost.

The Obvious Definition.   One paper on Marx's *Communist Manifesto* began, "Society is defined as a voluntary association of persons for common ends, and government, which exists in society, is defined as the organization or agency through which a political unit exercises authority." Nothing new or interesting in that.

Facts Nobody Needs to Be Reminded Of.   A paper on Harry Truman's foreign policy need not begin, "Harry Truman, who served as president of the United States." This is tedious.

Platitudes.   Too many essays begin with sentiments such as "The processes of life are awe inspiring" or "Despite thousands of years' experience of the horrors of war, we seem no closer to controlling our destructive impulses" or "Poetry can be important to our lives." True statements all, but hardly promises of an exciting essay.

Apologies and Excuses.   "Ricardo's economic theories are extremely difficult to explain, but I will do the best I can" does not increase the reader's confidence in the writer. And "This essay will be short, because I began it only five hours before it was due" may seem clever to the writer, but it probably will not amuse the instructor. Some apologies and excuses are honest expressions of insecurity; others are mere manipulations. Spare the reader both.

Tips for Your Opening Paragraph

- Remember that the goals of a beginning are to get the reader's attention, to identify the central issue, and to create the tone. Make your first paragraph as inviting as you can.
- Remember that your first sentence is perhaps the most important in your essay.
- Don't dawdle — get started.
- Choose the form that suits your subject and your style. A funnel is a good way to begin, but it is not the only way.
- Avoid obvious definitions, well-known facts, platitudes, apologies, and excuses.

EXERCISES FOR YOUR OPENING PARAGRAPH

1. Here are four thesis statements, each of which sets forth a controversial or unpopular position:

   In light of the recent upswing in violent crime, police officers should be allowed more latitude in making arrests.

   Plaintiff lawyers are to blame for putting doctors out of business with their high malpractice suits.

   American children are growing up largely ignorant of the way the federal government functions.

   Minority children need more scientists and intellectuals and fewer athletes and musicians as role models.

Choose one statement and compose an opening paragraph for an essay arguing for or against that thesis. Your paragraph can be as long or short as you please, but it must start with a provocative or attention-grabbing sentence that employs one of the strategies outlined in "The First Sentence" and end with the thesis statement.

2. Find a recent essay of yours and examine the opening paragraph. Is it effective? What do you think of the first sentence and the way the paragraph unfolds? Revise your paragraph to improve it.

3. Exchange your revised opening from Exercise 2 for a classmate's. Write a paragraph comparing the effectiveness of the two. Now write a final version of your opening, incorporating the good ideas from both.

YOUR CONCLUSION: FINISHING IN STYLE

We won't claim that your concluding paragraph is as important as your opening one—if you don't give your readers a good start, they probably won't make it to the end. Nonetheless, it is crucial, for it is your last chance to make a good impression. Make it as effective as you can.

A conclusion has three goals:

to make one last effort to convince the reader

to suggest larger implications than you could reasonably assert before you presented your evidence

to provide a satisfying sense of closure

Ending on the Right Note

When so much is riding on your essay, you do not want to leave the impression of limping or skulking off. You want to appear dynamic and confident, fully engaged and in control. Without appearing smug, you want to be seen—figuratively, of course—brushing the dust off the palms of your hands after a job well done.

To achieve this poise, follow two general rules: never apologize and never brag. If a writer apologizes, the reader is very apt to think the whole journey through the essay has been a waste of time. And when a writer brags that he or she has proved a large notion or accumulated a great deal of information, the reader is apt to be annoyed— and inspired to find holes in the argument and faults with the writing. Be honest and modest: don't claim more than your argument fully justifies. A concluding tone of judicious assurance can finish off your essay in style.

The Larger Implications

If you have done your job in the middle of the essay—developing your argument while staying close to the thesis—by the end you should be ready to push your thinking—and your reader's—a little. After all, what you have said surely has some importance beyond the limits of your thesis. You should now be able to tell your reader how the thesis opens a window on a larger idea.

A student in an art history class was asked to write a paper on painting. She narrowed the topic to her favorite painter, Vincent van Gogh, and then to a favorite painting, *Chair and Pipe*. Her thesis was "The physical quality of van Gogh's brushstroke emphasizes the concrete and material reality of his subject." Through the body of the paper she analyzed the painting. In her last paragraph she wrote that *Chair and Pipe* may have led other painters to employ similar techniques reflecting the density of their subjects. She did not have to prove this observation; she only had to suggest it. Her analysis gave her the right to this larger observation.

In a criminal justice class, a student wrote an essay arguing for automatic jail sentences for anyone driving with a blood alcohol count of over 0.5 percent. In the body of the paper, she carefully presented and analyzed information on both sides of her subject. She discussed the effects of the alcohol count on the nervous system, the experience of countries with stringent laws, the increase of alcohol consumption, and the increase in teenage drinking. She admitted negative implications. In her conclusion, she stated that despite problems, the compulsory jail sentence was worth a try. That assertion would hardly have surprised an attentive reader—it was probably assumed in the writer's thesis. But this writer wanted to go beyond the thesis and make an impression on her reader, and so she enlarged her argument:

> Many Americans seem willing to forbid smoking in public places, to insist that guns be prohibited, and to re-institute a nationwide speed limit of 55 miles per hour. Surely the time is right to go after the deadliest killer of them all—driving under the influence.

By shifting the focus to other kinds of socially dangerous behavior, she provided some thought-provoking analogies and expanded the implications of her paper. And she left a strong impression.

An accomplished conclusion, then, is often more in-depth than the essay. It sets the thesis in a larger context, and that larger context helps to clinch the argument, for then the reader understands the importance of the ideas.

Pitfalls to Avoid

A good conclusion adds to an essay; a bad conclusion detracts from it. Many last paragraphs, unfortunately, seem mechanical, embarrassed, lazy, or frenzied. Here are the major pitfalls you should try to avoid in your endings.

The Wastebasket Ending.   Some writers sweep up all the overflow points they could not fit into the body of an essay and present them in the last paragraph. In an essay on the founding of Israel, a writer concluded: "The Palestinians are Sunni Moslem. The Sunnis are one of the great divisions in Islam, the other being Shiite. The two groups separated over the succession to the leadership of Islam following the death of Mohammed." Those facts might have been interesting if the writer had developed them in the essay, but tacked on in the last paragraph, they only confuse the reader. Don't throw into your conclusion bits and pieces that didn't fit elsewhere.

The Fade-Out.   Have you noticed how some people can tell a fascinating story but seem to lose heart as they get to the end and let their voices dwindle away? Some writers end essays that way. The following concludes a very good essay on how children learn to use language: "Researchers have so much more to discover in this area that I have to admit that we have only scratched the surface. Whatever we say now will be superseded very soon." Those last sentences seem to say, "Maybe this wasn't worth writing after all. Sorry I took your time." An essay should end on a note of confidence.

The Wild Surmise.   We have noticed that when students fear that their essays are not important enough, they often write a concluding paragraph that leaps far beyond the evidence to a grandiose pronouncement. The concluding paragraph of an otherwise excellent essay on Zairean bureaucracy suddenly claimed, "From this we see the utter futility of tying aid to underdeveloped nations to the adoption of Western standards." All because of limited experience in Zaire? How much better it would have been to conclude with "If the Zairean experience is typical of the Third World, perhaps we ought to re-evaluate the strings we attach to our foreign aid." Qualified claims are better because they are so much likelier to be acceptable.

The Mirror Image.   The mirror image is perhaps the most common error students make in endings. The writer repeats the thesis and summarizes the main point of each paragraph, as in this example:

> As I said, professional athletes should be allowed to participate in the Olympics. They would add quality to the games. The hypocrisy now rampant would decrease. The nations that provide their athletes with "government jobs" would no longer enjoy an advantage. We should act immediately to change the Olympic rules.

This kind of conclusion is dull and mechanical. If you have done your job in the body of the essay, you do not need to repeat the whole argument in the last paragraph. The best conclusions carry the thought not backward but forward.

The conclusion can be one of the most effective parts of your essay. Let it be an elegant and creative farewell.

Tips for Your Conclusion

- Pay as much attention to your closing as to your opening.
- Keep in mind the three goals of an essay's conclusion: to make one last effort to convince the reader, to suggest larger implications than you could reasonably assert before you presented your evidence, to provide a satisfying sense of closure.
- Avoid the wastebasket ending, the fade-out, the wild surmise, and the mirror-image closing.

EXERCISES FOR YOUR CONCLUSION

1. Here are the last paragraphs of three professional essays:

    "Like bone to the human body, and the axle to the wheel, and the song to a bird, and air to the wing, thus is liberty the essence of life," José Martí, the Cuban poet and patriot, wrote. "Whatever is done without it, is imperfect." (William Pfaff)

    As black people go moving on up toward separation and cultural nationalism, the question of the moment is not which dialect, but which culture, not whose vocabulary but whose values, not *I am* vs. *I be,* but WHO DO I BE? (Geneva Smitherman, "White English in Blackface, or Who Do I Be?")

    So I will try here to be exact. I wish my father had done more headlong, more elegant inventing. I believe he would respect my wish, be willing to speak with me seriously about it, find some nobility in it. But now he is dead, and he had been dead two weeks when they found him. And in his tiny flat at the edge of the Pacific they found no address book, no batch of letters held with a rubber band, no photograph. Not a thing to suggest that he had ever known another human being. (Geoffrey Wolff, *The Duke of Deception*)

    Can you tell what each essay was about? What hints do you find? What techniques did each author use to make his or her ending more effective? What do you think of the last line of each paragraph?

2. Exchange with a partner a recent essay without its concluding paragraph. Write a conclusion for your partner's essay. Then compare your conclusion and your partner's for each essay. What are the weaknesses and strengths of each closing? Which suits the essay better? Write a paragraph analyzing the differences.

THE TITLE:
ISSUING THE INVITATION

The title is probably the last thing you write for an essay, but it is the first thing the reader sees, and it ought to be attractive. No title at all or something like "Assignment 3" or "Second Sociology Paper" is pretty unappealing. Even "Hemingway's *The Sun Also Rises*" or "The Albigensian Heresy" won't arouse a reader's wild enthusiasm. These titles are too broad and shapeless.

You need a title that says, "I know something interesting—come and find out." A title like "Why Nothing Is 'Wrong' Anymore" or "Running and Other Vices" or "Shakespeare without Tears" intrigues readers and even softens them up to enjoy the essay. Even "Authorial Intervention in *The Sun Also Rises*" and "The Albigensian Heresy and the Rise of Preaching" tell something about their essays and provide the reader with an entryway.

A title should be an honest advertisement. Something cute and snappy is fine as long as it is relevant and appropriate. When "Three Months Behind Bars" turns out to refer to a summer spent mixing drinks at a fancy restaurant, some readers may smile, but some may feel tricked. Similarly, a serious essay shouldn't have a frivolous title. If, for example, the subject is geriatrics, a title like "Everything You Always Wanted to Know about Death—But Were Afraid to Ask" would offend many people.

A well-chosen title will indicate not only the subject but also the tone of the essay. Think for a moment about what your expectations are for these titles: "A Dog's Eye View of Man," "Hypocrite Hit Parade," "The Reach of Imagination." Which essay would you expect to be the most serious? Which would you expect to be confrontational? Titles can—and in these examples do—represent both the thinking and the approach of the essay.

You can find titles in a variety of places. Sometimes a title will come from within your essay. A nice turn of phrase or a recurrent theme may say it all. Or you might pull a quotation out of the text or the subject you are writing about: "I beg your pardon—I know exactly what to think" comes from Jane Austen's *Pride and Prejudice* and could serve as the title for a study of the character who made this statement. General Douglas MacArthur said "I shall return" when he was forced to leave the Philippines at the beginning of World War II; that quotation would nicely introduce a paper on the Battle for the Philippines.

Sometimes you can find a good title outside your immediate subject. Hundreds of writers have used the Bible and Shakespeare as sources for titles. Peter Cohen wrote *The Gospel According to the Harvard Business School;* his ironic title tells much about his approach. If you were writing about the difficulty of starting college, you might find a title in the words of the Latin poet Virgil: "Look with favor upon a bold beginning." Some writers use twists on an old saying, such as "Father Knows Best" for an essay on priests in today's culture, or a phrase from a song, such as "My Country 'Tain't of Thee" for an essay on pollution. In short, you can find a title anywhere.

Tips for the Title

- Choose a title that is inviting and appealing.
- In devising a title, think about both the content and the tone of your essay.
- You can find a title in your essay, in the work or subject you are discussing, in literature, or even in popular sayings.

EXERCISES FOR THE TITLE

1. Match the description of an essay in column A to the corresponding title in list B. Why did you make the match you did?

A	B
Suggests that the English people fight famine by dining on Irish babies	1. The Importance of Being Ordinary
Compares the tools and methods of different plastic surgeons	2. Was Paul Revere a Minute-Person?
Details a month in the life of a professional art appraiser	3. A Modest Proposal
Draws up a program of absolutely essential education	4. The Cutting Edge
Argues that we should not change our use of English just to avoid sexism	5. In the Eye of the Beholder
Discusses how the rich and famous try to be just like other people in order to improve their public image	6. Is There Any Knowledge That a Man Must Have?

2. Here is a partner exercise. Write an essay that describes eating, compares people who listen with people who watch, or discusses your personal tastes in humor. Then give it to your partner to title. Do you think the title works? Does it capture the essence of your essay? Why or why not?

3. Devise new titles for the last three essays you have written. Ask a partner to judge whether the new titles or the old are better and to state why. Do the same for three of your partner's essays.

10

The Sentence from
Many Angles

Backward ran sentences until reeled the mind.
— WOLCOTT GIBBS (1902-1958)
AMERICAN WRITER AND HUMORIST

You could not write an essay, you could not write a paragraph, indeed you could not express a thought at all without sentences. You could say a word, and thus denote an object or even identify a concept, or make a sound to suggest a feeling, but you could not say anything about that thing or concept. A sentence expresses the basic unit of thought. By its construction, it discriminates among ideas and signals what is important. Its very form affects its meaning.

Some writers seem to think sentences exist fully grown somewhere in the mind and will come when called. It isn't that easy. Sentences don't write themselves: we have to do the work. Words are in our heads, but we have to put them together to make a whole thought.

In this chapter we will consider the sentence under two main headings:

Structure: A sentence is something you put together. How you put it together always affects its sense and impact. We will examine various ways of assembling sentences and the effect different structures have.

Quality: Writers of good sentences work for three main qualities. They work for emphasis—they manage the force or intensity of expression to make the sentence memorable or impressive. They work for

251

economy—they pack the most meaning into the fewest words. And they work for variety—they mix up different kinds and lengths of sentences to keep the reader interested.

Thinking critically is all-important with sentences. Good writers concentrate furiously on both what a sentence says and how it says it. Good thinking, good sentences, and vice versa. Let us start thinking about sentences by starting with the basics of sentence grammar and syntax.

PARTS OF A SENTENCE: THE BASIC THOUGHT

Deep in every complete sentence there always exist a simple subject (S) and verb (V) and frequently a direct object (O) or a complement (C). These elements compose the spine of the sentence.

S	V	O/C
Mona Lisa	smiles.	
Raccoons	harassed	farmers.
Sugar	is	sweet.

The *subject* is the topic of the sentence. *Mona Lisa* is the subject of the first sentence. The *verb* indicates an action or state of being. *Smiles* indicates the action of the first sentence. The *direct object* receives the action. *Farmers* received the harassment in the second sentence. The *complement* indicates a state of being of the subject by naming, identifying, or describing the subject. In the third sentence, *sweet* describes *sugar.*

When the verb *requires* a direct object to complete its meaning, as in "Raccoons harassed farmers," we call that verb *transitive;* when the verb does not require a direct object, as in "Mona Lisa smiles," we call it *intransitive. Linking verbs,* such as *be, become, look,* and *seem,* carry the complement back to the subject. In "Sugar is sweet," the verb *is* carries the sweetness back to the sugar.

Some sentences contain both an indirect object (IO) and a direct object. The indirect object indicates to whom or for whom the action was done.

S	V	IO	O
The hamburger	cost	us	money.

Spines provide the substructure for thought, and often they are all we need. "I love you," "War is hell," and "Shut your mouth" hardly require embellishment.

MODIFIERS:
ENRICHING THE THOUGHT

Usually we want to go beyond the simple statement to ask subtle questions, voice reservations, describe in detail what we see, give complicated commands, explain with precision. The unembellished subject-verb-object/complement will seldom convey a complex meaning.

Here is an unembellished sentence:

The people supported a law.

We can enrich it by adding adjectives, adverbs, phrases, or clauses.

Long before pollution reached international proportions, the people *of Dortmund, Germany,* supported a law *making public health a higher priority than any other political consideration.*

Although still there, our original sentence is hardly recognizable, for now we have added modifiers that explain, qualify, and amplify the central thought. We know when the people passed the law, where they lived, and what the law said.

Adding Adjectives and Adverbs

We can hang a modifying word on any part of the spine. Suppose our sentence is

Raccoons harassed farmers.

We can make this sentence more pictorial and more exact by adding an adjective to modify the nouns or an adverb to modify the verb.

The *marauding* raccoons harassed the farmers.
The raccoons *gleefully* harassed the farmers.
The raccoons harassed the *hot-tempered* farmers.

We can combine these possibilities and write a fairly lively sentence.

The marauding raccoons gleefully harassed the hot-tempered farmers.

Now we have told our readers more about the raccoons, the harassment, and the farmers.

If we wish, we can add more than one adjective to any noun and more than one adverb to any verb.

Beautiful, mysterious Mona Lisa smiled slyly but sweetly.

Building with Phrases and Clauses

So far we have added fairly simple modifiers. But we can also attach more complicated modifiers—phrases and clauses—to sentence spines.

A *phrase* is a group of words lacking either a subject or a verb. We can hang phrases on any part of the spine.

> *Blue from the cold,* the mountain climbers plunged *into the Jacuzzi.*

> *To get even for the harsh and petty measures of the Roman officials,* the Visigoths rebelled *against Rome.*

We do have to be sure, though, that we hang phrases close to the words they modify. We might confuse the reader if we wrote

> The mountain climbers plunged into the Jacuzzi *blue from the cold.*

Is the Jacuzzi blue from the cold?

A *clause* is a group of related words containing both a subject and a verb. Clauses come in two varieties. One variety, called *independent,* can stand as a complete sentence.

> Babe Ruth started his baseball career as a pitcher.

The other variety, called *dependent,* cannot stand alone.

> After Babe Ruth pointed his bat at the center field bleachers

Although this clause contains a subject and a verb, it is not a complete thought, and it needs an independent clause to support it.

> After Babe Ruth pointed his bat at the center field bleachers, *he hit a home run.*

Dependent clauses, like phrases, can be attached to any part of the spine.

> The conquistador Balboa, *who was the first European to view the Pacific from the Western Hemisphere,* claimed the entire Pacific coast for the Spanish crown.

> *While he was preparing an expedition to Peru,* Balboa was accused of treason.

Again like phrases, clauses must be placed close to the part of the spine they modify. We would confuse our reader if, for instance, we wrote

> General Lee presented his sword to the victorious General Grant, *which he had carried throughout the Civil War.*

Lee most certainly did not carry Grant throughout the Civil War, although the placement of the modifying phrase implies that he did. Placing the phrase immediately after the word *sword* would prevent a mis-reading.

> General Lee presented his sword, *which he had carried throughout the Civil War,* to the victorious General Grant.

Modifiers carry information, and where and how they carry it makes all the difference. We must follow the rules of syntax, grammar, and usage. And, of course, we must show restraint and choose our modifiers carefully. Piling on modifier after modifier can make near-gibberish of writing.

> On a cold and rainy January morning, in a fit of pique, and blue from the cold, marauding raccoons who had reconnoitered at dawn glee-fully harassed the furious, hot-tempered farmers, which was their way of getting even for harsh and petty measures.

The human mind simply cannot sort out so many ideas and images at once. A few well-chosen modifiers will make the point more clearly and forcefully. A single sharp image may have more impact than a lengthy description. Often a simple noun is better all alone. *Gorilla* hardly needs *hairy* or *scary*, and *howled* hardly needs *wildly*. If, however, the gorilla is *bald* and *simpering*, add the modifiers.

Tips for Modifiers

- Use carefully chosen modifiers to sharpen or enrich your thought.
- Place modifiers as close as possible to the part of the spine they modify.
- Show restraint: use only as many modifiers as the spine can easily carry and the reader's mind take in.

EXERCISES FOR MODIFIERS

1. Make these sentences livelier by modifying each at three places, using adjectives or adverbs.
   a. Mother wrote a book.
   b. Politics is absurd.
   c. The boss provided us with transportation.
   d. The crane hit the pavement.

2. Modify each of these sentences with both a phrase and a clause. (Make up attributes and events if you need to.)
   a. I study metallurgy.
   b. The hurricane destroyed the house.
   c. Sherman attacked Atlanta.
   d. The Spartans defeated the Athenians.

3. Modify each of these sentences by adding at least one adjective, one adverb, one phrase, and one clause.
   a. George Bush succeeded Ronald Reagan.
   b. Economics is dismal.
   c. The instructor flunked me.
   d. Sigmund Freud wrote *Interpretation of Dreams*.

   First, let yourself go. Make them as wild as you like. Then revise the sentences to make them acceptable for a school essay. But keep them lively.

4. Eliminate from these sentences all modifiers that are not absolutely necessary. Be ready to explain what you kept, what you deleted, and why.
   a. After a twenty-mile trek in the pelting rain, the American troops, weary
      and wet, wanted nothing more than a good meal, a full night's restful
      sleep, and, to protect them from the merciless elements, a dry place to
      sleep away from the rain.
   b. J. Fred Muggs was a hopping, screeching, hairy, funny, extremely intel-
      lectual chimpanzee with a constant habit of scratching his forehead
      every few minutes.
   c. Born in Ireland in the British Isles, the Irish writer Sean O'Casey wrote
      popular and successful dramatic plays such as *Juno and the Paycock* and
      Within the Gates, both of which were well received when they were per-
      formed onstage.
   d. If you asked me, I actually don't believe I would truly agree, although
      possibly I could be convinced to change my mind.

COORDINATION AND SUBORDINATION: SHAPING THE THOUGHT

Modifiers are only one way of shaping and directing sentences. Now
that we have seen how they work, we can begin to look at the others.
In this section, we discuss how to structure the sentence.

The Simple Sentence

The simplest construction is a simple sentence. It consists of a single independent clause.

The Irish elk is a deer.

Leonardo da Vinci invented the bicycle.

The simple sentence can express complicated ideas and contain a
good deal of information.

Woodrow Wilson, the twenty-eighth president of the United States, had
been a practicing lawyer, a professor of political science, president of
Princeton University, and governor of New Jersey.

The simple sentence can have a compound subject.

> *Sammy Baugh* and *the Washington Redskins* lost the 1940 National Football League championship to the Chicago Bears by a score of 73–0.

It can also have a compound verb.

> Woody Allen *wrote, directed,* and *starred* in *Annie Hall.*

Both these sentences contain only one independent clause.

The simple sentence can also come right out and say what is what. From it the reader can quickly pick up the main idea.

Young children use simple sentences almost exclusively. Their writing sounds like this:

> Dear Mom and Dad,
>
>   I am having a lot of fun at camp. We learned how to swim yesterday. Then we went on a hike. We got on top of a mountain. It was high. You could see a long way. I got dizzy. I like Counselor Howard. I don't like the food so much. Give Meatball a big kiss. Say hi to Grandma.
>
>   Love,
>   Patty

What gives such writing its charm—and makes it sound childish—is its way of putting the same emphasis on everything. Each sentence runs in a straight line, from locomotive to caboose. Patty writes with clarity and directness, all right—even Grandma will know Patty favors the dog, Meatball—but her prose lacks variety and depth. No one, of course, would criticize a nine-year-old for this kind of writing. Readers, however, expect mature writers to be able to use not just the hammer and the saw but all the tools of the trade. And they expect the right tool for the job.

Combining sentences is an important technique. When you join related ideas into a single sentence, you clarify their connection and identify what is important. And your prose will be more attractive and readable. Of course, the occasional pithy or even just appropriately direct simple sentence is a very useful tool. But knowing how and when to combine your sentences will add a finish to your writing.

Coordination

Rather than having a string of seemingly unrelated sentences, an older Patty could combine her simple sentences into compound sentences.

> We learned how to swim yesterday, and then we went on a hike. I like Counselor Howard, but I don't like the food so much.

A *compound sentence* contains at least two independent clauses and no dependent clauses. By combining simple sentences, Patty shows the relations between ideas. She points out how camp activity is structured and how one event immediately follows another. Finally, to express her experience more strongly, she combines a like and a dislike in one sentence.

This process is called *coordination*. When we coordinate sentences, we are saying that the clauses enjoy the same importance. They are costars and deserve equal billing.

By placing two independent clauses in the same sentence, we suggest that they are not only equal, but also so integrally connected that they must perform in the same show. The two independent clauses should reinforce each other, each thought benefiting from being coupled with the other.

> Give me liberty or give me death! (Patrick Henry)
>
> Candy
> Is dandy
> But liquor
> Is quicker.
>   (Ogden Nash)

If the two ideas are not closely related and of more or less equal weight, they should not be in the same compound sentence. When we hook together disparate ideas, our sentences tend to fly apart.

> Michelangelo painted the Sistine Chapel, and Pope Julius II was a great patron of the arts.

These two clauses have no apparent connection.

Even if both parts of the sentence treat the same subject, they may not mesh.

> Leonardo da Vinci painted *The Last Supper,* and he died in France.

The connection between these two ideas is too vague to justify putting them together—what has France to do with *The Last Supper?*—and we can hardly imagine a context in which the ideas would be equally important.

To show the connection between independent clauses, insert between them either a comma with a coordinating conjunction or a semicolon. (Without one of these devices, you would commit the error called a *comma splice*.)

Coordinating conjunctions *(for, and, nor, but, or, yet, so)* indicate the relation between the independent clauses. Each carries its own logic. You would not use *and* when one clause contradicts the other. You would not use *yet* when you meant *nor*. (An acronym for remembering the coordinating conjunctions is FANBOYS.)

Writers sometimes face the decision of whether to use a conjunction or a semicolon.

> The pollsters predicted a close election, but the smart money predicted a landslide.

> The pollsters predicted a close election; the smart money predicted a landslide.

Often this choice is a matter not of correct grammar but of intuition. The semicolon signals a closer relation between the two clauses. It rivets the reader's attention on the connection. Even if the comma and conjunction seem more natural to you, try a semicolon occasionally. It will give your clauses a tighter link.

Subordination

Prose consisting only of simple sentences and coordination can tire your reader and seem immature. Even though you may add interesting modifiers, the basic beat goes on until the reader marches off. When every idea is in an independent clause, the reader can't distinguish between what is more important and what is less.

Remember our tortured sentence about the raccoons and the farmers? Suppose we had presented the information this way:

> It was a cold January morning, and it was rainy too. It was dawn, and the marauding raccoons reconnoitered. They were blue from the cold, but they were piqued. They were determined to get even. The farmers' measures had been harsh; they had been petty. The raccoons harassed the farmers. The farmers were furious; they were a hot-tempered bunch. And, oh yes, the raccoons were gleeful.

This series of independent clauses fails to identify what is important and what is not. Everything comes at the reader willy-nilly. For all its silliness, our original involuted sentence makes better reading. Intelligent readers will make some educated guesses about the priority of each bit of information. But why should they have to do the work? It is the writer's responsibility to make the point clear and to indicate relative importance, to *subordinate* the less important ideas to the more important. As coordination indicates equal significance of ideas, subordination indicates that one idea is more significant than the other.

> Although it was a cold, rainy January morning, the raccoons were determined to get even with the farmers.

From this sentence the reader knows that the weather and time of day are less important than the raccoons' determination.

When we subordinate, we bring the main idea front and center in an independent clause and push less important ideas back into a dependent clause. The main idea should *always* appear in the independent clause. The subordinate ideas depend on and are secondary to that main idea and should be housed in a dependent clause.

> When I finally left the casino, I had lost my last dollar.

This sentence suggests that the main idea is losing that last dollar, expressed in the main clause. Had the main idea been leaving the casino, the writer would have put it in the main clause.

> After I lost my last dollar, I finally left the casino.

The writer could clearly improve the next sentence by subordinating one idea to the other:

> Hunger had finally driven him wild, and Big Foot Sam began to stalk the Milwaukee suburb looking for food.

There is nothing wrong here—except that there is no weighing of the ideas. Is the hunger more or less important than the stalking? And what is the connection between them? The intelligent reader figures out the meaning and silently rewrites.

> Because hunger had finally driven him wild, Big Foot Sam began to stalk the Milwaukee suburb looking for food.

You can have more than one subordinate idea in a sentence, and you can put them in different places, depending on meaning and style.

> Amelia Earhart, *who disappeared during an attempted round-the-world flight in 1937,* became a role model for many women *when she flew across the Atlantic in 1928.*

To join a dependent clause to the independent clause, use either a subordinating conjunction or a relative pronoun. (One of each appears in the Earhart sentence.) The subordinating conjunctions you are most apt to read and use are *after, although, as, because, before, if, in order to, since, so that, unless, until, when, whenever, where,* and *while.* Each of these indicates a particular relation between the dependent clause and the independent clause—what caused what, when, where, why, and how.

> *Although* he never learned to juggle, Raoul had a certain unwashed charm about him.

> The postman refused to deliver the mail *because* my Great Dane bit him on the rump and tore his britches.

(Caution: some of these words also function as prepositions in prepositional phrases—*before the vending machine, because of you, since Tuesday.* To identify a subordinate clause, look for both a subject and a verb.)

The relative pronoun ties the subordinate clause to a specific noun or pronoun, usually right next to it. The relative pronouns are *that, which, who, whom,* and *whose.*

> The question *that* this essay poses has baffled all the critics *who* have wrestled with it.

Some sentences contain both a subordinating conjunction and a relative pronoun.

> *Because* a small, barred window *that* looked down on the prison yard provided the only light in the cell, he could not read.

As these examples demonstrate, subordination can create flexible, energetic, precise, and subtle sentences. Subordinated sentences can be either *complex*—having one independent clause and one or more subordinate clauses—or *compound-complex*—having at least two independent clauses and one subordinate clause.

Tips for Coordination and Subordination

- Remember that too many simple sentences may sound childish.
- When two thoughts are equal and reinforce each other, coordinate them in a single sentence.
- Use subordination to convey the relative importance of thoughts.
- Put main thoughts in independent clauses and subordinate thoughts in dependent clauses.

EXERCISES FOR COORDINATION AND SUBORDINATION

1. Revise the following sentences as directed.
   a. The boss turned her back, and Carl and Tony stuck out their tongues. (Use subordination.)
   b. Margaret Mead was able to throw herself into tribal life because she possessed remarkable gusto. (Make into a simple sentence.)
   c. After he took a bite out of the Big Apple upon his arrival in New York, he was hooked. (Use coordination.)
   d. There is no other drink as potent as the zombie, and I know that from recent, painful experience. (Use subordination.)

   In a few sentences, discuss each change you made, stating whether it was an improvement or not, and why.

2. Revise the following to make subordinate sentences.
   a. I played the piano, and Mary sang.
   b. Galileo had artistic ability and might have turned out to be a painter or a musician.

    c. Williams voted for Phillips and so Phillips won the election.

    d. Many old people watch the actions of the young with nostalgia, regret, and sometimes horror, but few young people take an equally strong interest in the old.

    e. A history of philosophy and theology could be written in terms of grudges, wounded pride, and aversions, and it would be far more instructive than the usual treatment.

    f. She came up behind the man, and she looked gaunt in the gray, shapeless garment and the sunbonnet, and she wore stained sneakers.

3. Combine each of the following groups of sentences to make one sentence or at most two.

    a. Inflation most drastically affects the lives of people on fixed incomes. These people depend on Social Security. The Social Security laws provide for increased payment based on the cost of living. We should protect that part of the law.

    b. Each year, the swallows come back to Capistrano. They come in the summer. They are small birds. In flight they are graceful. Their plumage is an iridescent black or blue.

    c. The obelisk is a monument. It is four sided. Usually it is made of a single piece of stone. It tapers toward the top. In ancient Egypt, obelisks were dedicated to the sun god.

    d. The Mississippi is a mighty river. It is sometimes as thick and brown as mud. It curls like a snake in motion. It is one of the world's greatest waterways. Vast cities have been built on its banks.

    e. San Marco is a church in Venice. It contains beautiful mosaics of stone, glass, and gold. Its foundations are in watery soil. The air is damp. These factors threaten the permanence of the artworks. They also threaten the stability of the church.

    f. The channel catfish will eat almost anything. It is a scavenger. It is a predator. It can find food by sight and also by touch and taste with its fleshy barbels. You can bait your hook with minnows. You can also use frogs and chicken innards. Artificial lures attract the channel catfish. It is omnivorous.

EMPHASIS: STRENGTHENING THE THOUGHT

Some sentences should have punch; others should not. An essay that came on like gangbusters all the time would soon exhaust and irritate the reader. You want some sentences to end with a bang, some to start with a punch, a few to proceed evenly from start to finish. You want variety.

Ending with a Bang

All of us want occasionally to make a truly emphatic statement, to cue the trumpets and train the spotlights as the big point arrives. The big moment will very likely occur at the end.

> Take the money and run.

Reverse the order of the ideas and they lose that strong emphasis.

> Run after you take the money.

An English sentence generally wants to get somewhere. It wants to gather momentum as it travels.

> Beethoven had been deaf for five years when his Ninth Symphony was first performed.

This sentence is grammatically correct but hardly emphatic. Suppose it had been written this way:

> When his Ninth Symphony was first performed, Beethoven had been deaf for five years.

Here we have the same words, same ideas, same independent clause, same dependent clause, but the different order provides a greater impact. The notion of the great composer's deafness is not slipped in but slammed home.

One of the most important arts a writer can master is that of recognizing where to end a sentence. Each sentence has an element on which it should end: a word or idea after which further words are superfluous. Compare

> Michael Jordan never tires of shooting baskets all the time.

to

> Michael Jordan never tires of constantly shooting baskets.

The sentence should end, as Michael Jordan's jump shots do, with *baskets*. Compare

> If a behavior is not expressly forbidden in the Constitution, the courts of this land are obligated to allow it.

to

> The courts of this land are obligated to allow any behavior not expressly forbidden in the Constitution.

Did the second sentence seem clearer, stronger? That may be because it ended not on the weak *it,* but on the powerful *Constitution.*

Opening with a Punch

Although the ending is the most emphatic part of a sentence, the beginning is a close second. When you start your sentence with a strong idea, you step right out and say, "Here it is, folks—take it or leave it."

> The cold grave is the fate of humankind.

That sentence packs a wallop from the first word. To reverse it would be to weaken it.

> The fate of humankind is the cold grave.

Even for less stunning assertions, the opening can make a reader sit up and take notice.

> Be cheerful while you are alive.
> Stealing apples can lead to trouble.

Some writers muffle a strong opening idea in a construction that weakens the impact.

> There isn't anyone who can stop him now

is less emphatic than

> No one can stop him now

and

> It was frequently said that lust for applause was his worst fault

is bland compared with

> Lust for applause, it was frequently said, was his worst fault.

In this revision, the writer buried the least interesting idea in the middle.

> ### 🖥 Computer Tip
>
> When working on the computer, we usually type so quickly that main ideas come out first, followed by modifying phrases and clauses — for example, "The phone rings whenever I sit down to study." Instead of this *loose* structure, good stylists try to achieve *periodic* sentences — those that place modifiers first and end with the main clause. "Whenever I sit down to study, the phone rings." Better? more interesting? Avoid the word-processed sentence: don't start every sentence with the main thought first.

Even when you put your main idea at the end, start off with the second most important idea. Read these two sentences:

> Because every day the city sees the influx of thousands of people, Mexico City is a sprawling mess.
> Because thousands of people enter the city every day, Mexico City is a sprawling mess.

Sprawling mess is, of course, the most compelling idea in the sentence and rightly goes at the end. But *thousands of people* is the second most compelling and should have the second spotlight, the beginning.

Treating Equal Ideas with Equal Emphasis

So far we have seen sentences in which one idea dominates and therefore deserves the most emphasis. Now we turn to sentences in which two or more related or similar ideas deserve equal billing. We create such sentences by means of parallelism and correlatives.

Performing on the Parallel.   In parallel construction equal or similar ideas are presented in the identical grammatical form.

> I came, I saw, I conquered.

Follow Caesar's lead: put parallel ideas in parallel grammatical form. Parallel construction requires that all like elements be treated in the same manner. They should be expressed in the same grammatical construction, whether clauses or phrases.

Maintaining parallelism is particularly helpful in comparing and contrasting two things. Although the following example contains all the elements of a comparison, the writer has presented them in a fuzzy, unemphatic manner:

> The Sahara was a verdant region in 10,000 B.C., but seven millennia later you would have seen fewer lakes and forests.

Not only is this sentence limp, but also the reader must reorganize elements to figure out exactly what it says. The revision is clear and forceful.

> In 10,000 B.C., the Sahara was a verdant region, but by 3,000 B.C. it had become a desert.

Verdant region and *desert* offer a sharper contrast; starting each clause with a date makes the point clearer; repetition of the subject-verb construction underscores the comparison.

In constructing a list of complicated thoughts, we ignore parallelism at our peril, as the writer of this sentence discovered:

> The main priorities of Hitler's campaign were encouraging the German people, fewer debts, the subjugation of France, and he wanted to become the sole power in Europe.

This is a jumble. The reader has to get in there and straighten it out.

> The main priorities of Hitler's campaign were to encourage the German people, to reduce the German debt, to conquer France, and to become the sole power in Europe.

Now the reader will grasp Hitler's goals more easily.

Although in parallelism all parts must have the same construction, they need not all possess the same length or cadence. Here is a parallel sentence in which one element is much fuller than the other:

> Mississippi depends largely on agriculture, but Georgia depends not only on agriculture but also on business, commerce, and manufacturing.

Maintaining Your Balance.   Balance is a stylistic variation on parallelism. In a balanced sentence, the length and rhythm, as well as the grammatical elements, are the same in both parts. We could find no better illustrations of balance than in the orations of Brutus and Mark Antony over the body of Caesar in Shakespeare's *Julius Caesar*.

> As he was valiant, I honor him; but as he was ambitious, I slew him.

These balanced cadences emphasize Brutus's thoughts, and with them he sways the Roman crowd. In opposition, Antony uses the same technique with even greater effect.

> The evil that men do lives after them;
> the good is oft interred with their bones.

The reader here feels the exquisite and powerful tension of perfect balance—that of an elegant gymnast on the high bar.

We cannot write as Shakespeare did, but we can strengthen even our everyday sentences by balancing the ideas. A sentence like

> Although Stephen Douglas triumphed in the debates, the presidency went to Abraham Lincoln

can become

> Stephen Douglas won the debates, but Abraham Lincoln won the presidency.

Revised, this sentence is now balanced.

Joining with Correlatives.   When you are working out on the parallel bars or trying to balance on the high beam of a sentence, you can find help by turning to correlative conjunctions: *both . . . and, either . . . or, neither . . . nor, not only . . . but also, whether . . . or.* These pairs firmly tie two thoughts together by showing exactly how they are related.

> Both Charlotte Brontë and Virginia Woolf were English novelists.
>
> Either he would get his way, or he would not play.
>
> Neither screaming men nor rivers of blood could stop the war.
>
> Francis Bacon was not only a philosopher but also an essayist and a statesman.

When you use these pairs, you show that the two parts of your thought are equally important and you indicate how they are related. You can forge a stronger and more emphatic bond with correlatives than with the coordinating conjunctions, such as *and, but,* and so on.

Bonding carefully is both grammatically and stylistically important. When using correlative conjunctions, make sure the grammatical form of the first phrase or clause is repeated in the second. It is incorrect to write

Either you are part of the solution or part of the problem.

It should be

Either you are part of the solution or you are part of the problem

or

You are part of either the solution or the problem.

By using correlatives, you can strengthen grammatically correct but uninspired sentences. You can, for instance, change a rather dull sentence like

At Abu Simbel, Ramses II built an immense temple in his own honor and he built another one as an honor for Queen Nefertari

to the livelier

At Abu Simbel, Ramses II built not only an immense temple to honor himself but also one to honor Queen Nefertari.

Caution: The words *both, either,* and *neither* are not always correlative conjunctions; they can also function alone as pronouns or adjectives.

Because both played well, either side could have won, but neither was overwhelming.

Tips for Emphasis
- Remember that the place of greatest emphasis is the end of the sentence. The second most emphatic position is the beginning.
- When you express more than one important thought, put them in parallel grammatical form.
- Balance elements in a sentence to emphasize the equality of the thoughts.
- Correlative conjunctions tie thoughts together, but when you use one of the pair, you must use the other. Be sure the thoughts are expressed in the same grammatical form.

1. Change the following sentences so that the emphasis comes at the end.
   a. The airport is where I would like this taxi to take me.
   b. Virtually all agree that we must find a new source of fuel to be able to meet our increasing energy demands in the future.
   c. The paintings of Giorgione are enjoying a period of immense popularity because there is an exhibition attracting crowds at the museum.

2. Rewrite the following sentences so that the emphasis falls at the beginning.
   a. What it is that's important is doing your homework.
   b. A bad way to bring about change is mob rule.
   c. The languages of the Bantu and the Arabs combined to form Swahili.

3. Rewrite these sentences to emphasize the most important point.
   a. Born in the fifteenth century, Lucrezia Borgia had her second husband murdered, although she was the daughter of a pope.
   b. Pacifists, celibates, and egalitarians, the Shakers have virtually vanished as a religious group, although they were a relatively popular offshoot of the Quakers in the nineteenth century.
   c. Copper is a useful element because it is a good conductor of heat and is used in alloys such as brass and bronze, in addition.

4. Revise the following sentences to make them parallel, balanced, or both.
   a. Football players should be as respected as academic stars, and I think they also ought to be able to feel as good about themselves.
   b. People should save their money so that they can put it in investments of one kind or another, but money earning something would be important too.
   c. Although he thought he was probably extremely prejudiced, behaving in a fair manner was something he knew he was capable of doing.

ECONOMY: REDUCING THE VERBIAGE

Some people write as though they believe that the more words, the better the writing. Of course, that is not true. We have all read passages in which the writing sags from sheer volume of verbiage. In this section we discuss how to write a trim, economical prose.

Excess Weight

"Under the impression," said Mr. Micawber, "that your peregrinations in this metropolis have not as yet been extensive, and that you might have some difficulty penetrating the arcana of the modern Babylon . . . in short," said Mr. Micawber in a burst of confidence, "that you might lose your way. . . ." (Charles Dickens, *David Copperfield*)

Mr. Micawber takes twenty-nine words to say what he did finally say in six. He is a glutton for words. In contrast, good writers look for that one word that will do the work of ten. This restraint is much to their credit, for in English the longer and the more repetitious the statement, the weaker.

Here is a sentence from a student paper that is laboring under a great deal of excess weight:

> Carl Sagan opens up an area of interest to me with the content of his essay, which cites explanations of how monkeys can be observed to learn to communicate through the use of language.

Even the most physically fit reader would sweat under that load.

The writer put the sentence on a diet. If the area is *of interest to me,* then it is *interesting,* period. The *content of his essay* is nothing more than *his essay. Can be observed to learn* is unnecessary and confusing, because the focus is not on someone's observing, but on the monkeys' learning. *The use of language* is only a long way of saying *language.* So now the writer had

> Carl Sagan opens up an interesting area with his essay, which cites explanations of how monkeys can learn to communicate through language.

From thirty-four words down to twenty-two without losing a thing. With such success, the writer became a little bolder and began to change some verbs and nouns.

> In his essay, Carl Sagan explains how monkeys can learn to communicate.

Cites explanations became *explains.* Then she realized that *opens up an interesting area* could be tucked into *essay.* And she didn't need the uninteresting word *interesting.* The words *through language* were simply redundant. She was down to twelve words and a much more vigorous sentence.

In the next few pages, we discuss the kinds of surplus that you can easily jettison.

Blah Phrases.   Sometimes your prose will be invaded by blah phrases, groups of uninteresting words that contribute nothing to your sentence. Whenever you see tiny words in your sentences, beware. *It, that, of, do,* and many more are waiting to weigh down your sentences. They form flocks: *due to the fact that, in the event that, it is also of importance that, when it comes to, in the matter of, has to do with.* Flocks of tiny words can be a bad omen in writing. They burden your reader.

> Due to the fact that the death of the previous captain had to do with a quarrel over a black hen, the effect is that of providing a preview of what Marlow himself will face in the future.

We can eliminate many of these tiny words.

> Because the previous captain died after a quarrel over a black hen, Marlow understands what he will face.

Frequently, we can translate a flock of tiny words into a single one: *in the event that* can become *if,* *has to do with* can become *concerns,* and *when it comes to* can usually shrink to *when.* As in the example, *due to the fact that* can become the simple *because.*

Blah phrases do not necessarily consist of tiny words; they are often simply long ways of expressing things. Sometimes they conceal perfectly good ideas.

> Lincoln decided that he would go to Ford's Theater to see the play even though he had been somewhat disturbed by thoughts that there might be some kind of danger if he went.

We can often find energetic substitutes for these limp strings.

> Despite his premonitions of danger, Lincoln went to Ford's Theater to see the play.

In revising, we can often condense overlong modifying clauses or phrases—especially *who* or *which* clauses that end a sentence—into an adjective or shorter phrase with the same meaning and then embed that replacement elsewhere in the sentence. Finding an equivalent will sometimes take some imagination; just as often, though, it is quite easy.

> The emperor, who had been drinking to the point of intoxication, staggered here and there through Rome, until he eventually found a place to sleep in the garbage dump, which all the Romans used

can easily become

> The emperor, drunk and staggering, eventually slept in Rome's garbage dump.

Redundancy.   *Redundant* refers to words used when the meaning is clear without them. We culled this from a newspaper:

> We will do all we can to do everything in our power to see that the incumbent does not return to Capitol Hill as senator for another term.

We certainly got the point, but we could have gotten it more quickly and enjoyably if we hadn't had to push through unnecessary verbiage.

> We will do everything in our power to see that the incumbent does not return to Capitol Hill.

Repetition is not bad in itself and can sometimes come in handy. We may want to emphasize a point by repeating it, as in "I said no, No, NO!"—but we should be on our guard. Redundancies are useless repetitions; they creep into speech and once there are hard to extricate. How many times have you heard *the general public* instead of *the public, the stadium's total capacity* instead of *the stadium's capacity, personally I think* instead of just *I think,* or *my close personal friend* instead of *my friend?*

Redundancies appear in several guises. Often writers use a modifier for a noun or verb that already contains the modifier's meaning.

> Thomas Edison was the original inventor of the electric light bulb.

Inventor means "originator," and the only thing we call a *light bulb* is electric. We should settle for

> Thomas Edison invented the light bulb.

Sometimes writers pile on adjectives with the same meaning.

> She did not strike him as an open-minded, impartial, or objective judge.

These adjectives mean about the same thing. Any one alone is ample.

> She did not strike him as an impartial judge.

Occasionally an idea already implied in one part of a sentence is made explicit elsewhere.

> Unlike his friend Cassius, who seems to have made his decision quickly in comparison with Brutus, Brutus has made his decision slowly, as his opening words show.

Because this sentence obviously contrasts the two men, the phrase *in comparison with* is redundant. Nor is it necessary to spell out how both men acted. The writer can imply Cassius's quickness by focusing on Brutus's slowness.

> Unlike Cassius, Brutus has made his decision slowly, as his opening words show.

This problem is harder to identify and avoid than simple one-word redundancies; the best prevention is to pay close attention to the meaning of your sentence. Develop your "redundancy detector." Weed out useless repetitions in pursuit of spare, efficient English.

Long, Running Jumps and Expletive Openers.   Look for excess at the beginning of the sentence. Some sentences take a long run before leaping into the thought. This practice is especially common in papers on literature, history, or political science. In the following sentence, so many words run by that the reader would have to watch the replay to remember the subject:

> Clearly, the effect of free agency in the National Football League over the last several years was not conducive to the bankruptcy so many owners claimed to fear, for there are ample profits still being made.

The sentence improves with a shorter run.

> Despite claiming that free agency would bankrupt them, National Football League owners are still profiting greatly.

The problem of the long running jump is particularly acute in sentences that begin with a subordinate clause or a lengthy phrase.

> Even if it were true that you and your mate enjoy a perfect marriage, it would still be just as true that, if certain sociologists are to be believed, there are 125,000 other possible mates who would suit you just as well.

From the revision, we realize that the sentence contains an interesting idea.

> Even if you and your mate enjoy a perfect marriage, certain sociologists claim that 125,000 other possible mates would suit you just as well.

Many long, running jumps start with *It is* or *There are.* This opening is called the *expletive,* meaning that *It* or *There* acts as the formal (though not the real) subject of the sentence. Sometimes expletive openers are the most appropriate way to start a sentence. They are, for instance, wonderful for pointing out things that simply exist. The first line of Jane Austen's *Pride and Prejudice* is

> It is a truth universally acknowledged, that a single man in possession of a good fortune must be in want of a wife.

And sometimes no other opener can capture just the right mood.

> There is a tavern in the town, in the town. . . .

Frequently, however, the expletive conceals more than it clarifies.

> There were occasions when there was governmental agreement to intervene in currency markets and to intervene in a coordinated manner. There was some concerted intervention after January 31 and last week.

Without the expletives, the sentence is much clearer and shorter.

> On occasion the government agreed to intervene in currency markets in a coordinated manner. Some concentrated intervention occurred after January 31 and last week.

We can hardly talk without the expletive, for it gives us time to shape our thoughts. But when we write, and therefore have time to revise, we ought to cast away unnecessary verbiage, and that often means the expletive. We are not suggesting that you never use *It is* or *There are* —they have their uses. You just should not overuse them or fall back on them to avoid a little extra effort or thought.

Wasteful Constructions

The requirements of the thought should determine the size and construction of a sentence. Overextended, a sentence can appear awkward or even incomprehensible.

> When he was in the village, he saw the timbered houses, which had been built by the colonists, who brought the style from England, and they were now occupied by the aborigines, who had entered the village after the colonists had retreated.

In revising, the writer wisely broke the sentence in two.

> When he was in the village, he saw the timbered houses, built by the colonists in a style brought from England. Ever since the colonists had retreated, the aborigines had occupied the houses.

The passage gains in both clarity and strength. Never do violence to the complexity or subtlety of your thought, but when you can shorten and simplify, do so.

The English language offers numerous ways to compress thoughts without changing meaning. Sometimes you can move elements around and substitute a few words for a long clause.

> Dirty tricks in political campaigns are as old as the American republic, and they will probably be around until its end because they have frequently been effective when politicians have resorted to them.

Compressed, the sentence is easier to read.

> Frequently effective, dirty tricks in political campaigns are as old as the American republic and will probably be around until its end.

The writer combines the two independent clauses into one main clause. *Frequently effective* takes the place of *because they have frequently been effective when politicians have resorted to them*. The writer does not mention *politicians* in the revised sentence because the reader can assume the word from the main clause.

We can also use appositives to condense. The word *appositive* refers to a word or group of words placed beside a noun or noun substitute to supplement its meaning. In the sentence "Tom, a fat cat, chased Jerry, a sly mouse," both *a fat cat* and *a sly mouse* are appositives. Using an appositive is an important skill. It can take the place of a wordy clause.

> Paris, which is the largest city in all of France, was founded in the third century B.C. by the Parisii.

can become

> Paris, France's largest city, was founded in the third century B.C. by the Parisii.

Changing a dependent clause to an adjective phrase can often create a shorter, more energetic sentence.

> Philadelphia, which is called the City of Brotherly Love because it was founded as a Quaker colony, served as the American capital during the Revolution

can become

> Founded as a Quaker colony and called the City of Brotherly Love, Philadelphia served as the American capital during the Revolution.

You may have noticed that many of the changes we recommend in this section get rid of a *which* clause. As a general caution, beware the *which* clause, which is much overused, which is a shame, which is an example. *Which* clauses tend to inefficiency as well as windiness.

We are not suggesting you should excise all clauses that begin with *which*. Here, for instance, is an elegantly turned sentence:

> Punishment, which is inflicted by all civilized societies, is not a virtue but a necessity.

The *which* in this case emphasizes the idea that all civilized societies do punish, an idea the writer did not want buried. No serious writer could do without the word *which*. But when saving words, check your *which* clauses.

Tips for Economy

- Look for blah phrases and cut them out of your prose.
- Remove, delete, and get rid of redundancies, repetitions, and instances of saying the same thing twice.
- Beware of overusing expletive openers.
- Remember that the complexity of a sentence should be determined by the complexity of the thought.
- When you can shorten and simplify without distorting meaning, do it.
- Look for *which* clauses when you are searching for excess.

EXERCISES FOR ECONOMY

1. Reduce the following sentences to a minimum without losing sense.
   a. In view of the fact that she is a person who is likely to monopolize the conversational talk, men and women alike have experienced a wish to go elsewhere and in fact do go elsewhere when she is speaking.

b. It is unbelievable for you to say that if a person who smoked marijuana regularly did not fear that he or she might come into conflict with the law in an unpleasant manner and subsequently serve time in a jail, marijuana would very likely be smoked in public places more often than in fact it now is.

c. When people are a bit too quick to do things, it is a fact that they often end up making a mess of what they are trying to do.

d. It is a fact that many human beings, including both men and women, who stay up late at night seeking excitement in its very many guises and in all ways driving themselves a bit too much, may find that later in life their chances to live to a ripe old age have been in point of fact extremely curtailed.

2. Exchange with a partner two paragraphs from an essay you wrote for an earlier assignment. Revise each other's paragraphs for economy. Then revise your own paragraphs. Compare the revisions, and discuss the effectiveness of the changes.

3. Find two- or three-word substitutes for the italicized parts of the following sentences.

a. My father was *a person who was born and lived in Italy before he came to the United States.*

b. He *uses a lot of words that repeat each other.*

c. My mother married *when she was very young and in fact was not even twenty years old.*

d. Richard Nixon was *the thirty-seventh president of the United States and was the only president the people of this country ever elected who resigned.*

4. Using appositives and without losing information, revise these sentences to make them less wordy.

a. Auburn is a university in the state of Alabama, and it has an agricultural school and an architecture school.

b. Abraham Lincoln, who was a citizen of Illinois though he was born in Kentucky, was a lawyer who was elected the sixteenth president of the United States.

c. The Napa Valley, which is located just north of the city of San Francisco, is famous for many varieties of wine, which have been praised highly.

d. Emma Thompson, who is from England and is a talented actress, starred in the movie *Sense and Sensibility,* which was based on a Jane Austen novel with the same title.

VIGOR: MAKING PROSE ENERGETIC

Some writing seems crisp and energetic; other writing seems limp and tired. We have already dealt with some of the causes of limp, tired writing, such as imprecision and verbosity. Here we give direct advice on how to make your writing more dynamic.

Be Active

The verb makes things happen in your sentence. It builds muscle. It generates energy. If your sentence begins to sag, blame the verb. If it zings home its meaning, credit the verb. Nurture your verb as though the life of your sentence depended on it.

Active and Passive Voice.   English verbs come in two voices: active and passive.

> The fire fighter grabbed the hose.
>
> The hose was grabbed by the fire fighter.

The first sentence is in the active voice. The subject *(the fire fighter)* performs the action *(grabbed)*. The second sentence is in the passive voice. The subject of this sentence *(the hose)* receives the action *(was grabbed)*. The passive consists of the past participle of a verb *(grabbed)* preceded by some form of the verb *to be (was)*.

Good writers prefer the active voice most of the time. It is clearer and more direct, and it packs more punch. Also, it immediately identifies the actor.

> Amy Tan wrote *The Joy Luck Club*.
>
> Professor Beerbohm spilled coffee on my term paper.

We know exactly and immediately who did what. Passive voice tends to be unemphatic and wordy.

> *The Joy Luck Club* was written by Amy Tan.

It is sometimes evasive.

> Coffee was spilled on my term paper.

Thus does Professor Beerbohm escape blame.

Much official writing resorts to the passive voice, frequently erasing all signs of personal responsibility.

> It has been decided that farm subsidies must be decreased.

This sentence makes it sound as though a disembodied law of nature made this fiscal decision rather than the people responsible for legislation. If the writers recast their sentence in the active voice, they would have to admit that

> The congressional committee has decided to decrease farm subsidies.

Some student writers employ the passive because they think it sounds more important.

It is agreed by most scholars that the superego was meant by Freud to be portrayed as a force by which the id is prevented from getting what it wants.

Four passive constructions in a single sentence are not so much weighty as wooden. In an effort to remove all evidence of the passive, the student revised the sentence.

Most scholars agree that Freud meant to portray the superego as a force that prevents the id from getting what it wants.

She reduced thirty words to twenty-two and wrote a much clearer, more direct, more active, more enjoyable, and more informative sentence.

The passive voice is not, however, always bad. You should not tie yourself into a pretzel to avoid it. Sometimes it is awkward to state the subject of the sentence. If you just want to say

Los Angeles is well supplied with water

it would distort your meaning to twist the sentence into the active voice this way:

Canals, conduits, pipes, and a series of reservoirs supply ample water to Los Angeles.

When an important baseball game is canceled because of the weather, it is only natural to write

The game at Fenway Park was called on account of fog and rain

instead of

The chief umpire and the rest of the umpiring crew called the game at Fenway Park on account of fog and rain.

When used with finesse and restraint, the passive voice can even add variety to prose.

The slumbering household was slowly awakened by the twittering of tiny birds.

The problem is misuse. Pseudoscientific and pseudo-official prose is everywhere, tempting writers into the passive voice. Resist. Write in the active voice whenever you can.

Vigorous Verbs. Many dynamic verbs are vanishing into extinction. And some of the best are converting into nouns, leaving the work of sentences to weak, deflated verbs. In this sentence,

The police made an investigation into reports of explosions near the Capitol the writer has turned a fine verb—*to investigate*—into a noun—*investigation*—and the uninteresting verb *to make* has taken over the action. Result: more words, less action. The rewrite,

> The police investigated reports of explosions near the Capitol

saves three words and restores the action.

Some writers apparently abhor the powerful and direct use of good verbs. But how much stronger our prose would be if we changed

I have admiration for	to	I admire
You will show deference to		You will defer to
She is in need		She needs
They gave approval		They approved

Writers are sometimes seduced from specific verbs by fancy-sounding-general verbs, such as *interact, relate, impact,* and *deal with.* Unfortunately, in meaning almost anything, verbs like these mean almost nothing.

> I interacted with Alex yesterday.

What did the writer do with Alex? Did she kiss him? stab him? hand him a subpoena? All these would be *interactions,* but no one knows exactly what happened.

Likewise, *impact* as a verb has almost no impact.

> Mr. Smith's failure to meet his debt obligations has impacted on his reputation.

Was the effect good or was it bad? You can always replace *impact* with a more specific action.

> Mr. Smith's failure to meet his debt obligations has hurt his reputation.

Perhaps less blatant but still debilitating is writing that contains an abundance of general-purpose verbs, such as *go, seem, do, make, have,* and *become.* While useful beasts of burden, these verbs cannot carry the specific meanings that vivid prose demands. As much as possible, good writers choose verbs that tell exactly what the action was. This sentence badly needs a good verb:

> Ingesting plant fiber has a positive effect on the risk of heart disease.

Just what does *has a positive effect on* really mean here? Will the risk of heart disease increase or decrease? Is there a verb out there that will make the point more clearly? Perhaps *decreases* will do; it is certainly more active than *has* and tells us something more precise about that plant fiber.

Ingesting plant fiber decreases the risk of heart disease.

When you revise your prose, seek verbs with energy.

Not *to Be*.   You may have noticed that forms of *to be* crop up frequently in inactive sentences. This verb links the subject of the sentence to a word or words that describe the subject's condition.

> Max is a friendly Doberman pinscher. He really is.
>
> The town with the lowest zip code number in the United States is Agawam, Massachusetts.
>
> I am Gunga Din.

The little verb *to be* is one of the most necessary verbs in English. Many sentences would not be without it. For instance, you couldn't convey a complete thought by saying

> I hungry!
>
> The baby disgruntled!
>
> The bathtub overflowing!

With so many forms of *to be* around, however, writers can fall into the habit of using them for almost everything. Verb deflation frequently occurs because we use forms of the verb *to be* followed by a noun followed by a preposition.

> She was understanding of
>
> This episode is an example of

These phrases have lost the services of the vigorous verbs *understood* and *exemplifies*.

> We tend to overwork the verb *to be* in other ways as well.

> Demosthenes was a more effective speaker than Cato was.
>
> If it had not been for the unfair taxes the British imposed, there might not have been an American Revolution.

We can turn a static condition into an action by substituting for the verb *to be*.

> Demosthenes spoke more effectively than Cato did.
>
> Without unfair British taxation, the Americans might not have revolted.

Very long and complicated sentences often rely too heavily on forms of the verb *to be*.

> Stein is saying that American governing philosophy is in a situation where it is becoming an area that is under the domination of men who are not really sincere about what is good for the public, men who are

> attracted only by what is advantageous to them and to the special interests that it is their function to represent.

As this sentence shows, when a writer overuses the verb *to be,* other problems frequently emerge. The revision, short and to the point, eliminates many *to bes,* the passive voice, verbosity, and confusion.

> Stein maintains that the men who have dominated American governing philosophy care less for the public good than for their own advantage and that of the special interests they represent.

In revising a first draft, identify each occurrence of *to be* (don't forget to include *is, am, have been,* and other forms), and search for a better word. You won't be able to change every one (nor should you), but try especially hard to reword when you see bunches of circles.

Prefer People

Imagine being confronted with the following sentence:

> Renouncing a former state to obtain real existence is an adjustment requiring understanding of what is seen, comprehending its causes, and coping with it.

Can you figure out who is doing the renouncing, or who must adjust, understand, comprehend, and cope? The sentence is depopulated, yet the writer seems to be writing about human beings.

Now look at the revision:

> In order to renounce their former state and improve themselves, clients must understand how they perceive the world, why they perceive it that way, and how they can cope with it.

Although a little longer, this sentence is much clearer and more interesting. We know who is doing what.

Why did the writer depopulate that sentence? Perhaps he thought impersonal prose sounded more serious. But aren't you more interested in reading about what people do or have done to them? Wouldn't you rather read *The actress playing Hedda Gabler made the audience weep* than *The performance of the role of Hedda Gabler brought tears?* Even a small move toward putting people in a sentence can make a difference. People add strength and vibrancy to your sentences.

Impersonal writing can be both boring and confusing, as is this passage on how tennis players should choose the food they eat:

> Careful selection of foods containing all the proper nutrients is important for maintaining health and adequate energy. Whether food is prepared at home or eaten out, resistance to disease can be increased and energy rate maximized through careful nutritional food selection.

Tennis players, anywhere? Not a person within a mile of those sentences, although people ought to be doing almost everything in them. You have probably spotted some of the ways the writer has kept the passage impersonal: overuse of the passive voice, nouns where there might be verbs, too many *to be*s. It doesn't make you want to rush out and try the diet, does it?

A revision puts the people back where they belong.

> To stay healthy and full of energy, tennis players must select foods that contain all the proper nutrients. Whether they cook their meals at home or eat out, they can better resist disease and maximize their energy by carefully choosing nutritional foods.

We are not claiming that every sentence must contain a person. It would be absurd, perhaps impossible, to try to stick people into sentences such as

> Art is the accomplice of love. (Remy de Gourmont, 1858–1915)

or

> Land is immortal, for it harbors the mysteries of creation. (Anwar Sadat, 1918–1981)

When people are involved, though, good writers put the people in. And they put them in as human beings, not as abstractions or congregations. When speaking, we wouldn't say *members of the student body* or *members of the electorate*. We would say *students* and *voters*. We ought to follow this natural inclination when we write.

We can go a step further and use the good old names for occupations and professions. When we write *teacher* or even *professor,* we picture a human being, perhaps even someone we know, but when we refer to an *educator,* we imagine a faceless bureaucrat. When we write *lawyer,* again we picture a person, but when we say *legal advisor,* we don't even pretend a human being is concealed inside that gray eminence. Indeed, our prose takes on a slightly gray quality itself.

We don't advise you to make everything in your writing sound chatty. As we discuss in Chapter 12, there is a tone appropriate to college writing, and chatty it isn't. But neither is it depopulated. When possible and where appropriate, keep your sentences alive with people.

Say It Straight

Even with energetic verbs and people, prose can be flat and feeble. Often, the problem is indirectness. Many of us apparently like to hold off saying what we came to say or try to conceal our thought beneath a variety of indirect constructions. Just as English tends to move straight ahead from subject to verb to object, it also works best when it goes straight to the point. Our moral here is "Say it straight." Readers don't have time to play hide and seek with thoughts. You can help them understand your meaning.

We discuss here three bad habits that often block understanding.

Disclaimers. No doubt you have read *opinions to the contrary notwithstanding, it is conceivable* (or *arguable* or *possible*) *that one might say, an opinion might be hazarded that,* and phrases such as these. They may seem like security blankets, but they are more like smoke screens. Some of these disclaimers self-destruct if you think about them; our two favorites are *needless to say* and the immediately comic *needless to repeat.*

Weak-Hearted Negatives. As George Orwell pointed out in his essay "Politics and the English Language," overuse of the negative is a form of circumlocution— "talking around" your meaning. Orwell quotes this sentence:

> I am not, indeed, sure whether it is not true to say that the Milton who once seemed not unlike a seventeenth-century Shelley had not become, out of an experience ever more bitter in each year, more alien to the founder of that Jesuit sect which nothing could induce him to tolerate.

Once you untie all the negatives, you have the following (we think):

> Out of an experience more bitter each year, the Milton who once resembled a seventeenth-century Shelley had come to resemble the founder of that Jesuit sect which nothing could induce him to tolerate.

Less outrageous, but more frequent, is the use of the negative to fog a disagreeable opinion: *They did not honor their debts as they had promised* instead of *They reneged,* or *She did not play her clarinet very admirably* instead of *She played her clarinet abominably.* In each case, the first may sound more polite, but the positive is stronger and clearer.

Think of the statements *The president was not inarticulate* or *The book is not uninteresting.* The reader has to cancel out the double negative and even then cannot be sure what the sentences mean. Was the president articulate or only a cut above mumbling? Is the book interesting or just this side of the trash basket?

Euphemisms. Writers of euphemisms substitute neutral terms or agreeable words for words with strong or unpleasant associations. They say *salvage engineers* when they mean *junk dealers, remains* when they mean *corpse, fib* when they mean *lie,* and *water closet, comfort station, necessary room,* or almost anything else when they mean *toilet.*

Euphemisms sometimes spare feelings—to say *I'm sorry your mother passed on* might be gentler than to say *I'm sorry your mother died.* Too frequently, though, people slip in euphemisms to conceal meaning. Hitler used the term *rectification of the frontier* when he forced thousands of people to march miles from their homes; some government bureaus have referred to murder, execution, or assassination as *termination with extreme prejudice.* These phrases conceal the awful truth: Hitler uprooted large populations; someone killed someone.

You should try to say exactly what you mean in the most honest manner you can. Try to be graceful rather than crude, of course, but say it straight.

Tips for Vigor

- Prefer the active voice to the passive.
- Seek vigorous, fresh verbs, and avoid tired, general ones.
- Don't overuse forms of *to be.*
- Put people in any sentences in which they can fit.
- Avoid disclaimers, weak-hearted negatives, and euphemisms.

EXERCISES FOR VIGOR

1. Rewrite the following sentences to make them more vigorous.
   a. The decision was announced by the referee, and loud cheers were emitted by Jack Dempsey's supporters.
   b. Open-heart surgery will be performed on me tomorrow.
   c. Absconding with the family heirlooms was the accusation made against Señor Ortega by Señora Sanchez.
   d. Asia was overrun by Genghis Khan and the hordes of warriors who had been enticed by him to join his army.

2. Replace the weak verbs in these sentences with more energetic ones.
   a. He made a very tasty sauerbraten and then gave a party.
   b. My cousin went through India in eight days and then came home in a big hurry because she had a job to go to.
   c. Admiral Darlan, who had been the head of the French navy during the Second World War, seemed to become a different person when he became minister of defense in the Vichy government.
   d. My decision was to go to the head of the department and to make a strong case for a raise in what I got in my job.

3. Reread an essay you've written recently and circle every use of the verb *to be.* Then revise the whole essay, using *to be* as little as possible.

4. Revise the following sentences to make them more direct.
   a. One is not unwilling to hang-glide although one is not unfamiliar with the difficulties one may encounter.

b. When in the vicinity of vipers capable of making what might be called a fatal attack, I have a tendency to experience unpleasant emotions and to prepare to exit as quickly as possible, in a manner of speaking.

c. Once the animal custodian picked up the little dog, it was not unlikely that in a short period of time the underground engineer would be called in to perform, if he has not been intemperate with alcohol lately, though far be it from me to claim to know about his private habits.

11

Working with Words

When we write, we are always choosing words. Most of our words just appear on the page, without our quite knowing where they come from. Crucial moments arise in writing, however, when we consciously rack our brains for exactly the right word. *Diction* is the art of choosing that right word. It is the critical art of finding words that will present our thought exactly, clearly, and attractively.

Although words are neither good nor bad but only used well or badly, every word counts. We want to repeat that: every word counts, the ones that just appear on the page *and* the ones you worry over. Note the different meanings in these sentences:

A dog has fleas.

The dog had fleas.

The dog has the fleas.

Every single word, including the verb as it changes and the article *the,* carries specific meaning. In simple sentences like these, we have no problem. As the ideas become more complicated, however, so does the job of choosing the right words to fit them. As we write and revise, we fret over our choices, conscious and unconscious.

Writers have in common with musicians a reliance on their hearing. We have all known people with such perfect pitch that they can tell what note the doorbell hits when it rings, and we have all known people who sound as though they are moaning for help when they sing "Jingle Bells." Similarly, some people have a talent, a good ear, for words. They instinctively go for the right one at the right time. Most of us, however, are not so blessed. We often put the wrong preposition with a verb or derail a sentence with the wrong noun.

Like our ear for music, our ear for words can be trained. People who thought they couldn't carry a tune have learned to sing. And people who thought they could never be happy with pen in hand have learned to write well. This chapter should help you to train your ear and your eye for good diction.

Our first piece of advice is this: read and read and read some more. Read aloud. You should read in all directions, but be sure you read good writing. If you are a speed-reader, slow down and listen to the words. Try to feel their shape and size and strength and rhythm. Notice the company they keep. When an excellent stylist uses a phrase you have never used, say it aloud several times and use it in a sentence. Analyze a superb essay. If the words seem strange or awkward, write them down in a notebook. Try them out.

WRITING WITH PRECISION: SEEKING THE EXACT WORD

All good prose is precise. Good writers don't settle for a word that is nearly or almost what they mean. They want the exact word. As a soprano would be embarrassed to hit C-sharp when she meant to hit C, so a careful writer avoids words that do not communicate the precise meaning.

Connotation and Denotation

Most words have a number of different meanings or shades of meaning. Take the word *gross*. It derives from the Latin *grossus*, which meant "thick." It still means thick. But it has also developed many additional meanings. To accountants and economists, it means an overall total, as in *gross national product*. To merchants, it means twelve dozen of anything ordered. To many people, it means anyone big or overweight. To some, however, it means something disgusting.

Words both *denote*—indicate or point to something in the world— and *connote*—suggest a range of meanings surrounding that something. *Denotation* is the explicit meaning. *Connotation* refers to all that is associated with the word, the feelings and references it calls up.

Let's look at the word *government*. According to the primary dictionary definition, *government* means "an organization that exercises authority over a particular political unit." That is its denotation, on which everyone would agree. Its connotations vary, however. When some people think of *government,* they think of exorbitant taxes, corruption, and officials meddling in their private lives. To them the word connotes something bad. But when others think of *government,* they think of law and order, care for the poor, protection and security. To them, *government* connotes something good.

Connotation is composed of the suggestions and feelings that each word carries with it. It is molded by a word's history—is it from Old English, like *half-wit,* or from Latin and Italian via French, like *prestidigitation?* Each word has been shaped by the way people habitually use it. For instance, people have *hangovers,* but roofs have *overhangs.* Even a word's physical properties—such as sound and length—help determine its connotation. Think of *hide, smug,* and *rump* as opposed to *obfuscate, self-satisfied,* and *derriere.* Because of all these shades of suggestion, English has few if any exact synonyms, that is, words with precisely the same meaning. Brothers and sisters, yes, but no identical twins.

If a word has several near-synonyms, chances are that each, while denoting the same thing, will connote something slightly different. *Police officer* denotes the same thing as *cop, flatfoot,* and—to those who disliked them in the late 1960s—*pig,* but the connotation worsens with each synonym.

Word choice depends on the situation and the writer's purpose. Was the officer who gave you the speeding ticket a *slender police officer* or a *scrawny pig?* The first phrase has a touch of delicacy and respect; the second suggests you think you were framed and want to fight.

Simple choices, like that between *police officer* and *pig,* don't cause much trouble. When the words are more abstract or remote, however, diction becomes a fine art. Welfare recipients receive *handouts, payments,* or *entitlements,* depending on who is talking. We constantly read, hear, and use phrases such as *corporate welfare, affirmative action,* and *developing nations,* and words such as *materialism, socialism,* and *gay.* All are loaded with connotation.

We don't have a formula for choosing the right word every time. Good word choosers develop their skill through years of training. We do, however, have a few suggestions.

First, handle with care. Some words have acquired such a weight of meaning that no two people would agree on their proper definition; writers who use them without thinking risk confusing and misleading their readers.

Second, define your terms. If, for instance, your essay is on entitlement programs, don't assume that your reader will correctly interpret the phrase *safety net*. Fairly early in the essay, provide a definition: "By *safety net*, I mean a package of government benefits that would bring the recipient's income to the government-designated poverty level." (See "Definition: Establishing What a Word Means" in Chapter 8 for a discussion of definition.)

Finally, use your dictionary. It can help you choose the word with the right connotation.

Using Your Dictionary

The great dictionary maker himself, Samuel Johnson (1709–1784), said, "Dictionaries are like watches; the worst is better than none, and the best cannot be expected to go quite true." While it may not "go quite true," a good dictionary can be a writer's valuable friend, and most writers keep one close at hand.

You may be surprised at all you can find in a dictionary. It will give you preferred pronunciation—sometimes you have a choice, as with *pajamas* and *advertisement*. It will tell you where to divide between syllables—is it *in-nards* or *inn-ards?* It will provide synonyms and antonyms. If it is a fairly good dictionary, it will also trace the derivation of a word, whether it comes from Greek, Latin, Old English, or another language, and what prefix or suffix is appropriate for it—whether, for instance, we *legitimize* or *legitimate*.

The surprise about good dictionaries is that they can inform us about not only denotation but also connotation. The word *tolerate*, for example, has several meanings in most dictionaries: (1) to allow without opposing or prohibiting; (2) to recognize and respect the rights, opinions, and practices of others; (3) to bear or put up with someone or something not especially liked. Follow these denotations a bit and you will arrive at the word's various connotations: indifference, appreciation, mild hostility.

The *Oxford English Dictionary*, known familiarly as the *OED*, is a veritable education in itself. It contains nearly a half million English words and over a million and a half quotations illustrating their use at various times in history. It traces the development of words and their meanings in detail. Not many of us can afford to own this publication, but almost every library has a copy. Browse through the *OED* and learn more about the world of words.

Another storehouse of words is the thesaurus, popular with writers because it contains synonyms (and often antonyms). At this point, we want to flash a giant caution sign. A thesaurus is a good servant but a bad master. What it gives you are all the rough equivalents for your word; what it does not give are differences in connotation. Beware: a near-synonym may have the proper denotation but a wrong connotation.

Computer Tip

Be especially aware of the temptation to overuse the thesaurus when writing on a computer. Many word processing programs offer a thesaurus and a spell checker but not a full-fledged dictionary. Keep a dictionary by your computer.

Some writers are afraid of repeating a word, so they run to the thesaurus for a synonym. Or they fear that their vocabulary doesn't sound intelligent enough, and the next time *policeman* pops up in an essay on crime prevention, it appears as *constable* or *minion of the law*. Imagine a love letter:

Dear Laura,
    I have been sitting next to you all day and just can't believe how pretty you are. Your voice is like music, and your eyes are like moonlight. I know that beauty isn't skin-deep, for I saw you laughing at our teacher, which shows good sense. I think we could get on well together. Let me know what you think.
                                                    Love,
                                                    Name Withheld

Fearing that Laura would find his note unexciting, the writer scurried to his thesaurus. There, of course, he found all sorts of replacements for his plain words. The trouble was, the resulting stew of mismatched words would have sent even the most receptive Laura into paroxysms of laughter.

Dear Laura,
    I have been straddling you daily and simply cannot fathom how comely you are. Your vociferation approximates a sonata, and your peepers resemble lunar illumination. I comprehend that pulchritude isn't subcutaneous, for I ogled you sniggering at our pedagogue, which illustrates beneficent cranial capacity. I formulate in my mind that we would have a positive response to each other. Inform me of what you reason about.
                                                    Charity,
                                                    Name Withheld

Luckily for this writer, his pedant/instructor/educator intercepted the missive/epistle/correspondence and saved him some embarrassment/incommodity/loss of face, for which he was profoundly/deeply/intensely grateful.

If you use a thesaurus, use it along with—not in place of—your dictionary and your own imagination. Use it to remind yourself of what you already know—to draw out a word momentarily forgotten or to help you find a more exact word. Don't use it to inflate your language.

The Idiom

Do we go to town or downtown or uptown? Should we nurse our cold or nurture it or nourish it? When we are under the weather, are we out in the rain or inside the house? When we pass an exam, do we politely say hello? When a word is appropriate, and in what context, is a matter not of decree but of accepted usage—idiom.

Idiom refers to the way native speakers speak a language and good writers write it. Idiom is the customary way people put words together, the peculiar twist that a group gives to its language. Americans look under the *hood* of the car and put their tools in the *trunk,* while the British look under the *bonnet* and put their tools in the *boot.* Southerners say, "I'm fixing to eat supper," but a northerner might say, "I'm about to start dinner."

Idiom is the hardest part of a language to master. It does not follow rules the way grammar does. In answer to the question *Who wants to shampoo the Great Dane?* most of us will cry, *Not me*—bad grammar but good idiom. And *Cecil spent all his hardly earned cash* is good grammar but bad idiom.

If you grew up speaking English, its ins and outs are second nature to you. Even so, you may still be uncertain about some idioms. Again, use your dictionary if a phrase you have written does not sound right to you. Ask a roommate or classmate. And keep an ear out—not *on* or *in* or *at*—for the often irrational twists and turns that idiom takes.

Tips for Writing with Precision

- Know the difference between what a word denotes and the connotation it carries.
- Handle overloaded words with care.
- Define your terms to avoid confusing or misleading your reader.
- Use your dictionary for preferred pronunciation, meanings, syllabication, synonyms, antonyms, and derivation.
- Resort to a thesaurus with a critical eye and consult it along with —not in place of—your dictionary. Never use a thesaurus merely to avoid repetition or to inflate your prose.

████████ **EXERCISES FOR WRITING WITH PRECISION** ████████████

1. For each of the following pairs of synonyms, write a sentence in which either would fit: *hold/grasp, evening/dusk, throttle/choke, obsequious/humble, humiliate/embarrass, refuse/garbage, teeth/dentures, inebriated/drunk, crazy/insane*. Discuss the connotations and analyze how the sounds of these words do or do not reinforce their meanings.

2. For each of the following phrases, provide at least three synonyms that carry different connotations.
   a. unwillingness to change one's mind
   b. an object that costs less than one expected
   c. not telling the truth
   d. one's parent of the opposite sex
   e. a member of the House of Representatives

3. Go to a large dictionary, preferably the *OED,* and look up the following pairs of words: *empathy/sympathy, enormity/enormousness, notoriety/notoriousness, uninterested/disinterested, ensure/insure.* In a single paragraph, compare the meanings of each pair.

4. Practice using a large dictionary by investigating the derivations of the following words: *engineer, sarcasm, gossip, oxygen, circle, corespondent.* Write a coherent paragraph about two of them, tracing their meanings from their earliest usage to the present.

AN APPROPRIATE PROSE: LANGUAGE THAT FITS

All of us want our prose to express our sensitivity, our distinctiveness, and our taste. At the same time, we want what we say to fit both the reader and the subject. Yet we sometimes slip into language that does not express what we mean, let alone who we are, and is clearly inappropriate for the occasion. In the pages that follow, we examine ways to choose the right words and avoid sour notes.

Specific and General

The difference between the specific and the general is the difference between *Aunt Tabitha* and *woman,* or *bow tie* and *item of clothing.* A specific term refers to the individual item, the thing itself. A general term encompasses all the items of a kind or class.

These are not absolute terms but relative, a matter of degree rather than of opposites. *Bow tie* is not as specific as *purple polka-dot bow tie,* and *woman* is not as general as *living creature* or *thing.*

In the following lists, you can see increasing specificity:

crime, felony, murder, first-degree murder, the murder of a man in a purple polka-dot bow tie

food, meal, entrée, chicken Kiev, burned chicken Kiev, the chicken Kiev Aunt Tabitha burned last night

We need general terms to show relationships and concepts, and we need specific terms to appeal to the reader's senses and create exact images.

As our words become more specific, they sharpen and solidify the image in the mind of the reader. The reader can picture the prostrate body of the man in the bow tie, Aunt Tabitha weeping over the charred chicken. The more specific the language, the closer the reader will come to understanding what we mean. And to enjoying what we write.

Sometimes writers use general terms when something specific and pictorial would serve much better:

The official sent fire-fighting equipment to the scene of the fire.

A few specifics could make the sentence more visual, more interesting, more informative:

Governor Richardson ordered bulldozers, fire trucks, and air transport carriers to the forest fire near Smithville.

A sentence such as

Emperor Nero of Rome was obese

is correct, but

Emperor Nero of Rome weighed 360 pounds

is more vivid. *Obese* only skitters across the surface of Nero's fatness; the revision gives us the fat emperor pound for pound. A writer would bore us with

An official said that Biotechtronics suffered recently from financial problems

but might get us to read further with

The Biotechtronics CEO said that the company had suffered record-breaking losses in the third quarter, largely due to unanticipated health benefits costs.

Specific terms help our writing come alive for the reader, but we cannot always be discussing a particular chicken or a particular murder. We may want to discuss the qualities common to all chickens, or ideas about felonies in general, not just murder. The more complex the ideas and relationships we want to discuss, the more necessary are general terms.

To *generalize* means to think of a quality apart from a particular context and to construct an idea that will cover the individual items that share the quality. "Politics is the art of the possible," said Otto von Bismarck, generalizing from his experience as the first chancellor of Germany and saying a great deal about politics everywhere. "The beauty of the world has two edges," said the novelist Virginia Woolf, "one of laughter, one of anguish, cutting the heart asunder." The sentence is full of general ideas, such as beauty, laughter, anguish, ideas we can all understand. We cannot make serious statements without such words, and it would be absurd to try.

Good serious writers, however, ground the general in the specific. They explain difficult general ideas by reference to the specific. The evolutionary biologist Stephen Jay Gould handles general ideas as a scientist but grounds them in the concrete. In discussing Freud's idea that to ensure civilization, human beings must "renounce more and more of our innate selves," Gould writes,

> Freud's argument is a particularly forceful variation on a ubiquitous theme in speculations about "human nature." What we criticize in ourselves, we attribute to our animal past. These are the shackles of our apish ancestry—brutality, aggression, selfishness; in short, general nastiness. What we prize and strive for (with pitifully limited success), we consider as a unique overlay, conceived by our rationality and imposed upon an unwilling body. Our hopes for a better future lie in reason and kindness—the mental transcendence of our biological limitations. "Build thee more stately mansions, O my soul." *(Ever Since Darwin)*

Gould makes these complex ideas clear by using specific, familiar language. Having clarified what Freud meant, he can now refer simply to "Freud's argument." He concludes with a line from a once-popular poem by Oliver Wendell Holmes.

Once you have made your point clear, you will often use a general term to stand for that point. In a discussion of the fire in Smithville, for instance, you would not continue to say "bulldozers, fire trucks, and air transport carriers." You would just say "the equipment." First, however, be sure you bring your ideas out into the concrete world you share with your reader. Specific terms bring writing to life.

Qualifiers

Three kinds of qualifiers—vague, timid, loud—are often verbal fillers rather than informative elements in a written sentence. Often writers use words such as *very, actually,* and *really* to pump up adjectives. But these vague qualifiers frequently have the opposite effect. The unadorned

That rhinoceros was huge

suggests more hugeness than

That rhinoceros was really very huge.

How big is *very?* How real is *really?* It was huge, period. By overusing vague qualifiers, we diminish the power of language.

Cousins to the vague qualifiers are the timid qualifiers. How big is *a bit?* To what degree is *somewhat?* Is *a lot* the same as *a good deal,* or is it more like *much?* How much is *rather?* Like their kin, these words pop up almost unbidden. They may save you the work of being precise, but they can blur your writing. If we say *Our friend is somewhat of a hypochondriac,* do we suggest one major complaint a week or a dozen minor ones each day? You should not pretend to a certainty you do not possess of course, but use these qualifiers only when they convey your thought as precisely as possible.

Loud qualifiers also add verbiage without much meaning. "Oh wow! That is absolutely the most *fantastic* thing I ever heard! That's just *incredible!"*

The problem with constant emphasis, whether in writing or in speech, is that it fails to make distinctions. What did the person find so *fantastic* and *incredible?* Did someone rise from the dead? That is indeed incredible. Did a rich uncle die, bequeathing an island off the coast of Greece? That does sound like a fantasy. If, however, the writer just attended a movie, maybe it was only *good,* or—to be more informative—maybe *the acting was effective* or *the camera work helped convey the mood. Incredible*s and *fantastic*s do not tell what somebody thinks. "How was the movie?" "Fantastic!" "But how was the movie?"

Short Words and Long Words

Winston Churchill said, "Short words are best and the old words when short are best of all." Most great literary stylists agree. Yet some writers think that the more complicated and unusual the language, the more serious the thought. Windiness is not elegance, however, and difficulty is not profundity. It is no more elegant and profound to say *Precipitation appears imminent* than to say *It's going to rain.*

Many of the shorter, plainer words in English come from Old English: they preserve the Anglo-Saxon in our language, growling our practical and durable monosyllables: *house, thief, stone, want, help.* Such words are concrete, familiar, and useful. *I want to get an ice cream cone* is more direct and understandable than *I desire to procure a frozen gelatinous confection; want* and *get* are the functional words you need in this sentence, not the overdressed *desire* and *procure,* and that *gelatinous confection* sounds nauseating.

The thesaurus provides a list of synonyms for *get,* including *procure, secure,* and *acquire.* These words came into English later than *get,* via

Latin and French. Like most travelers of this route, they are longer than their Old English near-equivalent and have connotations that *get* does not. The dictionary tells us that *get* is a "very general term and may or may not imply initiative." *Procure,* however, suggests "effort in obtaining something"; *secure* implies downright "difficulty in getting"; *acquire* has it easy by comparison, implying "an addition to what is already possessed." Good writers would neither abandon *get* just to have more letters and syllables nor use *get* when they mean *procure* or *secure.*

Keep in mind this simple rule from George Orwell: "Never use a long word where a short one will do."

This does not mean that you must speak in Tarzanlike monosyllables. Longer is better when that is the clearest way to say something. Here is Orwell writing clearly but not in monosyllables:

> Now, it is clear that the decline of a language must ultimately have political and economic causes: it is not due simply to the bad influence of this or that individual writer. ("Politics and the English Language")

No one would call that sentence pretentious. The "long words" *(language, ultimately, political, economic, influence, individual)* are all familiar ones, and Orwell obviously used them because they are the ones he needed. No other words mean what those words mean.

If we used only one-syllable words, our essays would be about as subtle as telegrams. Long words often help us to be precise and to convey the right nuance.

> Karl Marx said that rich people keep poor people from being free

is direct, but

> Karl Marx's economic theories depict the efforts of the powerful capitalist classes to oppress the workers of the world

tells us more, and more exactly. *Capitalist classes,* for example, suggests more than just rich people, and *oppress* implies both action and purpose. The longer sentence is truer to Marx's thought. Orwell would have agreed with this corollary to his little rule: use a long word when it, and only it, is the word you need.

Another rule we think Orwell would have agreed with is this: when two words bear more or less the same meaning, select the one more familiar and natural to you and your reader. Prefer *limit* to *circumscribe, the rest* to *the remainder,* and *use* to *employ.* Remember that English has a great heritage of short, direct, familiar words. They are where the language began. When we need to be clearest in our writing, they are waiting for us.

Prioritizing Dejargonization

Technical terms emerge in every discipline. They take the place of lengthy descriptions or definitions. In law, we speak of *torts* and *liability* and *double indemnity;* in computer science of *graphical user interfaces, bits,* and *bytes,* and in economics of *balance sheets* and *cartels.* Of course, we must use the terms of the discipline we are discussing.

A problem emerges, however, when technical terms are used unnecessarily or inappropriately. Then they are *jargon,* a special language often unintelligible to anyone outside the group that devised it. Try to figure out this Hollywood jargon:

> The veepees and the exex of the new org were skedded to orb the Europix in an all-day sesh.

or this psychological babble:

> The process of representational guidance has been found to be essentially the same as response learning under conditions where an externally depicted pattern was followed by a subject who is then *directed* through an instructional process to enact novel *response* sequences.

Both these examples are comical, but some people will believe that the second is appropriate English because it sounds academic.

Often prose riddled with jargon is depopulated, and the passive voice dominates. Common words, such as *direct,* receive a special twist. The writer piles adjectives one on top of another in the interest of precision. Business writing can come up with some whoppers.

> Problem determination procedures indicated that parallel reciprocal mobility was supported by management options.

And we wouldn't want you to think that English studies is lagging behind in the jargon race.

> Plot is the structure of action in closed and legible wholes; it thus must *use* metaphor as the trope of its achieved interrelations, and it must *be* metaphoric insofar as it is totalizing.

Thus many writers abandon the common language and common usage in favor of a private language bewildering to outsiders and often incomprehensible even to other professionals. Jargon poses a threat to the most basic principle of writing: communication between people.

Whether you write about an engineering project, a painting, a computer program, you should try to avoid jargon. Always strive to write so that any literate person with an interest in the subject could understand you. Write in standard, vigorous English.

Giving Clichés the Kiss of Death

Clichés are a dime a dozen. Some people use them right off the bat, even though they may have a sneaking suspicion that brave souls would give them the cold shoulder. But make no bones about it, good writers have other fish to fry and could care less. That's the bottom line.

A cliché is a worn-out saying or expression, an expression we have heard so much that it no longer creates an image for us. The first time they appeared, the clichés in the preceding paragraph offered fresh images or fresh views. *The kiss of death,* for instance, was what Alfred E. Smith called it when he learned that William Randolph Hearst was supporting Smith's opponent in the election for governor of New York. Smith suggested that Hearst's help was like Judas kissing Jesus and would lead to political death. His opponent lost. At the time, the expression was fresh (fresh enough to go down in Bartlett's *Familiar Quotations*). Since then, however, overuse has exhausted it.

Most clichés start out as efforts to make an idea vivid. A speaker or writer puts a new twist on something to illuminate it. When the twist is pithy, others adopt it—we can imagine Smith's supporters chortling as they repeated *the kiss of death.* Even though the original context fades, the saying may struggle on, mechanically, thoughtlessly, pointlessly. Whenever fresh expression fails, out trots the cliché.

When people string several clichés together, the result can be hilarious: "He is one of those people who stand up and tell it like it is and make the powers that be pay through the nose whenever they have their turn at bat." "My target is to explore every avenue to relieve the bottleneck in our backlog of orders." The mind reels.

Another form of cliché is the trite expression. *Gone but not forgotten, easier said than done, better late than never, in a very real sense* are a few of the ubiquitous phrases out there enticing us into dreary prose. Platitudes such as "all's well that ends well" are likewise overused and meaningless. They may once have carried thought, but now they carry only yawns.

Akin to the trite expression is the automatic pairing of a noun with a particular adjective. In this group we find *solemn oath, heavy burden, foreseeable future,* and the slightly newer *sea change* and *fire storm.* The list could go on and on.

The attraction of clichés is that they are ready-made. Rather than struggle with a fresh image, we reach for the nearest cliché. Using them may be excusable in speech—we are often in a rush to get our opinion stated. Writing is different. We—and our readers—have time to examine our prose. When we state even the most imaginative and reasonable idea in clichés, it will seem flabby and vague. Precision in thought and energy in expression are the aims of good writing, and that means getting rid of clichés.

The Private Language of Our Crowd

Slang refers to the special and spontaneous language a group develops. Often it can revitalize and rejuvenate the standard language. It keeps English slightly off balance and prevents it from becoming rigid. Like the unmannerly, vital yokel who crashes the tea party, slang brings in energy. Terms such as *dis* when we mean *insult, wack* when we mean *crazy,* or *way* when we mean *extremely* can sometimes add vitality to what we say.

Slang is not universal or standard throughout society. People on different blocks in the same neighborhood—not to mention people on different coasts or people in different social or cultural groups—may use words to mean quite different things. *Get wasted* means drink too much, take too many drugs, or be killed, depending on where you are. In the 1960s *uptight* meant overly tense to whites and ready to go to blacks. The word *fag* has meant, at various times to various people, a servant, drudgery, a cigarette, and a homosexual.

Slang is often a signal that a person belongs to a certain group: youth, jazz lovers, the political left, the country club. Creating new words or giving old words new meanings helps form a group's identity. Although some slang expressions filter into everyone's vocabulary, they usually take a long time to do so, and by then the originators have probably gone on to other slang words, maintaining their group identity.

Occasionally slang achieves a desirable effect in writing.

> With their vote in the municipal runoffs, the residents of Bedford-Stuyvesant have told the all-white city council, "If you can't deal, you're history."

College writing generally requires a level of diction offensive to none and understandable to all. You should write *bewildered* rather than *freaked out, overwhelmed* instead of *blown away,* and *frustrated* rather than *bummed*—or are our examples already out of date?

Avoiding Sexist Language

We have all heard words that disparage the opposite sex or suggest sexual assault. Sometimes using these words is only the result of carelessness or a wish to appear part of the gang and tough. But often we must assume the speaker intends to express hostility, a need to feel superior, or a desire to inflict pain. Using such words seems to indicate the speaker's personal problems. Whether deliberately assaultive or a result of ignorance, these words have no place at all in writing.

Not all sexist language is overtly cruel and crude, however. Words such as *doll* and *stud* can be affectionately or admiringly intended. Even so, they carry connotations that to some suggest a less than fully human person, a plaything, an object. Innocent though many may find these terms, they often suggest disrespect for the opposite sex and almost always reflect slovenly writing habits. Like the harsher terms, they have no place in expository writing.

Sexist assumptions permeate our language. In the higher ranking professions, the male seems to be the norm and the female the aberrant. Without intending insult, many of us say *the lady veterinarian* or *the female lawyer,* although we would never say *the gentleman veterinarian* or *the male lawyer.* We tend to call the hypothetical doctor *he* and the nurse *she.* Positions of leadership and responsibility in many fields contain masculinity in their denotative words: *chairman, congressman, policeman, fireman.* Yet we know that women can and do hold positions of prestige and responsibility in these fields.

In addition, many grammatical conventions favor men and ignore women. Traditionally, it has been grammatically correct to say *A writer must choose his words carefully* or *To each his own.* Some people think these constructions suggest that the female was an afterthought, to be subsumed under the dominant category "male."

Some of our common expressions seem to support this bias favoring males. The rallying cry of the American Revolution—"All men are created equal"—seems to exclude women. Some people argue that the term *man* encompasses the entire species and that objections to its use are foolish. But others note that during the time of the Revolution the "equal" did not include women, for they were not allowed to vote or serve on juries, and a married woman could not dispose of her own property without the consent of her husband.

These usages reflected the society in which they grew, a society dominated and documented by males. The complaints that females may have had about the laws and the language would not have been well known or widely reported. Society has changed drastically, and so has language.

The English language is now, as always, in a state of flux, growing and adjusting to new perceptions. Recognizing that sexism has no place in intelligent prose, sensitive writers are trying to get rid of it. Unfortunately, sexism in language is much easier to criticize than to weed out, but we have five suggestions for writing nonsexist prose.

1. Avoid stereotypes about men and women. Treat both sexes with respect and appreciation, and treat individual people as individuals. Think of all the exceptions there are, for instance, to the stereotypes *insensitive men* and *irrational women.* (For more on stereotypes see "Opening the Mind" in Chapter 1.)

2. Keep your writing free of gender-determined words, from obscenities to apparently innocent terms like *man and wife. Man and wife,* for instance, suggests that women are an attachment.

3. Avoid sexist usage. Find broader, more inclusive terms for words that denote only males. Instead of *policeman,* say *police officer.* Instead of *chairman,* say *chairperson.* If that usage sounds awkward or condescending, say *chair* or *head.* The point, of course, is to avoid the implication that only males hold high positions.

4. Steer clear of what many people consider sexist grammar. When you write about a nonspecific person, an anyone, use the plural instead of the sexist masculine singular pronoun. In place of *A writer should choose his words carefully,* say *Writers should choose their words carefully.* Shifting to the plural means that you avoid the suggestion of sexism without resorting to either the ungrammatical *a writer should choose their* or the questionable *s/he.*

5. Be ever gracious and inclusive: on the rare occasions when you cannot avoid the singular, write the unobtrusive *he or she, him or her, his or hers.*

Tips for Appropriate Prose

- Be as concrete and specific as you can.
- Watch out for vague, timid, and loud qualifiers.
- Prefer short, slim words to long, fat ones.
- Avoid jargon; strive to write so that any literate person can follow your thought.
- Get rid of clichés.
- Keep slang out of your writing.
- Avoid sexist language.

EXERCISES FOR APPROPRIATE PROSE

1. Make the following sentences more concrete or specific.
    a. The creature took the food into the room.
    b. Attendance at secondary educational institutions has been correlated with participation in athletic endeavors.
    c. The woman took down the garment and concealed it about her person without the store personnel's awareness and then went to the escalator and descended.
    d. When exposure and malnutrition are present, support from various levels of government should be forthcoming.
2. Revise these sentences by removing jargon, clichés, and slang.
    a. Incrementally compatible programming will always impact on total management options.

    b. Although the horror movie freaked me out, I thoroughly enjoyed the evening, most particularly when I flashed on the fact that I cannot relate to that other dude because he does not give me ego reinforcement. That's when I decided to be up-front with you, sweetie pie.

    c. What you say may be true, but if I hear that bromide one more time, I will flip.

    d. The Bard of Avon was a great writer and had a mind like a steel trap.

3. For fun, construct two sentences using at least two of the following words in each sentence: *dialectical, functioning, heuristic, conceptualized, metonymy, partial need factor, systematized, reciprocal, time-phase, parameter, feedback, logistic, hermetic.* Be sure your sentences *mean* something. If you don't know the words, look them up in your dictionary.

4. Eliminate the sexist bias from the following sentences.

    a. Three students—a man and two girls—were murdered in their composition class because they had misplaced a modifier.

    b. The dean presented awards to both John Smith and Ellen Jones. Smith's was, of course, for athletics and Ellen's for art.

    c. When I went to the ladies' room, my escort went to the men's room.

12

Developing Your Own Style

Oh tain't what you do, it's the way that cha do it. . . .
Tain't what you say, it's the way that cha say it —
That's what gets results.
— SY OLIVER (1910-1995) AND
TRUMMY YOUNG (1912-1984)

Style is what the artist does with the raw material of the art, what the writer or the speaker does with the thought to be communicated. Every decision you make while writing—the words you select, the construction of sentences, paragraphing—will contribute to your style. In that sense, this book has been discussing style all along. In this chapter, however, we want to concentrate on the way that cha say it.

CHARACTERISTICS OF GOOD STYLE: BEST FOOT FORWARD

We cannot set up absolute standards for style. Some very good styles are simple and direct, some are florid, some are sinuous, some are muscular. The following passages, all excellent, demonstrate how varied good style can be:

302

To everything there is a season, and a time to every purpose under
   heaven.
A time to be born, and a time to die;
A time to plant, and a time to pluck up that which is planted;
A time to kill, and a time to heal;
A time to break down, and a time to build up;
A time to weep, and a time to laugh;
A time to mourn and a time to dance . . .
   (Ecclesiastes 3:1–4, King James Version)

It is difficult to imagine, with what obstinacy truths which one
mind perceives almost by intuition, will be rejected by another; and
how many artifices must be practiced, to procure admission for the
most evident propositions into understandings frighted by their nov-
elty, or hardened against them by accidental prejudice: it can scarcely
be conceived, how frequently in these extemporaneous controversies,
the dull will be subtle, and the acute absurd; how often stupidity will
elude the force of argument, by involving itself in its own gloom; and
mistaken ingenuity will weave artful fallacies, which reason can
scarcely find means to disentangle. (Samuel Johnson, *The Adventurer*)

When I was three and Bailey four, we had arrived in the musty
little town, wearing tags on our wrists which instructed—"To Whom It
May Concern"—that we were Marguerite and Bailey Johnson Jr., from
Long Beach, California, en route to Stamps, Arkansas, c/o Mrs. Annie
Henderson.

Our parents had decided to put an end to their calamitous marriage,
and Father shipped us home to his mother. A porter had been charged
with our welfare—he got off the train the next day in Arizona—and
our tickets were pinned to my brother's inside coat pocket.

I don't remember much of the trip, but after we reached the segre-
gated southern part of the journey, things must have looked up. Negro
passengers, who always traveled with loaded lunch boxes, felt sorry
for "the poor little motherless darlings" and plied us with cold fried
chicken and potato salad.

Years later I discovered that the United States had been crossed
thousands of times by frightened Black children traveling alone to their
newly affluent parents in Northern cities, or back to grandmothers in
Southern towns when the urban North reneged on its economic
promises. (Maya Angelou, *I Know Why the Caged Bird Sings*)

Well, evolution *is* a theory. It is also a fact. And facts and theories
are different things, not rungs in a hierarchy of increasing certainty. Facts
are the world's data. Theories are structures of ideas that explain and
interpret facts. Facts do not go away when scientists debate rival theories to explain them. Einstein's theory of gravitation replaced Newton's,
but apples did not suspend themselves in mid-air pending the outcome. And human beings evolved from apelike ancestors whether they
did so by Darwin's proposed mechanism or by some other, yet to be
discovered. (Stephen Jay Gould, "Evolution as Fact and Theory")

These four writers all treat an interesting subject respectfully and put their stamp on it. Though quite different in subject, they share several qualities.

They write with clarity. They follow the rules of the English language, match their nouns to their verbs, place their commas correctly, put their modifiers where they belong. They make appropriate word choices. When Samuel Johnson uses the word *artifice,* he brings all its connotations into the sentence—skill or ingenuity, clever expedient, or sly trick—and enlarges his meaning. When Maya Angelou narrates the story of her life, her colloquial language expresses both the innocence of youth and the maturity of a grown woman.

Proper organization and emphasis contribute to good style. Without the balanced cadence, the parallelism and the repetition, the passage from Ecclesiastes could have read something like this:

> Everything takes place at a given time. We are born at one time and we die at another time, just as planting takes place every spring and then farmers get their workers up early in the autumn because that's harvest time. Which brings me to a discussion of hunting.

Written that way, this passage would hardly have had such an immense effect.

A good stylist considers the reader. Had Stephen Jay Gould been writing for scientists, he would have assumed a more sophisticated background. Had he been writing for children, he would no doubt have used simpler terms. His language was appropriate for the readers of *Discover* magazine, where his essay appeared.

A good stylist expresses both personality and situation. Johnson, the great eighteenth-century stylist, treats a complex subject in a complex neoclassical style. Gould is a late twentieth-century American, and his prose sounds appropriately fresh and direct.

Because it appeals to our senses and emotions and intellect, a good style can be very persuasive. Read these three passage aloud:

> Any man's death diminishes me, because I am involved in mankind; and therefore never send to know for whom the bell tolls; it tolls for thee. (John Donne)

> Indeed, I tremble for my country when I reflect that God is just. (Thomas Jefferson)

> When anything gets freed, a zest goes round the world. (Hortense Calisher)

Sentences such as these move us physically—that is, the stately rhythms of Donne, the anxiety of Jefferson, the exuberance of Calisher excite our senses. Read Donne's sentence aloud again, listening to his music—hear the repeated *m*s and the two *toll*s like a death knell. The passages move us emotionally. Donne's statement is nobly affecting, Jefferson's plain terrifying, Calisher's full of hope. And, all three saying something very worth saying, worth thinking about for a lifetime, they move us intellectually.

What makes a style interesting? Economy. Vigor. Flair. Variety. The writing is down-to-earth and sincere without being ponderous. It has personality without self-preening. The most interesting style is the most interesting *you* that you can get on the page.

Tips for Characteristics of Good Style

- Think about the qualities and techniques that make a style clear, appropriate, and interesting.
- To learn how to develop a good style, observe and imitate what good writers do.
- Consider the reader.

EXERCISES FOR CHARACTERISTICS OF GOOD STYLE

1. Evaluate the styles of the following passages, from the works of professional writers. Write a paragraph in which you state your preference and why. What kind of person do you think each writer is? Justify your opinion by referring to the style of the selections.

   a. A word is dead
      When it is said,
      Some say.
      I say it just
      Begins to live
      That day.
         (Emily Dickinson)

   b. Some say the world will end in fire,
      Some say in ice.
      From what I've tasted of desire
      I hold with those who favor fire.
      But if it had to perish twice,
      I think I know enough of hate
      To say that for destruction ice
      Is also great
      And would suffice.
         (Robert Frost)

   c. The emphasis on skills was a response to what had been the major weakness of Peace Corps programs in the 1960s. There has always been a debate within the agency about whether its emphasis should be on socioeconomic development or cross-cultural exchange. In theory, one goal is as important as the other. In the 1960s, however, too many projects tended to focus on the second goal of the Peace Corps Act (the people-to-people aspect) and neglected the first goal (the supply of *trained* manpower). (Gerald T. Rice, *Twenty Years of Peace Corps*)

d. I am an invisible man. No, I am not a spook like those who haunted Edgar Allan Poe; nor am I one of your Hollywood-movie ectoplasms. I am a man of substance, of flesh and bone, fiber and liquids—and I might even be said to possess a mind. I am invisible, understand, simply because people refuse to see me. Like the bodiless heads you see sometimes in circus sideshows, it is as though I have been surrounded by mirrors of hard, distorting glass. When they approach me they see only my surroundings, themselves, or figments of their imagination—indeed, everything and anything except me. (Ralph Ellison, *Invisible Man*)

e. I am. I think. I will.

My hands . . . My spirit . . . My sky . . . My forest . . . This earth of mine. . . .

What must I say besides? These are the words. This is the answer.

I stand here on the summit of the mountain. I lift my head and I spread my arms.

This, my body and spirit, this is the end of the quest. I wished to know the meaning of things. I am the meaning. I wished to find a warrant for being. I need no warrant for being, and no word of sanction upon my being. I am the warrant and the sanction.

It is my eyes which see, and the sight of my eyes grants beauty to the earth. It is my ears which hear, and the hearing of my ears gives its song to the world. It is my mind which thinks, and the judgment of my mind is the only searchlight that can find the truth. It is my will which chooses, and the choice of my will is the only edict I must respect.

Many words have been granted me, and some are wise, and some are false, but only three are holy: "I will it!" (Ayn Rand, *Anthem*)

2. Choose a recent essay of your own and recast the first two paragraphs in the style of one of the above selections.

THE PERSONAL VOICE:
BEING THERE IN YOUR WRITING

We should not underestimate the importance of style. The way that we say or do something is distinct and makes even the most common thought or gesture our own. We hear a few bars of music and we say, "That's Brahms" or "That's Beethoven." We read a paragraph from a novel, and we may know it is by Faulkner, Woolf, or Hemingway. We read the inaugural addresses of John Kennedy, Richard Nixon, Ronald Reagan, and Bill Clinton, and even though the sentiments expressed are pretty much the same, we know whose speech each is. We know by the style. Style is the indelible signature of an individual's personality.

All saying much the same thing, some very important military commanders presented themselves in these statements:

> My first wish is to see this plague of mankind, war, banished from the earth. (George Washington, 1732–1799)

> There is many a boy here today who looks on war as all glory, but, boys, it is all hell. You can bear this warning voice to generations yet to come. I look upon war with horror. (William Tecumseh Sherman, 1820–1891)

> I know war as few other men now living know it, and nothing to me is more revolting. I have long advocated its complete abolition, as its very destructiveness on both friend and foe has rendered it useless as a method of settling international disputes. (Douglas MacArthur, 1880–1964)

> I hate war as only a soldier who has lived it can, only as one who has seen its brutality, its futility, its stupidity. (Dwight D. Eisenhower, 1890–1969)

These quotations all convey the same thought: war is bad. But the styles of the speakers differ, and so do our responses to them.

Read the quotations again. Which commanders attract you and which put you off? Would you like to know any personally? Which ones would you trust? Imagine for a moment that the statements involved complicated, arguable ideas about matters that affect you directly—say American troops abroad or national service. Judging purely by the style of these quotations, which commander would you be most apt to believe?

Too frequently, people think style is just so much verbiage to be slathered over thought like a rich coat of paint over wood. It isn't. It isn't filigree and curlicue added to substance. It isn't fancy packaging. It isn't decoration at all. Style is an integral part of the message. It is the voice of the writer in the message. When Sherman said, "but, boys, it is all hell," his very bluntness conveyed his personality as well as his attitude toward both subject and audience.

Look closely at Sherman's statement. The abrupt use of commas, representing pauses in his speech, rivets the attention, and then the word *hell* hammers home the simple message. The use of the word *boys* establishes a friendly, though paternalistic, relationship between Sherman and his audience, all former soldiers. By his choice of words, phrasing, and punctuation, Sherman has perfectly matched the language to his meaning. We hear his voice in his words. That is style.

Although some lucky few seem born with a distinctive writing style, most of us must work to get our personality into our writing. Improving our writing style is at least as hard as improving our guitar-playing style or our tennis-playing style or even our having-a-good-time-at-a-party style. And as with these, improvement results from observation, practice, and imitation. Don't be afraid of imitating—most professional writers imitated other writers they admired before developing their own style. And don't be afraid of trying and failing. You will get better if you are willing to write, rewrite, and rewrite again. (We have rewritten this chapter at least six times.)

Tips for Personal Voice

- Remember that words convey values and feelings as well as thoughts.
- Keep in mind that your style is the you that you present to your reader.

EXERCISES FOR PERSONAL VOICE

1. Analyze the personal voice in these passages written by professional writers. What kind of values and attitudes are implied by each passage? Write a paragraph for each in which you justify your opinion.

   a. For generations the machine and the garden have proposed contradictory goods to Americans. As the garden is more and more invaded, dug up, paved over, and polluted, we may, being adaptable, develop plastic lungs and stainless-steel bowels and learn to exist in the environment we have created for ourselves, as Stephen Benet's urban termites learned to sustain themselves on crumbs of steel and concrete. But it may also be that we will lose—are already losing?—touch with our humanity as we lose touch with the natural world. (Wallace Stegner, *One Way to Spell Man*)

   b. As always, paranoia reigns in movieland. To make a film is to make a choice which, should it be the wrong one, means the loss of a career. One evening I introduced the editor of *The New Yorker* to several hundred of the essential players, as stars and magnates of the largest magnitude are currently known. I quoted myself: "To be truly commercial is to do well that which should not be done at all." Silence like the tomb engulfed these words. But the commercialities have their own weird integrity, and their productions are often rather better than those of solemn *auteurs,* as "serious" directors are inappropriately known in these parts. (Gore Vidal, *Palimpsest*)

   c. Even as we grew up, my mother could not help imposing herself between her children and whatever it was they might take it in mind to reach out for in the world. . . . She did indeed tend to make the world look dangerous, and so it had been for her. A way had to be found around her love sometimes, without challenging *that,* and at the same time cherishing it in its unassailable strength. Each of us children did, sooner or later, in part at least, solve this in a different, respectful, complicated way. But I think she was relieved when I chose to be a writer of stories, for she thought writing was safe. (Eudora Welty, *One Writer's Beginnings*)

2. Revise these three sentences so that they express your personal voice. Change the words, add what you want, but retain the facts.
   a. The large boy took the little boy's football and threw it up in the tree, and I didn't like it.
   b. When people are surprised at the number of homeless, I am surprised at them.
   c. My first day of college was interesting.

TONE: THE VOICE FROM DEEP WITHIN

Perhaps the most important ingredient of style is tone, that is, the atmosphere or attitude the words convey. In speech, the way we say something—the tone of our voice—will telegraph our attitude, even if the words are neutral. Our voice indicates whether we are being sincere, bewildered, amused, or any of dozens of possibilities. To change the tone, we make small changes in pronunciation or pacing. For instance, the sentence *The college newspaper critic said this was the best movie of the year* could be sarcastic, pompous, innocent, deadpan, and so on— the difference depending on the subtle adjustment of tone.

Tone in writing is not as unconsciously or automatically achieved as tone in speech. A writer cannot "drip sarcasm" by anything as simple as modulating the voice. In writing, you have to change what you say. Choice of words, length of sentence, rhythm, punctuation all contribute to the atmosphere in which the ideas exist. They express an attitude toward the subject. (For more on tone, see Chapter 16.)

Finding the Right Tone

Too much writing today, unfortunately, sounds as though it issued from a vending machine—cold, detached, inhuman. Three sentences for a quarter. Some students actively seek tonelessness, believing that tone has no business in academia. That notion is mistaken. Tone in writing is a significant part of the message. That's why it is so important to get it right.

The right tone is one that expresses your feelings about the subject. After all, you are presenting *you* by your tone as well as by your ideas. If you feel passionately, you will want to express your passion. If you find the subject humorous, your writing shouldn't pretend that it's deadly serious. If you are ambivalent about the subject, your tone should suggest that ambivalence.

The right tone also respects the reader's feelings. If the subject arouses your passion, so probably does it arouse the reader's, perhaps on the other side. The best writers don't foreclose communication by ignoring the reader's own commitments and beliefs. Passion, yes; bullying, no. Humor, yes; ridicule, no. They adapt their writing to take into account the reader's equal right to an opinion.

Critical distance will provide a good test of a good tone. Put your essay aside for a while. When you come back to it, imagine that you are a recalcitrant reader, forced to read this essay. Does the tone seem appropriate for the subject? Does this writer look to be a reliable guide into the subject? Are you attracted by the personality behind the words? (Come on, be honest.)

Avoiding the Wrong Tone

Not all tones are acceptable in college writing or any kind of writing. Some can be downright unattractive. In this section, we will discuss six tones that you should keep out of your papers.

Flippancy.   When something is flippant, it indicates a disrespectful levity. Here is the opening of an essay on utilitarian philosophy:

> Suppose Jesus Christ had truly lived and suppose he had fallen in love with some Egyptian girl who jilted him for a pharaoh. Brokenhearted, he committed suicide before he could spread his word to the people. Now, by committing suicide, more grief was caused, and therefore the utilitarian must say that his act was immoral.

This flippancy is inappropriate to both the reader, the instructor, and the subject, serious and to some people sacred. With such a tone, almost no argument, however cogently reasoned, could salvage the paper. Flippancy can be fun to say or write—maybe fun to hear—but almost never fun to read. To be flippant about a subject indicates that we do not take it seriously. Instructors, and bosses, are unlikely to appreciate that approach.

Sarcasm.   Sarcasm is a contemptuous remark or taunt, often couched in words opposite to the speaker's real meaning.

> If only the rest of us misguided students were one quarter as intelligent as my roommate, what a brilliant student body we would be.

In an essay, sarcasm is even less attractive than flippancy. When you think of that word, don't you picture a sneering, superior look on someone's face? We do, perhaps because when we use sarcasm that is the way we feel. A sarcastic tone may create in the reader's mind that image of the writer.

Sentimentality. Sentimentality means forced or shallow feeling, and it is another tone to avoid. It is good to express feeling in our writing, of course, but only honest—not pumped up—feeling. Excessive sentiment in an essay casts doubt on both the thinking and the sincerity of the writer. When people overstate their feelings, their writing is apt to deteriorate. They begin to dredge up clichés and trite sayings to back up an emotion they don't have. In an essay opposing animal experimentation, a student wrote

> Tears spring to my eyes when I think of those helpless little mice.

We doubt those tears—we even doubt the mice.

Self-righteousness. Akin to sentimentality is the self-righteous, or holier-than-thou, tone. Some writing seems to suggest that the writer has a special claim to virtue. Often this tone is accidental. The following, from an autobiographical essay, was written by a modest but naïve young man:

> The well-being of my mind, body, and spirit is the result of my family life. My parents love and respect life. This love has inspired me to use my gifts to the height of their potential so that I perform at my best throughout my life.

Appreciating one's parents is a virtue, but a recognition that things are not always as they seem and no one is perfect would have added depth to this essay.

Belligerence. The belligerent writer comes right at the reader, chin thrust forward, fists doubled, like the schoolyard bully, threatening to beat up anyone who dares to disagree. We once read a letter to the editor of a college newspaper that began, "I just can't believe how ignorant and stupid some people are regarding the military. They just like to protest something in between hits of the old weed." Not many people would want to associate themselves with views expressed that way.

Some ideas are, of course, worth fighting for. It would be absurd not to show feeling about important issues, such as hunger in Africa, missing children in America, or the torture of animals. Indeed, honest indignation can contribute to effective argument.

There is a line, however, between belligerence and acceptable indignation, and that line should be carefully observed. State your opinion with a tone of indignation, but back it up with evidence. Do not bully us into agreement but respect us enough to want to persuade us with argument. The tone of the letter writer, in contrast, offers no evidence of argument but only more bullying: "Take my word for it or else."

Apology.   The opposite of belligerence, and equally inappropriate, is the apology, what might be called the po'-li'l-me tone. With this, the writer claims that he or she is modest, diffident, and hardworking and thus deserves special consideration.

> Even after reading T. S. Eliot's "The Hollow Men" five times, I could not figure it out. I know it is a great poem, and I realize I have not received the education necessary to understanding it.

Professors seldom give A for effort, and they never do when they realize they are being manipulated for a grade. They want ideas, not the writer hat in hand. Imagine Samuel Johnson saying "I know I don't know much, but . . ." Like Johnson, confidently say what you think.

Tips for Tone
- Read your work critically so that you can evaluate whether your tone is the one you want to convey.
- Avoid flippancy, sarcasm, sentimentality, self-righteousness, belligerence, and apology.

EXERCISES FOR TONE

1. Describe the tones of the following passages.
   a. Abortion is a vicious crime, and any person who encourages another person to have one is an accomplice in a murder and should be prosecuted to the fullest extent of the law.
   b. Males are so honorable by nature that they would naturally take the high moral position on this issue of abortion because of course it affects them so greatly and they have so much to lose if abortion is recriminalized.
   c. I don't care about the issue—what's one more aborted fetus or one more unwanted baby? People have always had abortions and people have always hated their children. The thing that amuses me is how excited people who are centuries past the childbearing years can get about this. Now that is worth pondering.
2. Revise the three statements in Exercise 1 to remove the offending tones.
3. Write six sentences, using a different unacceptable tone in each. Revise the sentences to make the tones acceptable.

WRITING WITH FLAIR:
RISKS THAT PAY OFF

Although much of our book has been prescriptive—do this, don't do that—we want you to be adventurous and courageous in your writing. Take chances, even if you risk failure. At that, you may be shaking your head: why should I take a chance of falling on my face? That question has four answers.

One, nothing communicates what we are and how we think more powerfully and completely than prose. It tells what we value and why.

Two, good writing leads to good thinking and vice versa. As you strive to interest your reader, you challenge your own thinking. Struggling to find a particular image or an exact phrase may open up a new range of thought.

Three, almost all A papers in the world possess personality and imagination. Aim high. Stretch toward excellence.

Four, writing with flair is more fun.

Although you should never sacrifice sense and integrity, you should actively seek the vivid. Indeed, vivid writing will often add to sense and integrity. The following three passages demonstrate some different ways of employing vivid language.

The first was written by a humorist who obviously enjoys his words.

> There is no question that there is an unseen world. The problem is, how far is it from midtown and how late is it open? Unexplainable events occur constantly. One man will see spirits. Another will hear voices. A third will wake up and find himself running in the Preakness. How many of us have not at one time or another felt an ice-cold hand on the back of our neck while we were home alone? (Not me, thank God, but some have.) What is behind these experiences? Or in front of them, for that matter? Is it true that some men can foresee the future or communicate with ghosts? And after death is it still possible to take showers? (Woody Allen, "Examining Psychic Phenomena")

The humor in this passage is provided by the sudden invasion of the absurd. Allen juxtaposes two different worlds, that of psychic phenomena and that of daily concerns. The incongruity of the two is unexpected and forces the reader to look at ideas anew.

The strength of the second passage comes not from the collision of ideas but from the strings of memorable images or mental pictures used to describe the prose of President Warren Gamaliel Harding.

> He writes the worst English that I have ever encountered. It reminds me of a string of wet sponges; it reminds me of tattered washing on the line; it reminds me of stale bean-soup, of college yells, of dogs barking idiotically through endless nights. It is so bad that a sort of

grandeur creeps into it. It drags itself out of the dark abysm (I was
about to write abscess!) of pish, and crawls insanely up the topmost
pinnacle of posh. It is rumble and bumble. It is flap and doodle. It is
balder and dash.

But I grow lyrical. (H. L. Mencken, "Gamalielese")

This passage is a feast of vivid writing. Mencken is certainly having fun,
and providing fun, but he is also expressing his strong opinion about
Harding's writing style.

Neither of these passages is particularly complicated. Both make
fairly simple points. But vivid language is not limited to the simple, as
you can see in the following passage:

> The current political debate over family values, personal responsibility,
> and welfare takes for granted the entrenched American belief that de-
> pendence on government assistance is a recent and destructive phe-
> nomenon. Conservatives tend to blame this dependence on personal
> irresponsibility aggravated by a swollen welfare apparatus that saps in-
> dividual initiative. Liberals are more likely to blame it on personal mis-
> fortune magnified by the harsh lot that falls to losers in our competitive
> market economy. But both sides believe that "winners" in America
> make it on their own, that dependence reflects some kind of individual
> or family failure, and that the ideal family is the self-reliant unit of tra-
> ditional lore—a family that takes care of its own, carves out a future
> for its children, and never asks for handouts. Politicians at both ends of
> the ideological spectrum have wrapped themselves in the mantle of
> these "family values," arguing over *why* the poor have not been able to
> make do without assistance, or whether aid has exacerbated their situ-
> ation, but never questioning the assumption that American families tra-
> ditionally achieve success by establishing their independence from the
> government. (Stephanie Coontz, "A Nation of Welfare Families")

Coontz brings an intriguing and complex point to life.

As you can see, good writing comes in many shapes, sizes, and colors—and can be the result of different intentions. Sometimes we forget
that with a little effort we too can write a prose that has more flair. Perhaps a few precepts can help to translate what we admire into what we
write.

Appeals to the Senses

The best writing is concrete and specific. Not all concrete and specific
writing, however, is vivid. Take this one:

> The child played ball on the sidewalk.

The sentence is both concrete and specific, but it is not particularly
vivid. In revising we wanted to create a picture, a mental image, in the
reader's mind.

First we visualized the subject: *boy* is more visual than *child*, but we thought harder about the image and tried to picture physical qualities. Then we turned to what the child was doing. We imagined as vividly as we could.

> The frizzy-haired little boy slashed line drives to himself off the brick wall.

We thought the reader could better see the boy when we described his frizzy hair. *Slashed* conveys a specific action: the stroke of the boy's arm. The brick wall completes the picture.

According to an ancient Chinese proverb, one picture is worth more than ten thousand words. But by using words, we can create a picture in the reader's imagination, as James Baldwin does here:

> [My father] looked to me, as I grew older, like pictures I had seen of African tribal chieftains: he really should have been naked, with war-paint on and barbaric mementos, standing among spears. (*Notes of a Native Son*)

By creating an exact image, Baldwin clearly illuminates his father's personality.

Unfortunately, dull language is as hard to fight in writing as crab-grass in a lawn. When we get the least bit lazy it springs up. This kind of sentence results:

> Many landmark residential structures were destroyed for redevelopment.

It is a sensible sentence and we understand it. But if we wish the reader to share our indignation, we need a more vivid image.

> To clear the way for a new glass box, the wreckers sledgehammered the Victorian mansions and reduced them to rubble and dust.

Now the reader hears the wrecking ball, sees the rubble, and can taste the dust. Only a redeveloper hoping to go unnoticed would be happy with that first version.

All things being equal, we would not recommend additional words. But if you want to appeal to your reader's senses, you may need more words. Brevity is not the only virtue of good writing.

Vivid writing is important for two reasons. First, it makes understanding easier and quicker for the reader. In the "Victorian mansions" example, the image of rubble and dust quickly tells the real damage. Second, vivid writing pleases readers. We all like to read about the world of sight and sound and smell and taste and touch.

Figurative Language

Most good writing contains figures of speech, that is, words and expressions not used for their literal sense. Writers make figures of speech by describing one idea or object in language that properly belongs to another. If we say

> Doubt crucified the president

we call on feelings and ideas the reader has about actual crucifixion to illuminate the painful experience of doubt. By comparing one thing to another this way, we can reveal a new world for our readers and often ourselves.

Not every idea or sentence needs a figure of speech—sometimes a simple, unadorned statement is effective. But if your sentence seems dry, flat, or unclear, make an effort to think of a simile, a metaphor, or an analogy to illuminate it.

Similes. A simile is an explicit comparison of one thing with another: the writer clarifies one idea or thing by claiming it is *like* another. A simile always includes *like* or *as*. In describing his father, James Baldwin said that people thought him ingrown "like a toenail." This simile conveys the isolated, pained, and disturbing old man. Here are more similes:

> During the swing, the golf club bends like a whip.
>
> Seen from a distance, the brightly dressed crowd in the market looked like a basket of summer fruit.
>
> Like a mysterious, fog-enshrouded island approached by explorers, atomic energy fascinated and frightened the scientists.

An apt and nicely shaped simile can not only paint a vivid picture but also illuminate an idea. Shakespeare's work is rife with similes that make pictorial the nonpictorial opinion or abstraction. Near the end of *King Lear,* the Duke of Gloucester expresses his despair at human existence.

> As flies to wanton boys, are we to the gods;
> They kill us for their sport.

The successful simile, like this one, is brief and to the point. You shouldn't try to keep a comparison rolling just because you can. It can become silly and tedious if carried too far. But you should occasionally enrich your prose with an apt simile.

Metaphors. A metaphor compares two things without making the comparison explicit: the writer illuminates the unfamiliar or mysterious by identifying it with the familiar. Two things, the metaphor suggests, are the same.

> A mighty fortress is our God,
> A bulwark never failing

wrote Martin Luther, suggesting in metaphor a characteristic of the deity.

> Religion . . . is the opium of the people

said Karl Marx, obviously not to be taken literally but as a negative image of religion.

"The metaphor is probably the most fertile power possessed by man," said the Spanish philosopher José Ortega y Gasset, relying on metaphor to make his point. A good metaphor lets us think and talk about the world in fresh ways by converting vague ideas into images.

Sometimes a longer metaphor can illuminate a complex situation. The following extended metaphor by the historian Barbara Tuchman describes marriage among ruling families of the Middle Ages:

> Marriages were the fabric of international as well as inter-noble relations, the primary source of territory, sovereignty, and alliance, and the major business of medieval diplomacy. The relations of countries and rulers depended not at all on common borders or natural interest but on dynastic connections and fantastic cousinships. . . . At every point of the loom sovereigns were thrusting in their shuttles, carrying the strand of a son or a daughter, and these, whizzing back and forth, wove the artificial fabric that created as many conflicting claims and hostilities as it did bonds. [The leading families of Europe] were all entwined in a crisscrossing network, in the making of which two things were never considered: the sentiments of the parties to the marriage, and the interest of the populations involved. (*A Distant Mirror*)

Because of Tuchman's use of weaving as a metaphor, her reader is able to understand how tightly connected the various families were and how important these connections were. By representing an abstraction in concrete terms, she achieves the persuasiveness of illustration. Moreover, her metaphor adds energy to ideas and observations that might otherwise have been dry or tedious.

Some people dismiss metaphors and similes as too "literary." They need not be, however. Politicians have frequently used them, as Theodore Roosevelt did when he recommended that the United States "Speak softly and carry a big stick." Athletes and sportswriters instinctively use metaphors when nicknaming the greats: Ted Williams is "the Splendid Splinter" and Michael Jordan "Air Jordan." Likewise, scientists often find that a simile or metaphor will help explain a difficult concept, as did Loren Eiseley when he titled an essay "The Ghost Continent" and another "The Angry Winter."

Analogies.   An analogy is an extended comparison, drawn point by point, between two things or ideas. Its purpose is generally to explain a complicated or remote phenomenon by reference to a more accessible one. The advantage of an analogy comes from its careful elucidation of an idea.

The Bible is full of analogies. The parable of the prodigal son is an example. In it Jesus discusses God's forgiveness of sinners by suggesting it is like a father's treatment of his wayward son. The remote idea of the deity is made clear by reference to the homely idea of the father.

As Sigmund Freud said, "Analogies prove nothing, that is quite true, but they can make one feel more at home." Because they do make readers feel more at home, analogies appear everywhere, even in instructions for using a soldering iron.

> Soldering is the joining of metal surfaces by a melted metal or metallic alloy. We can compare this roughly with the gluing of two pieces of wood. Instead of wood, the solderer joins two pieces of metal and instead of glue, he or she uses a melted alloy or metal that, like the glue, hardens and forms a bond.

Analogies can be surprising when used to compare things not obviously similar. In the sixteenth century, a band of thieves waylaid a parson and forced him to make a speech praising all thieves. At the height of his oration, he conferred high praise indeed, drawing an analogy between the thieves and Christ.

> I marvel that men can despise you thieves, since in all points (almost) you are like Christ himself. For Christ had no dwelling place; neither have you. Christ went from town to town; so do you. Christ was laid wait upon in many places, and so are you. Christ at length was captured; so shall you be. He was brought before the judges; so shall you be. He was condemned; and so shall you be. He was killed; so shall you be. He thereupon went to heaven—and that you shall never do.

That little twist at the end goes to show that even the best analogies should not be pushed too far—no two things are alike in all particulars (or they would be the same thing). The thieves must not have noticed, though, for according to the legend, "they went away well pleased." (See Chapter 6, Using Evidence, for more discussion of analogies.)

Changing the Pace

There may come a time in your writing when you want to take a chance and try something different, a style you haven't tried and don't see very often in your school reading. When that mood strikes, go ahead. Dive in. Here we describe three ways to vary the construction of sentences— inverting the natural order, using fragments, and modulating the beat.

Inverting the Natural Order.   A writer's natural inclination is to move through a sentence from subject to verb to object—along the way, of course, hanging modifiers on the spine. Most of the time, this is how you will construct your sentences. But occasionally you may want to try an unusual construction, such as

A genius he isn't.

By inverting the natural order, you undercut your reader's expectations and quicken his or her interest. Used sparingly, inversion can transform a bland sentence into a sharp one and add power to a thought. Compare

We shall always have the poor with us

with

The poor we shall always have with us.

Using Fragments.   A group of words set off as a sentence is a fragment if it lacks either a subject or a verb or if it contains a dependent clause but no independent clause.

Walking fast in order to get home by dusk.

The role played by Susan Sarandon.

Because I said so.

Although fragments are grammatical errors—complete sentences must contain both a subject and a verb—they sometimes appear in published works; we have used a few in this book. Employed rarely and carefully, a fragment can add a little zing to writing, as in this example.

> Had you gotten off the Harbor Freeway and driven into Watts before the 1965 riots, you would have seen the scars of official indifference. For Watts had been forgotten by those responsible for the city. On either side of the freeway you would have seen once-pleasant houses now with broken windows and crumbling walls, once-verdant gardens now junk heaps, a once-prosperous commercial area now half-occupied and wholly dilapidated. You would have seen teenagers—and adults—lounging against liquor stores, with absolutely nothing in the world better to do. What were the elements that turned their quiet lethargy into violent rebellion? *A very hot summer day. Some radio and television stations hungry for news. A handful of frightened police officers. A small event.*

When experienced writers use fragments, they prepare the ground so carefully that the reader understands the ideas very well and can supply the missing words without thinking.

An occasional and deliberately designed fragment can intensify a thought and add complexity to a paragraph. But you must take great care to lay the groundwork and make sure that your meaning is clear and your writing smooth. We have a peculiar rule for writing fragments: don't ever write a fragment unless you know you are doing it, and be sure the missing part is clearly and strongly implied.

Modulating the Beat.   Short sentences are fine. Short paragraphs are fine. They say what they came to say. Then they leave. They are clear. They are direct. They are efficient. They can be punchy. But they can become exhausting. Too many in a row will not do. Your readers will get irritated. They will put down your writing. You will lose them. Try again.

And so the time comes when you wish you had written not with more wit, for your words were clever enough; and not even stronger sentences, for short ones were as strong as an uppercut; but longer sentences, and paragraphs that took their time getting to their appointed end, fuller paragraphs that stopped every so often en route to consider not only where they had been but also where they were most likely to be going. However, and this is an important point, the simple act of writing at greater length, as tantalizing as it may be and as much as it seems to promise greater complexity of thought, wider command of all possible aspects of the subject matter, and that adroitness, that panache, that *je ne sais quoi* for which every writer strives, frequently fails to deliver and all too often becomes a way of stretching out the little you have to say over as many words as you can find to stuff into the paragraph or even the sentence in an effort to avoid having to come to the end of saying that little. Your readers will get irritated. They will put down your writing. You will lose them. Try again.

Add a little variety to your writing. Try not to have the same shape sentence after sentence, paragraph after paragraph. Include all four constructions: simple, compound, complex, compound-complex. Perhaps a fragment. Why not try an occasional question? Don't get stuck in one rhythm like a rutted phonograph record. Have some long sentences, some medium, some as short as a word.

Try a one-sentence paragraph.

Write a paragraph with its topic sentence in the middle, or at the end. Write a paragraph without an explicit topic sentence. Don't try to dazzle your reader with the brilliance and power of every sentence, but make sure your reader occasionally sits up and takes notice.

Tips for Flair

- Take some risks with your writing.
- Write to appeal to your reader's senses; make pictures as vivid as possible.
- Try for an occasional simile, metaphor, or analogy.
- Be a little adventurous: invert the natural order and try an occasional fragment.
- Change your pace by mixing up constructions, sentence length, and placement of emphasis.

1. Write a vivid sentence for each of the five senses to describe a specific experience.

2. Complete each of the following sentences with a simile.
   a. The bird's raucous song was like
   b. The entire team sprawled on the turf, looking like
   c. He hated tap dancing just as . . . hated
   d. For Napoleon, those winter months in Moscow were like
   e. Dealing with the Internet is like

3. Make an apt metaphor based on the following ideas.
   a. Lovers holding hands on a beach
   b. Pollution in the city during a rainstorm
   c. An old woman on a park bench on a cold winter day
   d. The state legislature during a heated debate
   e. The collision of two cars

4. Make an analogy for two of the following sets.
   a. The circulatory system and a college or university
   b. A lion and her cub and a teacher and her student
   c. The solar system and a family
   d. Crime in a society and chicken pox

   Remember that you are using the known to explain the unknown.

5. Revise a paragraph in an essay you wrote for an earlier assignment to include a simile, a metaphor, and an analogy.

6. Rewrite the following to give it variety.

   > The young people in our culture seem to be suffering from a lot of anxiety. This anxiety has many causes. The young people fear they will not have jobs. They won't be able to afford to own houses. Children are expensive. If they have them, will they be able to educate them? When they travel, they worry about terrorism and anti-American feeling abroad. Some people tell them they are lucky anyway. It is possible that they are lucky. But maybe they are not so lucky.

   Be sure to include one inversion, one fragment, and one question.

7. Now write a follow-up paragraph of an entirely different structure.

THE HIGH INFORMAL STYLE: THE RIGHT BALANCE

For work in college, seek to write in what could be called the *high informal style*. This style is high because it shows respect for the reader and for the subject. It observes the rules of argument and of etiquette, including correct grammar, syntax, and punctuation. It avoids silliness, breeziness, overfamiliarity, and vulgarity. And it allows room for your personal voice.

Seriousness does not mean "academic writing." As university instructors, we are particularly sensitive to this kind of writing. For centuries, academics have been pilloried and parodied for being precise to the point of pedantry and pomposity. Yet some of the best writing comes from academics. Henry Louis Gates, Jr., Helen Vendler, and Stephen Hawking are three professors who write with elegance, imagination, and personality. Look up some of their writing. They are well worth imitating.

Some writers, unfortunately, imitate the worst kind of academic writing, the kind that really is pedantic. They insert ten-dollar words when nickel ones would be better. They pile clause on top of clause, modification on top of modification, until their sentences and paragraphs teeter and collapse. Along the way, they are apt to lose touch with their thought and certainly with their own style. Imagine how baffled the instructor was when she read the following passage:

> If it were in my power to change one aspect of modern living, I would prioritize change in the capitalist ideology that is predominant socially at the present point in time. It is because of this ideology that pursuit of truly valued goals is prevented. Many settle for conditions that create the possibility of generating sufficient income for inordinate materialistic wants. Stifled by the deluding paradigm of materialism, individual hopes and dreams are stillborn, poverty is the norm while the wealthy survive, and many people are forced into molds that will reflect a wealthy lifestyle.

This sort of writing is not entirely the writer's fault. She was trying, too hard, to write the way she thought she was expected to write. And so she stumbled over awkward combinations of words, the complex ways of saying simple things, the strained effort to sound intelligent.

The high informal style shifts a little toward informality. It gives the impression of natural speech—without, of course, lapsing into error in form or diction. The writer's voice can still be heard.

In the revision, the writer relaxed and began to sound more like herself and less achingly formal and pretentious:

> If I could change one thing in the world, I would change the emphasis on materialism that I see today. Because of the rush to get rich, many people cannot pursue what they really find valuable in life, like teaching or farming or social work. Instead, many settle for being doctors, lawyers, bankers, not because these careers interest them, but because the salaries will provide material rewards. It is very sad to see the dreams and aspirations of so many people destroyed by the quest for money. But perhaps we cannot expect anything else in a world where the poor struggle or perish and the wealthy have much more than enough.

Writing like this preserves the high aspect of style—the need for respect and seriousness—and adds the informal, the personal, the sense that someone is talking. We know full well what this writer believes and cherishes. In her examples, she puts her stamp on the thought. An appropriate style is always a personal style. It should include not only your values but also your humor, your tolerance, your quirky way of viewing the world. A writer with style is a writer with power. Discover your own style, master it, and improve it.

Tips for the High Informal Style

- Seek a mixture of respect, seriousness, and informality in your style.
- A persuasive style appeals to the senses and emotions as well as to the intellect.

EXERCISES FOR THE HIGH INFORMAL STYLE

1. Review three of your previous essays. Be honest with yourself; look for words, phrases, or passages written in a "college paper style." Write down words and phrases that are unlike any you would normally use. Write down anything that sounds inflated. Write down any word or phrase taken from a thesaurus. When done, revise everything on your list. Try to achieve the "high informal style." Write a brief essay in which you discuss the difference your revisions made.

2. The following is a short list of writers many people find persuasive:

   Abraham Lincoln
   Margaret Thatcher
   William Bennett
   Cornel West
   William Safire
   Susan Faludi
   Robert Hughes
   Emma Goldman

   Choose one of the writers on this list and read some of his or her writing. Then write an essay in which you discuss the elements of your chosen writer's style that make his or her writing persuasive.

CASE STUDY: REVISING FOR STYLE

Although in reality, writers constantly make stylistic changes, most good writers dedicate some time, often near the end of the revision process, to style alone. They look at word choices, phrases, cadences. They check to be sure that the tone of their writing truly expresses their attitude toward the subject. Courtney Hough took a hard look at her essay on the poetry of Anne Sexton. Here we show how she revised this passage:

```
Anne Sexton's poetry expresses the speaker's life.
She writes her poetry in simple free verse. That makes it
fairly easy for the reader to understand. The topics of
Sexton's poetry are bold and interesting. They include
insanity, sins, confessions, sex, women's issues, and re-
lationship problems. These topics give the speaker a "bad
girl" image.
     Feelings of discontent are prominent in Sexton's poem
"The Abortion." The title of this poem alone can express
the troubled feelings of the speaker. Anyone who has dealt
with an abortion in even a remote way is likely to suffer
from perplexed feelings. Unlike most poems, the title of
this one perfectly describes the topic. "Someone who
should have been born/is gone." Sexton repeats this line
continuously throughout the poem, intensifying the feel-
ings of discontent surrounding the issue. The speaker
seems very upset with the whole ordeal even though it might
have been necessary. The final stanza of the poem reads:
          Yes, woman, such logic will lead
          to loss without death. Or say what you want,
          you coward . . . this baby that I bleed.
     The speaker is angry with herself for thinking she
was doing the right thing by getting an abortion. She
feels in her heart, though, that she was wrong and now it
is too late.
```

Hough's ideas had reached the page just as they came into her mind. While intelligent and clear, they needed some grooming to be worth reading. A little critical distance and she was ready to tackle the style.

She recognized that the very important first sentence was a general statement about Sexton's poetry, expressing neither the poet's approach nor her own response. She knew that the life Sexton writes about was very wild; sometimes Hough had felt she was peeping into private matters. Maybe a figure of speech would capture that. With a little thought, she wrote this:

```
Anne Sexton's poetry is a window that looks into its
speaker's whirlwind life.
```

She turned a plain statement into poetry.

So onward. A little critical thinking about the rather flat second and third sentences revealed a cause and effect relationship that would tighten the ideas:

```
Because she writes her poetry in simple free verse, a
reader can easily understand, or let's say look in on the
speaker.
```

By adding "look in," she tied this thought back to the first sentence, and we get a much better sense not only of the point but of Hough herself.

She took a closer look at her next three sentences, and saw that they had the exact same sentence structure, beginning with *the, these,* and *they.* By combining sentences and deleting unnecessary verbiage, she could make a much stronger, clearer statement:

```
Sexton's interesting and bold topics--insanity, sins,
confessions, sex, women's issues and relationship prob-
lems--give the speaker a "bad girl" image.
```

She paused long enough to decide that *interesting* was just an empty version of *bold* and that *women's issues* and *relationship problems* hardly qualified as bold. She deleted the unnecessary words.

The second paragraph, while containing much to like, left much to improve. The language was drab, almost emotionless, and hardly appropriate, given the plight of the speaker and the strength of Hough's own feeling. Words such as *discontent, perplexed,* and *upset* were timid and vague. Hough decided to replace them with more precise and powerful words, such as *anxiety* and *regret.*

Hough realized that the second sentence, "The title of this poem alone can express the troubled feelings of the speaker," simply wasn't accurate. She deleted it. She also deleted the fourth sentence: "Unlike most poems, the title of this one perfectly describes the topic." The title names the topic, yes, but she saw that it didn't describe this complex issue.

She then expanded the old third sentence to take into account some of the complexity.

```
Such reactions are understandable: anyone with even re-
mote experience with an abortion is likely to suffer
inner conflict, even when compelling reasons exist for
taking that step.
```

The next change was the use Hough made of the refrain, "Someone who should have been born/is gone," pointing out in the revision that it suggests the speaker's obsession and guilt. And, finally, finding the last sentences rather flabby, Hough combined them into an excellent complex sentence.

```
Although she pretended she was doing the right thing, she
feels in her heart that she did wrong and it is now too late.
```

Another break and a little more critical distance.

When Hough read the revised passage, she realized that though it was unquestionably improved, her own intense feelings about the subject—her personal voice—still did not come across. She went back through the essay sentence by sentence—adding more expressive words, such as *courageous,* and firming the cadence and the sentence structure—so that the tone expressed her understanding of the speaker's predicament. As she revised, she became aware that her own thinking was clearer and sharper—more proof, if it were needed, that writing is a form of thinking.

Here is the revised passage:

```
     Anne Sexton's poetry is a window that looks into its
speaker's whirlwind life. Because she writes her poetry
in simple free verse, it is fairly easy for the reader to
understand, or let's say look in. Sexton courageously
tackles bold topics--insanity, sins, confessions, sex--
often giving her speaker a "bad girl" image.
     Anxiety and regret are particularly prominent in
Sexton's poem "The Abortion." Such reactions are under-
standable: anyone with even remote experience with an
abortion is likely to suffer inner conflict, even when
compelling reasons exist for taking that step. Throughout
the poem, Sexton's speaker repeats the line "Someone who
should have been born/is gone," indirectly expressing her
guilt and obsession. The speaker suggests that the abor-
tion may have been necessary--but that thought does not
comfort her or make her decision seem any better. The
final stanza of the poem reads:
              Yes, woman, such logic will lead
          to loss without death. Or say what you want,
              you coward . . . this baby that I bleed.
The speaker is angry with herself for making excuses. She
calls herself "coward" as though punishing herself. Al-
though she pretended she was doing the right thing, she
feels in her heart that she did wrong and it is now too
late.
```

Perfection was still far off, but Hough was well on the way to increasing the command and impact of her writing.

PART FIVE

Putting It All Together
College Writing

13

Doing Research

Somewhere along the way it is going to happen. A teacher, an employer, or a colleague will ask you to study a topic thoroughly, gather information, and write a paper that communicates your research in an accessible form. A time-honored response is to wait until the last moment, then whirl in a frenzy to the library for two days, thence to the keyboard to bash out an overnight wonder. This method has a world of drawbacks. The results are almost always shabby. Worst of all, last-minute researchers waste a real opportunity to do something challenging and significant.

Modern researchers have a powerful arsenal of tools and techniques. The most powerful is still the mind, its interests, its way of seeing things. Research tells you almost as much about yourself as about your topic. That may be why so many people like doing it. Research has its own suspense, its close calls, its mystery trails, its revelations. Enjoy it.

Like any writing project, the research paper is a process. We will divide that process into ten stages and look at each in this chapter and the next. The stages are:

Choosing a General Subject

Compiling a Working Bibliography

Limiting Your Area of Research

Formulating a Tentative Thesis

Reading and Taking Notes

Restating Your Thesis

Preparing an Outline

Writing a First Draft

Documenting Your Sources

Revising and Writing the Final Draft

If these stages sound like repetitions of much of our book, all the better: a research paper requires us to combine all our critical and analytical skills with all our writing skills, from drafting and inventing to choosing words.

The order of these stages varies from project to project, but few research papers are written without involving all of them in some way. Some stages repeat themselves; research is a recursive rather than a linear process. Be ready to rethink your thesis many times, to return to the library again and again, to go back over steps you thought you had left behind.

CHOOSING A GENERAL SUBJECT

A research paper has to be about something. That seems perfectly obvious, but, strangely enough, some writers neglect this essential requirement. They circle a possible topic page after page, switch to another one, and perhaps somewhere near the end, discover what it was they should have been discussing all along. By then, of course, it is too late. The first step in writing a research paper is to choose the general subject you will study.

Research topics will come to you along different paths. Your instructor may explicitly define the topic or leave it as broad as possible.

Working with an Assigned Topic

When you are given a topic for writing, read the assignment carefully. You will want to stay within its limits. Look closely at the questions or statements your instructor provides. You may find clues in them to direct you. Here, for instance, is a research assignment for an African studies class:

> Examine studies done by Warner, Junker, Adams, and Edwards. Compare their thinking about black group stability on the basis of class, economics, and social structure.

Go straight to the command words, *examine* and *compare.* They lead to both the sources (the various studies) and the subject (*their thinking about black group stability*). The assignment even provides subheadings (*class, economics, and social structure*) that could help you organize your paper.

Here an instructor limits a topic in a different way:

> What in your opinion were the main causes of the Johnson administration's "failure" in Vietnam in 1964–1967? Argue for your opinion on the basis of references to documents, debates in the press, and major scholarly interpretations.

Rather than asking for an analysis of what scholars have written, this instructor wants you to defend an opinion. He has been unusually kind, providing not only the topic and a suitable strategy (cause and effect) but also a possible theme: *"failure."* Those quotation marks are asking you to define the term, perhaps even to disagree with the verdict that the administration's policy *was* a failure. The assignment also specifies a time frame (*1964–1967*) and three broad kinds of sources. It will be up to you to limit the topic further in your research paper. But again, the way the question is phrased has given some idea of how to begin.

Discovering Your Own Topic

Frequently you will have free rein to find your own topic. You might discover a topic in the form of a surprise in the course. In the assigned reading for a course on architecture, for instance, you might come upon this sentence:

> Now Jefferson's plan [for Monticello] prefigures that by Frank Lloyd Wright of the Ward Willitts house of 1902.

If you had never thought of Thomas Jefferson as an important architect, that might lead you to consider whether other architects were deeply influenced by him. Your research project would be your opportunity to find out. Or in a psychology class your lecturer may comment in passing that

> Apologists for the Roman Catholic Church have often been critical of Freudian forms of therapy.

If you want to know why, you may have a research topic.

Take pains to choose a subject area large enough to offer you interesting research but small enough to allow you to treat it fully. No single paper can cover the whole field of Chinese-American relations or American fiction in the twentieth century. Researching such a large, amorphous subject can be like trying to serve Jell-O with your fingers.

Begin thinking about your subject early. Go over your textbooks, notes, and assigned readings. Brainstorm. Free-write. Question yourself and the subject systematically. Write out a few ideas. Let your ideas ripen.

If you are a journal-keeper, research is an excellent opportunity to put your journal to work. As soon as you receive a research assignment, free-write for ten to twenty minutes each day on the general assignment. Keep a dated diary of all visits to the library, all classroom revelations, all bright ideas. Review your journal often.

You may have trouble brainstorming if you don't know much about a topic. In that case, off to the library immediately: crack open some encyclopedias and other general reference works on the subject. If your library has programs such as First Search or Infotrac, use them to get a general idea of articles and books written on your subject. Get some background. Talk to your instructor. See how the subject looks before trying to narrow it.

When you have found a subject, you will need to start narrowing it to a manageable size. Here are ways of narrowing the two broad subjects we mentioned earlier.

> Chinese-American relations
>> Chinese-American trade relations
>>> Chinese-American trade relations and intellectual property rights
> American fiction in the twentieth century
>> American short fiction in the twentieth century
>>> American short fiction in the 1920s

These topics are still too broad to write on, but they are a proper size for starting a research project.

Christina Gerke, who wrote the paper reproduced at the end of Chapter 14, had complete freedom in her freshman composition class to choose her research topic. She was also taking a course entitled Contemporary American Society, which had interested her in the changes taking place in America. She knew that this topic was far too broad for a research project, so she began to whittle it down.

> Recent changes in American society
>> Minorities and recent changes in American society
>>> Minorities and the educational system

Although her subject was still broad, she had enough direction to make her first sweep of the library.

COMPILING A WORKING BIBLIOGRAPHY

Once you have chosen a general subject, it is time to begin your library work. Notice that this is the groundwork for more extensive research later. You are scouting ahead, getting the lay of the land, so that when the time comes for the real journey to begin, you will know where everything is.

Your main aim during this first sweep, which will take a number of visits to the library, is to compile a working bibliography, or a list of the books, articles, and other sources to be consulted in your research. The working bibliography will help you come up with the list of works cited in your final paper. Many instructors also require that you submit a preliminary bibliography early in the research process, and this stage will help you compile one.

You will find titles and leads to sources in many of the places we discuss in this section; you will also find them in the bibliographies of the books and articles you consult. Each source will send you to more sources, and so your working bibliography will grow. Make your list using notecards—they are the neatest and easiest way (see a system for note taking in "Taking Notes," pages 356–62). Add to and delete from your working bibliography as you extend your research.

Time Management

You will want to use your research time as efficiently as possible. Here are five hints on how to do so.

1. Start early on all projects. A good rule of thumb is to start writing no later than halfway between the time you receive the assignment and the deadline. That means that your research should have been started well before then—certainly before a third of the time has passed. Remember that every step will take longer than you think it will. Do not rely on the pressure of an advancing deadline to squeeze a project out of you.

2. Make frequent two- or three-hour visits to the library. This method usually works much better than marathon sessions. First, it gives you more time to ponder what you find. Second, you will remember and understand more in shorter sessions than when you are fatigued, hungry, and under pressure—for instance, frantically researching at three o'clock in the morning during the last week of the term.

3. Since few of us are at tip-top form all day, do your most challenging and creative work at your best time, whether that is early morning or late evening. Search, read, and take notes then; review notes and drafts when you begin to run down.

4. If possible, schedule your research visits for the same time every day. Like you, your brain likes habits.

5. Find a place free of distraction for your work. If your dorm room is a popular conversation spot, avoid it. If the library is a social center, check out the books and flee. Take frequent short breaks; get a drink of water or just gaze out the window. But make the breaks short. Don't steal time from yourself.

Using Notecards

Here you are, in the best place at the best time, notecards and sources at hand. Yes, notecards. Even at this early juncture, you will want to retain what you read. Do not rely on memory. Take careful notes.

For each source you plan to consult in detail, make a *bibliography card*. This card will contain all the vital information about the source. Put down the author's last and first name, the title, the journal name (for articles), and all publication information (place, publisher, date). To save yourself work later, follow the MLA format for lists of works cited (see "Documenting Your Sources" in Chapter 14). Be sure you include the library call number. And in case you need to return to it, write down where you found the source—what list, bibliography, or subject heading. Put the author's last name in capital letters in the upper-left-hand corner of the card. Losing or garbling any bibliographic information could cost you time later—or even the ability to cite a promising source.

If your source is electronic—from an Internet news group, for example—record whatever information you can to help a curious reader get back to that source, and always print out the information you plan to use.

 Computer Tip

If you store your note entries on computer, follow the same form used in Figure 13.1. Input your entries in alphabetical order, starting a new page with each entry. That way, it will be easy to "flip through" your note entries using **Page Up** or **Page Down**. Print out your entire note file after each research trip, and copy that file onto a backup disk.

Figure 13.1 shows a bibliography card that Christina Gerke made during her research. Note that her entry is exactly as it might appear in a list of works cited.

Figure 13.1.   Bibliography Card

BERK

LB   *Berk, Ronald, ed.*
3060.62   <u>*Handbook of Methods for Detecting Test Bias.*</u>
H36   *Baltimore: Johns Hopkins UP, 1982.*
                  SUBJECT CATALOG: "Test bias — congresses"

We will discuss note taking in more detail in "Taking Notes," pages 356–62. Here we want to emphasize that you should always make a complete record of every source that you expect to consult in any extensive way.

The Modern Library

Although most research will rely on the written word, college and university libraries house more than stacks of books. Researchers now must know more than how to look up an article or a book title. CD-ROM and online databases; record, audiotape, and compact disc collections; microfilm and microfiche collections; Internet access, including the library's own home page; videotape collections; motion picture catalogs; and interlibrary loan services are among the many resources available.

If a researcher were studying the treatment of Japanese-American servicemen during the Second World War, the traditional and necessary first approach would be to amass the titles of relevant books and articles. But it is not hard to think of materials that would augment the information in printed sources: newsreels and photographs, audio- and videotapes of interviews with Japanese veterans, even online discussion groups devoted to this topic. This kind of research can aid the traditional kind in creating a fully rounded and persuasive project.

Therefore, *know your library*.

As early as possible in your education, take a tour of your school's main library and learn the locations of any other libraries on or near the campus. If your school offers guided library tours, take one. If your library offers informational pamphlets, read them. Detailed knowledge of a college or university library system would take a research project in itself, but you will find it useful to develop a general idea of what materials are where. You might not have planned to step into the campus geology library, for instance, but you may find it useful if you do a report on the San Francisco earthquake of 1906. Also, learn about other institutions affiliated with yours. Become familiar with your school's information network.

Oh, yes—know the hours the libraries keep. Save yourself disappointment later.

Finally, get to know the librarians. People are often a library's most valuable resource. Librarians have been trained to know their collections and other available resources and to help those who do not know them as well. Reference librarians are paid to answer your questions, so ask them. And circulation librarians can help you locate a book if you cannot find it on the shelf.

Primary and Secondary Sources

In the library you will find two classes of materials: primary and secondary sources. You will probably use both, but it is important to distinguish between the two.

Primary sources are the contemporaneous documents relating to a subject: letters, interviews, polls, eyewitness accounts, experiments, speeches, and surveys. To write an essay on the battle of Vicksburg during the Civil War, you could consult *The Official Records of the War of the Rebellion between the Armies of the United States and the Armies of the Confederacy,* which contains primary documents, including military orders. Most instructors want you to examine available primary sources at some stage in your research. You can even create your own primary sources when you conduct interviews or take polls. For a discussion of this topic, see "Being Your Own Source," pages 347–48.

Secondary sources are what other investigators have said about a subject. Douglas Southall Freeman's great tome *Lee's Lieutenants,* a scholar's informed study of the decision makers in Lee's army, is a highly useful secondary source on the battles of the Civil War. (For a discussion of how to evaluate and use the expert evidence that secondary sources represent, see Chapter 6, Using Evidence.)

Most instructors want you to consult whatever primary documents are involved with your topic, but do not ignore the helpful insights in secondary sources.

The Reference Section

The main library will probably be your research center, and its reference section will be an early stop. Here you will find overviews of virtually every subject and guides to getting right to the more detailed information. Start big. Consult general surveys of your topic. Once you get an overview, you will know much better what aspect you want to pursue. Encyclopedias are especially good for background reading; they can provide you with the main terms, controversies, and names and biographies of people in your subject. Even if you do not have a subject yet, you may find one while looking through general reference works. Among the many types of resources available in the reference section, we will describe nine that you will find especially helpful.

General Encyclopedias.   General encyclopedias offer broad overviews of a variety of topics. Under the entry for your subject you can find a capsule survey, including a list of books for further reading. General encyclopedias are *not* adequate in themselves as research sources. They may, however, be helpful first steps. Christina Gerke consulted encyclopedia entries for "Intelligence" and "Education" as a first step in her research. Among the best general encyclopedias are *Collier's Encyclopedia, Encyclopedia Americana, Encyclopaedia Britannica,* and *New Encyclopaedia Britannica.* Encyclopedias are increasingly available in CD-ROM form.

Specialized Encyclopedias.   Almost all fields have their own encyclopedias. These books can help you with definitions of special terms and recurrent themes within a subject. Gerke, for instance, looked in *The Encyclopedia of Education* for a discussion of educational testing. Here are some other specialized encyclopedias:

> *Encyclopaedia of Religion and Ethics*
> *Encyclopedia of World Art*
> *International Encyclopedia of Film*
> *International Encyclopedia of the Social Sciences*
> *McGraw-Hill Encyclopedia of Science and Technology*
> *Oxford Companion to English Literature*

Dictionaries.   Dictionaries offer not only spellings, etymologies, and histories of words but also rules of punctuation, indexes of foreign phrases, and lists of famous people and places. Dictionaries become important at many points in research. When Gerke needed a good, solid definition of *intelligence,* she consulted the dictionary, where she discovered that the word refers not to one thing but to many, including understanding, quickness, and wisdom. She realized that measuring intelligence would not be an easy task. The dictionary she consulted is generally viewed as the most comprehensive and scholarly in English, the *Oxford English Dictionary.* Also among the most wide-ranging and thorough is *Webster's Third New International Dictionary of the English Language.* (For more on dictionaries, see the discussion in Chapter 11 called "Using Your Dictionary.")

Biographical Works.   Biographical works contain brief, informative entries on prominent people, detailing their lives and achievements. Such directories exist for people living and dead, for particular countries, and for various fields. Some are periodicals, and some are updated every few years. Consult them if you want to know more about the people in your study, or if you wish to follow up on unfamiliar names. Gerke consulted *Who Was Who* to learn more about Alfred Binet, and *Who's Who in America* for more on Arthur Jensen, both influential figures in educational testing. Other valuable biographical works include

> *American Men and Women of Science*
>
> *Biography and Genealogy Master Index*
>
> *Biography Index*
>
> *Chambers's Biographical Dictionary*
>
> *Current Biography*
>
> *Dictionary of American Biography*
>
> *Dictionary of National Biography* (British)
>
> *International Who's Who*
>
> *Notable American Women*
>
> *Webster's New Biographical Dictionary*

Guides to Books.   Guides to books can tell you what is currently being published in your field. Two general guides are *Books in Print,* yearly lists of books by author, title, and subject, and *Book Review Digest,* which offers summaries of book contents and reviews. Both are now available on CD-ROM.

Atlases.   Atlases contain more than maps. They can help you locate unfamiliar place names and also give you extremely useful facts and statistics about topology, population, economics, and forms of government. There are atlases for the whole world, for single countries, for specific regions, for the oceans, and for the heavens. There are atlases for the modern world and for the ancient world. Here is a small sampling: *Historical Atlas of the World, National Atlas of the United States of America,* and the *Times Atlas of the World.* Many maps and atlases are available on CD-ROM and on the Internet, including weather and satellite maps.

Research Guides.   These books help you find the most important research in a particular field. They will not list or summarize every work—rather, they will give you overviews and commentaries on the broad sweep of research and scholarship, with examples and suggested reading. Research guides bear titles such as *Guide to the Literature of Art History* and *Philosophy: A Guide to the Reference Literature.* A good source list for the titles of research guides is the *Guide to Reference Books,* published by the American Library Association.

Yearbooks.   Yearbooks summarize the issues, events, and statistics of a given year. Many are connected with encyclopedias. They chronicle a year's major events. A few examples are *American Annual, Britannica Book of the Year,* and *Facts on File Yearbook.*

Almanacs and Gazetteers.   Almanacs, such as *The World Almanac and Book of Facts,* can be either compendia of broad, general information arranged by the days of the year or annual general reviews of statistics and facts of all kinds. Gazetteers, such as the *Columbia Lippincott Gazetteer of the World,* are geographic dictionaries. Both contain useful information.

If you cannot find the reference works you need, ask your reference librarian.

Book Files and Catalogs

If you spend some time doing patient and alert reading in the reference section, you will emerge with a list of authors and titles of books. You may well return to the reference section later as you learn more about your subject. But now you need to know which of these books the library has. The library's book files and catalogs are your next stop.

If you are not familiar with the following files and catalogs, take time to learn their location and their use. Many libraries now have catalogs in different forms, including online catalogs, card catalogs, CD-ROM databases, bound books, and microfilm or microfiche.

The Online Catalog

Most college and university library catalogs are now online. Learn your library's system. Your user-friendly monitor probably will present a menu like the following:

```
WELCOME

Please choose one of the following options:

L> Library Catalog
I> Interlibrary Loan
C> Connect with Other Libraries
D> Databases
S> Library Information and Suggestions
Q> Quit
Choose one (L, I, C, D, S, Q):
```

As you can see, online catalogs do more than list books.

Listing and searching for books, however, is what you will most often use catalogs for. If what you seek is on the shelves, the online catalog can tell you its location and status in a couple of keystrokes. Online catalogs can help you search for a book in several ways:

By author

By title

By keyword in a title

By subject heading

If you find a promising book, some catalogs allow you to **Look at Other Books Nearby**—an extremely useful way to create a list of books on similar subjects. (Remember, books are not the only items the online catalog contains. Many online catalogs will also help you search for articles in periodicals.)

In a bibliography on educational testing, Christina Gerke discovered a listing for "Smith, Frank, *Insult to Intelligence.*" She immediately went to her library's online catalog and selected **D** for databases and then **Find Author.** She then typed in the author's name and found the entry displayed in Figure 13.2. The subtitle told Gerke that this was a book worth consulting. The call number led her to the right floor of the library, then to the right shelf, then to the right book.

Before she went to the book, however, Gerke used her online catalog's **Find Subject** feature to find other books with the subjects *Teaching—United States; Learning, Psychology of;* and *Education—Aims and objectives.* Beneath each subject heading, her catalog listed book titles alphabetically. Searching this list gave Gerke more titles and call numbers. She was careful to make separate and complete notecards for each book and article she found interesting.

Figure 13.2   Find Author Screen

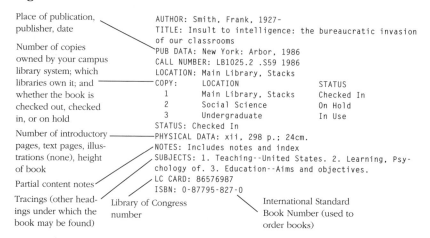

Place of publication, publisher, date

Number of copies owned by your campus library system; which libraries own it; and whether the book is checked out, checked in, or on hold

Number of introductory pages, text pages, illustrations (none), height of book

Partial content notes

Tracings (other headings under which the book may be found)

```
AUTHOR: Smith, Frank, 1927-
TITLE: Insult to intelligence: the bureaucratic invasion
of our classrooms
PUB DATA: New York: Arbor, 1986
CALL NUMBER: LB1025.2 .S59 1986
LOCATION: Main Library, Stacks
COPY:     LOCATION            STATUS
  1       Main Library, Stacks    Checked In
  2       Social Science          On Hold
  3       Undergraduate           In Use
STATUS: Checked In
PHYSICAL DATA: xii, 298 p.; 24cm.
NOTES: Includes notes and index
SUBJECTS: 1. Teaching--United States. 2. Learning, Psy-
chology of. 3. Education--Aims and objectives.
LC CARD: 86576987
ISBN: 0-87795-827-0
```

Library of Congress number

International Standard Book Number (used to order books)

Increasingly, online catalogs are becoming mini research centers. Many online catalogs offer you access to bibliographic databases such as Infotrac, First Search, *Books in Print,* the *Readers' Guide to Periodical Literature,* and *The MLA International Bibliography.* Some can connect you with newspaper indexes such as *The National Newspaper Index.* And some can link you to the catalogs of other libraries. Still others offer interlibrary loan and text reprint services; some allow you to access these services from home via modem. Find out what your library's system offers.

Card Catalogs

The card catalog lists each book the library owns on a separate card. The cards are arranged alphabetically by author, by title, and by subject heading. Each card provides the call number, by which you can locate a book on the shelves.

Figure 13.3 shows the "main entry," or *author card,* for Frank Smith's book *Insult to Intelligence* in the author-title catalog. The *title card* (see Figure 13.4) is exactly the same as the author card, except that it has the title at the top and is filed alphabetically by the first word of the title, not counting *a, an,* and *the.* The *subject card* lists the work alphabetically under the subject heading or headings shown on the author and title cards. The subject card for Smith under the heading *Education—Aims and objectives* also appears in Figure 13.4. Card catalogs also contain *reference cards,* which direct you to other related subject headings via a "See" or a "See also."

Figure 13.3   Main Entry Library Card

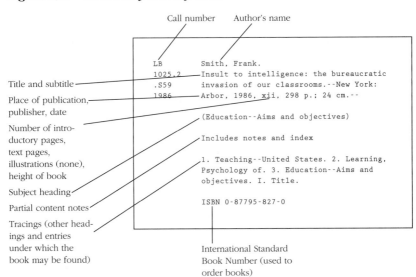

Figure 13.4   Title and Subject Library Cards

```
            Insult to intelligence.

 LB         Smith, Frank.
 1025.2     Insult to intelligence: the bureaucratic
 .S59       invasion of our classrooms.--New York:
 1986       Arbor, 1986.

                         EDUCATION--AIMS AND OBJECTIVES.
                 LB
                 1025.2     Smith, Frank.
                 .S59       Insult to intelligence: the bureaucratic
                 1986       invasion of our classrooms.--New York:
                            Arbor, 1986.
```

Subject headings can be a good lead in your research. If your library uses the Library of Congress classification system, the reference desk will have books called *Library of Congress Subject Headings,* which list all the subject headings most library catalogs use. Consult them to see the range of headings that may apply to your subject. If your library uses the Dewey Decimal classification system, consult the *Dewey Decimal Classification and Relative Index* for a directory of subjects. Many online catalogs offer a computerized version of this index. Once you have the headings, you can examine the catalogs to learn what your library has on the subject.

When using the files and catalogs, be a sleuth. Follow leads. Trace connections between ideas. When you know a few names, check under the authors' listings to see if they have written other books on the subject. Check subject headings under major key words you find in your study—*testing, educational psychology.* And do not forget to complement your search for books with an equally vigorous search for articles in periodicals.

Periodical Catalogs and Guides

The library's periodical catalog lists all the newspapers, newsletters, magazines, journals, and other periodicals the library owns. These catalogs may be available in print, on CD-ROM, or online. College writers sometimes avoid periodicals, probably because the process of finding books seems more familiar and less complicated. Locating an article is occasionally more difficult than tracking down a book, but the rewards can be great. Periodicals are rich, varied research sources. Their articles focus on very specific topics. They carry the latest scholarship and debate: you cannot ignore them if you want to know what people are thinking or learning *now*.

You can locate the issues you want in a general or specialized periodical index. Recent issues will be out on the shelves in what is often called the periodical room. Older issues are usually bound or stored on film and are located in a special section of the library. Both the indexes and the periodicals themselves may also be available on CD-ROM or online. Below we discuss some useful types of periodical guides.

General Periodical Indexes.   General periodical indexes are invaluable directories to articles. They are organized in different ways, alphabetically or chronologically, but it will take only a moment to figure out the organization. Two extremely helpful general indexes are the *Essay and General Literature Index* and the *Readers' Guide to Periodical Literature,* both available in either print or electronic form. Each of these sources contains a guide to its use and an explanation of the abbreviations employed. Find these helps and use them.

The *Readers' Guide* is a good starting point for research. It indexes articles in popular periodicals by year, by quarter, and by month, and it lists articles by author and by subject. Be careful with it, though—not all the periodicals it covers are authoritative. Check the title of the journal and the author's credentials (see "Recognizing Good Sources," pp. 335–56).

The CD-ROM version of the *Readers' Guide* is quickly becoming a mainstay of many reference rooms. Students and scholars find it a convenient and useful first step in their research projects. As with other CD-ROM and online databases, you tell the database what to search for, and it delivers a list of periodical sources.

Gerke consulted the *Readers' Guide* CD-ROM database and found the entries shown in Figure 13.5 by searching under the topic *Scholastic Aptitude Test.*

Newspaper Indexes.   As their name suggests, these books and electronic databases are indexes for articles published in newspapers. The all-time newspaper index is probably the *New York Times Index.* Other newspapers that offer indexes include the *San Jose Mercury News,* the *Wall Street Journal,* and the *Washington Post.* Especially exciting is the *National Newspaper Index,* a CD-ROM database available at many libraries. (It is also available on several online services.) This is an index of several great newspapers, including all of those just mentioned. *Facts on File* publishes a twice-monthly index of summaries of recent news, and NewsBank is a monthly index of 450 papers, available in print or on CD-ROM. Learn what your library owns and how to use it.

In the 1975 volume of the *New York Times Index,* Gerke found one of her sources (see Figure 13.6). At first she had looked under the heading *Scholastic Aptitude Test,* which referred her to the heading *Colleges*

Figure 13.5   Entries from the Readers' Guide Abstracts (on CD-ROM)

```
Author ──────────────────── AUTHOR: Seligman, Daniel
Article title ──────────────── TITLE: Testing . . . testing (alleged sexism in
                                       scholastic testing)
Periodical title, ───────────── SOURCE: Fortune (ISSN:0015-8259) v 115 p 153-4
volume number,                          May 11 '87
pages, date                     CONTAINS: illustration(s)

Includes main topic ────────── SUBJECTS COVERED:
and related subjects            Sex discrimination in education
                                Scholastic Aptitude Test
Detailed abstract ──────────── ABSTRACT: Genetic differences between males and females,
summarizes article              rather than discriminatory tests, most likely cause
                                males to perform better on SAT tests than females. As
                                explained by psychologist Robert G. Lehrke, men's


                           TITLE: A rejection slip for the SAT
                          SOURCE: Newsweek (ISSN:0028-9604) v 109 p 71
                                  April 27 '87

                         SUBJECTS COVERED:
                         Scholastic Aptitude Test
                         ABSTRACT: The Scholastic Aptitude Test (SAT), which is
                         required for admission into nearly 75 percent of four-
                         year colleges, has fallen upon hard times. Middlebury
```

and Universities—United States—Grading of Students. One article listed there sounded promising. To find it she went to the microfilm room of the library, got the spool that included the May 4, 1975, issue of the *New York Times,* located the proper section, and read the article. She thought the information well worth her search. She also checked under the same heading in volumes for other years: 1989, 1990, and so forth. You should check under the same heading starting in volumes for ten years in the past and work your way to the present.

Specialized Periodical Indexes and Bibliographies.   Specialized periodical indexes and bibliographies list articles and books in particular fields. They are a natural resource as your subject focus narrows and you need more specific information. Gerke consulted the *Social Sciences Index* and the *Education Index,* both of which yielded further leads. Almost every field has an index of periodicals. Here are a few:

> *Applied Science and Technology Index*
>
> *Art Index*
>
> *Business Periodicals Index*
>
> *General Science Index*
>
> *Humanities Index*
>
> *MLA International Bibliography*
>
> *Guide to U.S. Government Publications*

Figure 13.6   Entry from the New York Times Index

Main subject heading ——————————— **COLLEGES and Universities – United States – Finances – Cont**

Nathan Kolodney disagrees with Prof Richard Gambino's remarks on Jews in Dec 8 article on high cost of coll educ, · Ir, D 20,26:5

NY Times survey of NYC's fiscal crisis notes leading social scientists see parallel between that plight and plight of univ; notes costs have spiraled for colls, and tuition often exceeds full-time means of students, while full-time teaching load is 6-8 hours per week in many insts, with 4-month vacations; Yale Univ Prof Douglas Yates cites 'unconscious acceptance of past practice' (M), D 29,50:7

Subheadings and ——————————— •*Foreign Students.* **See** subhead Foreign Study
list of other relevant ·*Fraternities and Sororities.* **See also** names
subheadings

Pres Ford on Dec 31 signs bill containing amendment following up regulation on sex discrimination in educ activities issued by HEW; measure exempts from provisions membership practices of tax-exempt social fraternities and sororities (S), Ja 1,36:4

·*Grading of Students.* **See also** subhead US – Adult Education, Ag 3. Subhead US – Equal Educ, Ja 16. Subhead US – Student Activities, My 18

Jackson never graduated from hs; NCAA official Bill Hunt

Author's name ——————————— comments on increased violation of acad rules; King illus (M), F 7,22:3; Diane Ravitch article explores history,
Detailed summary ——————————— theory, purpose, value and other aspects of Scholastic Aptitude Test (SAT), which will be given this yr to some 1.5-million hs srs seeking to enter coll; notes supporters of tests view them as reliable indicators for predicting coll performance, while critics contend tests are racially and culturally biased; some educators concede tests may be culturally biased to extent that reading is culturally linked; many colls are now giving weight to other factors, such as depth of preparation and unusual personal qualities, in admitting students; modifications expected in some aspects of tests but prospects for future is that testing, evaluation

Date, section of the paper, and assessment on national basis will be a regular and
and page on which the pervasive aspect of educ policy; samples of typical
article begins. Note: you questions from SAT exams; student taking exam illus (L),
must consult the article My 4.VI,p12; Mrs Charles M Apt Ir on Diane Ravitch May
itself for the title and 4 article on College Entrance Examination Bd holds
pagination. manner in which exam dates are set militates against public school students; Ravitch replies; illus, Je 8,VI,p54; efforts on some coll campuses to do away with grade inflation, by

Abstracts.   Abstracts list journal articles in specific fields and offer brief article summaries. Reading the summaries does not take the place of reading the articles, but the summaries do tell you whether an article is what you want. *Abstracts in Anthropology, Historical Abstracts, Psychological Abstracts,* and *Science Abstracts* are among the abstracts you may find helpful.

Databases.   Although print databases are still in use, libraries have moved rapidly toward electronic databases, which usually are more comprehensive, more convenient, and more current than their print counterparts. *Online databases* are those you access on the Internet via computer and modem. Many libraries have computer terminals for this use; learn what your library has. There are thousands of online databases available. *CD-ROM databases* are stored either on small compact disks or on the library's main computer system, and they can be accessed at terminals throughout the library. As mentioned, online and

CD-ROM databases are updated much more frequently than are print sources; online databases keep their information the freshest. Some very useful bibliographic databases now available on CD-ROM include *Books in Print,* the *Readers' Guide to Periodical Literature,* and the *MLA International Bibliography.*

Many electronic databases, as well as many online catalogs, use Boolean logic, named after its inventor, George Boole. This simple system uses the words *and, or,* and *not* to define subject and title searches. You can use the words *and* and *not* to make your search term more specific. In researching the subject of standardized intelligence tests, Gerke first tried the term *intelligence,* and her database gave her a long, unusable list of everything written on the broad subject of intelligence. The subject *intelligence and testing* narrowed the search dramatically. *Testing not Jensen* allowed her to see a list of all works on testing—excluding those by Jensen and those mentioning him in the title. The word *or* allows you to expand a search. Part of Gerke's paper addressed college entrance examinations, so she did a search using *college boards or SATs;* her search turned up sources on both topics.

Other Library Resources

We have been discussing the main reference works your library offers. These will doubtless be somewhere on your itinerary, but they do not exhaust the library's resources. Depending on your research, you may have many other places to visit, including the following five.

Recent Acquisitions List.   Listings for recently purchased books and periodicals take a while to get into the library's catalogs. Thus, most libraries have separate up-to-date lists of relatively new materials, usually on computer printouts or microfiche. Consult these lists, especially if your topic concerns very recent events.

Microfilm Holdings.   Many libraries own microfilm copies of old and rare books, newspapers, and public and private documents. Many, for example, own microfilms of books printed in English before 1640. Usually, the online catalog entry or card in the author-title catalog will tell you whether a work is on microfilm.

Special Collections.   Because some library collections are marked *special,* you may be intimidated. Don't be. The books are there to serve you, and some of them can be quite helpful. For instance, in writing a paper about the history of Boston, you may find that one of your library's special collections includes a privately printed booklet about one of the city's earliest merchant families. Materials in special collections may be listed either in the author-title catalog or in separate catalogs.

Government Documents.   Many libraries have a special area in which they house government documents, that is, publications by various state, federal, and foreign governments. These documents are not as dry or narrowly focused as they sound. The U.S. government, for example, publishes material on everything from international arms negotiations to how to collect honey from bees. The *Congressional Record* is an unsurpassed primary source for what goes on in the U.S. Congress. The government documents area is definitely worth exploring. Most government documents are also available via the Internet.

Online Searches.   Many libraries subscribe to local, state, national, and world computer information services. If your library does not have the information you need, the reference librarian may be able to either obtain a printout of the needed material or tell you the name of the nearest place that owns it. Other services can suggest books on the same or a related subject; still others can give you cross-references along with related subject listings. Again, make it your business to know what your library has and how to use it.

Computers have revolutionized the process of making preliminary bibliographic searches. But such computer searches are *only* preliminary. Nothing takes the place of checking the stacks, paging through promising sources, and scanning recent periodicals.

Being Your Own Source

You need not limit yourself to material you can find in libraries. You can also generate your own primary source information.

Interviews.   You can interview people involved with your subject. Ask them about their experiences and what they know. One student's report on the social organization of a local Quaker congregation included interviews with elders and members.

There is an etiquette to interviewing. Some interviewers handwrite notes; others input them into laptop computers; still others use tape recorders. Always ask your interviewee for permission to use your technology of choice. Taping the interview can save time and allow you to devote more attention to the interview and less to taking notes. When you conduct an interview, have your questions written out in advance. Always offer to let interviewees listen to the tape later, or better yet, read a typed transcript of the interview. These courtesies will allow them to verify what they have said and thus lend more authority to your evidence.

Correspondence.   You often can get helpful information by writing to people involved with your topic, such as congressional representatives, your governor or mayor, or people in business, sports, or entertainment.

If you write a respectful, serious letter, the results can be surprising. One memorable research project on the Mercury astronauts was based in part on correspondence with John Glenn, Wally Schirra, and Alan Shepard. Be sure to leave ample time for an answer to your letter. E-mail accomplishes many of the same aims very quickly.

Polls.   One of our favorite essays included polls measuring audience response to three different performances of Henrik Ibsen's play *Hedda Gabler*. Unfortunately, polls are easy to get wrong. If you do not have experience with them, consult a friend or teacher who does. The better the instrument, the better the data. (For a brief discussion of polling, see Chapter 6, Using Evidence.)

Fieldwork.   Some researchers can go right out into the field to collect information. For a research paper on Indian burial grounds in the San Francisco Bay area, one student visited an archaeological excavation on the site of a planned subway station. Eventually, he started digging himself.

Experiments.   Much writing in the natural and social sciences is based on experiments the writer has conducted. To test extrasensory perception, a student designed a set of cards and asked all the students on his dorm floor to identify what was on the hidden side of each card. He analyzed the responses, and then, disappointed to learn that only chance was operating, he valiantly wrote up the experiment anyway.

Other Personal Experiences.   You can research your own experience or background. Did your family name change when your ancestors came to America? You could discuss when and how it changed in a paper on immigration history. Have you ever had to testify in court? Your experience could contribute to a paper on the legal system.

Personal experience has both its own authority and its own limitations. When using it, work especially hard for objectivity and relevance. You should be at least as careful when you are your own source as when you use library research. For a brief discussion of personal experience as evidence, see Chapter 6.

USING THE INTERNET IN YOUR RESEARCH

The word *Internet* is short for *interconnected networks,* and that is exactly what the Internet is: a world network of connected computers (called hosts) offering information, services, and still more connections to anyone who happens to come along. If you have access to a phone line, a modem, a computer, and the proper software, you can use the

Internet as a research tool. Here, we will look at some of the resources, some of the issues, and some of the problems.

What Kinds of Sources Are Available?

The Internet constitutes the largest reference room in the history of humankind. To make the most of it, familiarize yourself with what's out there by browsing for a few hours. It is also a good idea to read a reliable Internet reference guide (see our bibliography, pp. 565–66) to uncover a variety of excellent sites. Below we list some places to start. (The addresses given were current when this book went to press. Check all Internet address at your library's reference desk or via Gopher on the Internet.)

Library Catalogs. The catalogs of most major university and city libraries are now online. Some of these services allow you to search and retrieve text files. Many allow you to arrange interlibrary loans. Through Gopher, you can find a menu of libraries throughout the world and instructions on how to connect with their online catalogs (gopher:// libgopher.yale.edu). The reference staff of most libraries are easily available through either e-mail or the telephone.

Reference Works. On the Internet you can find dictionaries, atlases, books of quotations, biographical references—almost anything you can find in a good library reference room. A good starting place is the Reference Desk (http://dewey.lib.ncsu.edu). Another place to try is the Whole Internet Catalog (http://gnn.com/wic/wics/index.html).

Government Documents. Most government documents available in print are now available online, including the text of congressional bills (http:// thomas.loc.gov), census data (http://cedr.lbl.gov/mdocs/LBL_census.html), even the text of the Gettysburg Address (http://jefferson.village.virginia. edu/readings).

Databases. Thousands of databases are now available on the Internet. There are databases for almost every area of interest, from accounting (http://www.rutgers.edu/Accounting/raw/internet/internet.htm) and art history (http://rubens.anu.edu.au) to linguistics (http://www.sil. org/linguistics/linguistics.html) and popular music (http://american. recordings.com/wwwofmusic/).

Texts. The complete Bible (http://jg.cso.uiuc.edu/pg/lists/subject2. html), all of Shakespeare's writings (http://the-tech.mit.edu/Shakespeare/ works.html), and many other texts are available on the Internet. A good directory is the World Wide Web Virtual Library (http://sunsite.unc.edu/ ibic/guide.html).

Electronic Journals.   Hundreds of journals are now online. (Some are online versions of print journals; others are available only online.) You connect with them and read their contents, much as with a print journal.

Interactive Resources on the Internet: E-mail, Mailing Lists, Newsgroups, and Bulletin Boards

In addition to home pages, text, and graphics resources, the Internet offers a range of interactive resources—various ways of communicating with other people with shared interests. E-mail, mailing lists, newsgroups, and bulletin boards are the best-known examples.

E-mail can be a useful source of information. We know several students who have sent e-mail messages to scholars and other important figures in their fields, asking questions, requesting clarifications, and discussing possible paper topics. People generally consider e-mail less invasive than telephone or direct mail. We are pleased to report that, although not everyone replies nicely or replies at all, most who do respond have done so courteously and with interesting, usable insights. E-mail messages from reputable figures constitute exciting and original material.

A mailing list (also known as a discussion list) is best thought of as a *place*. People with a common interest (astronomy, athletics, motion pictures, rap music) sign on to a mailing list in order to discuss their shared interest and read what others have to say about it. If you send a message to a mailing list, that message is broadcast to all others on the list. In turn, you receive all other messages placed on the list. This system makes it a free-form forum.

Mailing lists can be useful but limited short-cuts for difficult research questions. Post a question on a mailing list in your specific area of research, and wait for the answers to come in. It will be up to you to check the accuracy of any information you receive.

Newsgroups and bulletin boards (also known as message boards) are similar to mailing lists, except that you do not receive any mail. Newsgroups are forums for people with shared interests. You connect with a newsgroup and read what people are saying. You can make your own contributions to the continuing conversation, go away, and return later to read the responses. Newsgroups are not usually anonymous; you can trace interesting contributions to their source by noting the e-mail address of the contributor.

Narrowing the Net

With millions of hosts, the Internet is far too large and shapeless even to conceive of, much less use, as a research tool. And there is no one road map for the whole thing. There are, however, ways to narrow your search for information. We suggest you learn about Gopher, the search service originated at the University of Minnesota. Similar services are the Wide Area Information Server (WAIS); Archie, Jughead, and Veronica; and Telnet.

The best-known attempt to organize the Net is the World Wide Web. Created in 1990 by the European Particle Physics Laboratory in Geneva, Switzerland, the Web links thousands of Internet hosts and services. For most people, the Web is nearly synonymous with the Internet. If you have America Online, CompuServe, Prodigy, or some other commercial service, chances are you already have easy access to the Web and pointers on how to find what you want.

What makes the Web so useful is that many of its hosts are connected to others by means of *hyperlinks*—a set of cross-referencing systems that allow you to "jump" to other resources (graphics, sounds, other Web hosts) from a particular place. For example, if you connect with the Virtual Louvre, you can jump to a list of painters, from which you can select da Vinci, and from a description of da Vinci you can jump to an image of the *Mona Lisa*. Through hyperlinks, you can surf your way to the information you need most.

Browsing is a great way to discover the Internet. When doing research, however, you want something more efficient than casual exploration. Below are three means of focusing your Internet searches.

Browsers, Directories, and Search Engines

A *browser* is a program that runs like a comb through the Internet, bringing back things of interest to you. Some browsers are better than others, and, since thousands of hosts go on- and offline every day, none has a list of every single Internet host. Your online service probably has a built-in Web browser; start with that.

Many browsers are in the form of *directories,* lists of Internet sites organized by topic. Three useful directories are Yahoo (http://www.yahoo.com), Web Voyager (http://webspace.com//~wvoyager), and the Whole Internet Catalog (http://neamet.gnn.com/wic/index/html). Like the Yellow Pages, a good directory can guide you from general topic to subtopic to subsubtopic until you find useful material. Directories are excellent starting points in Internet research.

Search engines are programs that help you find specific terms on the Internet. Instead of navigating by subject, you simply enter a term for which you wish to search. Three search engines we have found very useful are Alta Vista (http://www.altavista.digital.com), Lycos (http://lycos.cs.cmu.edu), and Infoseek (http://www.infoseek.com). And there are gigantic *metasearch engines* such as All-in-One Search Page (http://www.albany.net/~wcross/all1srch.html) or Savvy Search (http://www.cs.colostate.edu/~dreiling/smartform.html) that put several search engines at your disposal. Remember: most search engines will bring you back lists of Internet sites in which the term you choose (*Intelligence tests* or *SAT,* for example) is *mentioned,* not necessarily a page dedicated to that term.

You have to tell these programs what to look for, however; how you tell them is extremely important. If you connect with a search engine and ask it to look for *poetry,* it will bring you an unorganized, unusable list. Alta Vista obediently brought us back 90,000 host names. Not useful.

With many search engines, you can use Boolean logic to narrow your search, much as you can with databases. Run several searches, making your search titles as specific as possible. With each search, look through at least thirty items. If an item catches your interest, click on the address, and you will ride the hypertext magic carpet to that source.

Let the User Beware: Being Critical about Internet Sources

Wonderful as it is, much of the Internet is inappropriate for research use because verification of sources—an essential part of research—can be extremely difficult. Anyone can create a home page, newsgroup, or database, and the result is that this great information universe is also a whirling nebula of junk. (For a general discussion on evaluating sources, see "Recognizing Good Sources," pp. 355–56.)

Try to learn the background and aims of the people responsible for the information on any Internet source you use. If an address is given, send an e-mail message to the address and ask for references, perhaps even page numbers—and then check them. And prefer Internet addresses bearing the name of reputable sources: prefer the Oxford University Shakespeare Project to Bill's Ho-made Shakespeare Korner. Unless you can verify that your information comes from a reputable source and is accurate, it is all but worthless. Consult our bibliography on page 565 for a listing of current guides to the Internet that we find useful.

A good rule for using Internet information is to discard any source if:

you have neither the time nor the resources to verify it properly

the information is anonymous

a source is given but is difficult or impossible to trace

your inquiries about the information receive dismissive or obscure answers—or none at all

in the course of hyperlinking you run into questionable or inappropriate material, anything from jokes to pornography.

A good research guide, a critical stance, and a little experience will help you separate the dross from the gold.

LIMITING YOUR AREA OF RESEARCH

As you learn more and more about your subject, you will begin to see how it divides into parts. This will suggest ways to narrow the subject to exactly what you want to research.

One of the leading killers of research projects is an overly large topic. If you take on too much, you will not be able to shape your material effectively. If you neglect the research necessary to cover the topic, your ideas will lack the background or support they need. Your paper will be as deep as a teacup. You should aim to work on a topic small enough to cover well but challenging enough to be worth covering.

After Christina Gerke had scouted the reference works, the catalogs, the periodical indexes, and the Internet, she saw that her topic, *minorities and the educational system,* was far too broad. She brainstormed a list of attractive aspects of the subject.

> affirmative action in colleges
>
> busing
>
> changing populations in city schools
>
> Supreme Court decisions on minorities in education
>
> incorporating minority views into history
>
> the effects of standardized testing

She paused there. While compiling her working bibliography, she had discovered that standardized tests were a hot issue. People argued about what the tests measured, how they were designed, and what effects they had on future careers. There was obviously a good deal more to learn about testing, particularly about its effects on minorities.

By eliminating some possibilities and focusing more intently on others, Gerke narrowed her topic this way:

> Recent changes in American society
>> Minorities and recent changes in American society
>>> Minorities and the educational system
>>>> Standardized tests and their effects on minorities

As you read more and narrow your subject further, you no doubt will begin to identify controversies to be settled, causes to be traced, patterns to be explained, questions to be answered. While you consider the possibilities, ask yourself a series of questions about your direction and focus.

> Do I like this topic?
>
> Do I feel in control of it?

Do I have enough time to do thorough research on it?

Will I be able to find out enough about it in the sources available to me?

Will I find adequate support for my ideas?

Is the topic appropriate for the assigned length?

Is it too elementary?

Is it too technical?

Is it worth my while?

Will it interest my audience?

Know the answers to these questions before you write. Early in the project, your instructor may advise you on some of them.

FORMULATING A TENTATIVE THESIS

At this point, a tentative thesis can help you organize your thoughts and direct your research. A tentative thesis in a research project is like a working hypothesis in a scientific experiment. It is the "idea" the research will examine, so it serves as the basis for further investigation.

You may find it helpful to express your topic in the form of a question and your position as an answer. That answer can often be your tentative thesis. This is what Christina Gerke wrote:

QUESTION	In light of the effects of standardized tests on the careers of minority students, should educators continue to use the tests?
ANSWER	We should do away with standardized tests because they perpetuate prejudice against minorities.

Gerke was aware that her thesis was tentative and that her ideas might change by the end of the research process.

At this stage, don't lock yourself into a set proposition. The intensive search you are about to undertake may—probably will—uncover facts and opinions that will make you change your ideas. Welcome the opportunity to change your thesis as the material guides you.

We have so far been discussing the tentative thesis with an argumentative edge. Some research assignments, however, want you only to gather information and report it. Your report will still need an organizational thesis to give shape to your research. (For a full discussion of the organizational thesis for a report, see Chapter 15, Writing in All Disciplines: The Report.)

READING AND TAKING NOTES

Back to the library, tentative thesis in mind.

Here among the stacks, you will now read more intensively, collecting evidence to support, or correct, your tentative thesis. Don't stint on gathering information. Search the stacks. When your research leads you to a book with a particular call number, look also at the books around it on the shelf. Perhaps they too will be promising sources. Page through a few books and evaluate them. Flip through your bibliography cards. Look for other books by the same authors. Follow interesting leads. Chase ideas through periodicals. Collect the details of your subject, the uncommon facts, the competing theories. Whenever possible, trace all references back to their original sources. You probably will not use everything you amass, but the more you know, the more confidence you will have when you sit down to write.

Recognizing Good Sources

A kind of reasonable panic may set in at this point. "I'm going to have 3,000 notecards! It could take weeks just to write everything down. How can I decide which materials are authoritative and which I can leave alone?"

Excellent question. Not all your sources are going to be good ones. Some will be popularizations, summaries, quick-and-easy presentations of topics you need to read about in depth. To sort out the useful from the fallible, test each book, article, or other source you find in these five ways.

Reliability of the Author.   Ask yourself whether you have seen the author's name in other references. Check his or her background in a biographical or bibliographic index. Consult the *Book Review Digest* for reactions to his or her writings. Ask the reference librarian or your instructor for help.

Quality of the Periodical, Publishing House, or Online Source.   Try to get a sense of which periodicals are truly authoritative for your topic. *Time* magazine offers mostly glossy and simplified versions of events. A *Time* account of recent heart transplant techniques would not be nearly as detailed and reliable as one in the *New England Journal of Medicine*. *Scientific American* is a respected science magazine, but it is hardly as authoritative as the more scholarly *Nature*. For books, assess the publishing house. Is it a university press or one of the well-established trade houses? Have you heard of it before? Have you seen it in other references? Again, ask your reference librarian or your instructor. The Internet poses special difficulties in this regard. If you have found your source via a reference librarian, an online service, or a guidebook, chances are that the source is reliable.

Currency of the Material. Check dates of all sources. With most topics, especially current issues, you will want sources as up-to-date as you can find. Suppose your topic is the economy of Pakistan. Pakistani politics and external relations are changing so rapidly that few books more than five years old will be authoritative. Some topics, of course, have standard references that are quite old. Sir James Frazer's *The Golden Bough,* for instance, is still a classic source in anthropology, although it was first published in 1907. But even in a relatively established field, such as Elizabethan drama, most authoritative studies are less than thirty years old. If a source seems out of date, look for newer material.

Completeness of the Presentation. Look for both detail and comprehensiveness. Do not rely wholly on summaries. Prefer Professor Y's original journal article to a brief excerpt from her informal posting on an online message board. For clues to the completeness of a source, check the title and subtitles, the length, the table of contents, chapter headings and subheadings, the bibliography, and the index.

Slant or Bias. Some sources have a bias arising from politics, nationality, the methods of research used, or the sponsors of the study. Books or articles out of the conservative Hoover Institution or the Heritage Foundation may have a different slant from those out of the liberal Brookings Institution or Common Cause. We are not suggesting that you should ignore works from these organizations. That would be foolish, for they can be useful and scholarly. But whatever you consult, be alert to bias. Read prefatory chapters carefully: authors sometimes bring their affiliations and their prejudices to light at the beginning of a work. Notice the tone: does it seem judicious? Look also for a balance between opinion and substantiation. Is opinion clearly and consistently distinguished from fact? If so, the source may be a responsible one; if not, you should have your doubts. Internet sources may take somewhat more work to check, but many are reachable through hyperlinks, e-mail, and the telephone, and they usually are happy to furnish information about the origins, viewpoints, and aims of their organizations.

Taking Notes

Never sit down with any source until you are prepared to take notes. Taking notes on what you read serves two purposes: it helps you store information for easy recall, and it helps you organize your essay. You will reap these benefits only if you gather and arrange your notes carefully. Review Chapter 3, Critical Reading, and apply the principles there to any source on which you take notes.

We all have our own ways of taking notes, and no system in this or any other book can guarantee brilliant results. The following suggestions, however, have worked well for many people.

Take notes on notecards. Although some people use sheets of paper when they take notes, we think notecards are a more efficient way to store information. They are flexible: you can move them around in a pack as you wish, and, as you will see, you can group them to help you shape your essay. Unlike bibliography cards, which contain factual information about the works consulted, notecards remind you of the *content* of sources.

🖥 **Computer Tip**

If you take notes on a laptop, follow the same format as in Figure 13.7: use one page per note, and store all notes in a file different from your bibliographic notes file.

Whenever you find something interesting or significant—a quotation, an idea, a piece of information, a reference, a picture, a statistic, a graph—make a note of it on a notecard. Develop notecards on all the sources you consult in any depth.

Use one card for each major point. Avoid covering cards with too many notes; otherwise you will not be able to file them efficiently. It is much better to make a separate notecard for each point. In the upper-left corner, write the author's name. In the upper-right corner, write the topic of the note in a key word or short phrase. Never forget to write down the *exact* location of the noted material, whether it be page number, Internet address, or electronic database location. You may well need to find your way back to important information; you may well need locations for documentation later. In the notecard in Figure 13.7, Christina Gerke used the key phrase *minority performance.*

File each notecard under the key word or phrase. As you accrue notes, you will be compiling stacks of cards on the various aspects of your subject. They will all be together when you need them. Under each key word or phrase, alphabetize your notecards by the author's last name. If the author is anonymous, use the first word of the title of the source. This will be helpful later when you want quick access to specific points; you can go directly to the exact spot in the stack.

Keep your cards grouped together with rubber bands. You may want to use different colors or sizes of cards to keep notecards separate

Figure 13.7   Key Phrase Notecard

Berk   *Minority Performance*

*183–184: minority students give answers that are right
for them but show up wrong on tests*

from bibliography cards. Three-by-five-inch cards will be adequate for bibliography cards, but use four-by-six-inch cards for notes, because they have more room. Edit your notes frequently—that is, delete old or useless sources often.

There is no rule for how many notecards are enough, although you can usually tell when your research is skimpy. An old high-school rule of thumb says, with some reason, that forty is a lower limit for a ten-page paper. It is not unusual, however, to get into the hundreds. Do not be afraid of a rich supply.

What kinds of notes should you take? You have three choices, and you should probably use them all:

> *quotation*—a precise, word-for-word rendering of the author's original statement
>
> *paraphrase*—a rendering that follows the order and emphasis of the author's original statement but puts it in your own words
>
> *summary*—a concise, condensed presentation of the essentials of the author's original statement.

Quotation. Sometimes an author will make a point with such eloquence or authority that you will want to write down the exact words. Don't misquote. Carefully spell and punctuate exactly as the author did, and put quotation marks around the material. If you decide you do not need the entire quotation, indicate where you have omitted any words (see "Integrating Quotations into Your Text," pp. 367–70). After you complete the transcription, proofread your card against the text, and be sure to write down the exact page numbers or locations. This may seem time-consuming, but it will save you grief later.

Sometimes you will quote a passage because of its particular aptness or authoritativeness. In an article by George F. Madaus, Gerke found a passage that expressed fears similar to her own about standardized tests. She had already made a bibliography card for Madaus, so now she made a notecard on which she quoted this passage exactly (see Figure 13.8).

At other times you may wish to quote a passage because of the way in which it is phrased, for the language as well as the content. While reading Andrew J. Strenio's *The Testing Trap*, Gerke found a passage that she knew immediately was worth writing down word for word. Strenio was arguing that many people have the right skills for a job yet would do poorly on a standardized test on such skills.

> Can't you just see Richard Petty asking an applicant for one of his racing crews to take a standardized test on internal combustion engines? Or Red Auerbach telling Larry Bird to quit the Celtics until he scores well on a standardized test about passing lanes in basketball?

Right away she made a bibliography card and a notecard with the quotation on it.

If the material you are quoting is lengthy, you may wish to photocopy it—especially if you can't take the source out of the library, as with noncirculating journals, reference books, and special collections materials. If working online, you can simply print out the material you

Figure 13.8   Quoted Passage Notecard

Madaus   "Effects of Tests"

"The more one knows about the technology of testing, the more one realizes the potential for harm when a test score is used as the sole or primary criterion on which to make an important decision affecting an individual's future."

(93)

wish to use. Make sure to record all the information you'll need to document the source you're copying or printing out. Record this information both on a bibliography card and at the top of the first page of the material.

Photocopying and printing out have three important limitations. First, the cost can add up. Second, copyright laws govern the amount of material you may take and the purpose for which you may use it. The library staff should know the laws and be able to advise you. Third, photocopying and printing out let you take only the material with you—they are no substitute for thinking critically and taking careful notes.

Quote only when the elegance, forcefulness, or authority of the author's original words is absolutely essential. When *what* the author says is more important than *how* the author says it, you may wish to paraphrase or summarize.

Paraphrase.   Paraphrasing is a useful way to make an author's ideas accessible to a reader. Paraphrasing information is also useful to you in two ways. First, it helps you get a handle on the material and preserve your understanding. Second, because the paraphrase is already in your own words, you can easily work it into your first draft. It represents much of the analysis and context that your final paper will offer. Paraphrase whenever an idea or passage seems important but the exact wording is not essential or a good idea is couched in difficult language.

A good paraphrase must be faithful to the content and order of the original while being expressed in completely different language. Therefore, when paraphrasing, follow the author's thought closely but recast it in your own words; your version will be about as long as the original. But it will probably take longer to write a paraphrase than it will to quote the original because paraphrase includes analysis and translation.

In her research, Gerke read a particular passage that struck her as important.

> The systematic testing of school children that began in Britain in the early years of the present century was closely linked with an influential eugenics movement, primarily motivated by a fear of uncontrolled fertility and inherited intellectual inadequacy in the poorer classes. The preferred solutions to what in those days was seen as a potential threat to the race were usually birth control and sterilization. (Frank Smith, *Insult to Intelligence: The Bureaucratic Invasion of Our Classrooms*)

Gerke liked the point but did not feel that the language merited direct quotation. So she wrote her own version (see Figure 13.9).

Do not let the author's language sneak into your paraphrase. If, however, you are struck by a phrase of the author's, jot it down at the bottom of the card but enclose the phrase in quotation marks. Include exact page references for all paraphrases.

Figure 13.9   Paraphrased Passage Notecard for Smith Passage

Smith   Insult

Testing began in Britain early in the twentieth century because of a eugenics movement that was founded on the
idea that the poorer classes were inferior and that the
growth of these classes threatened the purity of the upper
classes. The spread of such inferiority could be checked by
birth control and sterilization.   (132–133)

Summary.   If you don't think you will need the author's exact words or an extensive paraphrase, summarize your findings. Summary fits meaning into a smaller space; it is the art of distilling the essential. You might condense a whole paragraph into a few words, a whole page or section into one or two sentences. Good summaries are accurate (they faithfully represent the main points), comprehensive (they don't miss any main points), and independent (they do not rely on the original at all for order, emphasis, or wording). They concentrate exclusively on meaning.

The author of the original must define terms and provide illustrations, prove or explain ideas; however, the summary captures only the main ideas in as few words as possible. This may require combining snippets of ideas from different parts of a passage. It most certainly will require ignoring interesting details.

Here is an example of a passage and its summary.

> One difference between war and football, though, is that there is little or no protest against football. Perhaps the most extraordinary thing about the game is that the systematic infliction of injuries excites in people not concern, as would be the case if they were sustained at, say, a rock festival, but a collective rejoicing and euphoria. Players and fans alike revel in the spectacle of a combatant felled into semiunconsciousness, "blindsided," "clotheslined," or "decapitated." I can remember, in fact, being chided by a coach in pro ball for not "getting my hat" injuriously into a player who was already lying helpless on the ground. (On another occasion, after the Stampeders had traded the celebrated Joe Kapp to BC, we were playing the Lions in Vancouver and Kapp was forced on one play to run the ball. He was coming "down the chute," his bad knee wobbling uncertainly, so I simply dropped on

him like a blanket. After I returned to the bench I was reproved for not exploiting the opportunity to unhinge his bad knee.) (John McMurtry, "Kill 'Em! Crush 'Em! Eat 'Em Raw!")

SUMMARY

```
Football players are encouraged to inflict as much injury
as possible, and no one complains.
```

McMurtry's original is intelligent, humorous, and horrifying, but in this case the main idea counted most, and a sentence was enough.

When summarizing, be sure to indicate on your notecard exactly where you found the summarized material: you may decide to go back to get the precise language, and in any case you want your reader to know where you found the information. For one method of writing a summary, see "The Précis" in Chapter 15.

We discuss plagiarism in more detail under "Documenting Your Sources" in Chapter 14. Here we want to point out that good notes can protect you from that worst of academic problems. Record all information accurately. Put quotation marks around *all* quoted material. Identify whatever you paraphrase or summarize. If while taking notes you get your own idea on the same subject, write your idea on the same notecard, but put it in brackets or write it with a different colored pen. Don't intermingle your thoughts and the original. That would create trouble.

RESTATING YOUR THESIS

Now you are back from the stacks with plenty of notes and a much better understanding of your topic. You should be able to tell at this point whether your tentative thesis needs modifying. The temptation will be strong to ignore contrary or qualifying evidence and start writing immediately. Beware: do not defend a thesis that should be changed. Instead, interrogate it in the light of your research.

Do you still believe it?

Does your research amply support it?

Should you modify it in any way?

In the light of her research, Christina Gerke had begun to question her tentative thesis, which had been

We should do away with standardized tests because they perpetuate prejudice against minorities.

This statement now seemed to her too extreme. Her research did not fully support it. After her reading she thought that some tests had value and that the bias in them was often accidental. During her research she had asked herself more probing questions, such as *Why* are the tests harmful to minorities? And from her reading she had developed an answer: they are harmful because a low score on a test can determine much of a person's future. Her revised thesis shows how research had refined her ideas.

> Standardized tests often shape the course of people's lives, not to mention their self-image and their society's image of them. Since there is still so much controversy about standardized tests, employers and institutions should place less emphasis on test performance as a criterion for admissions and hiring and more on aptitude and personal characteristics.

Gerke had gone from an ill-defined general feeling to a refined and arguable thesis, one that mattered to her and would guide a rich essay.

Examine your thesis, write it out, and be sure it is clear. If you are in doubt, state it to someone else. The response should tell you a great deal. Be sure it is worth arguing. Be sure you have time and space to do it justice. Take time to reconsider the thesis at least once during each day of work.

PREPARING AN OUTLINE

You and your project are still together after all these trials. Now you have a thesis and a mass of research to mold into some shape. A first step toward that goal is to make an outline. This will help you in three ways.

> It will put your argument or exposition down on paper for the first time.
>
> It will force you to organize and develop your material.
>
> It will carry you a long way toward your completed essay.

Think of your outline as an opportunity to combine each of your ideas with relevant evidence or background and to place each idea in its proper relation to your other points.

To devise an effective outline, you should have completed your research and have your notecards stacked in order, your authorities and accurate quotations at your elbow. Now is the time to think carefully about your approach to the subject.

First, go through all your notecards. Note which topics have grown largest. Make a scratch list of the main points that emerge. Try arranging your notes into piles according to these important topics. Look for a natural form for your discussion. If the organization "wants" to go in a certain direction, follow it and see how it works. Think about where you might employ different strategies: description, process analysis, cause and effect, comparison and contrast, definition (see Chapter 8, Structure and Strategies of the Paragraph). Determine what will be the crucial parts of your paper. Write a few trial outlines.

🖥 **Computer Tip**

If you prepared your notecards on a computer, you should print them out and arrange them as if they were handwritten notecards. Don't try to do all your organizing on-screen.

Christina Gerke decided to begin her paper with general background on standardized tests, move to an overview of the controversy, and then present her thesis. Later, she could treat the debate in more detail and present one test—the Scholastic Aptitude Test—as a case study. Her outline, which appears just before her paper in the next chapter (see pp. 405–07), reflects this organization.

For an assignment as large as a research paper we recommend that you devise a formal outline—that is, an outline that presents the shape and direction of your paper as exactly as possible. (See Chapter 5, Putting Words on Paper, for a full discussion of outlining.) Many instructors require that students submit an outline at some stage of research, so be sure you know what is expected of you.

Once you have made your outline, go back to your notecards. Working by the topic key words and phrases, organize your cards according to the outline. If a note pertains to your conclusion, it belongs on the bottom of the pile; if it pertains to your introduction, it belongs near the top. Once you have your notes in order, reading through them ought to be like surveying a compressed version of your paper. Do not worry about having too much material. As writing proceeds, you can decide which pieces of support you need most. It is far easier to cut excess material than it is to search for new sources at the last moment.

The research project's most important elements—organization, argument, evidence—should all be there when you finish a good outline. Even now, much about your outline may be provisional. Problems may stick out. You may see that one part needs more work or that one of your main points is out of place. Many writers find it painful to sit down, bash out the shape of the argument, and arrange all the evidence without writing the paper at the same time. But correcting problems in an outline is more efficient than trying to fix a finished product. A little work ahead of time will make things easier later.

WRITING A FIRST DRAFT

Once you have an outline and notecard order that seem to work, you are ready to begin writing your first draft. With something as complex as a research paper, you won't get everything right—ideas, references, commas—the first time. The whole point of the first draft is to be flexible. You may find, for example, that your outline, so painstakingly thought out, doesn't work in all parts. Some of your most cherished ideas may go up in smoke. Some may require more research. You may even need a different thesis, a whole new approach. Take all such discoveries with good humor: the purpose of a first draft is to help you figure out what you want and need to say. Nothing characterizes research more than global revisions at every stage.

Two issues will be especially important to you at this stage: using your evidence and integrating different sources.

Using Your Evidence

In an argumentative project, your ideas make your paper go; they make it new and worth reading. But assertion of opinion—no matter how brilliantly phrased or original—is not enough. You must show how you arrived at your ideas, or why they are justified. That is why you did all that research. When you provide appropriate evidence, you allow your reader to make an educated decision about the validity of your argument.

Let your reader review all the evidence. Don't suppress information contrary to your thesis. Presenting the opposition and responding to it can only strengthen your argument. (For a discussion of how to construct a complete argument, see Chapter 7, Making the Argument.)

In the section on note taking, we discussed the differences among quoting, paraphrasing, and summarizing. Here we discuss when and how to incorporate these techniques into a paper.

Quotation. When should we include quotations in essays? Here is what a great language expert says:

> A writer expresses himself in words that have been used before because they give his meaning better than he can give it himself, or because they are beautiful or witty, or because he expects them to touch a chord of association in his reader, or because he wishes to show that he is learned and well read. Quotations due to the last motive are invariably ill-advised. (H. W. Fowler, *A Dictionary of Modern English Usage*)

Almost all research contains quoted material because it makes such good evidence. For example, quotations can help you amplify or clarify a point, as this one does:

> Baseball players have an unusual approach to language, as
> in Yogi Berra's famous line, "The game isn't over till
> it's over" (Bartlett 903).

In the examples given here, the parenthetical reference after the quotation follows the Modern Language Association's system for documenting sources. Other systems of documentation are discussed in the first appendix.

Or quotations can prove a specific point or attach weight to a theory or opinion, as this one does:

> Mothers in Japan take on the role of educational disci-
> plinarian, making certain that their children succeed in
> school. "Hence," as one Japanese writer observes, "the
> mother encourages, scolds, bribes, and does anything else
> that might help her child study" (Tanaka 68).

If you are using a short quotation, you can include it in the text, enclosed in quotation marks.

> Perhaps it would be best for everyone to follow William
> Least Heat Moon's advice and "Beware thoughts that come
> in the night" (3).

When you have quotations of more than four lines, however, make them easier to read by setting them off from the text, indented ten spaces from the left margin, double-spaced, and without quotation marks, as Christina Gerke does in this passage:

> Sometimes it is difficult to ascertain exactly what
> qualities the tests actually measure. Scientists do not
> yet agree on a single definition of the word intelligence,
> for example, and as the meaning of the word changes, so
> do the tests that try to measure it ("Brave New World").
> Furthermore, a test item designed to measure one ability
> may actually test different abilities in different people.
> This accidental shifting can occur in something as simple
> as a spelling test, as John R. Bormuth explains:
>
>> Asking for the spelling of a given word may re-
>> quire a student who was previously drilled on
>> the word merely to recite from rote memory a
>> string of letters but require a student who was
>> not taught this word to analyze it into syl-

```
lables and phonemes and then to apply his phon-
ics knowledge to the task. (23).
```
```
Consequently, a test item aimed at a specific ability
(phonics knowledge) tested something quite different
(ability to memorize).
```

Note that Gerke does not sprinkle her work with unexplained quotations; she shows the reader the reason for her reference. She makes clear how the quotation supports her opinion.

Integrating Quotations into Your Text.   When you are using a writer's words, you must be careful to fit those words into your own writing. Here are four suggestions on how to integrate quotations gracefully into your own text.

1. *Give the source's full name when you first refer to that source.* No acknowledgment is clearer than the kind you make in the text itself. Include the person's credentials if possible. Gerke did just that in a passage from her research paper.

```
For example, Harvard University's Arthur Jensen, noted
and controversial expert on standardized tests, claimed
that the overall difference between whites and blacks
is 15 points, and the gap between rich and poor is
12 points (44).
```

Jensen is surely a big name in the field. Mentioning his name and credentials added authority to her evidence.

2. *When possible, give some background to your quotations.* Transition from your text to quoted material and back will be easier if you suggest the topic of the coming quotation.

```
Against those who charged that women had not proven them-
selves especially virtuous, Mary Wollstonecraft Shelley
wrote, "It is vain to expect virtue from women until they
are in some degree independent of men."
```

3. *Fit quotations into the grammatical structure of your sentence.* A quotation that doesn't fit is as awkward as if you had made the error yourself. Note the difference between the following examples:

ORIGINAL PASSAGE

Black women are called, in the folklore that so aptly identifies one's status in society, "the *mule* of the world," because we have been handed the burdens that everyone else—*everyone* else—refused to carry. [Alice Walker, "In Search of Our Mothers' Gardens," *The Norton*

Anthology of Literature by Women, ed. Sandra M. Gilbert and Susan Gubar. New York: Norton, 1986: 2378]

AWKWARD QUOTATION

```
Today, according to Alice Walker, the black woman "are
called, in the folklore that so aptly identifies one's
status in society, 'the mule of the world'" (2378).
```

In this instance the writer's subject (*woman*) does not agree with Walker's verb (*are*). Such problems are usually easy to correct. Here are four ways to fit your sources' words in with your own.

a. Change your sentence structure to fit the quotation.

```
Alice Walker's view of the plight of the black woman is
clear: "Black women are called, in the folklore that so
aptly identifies one's status in society, 'the mule of
the world'" (2378).
```

b. Use only a part of the quotation.

```
Today, according to Alice Walker, the black woman is
called "'the mule of the world'" (2378).
```

c. Change or add material in the quotation by using brackets. Brackets tell the reader that you are adding words of your own to clarify the quotation or smooth the transition between it and your own prose.

```
According to Alice Walker, the black woman has been taken
for granted "because [she has] been handed the burdens
that everyone else--everyone else--refused to carry"
(2378).
```

d. Delete words from the quotation by using ellipses.

```
Alice Walker explains that "black women are called . . .
'the mule of the world'" (2378).
```

Use brackets and ellipses sparingly. If you change too much, the quotation will no longer be a quotation.

4. *Identify and introduce quotations smoothly; use a variety of methods.* There are plenty of acceptable and elegant ways to work a quotation into a sentence. Here are four ways you should master.

INTRODUCTION AND COLON

```
Alice Walker identifies one main reason black women have
been denigrated in folklore: "we have been handed the
```

```
burdens that everyone else--everyone else--refused to
carry" (2378).
```

INTRODUCTORY PHRASE

```
According to Alice Walker, black women have "been handed
the burdens that everyone else--everyone else--refused to
carry" (2378).
```

Other introductory phrases include "In Alice Walker's view," "For Alice Walker," and so forth.

SUBORDINATION USING *THAT*

```
In the face of racism and antifeminism, Walker declares
that "black women have been called . . . 'the mule of the
world'" (2378).
```

The word *that* subordinates the rest of the sentence. The same thing goes for quotations as well. When using *that* as a way into a quotation, you may lowercase the first letter of the quoted material whether or not that material begins a complete sentence.

INTERRUPTED QUOTATION

```
"We have been handed the burdens," declares Walker, "that
everyone else--everyone else--refused to carry" (2378).
```

Here is a very experienced book reviewer using quotation confidently and with great variety. He is quoting from the American poet Wallace Stevens's journal entries about Stevens's hometown of Reading, Pennsylvania. Note how smoothly the writer has interwoven his own commentary with Stevens's original.

> Coming home from Harvard for Christmas of 1898, he wrote in his journal, "The city was smoky and noisy but the country depths were prodigiously still. . . . Coming home I saw the sun go down behind a veil of grime." The journal entries balloon when he is back in Berks: "Country sights both purge and fill up your fancy," he notes, and says, having described a raindrop slipping from leaf to leaf of a clematis vine, that "it was certainly a monstrous pleasure to be able to be specific about such a thing." Paragraphs are devoted to local botany and atmospheric effects; he ends one entry "Salut au Monde!" and another "The splendor is almost too great: things seem a little overdressed, a little overdone." (John Updike, "The Heaven of an Old Home," review of *Souvenirs and Prophecies*)

Paraphrase.   If a paper contains excessive quotation, a reader will suspect that the writer has not fully digested the material, has few ideas of his or her own, or is showing off. Your instructor wants to know whether you have understood the information and what you can do with it. A quotation may indicate that the information has been swallowed whole. A paraphrase means you've chewed the information.

You may need to help your reader understand difficult material. You have no doubt read much more of the author's work than your reader has, at least recently, and you have grown accustomed to the way the author presents ideas. Furthermore, you are more familiar with the context in which the material appears. Since you can't possibly reproduce the entire text, you need to break out the ideas and put them in language that doesn't require that context.

A paraphrase must be acknowledged—even though the words are yours, the ideas still belong to the author. To start a paraphrase by identifying the source provides a context and is a courtesy to the reader. No one wants to have to go back and reread in the light of a late-arriving source. If Gerke had paraphrased the quote shown in Figure 13.8, for example, she might have said

> According to Madaus, test scores have the "potential" to
> hurt students when educators use the scores as the only
> or the most important basis for making decisions that can
> influence the students' futures. (93)

Notice the quotation marks around "potential": any important word or phrase used in the original must be identified. To signal the end of the paraphrase, immediately cite the exact reference in a note.

Summary.   Much of a research paper will be summary. In fact, such an essay could be viewed as an interpretation of a compendium of summaries sprinkled with quotation and paraphrase. You probably won't use quotations or paraphrases nearly so much as summaries. In some ways, summarizing ideas is more fraught with peril than quoting because it *seems* so easy that we becomes careless.

When summarizing, you still need to cite important ideas that you obtained from a source. Gerke, for example, may have summarized the Madaus passage instead of quoting or paraphrasing:

> The use of test scores to determine students' futures is
> potentially harmful. (Madaus 93)

Integrating Different Sources

As you write, you may be pulling information from books, articles, and other sources much separated in time and different in style and point of view. One of the most delicate tasks in writing your first draft is that of weaving these various sources into your argument. Here are three tips on this process.

1. Make sure your sources exactly support your claim. One student paper contained the following passage:

```
Many researchers are in favor of teachers retiring when
they reach age sixty-five. According to the National Bu-
reau of Statistics, there are no teachers over eighty-
five now active in the United States (123).
```

Interesting fact, but it does not really fit the claim. Putting the two together will confuse the reader. Resist the temptation to plug in a reference because it is "close" to your own thought. Close gets no cigar.

2. When you use more than one reference to back up a point, compare the references closely to make sure they truly agree.

In her first draft, Christina Gerke wrote this passage:

```
Another challenge points to the difficulty of ascertain-
ing exactly what qualities standardized tests actually
measure. Scientists do not yet agree on a single defini-
tion of the word intelligence, for example, and, as the
meaning of the word changes, so do the tests that try to
measure it ("Brave New World"). H. J. Eysenck, a promi-
nent expert in the field of human intelligence, suggests
that since we lack a better definition, intelligence is
what is measured in IQ tests (78). It is also possible
that a test item designed to measure one ability will in
reality test different abilities in different people.
```

Her first reference was indeed appropriate, but her second did not really agree with it. The paragraph treats the problem of "ascertaining exactly what qualities" the tests measure. Eysenck's quotation threatens to derail the paragraph into a discussion of how *intelligence* is defined. In the end Gerke decided to drop it, much as she wanted this expert to appear in her paper.

Some writers put in references out of desperation or the desire to appear informed. But you should never use a reference you don't need. Every reference should push your point forward, not merely add to what you have already established. No amount of padding will hide shoddy research or inconsistent research.

3. Be sensitive to the way passages are worded, to the context from which you have taken material, and to the background and point of view of the author. If you weave together uneasy companions, the result

will be a strange paragraph, one that may confuse the reader because its pieces of evidence do not follow directly from one another.

The following three suggestions should help you pick and choose among your sources:

> Prefer the concrete—facts, statistics—to the general.
>
> Choose firsthand accounts over second- and thirdhand ones.
>
> Prefer recent sources to older ones.

As you add body and detail to the skeleton of your outline in your first draft, you may very well find—no surprises here—that you need to make further modifications. Enjoy your first draft, but treat it as the first version of what will eventually be a solid, polished piece of writing.

Tips for Doing Research

- Choose a general subject that is both interesting and specific enough to cover adequately in your research paper.
- Be aware of all the materials that your library offers, including books, periodicals, reference works, online catalogs, and Internet resources.
- Carefully compile a working bibliography as a basis for later research.
- Use Internet sources with care; verify all authors and information.
- After initial research has helped you narrow your topic, formulate a tentative thesis. Be ready to change your tentative thesis at any time.
- Read sources critically. Evaluate sources according to the reliability of the author, the quality of the publisher or online source, the currency of the material, the completeness of the presentation, and slant or bias.
- Take careful notes.
- Quote directly if a passage is unusually striking in aptness, authoritativeness, or phrasing.
- Paraphrase when the content of a passage is more important than the wording, or when an important idea is couched in difficult language.
- Summarize passages in which only the main points are essential.
- Restate your tentative thesis often.
- Prepare a formal outline for any extended research project.
- Use your evidence critically. Remember the criteria for good evidence and the rules of argument.
- Integrate quoted material smoothly with your own writing. Use a variety of methods to introduce quotations.

▬▬▬▬ **EXERCISES FOR DOING RESEARCH** ▰▰▰▰▰▰▰▰▰▰▰▰▰

1. The following is a treasure hunt. Find the answers to these questions by consulting the appropriate source in your library or on the Internet. When you have located each answer, report on how you found it and in what source. State what sent you to that source in the first place.

   What country produced the largest amount of chromium in 1968?
   What did movie critics say about *The Jazz Singer* when it first appeared?
   How did people do the Big Apple?
   How and when was Tanzania formed?
   Who won the Nobel Prize for Literature in 1995? 1955? 1905?
   Where did the word *swastika* come from?
   Who was the last man Don Larsen faced in his perfect game in the World Series, and how did Larsen get him out?
   Who was the second person to walk on the moon?
   What was a rumble seat?
   Why do some Americans say "Gosh!" and "Gee Whiz!"? When did these expressions originate?
   Which country has the oldest continuously operating form of government?
   What was the worst zeppelin crash in Europe's history?
   Name all the members of the present cabinet and report on what they did before becoming cabinet members.
   Who were the members of the Miles Davis Quintet, and why were they important?
   Does either Neptune or Uranus have any moons?
   Name four cannibal tribes.

2. Look up one of the following names and give a short account of the person's life. Where did you find the information, and why did you go there?

Sigrid Undset	Gabriela Mistral
Napoleon Lajoie	Elizabeth Blackwell
Alessandro di Mariano Filipepi	Bessie Smith
H. Rap Brown	Harun al-Rashid
Yevgeny Yevtushenko	Bahaullah
Le Corbusier	William Wheeler

3. Find and present an example (through a recording, photocopy, still photograph, plot summary, short excerpt, or other means) of five of the following. Discuss the creators and what makes the works distinctive. Finally, discuss how you found your information. What sources did you use?

a song by John Dowland	a sculpture by Constantin Brancusi
a painting by Georgia O'Keeffe	a mural by José Orozco
a photograph by Edward Steichen	an invention by Thomas Edison
a movie starring Ingrid Bergman	a theory by John Maynard Keynes
a newspaper article by Damon Runyon	a discovery by Mary Leakey
an essay by Jessica Mitford	an opinion by Ruth Bader Ginsberg
a discovery by Louis Pasteur	a poem by Elizabeth Bishop
a concerto by Ellen Zwick Perry	a study by Mary Douglas

4. Imagine that you are doing a research paper on the presidency of John F. Kennedy. What would you take notes on in this passage? What would you quote, paraphrase, or summarize? Why?

   > Kennedy was called an intellectual very seldom before 1960 and very often thereafter—a phenomenon which deserves explanation.

One cannot be sure what an intellectual is; but let us define it as a person whose primary habitat is the realm of ideas. In this sense, exceedingly few political leaders are authentic intellectuals, because the primary habitat of the political leader is the world of power. Yet the world of power itself has intellectual and anti-intellectual sides. Some political leaders find exhilaration in ideas and in the company of those whose trade it is to deal with them. Others are rendered uneasy by ideas and uncomfortable by intellectuals.

Kennedy belonged supremely to the first class. He was a man of action who could pass easily over to the realm of ideas and confront intellectuals with perfect confidence in his capacity to hold his own. His mind was not prophetic, impassioned, mystical, ontological, utopian or ideological. It was less exuberant than Theodore Roosevelt's, less scholarly than [Woodrow] Wilson's, less adventurous than Franklin Roosevelt's. But it had its own salient qualities—it was objective, practical, ironic, skeptical, unfettered and insatiable.

It was marked first of all, as he had noted to Jacqueline, by inexhaustible curiosity. Kennedy always wanted to know how things worked. Vague answers never contented him. This curiosity was fed by conversation but even more by reading. His childhood consolation had become an adult compulsion. He was now a fanatical reader, 1200 words a minute, not only at the normal times and places but at meals, in the bathtub, sometimes even when walking. Dressing in the morning, he would prop open a book on his bureau and read while he put on his shirt and tied his necktie. He read mostly history and biography. . . . His supposed addiction to James Bond was partly a publicity gag, like Franklin Roosevelt's supposed affection for "Home on the Range." Kennedy seldom read for distraction. He did not want to waste a single second. (Arthur M. Schlesinger, Jr., *A Thousand Days*)

5. Summarize the following passage. After writing your summary, discuss what you left out, what you left in, and why. What problems did you encounter putting the passage into your own words? How does your summary compare with the original in terms of clarity and comprehensiveness?

Are viruses very simple forms of life? Can they give us clues to the nature of a precellular living system of which no fossil is likely to remain? As information increases on the nature of viruses and, in particular, of their relationships with host cells, this interpretation of viral origins seems less and less likely. Viruses are able to reproduce and to make their protein coats only because they are capable of commandeering the enzymes and other metabolic machinery of the host cell. Without this machinery, they are as inert as any other macromolecule, lifeless by many criteria. It seems more likely that viruses are cellular fragments that have set up a partially independent existence. (Helena Curtis, *Biology*)

6. You and a partner separately write a paraphrase of the following passage. If you come upon portions that are difficult or vague, work on the difficulty together. When you are finished, compare paraphrases. How well does each capture the content of the original? Which is more faithful to the author's original order? What problems did you encounter trying to stay away from the author's original words?

[A brief look at history] may suggest the mutual interdependence of the scientific revolution and the industrial revolution. Upon the one hand, modern industry *is* so much applied science. No amount of desire to make money, or to enjoy new commodities, no amount of mere practical energy and enterprise, would have effected the economic transformation of the last few centuries and generations. Improvements in mathematical, physical, chemical and biological science were prerequisites. Businessmen through engineers of different sorts, have laid hold of the new insights gained by scientific men into the hidden energies of nature, and have turned them to account. The modern mine, factory, railway, steamship, telegraph, all of the appliances and equipment of production, and transportation, express scientific knowledge. (John Dewey, "Some Historical Factors in Philosophical Reconstruction")

7. Read each of the following quotations, and then fit it into the types of introductions and sentence structures given.

To be an existentialist, one must be able to feel oneself—one must know one's desires, one's rages, one's anguish, one must be aware of the character of one's frustrations and know what would satisfy it. (Norman Mailer, "The White Negro")

a. The existentialist, according to Norman Mailer, must
b. Mailer called on the existentialist to know four things:
c. When speaking of the existentialist, Mailer said that
d. The existentialist should not only know his or her "frustration"; for Mailer, one should also
e. "[part of quotation]," said Norman Mailer, "[another part of quotation]"
f. Norman Mailer declared,

And we do not quite say that the new is more valuable because it fits in; but its fitting in is a test of its value—a test, it is true, which can only be slowly and cautiously applied, for we are none of us infallible judges of conformity. (T.S. Eliot, "Tradition and the Individual Talent")

a. Eliot did not claim that [part of quotation], but instead he claimed that [other part of quotation]
b. The reason that we must be cautious in judging the new, says Eliot, is that
c. Eliot called the test of conformity [use ellipses to omit words from the quotation]
d. No one can ever be completely confident of his or her taste in the new because he or she is only a [use brackets to work quotation into sentence]
e. Eliot believes that the best test of something new is its

14

Writing Research

And time yet for a hundred indecisions,
And for a hundred visions and revisions
— T. S. ELIOT (1888-1965)
AMERICAN POET AND CRITIC

Preparing a research paper for handing in involves not only the writing
but also precise documentation of your sources, revision, and careful
presentation of the final manuscript.

DOCUMENTING YOUR SOURCES

Documentation is an essential part of presenting evidence. You must
identify the source of every quotation, fact, statistic, graph, or opinion
about your subject that you include in your research paper. You must
tell your reader exactly where you got every bit of information that you
use. Further, you must list for your reader every source you have cited
in your paper. In short, you must thoroughly document your research.

You must do this for three reasons:

Documentation provides a guide for any reader who wants to study
your subject.

It indicates the extent of your research.

It gives credit where credit is due.

If writers document their sources sloppily or not at all, they disappoint curious readers and undermine confidence in the quality of the research. Worse, they run the risk of plagiarism.

Plagiarism

Plagiarism is the use without due acknowledgment of the thoughts, writing, scholarship, or inventions of another. In college and university writing, as in most other walks of life, people place great value on knowing what is theirs and what belongs to someone else. Therefore, plagiarism is a serious moral issue.

Plagiarism is often the result of carelessness or ignorance: sometimes a student does not fully understand the importance of the issue or does not know the right way to acknowledge sources. The remedy is to learn. Sometimes, however, people in full awareness submit as their own the ideas or work of someone else. Compare this passage from a book on fifteenth-century art with the way a writer used it in a paper on the same subject:

> **SOURCE**
>
> The diminishing role of gold in paintings is part of a general movement in western Europe at this time towards a kind of selective inhibition about display, and this shows itself in many other kinds of behavior too. It was just as conspicuous in the client's clothes, for instance, which were abandoning gilt fabrics and gaudy hues for the restrained black of Burgundy. This was a fashion with elusive moral overtones. (Michael Baxandall, *Painting and Experience in Fifteenth Century Italy*)

> **USE**
>
> ```
> At this time, western Europe was moving toward inhibition
> of display, which shows up in the diminishing role of
> gold in paintings as well as in many other kinds of be-
> havior, including the abandoning of gilt fabrics and
> gaudy hues in clothing. This fashion had moral overtones,
> though elusive.
> ```

In this case the writer has obviously used material belonging to another without crediting the source. He or she has used the same words and phrases, in only slightly altered form. This is plagiarism.

Even if you do not quote any of the words of a source, borrowing ideas can also be plagiarism. Compare this passage from an original source with its use in a paper called "The Psychology of Children's Play":

> **SOURCE**
>
> Just as for its growth an organ needs nourishment in proportion to its functioning, so each mental activity, from the most elementary to the

highest, needs for its development to be fed from without by a continuous flow, which [in the case of children's play] is purely functional,
not material. (Jean Piaget, *Play, Dreams, and Imitation in Childhood*)

USE

```
Children play as part of the normal process of growing
and developing. Like any bodily organ, the mind needs
constant nourishment and exercise as it grows. When chil-
dren play, they exercise and nourish the mind and assist
it in its growth.
```

These ideas may be in the writer's own language, but he or she has borrowed them from the source without acknowledgment. If the writer did
this knowingly and deliberately concealed the source, it is a kind of theft.

Here is the general rule for avoiding plagiarism and providing appropriate documentation: give enough information so that a reader can
examine the sources you have used.

Now, here are seven guidelines for applying the general rule.

1. When you incorporate into your paper sentences, paragraphs, or
apt phrases from the work of another, you must use quotation marks
around the borrowed words—or indent passages longer than four
lines—and you must identify the source. In the case of Baxandall's material about fifteenth-century painting, the writer should have credited
the source and put borrowed phrases inside quotation marks, like this:

```
According to Michael Baxandall, people in fifteenth-
century western Europe were tending toward an "inhibition
about display," which manifests itself in "the diminish-
ing role of gold in paintings" as well as in other cul-
tural practices, including "abandoning gilt fabrics and
gaudy hues" in clothing. As Baxandall says, "This was a
fashion with elusive moral overtones" (14).
```

2. When you rely on another person's ideas or train of thought but
change the actual words used or the order of the ideas—that is, when you
paraphrase—you still must acknowledge your source. To avoid plagiarism, the writer who borrowed from Piaget should have written this:

```
Jean Piaget claims that children play as part of the nor-
mal process of growing and developing. Like any bodily
organ, the mind needs constant nourishment and exercise
as it grows. He goes on to say that when children play,
they exercise and nourish the mind and assist it in its
growth (87).
```

Notice that Piaget is named in the text, not merely in a note. The material was Piaget's own, and he should receive clear and obvious credit. An opinion or an original interpretation of the facts—whether quoted, paraphrased, or summarized—should be part of the text; otherwise, it might appear that the writer doing the quoting is claiming the opinion.

3. When the material you use is widely known and generally available—that is, not an interpretation—you can acknowledge the source simply in a parenthetical reference rather than in the text. Christina Gerke acknowledges the sources of some facts in this way:

```
The French psychologist Alfred Binet originally formu-
lated his Binet scale of intelligence in 1905 to place
advanced and handicapped children in special schools
(Wardrop 8; Jensen 141-43).
```

4. When your ideas or opinions have been influenced in a **general** way by material you have read or lectures you have heard, you **must** also acknowledge your debt. In a paper on modern linguistics, a writer indicated the source of a borrowed idea in this fashion:

```
Paradoxically, linguists can no longer confine themselves
to language to understand how language works. They must
now take into account the time, the place, the speaker,
the listener, and the actual situation of each single ut-
terance. Mikhail Bakhtin's analysis of these sociolin-
guistic elements is exceptionally insightful (383).
```

5. When you rely on factual material gathered by another person, you must state this as well.

```
My discussion of Samoan marriage ceremonies will draw
heavily on Margaret Mead's Letters from the Field.
```

6. When you have benefited from another person's way of organizing material that is widely known, you must still acknowledge.

```
When researching the movies of Preston Sturges, I found
Simonson's History of American Film extremely helpful.
```

7. Finally, when you employ another writer's method of analyzing material, you must give credit where it is due.

```
If we agree with David Riesman's view of American society
in The Lonely Crowd, we can see that . . .
```

There are practical exceptions to the general rule, however. Some things are just common knowledge and it would be nearly impossible to acknowledge them. For instance, you need not identify a source for facts that almost everyone knows or could easily learn and that no one needs to prove.

Columbus sailed across the Atlantic in 1492.

The chemical symbol of water is H_2O.

Nor do you need to provide a source for an idea expressed by many people.

Hamlet is one of Shakespeare's greatest tragedies.

Hostility has existed between Israel and the Arab nations since Israel became a nation.

Err on the side of overacknowledgment, however. Be generous and open in giving credit for any source of help.

There are three common practices that also qualify as plagiarism. Avoid them in all the work you do.

1. *Never submit another student's paper as your own.* This practice is obviously unethical. Worse, it can actually harm both you and the other student. If you wish to use the ideas of a classmate or other student, do so and acknowledge the source. But submit work only you yourself have written.

2. *Never submit a paper that you have obtained from a "paper mill" or paper-writing service.* All instructors expect that the work you turn in is your own. Submitting a professionally written paper is simply putting up a false pretense. "Paper mills" cater to the worst aspects of people: their laziness, their eagerness to take the easy way out. Turning in a professionally written paper makes a mockery of the entire reason we teach and learn. Besides, most of the "paper mill" papers we have read have been awful. Have nothing to do with such papers: Do not use them, do not quote them, do not read them.

3. *Never turn in the same paper to more than one class.* This practice is simply plagiarizing yourself. Instructors expect original work. Do not turn in a paper you have written for any other class. Avoid using sections of such works as the basis for other papers. If you find yourself writing on a topic you have treated before, consider writing on something else unless you have something new to say. Ask your instructor for permission.

Every discipline has its own way of documenting sources. Many humanities researchers use the Modern Language Association (MLA) system; social scientists often use the system advocated by the American Psychological Association (APA); the natural sciences use a number system. Indeed, methods of documentation will vary somewhat from course to course. We will cover the MLA system of parenthetical references in this chapter. You can read about this system in more detail in Joseph Gibaldi, *MLA Handbook for Writers of Research Papers,* 4th ed. (New York: MLA, 1995), widely considered the arbiter on such matters. The MLA standard format for notes and bibliography and the author/ year or APA style appear in our second appendix, Other Systems of Documentation.

The MLA Documentation System

The MLA format uses parenthetical references that generally give the author's name and the page number after the quoted material. If readers want to know more, they can refer to a list of works cited at the back of the paper. In most cases this system allows you to acknowledge your sources immediately and in a relatively unobtrusive manner. We'll look first at how to present the list of works cited and then discuss how to handle references to these works in the text.

List of Works Cited. Your list of works cited should begin on a separate sheet at the end of your paper. This list will include *only books you actually cite in your paper, not all the books you consulted in your research.* Center the words *Works Cited* (not italicized) one inch from the top of the page and two lines above your first entry. Double-space all entries; arrange them alphabetically by author's last name or, when there is no author, by title.

In each entry give the author's or authors' names (last name first), the title of the work, and then the necessary publication information (explained below). The first line of each entry begins flush left; indent all lines after the first one five spaces. Skip two spaces after each period. Whenever italics are called for (as with book titles, for instance), we suggest that you underline. (Italic fonts are often hard to distinguish from normal-face fonts. Find out what your instructor prefers.) Continue to number your pages all the way through the list. See Christina Gerke's list of works cited at the end of her paper for a model (pp. 421–23).

🖥 **Computer Tip**

Some computer programs, such as Nota Bene, can build a list of works cited for you. If you don't have such a program, you can do it yourself by typing in entries for all sources you use extensively. Keep the list alphabetically as you go, or have the computer sort the entries for you at the end. Maintaining a list as you go will save time later.

In the following pages you will find examples of the kinds of references you will be most likely to use. Some preliminary notes to keep in mind:

a. Omit titles (Ph.D., M.D., and so forth) from an author's name.
b. Omit words such as *Company, Publishing,* and *Inc.* from a publisher's name. The words *University Press* are abbreviated UP, without any periods, even if they appear apart: Johns Hopkins UP, U of Pittsburgh P.
c. Always list the city in which the book was published—but list the state only if the city is obscure or is likely to be confused with another city with the same name: Oxford, MI; Athens, GA. (Use postal abbreviations for state names.) If several cities are listed on the title page, give the first.
d. Always list the date of publication. If a book has more than one copyright date, use the most recent.
e. Drop the word *The* from all periodical titles: *Los Angeles Times,* not *The Los Angeles Times.*
f. Abbreviate all months except May, June, and July.

Books by One Author.   Give the author's name, last name first; the title, underlined; and the city, publisher, and year of publication.

> Faludi, Susan. <u>Backlash</u>. New York: Crown, 1991.

Note the periods after the author's name, the title, and the year. The city name is followed by a colon and the publisher's name by a comma. If there is a subtitle on the title page, follow the title with a colon and capitalize the first letter of the subtitle.

> Smith, Frank. <u>Insult to Intelligence: The Bureaucratic
> Invasion of Our Classrooms</u>. New York: Arbor, 1986.

You should also record editors, translators, edition numbers, and volume numbers (see below and pp. 383, 386).

Multivolume Works.   If you have used two or more of the volumes of a multivolume work, put the number of volumes after the title, using the abbreviation *vols.*

> Knight, Alan. <u>The Mexican Revolution</u>. 2 vols. Lincoln: U
> of Nebraska P, 1990.

Editions.   An *edition* is a work by one person specially prepared for publication by another person. This second person, called the *editor,* is responsible for the text, the notes, and any other explanatory or accompanying material. To cite an edition, give the original author's name, the title, then the abbreviation *Ed.* and the name of the editor.

> Defoe, Daniel. <u>Robinson Crusoe</u>. Ed. Michael Shinagel. New
>   York: Norton, 1975.

Books That Are Part of a Series.   If the title page tells you that the book you are citing is part of a series, follow the book's title with the title of the series, neither underlined nor in quotation marks, and the book's number in that series. Use the abbreviation *Ser.* if the word *Series* is part of the series title, as it is here:

> Oquendo, Ignacio. <u>Spraygun Politics</u>. Southwestern Writers
>   Ser. 4. Los Angeles: Olmec, 1984.

Sacred Works.   The convention of underlining does not apply to sacred texts, such as the Bible or its books. For books in the Bible, be sure to specify whether they are in the Old Testament (abbreviated *OT*), New Testament (abbreviated *NT*), or Apocrypha. Omit *The Book of;* give simply the name or title associated with the book. Give full publication data for sacred texts, especially editors, edition, and page numbers, if you are citing individual books, chapters, or sections.

> Bible. Old Testament. Job. <u>New American Standard Bible</u>.
>   Chicago: Moody, 1995. 777-829.

Encyclopedias and Other Reference Works.   Include articles in dictionaries, encyclopedias, and other reference works in your list if you used them in your paper. If the article is signed, enter it under the author's name; if not, alphabetize it by its title. After either one, cite the title of the reference work. If the work arranges its entries alphabetically, omit the volume and page number. If the reference work is well known, you need cite only the edition (if stated) and the year of publication.
For a dictionary:

> "Cytotaxonomy." <u>Random House Webster's College
>   Dictionary</u>. 1995 ed.

For an encyclopedia:

> Kline, Katherine. "Alberto Giacometti." <u>Encyclopedia
>   Americana</u>. 1994 ed.

Prefaces, Introductions, Forewords, and Afterwords.   We do not suggest that students often cite these parts of a book, but when you use material from a preface or an afterword, you must give credit. Start the citation with the name of the author and the title of the part being cited—*Preface, Afterword,* and so forth—neither underlined nor in quotation marks. Follow with the title of the entire work. If the author of the part being cited is also the author of the complete work, follow the title of the work with *By* and the author's last name only. Follow the usual publication data with the page numbers of the part being cited (for prefaces, introductions, and forewords, these will often appear as lowercase roman numerals).

> Hoagland, Edward. Foreword. <u>Balancing Acts</u>. By Hoagland.
>   New York: Simon and Schuster, 1992. 9-10.

If the author of the part being cited is different from the author of the main work, follow the preceding form, except that after *By* give the full name of the author of the main work.

> Mudrick, Marvin. Afterword. <u>Persuasion</u>. By Jane Austen.
>   New York: New American Library, 1964. 241-54.

Articles in Daily or Weekly Periodicals. Start with the author's name, if you know it. Put the title of the article in quotation marks. Follow the title with the underlined title of the periodical. For periodicals that come out daily or weekly—including most newspapers and magazines—you need not give the volume number. Instead, give the exact date of publication, a colon, and then the page numbers followed by a period.

> McCarroll, Thomas. "Investors Rush the Net." <u>Time</u> 3 June
>   1996: 54-56.

Notice that the date appears as day, month, and year with no commas. Give all page numbers on which the article appears. If the article is not on consecutive pages, put a + after the first page number to indicate continuation on a later page.

> Washio, Ako. "Tough G-7 Road ahead for Tokyo." <u>The Japan
>   Times</u> 29 Mar.-4 Apr. 1993: 1+.

(Remember that although you would use the + in the list of works cited, you would use the exact page number in any citation in your text.)

If the newspaper numbers its pages with numbers and letters (A6, 11B, B-10, and so forth), show the page numbers exactly as they appear on the page. For an example, see page 389.

Articles in Monthly or Bimonthly Periodicals. If the periodical identifies its issues with the names of months, you need not give the volume and issue number. Instead, give the names of the months and the year.

If an issue is identified by two months, put a hyphen between their abbreviated names.

> Lyons, Donald. "Seventies Film Noir." Film Comment
>   July-Aug. 1993: 44-53.

Articles in Journals.   Use the same format as that for periodicals. If the journal uses *continuous pagination* throughout the annual volume (for example, if the first issue ends on page 413, the second issue picks up at page 414), simply follow the title with the volume number, the year of publication in parentheses, a colon, and then the page numbers.

> Eisenstein, Elizabeth. "The End of the Book? Some Per-
>   spectives on Media Change." The American Scholar 64
>   (1995): 541-555.

Some journals have *noncontinuous pagination*—that is, every issue begins with page 1. In that case, give the volume number, a period, and (without a space after the period), the issue number, then proceed as just described.

> Bean, Susan. "The Fabric of Independence." Parabola 19.3
>   (1994): 29-42.

Multiple Works by the Same Author.   When you have two or more entries for the same author, don't repeat the name, but type three hyphens and a period and complete the reference. List the author's works alphabetically by title.

> Theroux, Paul. The Kingdom by the Sea. London: Hamish
>   Hamilton, 1983.
> ---. Translating LA: A Tour of the Rainbow City. New
>   York: Norton, 1994.

Works by More Than One Author.   When you are citing a work by two or more authors, list the authors' names in the order in which they appear on the title page; this may or may not be alphabetical. Reverse only the first author's name, and type the rest out normally, separating names with commas.

> Packer, Nancy Huddleston, and John Timpane. Writing Worth
>   Reading: The Critical Process. 3rd ed. Boston: Bed-
>   ford, 1997.

If there are more than three authors, give only the first name that appears on the title page and follow it with *et al.,* a Latin abbreviation that means "and others." Do not underline *et al.* For the following work, the names on the title page were Elizabeth Waldeman, Allyson S. Grossman, Howard Hayghe, and Beverly Johnson:

```
Waldeman, Elizabeth, et al. "Working Mothers in the
    1970's: A Look at the Statistics." Monthly Labor
    Review Oct. 1979: 39-45.
```

Anonymous Works.   Sometimes the author of a work is not identified. For a book:

```
Primary Colors. New York: Random House, 1996.
```

For an article:

```
"Why the Troops Should Go." New Republic 18 Dec. 1995:
    7-8.
```

Works with Translators, Editors, or Compilers.   For translated works, begin with the original author's name and the title of the work, followed by the label *Trans.* and the name of the translator.

```
Chekhov, Anton. Three Sisters. Trans. Lanford Wilson. New
    York: Dramatists Play Service, 1984.
```

Some works have no author but have been assembled by an editor or compiler. Begin citations for such works with the title, followed by the label *Ed.* or *Comp.,* whichever is applicable, and the editor's or compiler's name.

```
Dear America: Letters Home from Vietnam. Ed. Bernard
    Edelman. New York: Pocket, 1985.
```

Works in Anthologies or Collections.   For college papers you may often use works in anthologies or collections. For such sources, give the name of the author of the anthologized work, the work's title, and then the title of the anthology or collection. Then give the name of the editor or compiler, preceding that name with *Ed.* or *Comp.* (Even if there is more than one such person, as in the following example, use *Ed.* or *Comp.*) After the place, publisher, and date, give the page numbers on which the work appears. (Don't count page numbers of introductions or notes.) Here are several such entries:

ESSAY

Hansberry, Lorraine. "In Defense of the Equality of Men."
The Norton Anthology of Literature by Women: The
Tradition in English. Ed. Sandra M. Gilbert and
Susan Gubar. New York: Norton, 1985. 2058-67.

Many anthologies have more than one volume. If you are using only one volume of a multivolume anthology, place the number of the volume you are using immediately after the name of the editor(s) or compiler(s):

Camus, Albert. "The Guest." Norton Anthology of World
Masterpieces. Ed. Maynard Mack et al. Vol. 2. New
York: Norton, 1992. 1900-1910.

You may also place the total number of volumes at the end of the entry. You *must* do this if you are using two or more volumes of the same multivolume anthology. In the following example, the writer was using both volumes of the *Anthology of American Literature.* Earlier, she had cited a piece by Thomas Jefferson from volume 1. Now she had to cite a Sylvia Plath poem found in volume 2 of that anthology:

POEM

Plath, Sylvia. "Lady Lazarus." Anthology of American Literature. Ed. George McMichael. Vol. 2. New York:
Macmillan, 1989. 1802-1804. 2 vols.

If the anthology has more than three editors, give the first editor's name, a comma, and then *et al.,* meaning "and others."

PLAY

Jonson, Ben. Volpone, or The Fox. The Norton Anthology of
English Literature. Ed. M. H. Abrams, et al. 5th ed.
Vol. 1. New York: Norton, 1986. 1114-208.

The edition number of an anthology is very important because anthologies change greatly from edition to edition. Place the edition number after the name of the editor or editors. Use abbreviated ordinal numbers (*1st, 2nd, 3rd,* and so forth) and the abbreviation *ed.* for "edition." The following short story was found on pages 1103–1106 of the fourth edition of the anthology.

SHORT STORY

Paley, Grace. "A Conversation with My Father." The Story
and Its Writer: An Introduction to Short Fiction.

```
    Ed. Ann Charters. 4th ed. New York: Bedford-St. Mar-
    tin's, 1995. 1103-1106.
```

Underline the titles of longer works (novels, epic poems, and plays) even when they are part of an anthology, as with the epic poem *Paradise Lost* in the following example:

```
Milton, John. Paradise Lost. John Milton: Complete Poems
    and Major Prose. Ed. Merrit Y. Hughes. New York:
    Odyssey, 1957. 173-206.
```

Works by Corporate or Institutional Authors.   Many publications have no individual author but are of group or corporate origin. In such a case, enter the name of the originating body as the author's name.

```
American Medical Association. AMA Pocket Guide to Sports
    First Aid. New York: Random House, 1993.
```

If a corporate or institutional name also appears as publisher, you may abbreviate it the second time.

Government Documents.   A special group of works by corporate authors are documents put out by the U.S. government. These are especially tricky entries. If the individual author is not known (usually the case), treat the government agency as author. State the name of the government first—that is, the state or country of origin—and then the name of the agency. You may use common abbreviations such as *Dept.* and *Cong.* if the context makes their meaning clear. Then give title, place, publisher, and date as for other book entries.

```
United States. Environmental Protection Agency. Facility
    Pollution Prevention Guide. Englewood, CO: Global
    Professional, 1992.
```

Make your citation as specific as possible. If a source is published by an agency within an agency, mention all the agencies in descending order of hierarchy.

```
United States. Dept. of Health and Human Services. Public
    Health Service. Centers for Disease Control. Under-
    standing AIDS. Rockville, MD: HHS, 1988.
```

Again, if the same agency is both author and publisher, as it is here, abbreviate the name of the agency the second time it is mentioned.

Pamphlets.   Treat a pamphlet the same way you would treat a book. Give the author, if known; otherwise, begin your entry with the title, underlined.

> Boden, Talbot. Identifying Desert Rocks. San Francisco:
>   Hiker's Aids, 1980.
>
> Is Your House Burglar-Proof? Washington, DC: Crimewatch,
>   1956.

Editorials.   Cite editorials by giving the author's name, the title of the editorial in quotation marks, and then the label *Editorial,* neither underlined nor in quotation marks. Then give the information as usual for periodicals.

> Friedman, Thomas. "A Time for Anger." Editorial. New York
>   Times 26 June 1996: A18.

(Note that the page number is A18, as it appeared in the newspaper.) Some editorials have neither authors nor titles. Then your task is simple.

> Editorial. The Arizona Republic 26 May 1996: H4.

Letters to the Editor.   For letters to the editor, begin with the author's name and the label *Letter,* neither underlined nor in quotation marks. Then give publication data and page number. If the letter is in reply to another letter, follow the author's name with the label *Reply to letter of . . .* , then give the name of the author of the initial letter.

> Watson, Steve. Letter. The Boston Globe 3 May 1996: 14.
> Ghoti, Frank. Reply to letter of Dan McGrath. New York
>   Times 22 May 1988: 17D.

A Published Interview.   If you are citing a published interview, start with the name of the person interviewed. Follow with the title of the interview, if any, in quotation marks, or underlined if the interview takes up the whole work. If there is no title, simply write *Interview,* without underlining or quotation marks. If you know the name of the interviewer, place it after the title, preceded by *By.* Then continue the entry as usual.

> Updike, John. Interview. By John Timpane. West 1 May
>   1988: 4.

A Personal Interview.   If you are citing an interview you have done, give the name of the person interviewed, a label stating the kind of interview (*Personal interview, Telephone interview, Interview by question-*

naire), and the date, using the order day, month, year. If you did a personal interview with Margaret Thatcher on June 7, 1994, the citation would read this way:

```
Thatcher, Margaret. Personal interview. 7 June 1994.
```

A telephone interview with Earvin Johnson on January 24, 1993, would be cited this way:

```
Johnson, Earvin. Telephone interview. 24 Jan. 1993.
```

For some advice on how to conduct personal interviews, see "Interviews" in Chapter 13.

Printed Material from a Computer Service.   Computer services such as DIALOG or Mead can now give you printouts of abstracts, articles, and other information in many fields. Treat material from computer services as you would any other material. Give the complete original reference (you'll find it on the printout), and add the name of the computer service and the service's identifying numbers for the material cited.

```
Castro, Janice. "Spanglish Spoken Here." Time 11 July
    1988: 53. Infotrac, Number A6474356.
```

Material from an Information Service.   Again, treat material from an information service such as the Educational Resources Information Center (ERIC) as you would any other material, but add the name and identifying numbers of the information service at the end.

```
Fuhrman, Susan, ed. Designing Coherent Education Policy:
    Improving the System. San Francisco: Jossey-Bass,
    1993. ERIC ED 359626.
```

Periodical Sources from Databases.   Many of us now find periodical sources via CD-ROM retrieval systems such as First Search, Pro Quest, or Infotrac. Always note that fact in your citations. Give the author, the title, the source, the date of the entry, the page numbers, the title of the database, the name of the medium, the name of the vendor, and the date of publication of the database.

```
Janisson, Gabriel. "Germany's Biotech Comeback." Business
    Week Sept. 1994: 78+. Infotrac: Magazine Index Plus.
    CD-ROM. Information Access. Dec. 1994.
```

Infotrac: Magazine Index Plus, the title of the database, is treated like the title of any major self-contained work. Information Access is the publication company.

Entries from CD-ROM Encyclopedias.   Entries in encyclopedias often are unsigned, as with this entry from a popular CD-ROM encyclopedia:

```
"Aaron, Hank." The New Grolier Multimedia Encyclopedia.
     CD-ROM. Multimedia PC. 1993.
```

The date of publication may appear on the title page of the database, in accompanying print materials, or (as in this case) on the disk itself or the CD jewel case. If you are unsure of the city or date of publication, ask your reference librarian for help.

Sample Entries for Online Sources

With online sources such as those on the Internet, the idea is, as always, to give enough information for interested readers to find your source if they wish. Give the author's name, the title of the work, the title of the source (database, home page, and so forth; give the title as it appears on the title line on your screen), the publication medium (Online), the name of the service or network you used to gain access (America Online, CompuServe, Nexis, and so on), and the date of access. We suggest you also include the URL or Internet address. Below are some examples.

Electronic Journals.   You may often use online versions of newspapers or electronic journals. Here is a common citation form for such articles:

```
Callicott, J. Baird. "Intrinsic Value in Nature." Elec-
     tronic Journal of Analytic Philosophy 3 (Spring
     1995). Online. Prodigy. 23 Mar. 1996.
     http://www.phil.indiana.edu/ejap/ejap.html
```

Note that this journal gave an issue number and date; always give these if provided. If you do include the Internet address, put the entire address on a line by itself to avoid confusion. Do not put a period after the address. If the Internet address is longer than one line of type, try to break the address after slashes or periods.

Articles from Online Newspapers.   Give the author, the title, the name of the source, the word *Online,* the name of your service or network, and the date.

```
Safire, William. "Commentary: New Mandate of Heaven." New
     York Times Online. Online. Lexis. 20 Mar. 1996.
```

Home Pages.   Give the titles of your sources (underlined) as they appear on the title line. The titles of smaller works within larger works are enclosed in quotation marks. Here again, include the word *Online* and the name of your service. Also, since information on the Internet changes so rapidly, document the date on which you visited the site, and print out a hard copy for reference. Here is a poem found on an Internet home page:

```
Roberg, Robert. "The Way Up Is Down." Robert Roberg's
     Home Page. Online. America Online. 25 Mar. 1996.
     http://www.coedu.usf.edu/~roberg/poetry.html
```

Anonymous home pages are treated much the same as any other anonymous source. On March 22, 1996, we used America Online to reach the home page of the Woods Hole Oceanographic Institution. There we found a "Construction Update." Here is how we cited the update:

```
"Construction Update." Woods Hole Oceanographic Institu-
     tion http Server. Online. America Online. 22 Mar.
     1995.
     http://www.whoi.edu
```

We found the text for a Senate health care bill by accessing *Thomas,* an information source run by the Library of Congress on the Internet. The title line across the top of our screen read *Thomas: Legislative Information on the Internet.* We used that as our title and came up with this entry:

```
U.S. Congress. Health Care Coverage and Affordability Act
     of 1996. H. R. 3103. Thomas: Legislative Information
     on the Internet. U.S. Library of Congress. Online.
     CompuServe 25 Mar. 1996.
     http://thomas.loc.gov
```

E-mail Messages.   Give the name of the author, the title or subject of the message (if any; many e-mail messages have titles beginning with "Re," short for "regarding"), the name of the addressee (if you are the addressee, write "E-mail to the author" followed by a period), and the date.

```
Wentworth, Claude. "Re: Standardized Testing." E-mail to
     the author. 12 Apr. 1992.
```

Keep copies of any e-mail messages you cite in your papers in case anyone asks to see them.

Postings from Newsgroups or Mailing Lists.   Give the name of the author, the date of the posting, the words *Online posting,* and the title of the newsgroup or forum (using words such as *Newsgroup* or *Forum),* followed (without a comma) by the Internet address, the name of your network or service, and the date you read the posting, which often will be different from the date of the posting itself.

> Setton, Ruth. "Re: Suleika." 14 Jan. 1991. Online post-
> ing. Newsgroup rec.arts.poems. Usenet. 23 May 1991.

Sample Entries for Other Sources

Films.   Citations for films usually begin with the film's title, underlined, followed by the director's name (preceded by the label *Dir.*), the name of the distributor, and the year. Separate distributor and year with a comma.

> It Happened One Night. Dir. Frank Capra. Metro-Goldwyn-
> Mayer, 1934.

If you wish to emphasize the contribution of a particular person, you can begin with that person's name and his or her contribution.

> Attenborough, Richard, actor. Jurassic Park. Dir. Steven
> Spielberg. MCA/Universal, 1993.

Radio or Television Programs.   Cite radio or television programs by giving the title of the broadcast (underlined), the name of the network (if known), the call letters and city of the local station (separated by a comma), and the date of the broadcast.

> Day of the Barricades. National Public Radio. WNYC, New
> York. 13 May 1988.

If you are citing a particular episode of a series, give the name of the episode in quotation marks, the author's name (preceded by the label *Writ.*), if known, then the series title (underlined), followed by network (if known), call letters, city, and date.

> "Common Pursuit." Writ. Simon Gray. Great Performances.
> PBS. 9 Nov. 1992.

In general, give information that is as detailed as possible, emphasizing the person whose contribution you are citing. The following entry cites the work of the writer of a particular episode of a television program and includes the names of the director and producer.

> Kinoy, Ernest, writ. "Chernobyl: The Final Warning." Dir.
> Anthony Page. Prod. Philip Barry. TNT. 22 Apr. 1991.

Recordings.   If you are citing a commercially available recording, you should usually begin your citation with the name of the *person* whose contribution you wish to cite, whether it be the writer or composer of the work, the artists involved, a conductor, or a producer. You will *always* include the title of the work, the artist or artists involved, the manufacturer of the recording, the catalog number (exactly as it appears on the cover of the recording), and the year of issue, if known. (If the year is not known write *n.d.* for "no date.") Follow the manufacturer and catalog number with commas.

```
Berlioz, Hector. Symphonie fantastique. op. 14. Cond.
     Leonard Bernstein. New York Philharmonic. Columbia,
     MS /278, n.d.
```

If the recording is a collection or anthology and you wish to cite a single work, enclose the title in quotation marks if the work is short, underline it if the work is long, and do neither if the work is identified only by form, number, or key.

```
Jordan, Stanley. "Return Expedition." Magic Touch. Stan-
     ley Jordan. Blue Note, CDP 7 46092-2, 1986.
Bach, J. S. Concerto for Violin and Orchestra in E Major.
     J. S. Bach Violin Concertos. St. Petersburg
     Soloists. Audiophile Classics, APC 101.021, 1994.
```

Using References in Your Text

To follow the MLA format, document sources in your text by inserting a short acknowledgment in parentheses. Usually, the author's last name and a page number are enough. We are basing this section on the *MLA Handbook,* especially on pages 183–205 of that book, so a reference is in order (Gibaldi 183–205).

We just gave it. Notice that there is no comma between the author's last name and the page number. Close the parentheses before a period or comma. If you are crediting a longer, indented quotation, skip two spaces after the concluding punctuation mark and give the reference. Christina Gerke does this in this passage from her paper:

```
Educator George F. Madaus writes,
        The more one knows about the technology of
        testing, the more one realizes the poten-
        tial for harm when a test score is used as
        the sole or primary criterion on which to
```

```
make an important decision affecting an in-
dividual's future. (93)
```

Because she mentions Madaus in the text before the quotation, Gerke needs to give only the page number in parentheses. Note that the reference comes outside the terminal punctuation and on the same line. If her readers want to know more, they can refer to her list of works cited; there they would find

```
Madaus, George F. "NIE Clarification Hearing: The Nega-
    tive Team's Case." Phi Delta Kappan Oct. 1981:
    92-94.
```

Whenever Gerke refers to Madaus, she simply uses the brief parenthetical reference and the appropriate page number.

Place such references at natural pauses in your sentences—usually at the end of the sentence, or the end of the phrase or clause that contains the cited material—and as close to the material as possible.

If the names of the authors of your sources already appear in your text, you need only give the page number in your reference. Here is another example from Gerke's paper.

```
Robert L. Green and Robert J. Griffore write, "The nega-
tive aspects of testing procedures are especially appar-
ent with respect to racial minorities" (25).
```

We recommend that you mention the names of important sources *often.* Your readers can find the names of the authors in the text, and complete information is always waiting for them in your list of works cited.

Common Kinds of Parenthetical References

Works by One Author. As mentioned, include the author's name and page number. The following example is straightforward.

```
Play, after all, is the way the growing mind gets nour-
ishment (Piaget 87).
```

Works by More Than One Author. For sources with two or three authors, give the last name of each in the same order as on the title page of the book.

```
Platypuses are bizarre holdovers from ancient animal
forms (Stein and Ahmad 223).
```

For sources with more than three authors, give the first author's name as it appears on the title page, then write *et al.* and give the page number. Thus, for the work with four authors that we cited on page 386, the text citation would be

```
As of March 1978 one of every five families with children
under the age of eighteen was maintained by a parent who
was separated, divorced, widowed, or never married
(Waldeman et al. 45).
```

Notice we kept only Waldeman. If you use a single name as a reference to a multiauthored source, use it also in your list of works cited.

Anonymous Works.   If the work lists no author, simply give a short title—usually the first main word of the title—in the reference. If your source is a book, underline the word or words from the title.

```
Today's lifeguards not only must know how to swim but
must be able to differentiate among many different kinds
of suntan lotion (Swimmers 56).
```

If your anonymous source is an article, put the title in quotation marks.

```
In short, a diet of cotton candy is detrimental to the
health of most rodents ("Effect of Cotton Candy" 6).
```

Multiple Works by the Same Author.   If you refer to more than one work by the same author, simply give the author's name, a short title of the work referred to, and page number.

```
Meaning is often lost in transit (Derrida, "Séance" 203).
Our final destination is often displaced in the search
for something else (Derrida, Grammatology 99).
```

The first reference is to an essay and the second to a book, both by Jacques Derrida. For clarity we separate the author's name from the title of the work with a comma.

Multiple Works in a Single Reference.   If you want to support a point by referring to more than one work, separate the references by a semicolon within the parentheses.

```
Like the hippies of the 1960s, the yuppies of the 1980s
were largely a creation of the press ("Bogus Order";
Nesbitt 6-18).
```

If you need to refer to three or more sources (a rare event for most college writers), use a footnote or endnote in the text of your paper.

> American teenagers now reach puberty at an average age
> of 11.5 years, much earlier than at any time in this
> century.[1]

The corresponding note would look like this:

> [1] Crossbeck 178; Delahay 42; Montemayor 788.

Place these notes on a sheet of paper *before* your list of works cited. Such notes can also be used for explanation and cross-referencing, but use them sparingly. See the two endnotes in Christina Gerke's paper, page 420.

Multivolume Works.   For a text reference to a multivolume work, show the volume number with an arabic numeral followed by a colon and the page number.

> Though the two never met, Tolstoy admired Dostoyevski
> (Scherrol 2: 77).

Works by Corporate Authors.   Some publications have a corporate author whose name is quite long. You may put that name in parentheses, but it is better to cite the title of the work and the name of the originating body in your text, followed by the page number in parentheses.

> In its newsletter, The Backyard Apiary, the National Con-
> gress of Independent Beekeepers reported a slight rise
> in the number of neighbors who sued members over bee
> stings (44).

CD-ROM and Online Sources.   Treat paginated sources in the standard fashion, giving the author's name followed by a space and the relevant page number(s).

> After thirty years in the shadow of the United States and
> Japan, German science has finally come into its own
> (Janisson 85).

When CD-ROM and online sources are unpaginated, your parenthetical references will contain only the author's last name or a short title.

```
One of the most interesting debates in philosophy today
is whether nature has any value in and of itself
(Callicott).
```

This practice, however, strikes many readers and writers as awkward or disconcerting. If you are one of them, simply refer to such sources directly in your text:

```
As the work of J. Baird Callicott makes clear, one of the
most interesting debates in philosophy today is whether
nature has any value in and of itself.
```

We recommend this approach also with e-mail or newsgroup references. Christina Gerke received a useful e-mail message from Claude Wentworth, an expert on standardized testing. Here is how she handled that reference:

```
In an e-mail message to me, Claude Wentworth describes
standardized tests as "extremely useful in categorizing
large numbers of people, but less and less meaningful as
you focus down to the individual student."
```

Literary References.   Most college papers on literature discuss a single work. In this case, establish the author and title of the work you are discussing early and then simply give page, chapter, act, or line numbers in your references. If you are writing about more than one work, give the author's last name and page number in your references as we just described, unless you mention the author or title in your text. In your list of works cited, give a complete entry for the edition you use of each work.

1. Novels. Put the page first, then the chapter (abbreviated *ch.*), in case your reader has an edition with different page numbers.

```
When Jo in Charles Dickens's Bleak House is asked where
his parents are, he replies, "I never know'd nothink
about 'em" (372; ch. 25).
```

2. Plays. Cite quotations from plays not by page number but by the division of the play—act, scene, line—in which the quotation appears. Give these divisions in arabic numerals separated only by periods. If you mention the name of the play in the text, you may omit it in the reference.

```
In Hamlet, the protagonist's most intense insight
occurs when he accepts his fate: "If it be now, 'tis not
```

```
to come; if it be not to come, it will be now" (5.2.
76-77).
```

3. Poems. For a poem, give line numbers cited in parentheses. Use the word *line* or *lines* in your first citation; once you have established that the numbers will indicate lines, use the numbers by themselves.

```
In John Donne's "The Good-Morrow," the speaker muses to
the loved one, "I wonder, by my troth, what thou, and
I/Did, till we lov'd?" (lines 1-2). Later, the poet says
that any idea he had of beauty before meeting his love
was only "a dream of thee" (7).
```

If you quote two or three lines of poetry, use slashes to separate them in the text. If you quote more than three lines, begin the quotation on a new line, indented ten spaces from the left margin. Break the lines exactly as they appear in the original.

If there are divisions (cantos, books, parts) in the poem you are quoting, give the division number before the line numbers.

```
When he sees what he has done, Milton's Adam gives one of
the most moving laments in Paradise Lost: "The more I
see/Pleasures about me, so much more I feel/Torment
within me" (9. 119-21).
```

Entire Works.   The best way to cite an entire work is to do so in your text.

```
The furthest development of the Russian novel is still
represented by Tolstoy's War and Peace.
```

Give a complete entry in your list of works cited for any entire works you cite.

Indirect Sources.   As we mentioned in "Primary and Secondary Sources" in Chapter 13, you should prefer firsthand sources to all others. Sometimes, however, you may be able to find only an indirect source, such as someone quoting someone else. If you quote or paraphrase material quoted in another source, put the abbreviation *qtd. in* (for "quoted in") before the indirect reference you cite in parentheses.

```
Even a compulsive worker like Harry Truman was heard to
mutter, "Even I need a day off once in a while" (qtd. in
Giuseppe 55).
```

Then cite the indirect source in your list of works cited.

> Giuseppe, Raphael. <u>Type A Personalities in American His-
> tory</u>. Seattle: Workplace, 1981.

REVISING AND WRITING THE FINAL DRAFT

Putting your research paper into final form will call on everything you have learned about writing: style, grammar, and punctuation; paragraphing, persuasion, and documentation; claim, evidence, and warrant. We hope you will refer to this book often in the course of rewriting. Be sure you reread the section "Revising: Getting the Writing Right" in Chapter 5.

Before typing the final draft, read your paper twice, first for content and then again for mechanical correctness. Do not try to read for both content and correctness at once. While hunting down an errant comma, you may miss a faulty warrant. One time-honored method of checking spelling is to start with the last word and read word by word backwards.

Try reading aloud too.

After you finish revising, you will prepare your final draft. Don't unleash a disheveled paper on the world. Turning in even the most closely reasoned and well-supported paper with incorrect spelling and poor grammar is like going out on a special date with dirty fingernails and greasy hair. If your instructor has given explicit directions regarding title page, binding, footnotes, and the like, follow them. Here are some standard guidelines:

1. Use $8\frac{1}{2}$-by-11-inch white bond paper. If you use continuous computer paper, remove the perforated sides and separate the pages.

2. Be sure the type is clear, dark, and black. Avoid inks and toners of unusual color, and always use normal, legible fonts. Be sure to left-justify the page, leaving the right margin ragged.

3. An inch below the top of the first page, even with the left-hand margin, type your name, your instructor's name, your course title and number, and the date on separate lines, double-spacing between each.

4. Double-space again and type your title in the center of the line. Do not underline the title or put it in quotation marks. Double-space between the title and your first line of text. Figure 14.1 shows the standard format for the first page of a research paper.

Cover sheets are not required for most research papers. We do, however, suggest that you use a cover sheet if you have included an outline for your paper. (That is what Christina Gerke did.) On a cover sheet, center your title about a third of the way down the page. Do not underline it or put it in quotation marks. An inch below the title, type

Figure 14.1   First Page of a Research Paper

Page number ¹/₂ inch below top of page

1

Name 1 inch below top

Christina Gerke

Professor Resnick

Subsequent lines double-spaced

English 102

2 May 1996

Title centered, neither underlined nor quoted. First line indented 5 spaces

The Standardized Testing Controversy

Standardized tests have become an American way of life. They now help determine who will be accepted to college; which students must take remedial classes and which may take advanced classes; who will make the best soldiers, civil servants, lawyers, state employees--even who may drive a car. According to James L. Wardrop, more than 200 million such tests are administered in the United States each year (16). It may come as a surprise, then, to learn that something so common is the subject of a national controversy.

Educators, psychologists, and experts in test

1-inch side margins

design stand on both sides of the debate. Advocates argue that standardized testing is still the best available method of assessing a person's abilities. They claim that existing tests are "not biased against minority groups" (Herbert) and are "valid predictors" of a person's future success (Eckland 12). In short, they see the tests as services to the community.

Opponents believe that the tests may do more harm than good. In their eyes, the tests fail to recognize the cultural diversity of our society. Constructed according to the styles and standards of the white, middle-class, male community, the tests, opponents say, are biased against minorities and less affluent whites. Robert L. Green and Robert J.

1-inch bottom margin

By followed by your name. An inch below your name, type your in-structor's name, the name and number of the course, and the date, each on a separate, centered line. On the first page of text, center the title (again, neither underlined nor in quotation marks) two inches from the top of the page. Begin the text two lines below the title. See Christina Gerke's paper (pp. 404–23) for the proper form for papers with cover sheets and outlines.

5. Number all your pages in the upper-right-hand corners, one-half inch below the top of the page and an inch from the right-hand edge. It is also a good idea to give your last name with the page number—for example, "Gerke 6"—from page 2 on.

6. Double-space your text. That includes long quotations, endnotes (if any), and list of works cited.

7. Leave one-inch margins at the bottom, top, and sides of each page.

8. Leave two spaces after any period or other end-of-sentence punctuation.

9. Make sure your references, endnotes (if any), and list of works cited follow the proper form. If you use endnotes, type them on a sepa-rate page, numbered as part of the paper. Center the heading *Notes* one inch from the top of the page. Double-space the notes. Indent the first line of each note five spaces from the left margin. The number of the note (corresponding to the raised number in the text) is raised a half-space above the note. For the proper format, see Christina Gerke's end-notes on page 420.

The list of works cited begins on a separate page following the text and endnotes (if any). The page is numbered as part of the text, and the heading *Works Cited* is centered one inch from the top of the page. En-tries are double-spaced throughout, with the first line of each entry even with the left margin and subsequent lines indented five spaces. Authors are listed alphabetically, with the first author's name inverted and addi-tional authors' names (if any) in normal order. Anonymous works are al-phabetized by the first important word of the title (not *a, an,* or *the*). See Christina Gerke's list of works cited on pages 421–23.

10. Use correction fluid if necessary, but retype a heavily corrected page or passage rather than submit anything sloppy or unreadable.

11. Fasten the pages together with a paper clip or a staple of ade-quate strength. Plastic binders and stiff cardboard can be a nuisance to your reader.

12. Keep all written work away from food and drinks, especially coffee, to which papers seem to have a magnetic attraction. Make a copy of your paper for safekeeping—of both hard copy and disk if working on a computer.

Computer Tip

If your instructor gives you format preferences, set up your document with those preferences in place before you input your text. Unless instructed otherwise, follow these guidelines: double-space and left-justify all text; leave one-inch margins on all sides; include running heads with your last name and page number on every page starting with page 2; and use normal fonts only. So that the type is dark and legible, make sure the toner, ink, or ribbon in your printer is fresh.

CASE STUDY: A SAMPLE RESEARCH PAPER

Here is a formal outline of Christina Gerke's research paper, followed by the paper itself. Notice that she uses the MLA parenthetical reference and list of works cited system of documentation.

Gerke includes a formal outline with her paper, so she uses a separate title page.

```
            The Standardized Testing Controversy




                       By Christina Gerke




                      Professor Resnick
                        English 102
                        May 2, 1996
```

Gerke ii

The outline is placed between the title page and the text. Gerke centers the title of the paper one inch from the top of the page. She double-spaces and types her thesis. This is a formal sentence outline.

Each major point of the outline corresponds to a part of the thesis. Each subdivision relates directly to the main division under which it appears.

The Standardized Testing Controversy

Thesis: Since there is still so much controversy
       about standardized tests, employers and
       institutions should place less emphasis
       on test performance as a criterion for
       admissions and hiring and more on aptitude
       and personal characteristics.

I. Standardized tests are a fact of life in the
   United States, but their design and effects are
   a matter of continuing controversy.

   A. They determine who graduates from high
      school, who attends the best colleges, who
      gets the best jobs, even who drives a car.

   B. Educators and experts disagree about their
      usefulness.

      1. Advocates say they are the best available
         instrument for assessing a person's
         abilities.

      2. Opponents charge that because the tests
         are biased, they may do more harm than
         good.

   C. This paper argues that employers and
      institutions should continue to use the
      tests, but they should de-emphasize them.

II. The controversy stems from the tests' social
    origin and social impact.

   A. The tests have replaced older prejudicial
      ways of choosing candidates for college
      admission and employment.

   B. Advocates praise the tests on two grounds.

      1. The tests have predictive value.

      2. They are reputedly fair.

   C. Opponents, however, point out bias in tests.

      1. Minorities score lower.

Outline pages are numbered with lower case roman numerals about a half-inch from the top of the page, in the upper-right-hand corner, beginning with *ii* (the first page is counted but not numbered). The pages of the text are numbered with arabic numerals, beginning with the first page.

2. Use of standardized English automatically discriminates against those for whom English is a second language and those who use dialects.

3. Most tests emphasize reading and vocabulary, both of which are culturally linked.

4. Test items can be "differentially attractive."

III. Because of further inherent problems in test design itself, critics doubt the ability of standardized tests to predict future perform-ance, and they question the tests' value in assessing knowledge.

A. Tests ignore personality factors that could influence a person's performance.

B. Candidates may be quite qualified for a position and still may perform poorly on tests.

C. It is sometimes difficult to ascertain exactly what the tests measure.

1. <u>Intelligence</u> is not clearly defined.

2. Tests may measure different abilities in different people.

IV. The Scholastic Aptitude Test (SAT) is a case study in the history and controversy surrounding standardized tests.

A. The SAT is the largest, most widespread standardized test.

B. Students' performance on the SAT may have more to do with which high school they attend than with their intelligence.

C. Minorities and the less affluent perform less well on the SAT.

Gerke iv

   V. Standardized tests may actually reinforce the subordinate position of minority groups.

     A. Low scores mean a limited future.

     B. Despite efforts to eliminate accidental bias, even minimum competency tests (MCTs) still maintain hierarchies that restrict candidates' future chances.

  VI. The shortcomings of standardized tests may undermine the efforts of teachers.

 VII. Still, standardized tests are useful within limits.

     A. In general, standardized tests can measure performance, predict future success, and indicate aptitude for various things.

     B. SATs can predict students' college success to some extent.

     C. It is useful, for better or for worse, to learn how to survive in a white, middle-class world.

VIII. We should not, however, rely on tests so much.

     A. They are overused, and they have too much power to determine candidates' futures.

     B. Some schools are already downplaying the tests in favor of other standards.

  IX. I propose that we adopt an "opportunity quotient" test.

     A. Such a test would compare a person's opportunity with his or her achievements.

     B. An "opportunity quotient" test would present a fairer and more comprehensive picture of a student.

Neither the introduction nor the conclusion is named as a separate part of the outline. Instead, Gerke includes sentences that describe the content of these sections.

Gerke 1

The Standardized Testing Controversy

Four-paragraph intro-
duction: one on gen-
eral background, one
for each side of the
controversy, and one
stating the thesis.

Standardized tests have become an American way
of life. They now help determine who will be accepted
to college; which students must take remedial classes
and which may take advanced classes; who will make
the best soldiers, civil servants, lawyers, state
employees--even who may drive a car. According to
James L. Wardrop, more than 200 million such tests

Since Wardrop is
mentioned in the text,
only the page number
appears in the paren-
thetical reference.

are administered in the United States each year (16).
It may come as a surprise, then, to learn that
something so common is the subject of a national
controversy.

Effective transition
from "national con-
troversy" in para. 1
to "the debate" in
para. 2.

Educators, psychologists, and experts in test
design stand on both sides of the debate. Advocates
argue that standardized testing is still the best
available method of assessing a person's abilities.
They claim that existing tests are "not biased
against minority groups" (Herbert) and are "valid

Gerke smoothly com-
bines material from
two sources with her
own writing. The ref-
erence to the Herbert
article has no page
number since the arti-
cle is one page long.

predictors" of a person's future success (Eckland
12). In short, they see the tests as services to the
community.

Opponents believe that the tests may do more
harm than good. In their eyes, the tests fail to
recognize the cultural diversity of our society.
Constructed according to the styles and standards of
the white, middle-class, male community, the tests,
opponents say, are biased against minorities and less
affluent whites. Robert L. Green and Robert J.
Griffore write, "The negative aspects of testing
procedures are especially apparent with respect to
racial minorities" (25). By failing to recognize
cultural diversity, they argue, test makers perma-
nently handicap large numbers of people whose poor
performances land them where they do not belong--

Gerke 2

in "slow" classes with restricted curricula and even more restricted opportunities.

> In her thesis paragraph, Gerke distinguishes her position from both sides of the debate. Her thesis promises a direction, raises some questions to be answered (*Why* should tests be deemphasized?), and commits the paper to argument.

My discussion will look at both sides of this issue in more detail but will not agree completely with either side. Standardized tests are useful, but they are also very powerful: test scores can affect the course of people's lives, not to mention their self-image and their society's image of them. Since there is still so much controversy about standardized tests, employers and institutions should place less emphasis on test performance as a criterion for admissions and hiring and more on aptitude and personal characteristics.

> In these paragraphs, Gerke gives readers background information. This section of the paper corresponds to II.A. in the outline.

In the past employers and institutions based their selections on factors such as a candidate's social class and family background. College admissions boards, especially those for private institutions, weighed these values more heavily than proven ability. Diane Ravitch points out that as late as the 1940s, admissions boards tended to select students from a small number of well-known public and private institutions (55). This practice, obviously unfair to deserving candidates from disadvantaged backgrounds, maintained the homogeneous nature of the colleges.

Standardized tests arose out of the prejudicial atmosphere of the early twentieth century. Testing began in Britain in the early twentieth century because of a eugenics movement that was founded on the idea that the poorer classes were inferior and that the growth of these classes threatened the purity of the upper classes. The spread of such inferiority could be checked by birth control and sterilization (Smith 132-33). At the same time,

however, there was a move toward standardization,
partly to correct such institutionalized prejudices.
The French psychologist Alfred Binet originally
formulated his Binet scale of intelligence in 1905 to
place advanced and handicapped children in special
schools (Wardrop 8; Jensen 141-43). Binet's test
began the long history of standardized placement
examinations.

Note how two differ-
ent sources are cited
in a single parenthet-
ical reference.

In the ninety years since, standardized tests
have often drawn praise as the most democratic
possible means of social selection because they aim
only to "predict performance in school and on the
job" (Herbert). Bruce K. Eckland, professor of
sociology at the University of North Carolina, gives
the standard defense:

Gerke establishes
the authority of her
source by giving his
credentials in her in-
troduction to the in-
dented quotation.

> There is no factor that has a stronger,
> more consistent effect in the college
> attainment process independent of
> race, social class, sex, or any other
> observed characteristic . . . than individual
> ability as measured by standardized tests.
> (12)

Long quotation in-
dents ten spaces from
left margin. Ellipses
indicate that some-
thing is omitted from
the original. Since
Eckland is already
mentioned, only the
page number appears
in the reference.

Advocates often seem to suggest that this ability to
predict exonerates tests from charges of bias. One
defender writes that the tests "can predict equally
well for members of minority groups as for nonwhites"
(Holden), as if this accuracy can somehow sidestep
the question of whether or not the prediction is
self-fulfilling.

Here and elsewhere,
Gerke analyzes and
evaluates her sources.
This appeal to reason
shows that she has
thought about Hol-
den's position and
has a response.

Yet the charge of test bias against minority
groups has become the central issue in the debate.
One consistent trend has proved most embarrassing
to those who favor standardized tests: in general,
minorities score lower on standardized tests than do

Gerke 4

middle-class whites. For example, Harvard University's Arthur Jensen, noted and controversial expert on standardized tests, claimed that the overall difference between whites and blacks was 15 points, and the gap between rich and poor was 12 points (44). Although these gaps have shrunk in the years since Jensen's announcement, differences between these groups seem to persist.

If such figures provide powerful evidence of bias, problems in the design of the tests are even more telling. One obvious example is the use of standard English in most tests. Peter Farb says that students for whom English is a second language, or those who speak a dialect such as black or Appalachian English, may have a handicap before they even sit down to take the test (162-63).

Further, many tests emphasize reading and vocabulary ability, which studies have shown to be culturally linked (Ravitch 54)--that is, a student from a background where reading is either unavailable or not encouraged will come to a standardized test at a great disadvantage. And some questions may similarly contain quite accidental bias. Consider this test question:

Collie is to dog as trout is to _____. The correct answer, of course, is <u>fish</u>, but if a student came from a background where people never used the word <u>trout</u>--or, more likely, used a slang or dialect equivalent instead--he or she would miss the question, not through lack of ability but, as Wardrop claims, through being different (53).

In the parlance of the experts, certain test items may have characteristics that "are differentially attractive" to different population

---

By suggesting that the next piece of evidence will be more convincing than the first, Gerke makes an effective transition.

In Gerke's first draft, the Farb information came later in the paper. In her revision she grouped it earlier with similar evidence.

Here Gerke closely paraphrases a passage from Wardrop. She carefully documents her source.

Gerke 5

This paragraph con-
tains a claim and a
lengthy quotation for
evidence. It then con-
cludes with a strong
warrant.

subgroups. As Janice Dowd Scheuneman, vice president

of the Eastern Educational Research Association,

states,

> Unexpected differences in item performance
>
> can occur as the result of . . . urban-rural
>
> distinctions, climatic differences, eco-
>
> nomic advantage or disadvantage . . .
>
> cultural characteristics or values . . .
>
> Spanish language heritage . . . black English
>
> dialects, and the interpersonal style and
>
> communication modes of different ethnic
>
> cultures. (185)

This means that a person's background shapes his or

her perception of the world.

A test constructed by a white, middle-class male

will necessarily reflect many of his norms and value

assumptions. Obviously, these may differ markedly

from those of a lower-class Hispanic woman, who may

be penalized for selecting answers that are true for

her. Her selection of different answers, however,

does not necessarily indicate that she lacks ability

or intelligence. Scheuneman gives the example of one

test of auditory discrimination in which children

were asked to select a picture of the object which

began with the same sound as a word given by the

teacher. In one item,

Gerke uses brackets
to insert material into
the quotation for
clarity.

> the key word was "heart," and the correct
>
> choice was [the picture of a] "hand." The
>
> first option, however, was a [picture of a]
>
> large, fancy car . . . called a "hog" in
>
> black dialect . . . this option, in fact, had
>
> drawn a disproportionately large number of
>
> black children. (183-84)

Gerke 6

Thus, although the answer was technically incorrect, the children demonstrated that they actually had the skill being tested. Such built-in inequities may not happen in most test items, but they do happen often enough to support the conclusion that standardized tests, while "highly perfected" (Ravitch 13), may not be humanly sensitive.

By referring to *bias* (the umbrella term for the first set of criticisms against the tests), Gerke makes a smooth transition to the next set.

Bias is not the only point of contention. The great selling features of standardized tests--their ability to predict future performance and their value in assessing knowledge--are now also under attack. In a report of the Committee on Ability Testing of the Assembly of Behavioral and Social Sciences, Alexandra K. Wigdor, study director of the committee, cites the

Gerke adds italics to emphasize a passage not originally stressed in the source. Her phrase *italics mine* in brackets immediately following the material indicates that this is her addition.

limited predictive powers of the tests . . . the constraints on assessment introduced by the very process of standardization [italics mine], the traditional concentration of the tests on a limited range of cognitive skills . . . and the inability of the tests to assess adequately other important characteristics such as motivation, creativity, or perseverance. (6-7)

Problems arise, then, whenever we try to measure people by a single yardstick. Standardization prevents tests from taking into account intangible differences among people, differences in personality factors, such as Wigdor's "motivation, creativity, or perseverance," that might be valuable or crucial to a

Gerke uses an e-mail message from an expert in the field.

person's success. In an e-mail message to me, Claude Wentworth describes standardized tests as "extremely useful in categorizing large numbers of people, but less and less meaningful as you focus down to the

Gerke 7

individual student." Most tests cannot address
aspects of character because test takers are often
confined to multiple choice answers ("Jensen's
Rebuttal"). Yet any truly predictive test must
measure such qualities, since what people lack in
strictly intellectual or cognitive abilities they can
sometimes offset with other abilities or with hard
work and dedication. The tests may therefore have
the serious shortcoming of ignoring significant
predictors of future performance.

Further, not all talented people are talented
test takers. Many people acquire skills informally
or by habit and are not skilled at recapitulating
their knowledge in a test environment. An extremely
skilled gardener could flunk a state examination, for
example, because he or she is semiliterate or poor
at mathematics. Such people can perform deceptively
poorly on a standardized test that is designed only
to produce a number. Critic Andrew J. Strenio says
that not accepting a talented individual because of
a low test score is like "Red Auerbach telling Larry
Bird to quit the Celtics until he scores well on a
standardized test about passing lanes in basketball"
(167).

Sometimes it is difficult to ascertain exactly
what qualities the tests actually measure. Scientists
do not yet agree on a single definition of the word
intelligence, for example, and as the meaning of the
word changes, so do the tests that try to measure it
("Brave New World"). Martha Fuentes-Cook, writing in
the Journal of Social Dynamics, believes that "as
long as such an important social determinant is based
on such a slippery term, there will be a structural
unfairness intrinsic to standardized tests

Here is a claim.

No warrant is neces-
sary for this, the first
piece of evidence.

Here is a second
piece of evidence.
The quotation that
follows makes the ev-
idence more specific.

Gerke found the
Fuentes-Cook article
through a CD-ROM
database.

Gerke 8

themselves" (66). Furthermore, a test item designed to measure one ability may actually test different abilities in different people. This accidental shifting can occur in something as simple as a spelling test, as John R. Bormuth explains:

> Asking for the spelling of a given word may require a student who was previously drilled on the word merely to recite from rote memory a string of letters but require a student who was not taught this word to analyze it into syllables and phonemes and then to apply his phonics knowledge to the task. (23)

The warrant explains how the evidence works with the claim. In fact, Gerke makes the warrant very detailed: it takes two sentences.

Consequently, a test item aimed at a specific ability (phonics knowledge) tested something quite different (ability to memorize). This shifting happened because of the different experiences of the students being tested, something that no test may ever fully take into account. If designers cannot limit what their questions test, their tests may not really identify specific abilities and test for them accurately and fairly.

The Scholastic Aptitude Test (SAT) is used as a case study of standardized tests.

Gerke follows an important term with its abbreviation in parentheses. In later references she uses just the abbreviation.

The title of the book is used when there is no author. If the title is very long, a brief form can be used.

Inequities occur on the largest scale in the largest, most standardized test of all. The Scholastic Aptitude Tests (SATs) evaluate high-school applicants to colleges and universities. Taking SATs has become a senior-year ritual for more than a million students every year (On Further Examination 1), and, despite the disagreements over their value, SAT scores are still very important parts of any college application. SATs aim to measure the student's innate capacity. However, SAT results may have more to do with one's school than with intelligence. In an article in New Republic magazine,

Gerke 9

Ann Hulbert says that "the SAT is in fact yet another exam that reflects the quality of the schools
students happen to attend, rather than a transcendent
test that measures some ambiguous 'aptitude' they
possess" (12). Certain schools gear the senior and
sometimes the junior year to preparing students for
the SATs; others run mock exams or hold classes on
how to use the multiple choice format to help
eliminate inaccurate answers. Thus, the SAT may
handicap people who have intelligence and potential
but have not attended schools with these programs.

Gerke uses the word
further to make a
smooth transition.

Further, the familiar gaps in average scores
exist between rich and poor and between racial groups
on the SAT as on other tests. Students from low-
income families average about 100 points lower on the
verbal and the mathematics parts of the test than
those from wealthier families. According to the
College Entrance Examination Board, blacks average
100 points below the overall average on the verbal
part and 115 points below on the mathematics (On
Further Examination 15).

This paragraph sum-
marizes the article
"Jensen's Rebuttal"
since only the main
sense of the article
was needed.

The great danger of the SATs and other standardized tests is that they may reinforce social
hierarchies by the simple fact that a low test score
is a social disadvantage. Because of their low test
scores, minority children have often been labeled
slow or retarded and placed in special schools or,
worse yet, have received no further education.
Studies show that such children grow up thinking they
are stupid and suffer further hardship, since with no
education they can expect fewer prospects in society
("Jensen's Rebuttal").

Even minimum competency tests (MCTs), which were
designed to reveal basic skill deficiencies so that

they could be rectified (Popham 91), may contribute
to the problem.[1] The aim behind these tests was to
eliminate the gap between racial and economic groups,
but the tests may reinforce class differentiation and
hold back deserving students.

The raised number refers readers to a content note at the end of the paper.

Once the system classifies people according to
test results, it tends to perpetuate and accentuate
the differences among them. Although students are no
longer rated "slow" or "fast" learners, Andrew R.
Trusz and Sandra L. Parks-Trusz discovered that a
specific number are classified as "pigeons," "hawks,"
or "eagles" according to their MCT scores (17). While
"eagles" learn the entire curriculum on which later
examinations will test them, "pigeons" are given only
a part of it, which causes them to fall further and
further behind. The rest of the story is familiar.
"Pigeons" could fail to earn a high-school diploma
and thus be cut off from further opportunities at
school and at work. The handicap of social labeling
could ensue: "remediation evokes labelling . . .
attaching a negative label to an individual's actions
causes the individual to develop a negative self-
image. The result is a self-fulfilling prophecy of
failure" (17). Though they are a result rather than a
cause of social assumptions, standardized tests begin
this circular pattern.[2]

Such shortcomings may make life harder for
teachers as well as students. At a time when teachers
are experimenting with new teaching methods, the
demands of standardized tests seem to undermine those
reforms. As Marilyn Bizar puts it, "Teachers are
being given a schizophrenic message: teach one way,
but your students will be tested another way." Monty
Neil and Joe Medinal of Fairtest, a testing watchdog

Gerke uses material from an Internet source, putting the author's name in her own text for clarity.

Gerke 11

organization, argue that the methods teachers use to raise test scores are "nearly the opposite" of those that really help students learn to be creative problem-solvers (qtd. in Bizar).

Despite these problems in design and social sensitivity, standardized tests have many uses. They can, in general, effectively measure performance. To some extent they can predict how well you or I will do in our future lives; within limits, they can also indicate our aptitudes for various things. For example, Scientific American reports that SAT scores are good predictors of how well high-school seniors will do in their first year in college ("Scores" 88). Test design has become a science to itself, and, as it develops, its products will improve. And even if the critics of SATs and MCTs are right, the political issue of bias by itself is not enough to justify doing away with testing. The world of work and school is, whether we like it or not, still largely white and middle class, and, until this changes, everyone needs to learn how to live and succeed in that world.

We should not, however, rely on standardized tests to the extent we do now. We should not use them to pigeonhole people, nor should we allow them to influence our opinions of them. Even such a proponent as Arthur Jensen admits that the tests are overused ("Jensen's Rebuttal"). Educator George F. Madaus writes,

> The more one knows about the technology of testing, the more one realizes the potential for harm when a test score is used as the sole or primary criterion on which to make an important decision affecting an individual's future. (93)

Gerke uses a parenthetical reference for an indirect source.

Gerke concedes that tests are valuable in certain ways. This concession will strengthen her thesis when she reasserts it in the next paragraph.

Gerke does not just string sources together; she uses her critical faculties and imagination to create a real argument.

The thesis is reasserted at the end, strengthened by the judicious qualifications in the previous paragraph.

Gerke 12

Tests may be able to suggest what this or that person's future might be like, but it would be wrong to
let them determine that future.

In a neat argumenta-
tive move, Gerke
notes that other insti-
tutions and people
think the way she
does. This point again
strengthens her thesis.

Some colleges and universities have already
begun to downplay applicants' test scores in favor
of "progressive validity indices" that balance SAT
scores with high-school grades, class rank, and the
quality of the high-school program (Ravitch 55).
Perhaps this practice will start a trend. Perhaps
parents, teachers, and administrators--who know
students as people--will concentrate on getting as
comprehensive a picture of each student as they can
and passing that picture on.

The conclusion steps
out of the argument,
now finished, and
makes a proposal,
well in keeping with
the tone and direction
of the paper. This
ending is a creative
way to finish the
paper.

Ironically, perhaps what we need is another
test--one for OQ, or "opportunity quotient." This
would compare the amount of opportunity in a person's
background with that person's achievements. The
motivated but disadvantaged student could score well
over 100, while the advantaged but only mildly active
student might score below. If this sounds whimsical,
it may only be because many of us are not used to
thinking in minority ways. An OQ test could reveal
people whose drive balances their handicaps in other

The paper ends with
a strong closing sen-
tence that appeals to
sympathy and humor.

areas. When they try for that job or that place at
Harvard, the Naval Academy, or the foreign service,
they should have a dossier that shows them not just
as a point along a scale but as a person with
potential.

Gerke 13

Notes

Note 1 gives additional information about the MCTs. Gerke originally included this material in the text, but she changed it to a content note so she could focus on her own argument.

Endnotes can also refer readers to additional sources of information, as in note 2.

1 Popham believes that MCTs will "restore meaning to a highschool diploma" (91), but opponents like Anderson and Pipho believe that "testing minimal competencies primarily affects low achieving students. . . . It can discourage those who are average or below" (212).

2 See Jaeger for more information about the relationship between standardized tests and student failure.

Gerke 14

Works Cited

Article with two authors.

Anderson, B., and C. Pipho. "State-mandated Testing and the Fate of Local Control." Phi Delta Kappan Nov. 1984: 209-12.

Book with two editors.

Austin, Gilbert R., and Herbert Gardner, eds. The Rise and Fall of National Test Scores. New York: Academic, 1982.

Berk, Ronald, ed. Handbook of Methods for Detecting Test Bias. Baltimore: Johns Hopkins UP, 1982.

Article found on the Internet.

Bizar, Marilyn. "Standardized Testing Is Undermining the Goals of Reform." Online. America Online. 7 Apr. 1996. http://www.ncrel.org/ncrel/mands/docs/4-2.html

Name of publisher is shortened.

Bormuth, John R. On the Theory of Achievement Test Items. Chicago: U of Chicago P, 1970.

Anonymous article, alphabetized by title.

"Brave New World of Intelligence Testing." Psychology Today Sept. 1979: 13.

Eckland's piece is a chapter in Austin and Gardner. Chapter title, in quotation marks, is followed by book authors' names and chapter page numbers. Book is cited in full earlier.

Eckland, Bruce K. "College Entrance Examination Trends." Austin and Gardner 9-34.

Farb, Peter. Word Play. New York: Knopf, 1973.

Article in a journal, found through a CD-ROM database.

Fuentes-Cook, Martha. "Reinforcing the Reinforcements: How the Word Intelligence Has Become a Tool of Kingmakers." Journal of Social Dynamics Fall 1994: 62-77. ProQuest. CD-ROM. UMI. 21 Mar. 1996.

Green, Robert L., and Robert J. Griffore. "Standardized Testings and Minority Students." Education Digest Feb. 1981: 25-28.

Herbert, W. "Ability Testing Absolved of Racial Bias." Science News 6 Feb. 1982: 84.

Holden, Constance. "NAS Backs Cautious Use of Ability Tests." Science 19 Feb. 1982: 950.

Hulbert, Ann. "S.A.T.s Aren't So Smart." New Republic
    20 Dec. 1982: 12+.

Jaeger, Richard M. "The Final Hurdle: Minimum Compe-
    tency Achievement Testing." Austin and Gardner
    223-46.

Jensen, Arthur. Bias in Mental Testing. New York:
    Free, 1980.

"Jensen's Rebuttal." Newsweek 14 Jan. 1980: 59.

Madaus, George F. "NIE Clarification Hearing: The
    Negative Team's Case." Phi Delta Kappan Oct.
    1981: 92-94.

On Further Examination. New York: College Entrance
    Examination Board, 1977.

Popham, W. James. "The Case for Minimum Competency
    Testing." Phi Delta Kappan Oct. 1981:
    89-91.

Ravitch, Diane. "The College Boards." New York Times
    4 May 1975, sec. 6: 12+.

Scheuneman, Janice Dowd. "A Posteriori Analysis of
    Biased Items." Berk 180-98.

"Scores." Scientific American Sept. 1978: 88+.

Smith, Frank. Insult to Intelligence: The Bureau-
    cratic Invasion of Our Classrooms. New York:
    Arbor, 1986.

Strenio, Andrew. The Testing Trap. New York: Rawson,
    1981.

Trusz, Andrew R., and Sandra L. Parks-Trusz. "The So-
    cial Consequences of Competency Testing." Educa-
    tion Digest Apr. 1982: 15-18.

Wardrop, James L. Standardized Testing in the
    Schools: Uses and Roles. Monterey: Brooks,
    1976.

First page number
followed by + indi-
cates article is not
paged continuously.

This anonymous
book is alphabetized
by the title.

Gerke 16

E-mail message sent to Gerke by Wentworth.

Article in a journal that paginates continuously throughout the year.

Wentworth, Claude. "Re: Standardized Testing." E-mail
    to the author. 12 Apr. 1992.

Wigdor, Alexandra K. "Ability Testing: Uses, Conse-
    quences, and Controversies." Educational Mea-
    surement: Issues and Practice 1 (1982): 6-7.

Tips for Writing Research

- Avoid plagiarism. Be generous in giving explicit acknowledgment to the sources of any ideas that you use in your writing. Give enough information so that the reader can examine the sources you have used.
- Learn and use the MLA parenthetical references and list of works cited format; it is a practical, unobtrusive system for acknowledging sources.
- Careful revision is especially important in a research paper.
- Prepare your manuscript carefully for submission; never turn in anything that is sloppy or illegible.

EXERCISES FOR WRITING RESEARCH

1. Go to the library (and other places!) and find an example of each of the following entries. Type out the entry exactly as it would appear in a list of works cited.
   a. a book with more than one author
   b. an article in a bimonthly periodical
   c. a poem in the second edition of an anthology
   d. a book of the Koran
   e. an edition of *King Lear*
   f. a book in a series
   g. a foreword
   h. a newspaper editorial
   i. a film
   j. a CD recording
   k. a television program
   l. an article published on the Internet

2. Do you know the correct MLA format for the preparation of the research paper? Try answering the following true or false questions. Use this book as a reference.
   a. Endnotes and lists of works cited pages are not numbered.
   b. First pages of text are numbered.
   c. There is a comma between the author's name and the page number in a parenthetical reference.
   d. Outlines are numbered in arabic numerals.
   e. Abbreviations are no longer used for entries in lists of works cited.
   f. The list of works cited includes all sources you have consulted.
   g. Your name should appear with the page number on every page beginning with page 2.
   h. It is all right to use computer printouts for research papers.
   i. Color printing and unusual fonts will liven up your paper and impress your reader.

    j. Long, indented quotations should be single-spaced.

    k. Binders and plastic folders are a good idea.

    l. If you cite the author's name before giving a quotation from that author, you need to give the author's name again in the parenthetical reference.

    m. When you indent a long quotation, you should place the parenthetical reference inside the terminal punctuation, just as you do in the text.

3. Write a research paper using at least three book sources, at least two periodical sources, and one electronic source (either database or Internet). Follow all the rules in this chapter for citation of sources and preparation of the manuscript.

15

Writing in All Disciplines: The Report

The fruits of the tree of knowledge are various; he
must be strong indeed who can digest all of them.
— MARY COLERIDGE (1861–1907)
ENGLISH POET

During your college career, and probably afterward as well, you frequently will be called on to write a report—that is, a brief reliable summary of a large body of information. Your history instructor might say,

> Write a four-page report on Fernand Braudel's *The Mediterranean and
> the Mediterranean World in the Age of Philip II*.

Thirteen hundred pages of a book in a few pages of report! Your work
is cut out for you. You want to give the reader a good idea of what is really in Braudel's book, but you must be brief. Your emphasis will be on
analyzing, summarizing, organizing, and conveying information. You
would perform pretty much the same tasks for chemistry lab reports and
for reports on new products for your boss.

The report differs from the argumentative essay in that it presents
material as objectively as possible, without focusing primarily on expressing an opinion. It differs from the research paper in not requiring wide-
ranging, original research. Rather, it tries to represent the knowledge and
research of others. In the society of writings, the report is plain and blunt.

Good writing, of course, matters in the report. How we say something determines whether or not our readers understand us and enjoy

our writing. But a report is only as good as it is clear, reliable, accessible, and sufficient. Although wit, metaphor, and imagery can help, they cannot substitute for these basic qualities.

As with other writing tasks, we go through a process when we write a report. We can divide this process into seven steps:

determining your scope

getting a handle on the subject

reviewing

devising an organizational thesis

outlining

writing

revising

Because we have spent most of this book discussing writing and revising, we will concentrate here only on the first five steps.

DETERMINING YOUR SCOPE

In report writing, determining the scope usually doesn't take very long. Your art instructor assigns a five-page paper on the career of the Russian painter Wassily Kandinsky, or your biochemistry instructor says, "Report on what's been written on the side effects of prednisone." Or your boss says, "We need a report on the performance of middle managers in the Marketing Division. Yesterday."

Scope, then, depends on purpose. Direct and simple as the stated purpose so often is, you still need to analyze it. Most teachers and most bosses leave some, maybe the largest part, of the assignment unspecified. What is the report supposed to accomplish? How wide a scope should you give it? Does that biochemistry instructor really want a summary of *all* the literature? all the journals? periodicals? drug company blurbs? Does the boss want to know exactly which middle managers are pulling their weight or how Marketing as a whole is doing?

The problem is what to include and how detailed and precise you should be. Aristole writes that audience, occasion, and purpose will tell you how long and how detailed to make your presentation. To see how these three factors function, read the following chart:

AUDIENCE	OCCASION	PURPOSE
Computer programmers	Annual Conference of Educational Computer Programmers	To give a background briefing on the changing role of computers in the classroom

AUDIENCE	**OCCASION**	**PURPOSE**
Your art class	Daily meeting	To introduce for discussion the work of Georgia O'Keeffe
Corporate directors and senior officers	Board meeting	To provide the basis for acquiring your main competitor for $150 million

In each case, audience, occasion, and purpose will help determine the length and detail of the report. Whenever you write, after all, you make certain assumptions about what your audience does and does not already know. If your readers are well informed, you may not need to dally with introductions and elementary issues; instead, you can begin at a sophisticated, detailed level. But if your readers know very little or have differing levels of expertise, those introductions and elementary issues may well be in order.

In the first example, the report need not be very long: the interested and educated audience probably needs only to be reminded of the usefulness of computers in the classroom. The words *background briefing* suggest that the large picture, rather than detail, is in order. In the second example, the report should provide an overview broad enough for an uninformed audience—your art class—to take in but with enough detail to give them a basis for discussion. In the third example, well, you had better be very careful and very thorough: the future of the company depends on the accuracy of your report, and so does *your* future. The directors will no doubt require a high level of detail before making such a momentous decision.

As a final word on length and level of detail, we want to share the best advice we ever heard uttered, by a tough advertising manager to her young employee about to write his first report: "Do a little more than they expect—but not a whole lot more."

GETTING A HANDLE ON THE SUBJECT

Once you know your audience, occasion, and purpose, you can begin to pull together the information for your report. Start off by scouting the topic. If you rush right in, you could get lost in the thickets. You need to know how far afield you should go. If you are reporting on a single book, read that book, and then check in some bibliographic dictionaries for information about the author (see "The Reference Section" in Chapter 13). Find out what reviewers and critics have said. If you are reporting on a fairly limited subject, such as the life and works of Georgia O'Keeffe, perhaps two or three sources will suffice. For some subjects, however, such as computers as educational tools, you may need to go to the library and look up many sources. And the Internet is waiting for you. (For a discussion of research processes, see Chapter 13, Doing Research.)

Whatever your project—be it a book report, a lab report, a progress report, or an accident report—take copious notes. You probably will not be able (or willing) to do your work twice—so do it once thoroughly. Note more, not less, than you think you need—you can toss what you don't need, but it is painful to find what you lack. And take careful notes. Write down authors' names, titles, publishers, dates, and page numbers for your sources. (For a discussion of quotation and paraphrase, see "Taking Notes" and "Using Your Evidence" in Chapter 13.)

But first comes analysis of the subject. In the pages that follow, we suggest some useful ways to analyze information.

The Précis

When instructors ask you to report on a book or passage, they are probably asking for a précis, that is, a concise summary or condensation. The point of such an assignment is to ensure that you have read the material and understand it. (If instructors also want an evaluation, they say so, and that usually will come in a paragraph or two after the précis.) In the working world, mastering the précis may help you condense material for someone who hasn't the time to read it in toto.

Here are ten steps for writing a précis:

1. Map the text before starting to read. (See "An Overview: Mapping the Text" in Chapter 3.)

2. After mapping, write out what you think the author's main point is. Doing this will help you to recognize and evaluate the main ideas.

3. Go back to the first paragraph and begin reading. Carefully. If it occurs to you that you did not identify the main point, restate it. You need that point to keep your reading on track.

4. Write a brief summary, on a notecard or separate sheet of paper, for each major idea. If the reading is short, summarize each paragraph in a note. For longer works, try to combine ideas even when they are spread over several paragraphs.

5. Make a page reference for each summary. You'll need this later.

6. Briefly note particularly significant or interesting supporting ideas so you can return to them. When the main ideas are very complex or unclear, be sure to note the supporting details that will clarify them.

7. Avoid direct quotation. Only when you translate the ideas into your own words can you be sure you understand them—and when you write your report, your instructor will want your words in order to be sure you understand the reading.

8. Retain the author's order, emphasis, and tone. By order, we mean the general arrangement of major points. You may well need to combine snippets of ideas from different parts of the piece—but adhere to the general arrangement. The same goes for emphasis. If a twenty-page essay on dog breeding devotes fifteen pages to training and only five to grooming, observe that general three-to-one ratio of discussion in your paraphrase. And it is essential to preserve the author's tone. If you don't, you will misrepresent the author and mislead your reader. Imagine a paraphrase that was serious when the author was only fooling, or vice versa. Remember—your reader depends on your summaries to convey what is actually in the work.

9. Avoid interpretations and evaluations. Keep your opinions to yourself. This is harder than it sounds. It is not merely a matter of not stating agreement or disagreement. Opinions may slip into the tone in which you couch your summaries. Be careful. An intrusion of your opinion will not only confuse you when it comes to writing but will also confuse the reader later.

10. Once you complete the reading, check your summary notes against the text and identify the contours of the argument.

The Pentad

The critic Kenneth Burke devised a set of five questions that offer a way of analyzing any piece of expository prose—newspaper, magazine, book, history text, primary document. These questions, derived from a method called the pentad, are fairly obvious, but asking them systematically can help you understand a text and thus begin a report.

1. *What does it say?* Summarize or paraphrase the article to get its main point.

2. *Who wrote it?* Check the bias, special interest, and expertise of the author and his or her biography if possible.

3. *In what source was it published?* Check the source's general reputation. Is it considered objective and reliable?

4. *When and where was it published?* Look at the source in regard to historical and geographic background, as well as its intended audience.

5. *What is its purpose?* Think about the immediate purpose as well as the ultimate and even ulterior purpose, if any. Read it again.

The Journalistic Method

Sometimes you may be reporting on events rather than on reading. If so, the journalistic method, mentioned in Chapter 4, provides a list of headings under which you can take notes or analyze your material into its most important elements. This method, used by beginning reporters, asks six questions: who? what? when? where? how? and why? By answering these questions, you gain control of the subject.

Suppose you were asked to report on the election of Richard Nixon to the presidency in 1968. Try asking the six questions:

Who? Richard M. Nixon, former congressman, senator, vice president; previously defeated for the presidency

What? won a contentious U.S. presidential election

When? in 1968, during the height of the Vietnam War and the attendant protests

Where? in all parts of the nation, though his victory margin was slim

How? most experts agree Nixon won because most voters thought he could end the war and bring back stability to society

Why? because the nation saw itself in the throes of upheaval and uncertainty and feared that opponent Hubert Humphrey would continue outgoing president Lyndon Johnson's policies

This analysis provides a structure for a report, complete with all the details, the numbers, the narratives, the explanations.

For events that do not involve people—volcanic eruptions, for instance—use the "headless" method: drop the Who? and answer the other five questions.

Format for Analyzing Raw Data

Scientists and social scientists often present their experiments and collections of data according to a format—that is, a generally accepted arrangement of the various aspects of the study. (Who "accepts" this arrangement? The community of other scientists. Again, audience is important.) Such a format can help you to get a handle on a large amount of raw data. Perhaps the most useful, and common, is this one:

problem or purpose
review of the literature
method
data
discussion/conclusion

Problem or Purpose.   In the "Problem" section, you set forth the problem you studied: What happens when I add this chemical to that and turn up the heat? What are the religious habits of the people of Abilene, Kansas? You will perhaps want to indicate the relevance of the problem to a larger field and how you differentiate it from similar problems. You might find it helpful to narrate or describe how you arrived at the problem and to define various terms. In some formats, this section is called "Purpose," but that is not much different; your purpose is usually to address the problem.

Review of the Literature.   In collecting your own raw data or performing experiments, you will sometimes be required to review important studies of the subject. (Ask your instructor whether a review of the literature will be required.) Reviews of the literature accomplish three things: they establish that the problem really is a problem, they let the reader know what research has been done in the field, and they establish that you are informed enough to undertake the study. The literature you review should be recent, authoritative, and well known in the field. When there are a great many studies, concentrate on those that are most authoritative and have most significance for your discussion. In general, give special emphasis to current research.

Method.   Your most important sections will be "Method" and "Data," because in them you will describe how you gathered the material and what you found out. Under "Method," you narrate how you went about your study, what steps you followed in what order. In lab reports, you describe how you designed your experiment; in a field study in the social sciences, you describe the interviews, polls, and quantitative techniques you used to amass your information. As a rule of thumb, this description should be detailed enough for someone else to follow exactly in your footsteps and (presumably) to arrive at the same conclusions.

Data.   The data section is all-important. In it you gather the information your study has produced. Don't interpret: report. Here is where you would tell that you changed lead into gold in the lab—or blew up six retorts and got tar in your test tube. Here is where you would present the statistics you amassed on church attendance in Abilene. Write your data section as objectively and clearly as possible. Only then will you know—and your ultimate reader believe—that your study has been responsibly conducted.

Discussion/Conclusion.   In the discussion section, you make sense of the data. You go beyond the sheer facts of the study to discuss their meaning and their importance. Here you might explain why you blew up the lab just as the lead was turning into gold, or why the people of Abilene are such big churchgoers. If in doing this analysis you discovered other lines of inquiry, this would be the place to mention them. In this section you may also incorporate quotations and compare your conclusions to those of others.

Here is an outline of a psychiatric study of depressed patients.

Problem: Some depressed people are merely depressed. But others have "psychotic depression"—that is, they not only are depressed but also have delusions or hallucinations. We wondered if such people were more or less likely to commit suicide than were people with simple depression.

Review of the Literature: [Reviews eight other studies—"by Guze and Robins, by Pokorny, by Weissman . . ."—that have defined and treated the problem.]

Method: We looked back over the files of all depressed patients who had committed suicide over twenty-five years at the Psychiatric Institute in New York. We classified them into a "depressed suicide group" and a "control group" of depressed patients who had not committed suicide. We further classed each group into those that had psychotic features and those that did not.

Data: Here is what our survey found:

	Psychotic Features	Nonpsychotic
Suicide group	10	4
Control group	9	19

Out of 14 suicides, 10 patients had psychotic features and 4 did not. In our control group of 28 patients, however, only about a third had psychotic features. We thus figured the odds ratio:

$$\text{Odds ratio} = \frac{10 \times 19}{4 \times 9} = 5.3 \text{ relative risk}$$

Discussion: A depressed patient with psychotic features is 5.3 times more likely to commit suicide than a depressed patient without such features. Patients with psychotic depression should thus be treated quickly and effectively, and they need to be watched more carefully if they are institutionalized. "Once hospitalized, the patients still require special suicide precautions and must be regarded with a high degree of caution, even when they appear recovered" (based on S. P. Roose et al., "Depression, Delusions, and Suicide").

Division and Classification

In addition to helping you develop your thoughts (see Chapter 8), division and classification can help you get a handle on a large topic. (Indeed, any of the strategies can be helpful.) Some subjects are so large that we need to break them down into smaller units. How impossible it would be for biologists to think about "living creatures" without breaking down the subject into the categories of kingdom, phylum, class, order, family, genus, and species! These categories help us sort out the myriad individuals according to similarities and differences.

The trick is to discover the most helpful way to break down a big subject. Suppose your history instructor asked you to report on the geography of Africa. What an enormous subject. Right off, you would divide the subject to make it more manageable: north, south, east, west, central. You would then gather data about each of these areas.

But as you gathered data you probably would begin to see more significant and revealing divisions. That Mali is in the west is not nearly so important as that much of it is desert. You might decide on a different division, one based on climate or terrain: the Sahara, the Sahel, the Congo region, the plains, and so on. Once you have divided up this enormous subject in a rational way, you will begin to see which parts of it you can report on.

COGITATING AND REVIEWING

Go over your notes early and often. We have had the experience of so intently jotting down notes that not one piece of information blowing by actually stuck to our brain. We might not have even been able to state the subject. But when we went over those notes, it all made sense. Once you have a pretty good handle on the subject, carefully review all your notes, card by card. After each review, sit back and cogitate.

Ask yourself these questions about the material:

What is the most significant aspect of the subject?

What are four or five other significant aspects?

What connections have I noted?

Can I find similarities with another topic?

Can I find recurring themes?

Is there a natural way to organize the information?

This is where the organizational thesis comes in.

DEVISING AN ORGANIZATIONAL THESIS

In "The Thesis" in Chapter 5, we pointed out the differences between the argumentative thesis and the organizational thesis. The argumentative thesis sets out the opinion or evaluation or view that the essay will attempt to prove. The organizational thesis does not focus primarily on an argument but rather establishes the writer's approach to the body of information. It says, "I have surveyed this material, and this is how we will travel over it." Your organizational thesis is your plan for the trip. It tells both you and your reader where you intend to go and what you intend to do along the way.

In the following pages, we discuss some possible forms the organizational thesis can take. Most reports will have a thesis that takes one of these forms.

Establishing Chronological Order

In writing about history or explaining how something happens, we quite naturally narrate events in the order in which they occur or occurred. An organizational thesis establishing chronological order lets the reader know the way we will organize this report, as this famous anthropologist does:

> The life of the day begins at dawn, or if the moon has shown until daylight, the shouts of the young men may be heard before dawn from the hillside. Uneasy in the night, populous with ghosts, they shout lustily to one another as they hasten with their work. As the dawn begins to fall among the soft brown roofs . . . (Margaret Mead, *Coming of Age in Samoa*)

Now we know that Mead will follow Samoan life through a typical day, from dawn to sunset.

Indicating Main Divisions

This is one of the simplest kinds of organizational thesis. It merely tells the reader how the subject will be divided and what the order will be.

> I will describe the society into which Virginia Woolf was born, offer an account of her life, and conclude with an annotated bibliography of major critical studies of her work.

This thesis statement plainly and bluntly informs the reader into what segments the material is divided and when to expect each segment.

Suggesting Recurrent Themes

As you study a topic, you will notice themes that arise again and again. Your stack of notes will be larger under certain headings than under others. Those large stacks indicate a recurring theme in your subject. Such themes can help you organize your thoughts. And when you encapsulate the recurrent themes in your organizational thesis, you tell your reader what is important.

After studying disputes over gun control laws, a student found that these themes kept popping up:

the constitutional right to bear arms

the necessity for owning guns in some parts of the country

how easy it is for anyone, including criminals, to buy guns

the relation between the crime rate and ownership of guns

He devised this organizational thesis for his report:

In this dispute, the question seems to be, Which shall be paramount: the individual's rights and needs or those of society as a whole?

Indicating the Means of Discussion

Often the most helpful bit of information is *how* the discussion will be conducted. Such a thesis provides the context within which the reader can evaluate the material. In the following, a musicologist explains how he will conduct a discussion of music in Africa:

In this chapter we will examine some of the general characteristics of African music, and we will draw heavily on the work of a few scholars who have made an effort to condense their broad experience into brief summaries. To illustrate these characteristics I will rely mainly on my own greater familiarity with Dagomba and Ewe drumming . . . (John Miller Chernoff, *African Rhythm and African Sensibility*)

Description of the subject, the sources, the kinds of examples, and the way they connect helps to orient the reader to the discussion that follows.

Defining the Subject

A definition often can point out the arrangement of an essay. In the following, the authors define their terms in order to tell us what they will and will not discuss:

No cheeses have such loyal supporters and such vociferous critics as the very strong cheeses such as Limburger, Liederkranz, Livarot and a half-dozen others, which have in common an aroma as unequivocal as a thunderclap. People who like them extol as virtues the very qualities that others deplore. Looking at Liederkranz that is *à point,* an enthusiast will see below its russet mantle the creamy, smooth cheese within—a cheese with something of the flavor of a Camembert or Brie intensified many times over. To him the flavor is robust, the aroma awe-inspiring. But to his opposite number, that aroma, in the words of Oscar Burdett, can "cling and penetrate with the tenacity of cigar smoke. Perhaps for this reason," he adds, "the puritan nose twitches in indignation." (Vivienne Marquis and Patricia Haskell, *The Cheese Book*)

The authors are not going to discuss cottage cheese or bologna, and they are going to tell us about those smelly cheeses.

Establishing the "Angle"

Webster's Ninth New Collegiate Dictionary defines the word *angle* both as "the precise viewpoint from which something is observed" and as "a special approach, point of attack, or technique for accomplishing an objective." Just as in journalism, in many reports it is essential to establish your angle—where you stand, what your special approach or attack will be—before you begin to tell your story. In the following paragraph the author establishes the angle of his essay:

> Since the mid-1970s, signs of Balkanization have arisen in France. Xenophobia, racism, and anti-Semitism are becoming more common, and the country's tradition of *laïcite* (secularism)—the radical separation of the state from all forms of religion—has been confronted with a revival of religious identities. The French republican model, with its twin universalist and assimilationist goals, appears more and more on the defensive. This is the context in which France has been debating immigration. (Sami Nair, "France: A Crisis of Integration")

The growing conflict of values is Nair's angle. That is enough to organize his view of France's immigration problems and give us an authoritative, detailed look.

Setting Up a Comparison

Sometimes you may be asked to compare and contrast two objects, two theories, two events, two proposals. Other times you may see that you can more brightly illuminate one subject by comparing it with a similar subject. In either case you need to set out for your reader what you will compare as well as suggest the attributes that will go into the comparison.

As we discussed in Chapter 8, The Structure and Strategies of the Paragraph, a comparison can be either item by item—that is, a complete presentation of one side before going on to the other—or attribute by attribute—that is, a thorough comparison of the two sides under one heading before comparing them under the next. Which method you will follow should be clear in the organizational thesis.

In an essay on the simultaneous invention of the telephone by Alexander Graham Bell and the obscure Elisha Gray, David Hounshell concludes his brief introduction with this clear statement of his organizational thesis:

> In the history of the telephone, the world of the professional and the world of the amateur appear at almost every turn, as will be made clear by a brief exploration of the two worlds, first Gray's and then Bell's. ("Two Paths to the Telephone")

Thus, Hounshell establishes what he will do—narrate the story of the two inventions—and how he will do it—complete one before going on to the other.

If you intend to compare attribute by attribute, that too should be clear from your organizational thesis.

> The Japanese and American economic systems might even seem superficially the same, except for the issues of incentives for savings, how government participates in overall economic decisions and protects various industries, and how tax burdens are distributed.

The writer established an attribute-by-attribute organizational thesis and could proceed to fill in the evidence.

Choosing the Right Organizational Thesis

The organizational thesis tells both you and the reader how the report will be organized. It provides the frame on which you can hang all the material you have gathered.

Here are some suggestions for crafting an effective organizational thesis.

1. Make it interesting and accessible. No matter how dull you think the subject, how automatic the assignment, rise to the occasion and catch the reader's interest. Avoid overly technical language, slang, facetiousness. Make the thesis readable so that the reader can get into the report and the harder, more complex issues with you.

2. Avoid overcomplicating your thesis. What the reader needs is a map, not a directory of gasoline stations and cafés along the way. If, for instance, the authors of the cheese book had included the name and locale of every strong cheese, along with some distinctions between strong cheeses and overripe cheeses, the reader would likely be confused. The authors take care of all that later in the report, where it belongs.

3. Be sure your thesis suggests all the major points of the paper. It need not state them by name but should suggest the range of the exploration.

Like the argumentative thesis, the organizational thesis should authoritatively sum up the entire scope of the discussion.

GETTING FROM THESIS TO OUTLINE

Once you have your organizational thesis clearly in mind, the next step is to outline your report (see "Developing, Organizing, Drafting" in Chapter 5). And where is all your evidence? Where are the major and minor points? In your notes, of course. Go through them, and identify the major ideas. Be relaxed about it: don't aim for a specific number, but if an idea seems important, hold on to it.

Now stack behind each of these major ideas any related smaller ideas. If, for instance, you were writing on the painting style of Frida Kahlo, you might have an important note dealing with Kahlo's idea of "painting a new reality." Under this card, you might file cards with entries on painting materials and cards with entries on subjects of Kahlo's paintings. Under each of these you might file cards detailing smaller ideas, for instance, "colors" or "Kahlo's dislike of the United States."

Go through your entire packet, and try to place every card. If something absolutely will not fit anywhere, don't throw it out—you may need it—but put it in a "Miscellaneous" stack. If that stack begins to climb too high, check your organizational thesis to be sure you really have selected the right road over this material—your road, after all, ought to pass by most of the major attractions. If your thesis doesn't allow for that, you probably need a new one. Don't be afraid of devising another thesis.

Once you have placed all your cards, take a fresh look at the major ideas. Are they all equally important? Are they mutually exclusive, or does one overlap another? Are there any obvious gaps between the ideas, or do they seem to cover the subject? Do you need more information about any of them? If everything is in order, try making an outline. With a strong outline and well-organized notes, your writing will be little more than filling in.

PARTING SHOTS

We want to close this chapter with three pieces of advice.

1. Your report, like any essay, should have a beginning, a middle, and an end. At the beginning provide the necessary background and define terms the reader needs at the outset. Then, of course, state your organizational thesis to tell the reader what is coming. Reports often become disorganized in the middle, so concentrate on those paragraphs. Follow your outline; include what it includes in the same order. If you find yourself discussing ideas not in your outline, go back and see whether you can fit them into the outline. If you can't, either drop the ideas or change the outline. At the end of reports, it is permissible—often required—to summarize your most important points. Even so, good conclusions give a sense of closure, of "wrapping up." Don't miss this chance to give your reader one last good grip on the subject. Never trail off in a whirl of loose ends.

2. Package your information; don't dump it. Each paragraph should be organized around a single idea, all sentences should relate to that idea, and the connections between ideas should be smooth and clear. Some report writers, unfortunately, treat paragraphs as little "information dumps." They simply unload a handful of information in each one, and it doesn't matter whether any is related or organized.

> Not all brain hemorrhages are fatal, although the brain tissue may be damaged. The rate of survival depends on age, concomitant health status of the patient, and other pre-existing factors. There may be some paralysis or loss of sensory capabilities. Hemorrhages are often caused by atherosclerosis. Along with cerebral infarctions, cerebral hemorrhages are a prime cause of stroke. A burst blood vessel floods an area of the brain. Cerebral infarctions are often caused by atherosclerosis too.

All are important bits of information, but when dumped out in a jumble like this, not much use to the reader. In the revision, the writer packaged the information. In one paragraph he combined the information on causation and pathology of hemorrhage, and in a second he discussed recovery.

> Cerebral hemorrhage is the bursting of a blood vessel that serves the brain. Like infarctions, hemorrhages are often caused by atherosclerosis, in which deposits inside the blood vessels constrict the passageway for blood. When this happens, the arteries may become hardened, lose their resilience, and become vulnerable to blockage or breakage. Along with cerebral infarctions, cerebral hemorrhages are a prime cause of stroke.
>
> Not all brain hemorrhages are fatal, although brain tissue damage is usually sustained. The rate of survival depends on age, concomitant health status, and other pre-existing factors. But even in patients who survive and apparently recover well, there may be some paralysis or loss of sensory capabilities.

Much better. You don't have to be a neurosurgeon to follow the discussion. (Actually, most neurosurgeons would find the original just as jumbled as we did.) Watch out for information dumps; they are especially common after the midpoint of an essay, when the writer, close to deadline, is working down to the end of the note pile.

3. Plan to revise. With a strong outline and well-organized notecards, you are well prepared to write, but even so you will find it difficult to get every idea firmly nailed in place. In your effort to get in all the information, you may find yourself writing, "Oh, yes, I forgot to say on page 3 that . . ." Reread your report most carefully from the midpoint on to scout out information dumps, loose ends, and gaping holes in the development. Remember, a report is only as good as it is clear, reliable, accessible, and sufficient.

Tips for the Report

- Let audience, occasion, and purpose determine the scope of your study.
- Take careful and detailed notes.
- To get a handle on the subject, consider using the précis, the pentad, the journalistic method, the ready-made format for analyzing raw data, or division and classification.
- At some point in your study, just sit down, review your notes, and cogitate.
- Formulate an effective organizational thesis that will tell your reader, and you, how you plan to cover the material.
- Based on your thesis, prepare an outline, and organize your notes around it.
- Make sure your report has a beginning, a middle, and an end.
- Don't just dump information, package it.
- Revise a report just as you would any other writing.

EXERCISES FOR THE REPORT

1. Here is a series of topics. Choose one and follow the process for writing a report outlined in this chapter. With the help of your classmates and instructor, determine your scope. Then review your subject, devise your organizational thesis, write, and revise.

   the trial of Socrates
   the Crédit Mobilier scandal, 1867–1872
   the Supreme Court's *Roe v. Wade* decision, 1973
   the Ethiopian famine, 1981–82
   how geese know it's time to fly south for the winter
   the career of photographer Margaret Bourke-White
   the North American Free Trade Agreement (NAFTA)
   the Sumerian epic *Gilgamesh*
   the trial of O. J. Simpson
   why superconductivity is important
   the career of American poet Robert Lowell
   the career of English anthropologist L. S. B. Leakey
   the construction of the Golden Gate Bridge
   the gypsy moth

2. Discuss how audience, occasion, and purpose would dictate scope and depth in the following reports:

   a report on the career of Arnold Schwarzenegger to be delivered orally for your physical training class
   a report on a new technique of laser surgery on the eye for a convention of the American Ophthalmological Society
   an end-of-term report on the fall of Communism for your class "Eastern Europe 1980–1995"

a report on your car crash last week for your insurance company

a report on the Super Bowl for the front page of the *New York Times*

a report on the toxic effects of a new drug for a committee of the Food and
Drug Administration that is considering that drug for public use

a report to the mayor on the moral profile of a policeman being considered for
the open position of chief of police

a report on the recent extraction of your wisdom teeth, for your mother, who
hasn't seen you in four months

3. Read one of the following essays and write a précis of it. Discuss the special
problems you encountered in writing your précis. What did you leave out?
What did you include? Why?

Walter Lippmann, "The Indispensable Opposition"
Karl Marx, "The Communist Manifesto"
Woody Allen, "My Speech to the Graduates"
Brigitt Brophy, "The Rights of Animals"
Richard Nixon, "The 'Checkers' Speech"
James Rachels, "Active and Passive Euthanasia"
Joan Didion, "Bureaucrats"
Alison Lurie, "Male and Female"

4. What methods of analysis—including the précis, the pentad, the journalistic
method, the format for analyzing raw data, or division and classification—
would work best with the following topics? Explain.

the patterns of college attendance by minority students
The Autobiography of Alice B. Toklas by Gertrude Stein
the changing place of protists in schemes of biological classification
the space shuttle disaster of 1986
starlings, grackles, and crows
methods of irrigating and fertilizing desert regions
the early childhood of the Unabomber
an experiment in which cats were trained to walk tightropes

5. Read each of the following organizational theses and discuss what it tells
the reader and what kind of report you expect based just on reading the
thesis.

A close look at what does actually take place may explain in large measure the un-
dertaker's intractable reticence concerning a procedure that has become his major
raison d'être. (Jessica Mitford, *The American Way of Death*)

Here, after all, were two forms of nature in collision: the elements and human nature.
Last Wednesday, the elements, indifferent as ever, brought down Flight 90. And on
that same afternoon, human nature—groping and flailing in mysteries of its own—
rose to the occasion. (Roger Rosenblatt, "The Man in the Water")

A definition that should really define [beauty] must be nothing less than the exposition of the origin, place, and elements of beauty as an object of human existence.
(George Santayana, "The Nature of Beauty")

Many now agree that the sexual revolution of the 1960s worked a profound change
on our society's family values and personal relationships. Certainly, the seeds of upheaval were present before that critical decade. But a major change that occurred in
the mid-sixties was an explicit rejection of the common values about sexual and family relationships that most Americans in the past had held up as an ideal. (George
Gallup, Jr., and William Proctor, *Forecast 2000*)

16

Reading, Interpreting, and
Writing about Literature

There are three points of view from which a
writer can be considered: he may be considered
as a storyteller, as a teacher, and as an en-
chanter.
> — VLADIMIR NABOKOV (1899-1977)
> STORYTELLER, TEACHER, ENCHANTER

Many of the most intense and moving moments in our lives have come
thanks to literature. It has clarified our thinking and feeling and changed
us in ways we cannot put into words. We have been entertained, taught,
and enchanted by it.

The challenges of literature are bracing. Responding to poems,
plays, novels, and stories calls for both sensitivity and clarity. It demands
an open mind as well as close attention. Yet far from "taking the fun out
of literature," accepting its challenges increases both our understanding
and our enjoyment.

In the pages that follow, we treat the study of literature as a three-
part process of reading, interpreting, and writing.

READING LITERATURE

Reading literature is different from reading a textbook, editorial, or essay. If you tried to use the eight questions in Chapter 3, Critical Reading, on Albert Camus's *The Plague,* T. S. Eliot's *The Waste Land,* or Anton Chekhov's *The Three Sisters,* you would not have much success. Literature does not follow the rules of argument. Rather, it presents a version of the world as the writer imagines it. And it presents this world in a language that is important for itself as well as for what it conveys. To get at the world of the writer and the beauty of its language, the eight questions offer little help.

So—how should you read a poem, a play, a novel, or a short story?

First of all, you should respect the world the work describes. Literature is always a product of a particular time and a particular place. Good readers try to view a work within its own context. Of course, no reader can wholly escape being culture bound; our customs and codes of behavior are too firmly planted. But good readers try to control the bias of their own class and era. They recognize that though values may be eternal, their expression is finite and various. Social relationships may be different. Definitions of acceptable behavior may have changed.

Plan to read any work of literature more than once. If you read an expository or argumentative essay carefully, you may well get much of its meaning with one pass—few would read an editorial twice. But literature will not yield its fullness of meaning in one reading. On the first reading, simply read. Don't try to be critical. Give yourself up to the work. Let it possess you.

When reading a poem, read aloud, slowly. Let the rhythms of the poem control the tempo and cadence of your reading. Listen to the music of the poem. Get a friend to read it with you. Never confine a poem to your head. Perform it and listen to the performance. As you read, think about the words themselves, their denotations and their connotations and how they join with the music to create the total effect.

When reading longer works, set aside at least one, preferably two, hours for uninterrupted periods of reading. Dive in and stay in until you get the feel of the work. Whenever you pick it up, give yourself time to settle in. If you only read piecemeal, five pages at a time, you may end up with a piecemeal view of the work.

Keep your mind open during the first reading. Don't try to make the story or poem mean what you expect; let it show you its own meaning. Literature is often startling, outraging, and bewildering. It may ridicule or deny your most cherished beliefs. Do not reject it: learn from it.

On this first reading, don't take notes. They are apt to break your connection with the work by introducing the critical element. If something strikes you, pencil a little check in the margin or circle a phrase (unless it's a library book). Later you can return to these spots to make full notes.

Warning: no one can skim a piece of literature and expect to get much out of it. You may learn some facts, but you cannot comprehend the quality of the work. Nor can you get much when you rely on the assessments or interpretations of others. There are notes, summaries, and shortcuts on the market today that promise a quick way through novels, plays, and poems. They, too, give facts, but the one thing these shortcuts can never give you is the work itself and your own response to it. There simply is no substitute for a sensitive reading of the text. Don't cheat yourself.

When you have finished this first reading, meditate on what you have read. Think about the ideas, the events, the language. Write a short paraphrase, like these, of the main concern of the work—or your main response to it.

> This poem is about the anguish of unrequited love and how its not being returned makes the loved one more attractive.

> There are a lot of marriages in this novel, but not all are happy because the people are silly or too selfish to adjust.

Thorough readers have been performing such exercises for centuries: they help firm one's hold on the material.

Now reread the work. This time, annotate the text. Write notes on notecards or in a separate notebook. If you scribble all over your book, your notes will stay unorganized, and you may not be able to find them again. If you strongly prefer to make marginal notes as you read, we urge you to transfer your notes into a separate notebook later to better organize and understand them.

If the work is long, summarize each chapter. If it is short, paraphrase the whole thing. When you come across one of your checks or circled passages, analyze what struck you the first time. Don't hesitate to go back and forth, to compare different sections. Pause at important junctures. If the characters are confusing, make a list of them. If the language strikes you as unusual, describe its qualities. Take special note of whatever you find arresting. Make exact page references. Frantically searching back and forth for a particular quotation is a waste of time and energy.

General Topics in Literature

What do we look for when we read literature? Literature is so rich that no discussion could possibly cover it. In this section, however, we deal with three important elements common to all literature: theme, language, and symbolism. (Later we will discuss special topics in fiction and poetry.)

Theme.   A literary work expresses the values of the writer and his or her ideas about the human condition. These values and ideas are rarely simple or obvious. A work of literature cannot be reduced to a simple moral. Nor can it be treated as a philosophical or sociological treatise, although the writer's opinions about philosophy and society may be expressed in the work. Usually, the reader is left with a sense of the point or meaning of a work. Examples of themes might be frustrated desire in Emily Brontë's *Wuthering Heights,* the cost of obsession in Herman Melville's *Moby-Dick,* or the alienation of modern life in T. S. Eliot's *The Waste Land.*

The themes we've identified do not come close to exhausting the subject of theme in these works. Other readers might focus on different meanings. They might find that for them, the most important idea in *Wuthering Heights* is the destructive power of sexual passion or that *Moby-Dick* is about the universe's indifference to human aspiration and *The Waste Land* about redemption and eternal life.

Read Vikram Seth's short poem "All You Who Sleep Tonight" and think about its theme.

> All you who sleep tonight
> Far from the ones you love,
> No hand to left or right,
> And emptiness above—
>
> Know that you aren't alone.
> The whole world shares your tears,
> Some for two nights or one,
> And some for all their years.

One reader might say that the theme is the pain of loneliness. Another might say that Seth is talking about the possibility of human fellowship. Still another reader . . . but you get the point: there is no single theme to be ferreted out. Readers bring different experiences and different needs and thus find different ways of looking at the meaning of a work.

Themes change and develop as a piece of literature unfolds. In the first section of *The Waste Land,* for example, Eliot conveys the attractiveness of death and the ugliness of contemporary life and closes the fifth section with the idea of redemption through Christianity. As you read great literature, note what changes the theme undergoes and what significance it has either in the world of the work or in your world.

Language.   We've discussed language throughout this book (what else is writing but language?), but we want to discuss it directly in this section because the way language is used is truly the heart and soul of literature. Many people believe that literature makes its impact more through the imagination than through the intellect and that the power of the writer's imagination resides in conjuring images that stimulate the reader's own image-making capacity. The writer strings words together to make images that trigger the reader's memories and sensations of sight, sound, taste, and so on. Identifying, responding to, and appreciating imagery is one of the great pleasures of reading literature. The word *imagery* can refer to pictures, but it is most commonly used to denote the sum of sensual language in a work—the vivid individual images as well as figures of speech.

The following literal description comes from "Boule de Suif" by Guy de Maupassant. In this story, a woman named Butterball eats while those around her are very hungry:

> Butterball took a chicken wing and proceeded to eat it very daintily, now and then taking a bite of one of those little *Regence* rolls, as they were called in Normandy.
>
> All eyes were drawn to her. The aroma of chicken spread, expanding nostrils, filling mouths with an overabundance of saliva, and making jaws contract with a painful sensation under the ears.

Because this passage triggers our own experiences of hunger, we can appreciate better what is happening in the story.

Several senses are involved in this stanza from Robert Browning's "Meeting at Night":

> Then a mile of warm sea-scented beach;
> Three fields to cross till a farm appears;
> A tap at the pane, the quick sharp scratch
> And blue spurt of a lighted match,
> And a voice less loud, through its joys and fears,
> Than the two hearts beating each to each!

The following description comes from Conrad's *The Heart of Darkness:*

> Marlow sat cross-legged right aft, leaning against the mizzen mast.
> He had sunken cheeks, a yellow complexion, a straight back.

The reader *sees* Marlow, his crossed legs, his yellowed skin, his straight back. But this passage provides more than Marlow's physical being: it conveys the impression of Marlow as a serious and important human being. Conrad is painting a moral portrait by means of concrete detail. Nothing in good literature is wasted: no matter how apparently mundane, the words matter.

Literature achieves many of its effects through startling figures of speech, such as *similes* and *metaphors*. A simile is an explicit comparison of two things, usually using *like* or *as* as a bridge. Archibald MacLeish's poem "Ars Poetica," which we reprint and discuss in "Special Topics in Poetry," is a series of similes.

> A poem should be palpable and mute
> As a globed fruit. . . .
>
> A poem should be wordless
> As the flight of birds.

Similes occur in fiction also, as you will see when you read Isaac Babel's "My First Goose" in "Special Topics in Fiction." In describing the commander, Babel writes that

> His long legs were like girls sheathed to the neck in shining riding boots.

Rather than making an explicit comparison, metaphor draws an identity between two things. Toward the end of "Ars Poetica," MacLeish describes the experience of grief in metaphoric terms.

> For all the history of grief
> An empty doorway and a maple leaf.

We find metaphors in fiction too, including this one in "My First Goose" of a man unable to concentrate on what he reads:

> the beloved lines came toward me along a thorny path and could not reach me.

Metaphor's power comes from its unspokenness: it draws us into the possible likenesses between things we had previously assumed were unalike.

We have more to say about similes and metaphors in "Figurative Language" in Chapter 12.

Tone is the atmosphere a writer creates by the way he or she uses language. It often indicates an attitude toward the subject or the reader. It provides the emotional context of a work and determines the voice in which we read. Here is the opening sentence of Edgar Allan Poe's "The Fall of the House of Usher":

> During the whole of a dull, dark, and soundless day in the autumn of the year, when the clouds hung oppressively low in the heavens, I had been passing alone, on horseback, through a singularly dreary tract of country.

Poe's choice of words, with all those dull *d* and ugly *u* sounds, and the slow, ponderous cadence, made slower by commas, create an atmosphere heavy with threat. It would be nearly impossible, certainly silly, to read that passage in a fast voice. Solemn and ominous, the tone shapes our responses.

Here is a paraphrase of the passage: "It was late afternoon and the day was overcast and I was out for a ride." The facts are there. All that's missing is the quality of Poe's voice that makes this story literature. Tone is what cannot be paraphrased.

One very common tone in literature is *irony*. Irony expresses the disparity between opposites: appearance and reality; the ideal and the real; the literal and the implied; the ostensible meaning and the implicit meaning; what we say and what we mean. Think of the many times you use irony in your daily talk. If someone rams your car, you might say, "That's just great." No one standing by would misunderstand your tone.

You will find all kinds of irony in literature. When J. V. Cunningham in "Dr. Drink" writes

> All in due time: love will emerge from hate,
> And the due deference of truth from lies.
> If not quite all things come to those who wait
> They will not need them: in due time one dies

the disparity between the overly optimistic, even smug, tone and the almost brutal reference to death in the last line calls attention to the difference between platitudes and reality, providing a double perspective on our hope that everything will work out. Irony often lends itself to humorous effects. Grace Paley opens her story "The Loudest Voice" this way:

> There is a certain place where dumb-waiters boom, doors slam, dishes crash; every window is a mother's mouth bidding the street shut up, go skate somewhere else, come home. My voice is the loudest.

The irony of the tone is carried through in the plot: Jewish children play leading parts in a school Christmas play.

Sometimes a reader knows something the characters don't know and therefore understands the deeper significance of words and deeds. This situation is called *dramatic irony*. Perhaps the most famous example of this knowing occurs in Sophocles' *Oedipus the King*. The audience knows that Oedipus, by a terrible series of mischances, has slain his father and married his mother. Unaware of these facts, Oedipus wants to discover the truth, and he cries, "I shall not cease until I bring the truth to light." The audience's prior knowledge of what his search will reveal makes his endeavors appear ironic.

Symbolism.   A symbol is a sign standing for something else. By means of the sign, we infer significance beyond mere physical properties. A symbol is a physical representation that expresses a deeper significance. The thirteen stripes of the U.S. flag symbolize the original colonies, and the fifty stars symbolize the fifty states. The flag itself, then, symbolizes the United States.

This kind of symbol is called a *constructed symbol,* that is, a symbol that people agree will represent a particular idea. Some symbols, however, seem to emerge without thought or plan. Trees quite naturally suggest life and growth, just as the sun suggests heat and lightning suggests sexual passion. In a film, the leaves of a calendar turning symbolize time passing.

Literary symbols call forth from the reader connotations and associations that illuminate a work. When Hamlet holds up Yorick's skull, that skull stands not just for the remains of a human being but also for death, the certainty that it will come to everyone, including Hamlet, including us. We are reminded of our own mortality. This image casts a light forward over the rest of the play, over everything that Hamlet does and says.

Though all description contributes to the overall effect, not every physical property is a symbol. The shovel the grave digger wields is just a shovel for digging the grave. Shakespeare does not ask us to notice it, to pause over it, to carry it with us through the play as we do the skull. A literary work is full of details, and not all of them are symbolic.

So how can you tell when an image is a symbol? Sometimes the environment of a work will indicate which images you should see as symbolic. When Hamlet holds up Yorick's skull, he is standing beside an open grave debating death with a grave digger. Shakespeare focuses us not on the dirt or the shovel but on that skull and thereby insists that we think about Hamlet and death. You would have to try hard to miss the symbolic function of Yorick's skull in these surroundings.

Repetition of an image suggests a symbolic function. In *Moby-Dick,* the whale and its whiteness are everywhere and on everyone's mind: that whale is obviously much more than a physical reality. Exacting such a great cost from the crew of the ship suggests its enormous symbolic significance.

Often, recognizing shared experiences can lead to an understanding of a symbol. When you see a human skull you can hardly avoid thinking of death. When T. S. Eliot wonders, in "The Love Song of J. Alfred Prufrock," "Do I dare to eat a peach?", we recognize that it is hardly a brave act to eat a peach, and so we may conclude that the peach is symbolic, that Eliot is suggesting that even innocent acts can be threatening in our time.

When a writer includes a particularly jarring or unexpected description, we can usually assume that the image is more than just a physical thing. In "My First Goose" (see p. 451), the narrator says that the commander's "long legs were like girls sheathed to the neck in shining riding boots." This sexualized image is so unexpected, so peculiar, that we pay attention and see that it symbolizes the narrator's excessive admiration for the Cossacks. This symbol bathes the rest of the story in a brilliant light.

Special Topics in Fiction

In addition to theme, language and symbolism, each kind of literature has its own concerns and terms to be mastered. To prepare for our discussion of the four major elements of fiction—plot, character, setting, and point of view—please read Isaac Babel's "My First Goose." Don't forget to give yourself to it on the first reading and then go back to make notes.

My First Goose
Isaac Babel

Savitsky, Commander of the VI Division, rose when he saw me, and I wondered at the beauty of his giant's body. He rose, the purple of his riding breeches and the crimson of his little tilted cap and the decorations stuck on his chest cleaving the hut as a standard cleaves the sky. A smell of scent and the sickly sweet freshness of soap emanated from him. His long legs were like girls sheathed to the neck in shining riding boots. 1

He smiled at me, struck his riding whip on the table, and drew toward him an order that the Chief of Staff had just finished dictating. It was an order for Ivan Chesnokov to advance on Chugunov-Dobryvodka with the regiment entrusted to him, to make contact with the enemy and destroy the same. 2

"For which destruction," the Commander began to write, smearing the whole sheet, "I make this same Chesnokov entirely responsible, up to and including the supreme penalty, and will if necessary strike him down on the spot; which you, Chesnokov, who have been working with me at the front for some months now, cannot doubt." 3

The Commander signed the order with a flourish, tossed it to his orderlies and turned upon me gray eyes that danced with merriment. 4

I handed him a paper with my appointment to the Staff of the Division. 5

"Put it down in the Order of the Day," said the Commander. "Put him down for every satisfaction save the front one. Can you read and write?" 6

"Yes, I can read and write," I replied, envying the flower and iron of that youthfulness. "I graduated in law from St. Petersburg University." 7

"Oh, are you one of those grinds?" he laughed. "Specs on your nose, too! What a nasty little object! They've sent you along without making any enquiries; and this is a hot place for specs. Think you'll get on with us?" 8

"I'll get on all right," I answered, and went off to the village with the quartermaster to find a billet for the night. 9

The quartermaster carried my trunk on his shoulder. Before us stretched the village street. The dying sun, round and yellow as a pumpkin, was giving up its roseate ghost to the skies. 10

We went up to a hut painted over with garlands. The quartermaster stopped, and said suddenly, with a guilty smile: 11

"Nuisance with specs. Can't do anything to stop it, either. Not a life for the brainy type here. But you go and mess up a lady, and a good lady too, and you'll have the boys patting you on the back." 12

He hesitated, my little trunk on his shoulder; then he came quite close to me, only to dart away again despairingly and run to the nearest yard. Cossacks were sitting there, shaving one another. 13

"Here, you soldiers," said the quartermaster, setting my little trunk down on the ground. "Comrade Savitsky's orders are that you're to 14 take this chap in your billets, so no nonsense about it, because the chap's been through a lot in the learning line."

The quartermaster, purple in the face, left us without looking back. I raised my hand to my cap and saluted the Cossacks. A lad with long straight flaxen hair and the handsome face of the Ryazan Cossacks went over to my little trunk and tossed it out at the gate. Then he turned his back on me and with remarkable skill emitted a series of shameful noises.   15

"To your guns—number double-zero!" an older Cossack shouted at him, and burst out laughing. "Running fire!"   16

His guileless art exhausted, the lad made off. Then, crawling over the ground, I began to gather together the manuscript and tattered garments that had fallen out of the trunk. I gathered them up and carried them to the other end of the yard. Near the hut, on a brick stove, stood a cauldron in which pork was cooking. The steam that rose from it was like the far-off smoke of home in the village, and it mingled hunger with desperate loneliness in my head. Then I covered my little broken trunk with hay, turning it into a pillow, and lay down on the ground to read in *Pravda* Lenin's speech at the Second Congress of the Comintern. The sun fell upon me from behind the toothed hillocks, the Cossacks trod on my feet, the lad made fun of me untiringly, the beloved lines came toward me along a thorny path and could not reach me. Then I put aside the paper and went out to the landlady, who was spinning on the porch.   17

"Landlady," I said, "I've got to eat."   18

The old woman raised to me the diffused whites of her purblind eyes and lowered them again.   19

"Comrade," she said, after a pause, "what with all this going on, I want to go and hang myself."   20

"Christ!" I muttered, and pushed the old woman in the chest with my fist. "You don't suppose I'm going to go into explanations with you, do you?"   21

And turning around I saw somebody's sword lying within reach. A severe-looking goose was waddling about the yard, inoffensively preening its feathers. I overtook it and pressed it to the ground. Its head cracked beneath my boot, cracked and emptied itself. The white neck lay stretched out in the dung, the wings twitched.   22

"Christ!" I said, digging into the goose with my sword. "Go and cook it for me, landlady."   23

Her blind eyes and glasses glistening, the old woman picked up the slaughtered bird, wrapped it in her apron, and started to bear it off toward the kitchen.   24

"Comrade," she said to me, after a while, "I want to go and hang myself." And she closed the door behind her.   25

The Cossacks in the yard were already sitting around their cauldron. They sat motionless, stiff as heathen priests at a sacrifice, and had not looked at the goose.   26

"The lad's all right," one of them said, winking and scooping up the cabbage soup with his spoon.   27

The Cossacks commenced their supper with all the elegance and   28
restraint of peasants who respect one another. And I wiped the sword
with sand, went out at the gate, and came in again, depressed. Already
the moon hung above the yard like a cheap earring.

"Hey, you," suddenly said Surovkov, an older Cossack. "Sit down   29
and feed with us till your goose is done."

He produced a spare spoon from his boot and handed it to me.   30
We supped up the cabbage soup they had made and ate the pork.

"What's in the newspaper?" asked the flaxen-haired lad, making   31
room for me.

"Lenin writes in the paper," I said, pulling out *Pravda*. "Lenin   32
writes that there's a shortage of everything."

And loudly, like a triumphant man hard of hearing, I read Lenin's   33
speech out to the Cossacks.

Evening wrapped around me the quickening moisture of its twi-   34
light sheets; evening laid a mother's hand upon my burning forehead. I
read on and rejoiced, spying out exultingly the secret curve of Lenin's
straight line.

"Truth tickles everyone's nostrils," said Surovkov, when I had   35
come to the end. "The question is, how's it to be pulled from the heap.
But he goes and strikes at it straight off like a hen pecking at a grain!"

This remark about Lenin was made by Surovkov, platoon com-   36
mander of the Staff Squadron; after which we lay down to sleep in the
hayloft. We slept, all six of us, beneath a wooden roof that let in the
stars, warming one another, our legs intermingled. I dreamed: and in
my dreams saw women. But my heart, stained with bloodshed, grated
and brimmed over.

Plot.   We call the structure and order of events in a work of fiction *plot*.
The novelist E. M. Forster differentiates a plot from a story:

> A story is a narrative of events arranged in a time sequence. A plot is
> also a narrative of events, emphasis falling on causality. "The king died
> and then the queen died" is a story. "The king died, and then the
> queen died of grief" is a plot. . . . Consider the death of the queen. If it
> is in a story, we say, "and then?" If it is in a plot, we ask, "why?"

Unlike a story, a plot, Forster says, demands not only curiosity but "intelligence and memory also." The writer should "leave no loose ends.
Every action or word ought to count. . . . It may be difficult or easy, it
may and should contain mysteries, but it ought not to mislead."

Plot is, then, not just a simple chronology. It focuses on the chain of
causation, on the connection between events and what forces bring the
events about. We could summarize the plot of "My First Goose" this
way:

> In the early 1920s in Russia, a young soldier joins a division of
> rough Cossacks. As an intellectual, he does not fit in. He is ignored or
> ridiculed. To prove himself and earn a place among the soldiers, he

bullies an old woman and kills her goose for his dinner. Although he is then accepted, this incident leaves him ashamed and uneasy.

This construction is fairly typical. It begins with a character in a situation, introduces a complication, and then proceeds to a resolution.

Plots do not always move in such a straight line. They may contain flashbacks, or events from the past, as well as foreshadowing, or hints of future events. The action may be interrupted for explanations, events may be seen from different viewpoints. But many stories observe the so-called three unities of action, time, and place. "My First Goose" observes these unities: the action is continuous, limited to a single location, and occurs over a short period of time.

Fiction is generally composed of a mixture of exposition and scene. The reader is told the exposition. The reader witnesses the scene. The exposition provides the background and context of the scene. The scene—composed of dialogue, gesture, and action—provides the drama. "My First Goose" is largely dramatic, but Babel includes exposition at certain points. Rather than writing out exactly what the narrator read aloud to the soldiers, for example, Babel summarizes the reading. With that information as background, the story moves on to its climax.

To get a firm grasp of a story, look at the plot first, especially at the beginning. Master the chain of causation. Locate the turning points. Summarize the whole work. Although it cannot be an essay, a summary can be a first step toward understanding the story.

Character. Sometimes when we read, we feel as though we have come to know another spirit and that we have experienced what that spirit has experienced. One of the great mysteries of literature is how a writer creates through words what feels like a real human being. No one can truly explain the miracle of characterization, but in the paragraphs that follow we attempt to identify some of the means writers use.

Sometimes the narrator will *tell* us something about a character, as in this passage from "My First Goose":

> The steam that rose from [the cooking pot] was like the far-off smoke of home in the village, and it mingled hunger with desperate loneliness in my head.

We also learn about a character from associated emblems: we know the narrator by means of the specs, the newspaper, the trunk, *Pravda*. Often a writer will give a minor character a defining emblem. One might say that the flaxen-haired youth in "My First Goose" was defined by his peculiar behavior.

What the character does and says is extremely important. Henry James asks, "What is character but the determination of incident? What is incident but the illustration of character?" A character is what he or she says and does. We are left in no doubt about the commander's opinions, his prejudices, and his arrogance when he says, "Oh, are you one of those grinds? Specs on your nose, too! What a nasty little object!" As for the narrator, we come to know him through both his willingness to violate his own nature to get close to the Cossacks and his subsequent anguished thoughts.

And at least as important in characterization is the way language is used to create the tone, the imagery. When the narrator says, "[The Cossacks] sat motionless, stiff as heathen priests at a sacrifice," we realize that the narrator is experiencing an almost religious awe in the presence of the soldiers. The narrator's tone changes over the course of the story from the admiring description of the commander to "The moon hung above the yard like a cheap earring." The changes provide a deeper insight into just how complicated the narrator is.

Setting.   In early fiction, writers described setting at some length, perhaps because people traveled very little and wanted to know about other places. Writers still provide setting, of course, but more cursorily. They don't dwell on the physical description. Anton Chekhov said, "You will evoke a moonlight night by writing that on the mill dam the glass fragments of a broken bottle flashed like a bright little star and that the black shadow of a dog or wolf rolled along like a ball." Short story writers like Chekhov have followed this credo more than have novelists.

Nonetheless, all the events in fiction happen within a time, a place, and specific social circumstances, and in order to be firmly in the work's reality the reader needs to know its context. The context may come from a small detail, such as reading a newspaper containing a speech by Lenin. Or a metaphor or simile might provide the context. When Babel writes, "The Cossacks commenced their supper with all the elegance and restraint of peasants who respect one another," we gain an understanding of the social situation, the camaraderie, in which the narrator finds himself. Sometimes a writer simply states the context, as Babel does when he writes, "Before us stretched the village street. The dying sun, round and yellow as a pumpkin, was giving up its roseate ghost to the skies."

Like all the elements in a fictional work, setting helps to determine meaning. The meaning of "My First Goose" depends on setting: a Russian village during the chaotic 1920s, when the Communists were battling to gain full control of the country. Babel does not stop to explicate the setting, but he provides enough for the reader to discern the unsettled state of life in the story and the various relationships. In the foreground are the tensions of a violent, confusing time—a time in which a sensitive person brutally kills a goose. The setting helps to illuminate the meaning of the story. This story could not have taken place in, say, San Francisco in the 1990s.

Point of View.   Stories have a storyteller, a narrator, who tells us what happens and sometimes even interprets the events. Because these storytellers are our only source of information, knowing their point of view is important. *Point of view* refers to the angle from which the story is told, the place from which the reader is allowed to see events. Is the storyteller a participant or only a reporter? Are we allowed to know what one person thinks, or many, or none? Are we close to the action or far from it?

Although there are other possibilities, point of view is generally either first person or third person. In *first person,* we see events through the eyes of a single character. This *I* may be the major character or only a witness or observer. In "My First Goose," he is the major character, that is, the one on whom the events register and to whom they matter most. In other works, such as F. Scott Fitzgerald's *The Great Gatsby,* an *I* describes what happens to someone else.

In *third-person* point of view, the storyteller is in no way a participant, although sometimes he or she will interrupt a story to make a judgment. Some third-person storytellers, called *omniscient narrators,* know everything and can move from past to present and from the mind of one character to the mind of another. Other third-person storytellers are *limited narrators,* confined to one character's consciousness. This is not necessarily a loss: though we know only one mind, we know it intensely and immediately. Occasionally, the storyteller is a *direct observer,* reporting only what can be seen or heard. This point of view creates a story resembling drama in that there is no interpretation of events or attempt to probe a character's mind. The reader, watching and listening, is like a fly on the wall.

Always note the point of view in a work and pay attention to how it colors your feelings about what happens. Just for fun, try imagining "My First Goose" told by an omniscient narrator who can go into the minds of the Cossacks and the old lady. Do you think that would have made a better story?

Later in this chapter we will use "My First Goose" as an example of how to prepare to write a literary essay.

Special Topics in Poetry

Poems sometimes tell stories that contain characters, plots, and points of view. And poems are as rich in theme as they are in symbolism, imagery, metaphor, and unusual uses of language. Careful readers notice these aspects when reading poems. They also attend to poetry's special domain: the intense world of musicality. In the pages that follow, we discuss this world expressed in rhythm, music, and rhyme.

Before going on, please read aloud, reread, and take notes on this poem by Archibald MacLeish.

Ars Poetica

A poem should be palpable and mute
As a globed fruit.

Dumb
As old medallions to the thumb,

Silent as the sleeve-worn stone   5
Of casement ledges where the moss has grown—

A poem should be wordless
As the flight of birds.

A poem should be motionless in time
As the moon climbs,   10

Leaving, as the moon releases
Twig by twig the night-entangled trees,

Leaving, as the moon behind the winter leaves,
Memory by memory the mind—

A poem should be motionless in time   15
As the moon climbs.

A poem should be equal to:
Not true.

For all the history of grief
An empty doorway and a maple leaf.   20

For love
The leaning grasses and two lights above the sea—

A poem should not mean
But be.

Rhythm.   Rhythm in a poem is created by alternating strong and weak
stresses on syllables in a line. When you read a line of poetry aloud, you
can always feel the rhythm.

> A poem should be palpable and mute
> As a globed fruit

The stresses force you to attend to certain words and phrases. When
you read the lines just quoted, you will hardly be able to ignore the
words *mute* and *globed*.

Often a poem will repeat a rhythmic pattern. The word *meter* refers
to this measured repetition. MacLeish's line

> A poem should be palpable and mute

contains a regular alternation of stressed and unstressed syllables, beginning with an unstressed syllable.

Critics often identify unstressed syllables with a ˘ and stressed syllables with a ˊ. If we used these marks on MacLeish's line, it might look like this:

Ă pŏém shóuld bĕ pálpăblé ănd múte

We call this a *metered* line. Each kind of metrical pattern has its own name, depending on the number and arrangement of stresses. (Handbooks on poetry will provide you with detailed information about these patterns.)

Rhythm does more than make reading delightful. It can tell you which words and ideas a poet intends to emphasize. Putting the stress on the word *globed,* for example, emphasizes the fruit's physical reality.

"Ars Poetica" plays many games with rhythm and meter. Read these two lines aloud:

Dumb
As old medallions to the thumb

That solitary, surprising word *Dumb* has a curious sense of finality to it, in part because it hitches the rhythm up short. MacLeish plays off the short one-syllable line against the next longer and more regular line and then comes down hard on *thumb.*

Now read this pair of lines aloud:

Leaving, as the moon behind the winter leaves,
Memory by memory the mind—

You may feel an almost hypnotic rhythm, regular and gradual. And perhaps that will remind you, as it has many readers, of the way the moon climbs in the sky.

Although all poetry has rhythm, not all poetry has meter. Since the mid-1800s, poets have increasingly turned to what is called *free verse,* poetry that does not repeat any rhythmic pattern. Even when reading free verse, however, you should listen for the rhythms that reinforce the meaning. Two lines from a poem by Walt Whitman show the importance of rhythm in free verse; read them aloud.

Out of the cradle endlessly rocking,
Out of the mocking-bird's throat, the musical shuttle

In these lines you can hear the rhythms of the rocking cradle and of the mockingbird's song. Words alone would not have made them real; words and rhythm together do.

Music.   The general term *music* covers the way a poem sounds. In the line

Twig by twig the night-entangled trees,

you can hear the *t* sound repeated. Such repetition of consonant sounds is often called *alliteration*. Again, the purpose is more than sound: the poet uses alliteration to point to objects or feelings in the lines. The repeated *t* sound calls up the physical reality of the twigs and trees.

The repetition of vowel sounds is often called *assonance*. In these lines, MacLeish repeats the sound of a long *e:*

> The leaning grasses and two lights above the sea—
>
> A poem should not mean
> But be.

These long *e*'s create a feeling of continuity between the physical world and the poem, which is MacLeish's point. Assonance can also slow the pace of a line. Notice how this line moves:

> Leaving, as the moon behind the winter leaves.

Because of all the long vowel sounds, the line is as slow as the moon itself. This combination of sounds drives the image home. Read the following lines aloud again slowly, shaping your lips around each word, dwelling on the sounds:

> A poem should be palpable and mute
> As a globed fruit.

The combinations of sounds can make you feel as though you were holding the globed fruit in your hand, weight, smoothness, and all.

Rhyme. When two words terminate in the same sound, they rhyme: *mute/fruit, dumb/thumb, stone/grown.* Most traditional rhymes in poetry happen at the ends of lines and are called *end rhyme,* as here:

> For all the history of grief
> An empty doorway and a maple leaf.

But frequently poems contain *interior rhyme,* as in these lines written by Gerard Manley Hopkins:

> I caught this morning morning's minion, king-
>   dom of daylight's dauphin, dapple-dawn-drawn Falcon, in his riding

Sometimes rhyming sounds are not exactly alike, but are approximate. These are called *slant rhymes.*

> A poem should be wordless
> As the flight of birds.
>
> A poem should be motionless in time
> As the moon climbs.

Like rhythm and music, rhyme directs us to what is important in a poem—the connection, for example, between *grief* and *leaf* and between *wordless* and *flight of birds.*

INTERPRETING LITERATURE

Once you have thoroughly read a work, interpreting it will come naturally. To interpret a work of literature, you say what you think it means, how it achieves that meaning, what values it expresses, what effect it has on the reader, and how it creates that effect. You look at the world the writer presents and at the artistry of the presentation. The aim is both to understand the work and to appreciate the achievement.

Responsible Interpretation

An odd rumor is going around about interpreting literature, namely, that all opinions are equally valid: "You can see whatever you want to see in it. You can say just about anything." There is some truth in that—but not much. The range of possible interpretations, whether of poetry or fiction, is indeed large, but it is not infinite. Flights of fancy may be fun, but they usually contribute little to understanding the work.

When MacLeish writes

Dumb
As old medallions to the thumb,

Silent as the sleeve-worn stone
Of casement ledges where the moss has grown—

you could perhaps claim that the medallions are portraits of knights from old castles and that the poem is about the decline of the British Empire. But such an unlikely interpretation is useless. It strays too far from the text.

Some readers seem to believe that literature, particularly poetry, contains some hidden meaning, and that interpretation is the deciphering of a riddle. It is true that the significance of a great work is seldom found on the surface. We have to think about it. But literature is not a riddle, and interpretation has little in common with doing crossword puzzles.

One important way in which interpretation is different from doing crossword puzzles is that the puzzles have correct answers, to be published next Sunday. There are facts about literature too. *"Hamlet was written before The Tempest"* is a statement of fact. About meaning in literature, however, there are no absolutely right answers—nor any that are completely wrong. Few writers provide a key to fix a work's meaning forever. Even when a writer does say what a work is about, that is only one interpretation. There will be others, probably just as illuminating. (This may sound like a paradox, but it is true. Virtually all writers acknowledge that there is much more to their work than they have consciously put there.)

Our job as interpreters is not to invent the fanciest answers we can or to discover a secret, but to articulate the meaning of a work.

When interpreting literature, keep two principles in mind.

First, the interpretation must fit the facts. A sound interpretation will not be contradicted by any element or event in the work. In interpreting the lines about the medallion in MacLeish's poem, you can't assert that the poem is about the British Empire when all the evidence points to its being about poems.

Second, the interpretation must be comprehensive. It should account for much of the work and should not neglect any important parts of it. Again, in interpreting MacLeish's poem, you would hardly neglect the facts of rhyme, music, and rhythm. Nor would you ignore the fact that MacLeish illuminates what poetry should do by reference to many physical objects. In "My First Goose," focusing extensively on the violent act and ignoring the narrator's anguish would badly distort the interpretation.

Bases for Interpretation

The question is, On what shall we base our readings? There are two possible bases for interpretation: factual analysis and informed speculation.

Factual Analysis. Good interpreters start with the facts of the text and stay close to them. Their readings are plausible because their insights are grounded in the text. Interpreters of MacLeish's poem, for instance, might begin with the fact that the poet refers to physical objects to illuminate what poetry should do. And in elucidating, they would stay close to that idea and use the text to prove it: "He uses fruit, medallions, trees . . ."

The most conservative interpreters stick exclusively to the text. They analyze *only* the facts of the work. In interpreting MacLeish's poem, for instance, a cautious interpreter might discuss the rhyme scheme, the rhythm or assonance, or the repetition of images.

In an essay on *Othello,* a conservative interpreter began this way:

> Iago is the most important character in *Othello,* as we can tell by an examination of the number of lines he speaks and the amount of stage action given to him.

To support her thesis, she went on to present a statistical analysis of the play's lines and action.

The possibilities for this kind of interpretation are large. Facts exist in plots and characters: what actually happens and what causes it; the names, ages, social standings, traits, and number of characters, and how these influence the plot. We can interpret aspects of the setting: whether it is rural or urban, domestic or foreign; whether the time is the present or the past. We can also base interesting interpretations on the physical makeup of the work: number of pages and lines; features of rhythm, meter, sounds, rhyme; use of verbs, nouns, adjectives.

Informed Speculation.   Often interpretation goes beyond the facts to what could be called informed speculation. It is informed because it starts with the facts of the text; it is speculation because it goes beyond the facts to the possibilities they imply. Informed speculation ventures opinions on the meanings behind the words.

Do not worry if you feel insecure about this approach to interpretation. Everyone, no matter how experienced, feels some uncertainty, some risk. It is obviously safer to discuss a rhyme scheme or the use of alliteration than it is to speculate on what the rhyme and alliteration are telling us. When we speculate, we run the risk of being wrong—but we gain the power of offering fresh insights into a work. In any case, informed speculation about a work is a very fine way to know literature.

In speculating, we build arguments not on hard evidence but on connotations. Read the following two lines from "Ars Poetica":

> A poem should be motionless in time
> As the moon climbs.

At the most concrete level, there are sounds: long *o* sounds and *i* sounds that take time to say. These are lines no reader can rush. An alert interpreter wrote,

> The long sounds in these two lines slow the lines down and direct us
> to the long, slow climbing of the moon, a climbing that is so gradual
> that it indeed appears motionless.

That is a lovely reading. It has speculated on the level of *the physical facts about the poem*. But there are other levels of speculation.

A second level involves speculation about *the literal meaning of the lines*. Take the poet absolutely literally.

> A poem should be motionless in time
> As the moon climbs.

Now, what does that mean? An alert speculator might write,

> But that is a contradiction. To climb is to move in time. The moon is
> never really motionless; it only seems that way because its passage is
> so gradual.

And this might naturally lead us to a third level, in which we speculate about *implications:*

> Perhaps MacLeish knows all along that a poem must move in time. Even reading it takes time, after all. Why does he make this apparent contradiction? For one thing, it seems to imply that there is something in the way the moon moves that defies our ordinary sense of motion. Try as we might, we can't see it move, even though we know it does. Perhaps MacLeish wants the poem to defy our ordinary sense of motion too—always to have something that we can't quite grasp, that eludes our demand for clear-cut certainty. And, of course, he, like many poets, probably wants the poem to seem as permanent, changeless, and inevitable as the natural world.

We are not talking about sounds or about words now but about implications. On the second level we asked, What do these lines mean? and on this one we asked, What is the significance of saying something like that? Note that we have not strayed very far at all from the poem. Those two lines are standing by waiting for us to reread them in the light of this new speculation. (We can press even further: Should a poet *want* a poem to be as permanent, changeless, and inevitable as the natural world?)

We might discuss a work's ideas *as* ideas or build our argument on appeals to shared experiences—as we did with our description of the moon climbing. We could analyze our impressions (why *does* the moon seem to stand still?) or evaluate the author's methods. And always we must identify those places in the text that give rise to our response.

With this kind of interpretation, our intelligence intersects with the text and brings forth fresh meaning.

CASE STUDY:
SPECULATING ABOUT A POEM

In a class called "Poetry and Poetics," Ines Echevarria was asked to write an essay on a poem from the course textbook. She chose Robert Frost's sonnet "The Silken Tent" because, though very challenging, something about it resonated with her. Here is the poem:

> She is as in a field a silken tent
> At midday when a sunny summer breeze
> Has dried the dew and all its ropes relent,
> So that in guys it gently sways at ease,
> And its supporting central cedar pole,

That is its pinnacle to heavenward
And signifies the sureness of the soul,
Seems to owe naught to any single cord,
But strictly held by none, is loosely bound
By countless silken ties of love and thought   10
To everything on earth the compass round,
And only by one's going slightly taut
In the capriciousness of summer air
Is of the slightest bondage made aware.

Echevarria read the poem aloud twice. Her next move was to turn on her
computer and, with the poem right beside her, begin inputting her
thoughts. Her method could be called "controlled freewriting," in that she
allowed herself to stop and return to the poem even in mid-thought.
Below is the process she went through to arrive at a thesis. In the margins
we have annotated her work to suggest steps in any workup of a poem.

The whole thing is one long, snaky sentence. Must be   1
a reason.

Seems to be comparing a woman ("she") with a tent. A   2
tent? A strange comparison for a woman.

Write out your first impressions of the poem.

The tent is silk. Silk is rare, flexible, very   3
light--surprising for a tent to be made out of it. Tents
are usually made of heavy fabrics.

At first I thought the poem was a metaphor, but   4
Frost begins with "She is as in a field a silken tent" so
that makes it one big simile. But you forget that little
"as"--it's even sort of hard to read--so the impression
you get is it's a metaphor.

Read it aloud again.

I don't quite get the poem yet, but I'm getting   5
there. Better read it again.

Simile or metaphor, it's a comparison. One side is   6
a tent, a silk tent, the kind you put up during a summer
celebration, not to go camping in. It's just a light
shelter from the sun.

Follow ideas that strike you.

The other side of the comparison seems to be a   7
woman. I know nothing about her, though I sort of like
her already. The poem says she's like the tent.

Account for your general impressions. Note details.

Interesting, unusual comparison. Original. General   8
impression is airy, sunny, light. Well, we're in "a
field," which is open, not a forest, which is confined.
As for sunny, Frost tells us there's a "sunny summer

breeze." Silk is light, delicate, yet flexible and most
of us like people who are light, delicate, yet flexible--

Underline or boldface
particularly important
observations.

women but men too. The ropes are loose. Now I'm getting
more of the comparison. The tent is supported by ropes,
but so delicately, no one can tell--it's as though the
tent stands by itself. The ties "relent"--meaning they
loosened as it got sunny and breezy and the dew dried.
So maybe Frost is saying people might start out stiff
but relax (relent) as time goes by.

The poem keeps reminding us that the tent needs the   9
ties. That is, the woman stands not by herself but by all
those tiny little ties. The guys. (Double meaning?) They
support her "cedar pole," "the sureness of the soul,"
which ensures that she stands upright, pointed
"heavenward."

Interesting how the woman is "loosely bound" but   10
seems to "owe naught" to any one thing, though the ties
are "slightly taut." Whoa. "Slightly taut" repeats
"loosely bound"! Also "silken tent" and "silken ties."
And what about using "cords," "ropes" and "ties"
interchangeably?

Lots of good metaphors in this poem. I especially   11
like "central cedar pole" that "signifies the sureness of
the soul." Suggests strength, good firm support.

Identify important
words, metaphors,
repetitions, figures of
speech; analyze and
interpret them.

Her "ties" are to "everything on earth." I'm be-   12
ginning to like this woman more. She's sure of herself.
She's connected to or pointed to "heavenward"--which you
could do a lot with. Frost says that "silken ties of love
and thought" tie us to things we cherish. Yes. They tie
this woman lightly, loosely--yet they do connect her
and their combined pulls help her stand. Stand upright?
Support her soul? What kind of pulls are they? Is this
poem about power? Maybe I'm getting closer. I know the
subject of power over women is a big one. The tent/woman
is "made aware" of "bondage."

Maybe it's power, but this woman seems quite con-   13
fident ("sureness of the soul"). Women who are sure of
themselves are interesting. Yet people seek to put claims
on women, and often place them in positions where they

are ashamed to assert themselves, as if being sure of themselves denies others their rightful claims. But this woman seems sure of herself--whatever bondage she may have is slight--yet she is tied, by "love and thought."

Speculate with regard to your own experience; write out what the images suggest to you. Argue with the piece.

NOT by coercion or force. These bonds, these ties--   14
the writer is really trying to let us know these are good things. Love and thought. Whose love and thought? Her own, I hope, but I look at the poem and I can't really tell. It could be other people doing the loving and thinking. It's ambiguous. But the poem is saying those things aren't too restricting.

Consider alternative interpretations.

If I were a certain kind of person, at this point   15
I'd say bondage is bondage, and no amount of apology and explanation can change that. This woman is stationary--so what if she points heavenward? She isn't going anywhere. I'd be willing to bet the poem was written by some guy who's trying to convince himself that being tied is a good thing. Who tied her? Another woman? Not that I can find. This is a woman imagined by a man to suggest an ideal of the self-actualizing female, but what it's really putting forward is just another image of the girl stayed put.

Listen to what you really think.

But that's not what I really think. What I really   16
think is that what gives the tent/woman shape and strength is the tension created by the lines that secure it to the earth, and that cedar pole. The cedar pole stands upright, not because of any one of the ties, but because it is a product of:
a. the "sureness" suggested by the staunch phrase "its supporting central cedar pole," in which the a and r sounds connote strength (to me at least). That impression is helped along by words denoting support, centeredness, and the strength of cedar.
b. the combined teeny pulls of the "ties" so that the tent "gently sways at ease." If any "single cord" pulls tight it's only by "the capriciousness of summer air," which suggests a light, transitory tug, not strong or lasting. No gale force winds here.

Well, all in all I'd say the tone is definitely   17
admiring. This speaker admires the way the woman stands
for and by herself. He likes her inner strength, a
"center"-ing in the earth balanced by a pointing toward
heaven--<u>suggesting maybe a grounding in both the flesh
and the spirit</u>. She's not likely to fall on this summer's
day.

Follow your ideas to their logical conclusion.

But the idea is paradoxical. How can she stand for   18
herself if she is bound to others? Well, the self is
something expressed, something exchanged, and you need
others for that. We have no important self apart from
others. That's something I believe, and I think it's one
of the reasons I like this poem. Even so, I prefer people
who are independent. To be ourselves, we have to be able
to be alone and make it on our own. So there's the
paradox.

Be alert to what most interests you.

The speaker is honest about this issue. There is no   19
utter freedom--the self is a product of tension, of pulls
between self and others, between heaven and earth, flesh
and spirit. For this woman, the ties provide shape and
security even as they "relent." A lot of the language
lets us know this is ultimately not a serious loss of
freedom: "capriciousness," the variations on "slight,"
the phrase "loosely bound" (sort of an oxymoron) and especially the light affectionate tone. The speaker seems
grateful to the woman for the "countless silken ties of
love and thought" with which she is so loosely bound. She
can be independent yet allied to "everything on earth the
compass round."

Write out your thesis and refine it.

That last paragraph contains my thesis: 20

> In "The Silken Tent," Robert Frost explores the
> paradox of being independent yet connected to other
> things and people. Although obviously bound to others,
> this woman expresses her independence, her sureness of
> soul, through her ties, which give shape and security.
> The combined pull of these ties actually contributes to
> the speaker's sense that this woman is herself and only
> herself.

If possible, set up a
conclusion as the
essay's target.

```
        I can see an interesting conclusion about this poem    21

as an image of the "good" woman. That image isn't without

problems. After all, the tent is too light to survive a

real storm. But in suggesting that there are constructive

ways of balancing self and bonds to others, the poem also

suggests that love and thought, while they compromise us,

do not compromise us totally.
```

WRITING ABOUT LITERATURE

When we turn our understanding and enjoyment of literature into writing, we stake out a claim on the work. In accounting for our thoughts and reactions, we take possession of the work. It becomes more deeply and securely ours. Writing about literature, then, is an opportunity to experience more profoundly the art of the writer.

Before writing, revisit the text and your notes. Return to high points, arresting language, themes that attracted you. Listen to your inclinations, the likes, dislikes, confusions, or enthusiasms that have stayed with you. To arrive at what you want to say, use your favorite form or forms of invention — freewriting, directed questioning, clustering.

CASE STUDY:
WRITING ABOUT FICTION

After her controlled freewriting, Echevarria had a thesis that asked *how* and *why*. She had a conclusion toward which to aim. And she had made herself so familiar with the poem that she could back up with solid evidence every point she wanted to make.

The best-kept secret about papers on literature is that they are argumentative. When you write about a poem, a play, or any literary work, you argue for your interpretation. The following case study is a description of the process Tripti Thomas went through to write a short essay on "My First Goose" (p. 451). The essay follows the description.

Thomas could not tackle such a rich, complex story without being analytical. Without breaking it into its parts, she would have been unable to say anything significant about it. ("It was great." "It was boring." "It was fun to read.") As she read, she kept in mind literary topics such as plot, character, setting, point of view, theme, symbolism, and language.

Thomas was particularly drawn to the central figure in the story, the lonely, idealistic young man who kills the goose. But she didn't want to force a thesis, and so she reread the story. When we read literature, we have to go through the same steps over and over, from reading to making notes to thinking to reading to making notes to thinking. Nothing appears in the exact same light twice. Thomas, for example, saw the action, the commander's laughter, and the actual killing differently each time she read the story. That is what makes literature great: it is inexhaustible.

Thomas noted the protagonist's characteristics: his admiration for Savitsky, his intellectuality, his desperate loneliness. She saw how he responds to the Cossacks, scrambles to gather up the contents of his broken trunk, pushes the old lady, kills the goose. After another reading, she listed several more events: the Cossacks shaving each other, the narrator reading Lenin's speech.

Having made a list of characteristics, some writers would simply plow through the items, devoting a paragraph to each until the bottom of the list announced the end of the paper. That kind of paper would be mechanical to write and boring to read. Thomas wanted to avoid the trap of writing a mere "character study." Instead, she wanted to account for the character's place in events and how he illuminates human experience.

From character, she naturally moved to thinking about the plot. Now she confronted a second trap: plot summary. The instructor, after all, has read the story and need not be told what is in it. Lengthy plot summaries are a waste of everyone's time. What an instructor wants is critical judgment, and that's what Thomas wanted to provide.

She found herself rereading the scene in which the narrator kills the goose, and she asked herself why he does so. True, he's hungry, but there is more than that. To get at it, she tried some freewriting:

```
The way the narrator crushes the goose with his boot and
digs into it with his sword, is too vicious to really
have anything to do with that goose or being hungry. He
seems sensitive, not like the other soldiers or they
wouldn't ostracize him, but then this violent act. He be-
comes just like them, as though he has given in to the
brutality around him.
```

Through rereading and analyzing, she moved closer to a thesis. She went back to the story to refine what she meant by "the brutality around him." The story seemed to contain all sorts of brutality, mostly implied: the commander's insolent power, the jokes about the spectacles, the quartermaster's remarks about women and soldiers, the flaxen-haired youth's insulting behavior. She had learned from reading a little about Babel that he had fought with the Red Army in a time of violence and upheaval. Those facts might help to account for the brutality that seemed to be behind every act.

With each reading, Thomas learned new things and could put them more firmly together. Eventually she had something significant to say about the story:

> In "My First Goose," Babel uses the tale of one young man's particularly brutal self-induction to demonstrate the influence of environment on human beings.

Thomas's analysis of the character led to the plot and on to a reexamination of the killing scene, and that led to her thesis. This thesis promised to show how and why the narrator capitulates to the brutality of his surroundings.

Thesis in hand, she then returned to the text and her notes. She determined the major supporting points and grouped important pieces of evidence from the text under each. This prepared her to discuss the story's ending. She recognized how important was the last line: "But my heart, stained with bloodshed, grated and brimmed over." That sounded an important note: capitulating to violence has a cost.

Here is Tripti Thomas's essay.

The Lad's All Right

The rites of initiation are always revealing, seldom forgettable, and often painful. In his short story "My First Goose," Isaac Babel uses the tale of one young man's particularly brutal self-induction to demonstrate the influence of environment on the human being. To earn these four casual words of approval, "the lad's all right," a seemingly gentle neophyte commits a violent act against the violent backdrop of war. 1

The story hints at the theme of initiation even before it begins. The title of the tale, "My First Goose," implies that the "slaughtered bird" will be the first in a series of violent acts the protagonist does to gain approval. Once the plot of the story emerges, so does the significance of the goose, a metaphor for everything (physical and abstract) that will henceforward be sacrificed by the narrator on the altar of adjustment and conformity to his new environment. The ritualistic quality of the moment is intensified by the attitude of 2

the Cossacks who sit "around their cauldron . . . motionless, stiff as heathen priests at a sacrifice." They
feign disinterest, but are fully aware of the first
bloody offering that lies, "white neck . . . stretched out
in the dung, the wings" twitching, at the feet of one who
aspires to their ranks. The choice of the goose as a
symbol is thus grounded in the reality of the narrator's
initial experience in his new environment, that is, his
initiation into it.

Deeming the protagonist an "aspirant" to the crude   3
ranks of the Cossacks would, at first, come as a surprise. If we disregard for a moment the implications of
his act, we are left with the impression of a young man
far removed from, and far superior on several levels to
the Cossacks. Here is a young man of enough aesthetic
sensitivity to find wonder and poetry in the figure that
his commander's body cuts and of enough academic sensibility to have "graduated in law from St. Petersburg
University" and to be taking an interest in the intri-
cacies of Lenin's manifestos. Moreover, his initial pas-
sivity in the face of ridicule suggests he is at least a
gentle person. So does the "loneliness in [his] head"
and a homesickness so profound that it transforms the
evening itself into "a mother's hand [laid] upon [his]
burning forehead."

These implied social, intellectual, and spiritual   4
characteristics stand in sharp contrast to those of the
Cossacks. It is precisely this contrast that Babel uses
to illustrate his point. The Cossacks and the environment
in which they are brought together are characterized by
vulgarity and brutality.

It is the war itself that is responsible for the   5
environment. The military personalities in this story
seem to thrive on their situation and produce personal
manifestations of brutality, the most obvious examples
being the ruthlessness of the commander, demonstrated in
his threatening note to Chesnokov, and the crudity of the
Cossacks, epitomized by their flatulent welcome of the

narrator and further underscored by the cruel treatment
he receives at their hands.

    The central act then comes as a jolt. It violently   6
bridges the gap that Babel has set up, by means of this
contrast, between the protagonist and his environment.
When he slaughters the goose and needlessly bullies a
helpless old lady, he is rapidly catapulted into the
other camp. His actions signal his aspiration to join
forces with the Cossacks. With the quartermaster's crude
advice fresh in his mind, he commits deeds far beneath
himself in an attempt to prove to the Cossacks that the
"specs on [his] nose" belie his inability to be one of
them, that he can sink to their level and paradoxically
become "worthy" of their approval. He kills the goose
because he finds it expedient to do so. He capitulates,
submitting with a brutal act to a brutal environment, and
thus Babel's point is proven.

    Once the young man is accepted by the Cossacks, he   7
indulges in a slightly feverish exultation. At this point
it becomes difficult for us to avoid passing a moral judgment. Apart from his shameful desertion of principles,
there remains the needless pain he has inflicted on those
weaker than himself. Perhaps on purely human grounds,
on the grounds of humanity's often shameless but necessary submission to the instinct of self-preservation,
we may excuse the young man. But can the young man excuse himself?

    The tale that he tells is one steeped in regret and   8
self-reproach. As night falls upon his first day at a
military outpost, the narrator falls into a fitful sleep,
his heart "stained with bloodshed, grat[ing] and brim-
m[ing] over." Though he dreams of women and conquests,
there are other things on his mind, thoughts that are not
made explicit. Perhaps it is his military career that
preoccupies him, one that stretches out ahead in an
interminable path of compromises, the tone and mood of
which he has set by butchering a goose. Perhaps he
recognizes that on this path he will perpetually be
plagued by the feeling of having something to expiate.

Some Do's and Don'ts

Let the structure of your argument take priority over the structure of the text. Too many papers start with line 1 or Chapter 1 and plow through straight to the ending. If you simply follow the text, your argument will have no shape or direction. Organize your argument first, and then arrange your notes and evidence to fit that organization.

Use the language of the text as your evidence. Nothing persuades quite so quickly and thoroughly as the text itself. Sometimes you may need to summarize or paraphrase a section for convenience or clarity, but when you can use the author's own words, do so.

Tie each piece of evidence in to your discussion. Warrants are essential in all papers on literature. Some writers pile on quotations without showing how they apply to the argument, as here:

> "Ars Poetica" tries to be the things it portrays. In the first two lines, "A poem should be palpable and mute/As a globed fruit," there are many *p* and *b* sounds.

Not so fast. What is the connection between the claim and the evidence? Until the writer shows *why* those sounds prove the claim, she will not carry her point.

> "Ars Poetica" tries to be the things it portrays. One of the ways it does this is with sound. In the first two lines, "A poem should be palpable and mute/As a globed fruit," there are many *p* and *b* sounds. These sounds force the reader to work the mouth and give the impression of real weight and texture.

This is the form the warrant takes in literary papers—the demonstration that the evidence fits the claim.

Do not praise the text or the author, no matter how great they are. One of the rewards of studying literature is the constant discovery of brilliant insights and technical mastery. But, then, everybody already knows that Honoré de Balzac, Thomas Mann, and Virginia Woolf are "great." Concentrate, rather, on showing how they achieve their great effects.

Write in the present tense. By convention, one writes as though the events of the poem, play, novel, or story are taking place in the present.

> When the old lady says, "I want to go and hang myself," the narrator responds by pushing her in the chest.

Give your own interpretation, not that of professional critics. Most instructors want to know what *you* make of the text. Books of criticism can help to illuminate a difficult text, but use them with great care. Do your own reading and build your own opinions. Exceptions to this rule are the book report and the research paper. But for interpretive essays on literature, *do not let experts do the thinking or writing for you*. Ask your instructor for suggestions on how to use the experts. And always acknowledge all sources that contributed to your essay.

Tips for Reading, Interpreting, and Writing about Literature

- Give yourself to the reading the first time through and make your notes on the second reading.
- Remember that theme, symbolism, and language are concerns in nearly all literary works.
- When reading fiction, think about plot, character, setting, and point of view.
- Read poems aloud, and, as you do, think about rhythm, music, and rhyme.
- Make sure your interpretation fits the facts and does not neglect major aspects.
- Try to go beyond factual analysis to an informed speculation about the meanings in the work.
- Identify what interests you most, and use that as a basis for your analysis.
- Develop an essay on literature as you would other argumentative essays, with a thesis, evidence, and warrants.
- Avoid mere character studies and plot summaries.
- Let the structure of your argument take priority over the structure of the text you are interpreting.
- Stay close to the text: the best evidence is the author's own words.
- Do not praise the author.
- Write in present tense.
- Remember that your instructor wants your own critical judgment of the work.

EXERCISES FOR READING, INTERPRETING, AND WRITING ABOUT LITERATURE

1. Read the following sonnet by William Shakespeare and write an essay in which you first describe the situation presented and then argue for what you believe to be the central anxiety in the speaker's mind. What is the origin of the anxiety? Has the speaker taken any steps at the end of the poem to address his problem? Back up your argument with detailed references to the poem's language, rhythms, and any other technical or thematic material you believe supports your thesis.

Sonnet 138

When my love swears that she is made of truth,
I do believe her, though I know she lies;
That she might think me some untutored youth,
Unlearnèd in the world's false subtleties.
Thus vainly thinking that she thinks me young,
Although she knows my days are past the best,
Simply I credit her false-speaking tongue;
On both sides thus is simple truth suppress'd.
But wherefore says she not she is unjust?
And wherefore say not I that I am old?
O, love's best habit is in seeming trust,
And age in love loves not to have years told.
Therefore I lie with her, and she with me,
And in our faults by lies we flattered be.

2. Analyze the language and symbolism of the sonnet in Exercise 1. Are there metaphors, similes, vivid images? Which words are symbols, and for what ideas?

3. Take the last two lines from the sonnet in Exercise 1 and try writing a paragraph in which you speculate on the three levels—the physical facts, the literal meaning, and the implication. If you feel brave, press one step further, to the implication of the implication. Exchange your paragraph with a partner's and compare.

4. Choose one of the following short stories and identify its central symbol. What makes this symbol significant? What relation does it have to the story's main theme?

   Delmore Schwartz, "In Dreams Begin Responsibilities"
   John Steinbeck, "Flight"
   Nathaniel Hawthorne, "Young Goodman Brown"
   Flannery O'Connor, "A Good Man Is Hard to Find"
   Ernest Hemingway, "The Snows of Kilimanjaro"

5. Analyze the use of point of view in the story you selected in Exercise 4. Write a paragraph describing the advantages or disadvantages of that point of view. Now write another paragraph analyzing the effect a change in point of view would have had.

6. Choose another one of the stories listed in Exercise 4, and write a three- or four-page essay about it. At the end, append a description of where you started your analysis and what route you followed to arrive at your thesis.

17

The In-Class Essay
Examination

Why didn't I know enough of something?
— ELIZABETH BISHOP (1911–1979)
AMERICAN POET

When your instructors require an essay examination in a course, they generally have two purposes in mind. First, they want to know how much you have learned about the materials and concepts of the course and how well you can use them. Their second purpose is more educational than evaluative: they want you to synthesize your knowledge and thus to understand it better and possess it more securely. Using knowledge is a superb way of making it yours. An essay exam, then, can be a great learning experience.

Essay exams take many formats. They can last from one to four hours. They can be open- or closed-book. They can consist of several short questions or a single long one. They have in common a premium on time. You must organize information quickly and respond clearly and concisely to the questions posed. Ease in writing in-class essays depends largely on your knowledge of the material and on your physical and mental state at the time of the test. We hope the advice in the pages that follow will help you to get the most out of yourself.

STUDYING FOR THE EXAM

When studying your notes, look for broad themes and patterns. Differentiate major ideas from supporting points. Analyze how the major points are related and how the evidence supports them. Notice changes and developments.

You may find it helpful to consolidate class notes and reading notes by transcribing them in an orderly way. The act of writing down the information is an excellent reviewing technique. In addition, when you group the information, you improve not only your grasp but also your memory.

A good method for consolidation is to put the basic themes of the course across the top of a sheet of paper as column headings and to list the major divisions of the subject down the left-hand margin. In a Western civilization course, for example, you might put major concerns—justice, religion, ethics—across the top and put various philosophers—pre-Socratics, Plato, Aristotle, Cicero, and so on—down the side. Under each topic, you would write out the ideas of each philosophical approach. You could then easily compare the major ideas of the course.

As you study and organize your notes, think about what areas of the subject the instructor favored. Try to anticipate test questions. In the Western civilization course, for instance, you might anticipate a question like this one:

Compare Plato's idea of justice with that of Cicero

or

In what ways is Augustine's idea of freedom a purely Christian concept and in what ways is it a continuation of the Greco-Roman idea of freedom?

Questions, even ones you invent, can help you structure your studying. You may find it both reassuring and informative to share this process with a friend in the class who might have different ideas about the subject.

As you identify probable areas the test will cover, think of major issues and supporting ideas. If, for instance, you think the instructor is particularly keen on the idea of justice, look closely at your reconstructed notes on that subject and know what you think about it. If a major theme remains vague to you, reread the textbook or the original material. Try to arrive at the exam with ideas that tie the course together.

If your test is open-book, review your syllabus and class notes to see which sections of your readings were covered in class. Flag for easy reference sections of the book that were heavily emphasized. Write down page numbers of especially important quotations and sections that came up in class. Remember that an open-book exam doesn't mean you don't need to study; in fact, you may be graded harder since you have your references in front of you.

Avoid anxiety as much as possible. Think about the examination not as just a test but also as a learning opportunity. When you can view the exam as intrinsically worthwhile rather than as an ordeal, you will reduce the concern you feel about it. While studying, try to maintain your usual habits of eating and sleeping. Staying up late, missing meals, or ingesting large amounts of coffee or other stimulants can upset both your memory and your thinking patterns. Cramming may push the information you already know out of your mind. Try to take the pressure off. Before the exam, get a good night's sleep. Eat a full breakfast—your brain needs fuel just as your body does.

Immediately before the test, read over your summary notes. Don't try to cram in facts: just remind yourself of patterns and themes. At this point, do not rehearse questions with others. It is too late for that to serve any purpose, and if someone brings up a subject you have not anticipated, it will no doubt increase your anxiety.

Arrive for the exam on time and fully equipped with pens or pencils and scratch paper. Bring a watch with you. Keeping track of time is essential, and you cannot count on a clock or instructor to do it for you. If you have a free choice of seats, sit away from distraction—doors open to the corridor, windows that look out on busy thoroughfares, even other students who might want to socialize.

Relax. If you feel nervous, try one of these methods for relaxing: either breathe in until your lungs are full, add another quick breath, breathe out slowly, and repeat the process several times, or consciously relax each and every muscle of your body, beginning with your little toes. (The first time you try this, you may laugh, which is relaxing in itself.) Clear your mind.

TAKING THE EXAM

Well prepared, confident, and relaxed, you will be ready, perhaps eager, to show what you know when the instructor says "Go."

When you receive the question sheet, read the instructions and all the questions slowly and thoroughly. Take the time to understand what is expected. Listen to all verbal directions. If you have any problems of interpretation, ask the instructor right away. Know when the test starts and when it will end. Synchronize your watch with the instructor's.

Organizing Your Time

Know exactly how much credit you will receive for each answer and allot your time accordingly.

Start with the question you feel most ready to answer. Not only is this encouraging and even soothing but also it taps right in on your best ideas. As you write about something you feel fairly confident of, ideas about other questions may occur to you. Be sure to keep your scratch paper handy so that you can jot down these ideas.

For open-book exams, don't waste time thrashing through the book for a marginal quotation. Your book should be flagged for quick reference to supporting evidence, but you shouldn't depend on its contents for the heart of your essay.

Noting Significant Words in the Question

Pay close attention to all command words, key words and phrases, and texts mentioned in each question. These tell you what to do and often how to do it. Keep in mind the development strategies (pp. 187–90) as ways to flesh out your answer.

Command Words.   Command words tell you exactly what the instructor wants you to do: *compare, define, demonstrate, evaluate, isolate, trace,* and so on. These are the action verbs in the question. You might, for instance, receive this instruction in a sociology class:

> Define *individualism* in America and trace the development of this concept.

This question asks something specific of you: to *define* individualism (identify the meaning of the term) and to *trace* its development (show its origin, its history, and its present application). Remember that you must perform both tasks. Doing just one will answer only half of the question. It does not ask you to compare American individualism with something else or to evaluate it. Be sure you know and follow the exact command.

Some command words—*discuss, explain, explore, describe*—are more general; they put you on your own. In answering a question that uses one of them, you will have to figure out whether to define, compare, evaluate, and so on. In an American history class, you might be asked to respond to this kind of open-ended question:

> John Adams estimated that one-third of the colonists were loyal to the British Crown during the American Revolution. Discuss the treatment of these loyalists during and after the Revolution.

Don't just start free-associating about the loyalists. Even when the instructor does not tell you exactly what to do, you still must construct a reasoned, organized answer. Figure out your own commands. Here, you might identify who the loyalists were according to economic class, occupation, and geographic location. Then you might trace their history and their fate. Finally, you might analyze their motives and the motives of those who, in punishing them, confiscated their property.

Key Words and Phrases.   With or without clear commands, a question may contain a key word or phrase that can help you organize your answer. This question certainly does:

> What was the origin of the Monroe Doctrine? Examine three occasions before 1900 on which this doctrine was invoked.

The key words and phrases are, of course, *origin, Monroe Doctrine, three occasions* and *before 1900*. They strongly suggest a course for a response: define the doctrine, summarize its origin, then turn to the period in question and select the three occasions. With each occasion, you might say why the doctrine was invoked and what the result was. You might conclude with an evaluation of the doctrine's effectiveness as an instrument of foreign policy in the nineteenth century.

If the key words in a question need definition, define them early and go right to a discussion of why they are significant. Then you can use that definition and evaluation as a basis for your entire answer.

References to Texts.   If the question mentions an author or a text, note them and prepare to treat them specifically in your essay. The instructor is providing you with a focus. Here is a question for a linguistics class that provides a sharp focus:

> Continental linguists criticize Noam Chomsky's theories of language on the ground that they are based on the behavioristic tradition of J. B. Watson and B. F. Skinner. With reference to Chomsky's *Language and Mind* and to Skinner's *Beyond Freedom and Dignity,* evaluate this criticism.

In answering, you would look first at the command word, *evaluate.* That word calls for a balanced response, neither enthusiastic agreement with nor dismissal of the criticism. You should express your own opinion, but the command asks you to be alert to both sides. Next, you would turn to the key words, *criticism* and *behavioristic tradition.* You would probably define *behaviorism.* Then you would pick up on the authors and texts mentioned. You would describe Chomsky's theories and relate them specifically to those of Watson and Skinner. You would include pertinent analyses of *Language and Mind* and *Beyond Freedom and Dignity.*

Fully understanding the question and identifying the important words in it can carry you a long way toward a persuasive answer.

Shaping Your Answer

The first moments of your exam are important. Once you understand what the question asks, start thinking. It is sheer folly to begin writing your answer the moment the gun goes off. Some good test takers use up to a quarter of the exam time to organize their thoughts before they write their answer. They then have a good idea of what to write and can be cool and collected when they begin.

Remember: an essay examination asks you to write an essay, and an essay has a thesis. Your instructor does not want a mess of unsorted facts or a list of vague feelings. Though the conditions of an exam are somewhat different from those of the usual essay, you can apply much of what you have learned in *Writing Worth Reading.*

Take the first few minutes to formulate your thesis. Use that scratch paper. Employ any of the invention devices. Brainstorm. Free-write. Write down your thesis.

Spend the next few minutes organizing. Make a scratch list of everything pertaining to the question. Don't waste time trying to retrieve something you can't remember. Either it will surface or it won't, and it is more likely to if you don't force it.

Turn your scratch list into an outline. Sort out the major ideas. Be ruthless: by combining, condensing, or discarding, reduce your list of major points to three or four. These will be the prominent subheadings under your thesis. Put these points in proper order. If the question lends itself to chronological treatment, as does the one regarding the Monroe Doctrine, use that organizing principle. Otherwise, arrange your answer either according to the order of the relay race, with the second strongest point first and the strongest last, or in ascending order of climax. What you want, of course, is to end on a strong note. (See "Coherence" in Chapter 8 for a discussion of ordering points.)

Flesh out your points. Virtually all graders prefer specific essays to general ones, the concrete to the abstract. The more specific your answers, the better. As you go over your scratch list, identify the support for all your major points. This is a good time to make sure you have included the major points and the evidence for them.

Writing Your Answer

Write legibly. Illegible handwriting is worse than useless; it is a positive irritant. Use conventional mechanics. Write an economical, plain, direct prose.

If you are using a blue book, skip lines and write on only one side of each page. That way, if you want to add something later you can put it in the empty line or on the blank side of the opposite page with an arrow showing where it fits. The grader will not mind incorporating the new material if its place is clearly designated. In any case, double-spaced writing on one side of the page generally makes reading easier.

Write a brief introduction that contains the general area you will cover in your answer, as well as your thesis. A good place for your thesis is in the last sentence of the introduction; it doesn't hurt to underline it for emphasis. Don't restate the question. That not only wastes time but also can irritate the grader. A strong thesis will tie your discussion firmly to the question.

Now you are ready to move into your answer. Check the remaining time. Plan so you have ample time to spend on the important points. You don't want to be gasping for breath as you leave a question.

Make paragraph breaks at important pauses. Write emphatically. Do not be afraid to underline your major point in each paragraph. Construct each paragraph with claim, evidence, and warrant in mind. Your claim will be the major point of the paragraph, perhaps stated as a topic sentence. Support each point with evidence: example, quotation, paraphrase, statistic, or what have you. Be sure you have at least one piece of evidence, and preferably more, for each point. We have never heard an instructor complain of too much evidence in an exam. And clearly tie the evidence to the claim with a short discussion, or warrant.

Write confidently. If a new idea about the subject strikes you, write it. Great revelations can come in the pressure cooker of the essay exam. But don't be diverted from your overall structure. You simply do not have time for digressions or stray points. Discipline is important. Keep the question clearly in mind. If you are to compare and contrast A and B, do not spend 90 percent of your time on A, and do not throw in C.

Leave yourself a few minutes for a conclusion. Ending in style will help any essay. Reiterate what you have said, but try to wrap up the essay with an observation that indicates the importance of what you have written. Your conclusion need not be long, but it ought to have a feeling of finality. Here is the conclusion to an essay analyzing George Washington's warning against getting involved with "foreign entanglements":

> The new United States was still wary from its war with England, and its first president understandably insisted that the country make its own way. But countries cannot exist in a vacuum, and, as the rest of U.S. history has shown, no country can keep out of foreign entanglements for long.

If you can, close each essay answer with a good authoritative last line. (See "Your Conclusion: Finishing in Style" in Chapter 9 for more on closing lines.)

If you run into trouble during the writing, don't panic. To get those juices flowing again, try freewriting on scratch paper.

Adding, Reviewing, Polishing

Leave time to review the whole exam. Use the blank sides of your blue book pages for new ideas or clarifications. Don't forget those arrows to indicate insertions: the grader won't want to reconstruct the order of your ideas. If you run out of space on the nearest blank page, go to the end of the book.

When reviewing, read your work critically, as though you were the grader. Try to catch inconsistencies, incoherent sentences, unfulfilled promises in your essay. Check your grammar and syntax. But don't make your paper look as if armies of pens and pencils had been in combat over it. Make sure your essay is presentable; then hand it in.

CASE STUDY:
AN IN-CLASS ESSAY EXAMINATION

The following answer was written by Jeri Shikuma in response to the question

> Drawing on readings and lectures, discuss (1) whether (and in what sense) you think Americans are individualistic, and (2) the possible *causes* and *consequences* of that individualism in America's religious origins, stratification patterns, and forms of political power.

Notice how she responds to the command words. In the first paragraph she sets up her thesis and the major topics she will pursue. After the brief introduction she gets right into her argument. Each following paragraph takes up a topic. She carefully develops evidence and always ties it to the claim. She has a strong conclusion. Notice how she bolsters her judgments by reference to sources.

> Individualism has characterized America since its beginnings with the idea of the rugged individualist. This individualism has grown and influenced America's stratification patterns as well as its forms of political power.
>
> Americans are individualistic in the sense that they place a great deal of importance on being unique and offering something special. This is manifested in art as well as commerce. Many great American novels portray a hero who must stand alone, outside society, to fight for justice. One such is Herman Melville's *Billy Budd*. Captain Vere accepts the responsibility as well as the loneliness of his command as he sends Billy to his death. Individualism, according to Blumberg, is even manifested in America's architecture. Isolated apartments and one-occupant flats emphasize the individual alone. Even the stress on the nuclear family—mother, father, children—is in opposition to the wider society.
>
> This individualism was probably founded at the very beginning of the nation with the arrival of the Protestants. According to Weber, the Protestants were deeply ingrained with the sense of the individual alone in the world, and they placed a high importance on individual acts. Calvin's idea of God's being so transcendent that he never interferes with one's life led the Calvinists to believe that they were alone on earth, with no one to turn to for help. Furthermore, because their

afterlife was predestined for either salvation or damnation—though they did not know for which—the Doctrine of Proof, in which their proof of salvation showed in their actions, made individual actions very important. Thus, the Protestants, and particularly the Calvinists, perpetuated an ethics of rational, systematic self-evaluation, which grew into a general idea of individualism.

This individualism has permeated every aspect of society. In politics, it manifested itself in pluralistic theories advocating particularistic interests as essential for the health of democracy. To theorists, the pursuit of personal, particular interests in the political arena keeps society from being split down the middle and thus prevents class conflict and, in the long run, tyranny. Mobilization around special interests also prevents deep ideologies from forming and promotes compromise.

Furthermore, individualism has affected stratification patterns. People are inherently different, and, in society like that in America in which these differences are exploited, stratification is inevitable unless the society directly tries to prevent it through redistributive means. Indeed, as Black said, the idea of individualism in the sense of inherent differences is essential for the justification and legitimation of inequality. Upper-class people can say they have privileges and advantages because they are inherently more capable. The idea simultaneously placates the lower classes by making them feel that they are on the bottom not because of any unfair system but because of human nature. It also lets them feel that they may rise in society if they really try and make the most of their unique talents.

Thus, individualism has been a very prominent force in shaping American society. And though people seem to be caught up in issues of society as a whole, such as unemployment and homelessness, individualism is still important. As Tocqueville recognized in the early nineteenth century, individualism is a deeply ingrained characteristic of American life.

SHORT ANSWERS

Short-answer essay questions require a different strategy from that used in long essays. Scan the identification section of the test. Note the number of questions and the credit you will receive for each one.

Spend the most time on questions that have the highest number of points. You can afford to botch or omit a five-point question, but not a thirty-five-point one.

Work on questions you know first; save harder ones for later. Generally, people write more easily and quickly on questions about which they feel confident, and much more slowly when they are uncertain.

Write short answers as crisply and specifically as you can. Some instructors want the *shortest* answer possible, and some will stipulate that complete sentences are not necessary. Again, make sure you know what your instructor expects. In any event, vague or general answers lose points. Recall what was said in class about the question at hand. What points did the instructor repeat? What important distinctions or details will he or she probably want to see? Here are two short essay examination answers to a question worth ten points. The first answer, brief and very general, received four points, and the second, more specific one received the full ten.

QUESTION	Identify the term *oxymoron*.
ANSWER 1	Oxymoron is a figure of speech used in poetry where two words contradict.
ANSWER 2	Oxymoron is a poetic figure of speech in which two terms seem to contradict. *Seem* is the important word, because although the two words may contradict, together they make a paradox. An example is *loving hate*. The two words seem to contradict, except that there are so many times when love involves feelings close to hatred that the oxymoron makes sense.

Tips for the In-Class Essay Examination

- Make summary notes of lectures and reading.
- Anticipate the questions or at least the probable areas to be covered.
- When preparing for an open-book exam, review your syllabus and notes for key readings, and flag your book or books for quick reference.
- Get a good night's sleep, and eat a full breakfast before the test.
- Avoid anxiety by breathing deeply and steadily or consciously relaxing each muscle.
- When taking an open-book exam, use your book or books for quotations and support, but don't overrely on them.
- Pay attention to command words, key words and phrases, and texts mentioned in the test question.
- Before beginning, formulate a thesis and organize your answer.
- Write legibly and use conventional grammar, syntax, and mechanics.
- Construct paragraphs with claim, evidence, and warrant in mind.
- Save time for writing a conclusion and adding, reviewing, and polishing.
- Make short answers direct, emphatic, and as specific as possible.

EXERCISES FOR THE IN-CLASS ESSAY EXAMINATION

1. Read these hypothetical essay examination questions. Focus on the command words, key words and phrases, the texts mentioned, the way the questions are put, and any other clues to possible organization. What is each question asking for? How would you organize an answer to it?

   a. Ten days before the San Joaquín revolt of 1886, the duke of Calabria said, "The people will never revolt. They depend too much on us." To what extent did the people of San Joaquín depend on the nobility? Trace the causes of revolt, with reference to Smith's *Urban Armies of Italy*.

   b. Discuss the major differences between a hunter-gatherer society and an early agrarian society.

   c. Design a program that uses positive reinforcement to help you cure yourself of some undesirable habit. Refer to the steps given in Gibson and Baker.

   d. Would the Athenian citizens have considered the American form of government a democracy? Why or why not?

   e. Read the following passage. Keeping in mind all we have read and learned about American stylists, say whether the passage was written by Faulkner, Fitzgerald, or James. What aspects of the style led you to make this identification?

      But for the moment she was so happy, so lifted up by the belief that her troubles at last were over, that she forgot to be ashamed of her meager answers. It seemed to her now that she could marry him without the remnant of a scruple, or a single tremor save those that belonged to joy.

2. Your instructor will design an essay examination based on a selection the class will have read in preparation. Before actually taking the exam, the class will discuss how to respond to the question, what clues might help organize the answer, and what the instructor is looking for. The instructor will not confirm or deny anything: the class must reach a consensus before writing.

PART SIX

The Nuts and Bolts
A Handbook of Grammar, Punctuation, Mechanics, and Usage

18

Basic Grammar

Grammar, which knows how to control even kings.
— MOLIÈRE (1622-1673)
FRENCH DRAMATIST

Grammar deals with the forms and structures of words and with their conventional arrangements in phrases, clauses, and sentences. In this chapter we discuss key grammatical terms.

THE PARTS OF SPEECH AND THEIR FUNCTIONS

Nouns

A **noun** is the name of a person, place, thing, condition, or idea, everything from Mrs. Smith to catfish, from honesty to Albania. **Proper nouns** name a particular person, place, or thing: *Caesar, Utah, Coca-Cola.* **Common nouns** name general categories: *politician, state, soft drink.* **Collective nouns** name a number of individuals considered as a single entity: *congregation, covey, jury.* **Concrete nouns** refer to tangible things: *iron, telephone, fingernails.* **Abstract nouns** refer to conditions, states, and ideas: *health, consciousness, technology.* A **noun substitute** is a word or phrase that functions as a noun: *Driving fast* is dangerous.

Pronouns

A **pronoun** is any word that stands for a noun or noun substitute. In the passage *Maud shot the sheriff. She shot him with a .44, she* stands for Maud and *him* stands for sheriff. Words such as *I, each, him, that,* and *which* are all pronouns.

Every pronoun must have an *antecedent*—a specific noun or noun substitute to which it refers. The pronoun must agree in person, number, and gender with its antecedent. In *Maud bought her gun from outlaws when they blew into town, her* agrees with the antecedent *Maud,* and *they* agrees with *outlaws.*

Pronouns come in many varieties and perform many functions.

Personal pronouns refer to a specific person or thing. Examples of personal pronouns are *I, you, him, hers, it, we, theirs.* (See "A Special Word about Pronoun Case" on page 491 for more on personal pronouns.)

Relative pronouns are *who, whom, whose, that,* and *which.* These pronouns introduce a subordinate clause and relate it to a noun or noun substitute in the main clause.

> Sam, *who* had never ridden a Brahma bull before, won the rodeo *that* took place in Amarillo.

Who introduces the subordinate clause *had never ridden a Brahma bull before,* and *that* introduces the subordinate clause *took place in Amarillo.*

When the antecedent of the relative pronoun is an animate object, use *who, whom,* and *whose. Sam,* an animate object, is the antecedent of the *who* clause. Use *which* or *that* when the antecedent is an inanimate object. *Rodeo,* an inanimate object, is the antecedent of the *that* clause. (See the Glossary under *"that, which"* for a discussion of when to use *that* and when to use *which.*)

Intensive and **reflexive pronouns** are *myself, yourself, himself, herself, itself, oneself, ourselves, yourselves, themselves.* An intensive pronoun emphasizes a noun or noun substitute.

> I *myself* witnessed the dastardly crime.

It stands beside the noun because it is part of the noun. A reflexive pronoun indicates that a subject is acting upon itself.

> Judas hanged *himself.*

The pronoun follows the verb because it is the direct object.

Demonstrative pronouns are *this, that, these,* and *those.* These pronouns point at the noun and make the reference unmistakable.

> *Those* plants are poisonous; *these* are edible.

Indefinite pronouns include *all, any, anyone, each, either, everyone, few, most, nobody, none, no one, some, somebody,* and *someone.* These pronouns refer to people or things generally rather than specifically.

> *Nobody* loves me, *everybody* hates me; I'm going out in the garden and eat worms.

Reciprocal pronouns are *each other, each other's, one another,* and *one another's.* They express a mutual relationship. Use *each other* when referring to two people, *one another* for more than two.

> Although we are told we should love *one another,* those two hated *each other.*

Interrogative pronouns are *what, which, who, whom,* and *whose.* These pronouns introduce questions.

> *What* on earth are you doing?

A Special Word about Pronoun Case.   The form a personal pronoun or a relative pronoun takes will depend on **case,** that is, on the pronoun's function in the sentence. English observes three cases:

> **subjective**—when the pronoun functions as the subject of the verb: *She* shot the sheriff.

> **objective**—when the pronoun functions as the direct or indirect object of the verb: Maud shot *him* and then gave the gun to *me.*

> **possessive**—when the pronoun shows either ownership or association: It was *my* gun, unfortunately.

Here are the cases for all personal and relative pronouns:

SUBJECTIVE	OBJECTIVE	POSSESSIVE
I	me	my, mine
you	you	your, yours
he, she, it	him, her, it	his, her, hers, its
we	us	our, ours
you	you	your, yours
they	them	their, theirs
who, that, which	whom, that, which	whose, of which

Most of us use the correct form unconsciously most of the time, but in the following paragraphs we discuss some particularly tricky usages.

1. Selecting the correct case for the verb *to be* can be tricky. We may naturally say

> Was it him? It wasn't me.

But for the high informal writing style, use the subjective case.

> Was it *he?* It wasn't *I.*

2. *Who* and *whom* can cause trouble. If the relative pronoun is the subject of a verb, then the pronoun should be in the subjective case.

> Do you know *who* ate all the pickles?

Who is the subject of the verb *ate.*

If the relative pronoun is the direct or indirect object of the verb in the subordinate clause, then the pronoun should be in the objective case.

> Do you know from *whom* they were stolen?

If the relative pronoun shows possession or association, use *whose* when the antecedent is an animate object.

> It was Old Dog Tray *whose* smell permeated the car.

If the antecedent is inanimate, use *of which* for the possessive.

> The fire, *of which* the source was old rags, raged through the night.

3. Be careful with compound subjects or objects. Be sure that all parts are in the correct case.

> He must not let ill will grow between *him* and *me.*
>
> Professor Krantz and *I* disagreed about my grade.
>
> The judge gave the lawyer, the defendant, and *me* a lecture.

To test whether the compound subject or object is in the correct case, read the sentence as if the problematic pronoun were not part of a compound.

> Me disagreed about my grade.
>
> The judge gave I a lecture.

4. When using a pronoun to modify a gerund (that is, a verb or verb phrase functioning as a noun, see p. 501), use the possessive case.

> *His* acting made me laugh.
>
> He adores *my* having fun.

Nouns modifying gerunds also take the possessive case, as in

> Martin Luther objected to the *clergy's* selling priestly offices.

5. Making a comparison using the word *than* followed by a pronoun can be confusing. The case depends on whether the pronoun is the object of the preposition *than* or the subject of an unspoken but understood verb. To test this, fill in the silent words.

> He loved her more than [he loved] *me.*
>
> He loved her more than *I* [loved her].

6. Writers are sometimes confused by a pronoun acting as an appositive—that is, placed right beside a noun or noun substitute to provide additional identification.

> *We* Americans have an "omnipotence complex."

The appositive takes the same case as the word it stands beside. *Americans* is the subject of the sentence, and therefore the pronoun must be in the subjective case.

> This "omnipotence complex" has injured *us* Americans.

Now *Americans* is the direct object of the verb *injured,* and therefore the pronoun takes the objective case. To test for correctness, read the sentence with the appositive pronoun only.

> This "omnipotence complex" has injured we.

EXERCISES FOR PRONOUNS

1. For each of the following sentences, choose the correct word in the parentheses.
   a. We looked forward to (them, their) coming home at Christmas.
   b. Men generally misunderstand (we, us) women.
   c. (We, Us) men are largely misunderstood by women.
   d. We (ourself, ourselves) are happy with the election's outcome.
   e. All the basketball players got in (each other's, one another's) way.
   f. The most valuable player award went to the entire team, including (I, me, myself).
   g. Just between you and (I, me, myself), she has bad breath.

2. Correct the following sentences for pronoun errors, if any.
   a. The woman never regretted hiring we students.
   b. The strike whose cause was low wages ended peacefully.
   c. My sister who lives in England wrote a letter to Mother, Father, and I.
   d. Here is a painting about which much should be said.
   e. Me and Eddie both participated in the track meet, but he pole-vaulting was funnier than me trying to high-jump.
   f. The man that tried to hang-glide last Saturday is doing nicely in the hospital, but the doctor that attended him is worried. So are his wife and me.
   g. I know of three movie stars who Goldwyn discovered in drugstores.

Verbs

Verbs express actions, processes, or states of being.

> He *ran* outside when the object *appeared* in the sky, but she *was* horrified.

Verbs are the energy at the center of all sentences.

Kinds of Verbs.   We classify verbs according to whether they take a direct object or a complement or help other verbs to perform.

Transitive verbs take a direct object.

The lion *ate* the wildebeest.

Intransitive verbs describe activities and states without an object.

Queen Victoria *sneezed* and the empire *trembled.*

Linking verbs act as equal signs between nouns and their complements, that is, words that complete the meaning of the sentence.

William *is* a clown, but he *appears* miserable.

To be is the most frequently used linking verb; other common ones are *appear, become, feel, look,* and *seem.*

Auxiliary verbs, also called helping verbs, join with the infinitive, past participle, or present participle of a verb to form a verb phrase.

The new phone book *has* arrived. It *has* helped us all in the past.

The verbs *to be* and *to have* are the most common auxiliaries. (*To be* also functions as a linking verb.) Other auxiliaries are *can, could, do, may, might, must, need, ought, should, would.*

Verb Forms.   The principal parts of the verb are the *infinitive,* the *past tense,* and the *past participle.* Changes in verb form rely on these basic parts. To form the past tense and the past participle of regular verbs, add *-d* or *-ed* to the infinitive.

INFINITIVE	PAST TENSE	PAST PARTICIPLE
help	helped	helped
traverse	traversed	traversed

Sometimes the present participle is considered a principal part of the verb. It is formed by adding *-ing* to the infinitive (*helping, traversing*).

Many English verbs are irregular, and ways of forming their past tenses and past participles vary greatly. An internal vowel may change (*arise, arose, arisen*), a consonant ending may be added (*fly, flew, flown*), the past tense or past participle may have two acceptable forms (*awoke, awaked; awaked, awoken*). Consult your dictionary when you are uncertain of verb forms.

Tense.   Tense refers to time. All verbs change according to when the action occurs, how it is related to another action, and whether it is continuous.

The **simple tenses** are present, past, and future. *Present tense* indicates current action.

She *sings* well.

Past tense indicates completed action.

She *sang* that song last night.

Future tense indicates action that will be completed later.

She *will sing* it again tomorrow.

To form the future tense, combine the infinitive of the verb with the future tense of *to be*.

The **perfect tenses** indicate an action that was or will be completed after another action. *Present perfect* indicates past action continuing up to the present.

She *has sung* that song every night.

Past perfect indicates action completed before another past activity.

She *had sung* it nearly fifteen hundred times before her big break came.

Future perfect indicates action expected to be completed later.

By July 4, she *will have sung* that song to a million people.

The perfect tenses are formed by combining the past participle of the verb with the present, past, or future tense of *to have*.

The **progressive tenses** indicate ongoing action.

She *was singing,* she *has been singing,* she *will be singing,* she *is singing* her life away.

These tenses can indicate ongoing actions past, present, or future. They are formed by combining the present participle of the verb with the appropriate form—present, past, future—of *to be*.

Be consistent with your tenses. Sudden and incorrect shifts can confuse and irritate the reader.

> **INCONSISTENT**   After Robespierre initiated the Reign of Terror, he controls the revolution and has Danton guillotined.

Because *initiated* is in the past tense, the other verbs should also be in the past tense.

> **REVISED**   After Robespierre *initiated* the Reign of Terror, he *controlled* the revolution and *had* Danton guillotined.

Voice.   English has two **voices,** active and passive. In **active voice,** the subject of the sentence performs the action.

The diva *sang* an aria from *Aida*.

In **passive voice,** the subject of the sentence receives the action.

> Even the stagehands *were moved.*

See "Be Active" in Chapter 10 for more on active and passive voice.

Mood.   The **mood** of the verb tells us whether the speaker views the action or state expressed in the sentence as fact, question, command, or likelihood. English has four moods. The **indicative mood** makes an assertion.

> She *will win* the race.

The **interrogative mood** asks a question.

> *Did* she *win* the race?

The **imperative mood** issues a command.

> *Win* that race!

The **subjunctive mood** has several functions. It can express a wish—

> I wish I *were* running,

a statement contrary to fact—

> If I *were* you, I *would run* faster,

a remote possibility—

> I *might get* in shape someday,

and a command—

> I *demand* that your laughter *be* stopped.

This form is slowly dying out in English, but careful stylists still use it.

EXERCISES FOR VERBS

1. Write two sentences using a transitive verb, two using an intransitive verb, two using a linking verb, and two using an auxiliary verb.

2. Provide the appropriate form of the verb for each sentence in this paragraph.

   > Before the snows have melted, my neighbor (to plant) his garden. He (to work) in his garden every day. He always (to have) tulips and daffodils by April. By the middle of May, the tulips (to begin) to droop. One year, however, they (to bloom) still in June. When he (to work) during the hot summer months, I am often afraid he (to suffer) heat stroke. I think he (to like) flowers.

3. Write sentences for all the different moods using a single verb (such as *to race*).

4. For the following sentences, identify the tense and voice of the verbs.
    a. Viewers of this program were dazzled by his performance.
    b. The quotation came from the *New York Times*.
    c. Studying the acquisition of language is instructive.
    d. You will be happy with his speech.
    e. Playing serves several functions in children.
    f. Coffee has sometimes been thought a cause of headache.
    g. Medicine is not yet considered a science.
    h. In April, she will have served as mayor for ten years.
    i. A surprising conclusion was drawn from the evidence.
    j. You will need a derrick to remove your car.

Adjectives

Adjectives are words that modify nouns or noun substitutes.

> It was a *brilliant* idea to build a *gravel* road.

They answer the question What kind of person, place, or thing is this? They also tell us how many people, places, and things there are.

> *Innumerable* bumblebees chased the *four* children.

They sometimes follow a linking verb and modify the verb's subject.

> The night was *bright,* and the horse looked *blue* in the moonlight.

The articles—*a, an,* and *the*—are also adjectives. *The* is the **definite article** and is used to refer to a definite, known thing.

> *The* book was torn by *the* baby.

A and *an* are **indefinite articles** and are used to refer to nonspecific things. *A* precedes nouns that begin with consonants, and *an* precedes nouns that begin with vowels.

> To some people *a* rat is less repulsive than *an* eel.

One exception occurs before nouns that begin with a long *u* sound; these take *a* as their article.

> Although you may think it *an* underhanded trick, it is *a* universal practice.

To some Americans, the phrase *an historical event* sounds and looks right. If it sounds natural to you, use it. Generally, however, Americans do not use *an* before *h.*

Comparative and *superlative* refer to the degree to which a person, place, or thing possesses an attribute. When a person, place, or thing possesses an attribute more than another does, the adjective is in the *comparative* form.

> My daddy is *stronger* than your daddy.

When a person, place, or thing possesses all of an attribute or possesses it in greater degree than does any other in a group of three or more, the adjective is in the superlative form.

My daddy is the *strongest* daddy in the world.

Most adjectives simply add *-er* for the comparative and *-est* for the superlative. Some, however, change form with degree (*good, better, best*). And some adjectives of two or more syllables require *more* or *most* to indicate their comparative or superlative form.

Chocolate is *more delicious* than vanilla; it is the *most delicious* flavor.

When in doubt, check your dictionary.

Adverbs

Adverbs modify verbs, adjectives, and other adverbs. They indicate how, when, where, why, how often, and in what manner. Most adverbs end in *-ly* (*swiftly, intelligently*), but some do not (*very, beyond*).
Like adjectives, adverbs may be compared, but unlike most adjectives, they require the terms *more* and *most* to signal their comparative and superlative forms.

She ran *more swiftly* than I did, but I dressed the *most elegantly* of all the campers.

EXERCISE FOR ADJECTIVES AND ADVERBS

Choose a passage of fifty words and underline all the adjectives and all the adverbs. Provide the comparative and superlative forms for all the words you have underlined.

Conjunctions

Conjunctions join words, phrases, and clauses. **Coordinating conjunctions** join equal ideas.

Bill and Phil hated the movie, *but* they liked the popcorn.

You can remember the coordinating conjunctions by remembering *fanboys—for, and, nor, but, or, yet, so.*
Subordinating conjunctions join a dependent clause to an independent clause.

If you hurry, you will catch the train.

Some common subordinating conjunctions are *although, because, if, since, unless, whenever, whereas.*

Correlative conjunctions are pairs of conjunctions that help balance the sentence and relate different parts of it to each other.

Either you leave *or* I leave.

The correlative conjunctions are *both/and, either/or, neither/nor,* and *not only/but also.* The same grammatical construction must follow both elements of the pair.

Caligula *not only* destroyed the pride of the Romans *but also* wasted Rome's resources.

Conjunctive adverbs provide a logical link between two independent clauses.

You misbehaved, and, *therefore,* you will have no supper.

We guarantee nothing; *however,* we hope to please.

Some common conjunctive adverbs are *however, moreover, nevertheless, therefore, thus,* and phrases such as *on the contrary.* Set them off with punctuation. Other punctuation is exactly as if the conjunctive adverb were not there.

EXERCISES FOR CONJUNCTIONS

1. Write seven sentences, using a different coordinating conjunction in each.
2. Write five sentences, using a different subordinating conjunction in each.
3. Write four sentences, using a different pair of correlative conjunctions in each.
4. Write four sentences, using a different conjunctive adverb in each.

Prepositions

A **preposition** ties a noun or noun substitute to another word in the sentence. In

The baseball rolled *into* the sewer,

the preposition *into* ties the sewer to the baseball. Constructing a complete list of prepositions would be nearly impossible—and certainly unnecessary. They range all the way from the common ones, such as *in, to,* and *with,* to rarer compound prepositions, such as *inasmuch as* and *on behalf of.* A preposition and its object form a **prepositional phrase.** Such phrases function in several ways. They can serve as adjectives to modify nouns.

John Maynard Keynes conceived a passion *for the ballerina with the long, beautiful legs.*

They can serve as adverbs.

> *On VJ Day,* Americans danced *in the streets.*

They can also serve as nouns.

> *In the streets* was the place to be that day.

Prepositions can combine with verbs to create multiword verbs.

> She can't *put up with* a man who won't *give up on* a car that always *falls apart.*

Unfortunately, prepositional phrases tend to pile up in a sentence, as in E. B. White's famous burlesque:

> What did you bring the book I can't stand to be read to out of up for?

When prepositions pile up, rewrite the sentence.

EXERCISES FOR PREPOSITIONS

1. Write three sentences in which the prepositional phrases function as adjectives, three in which they function as adverbs, and three in which they function as nouns.
2. Write five sentences that have more than one prepositional phrase.

Interjections

Interjections express feelings, not thoughts. Words such as *gosh, hey, oh, ouch, pshaw, say,* and *well* are interjections. They never constitute sentences on their own and appear only rarely in high informal writing.

PHRASES, CLAUSES, AND SENTENCES

Phrases

A **phrase** is a group of related words that lacks either a subject or a verb or both. It modifies another word in the sentence or modifies the sentence as a whole.

> *Standing in the sunlight,* the man *in the red sweater* squinted *at the photographer.*

A **prepositional phrase** begins with a preposition and can act as an adjective, adverb, or noun. See the section "Prepositions."

A **verb phrase** is a verb expressed in more than one word.

> By this time tomorrow, Los Angeles *will have traveled* in a 27,000-mile circle.

See the section "Verbs."

A **verbal phrase** is a form of the verb used not as a verb but as another part of speech. An **infinitive phrase** is a verbal phrase that contains the infinitive, its object, and any modifiers. In *To err is human,* the infinitive *to err* serves as the subject of the sentence, a noun or noun substitute. The infinitive phrase can also serve as an adjective or adverb:

> The Yankees are almost always the team *to beat.* (adjective)
>
> Drew juggled three chain saws *to show his talent.* (adverb)

A **participial phrase** includes a participle, its object, and any modifiers. It functions as an adjective.

> Police were on the lookout for a man *driving a 1951 Hornet.*

A **gerund phrase** is the present participle used as a noun. It functions as either the subject or the object of a verb.

> *Rising early* is healthy, but how I hate *getting up.*

An **absolute phrase** modifies a whole clause or sentence, not just a single word.

> *Weather permitting,* we'll boat over the rapids tomorrow.

It contains a participle and a noun or pronoun. Usually, we drop the participle if the verb is *to be.* In the following example, it is not necessary to put *Being* before *Weary and hungry.*

> *Weary and hungry,* the field hockey team trudged homeward.

An **appositive phrase** is placed next to another word or phrase to provide pertinent elaboration of it.

> Clarence, *brother of Richard III,* was drowned in a barrel of malmsey.

Brother of Richard III is an appositive, providing apt information about Clarence. Using appositives can help you maintain a lean, vigorous prose. We have more to say about them in "Economy: Reducing the Verbiage" in Chapter 10.

Clauses

A **clause** is a group of words that contains a subject and a verb. Clauses can be independent or dependent. When they are **independent,** they can stand alone.

> *Volcanoes rumble before spewing.*

When clauses are **dependent,** they cannot stand alone.

> *Whenever volcanoes rumble*

The dependent clause requires an independent clause to complete its meaning.

> *Whenever volcanoes rumble,* the villagers begin to fret.

A dependent clause (also called a *subordinate clause*) begins with a subordinating conjunction (such as *although, if, whenever*) and can function as an adjective, adverb, or noun.

> The witch doctors, *whose geological training was slight,* said they had nothing to fear. (adjective)
>
> The villagers knew better *when the lava began to flow.* (adverb)
>
> *Whether they should flee* was the pressing decision. (noun)

Sentences

A **sentence** is a group of words that expresses a complete thought. It contains a subject and a verb. It indicates what happened to the subject or what the subject caused to happen. For a detailed discussion, see Chapter 10, The Sentence from Many Angles.

Sentences come in four constructions. A **simple sentence** contains one independent (or main) clause and no other clauses. It may, however, have a compound subject.

> Lewis and Clark explored the Northwest Passage.

It may have more than one verb.

> They tried and tried but could not find their way.

As long as it has only one independent clause, it is a simple sentence.

A **compound sentence** contains at least two independent clauses but no dependent clauses. The independent clauses can be joined either by a comma and a conjunction or by a semicolon.

> You take the high road, and I'll take the low road.
>
> Diplomacy without defense is folly; defense without diplomacy is madness.

A **complex sentence** contains only one independent clause and at least one dependent clause.

> When John Adams was president, his wife hung the family wash in the East Room of the White House. (dependent-independent)
>
> On the other hand, George Washington, who preceded Adams in the presidency, never occupied the White House. (independent interrupted by dependent)

A **compound-complex sentence** contains two or more independent clauses and at least one dependent clause.

Men over age thirty-five should have a medical checkup regularly even if they are feeling fine, and they should begin to cut down on the sugar, salt, and cholesterol in their diet. (independent-dependent-independent)

In addition, sentences can be distinguished according to when the main idea is completed and where the emphasis falls. A sentence is called *loose* or *cumulative* when the main idea is introduced at or near the beginning and then modified by less important elements. The information piles up along the way in a rather casual and unemphatic fashion.

> Bats are obliged to make sounds almost ceaselessly, to sense, by sonar, all the objects in their surroundings. (Lewis Thomas, *The Lives of a Cell*)

This kind of sentence is very natural to speech, when we usually start with a subject and amplify it as thoughts occur to us.

A sentence is called *periodic* when the main idea is not completed until the end. Along the way, less important elements—modifiers, subordinate clauses, and the like—are presented, but the emphasis comes at the conclusion.

> No matter how many areas of the world the British colonized, the jewel in the crown was always India.

Most good writers combine these two forms, using the periodic to make a particularly important point.

EXERCISES FOR PHRASES, CLAUSES, AND SENTENCES

1. Identify the various kinds of phrases in the following passage.

   > Like ill-trained shamans, rock singers manipulated the energies they could scarcely keep in tow. This was closely akin to their self-destructive streak; they loved putting their heads in the lion's mouth, and several were dead before the sixties ended. Janis Joplin was particularly naked in her vulnerability to the audience, in her visible need of them. (Morris Dickstein, *The Gates of Eden*)

2. Write a sentence containing one of each kind of phrase.

3. Identify the various kinds of constructions in the following passage and determine which sentences are loose and which are periodic.

   > Anyone who has observed a dog doing his neighborhood rounds and leaving his personal mark on each convenient post will have already guessed how the wolves marked out *their* property. Once a week, more or less, the clan made the rounds of the family lands and freshened up the boundary markers. . . . This careful attention to property rights was perhaps made necessary by the presence of two other wolf families whose lands abutted on ours, although I never discovered any evidence of bickering or disagreements between the owners of the various adjoining estates. I suspect, therefore, that it was more of a ritual activity. (Farley Mowat, *Never Cry Wolf*)

4. Change the following passages as directed.

   a. Into a simple sentence: Thomas Marshall, who was vice president under Woodrow Wilson, said, "What this country needs is a good five-cent cigar."

   b. Into one complex sentence: Chinese chefs serve food in bite-size pieces. Bite-size pieces cook faster. That saves fuel.

   c. Into a compound sentence: Money is the root of all evil. Few people bury it or burn it.

   d. Into a compound-complex sentence: My uncle said he had a terrific television show to watch, and he insisted on turning to another station, and then he sat in his big green easy chair; he was snoring in five minutes.

5. Construct two loose sentences and two periodic sentences.

19

Problems in Sentences

since feeling is first
who pays attention
to the syntax of things
will never wholly kiss you
— E. E. CUMMINGS (1894–1962)
   AMERICAN POET

SUBJECT-VERB AGREEMENT

The verb of a sentence must agree in number and person with the subject.

The scarlet macaw lives in the jungles of South America.

The singular noun *macaw* takes the singular verb *lives*.

Macaws have long tails and large hooked beaks.

The plural noun *macaws* takes the plural verb *have*.
Subject-verb agreement can become complicated. Here are some difficult constructions and the rules that govern them.

1. Intervening words: subject and verb must agree even when other words come between them.

> The sight of red and blue macaws thrills the spectator.

Sight is the subject, and *thrills,* the verb, must agree with it, even though *macaws,* a plural noun, is next to the verb. An *intervening clause* with a plural verb can be quite confusing.

> The sight of red and blue macaws, which are the largest of all the parrots, thrills the spectator.

Sight is still the subject, and *thrills* agrees with it.

Phrases beginning with prepositions (*along with, as well as, in addition to, like*) are never part of the subject and cannot affect the verb.

> President Johnson, as well as Presidents Truman and Kennedy, was once a senator.

What applies to Johnson also applies to the other two, but Johnson alone is the subject, so the verb is singular.

2. Collective nouns: words like *committee, family, group, jury,* and *team* take a singular verb when you want to emphasize the group as a whole.

> The jury has decided.
> The family agrees about religion.

These collective nouns take a plural verb when you want to emphasize separate entities.

> The jury are in there arguing about the verdict.
> The family disagree, however, about sex and politics.

Apply the same rule and reasoning to *majority of, mass of, number of,* and other references to quantity or size. They take the singular to emphasize the totality and the plural to emphasize the separate entities.

> The number of mistakes is sometimes disheartening.
> But the majority of people make them.

3. Compound subjects: when the parts of a compound subject connected by *and* are viewed as separate entities, the verb should be plural.

> Harpo and Groucho are my favorites of the Marx Brothers.

When the parts of a compound subject are viewed as a unit, the verb should be singular.

> Peanut butter and banana is my favorite snack.

When a compound subject is joined by *nor* or *or,* the closer subject determines the verb.

> Either the Brownie Scouts or Ms. Peabody was lying about the rampaging bear.
>
> Either Ms. Peabody or the Brownie Scouts were lying about the rampaging bear.

When this rule leads to an awkward construction, rewrite the sentence.

> **AWKWARD**   Either Clara or I am the worst tennis player on the team.
>
> **REVISED**   Either Clara is the worst tennis player on the team or I am.

4. Numbers: numbers that act as a unit take a singular verb.

> Ninety-five cents is too much to pay for a soft drink.

Numbers viewed as individual items take a plural verb.

> Ninety-five dogs in the kennel were barking.

5. Singular words in plural form: some words ending in *-s* that refer to a single item or idea take a singular verb.

> Mumps is usually a childhood disease.

But some take a plural verb.

> Scissors are hard to sharpen.

Idiom controls the form. Consult your dictionary.
Some words ending in *-ics* will be singular in one context but plural in another.

> Statistics is a branch of mathematics.
>
> Statistics are not always reliable.

In the first example, *statistics* is singular because it refers to a body of knowledge viewed as a unit. In the second, it is plural because it refers to items viewed separately.

6. Noun substitutes: when the subject of a sentence is a phrase or clause used as a noun substitute, the verb is always singular.

> *Smuggling parrots* has become a lucrative business.
>
> *Why the smugglers persist* is hardly puzzling.

Smuggling parrots is the subject of the first sentence, and *Why the smugglers persist* is the subject of the second. Both require singular verbs.

When, however, two or more noun substitutes are the subject, the verb is plural.

> Smuggling parrots and selling them are violations of the law.

7. Linking verbs: a linking verb (*appear, be, feel, look, seem, smell,* and so on) agrees with its subject, not with the noun or pronoun that is the subject's complement.

> Pink cockatoos are an Australian native.

Pink cockatoos is the subject; *Australian native* is the complement.
  In sentences that begin with *There* or *Here* followed by a linking verb, the verb agrees with the real subject following the verb.

> There is a tavern in the town.
>
> There are many customers.

8. Relative pronouns: the singular or plural status of the relative pronouns *that, which, who, whom,* and *whose* is determined by their antecedent, the noun to which they refer.

> Most readers like *novels* that *have* a happy ending.

The antecedent of *that* is *novels,* and so the verb is plural.

> Most readers like a *novel* that *has* a happy ending.

Now the antecedent is *novel,* so the verb is singular.
  A problem may arise when the word *one* appears in the sentence.

> Thomas Mann was one of the German intellectuals who were willing to stand up to Hitler.

Who refers to *German intellectuals* and takes a plural verb.

> Mann was not the only one of the German intellectuals who was willing to stand up to Hitler.

Who now refers to *one,* a singular pronoun, and takes a singular verb.

9. Indefinite pronouns: indefinite pronouns, such as *any, each, either, everybody, someone,* and so on, generally take a singular verb.

> Everyone loves fudge.

A few indefinite pronouns (*all, any, few, none, some*) can take either a singular or a plural verb, depending on whether they refer to individual items or the group as a whole.

> Some fudge has nuts.
>
> Some people make themselves sick gorging on it.

Careful stylists generally prefer the singular when using *none,* and always use the singular when using *no one.*

> None was more gluttonous than William, who ate two pounds.
>
> No one was surprised when he got so sick.

EXERCISES FOR SUBJECT-VERB AGREEMENT

1. In the following sentences choose the correct word in the parentheses to make the subject and verb agree.
   a. The list of books (stays, stay) on my table.
   b. The committee (reviews, review) applications at night.
   c. Neither the coach nor the players rewarded (himself, themselves) for the victory.
   d. The collections of antique silver (shows, show) taste.
   e. Either the guards or the warden (was, were) responsible for the trouble.
   f. When measles (is, are) epidemic, I keep my children at home.
   g. The ethics of all who hoard vaccine (is, are) under scrutiny.
   h. She was one of those brainy people who also (loves, love) sports.
   i. The couple living next to the Bishops (drinks, drink) too much.
   j. Each one of the dogs that belonged to Jennie Vickers (has, have) fleas.

2. Correct any mistakes in subject-verb agreement in the following sentences.
   a. His collection of spiffy sports cars were impressive.
   b. The family is fighting viciously over the will.
   c. No one in all the display rooms were surprised at the brilliance of the artists.
   d. He is one of the salesmen who, having sold over a million dollars in policies, are going to Hawaii.
   e. Everybody clapped and were happy.
   f. Neither his clothes nor the car were paid for.
   g. The sound of the dogs, who barkcd all night, have driven her to distraction.
   h. Tommy, along with all his friends, are going to the circus.
   i. A favorite creature of mine are koala bears.
   j. How the accountants manage on April 15 are puzzling, but preparing income taxes is a laudable occupation.

PRONOUN-ANTECEDENT AGREEMENT

As we said earlier, a pronoun must agree in person, number, and gender with its antecedent, that is, the noun or noun substitute to which it refers.

> Dachshunds require special care because of their long backs.

The pronoun *their* matches in person and number its antecedent, *dachs-hunds.*

Our male dachshund requires special care because of his back.

The pronoun *his* matches in person, number, and gender its antecedent, *our male dachshund.*

Occasionally, a pronoun will precede its antecedent in a sentence.

While performing his tricks, the elephant fell on his nose.

Here we discuss four potentially confusing constructions.

1. Antecedents joined by *and* usually take a plural pronoun.

As Fido and Rover ate, they snarled at each other.

2. Antecedents joined by *nor* or *or* take singular pronouns when both parts of the antecedent are singular.

Either the flanker or the tight end missed his assignment.

When one of the nouns is plural, the closer noun determines the pronoun.

Neither the coach nor the players admit their mistake.

To avoid an awkward construction, put the plural noun closer to the verb.

AWKWARD	Neither the Brownies nor Ms. Peabody was able to find her way home.
REVISED	Neither Ms. Peabody nor the Brownies were able to find their way home.

3. A pronoun referring to a collective noun (such as *audience, committee*) should be singular when the emphasis is on the group as a whole.

The committee has its proposal ready.

The pronoun should be plural when the emphasis is on individual entities within the group.

The audience are slowly taking their seats.

4. Indefinite pronouns (*everyone, none, some*) are usually treated as singular and take singular pronouns.

No one eats her lunch before noon at Miss Blaine's School.
Each of the boys appears in his uniform on Fridays.

Sometimes, however, an indefinite pronoun suggests more than one and should be treated as a plural.

Some of the teachers eat their lunch alone.

When treating the indefinite pronoun as a singular, writers have traditionally used the generic *he, him, his*.

Everyone has his faults.

Many, however, have come to consider this usage sexist. To avoid the problem, recast your sentence.

All have their faults.

(For a general discussion of sexist language, see "Avoiding Sexist Language" in Chapter 11.)

EXERCISES FOR PRONOUN-ANTECEDENT AGREEMENT

1. In the following sentences, choose the appropriate pronoun in the parentheses.
   a. Neither Brecht nor Beckett typed (his, their, theirselves) manuscripts.
   b. The awards committee split (its, their) award between Conklin and Dumanian, and the chair asked each winner to express (her, their) appreciation.
   c. The family quarreled with one another because of (its, their) religion.
   d. Some of the members voiced (its, his, their) personal convictions.
   e. Either the manager or his assistants missed (his, their) chance to correct the error.

2. Correct any mistakes in pronoun-antecedent agreement in the following sentences.
   a. To sail in the Americas Cup, every member of the crew must do their job.
   b. The family sat down to their Thanksgiving dinner.
   c. Neither the Contras nor Ortega likes the proposal.
   d. All the meat was ground up and the sausages put in its cases.
   e. Charles and the Parkers driving home in his car really took their sweet time.
   f. Each member of the committee wanted to put forward their individual proposals.
   g. Either the secretary of state or the secretary of defense failed to assume their responsibility.

PRONOUN REFERENCE

A pronoun should refer specifically and unmistakably to one and only one antecedent.

Lincoln would have had a difficult time in his second term because his cabinet had turned against him.

All the pronouns in this sentence clearly refer to Lincoln. Unclear antecedents can cause the reader to misread the sentence. The following rules will help you avoid this kind of misreading.

1. When you use more than one noun or noun substitute to which the pronoun could refer, double check to make sure the reference is unmistakable.

> UNCLEAR   After Schmeling fought Louis, he was never the
>   same.

The pronoun *he* could refer to either boxer.

> CLEAR   After he fought Louis, Schmeling was never the
>   same.

Now the pronoun can refer only to Schmeling. The writer revised the sentence so that the second noun is not mentioned until after the pronoun reference is established.

2. When a group of words intervenes between the antecedent and the pronoun, the reference may be unclear.

> UNCLEAR   The jury was served doughnuts in the lunchroom
>   that tasted stale.

The lunchroom, we assume, is not what tasted stale. Reframing the sentence so that the pronoun is beside its antecedent clears up the problem.

> CLEAR   In the lunchroom, the jury was served doughnuts
>   that tasted stale.
>
> UNCLEAR   The lawless and intuitive character of modern art is
>   a familiar theme that Professor Longstreth delights
>   in criticizing.

Does Professor Longstreth delight in criticizing the theme, or in criticizing the lawless and intuitive character of modern art?

> CLEAR   The lawless and intuitive character of modern art
>   that Professor Longstreth delights in criticizing is a
>   familiar theme.

Now the pronoun stands beside the subject that is its antecedent. It could not be thought to refer to *theme.* If the writer had intended the clause to modify *theme,* he or she might have put it this way:

> CLEAR   The lawless and intuitive character of modern art is
>   a familiar theme, a theme that Professor Longstreth
>   delights in criticizing.

Repeating the noun *theme* makes the statement unambiguous. Don't be afraid of repeating a word in the interest of clarity.

3. A pronoun should refer to the subject of the previous clause, as this one does:

> New models had arrived at the showrooms, and they were all different colors.

We know that the models, not the showrooms, were different colors. When the pronoun refers not to the subject but to some other part of the clause, however, we may be confused.

> **UNCLEAR**   If your children refuse to eat their vegetables, slice them up and hide them in a savory beef pie.

What, we may well ask, is to be sliced up? Does the pronoun refer to the subject of the clause, *children,* or to the last noun in it, *vegetables?*

> **CLEAR**   Slice up the vegetables and hide them in a savory beef pie if your children refuse to eat them.

The writer has saved the children from a horrible fate.

4. Avoid confusion with demonstrative pronouns, such as *this, that, these,* and *those,* particularly when they begin a sentence.

> **UNCLEAR**   Otto nibbled at the frosting and finally took a little slice of the wedding cake and began to eat it. This so angered the bride that she dumped the whole cake on his head.

What angered the bride? the nibbling? taking a slice? eating it?

> **CLEAR**   Otto nibbled at the frosting and finally took a little slice of the wedding cake and began to eat it. Seeing him eating it so angered the bride that she dumped the whole cake on his head.

When using a demonstrative pronoun, be sure its reference is clear.

5. Avoid problems in vagueness with the ubiquitous *it.*

> **UNCLEAR**   The sheepdog sniffed the Chihuahua, and then it went to sleep on its side.

Which dog went to sleep? And did it go to sleep on its own side or on the other dog's side?

> **CLEAR**   The sheepdog went to sleep on its side after sniffing the Chihuahua.

6. Do not use a pronoun with an unstated antecedent.

> **UNCLEAR**   At the New York Stock Exchange, they buy or sell securities listed on that exchange only.

Who is *they?* There is no antecedent.

> **CLEAR**   At the New York Stock Exchange, traders buy or
>   sell securities listed on that exchange only.

Antecedents implied in adjectives, adverbs, or possessives can also be confusing.

> **UNCLEAR**   She laughed raucously, and that unnerved him.

Raucously is an adverb and cannot function as an antecedent.

> **CLEAR**   Her raucous laughter unnerved him.

> **UNCLEAR**   Tommy Manville was a much-married millionaire.
>   It was usually to starlets and dancers.

Much-married is an adjective and cannot serve as an antecedent for *it.*

> **CLEAR**   Tommy Manville was a much-married millionaire.
>   Usually he married starlets and dancers.

In almost all problems of reference, the reader can figure out the meaning, but the writer should make it clear.

EXERCISE FOR PRONOUN REFERENCE

Rewrite the following sentences to correct any problems in pronoun reference and to clarify the meaning you think the sentence has.

a. After Clarence overdosed on hot fudge while Rudolph ate peanut butter, he never trusted him again.

b. We all ordered chicken at the North Beach restaurant that had a tasty red sauce over it.

c. I have never seen a mother totally reject her daughter, no matter how angry and even humiliated she was.

d. I have never seen a mother totally reject her daughter, no matter how dissolute and degenerate she was.

e. If you compare the morals of people today with those of the most devout and enlightened people of the Middle Ages, you will see that they fall short.

f. When the players persist in breaking all the rules, change them.

g. The students in the dormitories made such messes on the floors of the dining rooms that Mrs. Hassenfuss had the staff hose them down and sweep them out.

h. In the women's dressing room, they often leave wet towels on the floor, and I have to nag at them.

i. Liz Taylor has lost thousands of pounds. It can't be either healthy or fun.

j. Getting into medical school isn't easy. They have to do well in college and on their MCATs.

COMMA SPLICES AND FUSED SENTENCES

Independent clauses of a compound sentence are joined either by a conjunction and a comma or by a semicolon.

Brutus was careful, but Cassius was cunning.

Jack Sprat could eat no fat; his wife could eat no lean.

When two independent clauses are joined by a comma alone, the error is called a *comma splice.*

COMMA SPLICE   I sauntered happily down Connecticut Avenue, it reminded me of my old neighborhood.

Expecting a dependent clause or a phrase to follow a comma alone, the reader may misread. To correct the problem, the writer could add a conjunction or replace the comma with a semicolon.

REVISED   I sauntered happily down Connecticut Avenue, for it reminded me of my old neighborhood.

When two independent clauses are joined by no internal punctuation at all, the error is called a *fused* or *run-on sentence.*

FUSED   Sudan is the largest country in Africa its land mass is larger than California's.

Absence of punctuation forces the reader to rethink the sentence to figure out the meaning. A comma and a conjunction or a semicolon will do the trick.

REVISED   Sudan is the largest country in Africa; its land mass is larger than California's.

The comma splice and the fused sentence can also be corrected by making two sentences.

REVISED   I sauntered happily down Connecticut Avenue. It reminded me of my old neighborhood.

EXERCISE FOR COMMA SPLICES AND FUSED SENTENCES

Correct the errors in the following sentences.
a. Walt Whitman's *Leaves of Grass* was poorly received its reception subjected Whitman to embarrassment.
b. When he was a senator, Nixon's votes on domestic affairs were conservative, his votes on foreign affairs were more liberal.
c. People call Salinas, California, the lettuce capital of the world also many artichokes are grown in the area.

    d. Jefferson and Adams wrote the Declaration of Independence, they died
       on the same day.

    e. Comma splices and fused sentences are a problem, they catch us unawares.

    f. These articles and essays provide an education, it is a humane and even
       entertaining one.

    g. The water for the Genoan fountains came from aqueducts, the water
       also powered the mills nearby.

    h. The grain in Sri Lanka is broadcast over cleared fields they are fertilized
       with ashes.

    i. Long ago, salt was used as money in parts of Africa, rain could be a
       disaster.

    j. Population increases come in spurts there was a prolonged rise in the
       late Middle Ages.

SENTENCE FRAGMENTS

From time to time we are all guilty of careless writing. We have a
thought, and, before it is completed, another intervenes and knocks the
first off the track. The result can be the error called a *sentence fragment.*
A sentence fragment lacks either a subject or a verb or contains a dependent clause but no independent clause.

> The building designed by Frank Lloyd Wright
>
> Walked fast in order to get home by dusk
>
> Because I said so

Not complete sentences, these are not complete thoughts. What is being
said about the building? Who was walking home, and what about it? Because you said so, what? The thought is fragmented, left hanging in midair.

    Sometimes you can catch fragments by reading aloud. A sentence
lacking either a subject or a verb will sound flat and toneless. A sentence that is only a moorless dependent clause will sound unfinished.

    For a discussion of the proper use of a fragment, refer to "Using
Fragments" in Chapter 12.

EXERCISES FOR SENTENCE FRAGMENTS

  1. Identify the fragments in the following brief passages.

    a. The Seine was seldom used for anything but commerce. Although some
       sightseers on Sundays going to Saint-Cloud.

    b. There is less consumption of beef. But more of fish and chicken. Many
       people have become vegetarians.

    c. He was exhausted and his feet hurt. His shoulders and calves as well,
       having run so very far. Sitting down felt good. Then getting up and run-
       ning on.

    d. When she opened the letter she found a check for one hundred dollars from her aunt. Thinking that it was quite a lot of money for a birthday present when she turned sixteen. She laughed.

    e. These times that try men's souls. Said Thomas Paine.

    f. East German money had a picture of happy schoolchildren on one side. A picture of Goethe on the other side.

    g. This essay is by far the most important I have written. Because it runs counter to prevailing opinion.

    h. Plato says the youth of Athens taught games and songs and dancing to the very gods themselves. Apollo, Athena. Plato wasn't too interested in literary studies. Rather, in poetry, largely for the sake of the music.

    i. I have learned much in school. If, indeed, because people have forced me to study subjects in which I had no natural interest.

2. Rewrite this passage so that there are no sentence fragments.

> Beyond the maze of alleys was an indoor market. Women guarded the tables. Loaded with fruits, vegetables, and melons. They chatted and nursed babies. Their social life. The mounds of produce came from the big local plantations. A false but incredibly vivid illusion that all was abundance in that poor country.

MODIFIERS: MISPLACED, SQUINTING, AND DANGLING

When we don't make it clear which word a modifier is related to, we run the risk of confusing our readers. The three types of unclear modifiers are misplaced, squinting, and dangling.

1. Misplaced modifiers: a modifier is misplaced if it seems to apply to the wrong word in the sentence.

MISPLACED	Gooey, sticky, and sweet, my friend Celeste put the finishing touches on the Baked Alaska.

At first glance, we have to assume the writer is calling Celeste "gooey, sticky, and sweet." What a friend! But perhaps he meant the Baked Alaska.

REVISED	My friend Celeste put the finishing touches on the gooey, sticky, and sweet Baked Alaska.

Sometimes we have to snicker at the effect of a misplaced modifier.

MISPLACED	Coming around the corner, the Empire State Building stood before the newly arrived immigrants, then the tallest in the world.
REVISED	The Empire State Building, then the tallest in the world, stood before the newly arrived immigrants coming around the corner.

In the revision, the modifiers are placed close to the items they modify, and the meaning is clearer, though not so amusing.

> **MISPLACED**   People should not toy with knives and forks who are eating their supper.
>
> **REVISED**   People who are eating their supper should not toy with knives and forks.

2. Squinting modifiers: some modifiers straddle a sentence and seem to "squint" in both directions. The reader cannot know which part of the sentence such a modifier belongs to.

> **SQUINTING**   That he cleaned up the car thoroughly pleased her.

Did he thoroughly clean up the car, or was she thoroughly pleased?

> **REVISED**   That he thoroughly cleaned up the car pleased her.
> That he cleaned up the car pleased her thoroughly.

Some adverbs (*just, merely, only, simply,* and so on) often seem to float blithely through a sentence, whimsically dropping between any two words they fancy. *Only* is particularly capricious. Think of all the places it could fall in this sentence.

> I have eyes for you.

Be sure to place these adverbs firmly and unambiguously.

> I have eyes for only you.

Sometimes a long phrase or clause will squint badly.

> **SQUINTING**   The coach said while the game was in progress he would make no substitutions.

Did the coach make the statement before or during the game?

> **REVISED**   The coach said he would make no substitutions while the game was in progress.
>
> While the game was in progress, the coach said he would make no substitutions.

3. Dangling modifiers: if a sentence simply lacks the word the modifier is supposed to modify, that modifier is dangling.

> **DANGLING**   Before riding the horses, all pets should be tethered.

Reading a sign like that, we do a slight double take: the *pets* will be riding the horses? Then we rewrite the sentence.

> **REVISED**   Before riding the horses, riders should tether all pets.

Most of the time, the dangling modifier occurs because the writer has not brought the modified term forward from the previous sentence.

DANGLING   We went to the Smiths' last night. The evening passed pleasantly, eating candy and playing music.

Eating candy and playing music dangles because the writer has left *we* in the previous sentence.

REVISED   We went to the Smiths' last night. We passed the evening pleasantly, eating candy and playing music.

<hr>

EXERCISE FOR MODIFIERS

Rewrite the following sentences to make clear which words the modifiers modify.

a. While telling a joke to friends, a boa constrictor coiled menacingly over Conroy's head.

b. Rationing food and experiencing nightly air raids, the war was extremely difficult for the British.

c. Some say the German people had themselves only to blame.

d. Listening to the glorious voice of Leontyne Price, the opera *Aida* was a marvelous occasion.

e. Second-guessing the coach's strategy, a football game can be a Monday morning social encounter.

f. More than a millennium and a half before Evelyn Waugh wrote *Brideshead Revisited,* amid the pagan influence of late antiquity, Augustine defined the very theology on which Waugh based his beliefs.

g. Eerily similar to my own experience, my friend returned to her car to find an old lady sitting in the front seat.

h. Whatever happens, I only want the best for you, not your other boyfriend.

i. Sugarcane appeared as a common food during the sixteenth century only of the rich.

j. The instructor said during the exam no one should look at either notes or the textbook.

<hr>

PARALLEL CONSTRUCTION

1. When thoughts are parallel, express them in the same grammatical construction.

To be Italian is to be fortunate.

By so doing, you not only indicate the connection between the thoughts but also create a more vigorous prose. When, in contrast, you present similar or equally important ideas in grammatically different forms, you make reading more difficult and less interesting. Compare these two sentences:

> **NONPARALLEL**   France's foreign policy irritates the British because of its arrogance and it is chauvinistic.

> **REVISED**   France's foreign policy irritates the British because of its arrogance and its chauvinism.

Ideas in parallel form are more easily grasped. Be particularly careful in constructing a series of equal parts. Whatever form you use for the first part, repeat for each subsequent part.

> **NONPARALLEL**   Use epoxy to fix broken dishes, for patching cracked glass, if your favorite knickknack is broken, and as a sealant for almost any broken surface.

In this example each item has a different grammatical construction— and the result is a mess.

> **REVISED**   Use epoxy to fix broken dishes, to patch cracked glass, to repair a favorite knickknack, and to seal almost any broken surface.

Sometimes in keeping a list parallel, you will need to repeat a word to maintain clarity.

> **UNCLEAR**   We chased the fox through the woods, the hills, the creek, and a dozen trees.

At first we thought the chase was through the hills, through the creek, and through a dozen trees.

> **REVISED**   We chased the fox through the woods, over the hills, over the creek, and up a dozen trees.

Writers can commit more grievous errors than repetition—confusion for one.

2. When you use a coordinating conjunction, be sure you have the same grammatical construction on both sides.

> **NONPARALLEL**   The woman hated all kinds of music but who loved painting.

In this construction *who loved painting,* a dependent clause, is in a different grammatical form from *The woman hated all kinds of music,* an independent clause.

> **REVISED**   The woman hated all kinds of music but loved painting.

3. When you use correlative conjunctions (*both/and, either/or, neither/nor,* or *not only/but also*), use the same form following each member of the pair.

NONPARALLEL   Either he is a genius or a fraud.

In this example, *either* is followed by an independent clause, but *or* is followed only by a noun. Both should be followed by the same grammatical form.

REVISED   Either he is a genius or he is a fraud.

He is either a genius or a fraud.

EXERCISE FOR PARALLEL CONSTRUCTION

Rewrite these sentences to make the thoughts parallel.
a. For years, Ryan had three things on his mind: watching out for his brother's temper tantrums, what his friends thought of him, and he wanted to break away from his overprotective mother.
b. Many consider Titian the greatest Venetian painter, but some thinking Tintoretto achieved equal greatness.
c. Either the instructor knows his subject or should be fired.
d. Not only was Jimmy Carter a farmer but an engineer.
e. The mechanic told Mrs. Filoli that the spark plugs ought to be replaced, she needed a new fan belt, and relining the brakes for the car to run well.
f. You will either pay your rent or you will have to move.
g. Some historians believe the major reason the British colonized Australia was to head France away from India, but sending criminals to get rid of them according to other historians.
h. She had many plans: to travel to China, getting married and having a family, and she had a legal career in mind.
i. The rich were quite aware of fashion in the sixteenth century: women not only wore short stilts to protect themselves from the muddy streets, which fashion had first appeared in Venice, the mantilla from Spain, and they also wore many jewels as well as ruffs of fine lace.
j. To linger over dinner having a fine glass of wine at hand is what can make a person glad to be alive.

20

Punctuation

No steel can pierce the human heart so chillingly as
a period at the right moment.
                    — ISAAC BABEL (1894-1941)
                      RUSSIAN WRITER

When you use periods, commas, semicolons, and other punctuation,
you are instructing your reader on how to read your work. Punctuation,
therefore, isn't an afterthought or window dressing; it is your practical
partner in the effort to be clear. Careful punctuation gets your message
across; careless punctuation hinders communication.

ENDINGS

Periods

Periods mark off the endings of sentences. They tell your reader, "This
is the end of a complete thought." They also signal abbreviations:
Gov., St. Augustine, Ibid., reg. U.S. Pat. Off. (See "Abbreviations" in
Chapter 21). And they mark off letters and numbers in outlines and figures: *A. Endings.*

Exclamation Points and Question Marks

The exclamation point tells your reader that your sentence is emphatic; the question mark, that it is a question.

> I see a ghost! Or is it my kid brother in a sheet?

In formal prose, use exclamation marks stingily. They are all right in quotations.

> When Shelley writes "Oh world! Oh life! Oh time!" he tells us . . .

They are also proper in the rare situation that calls for dialogue.

> Newspapers are like a neurotic friend ever at your elbow who cries, at every event whether large or small, "What a decision! What a cataclysm! This is unprecedented!"

But let your own sentences be emphatic without bullhorns.
Never double end punctuation. You would not, for example, write

> Who wrote *What Price Glory??*

One question mark is ample.

COMMAS

You will use commas more than any other punctuation mark. They tell your reader how to read your sentences. Commas have many uses. Here are the eleven you will encounter most often.

1. Before coordinating conjunctions: use a comma before a conjunction that connects two independent clauses, that is, before the *and, but, for,* and so on in a compound sentence.

> He liked sports, but he never exercised.

2. In a series: use a comma between all elements in a series of three or more nouns, verbs, or phrases.

> The pen, the pencil, and the typewriter all failed her.
> She whistled, tap-danced, and yodeled better than her mother.
> Playing jacks, eating candy, and chatting with friends occupied her days.

3. Between coordinate adjectives: coordinate adjectives are adjectives you can arrange in any order without changing the meaning.

> Here we are at the lush, moist, comforting oasis.

Not all adjectives in a series are coordinate, however. The adjective next to the noun sometimes combines with the noun to form a unit, and the other adjectives modify the whole unit.

> Early fliers hated the long, weary dawn patrols.

Dawn and *patrols* cannot be separated; *long* and *weary* modify *dawn patrols*. To check whether you are dealing with coordinate adjectives, see if an *and* can logically be placed between the last two adjectives:

> Here we are at the lush and moist and comforting oasis.
> Early fliers hated the long and weary and dawn patrols.

If you can't logically place *and* between adjectives, don't put a comma there.

4. After introductory material: use a comma to set off an initial long phrase or dependent clause from the main part of the sentence.

> Because of the coldest frost in thirty years, half of Florida's orange crop was lost.
> After I had swum across the Amazon River, I dried my hair.

The comma tells the reader to pause and not to run the thoughts together. You can, however, omit the comma after a very short introductory phrase.

> After swimming I dried my hair.

When in doubt, use your ear, and put the comma at the pause.

5. In quotation: use a comma to separate a direct quotation from its attribution, whether the attribution is at the end, at the beginning, or in the middle.

> "We are not amused," said the queen.
> The king asked, "Who is not amused?"
> "Who," asked the court jester, "wants to know?"

6. For nonessential information: use commas to tell the reader whether information is or is not essential to the meaning of the sentence.

Use a comma to set off words, phrases, or clauses that provide nonessential information (also called *nonrestrictive elements*).

> Harry's wife, Deirdre, was named den mother of the year.

Because Harry has only one wife, the name *Deirdre* is not essential to understanding the sentence and so is set off by commas.

Do not use commas to set off words, phrases, or clauses that provide essential information (also called *restrictive elements*).

As a result, Harry's son Russell became an Eagle Scout.

Because Harry has two sons, the name *Russell* is essential to the meaning of the sentence and therefore should not be set off by commas.

In the following sentence, the commas make a great deal of difference:

All the test pilots, who drink too much, will be grounded without pay.

All the test pilots who drink too much will be grounded without pay.

When *who drink too much* is set off by commas, the sentence means that (1) all tests pilots drink too much, and (2) all will be grounded without pay. When *who drink too much* is not set off by commas, the sentence means that (1) at least some test pilots do not drink too much, and (2) only those who do will be grounded.

7. With parenthetical and interruptive elements: all sorts of expressions and words pop into the middle of a sentence to interrupt. Mark them off with commas.

ASIDES	The emu lives, if you want to call it that, in Australia.
INTERJECTIONS AND EMPHATIC ELEMENTS	The emu, that flightless bird, runs rapidly.
	Well, no, it is not soothing to look at because its neck is, after all, four feet long.
CONJUNCTIVE ADVERBS	Moreover, it is almost extinct.
	Its cousin the ostrich, however, is protected for its feathers.
NOUNS OF DIRECT ADDRESS	What do you think of Mr. Steinbrenner, Mr. Winfield?

For other ways to set off parenthetical and interruptive elements, see "Parentheses and Dashes."

8. Between titles and names: use commas to separate names from titles that follow, such as *Jr., M.D., Ph.D., Inc.,* and *Ltd.*

Harry Horvath, Jr., and his wife, Deirdre Failin Horvath, M.D., are joint owners of Horvath Chinchilla Farms, Inc.

9. After place names: use commas after both city and state.

Every year Aunt Hepzibah leaves her boardinghouse in Bent Twig, Wyoming, to visit Harry.

10. For day and year: use commas to set off the year. Do not use commas to set off only the month and year.

On December 7, 1941, the Royal Japanese Air Force bombed Pearl Harbor, and the war ended in August 1945.

11. In long, complicated sentences: use commas to prevent misreading. When a long, twisty sentence threatens to leave your reader behind, you can sometimes break it into readable hunks with a considerate comma.

> In my opinion, aerobic exercise helps develop thick, muscular calves, and minds that are well rested and alert.

Because of its structure, this sentence would not automatically get a second comma. As you can see, however, without that comma, we would have thick, muscular minds, as well as calves that are well rested and alert. But be careful to avoid using commas ungrammatically or indiscriminately.

■■■■■■■ **EXERCISE FOR COMMAS** ■■■■■■■■■■■■■■■■■■■■■■■■

> Add commas at the appropriate places in the following sentences and then state the governing rule for each comma you add.
> a. The intelligence that a man has and most other animals lack at least according to experts lies in the power of language.
> b. Freedom of speech guaranteed by our Constitution is important for without it we would not learn of new not necessarily popular or conventional ideas.
> c. In my long association with books and libraries I have made many friends across the centuries.
> d. Being a tall lithe handsome redheaded talented tennis player she was greeted enthusiastically by hopeful ambitious tournament managers who believed she could draw audiences for their tennis tournament.
> e. Tea which came into Europe from China with the Portuguese did not catch on at once because of its exotic flavor.
> f. I was born on July 30, 1972 in the little town of Oneonta Alabama making my parents Andy and Mary Braudel very happy.

PARENTHESES AND DASHES

Two other ways to mark off parenthetical elements are parentheses and dashes. Each has its own function.

Parentheses

Parentheses are more emphatic than pairs of commas because they decisively block off the material between them.

> Years from now (and not too many years at that) the sexual revolution will seem as corrupt as the double standard that preceded it.

Parentheses are a cue to the reader to lower the voice, so to speak. Don't overuse parentheses; no one likes a constant whisperer. Enclose material within them that may be interesting but is really a digression.

> Present at Yalta were Joseph Stalin, Franklin D. Roosevelt (who would be dead within two months), and Winston Churchill.

Many people are uncertain about how to punctuate when parentheses are present. Here are four guidelines.

1. When the parentheses are within a sentence, punctuate the sentence exactly as if the parentheses were not there.

> Debate used to rage about whether the dog or the cat is smarter (not an unimportant topic for some of us); opinion now leans in favor of Fido.

Be sure not to put the sentence's punctuation inside the closing parentheses.

INCORRECT	Sixteen ounces is the equivalent of 454 grams (a ratio of 28.37 to 1.)
CORRECT	Sixteen ounces is the equivalent of 454 grams (a ratio of 28.37 to 1).

2. When a complete sentence stands by itself in parentheses— that is, when it is not inside another sentence—the period falls within the parentheses.

> Saying the dog is smarter than the cat does not devalue the latter in the eyes of cat fans. (It is doubtful whether anything could.)

In an occasional bizarre case a complete and parenthesized sentence can fall within another sentence. In such a case, omit both the initial capital letter and the terminal punctuation for the parenthetical sentence.

> Beekeeping is hazardous (you always risk being stung) but rewarding.

3. Use parentheses when appropriate to enclose acronyms, dates, or numbers.

> Walter Reuther founded the United Auto Workers (UAW).
>
> John Updike's *In the Beauty of the Lilies* (1996) received excellent reviews.
>
> He comes from Cleveland, Tennessee (pop. 26,415), not Cleveland, Ohio (pop. 573,822).

4. If you like the way they look, use parentheses to set off numbers in a numbered list.

(1) Name
(2) Address
(3) Occupation

Dashes

Even more emphatic than parentheses are dashes. They indicate not whispers but shouts.

> Although William Howard Taft was obese—a dinner guest once inquired whether he was expecting—he lived to be seventy-three years old.

Framed by dashes, this joke emerges loud and clear.

1. Use the dash—sparingly—to indicate interruptions, informal breaks in construction, or special emphasis.

> My best friend—my dog Kent, I mean—has left me forever.
>
> Muhammad Ali—then known as Cassius Clay—won an Olympic Gold Medal in 1960.

2. In typing, form the dash with two hyphens. Don't leave a space on either side, and do not use any commas, colons, semicolons, or parentheses adjacent to a dash—the dash is the only punctuation needed. When you use a dash before the final element in a sentence, close with the usual period.

> Caesar loved Cleopatra—but not as much as she thought.

Like the other components of writing, these emphatic markers become meaningless if you overuse them. Save them for special occasions.

EXERCISE FOR PARENTHESES AND DASHES

Place either parentheses or dashes at appropriate places in the following sentences. Explain briefly why you chose the material you did to set off and why you chose either parentheses or dashes.

a. Cinema has its own traditions and techniques similar to those of the novel but its history is of course much shorter and more dramatic in the rate of change.

b. Rolf Hochhuth's play has been the occasion for disagreement indeed for riots because it shows not merely suggests that Pius XII did not oppose the Nazis very vigorously.

c. Most of us wear masks most of the time and our lives are blighted.

d. At this date April 20, 1988, the National League West leader is Los Angeles won 9 and lost 4 and the National League East leader is Pittsburgh won 9 and lost 3.

e. After the twelfth century when fireplaces were first built into the wall cooking was done on the hearth with the family huddled close by.

SEMICOLONS

A semicolon announces a pause in the thought in a sentence. In the strength of pause it is exactly halfway between a period and a comma, and to indicate it a period sits on top of a comma. You can use this pause in two ways.

1. Between independent clauses. Use a semicolon to indicate a close connection between independent clauses.

> The pollsters predicted a close election; the smart money knew otherwise.

Used this way, the semicolon tightly holds together two or more complete thoughts. It indicates strong likeness or balance.

> He loved biology; he hated English; he was indifferent to languages.

The semicolon is also effective in suggesting a clash or contrast.

> He endured her for her money; she worshiped him for his soul.

You must have independent clauses on both sides of the semicolon in these constructions.

2. When you have a series of items that have internal punctuation, use the semicolon to separate the items clearly. This use of the semicolon is less common but no less useful. Here too the semicolon connects equal elements.

> At the party we saw Sam, the electrician; Tim, the magician; Bill Jones; Wanda Everts, the land, sea, and air endurance champion of England, China, and Wales; and Evert's dog, Spence.

Without semicolons, this sentence would be hopelessly confusing.

By all means learn to use semicolons; they will add subtlety and grace to your style. Do not overuse them, however, or their power to balance and connect will evaporate.

COLONS

The colon is the vaudeville punctuation mark. Its task is to introduce with a certain fanfare. It says, Here it is, folks! Here are the most common uses of the colon.

1. To introduce a series or a list.

> Kate visited three cities in Ohio: Akron, Columbus, and Toledo.

2. To introduce a short quotation.

> Eisenhower said it more than once: "I shall go to Korea."

3. To introduce, and thus emphasize, a single element.

> This element may be as short as a single word.

> When he asked to borrow money, I knew what to say: No.

The element introduced may be a phrase.

> There in the doorway stood something I never dreamed I'd see: my grandfather in a gorilla suit.

The element introduced may be another independent clause.

> Jealousy serves only one purpose for humanity: it alienates people from those they most dearly love.

Many careful stylists do not capitalize after a colon used in this way, except for proper names: what follows the colon is not a new thought but an extension of the existing one.

The colon has formal uses, too.

4. To introduce a long quotation set off from the text. (See "Integrating Quotations into Your Text" in Chapter 13 for a discussion of how to present long quotations.)

5. To introduce the body of a letter after the salutation in formal correspondence.

> Dear Senator Boxer:

6. To separate the title and the subtitle of a book.

> *Madness and Civilization: A History of Insanity in the Age of Reason*

7. To separate city and publisher in lists of works cited.

> New York: Knopf

8. To separate chapter and verse in biblical citations.

> Jeremiah 21:3

Note that there is no space after the colon in this use.

9. To separate hour and minutes in reporting time.

> It is 9:43 a.m. as I write this.

There is no space after the colon in this use either.

━━━━━ **EXERCISE FOR SEMICOLONS AND COLONS** ━━━━━

Place semicolons and colons in the following sentences, and explain your decisions for each.

a. The rain had stopped the sun was out the picnic was on.

b. On Christmas morning I received the present I had always longed for the *Encyclopaedia of Religion and Ethics.*

c. Americans were thrilled by General McAuliffe's defiant response to the demand for surrender at the Battle of the Bulge "Nuts!"

d. The early twentieth century produced a spate of fine writers who were expatriates Thomas Mann a German who lived his last years in Switzerland James Joyce an Irishman who lived in Trieste, Paris, and Zurich and Ernest Hemingway an American who spent much of his adult life in France.

e. I have four favorite things pistachio ice cream cowboy movies playing golf and my gerbil Patsy.

f. This production of *A Midsummer Night's Dream* has a most unusual aspect the same person plays Puck and Oberon.

g. Sanity permeates the literature of the eighteenth century insanity permeates the literature of the twentieth.

h. The whole thing was a mess Tim loved Sue Sue loved Craig Craig loved Carol Carol loved Tim.

APOSTROPHES

Apostrophes serve two important functions: to form possessives and to mark contractions.

1. To form the possessive of nouns and indefinite pronouns. Apostrophes used in this manner signify ownership or association.

To form the possessive of a singular noun or indefinite pronoun, add an apostrophe followed by an -*s*.

Lincoln's beard

the cat's meow

Amos's bee sting

the business's employees

everybody's favorite

To form the possessive of a plural noun not ending in -*s,* add an apostrophe followed by an -*s*.

the children's squeals

the Men's Glee Club

To form the possessive of a plural noun ending in -*s,* add only an apostrophe.

the Mohicans' war cry

the girls' crazy hats

the Joneses' dinner party

To form the possessive of a noun composed of several words, add the -'*s* only to the last word.

my brother-in-law's haircut

To show possession by more than one individual, add an apostrophe followed by an -*s* only to the name of the last individual if the possession is joint.

Harpo and Groucho's brother was named Zeppo. [The brother belongs to both.]

To show possession by more than one individual, add an apostrophe followed by an -*s* to each individual's name if possession is separate.

Harpo's and Groucho's careers were brilliant. [Each has his separate career.]

Avoid awkward possessives by using *of* or other prepositional constructions.

AWKWARD	After the collision, the Williamses' Acura was ruined.
REVISED	After the collision, the Acura owned by the Williamses was ruined.

2. To show contractions. Used in this manner, the apostrophe shows where you drop letters to contract two words into one. Words frequently *elided,* as this is called, are *can, do, does, have, is, not, will.*

If I can't find my algebra book, I'll flunk.

For the most part, contractions are still limited to informal prose and dialogue. Careful stylists keep them to a minimum. High informal prose should not sound chatty or breezy.

BREEZY	Japan couldn't've conquered the whole of Asia because it didn't have the resources.
REVISED	Japan could not have conquered the whole of Asia because it did not have the resources.

You should, however, use contractions when the full form would sound awkward.

| AWKWARD | Is this not the same as claiming that Japan would have been defeated even without the United States? |
| REVISED | Isn't this the same as claiming that Japan would have been defeated even without the United States? |

Tiny confusions and mistaken identities plague contractions. The contraction *it's* is often mistaken for the possessive pronoun *its*. There is no apostrophe in the possessive. In the contraction, the apostrophe marks the spot where the *i* in *is* is missing.

INCORRECT	Corsica is French, but its often rebellious.
CORRECT	Corsica is French, but it's often rebellious.
INCORRECT	It's main exports are olive oil, wine, and citrus fruits.
CORRECT	Its main exports are olive oil, wine, and citrus fruits.

Much the same confusion occurs in using *your* and *you're,* and *their* and *they're.* In both cases the first is a possessive form of a pronoun (*you* and *they*), and the second is a contraction of two words (*you are* and *they are*). Perhaps three correct sentences will make the differences clear.

Our beagle always knows when it's time for its dinner.

Your taxi will arrive in five minutes if you're lucky.

They're trying to find their lottery tickets.

You should avoid cutesy apostrophes in your writing. *Steak 'n' eggs* is *steak and eggs, a little bit o' soul* is *a little bit of soul.* Even *rock 'n' roll* suffers little when written *rock and roll. Three o'clock,* however, is standard; most of us do not know that it is a contraction for *three of the clock.*

Do not use an apostrophe before the *-s* to form the plural of abbreviations, capital letters, words used as words, or specific decades unless the *-s* alone would be confusing.

His high Cs are sharp, but his low Fs are delicious.

It will take sixteen IBMs to compete with one of our EECs.

In some ways, the 1890s were similar to the 1920s.

If, however, the *-s* alone might be confusing, precede it with an apostrophe.

He had difficulty pronouncing S's, A's, and I's.

Here are the do's and don'ts of the apostrophe.

▬▬▬▬▬▬ **EXERCISES FOR APOSTROPHES** ▬▬▬▬▬▬▬▬▬

1. Place an apostrophe where appropriate in the following sentences, and be prepared to explain what you have done.
   a. I didnt believe Id flunk because its not that hard a course.
   b. The boys game wasnt over until Billy Billings ball bounced over the players heads. Its bounce was at least fifty feet and now its gone for good.
   c. The editor-in-chiefs hat sits on the back of his head, and when Im angry its tempting to knock it off.
   d. The company lost its suit in court because its case was so weak.
   e. Its anybodys guess whether the Joneses summer house withstood the tornado, but my brothers-in-laws place was completely demolished.

2. Correct any mistakes in placing apostrophes in the following passages, and add any apostrophes that are needed.
   a. My friend James father hunts quail and hes taking James' with him this weekend. There staying at you're uncles. Im of two minds about there plans but they're going anyway.
   b. Fortunately no one was home when the Hopkinses' houseboat blew up the other night because it's safety valve melted. I called the Hopkins's but their staying at Mrs. Hopkins' sister-in-law's. They're new houseboat won't be ready until June. By then itll be nice weather.
   c. I read in Montaignes essay's that sin "dwells in us as in it's own home." He says it's a rare person who conducts life well and they're few men admired by there households. Id like to know you're opinion. Mine is that Montaigne's a bit cynical.

PUNCTUATION OF QUOTATIONS

In this section we discuss when to use quotation marks and how to punctuate with, in, and around them.

Quotation marks have many uses; we'll focus on three.

1. Use quotation marks when you quote the words of others.

Nixon said, "I am not a crook."

In this example, a comma follows the attribution. When writers use the word *that* to introduce the quotation, no comma is necessary:

Nixon said that he was "not a crook."

Refer to "Integrating Quotations into Your Text" in Chapter 13 for ways to introduce and use quotations in your writing.

2. Use quotation marks to indicate titles of short works.

POEMS	T. S. Eliot's "Ash Wednesday" is my favorite poem.
STORIES	Eudora Welty wrote "Why I Live at the P.O."
CHAPTERS	Chapter 22 is titled "German Folklore."
ESSAYS AND ARTICLES	I read Montaigne's "Of Idleness."
SHORT MUSICAL COMPOSITIONS	The band played "Send in the Clowns."
EPISODES IN TELEVISION SERIES	I saw Jimmy Smits in "NYPD Blue."

Titles of other kinds of works require italics. See "Italics" in Chapter 21.

3. Use quotation marks around a slang word to show that the use is not standard.

After all the dancing, everybody at the party was "beat."

Sometimes writers use quotation marks to indicate irony or distaste.

He was one of the "beautiful people."

If you use such a word a second time in the work, don't use quotation marks: continued use of the word indicates that you have adopted the initial usage and are treating it as standard in this context. The point is, you can't have it both ways: you can't use a word and also dissociate yourself from the usage by enclosing it in quotation marks.

Punctuation marks seem to congregate around quotations. Five standard practices will ease the guesswork involved in how to use them.

1. For a quotation within a quotation, use single quotation marks.

Harry said to Deirdre, "When I said, 'Life would be easier if I were not married,' I was only speaking figuratively."

2. In American writing, periods and commas always come inside quotation marks, whether they are part of the quotation or not.

When we speak of "the next wave," we mean the same thing our grandparents meant when they said "the latest thing."

3. Colons and semicolons fall outside quotation marks.

I mean three things when I say "junk food": hamburgers, potato chips, and Twinkies.

4. Place a question mark or an exclamation point inside the quotation marks if it is part of the quotation. Place it outside if it is not part of the quotation.

Betty Rollin wrote "Motherhood: Who Needs It?"

But who wrote "Three Kinds of Thinking"?

5. When quoting a complete sentence, capitalize the first word.

> We can sympathize with King Lear when he cries, "How dost, my boy? Art cold?"

Do not capitalize if you introduce a short complete sentence with *that* or a similar construction.

> When Mark Twain tells us that "training is everything," we should believe him.

Do not capitalize the first word if you are quoting a fragment.

> By "different but equal," women's rights advocates still mean "equal."

Finally, when the attribution comes in the middle of a quoted sentence, do not capitalize after the interruption.

> "The only animal ever to be recorded as having been killed by a meteor," Professor Frohling said, "was an Egyptian dog."

ELLIPSES

Ellipses—that is, spaced periods in the body of a quotation—indicate that material has been omitted. They should never be used to change a meaning, but they can help to shorten a long passage that contains material not directly relevant to your purpose.

Here is a passage in which Charles Darwin extols the lowly worm:

> Archaeologists ought to be grateful to worms, as they protect and preserve for an indefinitely long period every object not liable to decay, which is dropped on the surface of the land, by burying it beneath their castings. Thus, also, many elegant and curious tessellated pavements and other ancient remains have been preserved; though no doubt the worms have in these cases been largely aided by earth washed and blown from the adjoining land, especially when cultivated. The old tessellated pavements have, however, often suffered by having subsided unequally from being unequally undermined by the worms. Even old massive walls may be undermined and subside; and no building is in this respect safe, unless the foundations lie six or seven feet beneath the surface, at a depth at which worms cannot work. It is probable that many monoliths and some old walls have fallen down from having been undermined by worms. (Charles Darwin, *The Formation of Vegetable Mould, Through the Action of Worms, with Observations on Their Habits*)

By placing ellipses where text has been deleted, you can quote just a part of this passage and still convey its point.

In extolling lowly worms, Darwin says that "they protect and preserve . . . every object not liable to decay . . . by burying it beneath their castings," thus preserving ancient remains. Darwin points out the negative side to this activity, however: "Even old massive walls. . . . have fallen down from having been undermined by worms."

1. If the deleted material comes in the middle of the sentence, use three spaced periods.

Darwin says, "They protect and preserve . . . every object not liable to decay."

2. If the deleted material includes the end of a sentence, use four spaced periods.

"Even old massive walls. . . . have fallen down."

3. Never use ellipses in place of a colon to introduce or set off material.

INCORRECT   After miles of wandering, they stood before it . . . the sea.

4. And finally, never use ellipses to fade in or out of a sentence.

INCORRECT   Sunsets are beautiful . . .

OTHER PUNCTUATION

Two relatively rare punctuation marks are brackets and virgules.

Brackets

Whenever you have to change a quotation to fit your context, enclose your words in brackets to indicate the changes.

ORIGINAL   Darwin says that "a weight of more than ten tons of dry earth annually passes through their bodies. . . ."

REVISED   Darwin says that "a weight of more than ten tons of dry earth annually passes through their [the worms'] bodies."

Warning: Overuse of this form will annoy your readers.

Virgules

1. The virgule, commonly called the *slash,* is used to show that several possibilities are equally appropriate.

King James was a gypsy/god/king.

2. It is also used to show line breaks in poetry when the lines are not indented but are continuous in the text.

When T. S. Eliot writes, "set down/This set down/This," the sense of dislocation is breathtaking.

EXERCISES FOR PUNCTUATION

1. Punctuate the following sentences according to proper form.
   a. Heideggers work is difficult I had to read every paragraph several times.
   b. Who was that person shouting help help help outside the police department at six oclock this morning
   c. Her presence her regal walk I mean communicated to us all a sense of confidence poise and financial well-being
   d. Even when I am showered clothed and fed I still have trouble facing up to the mornings most frightening task shaving
   e. Somewhere in a run-down garret in the Spanish-speaking part of Ecuador the most gung ho yodeling choir in the world is practicing for tomorrow nights world championships
   f. All I said to the teacher Bill said was Why are you flunking me you old crow
   g. If you have no money welcome to the club if you do have some lend me five dollars until tomorrow
   h. Monique found three curious items in her grandmothers hope chest a white silk dress still wrapped in the tissue in which it was bought a pair of dancing slippers seemingly made of glass and a jeweled tiara covered with hundreds of fake amethysts
   i. Oh gosh this is great
   j. The black-footed albatross also known as the gooney bird can fly well but has terrible trouble with takeoffs and landings
   k. He reached into the aquarium and you won't believe this swallowed both goldfish whole
   l. Sometimes I go crazy with all the NFLs NBAs and USHLs don't you
   m. Long before he had told her he would marry someone else

2. Restore the proper punctuation to the following paragraph. Read the paragraph aloud as a first step.

   To this day we cannot understand how a great civilized nation or at least a considerable part of it could in the twentieth century succumb to its fascination with a ridiculous complex-ridden petit-bourgeois man could fall for his pseudoscientific theories and in their name exterminate nations conquer continents and commit unbelievable cruelties Positivistic science Marxism included offers a variety of scientific explanations for this mysterious phenomenon but instead of eliminating the mystery they tend to deepen it For the cold "objective" reason that speaks to us from these explanations only underlines the disproportion between itself a power that claims to be the decisive one in this civilization and the mass insanity that has nothing in common with any form of rationality (Vaclav Havel, "Thriller")

21

Mechanics

Always do right. This will gratify some people and
astonish the rest.
                    —MARK TWAIN (1835–1910)
                         AMERICAN WRITER

With punctuation we mark and divide sentences; with mechanics we
treat things such as abbreviations, capitalization, italics, numbers, and
hyphens. Mechanics are conventions—general and often unspoken
agreements about basic procedures—that all writers observe. Your
reader will expect you to follow these conventions and may be confused if you deviate from them or are inconsistent. All careful writers
learn the proper mechanics to keep their writing clear and correct.

ABBREVIATIONS

Some abbreviations, which we have grouped in three categories, are
standard.

**1. Abbreviate many titles and terms—such as *Dr., Mr., Mrs., Ms.,
M.D., Ph.D., A.D., B.C., A.M., P.M., Hon., Msgr., Rev., St., Jr.,* and *Sr.***

2. Abbreviate institutional names as appropriate, and note that most are now written *without* periods: *AFL-CIO, EEC, EPA, GNP, IBM, NAACP, TWA.*

If your reader may not know what the abbreviation stands for, write the name out the first time you use it, and follow it with the abbreviation in parentheses.

> The journalist's assignment was to cover the Environmental Protection Agency (EPA).

Now you could use EPA throughout the rest of the essay. (By contrast, IBM is so universally known as *IBM* that many people would not recognize *International Business Machines*.)

Keep abbreviations to a minimum. Clumps of letters and periods make your writing read like a ticker tape. If your audience uses these abbreviations as part of its language, use them. Careful stylists, however, never use *TV* for *television*.

3. Abbreviate figures and some items in footnotes: *ed., fig., ft., p., sec.*

American practice is tending away from abbreviations in footnotes and figures, although *ed.* for "editor" and (less so) *p.* and *pp.* for "page" and "pages" are still common. (See "Documenting Your Sources" in Chapter 14 for explicit information on documentation.)

Generally speaking, don't abbreviate days, months (except in lists of works cited), cities, states (except in addressing envelopes), business designations (such as *company, incorporated,* and *limited*), units of measure (such as *ounce, pound, liter, meter, inch, foot, pint, gallon*), or Latin words and phrases (such as *versus* and *et cetera*).

CAPITALIZATION

Every sentence should, of course, begin with a capital letter. This indicates that you are starting a new thought. The capital has additional uses. We have summarized the uses and misuses in three rules.

1. Capitalize the first letter of each word except internal prepositions and articles in the following categories.

PROPER NAMES	Jane Doe
SPECIFIC PLACES	Mongolia

WORKS OF ART AND ENTERTAINMENT:

BOOKS	*The Agony and the Ecstasy*
MOVIES	*Star Wars*

PLAYS	*Hedda Gabler*
PAINTINGS AND SCULPTURES	*The Last Supper, The Thinker*
TELEVISION SHOWS	*Good Morning America*
RADIO SHOWS	*All Things Considered*

NOTABLE OBJECTS AND GROUPS:

SHIPS	*Queen Elizabeth II*
PLANES	*The Spirit of St. Louis*
FAMOUS STRUCTURES	Golden Gate Bridge
ORGANIZATIONS	United Auto Workers
INSTITUTIONS	Lehigh University
RELIGIONS	Roman Catholic
ETHNIC OR NATIONAL GROUPS	Ute Indians
LANGUAGES	French, Swahili

MARKS ON THE CALENDAR:

DAYS	Wednesday
MONTHS	April
HOLIDAYS	Passover

HISTORICAL ITEMS:

ERAS	Middle Ages
DOCUMENTS	Magna Carta
EVENTS	Civil War

SACRED BEINGS AND TERMS:

DEITIES	God, Allah
SACRED PERSONS	Buddha
SACRED SCRIPTURES	the Koran

Capitalize titles when they precede proper names.

> Senator Olympia Snowe comes from Maine.

Do not capitalize titles that stand alone or titles that come after the proper name.

> Olympia Snowe is the senator from Maine.
> Being a senator is hard work.

An exception to this rule is complete titles of very high and special rank.

> William Rehnquist is the Chief Justice of the United States.

2. Do not capitalize the first letter of words in these categories.

SEASONS	winter
GENERAL GROUPS	the middle class
ABSTRACTIONS	love, art, nature

3. Be aware that some words appear both capitalized and uncapitalized, depending on their use.

Capitalize names of regions.

> New Orleans is the gem of the South.

But do not capitalize directions.

> Go west, young man.

Capitalize names of college courses and departments.

> I think Anthropology 119 is the best course offered by the Department of Anthropology.

Do not capitalize the names of general subjects.

> I love anthropology, but I don't like mathematics.

ITALICS

1. To indicate italics on a typewriter, underline the material. Use italics for titles of

BOOKS	*War and Peace*
PERIODICALS	*Scientific American*
NEWSPAPERS	*San Jose Mercury News*
MOVIES	*Braveheart*
PLAYS	*Much Ado about Nothing*
TELEVISION PROGRAMS	*Seinfeld*
LONG MUSICAL COMPOSITIONS	*Resurrection Symphony*
FOREIGN WORDS OR PHRASES	*sine qua non*

2. Use italics to indicate that you are using a word as a word.

When he says *language,* it sounds like music.

Avoid underlining and italics as a way of emphasizing. Writers who are fond of exclamation points also like italics, for with *them* they can *emphasize* every word they think is *crucial.* Let words stand without artificial emphasis. Give your sentences their own punch, and the reader will see the emphasis *without* being *pushed* by shouting, insistent *italics.*

NUMBERS

1. Use figures (2, 98, 92837) for addresses, dates, page numbers, divisions of books, scores. For other usages in nonscientific writing, use figures only for numbers of more than two words.

He was twenty-nine.

My grandfather died at 112.

2. Either spell out all the numbers in a sentence, *three of the six,* or use figures for all, *3 of the 6.* Don't mix the forms.

3. Spell out any number that begins a sentence.

One hundred and twelve years is a long time to be alive.

HYPHENS

The hyphen is used either to join words or to separate syllables.

1. To join words. Use hyphens to join multiword adjectives that precede the word they modify and multiword nouns.

Harry was a devil-may-care philosopher-poet who claimed he had many out-of-town speaking engagements.

When multiword adjectives follow the noun they modify, however, do not hyphenate them.

Yet he claimed he had many speaking engagements out of town.

There is no hard-and-fast rule governing when to hyphenate compound words. Check the dictionary. If it does not have the entry you seek, write the words without a hyphen.

2. To separate syllables. Use hyphens to show where words have been divided at the end of a line.

Houdini was not only an escape artist but also a prestidigitator.

If you type carefully, you should not need to divide words often. Most word-processing programs have a "word-wrap" function that automatically takes care of word division. Never divide one-syllable words, and divide longer words only at a syllable break. Check words in your dictionary to determine where these breaks occur. When you must divide a word, the last thing on the line should be the hyphen.

> Harry retired to Pocatello for a long rehabilita-
> tion because he had just completed a book.

Avoid breaking a word in a way that leaves only one or two letters on either side.

> If you do, the letter will look quite a-
> lone, and furthermore it will look sil-
> ly.

3. Use hyphens to attach certain prefixes to certain root words. The prefixes *ex-*, *self-*, and *all-* are attached by hyphens to the roots.

> Her all-encompassing dislike for her ex-husband is self-evident.

If the root word is capitalized, attach the prefix to it with a hyphen.

> She could not decide whether she was a pre-Socratic or a postmod-
> ernist.

When two prefixes apply to the same word, use a hyphen and a space after the first prefix and attach the second prefix to the word.

> She studied both micro- and macroeconomics.

More often than not, prefixes are joined to their root without benefit of a hyphen. When in doubt, use your dictionary.

4. Use a hyphen to join words that form certain compound nouns.

> daughter-in-law
>
> editor-in-chief
>
> reporter-at-large

Some compound nouns are not joined by hyphens, for instance, *vice president*. Keep your dictionary handy.

5. Use hyphens to indicate fractions and compound numbers.

> three-fourths
>
> twenty-nine

███████ ■ **EXERCISES FOR MECHANICS** ██████████████████████████

1. Edit the following sentences for proper form for abbreviation, capitalization, italics, and numbers.
   a. in the winter of '65, people in the midwest were far colder than people in the atlantic states because of a wintry arctic blast.
   b. albert appeared on claudia's doorstep last thursday night, whispering sotto voce, "Come with me to the casbah—or at least to cinema five. they're showing tracy and hepburn in woman of the year."
   c. in the epic poem gilgamesh, written down around 2000 bc, a sumerian king, gilgamesh of erech, prays to his patron goddess ishtar, and travels to the land of the dead in search of his friend enkidu.
   d. yesterday I read melville's whaling novel, moby-dick, hemingway's short story with the lean and revealing dialogue, hills like white elephants, and the new popular mechanics.
   e. when senator gass asked tommy what he wanted to be when he grew up, tommy said he wanted to be a senator just like him and serve in congress.
   f. jack meridge, lld, phd, was first a lawyer for the afl-cio, but then he hooked up with the nfl and the cia, which eventually led to a job with rev harold haines, a leader of the naacp.
   g. is twelve midnight am or pm?
   h. 30,000 buffalo took an average of 5 months to migrate from their winter pastures in new mexico to their summer pastures in montana.
   i. at the salt in geneva the ambassador from the united states and the ambassador from the ussr discussed the abm program and the deployment of medium-range icbms and ss-x-25's.

2. Restore proper mechanics to the following passage.

   on tonight's episode of houston, dr van slyke discovers fifi's plan to sell his ocean liner, the willie mays, to throckmorton gotrocks, jr, the sixty seven year old former tree surgeon and stunt pilot, in exchange for an autographed copy of his poem, how green the face, six prize st bernard dogs, and 22 us savings bonds. meanwhile, senator rex smith has telephoned his brother roy, governor of the state, to see if he can get free tickets for the exclusive performance of gershwin's porgy and bess, being given by the houston light opera company at the civic center opera house. tonight's episode is based on the short story the big swap by lily upmeier, phd, and is soon to be made into a feature length motion picture, to be titled grope for gold.

22

Glossary of Usage

"When I use a word," Humpty Dumpty said in a rather scornful tone, "it means just what I choose it to mean — neither more nor less."

"The question is," said Alice, "whether you can make words mean so many different things."

"The question is," said Humpty Dumpty, "which is to be master — that's all."

— LEWIS CARROLL (1832–1898)
ENGLISH WRITER

No one could hope to untangle all the snarls in American usage. In this section, however, we offer advice on how to avoid the common errors. We treat troublesome words that sound alike but have different meanings, words that are frequently used incorrectly, quandaries you may often find yourself in when choosing a word. When we have also discussed the problem in the text, we indicate a reference.

a, an   Use *a* before words beginning with a consonant sound and *an* before words beginning with a vowel sound. Check "Adjectives" in Chapter 18 for a further discussion.

accent marks   Accent marks are part of the word and must be used where they are called for, as in *cliché*. Consult your dictionary.

accept, except   *Accept* means "to receive" or "to agree to": *Hirohito finally accepted defeat. Except* as a verb means "to leave out" or "to make exception of" and as a preposition means "excluding": *The ravages of war do not <u>except</u> children, the aged, or the feeble. Everyone got out alive <u>except</u> the cat.*

adverse, averse   *Adverse* is an adjective meaning "hostile" or "unfavorable": *The <u>adverse</u> effects of alcohol include headache and nausea. Averse is an adjective meaning "reluctant" or "in opposition": Repeated hangovers soon made him <u>averse</u> to drinking alcohol.*

advice, advise   *Advice* is a noun meaning "counsel": *Bill went to his broker for <u>advice</u> on the stock market. Advise is a verb meaning "to give counsel": But Bill's broker was unable to <u>advise</u> him.*

affect, effect   *Affect* as a verb means "to influence" or "to pretend to have": *The oil slick did not seriously <u>affect</u> the beach. Professor Honnicutt <u>affected</u> a Boston accent. Effect as a verb means "to bring about" or "to cause to happen" and as a noun means "result": Diplomats are trying to <u>effect</u> a peace in Lebanon. The injections had no <u>effect</u>.*

aggravate, irritate   These words are not synonyms. *Aggravate* means "to make worse": *Running in the sprints, Lewis <u>aggravated</u> his hamstring injury. Irritate means "to make impatient or angry": My little sister <u>irritates</u> me.*

all, all of   When modifying a common noun, use only *all*: *<u>All</u> the world's a stage.* When modifying a proper noun or a pronoun, use *all of*: *When <u>all</u> his teeth were pulled, <u>all of</u> Hollywood cried.*

all ready, already   *All ready* is an adjective meaning "prepared": *We're <u>all ready</u> to dance. Already is an adverb meaning "prior in time": Sven had <u>already</u> cooked dinner by the time we arrived.*

all right, alright   Use *all right; alright* is a misspelling.

allusion, illusion   *Allusion* means "reference to," as in *The "railsplitter" was an <u>allusion</u> to Lincoln. Illusion means "deception" or "mistaken idea," as in He is under the <u>illusion</u> that he is Napoleon.*

almost, most   See *most, almost.*

along with   Phrases introduced by *along with* are parenthetical and do not change the number of the verb: *The mayor, <u>along with</u> the comptroller and the city council, runs a tight ship.* See rule 1 under "Subject-Verb Agreement" in Chapter 19.

altogether, all together   *Altogether* means "entirely": *Einstein was <u>altogether</u> unprepared for the fame his discoveries brought him. All together means "as a group": Our family stood <u>all together</u> in the dining room for this snapshot.*

ambiguous, ambivalent   *Ambiguous* means "capable of more than one meaning or interpretation," or, more generally, "unclear or confusing": *His statement was ambiguous, and I wasn't sure what he meant. Ambivalent* means "feeling two ways (usually conflicting) about something": *I was ambivalent about the movie and so stayed home.*

among, between   See *between, among.*

amount, number   *Amount* refers to the bulk or quantity of something viewed as a whole: *I have had an adequate amount of back talk from you. Number* refers to something viewed as separate units: *You have made a number of undeserved criticisms.*

and/or   Avoid this awkward construction. Decide whether you mean "and" or "or." If your sentence contains a third option, add *or both,* as in *We could not decide whether to go to India or China or both.*

ante-, anti-   The prefix *ante-* means "before": *Arlington is an antebellum mansion near Washington. Anti-* means "against": *If poisoned, find an antidote.*

anxious, eager   *Anxious* means "worried, uneasy, brooding": *Most students were anxious about the organic chemistry midterm. Eager* means "full of enthusiasm": *Few were eager to take the midterm.* Be careful not to use one when you mean the other.

anybody, any body, anyone, any one   *anybody* and *anyone* are single-word synonyms meaning "any person at all": *Anybody (or anyone) can be a star these days.* The phrase *any body* refers to any item of a particular group of bodies: *You students of surgery may dissect any body you find.* The phrase *any one* means "any single one of a particular group": *Can I choose any one of the cadavers, Professor?*

anymore, any more   *Anymore* (less commonly written as *any more*) is an adverb meaning "any longer" and is used in negative situations: *Annie doesn't live here anymore.* Avoid using it in positive constructions to mean "now" or "these days": *Vegetables are certainly expensive now* (not *anymore*). *Any more* usually refers to an addition: *I've had enough sass and don't want any more.*

apt, likely, liable   *Apt* means "having a tendency to": *I am apt to be forgetful. Likely* means "probable to happen": *I am likely to forget lunch dates. Liable* means "legally responsible": *If I don't repair that missing stair, I'll be liable for damages.* Writers sometimes incorrectly use *liable* when they mean *likely* in situations that have negative consequences: *I'm likely* (not *liable*) *to slip on icy sidewalks* is correct.

as   *As* can be a preposition, an adverb, or a conjunction. As a preposition, it means "in the role of": *As a cook, he would make a good tennis* *player.* As an adverb, it means "equally": *She would be just as miserable in Katmandu.* As a conjunction, it introduces an adverbial clause: *He smirked as he ate the goldfish.*

Poor *as* is much overused and abused. It is not a synonym for *because.* Prefer *Billy did not attend school yesterday because* (not *as*) *he had a cold.* It is not a substitute for *that.* Prefer *I don't know that* (not *as*) *I care who wins.* It is not a substitute for *to be.* Prefer *The president appointed her to be* (not *as*) *head of the SEC.* (*To be* is usually so strongly implied it may be omitted.)

as, like *As* and *like* are not interchangeable. *Like* as a preposition can be followed only by a noun or a noun substitute: *Do you think I look like Madonna? Like* should not introduce a clause. Use *as: Do unto others as* (not *like*) *you would have others do unto you.*

as best as, as well as *As best as* mixes up *as well as* and *the best that.* Use either of the latter two, as in *We did as well as we could* and *I danced the best that I could.*

awhile, a while *Awhile* (one word) is an adverb: *Let's rest here awhile. Awhile* cannot be the object of a preposition. *A while* is a noun phrase and can be the object of a preposition: *I will get moving again in a while.*

bad, badly *Bad* is an adjective that modifies nouns or noun substitutes; *badly* is an adverb. The problem arises with linking verbs, such as *feel, appear,* or *look,* that take the complement *bad: After eating the pound of chocolate, Hans felt bad* (not *badly*) *enough to call the doctor.*

being as, being that Avoid these colloquialisms. Use *because* or *since: Because* (not *Being as*) *I was ill, I could not attend your recital.*

beside, besides *Beside* means "by the side of" or "next to": *The Secret Service agents stood beside the president. Besides* means either "except" or "in addition to": *Besides her, no one volunteered. Three other students besides her received A's.*

between, among Use *between* for two things, *among* for three or more, or when the number is unstated: *Between you and me, I think this party stinks. He was first among equals.*

biweekly, bimonthly, semimonthly, semiannually As a prefix indicating time, *bi-* means happening every two periods of time. *Semi-* means happening twice in one period. *We meet biweekly, or every two weeks. We meet bimonthly, or every two months. We meet semimonthly, or twice each month. We meet semiannually, or twice a year.*

bring, take Someone *brings* something toward you and *takes* it away from you: *Bring me some antacid, and take away this awful soup.*

burst, bust   *Burst* is a verb meaning "to come apart forcefully." Its principal parts are *burst, burst,* and *burst: What will you do if I <u>burst</u> the balloon? I <u>burst</u> the balloon yesterday. I <u>had burst</u> another balloon a week before. Bursted* is incorrect. *Bust* and *<u>busted</u>* are slang.

can, may   *Can* indicates capability, as in *I <u>can</u> bench-press 300 pounds on a good day. May* indicates permission, as in *<u>May</u> I please have the salt?* or possibility, as in *I <u>may</u> need salt on my steak.*

can barely, can hardly, can't barely, can't hardly   Both *barely* and *hardly* carry negative implications: *I <u>can barely</u> swim and so <u>can hardly</u> save you. Can't barely* and *can't hardly* are double negatives and should be avoided.

cannot, can not   *Can not* is not the preferred form; use *cannot.*

can't help but   Careful stylists avoid using this colloquial phrase. Prefer *can't help* without *but* or *can't but* without *help: I <u>can't help</u> loving you; I <u>can't but</u> be pleased at that.*

censor, censure   *Censor* means "to scrutinize works for unacceptable material": *Some totalitarian countries <u>censor</u> private mail. Censure* means "to scold or criticize": *The Senate <u>censured</u> Joe McCarthy for his conduct.*

center around, center on   *Center on* means "to focus or concentrate on": *The FBI hunt <u>centered on</u> the town of Rome, New York. Center around* is illogical. Substitute *revolve around: The quest for freedom <u>revolves around</u> human dignity.*

cite, sight, site   *Cite* is a verb meaning "refer to": *To prove that the world is round, I need only <u>cite</u> that famous explorer Columbus. Sight* is a noun meaning "a view": *I'm sure Columbus found America to be a beautiful <u>sight</u>. Site* is a noun meaning "place" or "location": *Was Rhode Island the <u>site</u> of his landing?*

climactic, climatic   *Climactic* refers to a peak or high point: *Bogart's farewell to Bergman is the <u>climactic</u> love scene in Casablanca. Climatic* refers to weather: *His voice changed according to <u>climatic</u> conditions.*

compared to, compared with   *Compared to* suggests a similarity between two things not usually thought of together: *My boyfriend <u>compared me to</u> Jessica Lange. Compared with* suggests an analysis of differences and similarities: *His essay <u>compared</u> Roosevelt's presidency <u>with</u> Lincoln's under the headings of wartime leadership, intellectual ability, and personal integrity.* As an intransitive verb, *compare* always takes *with,* as in *Today's presidents just don't <u>compare with</u> yesterday's greats.*

complement, compliment   As a verb, *complement* means "to complete" or "to match," as in *The green sweater <u>complements</u> his green eyes.*

As a noun, *complement* means "a word or phrase that completes an idea": *"Sweet" is often the complement of "sugar."* As a verb, *compliment* means "to praise": *The mayor complimented the fire department's quick work.* As a noun, it means "a bit of praise": *"You've lost a ton of weight" doesn't sound like much of a compliment to me.*

compose, comprise   To *compose* means "to form the parts into a whole": *I composed a poem in praise of toothpaste.* The whole *comprises* or *consists of* the parts, as in *The Congress comprises [consists of] the Senate and the House of Representatives.* Careful stylists, therefore, would write *Twelve teams compose the National League* and *The National League comprises twelve teams.*

comrade, camaraderie   *Comrade* refers to a close companion or friend; *camaraderie* refers to the warm feeling between comrades. Note the different spellings.

conscience, conscientious, conscious, consciousness   *Conscience* is a noun referring to our sense of right and wrong: *My conscience hurt because I ate the whole cake by myself. Conscientious* is an adjective meaning "scrupulous, careful": *He was conscientious about homework and did it every night. Conscious* is an adjective meaning "aware of self and surroundings": *He was conscious of the lipstick smear on his cheek. Consciousness* is a noun referring to the state of being aware: *After the blow on her head, she lost consciousness.*

continual, continuous   *Continual* means "happening repeatedly": *His job as jackhammer operator gave him a continual headache. Continuous* means "uninterrupted or unbroken": *The Appennines form a continuous ridge of mountains.*

could of, should of, would of   Avoid all of these. They are incorrect ear-spellings for *could have, should have,* and *would have.*

council, counsel   *Council* refers to an administrative or legislative body, *councilor* to a member of that body, *Counsel* refers to advice or to a legal adviser, and *counselor* refers to anyone who advises. *Counsel* can also be a verb, as in *Gandhi counseled his followers to resist without violence.*

couple of   In formal English, use this phrase only to mean "two that are connected, a pair": *A couple of horses pulled the cart.*

credible, creditable, credulous   *Credible* means "giving sufficient reason to be believed": *After a vigorous cross-examination, the jury found her a credible witness. Creditable* means "worthy of praise or esteem": *Will Clark did a creditable job at first base. Credulous* means "ready to believe on slight evidence": *He was so credulous I convinced him I'd been to the moon.*

criterion, criteria   *Criterion* is the singular. *Criteria* is the plural. *Stamina is the main criterion for good running. Stamina and will are the main criteria for good running.*

datum, data   *Datum* is the singular form and *data* is the plural. *The data shows a 15 percent decrease* should be *The data show a 15 percent decrease.*

different from, different than   Many people say, and some write, *different than,* but careful stylists prefer *different from: Being a teenager is different from being an adult.*

differ from, differ with   *Differ* from means "to show unlikeness": *California bagels differ from Boston bagels in color and price. Differ with* means "to disagree with": *Oppenheimer differed with Teller over the hydrogen bomb.*

discreet, discrete   *Discreet* means "prudent" or "able to be silent": *He was so discreet about his poker losses that his wife never found out. Discrete* means "separate" or "distinct": *Each country has its own discrete culture.*

disinterested, uninterested   *Disinterested* does not mean "to have no interest" but "to have nothing personal at stake and thus to be impartial": *The dispute between Japanese and Soviet fishermen has been handed over to a disinterested Swiss arbitrator. Uninterested* means "apathetic," or "uncaring": *Deirdre took Harry for a fishing trip, but he was obviously uninterested.*

due to, because   Avoid using *due to* as a synonym for "because": *Because of* (not *due to*) *rain, the game was called.* Save *due to* for bill paying.

due to the fact that   This long running jump means "because." Use *because.*

each, every   *Each* means "one of a group": *Each carton of milk undergoes careful inspection. Every* refers to all members of a group: *Every writer wishes for fame.* Both take a singular verb.

effect   See *affect, effect.*

e.g., i.e.   These are abbreviations from Latin: *e.g.* stands for *exempli gratia,* which means "for the sake of example"; *i.e.* stands for *id est,* which means "that is." These Latin abbreviations are fading from use in formal writing. Stick to the English equivalents.

either, neither   Both of these words can function as an adjective, a pronoun, or part of a correlative conjunction. As an adjective, *either* means "one or the other": *Guard dogs stand on either side of the gate.* As an adjective *neither* means "not one or the other": *Neither dog has on a muzzle.* As pronouns, *either* and *neither* take singular verbs: *Either is enough to scare off burglars. Neither makes the postman cheerful.* As a correlative conjunction, *either* is followed by *or* and *neither* by *nor.* For further discussion, see "Conjunctions" in Chapter 18 and "Parallel Construction" in Chapter 19.

elicit, illicit   *Elicit* is a verb that means "to pull forth" or "to evoke": *Ted Williams's homer in his last time at bat elicited a huge roar from the crowd. Illicit* is an adjective that means "not allowed": *Ormsby was arrested for possession of illicit drugs.*

eminent, imminent, immanent   *Eminent* means "respected, high ranking, outstanding": *Ben Franklin was the most eminent statesman of his day. Imminent* means "impending": *An imminent storm darkened the horizon. Immanent,* a rare term of philosophy, usually means "inherent" or "resting within": *Romantic philosophers thought divinity was immanent in nature.*

ensure, insure   *Ensure* means "to make certain": *Tying Black Bart with a lasso ensured his detention. Insure* means "to get insurance for": *Lloyd's of London refused to insure the trombonist's lip.*

enthuse   Careful stylists avoid using this colloquial term in formal prose. Prefer *enthusiastic: New York City was very enthusiastic about baseball in 1955.*

everybody, every body, everyone, every one   *Everybody* and *everyone* are indefinite pronouns referring to all members of a group. Both take singular verbs: *When everybody plays well, everyone cheers loudly. Every body* is a phrase in which the noun *body* is modified by the adjective *every: You will find a heart in every body of every mammal.* In *every one,* the pronoun *one* is modified by the adjective *every: Every one has lungs as well.*

everyday, every day   *Everyday* is an adjective: *At five each morning, she rose to do her everyday chores.* The phrase *every day* acts as an adverb: *I see him every day.*

everywheres   Avoid this colloquial version of *everywhere.*

except   See *accept, except.*

explicit, implicit   *Explicit* means "stated outright": *I made an explicit offer to buy his car. Implicit* means "unstated but suggested": *Implicit in my offer was that he throw in the whitewall tires and a gallon of gasoline.*

farther, further   Use *farther* to express physical distance: *Is it farther to his house or to yours?* Use *further* to express abstract distance: *Newton probed further into the nature of the universe than any thinker before him.*

few, fewer, less, lesser   *Few* and *fewer* refer to countable items: *We have few friends, and with that attitude, we'll have fewer. Less* and *lesser* refer to a whole not divisible into individual countable units: *I have less money than you, but you are the lesser talent.*

firstly, secondly, thirdly   Prefer *first, second,* and *third: First, the economy is weak. Second, our foreign policy is in disarray. Third, the soda machine doesn't work.*

flaunt, flout   *Flaunt* means "to make an ostentatious display": *The Smiths flaunted their new car in front of the neighbors. Flout* means "to treat disrespectfully" or "to scorn": *The banker flouted convention by coming to the bank in jeans and sneakers.*

former, latter   These words can help avoid repetition. Use them only when you are referring to two things: *Mr. Hobson and his dog are so alike that I sometimes mistake the former for the latter.*

get, got, gotten   *Got* is the past tense of *get: Millions of Americans got their income tax forms in the mail yesterday.* The past participle of *get* is either *got* or *gotten,* hence the confusion. Either is acceptable English: *Have you got a tennis racket? I have gotten to bed late every night this week.*

Americans use *gotten* more often, especially to signal a progression: *The moral standards of the United States have gotten steadily worse.* We also use *got* in informal English as an intense form of *must: You have got to help us.* Our advice: don't overuse *get* in formal writing. Although it is a necessary verb, it can be an easy way out of the search for good verbs.

good, well   *Good* is a noun: *I stand for the true, the good, and the beautiful. Good* is also an adjective: *Wouldn't we all love to be good writers? Well* is an adverb: *She plays the bassoon well.* The problem arises, as with *bad* and *badly,* with linking verbs, such as *feel* or *sound,* which take *good* as a complement. *Whenever she ran ten miles, she felt good* (not *well*). In this sentence *good* modifies the subject *she,* not the verb.

good and   Avoid this colloquial equivalent of *entirely* or *very: You should be very* (not *good and*) *mad.*

hanged, hung   As past participles, the word *hanged* is used with people, and the word *hung* with objects: *In the old West, outlaws were hanged. Pictures are hung all over my house.*

hardly   See *can barely, can hardly, can't barely, can't hardly.*

have, of   Do not use the preposition *of* when you mean the verb *have: She shouldn't have* (not *of*) *done what she did.*

hopefully   *Hopefully* is an adverb meaning "in a hopeful manner" and modifies the verb, as in *The sick man waited hopefully for the doctor.* This means "As he waited, he was hopeful." The term is frequently misused: *Hopefully, we should arrive at the summit by two.* This means that when the climbers get to the top, they will be full of hope. The speaker meant *I hope we arrive at the summit by two.* Avoid using *hopefully:* its misuse is a pet peeve of many readers.

house, home   A *house* is an edifice; a *home* is an emotional entity in which you live: *A house is where the kitchen is. A home is where the heart is.*

however   This word means "in spite of" or "no matter": *We do not have the exact style you ordered; we do, however, have a similar one.* When used as a conjunctive adverb this way, *however* should be set off by punctuation. Never use this word in a clause beginning with *but:* that would be redundant. Careful stylists do not begin sentences with *however,* preferring to embed it near the verb.

human, human being   *Human* is an adjective: *Her dog had a human smile.* Although *human* is acceptable as a noun, careful stylists prefer *human being: Her dog was almost like a human being.*

i.e.   See *e.g., i.e.*

if, whether   In speech, we often say *I'll find out if he's home or not.* A better word here is *whether: I'll find out whether he is home or not. Whether indicates a choice or alternative. If indicates a contingency: If he doesn't shut up, I'll scream.*

imminent, immanent   See *eminent, imminent, immanent.*

impact   Avoid using this word as a verb. Prefer a more specific word: *Years of war depleted* (not *impacted on*) *the treasury of Venice.*

imply, infer   *Imply* means "to suggest" or "to indicate," as in *By shaking her head, she implied disapproval. Infer means "to conclude" or "to understand," as in *I inferred from her nodding that she agreed.*

individual, person, party, people   *Individual* emphasizes singularity or separateness: *Our government must protect the individual. Person* emphasizes the actual self or personality: *A person could develop a cough. Party* means a group of people assembled for a purpose: *Our party arrived fifteen minutes late. People* refers to a nation, congregation, class, or company: *Of the people, by the people, and for the people. People* is also used to refer to human beings in general: *People do the darnedest things.*

infer, imply   See *imply, infer.*

ingenious, ingenuous   *Ingenious* means "especially inventive" or "clever": *With an ingenious contrivance, King Frederick had the kitchen raised into his bedroom. Ingenuous* means "childlike" or "innocent": *When my daughter said I looked a hundred, I forgave her because of her ingenuous smile.*

irrespective, regardless, irregardless   *Irrespective* and *regardless* are synonymous and mean "whether taken into account or not," as in *We are all equal irrespective of sex, color, or creed. I am leaving regardless of her opinion. Irregardless* is incorrect.

is when, is where   Avoid these awkward constructions. Revise *A double elimination tournament is when teams losing twice are eliminated.* Prefer *In a double elimination tournament, teams losing twice are eliminated.*

it's, its   Because their appearance is so similar, these two words are often confused with each other. *It's* is always a contraction of *it is: It's lovely weather if you're a duck. Its* is a possessive pronoun: *My duck is looking for its bowl.* See "Apostrophes" in Chapter 20.

-ize verbs   Many verbs that end in *-ize* are essential, such as *organize* and *civilize.* Try, however, to avoid made-up *-ize* verbs that take the place of better verbs. Prefer *moisten* to *moisturize, finish* or *complete* to *finalize,* and *use* to *utilize.*

kind, kinds   *Kind* is singular and takes a singular modifier and verb, as in *This kind of novel bores me. Kinds* is plural and takes a plural modifier and verb, as in *these kinds of novels bore me. These kinds of novels* is incorrect. Some abstract words, however, such as *irony, beauty,* and *love,* come in different forms and can be used with the plural *kinds,* as in *There are many kinds of love.*

kind of, sort of   In formal writing, avoid using *kind of* and *sort of* to mean "to a degree" or "less than completely." If you cannot indicate the exact degree, prefer *somewhat* and *rather: Murray's poems are rather* (not *sort of*) *elusive. Kind* is never followed by *a. He is kind a tough* is incorrect.

lay, lie   *Lay* is a transitive verb and thus takes a direct object. Its principal parts are *lay, laid,* and *laid: That comedian will lay an egg tonight, just as he laid one last week, and just as he has laid one every night for the past five years. Lie* is an intransitive verb and thus does not take an object. Its principal parts are *lie, lay,* and *lain: I will lie on the beach today; I lay there yesterday, and I feel as though I have lain there all my life.*

lead, led   The verb *lead* becomes *led* in the past tense: *You lead me down the mountain today. I led you up yesterday.*

leave, let   *Leave* means "to depart"; *let* means "to allow." They are interchangeable only when both meanings apply, as in *Let* (or *Leave*) *me alone*.

lend, loan   Careful stylists use *loan* only as a noun, as in *The interest on the loan is 12 percent*. The verb is *to lend*, as in *Will you lend me a dime?*

less   See *few, fewer, less, lesser*.

liable   See *apt, likely, liable*.

like, as   See *as, like*.

loose, lose   *Loose* means "unbound" or "free from restraint": *Electricians traced the blackout to a loose wire*. *Lose* means "to become unable to find": *Don't lose your train ticket*.

lots, lots of, a lot of, a lot   These are all colloquial equivalents of *much, many*, or *a great deal*. Avoid them in your college writing: *Many* (not *a lot of*) *steamships sailed from Le Havre. Alot* is incorrect.

majority   Use this word to refer to more than half of a group of countable items: *The majority of voters stayed home*. Use words such as *most* when the subject cannot be divided into countable items: *Most of the sky is clear*.

may, can   See *can, may*.

may be, maybe   The phrase *may be* is the subjunctive of *is: The aliens may be laughing at us right now*. *Maybe* is an adverb meaning "perhaps": *Maybe they think our taste in clothes is strange*.

medium, media   *Medium* is the singular form: *Television is the fastest-growing news medium in the world*. *Media* is plural: *Newspapers and network news are the two most important news media*.

moral, morale   *Moral* is an adjective meaning "conforming to a standard of rightness or goodness": *Helping poor nations is a moral thing to do*. *Morale* is a noun meaning "mental or emotional condition": *After the Battle of the Bulge, Allied morale was high*.

most, almost   *Most* is an adjective meaning "the greater part": *Most people like finding hidden money*. *Almost* is an adverb meaning "close but not quite": *We are almost home*. They are not interchangeable. *I see him most every day* is incorrect.

nauseous, nauseating, nauseated   *Nauseous* and *nauseating* mean the same thing; that is, "causing nausea": *That wig is nauseating. I can't stand any more of his nauseous quips*. *Nauseated* means "feeling nausea": *She is a little nauseated after riding the Ferris wheel*. The sentence *That hotdog made me nauseous* means you were causing others to feel nausea.

none   *None* is almost always singular, as in *Of four candidates, none was female*. Treat *none* as a plural, however, when you wish to consider the members of the group as separate entities: *Of all the varieties of life on earth, none are hardier or more resourceful than the insects*.

nowheres   Avoid this colloquial equivalent of *nowhere*.

number, amount   See *amount, number*.

off, off of   *Off* is sufficient, as in *Get off my bunion*. Adding *of* is unnecessary.

OK, O.K., okay   Avoid these in your college writing.

on, upon   These words are synonyms. To many people, *upon* sounds pretentious.

on account of, because   *On account of* should be reserved for partial payment of a debt. Careful stylists use the shorter and more direct *because*.

one, you   *One* is the third-person impersonal pronoun: *One never knows where one stands these days*. *You,* the second-person pronoun, is often used in its place. *You never know where you stand these days*. Neither is perfect. *One* has the drawback of being associated with pretentious speakers; *you* has the drawback of being a little too chatty for formal prose. Careful stylists still prefer *one* although they use it sparingly. Sometimes it is simply better to say *I* when referring to your own experience.

only   To avoid confusion, place *only* in front of the word you intend it to modify: *Why did you buy only two bananas?* See "Modifiers: Misplaced, Squinting, and Dangling" in Chapter 19.

pair   Use a singular verb when you are considering the pair as a unit: *A pair of wild horses is hard to control*. Use a plural verb when you wish to indicate that the two elements of the pair are separate: *Our new pair of puppies are getting along well with each other*.

per   This Latin word means "for each." Prefer the English equivalent: *My Oldsmobile gets fifteen miles to a* (not *per*) *gallon. I sent the letter by* (not *per*) *Express Mail*.

percent, per cent, percentage   *Percent,* now used more commonly than *per cent,* must follow a numeral: *The bond paid 9 percent. Percentage* means "part" or "portion." Do not use it by itself to mean "a small part or portion." It requires an adjective to give it meaning: *A high percentage of injuries in football are to the knee*.

person   See *individual, person, party, people*.

phenomenon, phenomena, phenomenal   *Phenomenon* is a noun meaning "an observable fact or event": *A hurricane is a frightening phe-*

nomenon. *Phenomena* is the plural: *Hurricanes are frightening phenomena*. *Phenomenal* is an adjective meaning "extraordinary": *Her skill in doing calculus was phenomenal*.

plenty of   Careful stylists avoid using *plenty of* to mean a large number or amount: *Philip Johnson designed a great many* (not *plenty of*) *fine buildings*.

plus   Use *plus* only when adding numbers. Careful stylists never use it in place of *in addition to* or *and*.

precede, proceed   *Precede* means "to go before": *Women and children precede the men into the lifeboats*. *Proceed* means "to continue on": *Proceed directly to the boarding gate*.

presently   Use this word to mean "in a little while": *I'll return presently*. Do not use it to mean "now."

pretty   In formal writing, use for something pleasing or attractive, not to suggest size or degree. *Mr. Elton is rather* (not *pretty*) *drunk*.

principal, principle   *Principal* as a noun means "chief officer," as in *The principal sent Ralph home for keeping a frog in his book bag*. As an adjective, it means "foremost" or "most important": *Our principal objective is to defend the ridge until dawn*. *Principle* (note the spelling difference) is a noun that means "rule" or "truth": *The first principle of long-distance running is relaxation in the midst of arduous physical exercise*.

quote, quotation   *Quote* is a verb, not a noun: *Newspapers often quote rock stars out of context*. *Quotation* is the noun: *Reporters scramble to get good quotations* (not *quotes*).

real, really   *Real* is an adjective: *A real crocodile lay on the bank*. *Really* is the adverb: *It was sleeting really* (not *real*) *hard*.

reason is because, reason is that   *Reason is because* is a redundancy, although it is often seen: *The reason Hamlet waits so long to kill Claudius is because there is so much uncertainty in the court of Denmark* is incorrect. Use *reason is that*: *The reason Hamlet waits so long to kill Claudius is that there is so much uncertainty in the court of Denmark*.

regarding, in regard to, with regard to, as regards   All these words are synonyms for *concerning*. Avoid using *in regards to*, a cross between *in regard to* and *as regards*.

sensual, sensuous   *Sensual* means "preoccupied with bodily pleasures": *The voluptuous Polynesian women in Gauguin's paintings look sensual*. *Sensuous* means "appealing to the senses": *I love the sensuous colors in Gauguin's paintings*.

shall, should, will, would   *Shall* was once the correct future tense auxiliary for the first person (*I shall be home shortly*), but in American usage it is now reserved for emphasis (*I shall return*) or a request for an opinion or consent (*Shall we see each other again tomorrow night?*). For most purposes, *will* functions as the future-tense auxiliary for all persons. *Should* was once the past tense of *shall* but now indicates obligation: *He should occasionally volunteer to do the dishes. Would* was once the past tense of *will* but now indicates the conditional: *If she played softer music, I would attend her parties.*

should   See *shall, should, will, would.*

should of, should have   See *could of, should of, would of.*

sit, set   *Sit* is intransitive—that is, it takes no object: *Ever since I bruised my coccyx, I have found it difficult to sit. Set* is transitive—that is, it takes an object: *We set the piano in your kitchen.*

situation   This word is much overused and often unnecessary. Whenever possible, use a concrete word to indicate what the *situation* is: *Congress has done little to combat the worsening deficit* (not *worsening situation*).

so   This word can be an adverb, an adjective, or a conjunction. As an adverb, it usually means "in order to" or "to the degree": *She kept the door open so that she could hear the baby.* As an adjective, it is a vague intensifier. Careful stylists prefer *very* or *intensely: Denzel Washington is very* (not *so*) *good-looking.* As a conjunction, it indicates result: *The river is still cold, so the fish are still jumping.* Careful stylists avoid starting sentences with *so.*

somebody, some body, someone, some one   Both *somebody* and *someone* are indefinite pronouns meaning "an unspecified person": *Won't somebody* (or *someone*) *answer the phone? Some body* is a phrase meaning an unspecified body: *Some body of government ought to examine this problem. Some one* is a phrase that means "an unspecified one": *Some one of the guests committed the murder.*

someplace, somewhere   These two words mean "an unspecified place." Careful stylists prefer *somewhere.*

sometime, some time, sometimes   *Sometime* is an adverb that means "at an unspecified time": *Come up and see me sometime. Some time* is a phrase that means "an unspecified length of time": *I haven't seen jai alai for some time. Sometimes* is an adverb that means "occasionally": *Cockroaches appeared sometimes one place, sometimes another.*

somewheres   Avoid using this colloquialism in your writing.

sort of   See *kind of, sort of.*

split infinitives   An *infinitive* consists of *to* and the main form of the verb, such as *to deny*. To *split* an infinitive means to place an adverb or a phrase between the *to* and the verb (*to categorically deny*). When a writer places a long phrase between the *to* and the verb, the split infinitive can make comprehension difficult: *I want to categorically and without fear of contradiction from anyone deny all charges.* Some careful stylists strenuously object to any split infinitive.

stationary, stationery   *Stationary* is an adjective meaning "not moving or moved": *Scientists in antiquity once thought the earth stationary and the universe revolving. Stationery* is what we write letters on.

suppose to, supposed to   Use *supposed to* in your writing to indicate what is expected to happen: *The total eclipse is supposed to* (not *suppose to*) *begin tomorrow.*

sure, surely, certainly   Avoid using *sure* to mean "surely" or "certainly." *Sure* is an adjective that means "confident": *The scoutmaster was sure we were near the camp. Surely* is an adverb that means "without doubt": *Though cantankerous, Grandpa surely loved his family. Certainly* is even more assured: *He was certainly good at getting people to agree with him.*

take, bring   See *bring, take.*

than, then   Note the difference in spelling between these two words. *Than* introduces a comparison: *My father is stronger than your father.* When using *than* with a pronoun, be sure the pronoun is in the right case. One method of making sure is to fill in all the words: *He liked her better than [he liked] me. He liked her better than I [liked her].* See rule 5 under "A Special Word about Pronoun Case" in Chapter 18.

that, which   Use *that* to introduce clauses containing essential information: *The red hat that I lost yesterday was found.* I have other red hats; this sentence refers to the one I lost yesterday. Use *which* to introduce clauses containing nonessential information: *The red hat, which I lost yesterday, has been found.* I have only one red hat and therefore it is not essential to identify the hat further. The words *restrictive* and *nonrestrictive* are frequently used to make this distinction. See rule 6 under "Commas" in Chapter 20 for more on essential and nonessential information.

their, there, they're   *Their* is the third-person plural possessive: *The models put on their eyelashes. There* is an adverb of place: *I saw the baboon over there in the parking lot. There* can also introduce an expletive: *There wasn't a police officer to be found. They're* is a contraction of *they are: They're not eager to accost big animals.* (See "Apostrophes" in Chapter 20 for a discussion of correct usage.)

theirselves   Avoid this colloquialism.

this here, these here, that there, them there   Avoid these colloquial expressions.

through, thru   Use *through* in your writing. *Thru* is informal.

till, until, 'til   *Till* is acceptable, but *until* is preferable. *'Til* is incorrect.

toward, towards   Careful stylists prefer *toward.*

try and, try to   *Try to* is preferable: *Scuba divers should never try to* (not *try and*) *swim alone.*

unique   *Unique* does not admit of degree or comparison: a thing cannot be more or less or very unique, only unique. At all events, *unique* is much overused these days. It means "only one of a kind," "singular." Reserve it for things you have never seen the like of before.

upon, on   See *on, upon.*

use, utilize, utilization   *Utilize* is an overused *-ize* verb. Prefer *use: We must use* (not *utilize*) *every means at our disposal.* Similarly, prefer the noun *use* to *utilization: China condemned any use* (not *utilization*) *of biochemical warfare.*

use to, used to   Past tense is the preferable form when you mean "did habitually": *I used to* (not *use to*) *scream at horror movies.*

viable   The adjective *viable* means "capable of living or growing": *Anaerobic microbes are not viable in oxygenated environments.* Careful stylists avoid using it to indicate that something will work: *Hydroelectric energy is a practicable* (not *viable*) *alternative to nuclear power.*

well, good   See *good, well.*

where, where at, where to   In some regions of America it is quite common to hear *Where are you going to?* and *Where is the shoe at?* In writing, however, never use *to* or *at* after *where. Where are you going?* is sufficient.

whether   See *if, whether.*

which, that   See *that, which.*

would   See *shall, should, will, would.*

you're, your   *Your* is a possessive pronoun: *Your heart is in the right place.* Do not confuse it with *you're,* a contraction of *you are: You're coming to the show tonight, aren't you?* See "Apostrophes" in Chapter 20.

Bibliography of Internet Reference Guides

Other Systems of Documentation

Style Manuals and Handbooks in Various Disciplines

Bibliography of
Internet Reference Guides

Braun, Eric. *The Internet Directory*. New York: Fawcett, 1994.

Breeding, Marshall. *World Wide Web Yellow Pages*. Foster City, CA: Meckler, 1996. Updated annually.

Campbell, Dave, and Mary V. Campbell. *The Student's Guide to Doing Research on the Internet*. Reading, MA: Addison-Wesley, 1995.

Gale Guide to Internet Databases. New York: Gale Research, 1995. Updated annually.

Hahn, Harley. *The Internet Complete Reference*. 2nd ed. Berkeley, CA: Osbourne McGraw-Hill, 1996.

Harmon, Charles. *Using the Internet, On-Line Services, and CD-ROMs for Writing Research and Term Papers*. New York: Neal-Schuman Publishers, 1996.

Harris, Cheryl. *An Internet Education: A Guide to Doing Research on the Internet*. Belmont, CA: Wadsworth, 1996.

Kehoe, Brendan P. *Zen and the Art of the Internet: A Beginner's Guide*. Englewood Cliffs, NJ: PTR Prentice-Hall, 1993.

Krol, Ed. *The Whole Internet User's Guide & Catalog*. Sebastopol, CA: O'Reilly, 1994.

LaQuey, Tracy L. *The Internet Companion: A Beginner's Guide to Global Networking.* Reading, MA: Addison-Wesley, 1992.

Levin, Jayne, ed. *The Internet Federal Information Source: A Directory of Nearly 500 Federal, State, and Political Internet Sites, and How to Find and Use Them.* Washington, DC: National Journal, 1995.

Manger, Jason J. *The Essential Internet Information Guide.* New York: McGraw-Hill, 1995.

Morville, Peter, Louis Rosenfeld, and Joseph James. *The Internet Searcher's Handbook: Locating Information, People and Software.* New York: Neal-Schuman Publishers, 1996.

Newby, Gregory. *Directory of Directories on the Internet: A Guide to Information Sources.* Westport, PA: Meckler, 1994.

Pike, Mary Ann. *Using the Internet.* 2nd ed. Indianapolis: Que, 1996.

Rowland, Robin, and Dave Kinnamen. *Researching on the Internet.* Rocklin, CA: Prima, 1995.

Shea, Virginia. *Netiquette.* San Francisco: Albion, 1994.

Turlington, Shannon R. *Walking the World Wide Web.* Research Triangle Park, NC: Ventana, 1995.

Other Systems
of Documentation

THE MLA NOTES AND BIBLIOGRAPHY SYSTEM

Many college instructors still ask writers for notes and bibliographies in their papers. Practicality therefore dictates that you review the proper form for footnotes, endnotes, and bibliography. Instead of citations in the text, in this system you use raised numerals to direct your reader to references located either at the bottom of the page or on a separate page at the end of your paper.

Notes

Word processing programs can automatically create endnotes and footnotes. If, however, you type your papers, to indicate a reference, put an arabic numeral half a space up after the final punctuation of your sentence. Number your notes consecutively throughout the paper. If you prefer (or if your instructor requires) endnotes, list them on a separate sheet of paper just before the bibliography. If you use footnotes, be sure to leave enough space at the bottom of the page on which your reference occurs. Skip four lines after the last line of text; indent five spaces; type in the appropriate number and information.

Here are the note forms you will most often need.

Books by One Author.

    1 David M. Potter, <u>The South and the Sectional Con-</u>
    <u>flict</u> (Baton Rouge: Louisiana State UP, 1968) 12.

Books by More Than One Author.   Give the first and last name of each author in the same order as on the title page of the book, and then proceed with the entry.

    2 Alexei Abramowitz, Clarrisa Veer, and Thomas Ka-
    plan, <u>Cartels</u> (New York: International Library, 1977) 22.

For books with more than three authors, you may give the first author's name, followed by *et al.*

    3 Florence Sagforth et al., <u>Canyon Years</u> (Santa Fe:
    Illusions, 1982) 112.

Articles in Journals.

    4 Clair Schulz, "The Seat of Our Affections," <u>Verba-</u>
    <u>tim</u> 4 (1977): 3.

Articles in Other Periodicals.   For daily, weekly, or monthly periodicals (most newspapers and magazines), follow this form. Our model is from a newspaper, so it uses the newspaper's page number form.

    5 Anthony Lewis, "White Man's Lawyer," <u>New York</u>
    <u>Times</u> 6 June 1985: A27.

Repeated References to a Source.   If you have already referred to a source, do not repeat all the information in subsequent citations. Give the usual full information the first time.

    6 Oliver Sacks, <u>The Man Who Mistook His Wife for a</u>
    <u>Hat and Other Clinical Tales</u> (New York: Harper, 1985)
    95.

Thereafter, simply give the author's name and page number.

    7 Sacks 19.

If there are two works by the same author, give the author's name, a short title of the work, and the page number.

    8 Sacks, <u>Man</u> 36.
    9 Sacks, <u>A Leg to Stand On</u> 45.

Frequently, especially in book reports and papers on literature, you will refer to only one source in your paper. In this case, fully cite your source the first time; for each subsequent reference, however, you need not use a footnote or endnote. Just put the page number in parentheses *in the text,* followed by a period.

> The author goes on to say, "Here eight thousand mem-
> bers of the Oglala subtribe of the Sioux, or Dakota, live
> on land allotted to them by the government" (115).

Books with Translators.

> 10 Jean Genet, Our Lady of the Flowers, trans.
> Bernard Frechtman (New York: Grove, 1963) 130.

Books with Editors.   Some works by major authors have been edited by someone else. In such cases, put the original author's name, followed by the title, a comma, the label *ed.,* and the name of the editor, and proceed as usual.

> 11 Margaret Mead, Letters from the Field, ed. R. N.
> Anshen (New York: Harper, 1977) 58.

Sometimes collections or compilations have no author but have been assembled by an editor. Put the editor's name first, followed by *ed.,* then proceed.

> 12 Feldon Quinn, ed., Hollywood Writes: The Col-
> lected Graffiti of the Stars (Anaheim: Katella, 1977) 39.

When an author's work has been edited by one or several editors, give the author, the title of the work, then the names of the editor or editors, and proceed.

> 13 Harry Stack Sullivan, The Interpersonal Theory of
> Psychiatry, ed. Helen Swick Perry and Mary Ladd Gawel
> (New York: Norton, 1953) 156.

Anonymous Works.   For authorless works—pamphlets, newspaper articles, and so on—start with the title.

> 14 "The Bogus Order of Merit," New Republic 2 Apr.
> 1977: 6.
> 15 "The Effect of Cotton Candy on the Intestinal
> Fortitude of the Field Mouse," U.S. News and Information
> Service, n.d.: 8.

The abbreviation *n.d.* means "no date provided." The abbreviation *n.p.* would mean "no place of publication" or "no publisher provided."

Many instructors prefer slightly different forms for documentation. Make sure you know what your instructor expects.

Bibliography

If you use footnotes or endnotes, you may not need a bibliography or list of works cited. Check with your instructor for preference. The form for a bibliography entry is the same as that for the list of works cited. Your instructor may specify a heading such as *Bibliography, Selected Bibliography,* or *List of Works Consulted.*

THE AMERICAN PSYCHOLOGICAL ASSOCIATION STYLE

The American Psychological Association or APA style, most common in the social sciences, uses parenthetical text references. Instead of author and page number, however, the basic reference contains the author's last name and the year of publication. Page numbers are not always given because of the frequent necessity of referring to an article or a study as a whole. If you give a page number, precede it with *p.*

> Psychoanalysts have generally treated our pleasurable re-
> sponse to works of art as another example of the release
> of tension (Freud, 1956, p. 133).

Notice that in the APA system a comma goes between the author and the year. If the author's name appears in your text, you need only give the year and page number in parentheses.

> Freud, like many psychoanalysts before and after him,
> treated our pleasurable response to works of art as an-
> other example of the release of tension (1956, p. 133).

A list of references at the end of the paper contains complete information about each source.

Sample Text References

Here are the most common forms of reference within the text in APA style.

Books by More Than One Author.   When a book has two authors, always cite both names each time the reference occurs. If a book has from three to five authors, list all last names in the first reference; in subsequent references, use the first author's last name followed by *et al.*

For the first reference:

> Babies start smiling, laughing, and trying to converse at
> around three months (Miller, Haskell, & Golder, 1970).

Later in the text:

> Babies show a preference for bright, striking colors and
> well-defined patterns (Miller et al., 1970).

If a book has six or more authors, use the first author's last name followed by *et al.* for all references.

Anonymous Works.   Use a short title and the year for anonymous works.

> Cardiopulmonary resuscitation training is absolutely es-
> sential for the modern lifeguard (Swimmers, 1984).

Multiple Works by the Same Author.   When you cite two or more works by the same author, use the author's last name and the year.

> Psychoanalysis can be related to language (Edelson, 1972)
> and to the way in which dreams are generated in the
> sleeping mind (Edelson, 1975).

If an author has published more than one source in the same year, arrange the sources alphabetically by title and assign each one one a lowercase letter after the date (1979a, 1979b, 1979c, and so on); use these letters in your references.

Reference List

The reference list is preceded by the word *References* centered at the top of the page. Alphabetize entries by the author's last name, or by the first major word of the title if there is no author. Citations in the APA style differ from the MLA form in four major ways.

1. The APA puts the year immediately after the author's name.
2. The APA does not capitalize after the first word of a title—except proper names and the first word after a colon.
3. Where the MLA uses quotation marks—for titles of articles, chapters, or essays—the APA uses nothing.
4. The APA system uses only initials for authors' first and middle names and uses an ampersand (&) instead of the word *and*.

Books by One Author.

> Freud, S. (1956). Delusion and dream. Boston: Beacon
> Press.

Books by Two Authors.

> Phelps, E., & Drummer, T. (1985). Whale migration pat-
> terns and weather changes. Miami: Ourania.

Books by Three or More Authors.

> Miller, F. L., Haskell, J. K., & Golder, S. (1970). The
> growth of perception in the human infant. Edinburgh:
> Lanugo.

Books by Corporate Authors.

> National Association for Research into Parasitic Dis-
> eases. (1981). Schistosomiasis in the third world.
> New York: Harvey.

Anonymous Books.

> Swimmers for life. (1984). Huntington Beach: Nereid
> Press.

Books with Editors.

> Mead, M. (1977). Letters from the field, 1925-1975.
> (R. N. Anshen, Ed.). New York: Harper & Row.

Articles. In journals that paginate continuously throughout the year, use this form.

> Barnet, S. (1955). Some limitations on a Christian ap-
> proach to Shakespeare. English Literary History, 22.
> 81-92.

In periodicals that paginate each issue separately, follow this style.

> Gordon, G. (1985, May). Micro futures. Profiles, 2,
> 24-30.

In newspapers, follow this style.

> Lewis, A. (1985, November 8). White man's lawyer. New
> York Times, p. A27.

Style Manuals and Handbooks in Various Disciplines

The following is a brief list of suggested style manuals and handbooks in a variety of disciplines. Whatever major you choose, purchase the relevant style manuals and handbooks, learn the style, and follow it.

Agronomy

American Society of Agronomy. *Handbook and Style Manual for ASA, CSSA* [Crop Science Society of America] *and SSSA* [Soil Science Society of America] *Publications.* Madison, WI: American Society of Agronomy, 1984.

Biology

Council of Biology Editors. *CBE Style Manual: A Guide for Authors, Editors, and Publishers in the Biological Sciences.* Rev. 6th ed. Northbrook, IL: Council of Biology Editors, 1994.

McMillan, Victoria E. *Writing Papers in the Biological Sciences.* 2nd ed. Boston: Bedford Books, 1997.

Business

Brusaw, Charles T., Gerald Alred, and Walter Oliu. *The Business Writer's Handbook.* 4th ed. New York: St. Martin's Press, 1993.

Lesikar, Raymond V., and John D. Petit, Jr. *Report Writing for Business.* 9th ed. Homewood, IL: Richard D. Irwin, 1995.

Markel, Michael H. *Business Writing Essentials.* New York: St. Martin's Press, 1988.

Smith, Charles B. *A Guide to Business Research: Developing, Conducting, and Writing Research Projects,* 2nd ed. Chicago: Nelson-Hall, 1990.

Chemistry

Dodd, Janet S., ed. *The ACS Style Guide: A Manual for Authors and Editors.* Washington, DC: American Chemical Society, 1986.

Earth Science/Geology

Bates, Robert L., Marla D. Adkins-Heljeson, and Rex C. Buchanan, eds. *Geowriting: A Guide to Writing, Editing, and Printing in Earth Science.* 5th ed. Alexandria, VA: American Geological Institute, 1995.

Economics

See also "Business."

McCloskey, Donald N. *The Writing of Economics.* New York: Macmillan, 1987.

Officer, Lawrence H., et al. *So You Have to Write an Economics Term Paper.* East Lansing: Michigan State Univ. Press, 1985.

Engineering

See also "Technical Writing."

Michaelson, Herbert B. *How to Write and Publish Engineering Papers and Reports.* 3rd ed. Phoenix: Oryx Press, 1990.

Geography

Haring, L. Lloyd, and John F. Lounsbury. *Introduction to Scientific Geographic Research.* 4th ed. Dubuque, IA: Times Mirror Higher Education Group, 1992 (includes a section on writing geographic research reports).

History

McCoy, Florence N. *Researching and Writing in History: A Practical Handbook for Students.* Berkeley: Univ. of California Press, 1974.

Rampolla, Mary Lynn. *A Pocket Guide to Writing in History*. Boston: Bedford Books, 1995.

Law

Columbia Law Review, et al. *The Bluebook: A Uniform System of Citation*. 16th ed. Cambridge, MA: Harvard Law Review, 1996.

Oates, Laurel, Anne Enquist, and Kelly Kunsch. *The Legal Writer's Handbook*. Boston: Little, Brown, 1993.

Linguistics

Linguistic Society of America. "The Language Style Sheet." Published annually in the December issue of the *LSA Bulletin,* Washington, DC.

Literature

Achtert, Walter S., and Joseph Gibaldi. *The MLA Style Manual*. New York: Modern Language Association of America, 1988.

Gibaldi, Joseph. *MLA Handbook for Writers of Research Papers*. 4th ed. New York: Modern Language Association of America, 1995.

Mathematics

American Mathematical Society. *The Author's Handbook*. Providence, RI: American Mathematical Society.

Swanson, Ellen. *Mathematics into Type: Copy Editing and Proofreading of Mathematics for Editorial Assistants and Authors*. Rev. ed. Providence, RI: American Mathematical Society, 1994.

Medicine

Huth, Edward J. *How to Write and Publish Papers in the Medical Sciences*. 2nd ed. Phoenix: Oryx Press, 1990.

Iverson, Cheryl, et al. *American Medical Association Manual of Style*. 8th ed. Baltimore: Williams and Wilkins, 1989.

Modern Languages

See "Literature."

Music

Helm, Eugene, and Albert T. Luper. *Words and Music: Form and Procedure in Theses, Dissertations, Research Papers, Book Reports, Programs, and Theses in Composition.* Valley Forge, PA: European-American Music, 1982.

Holoman, D. Kern, ed. *Writing about Music: A Style Sheet from the Editors of 19th Century Music.* Berkeley: Univ. of California Press, 1988.

Nursing

Dowdney, Donna L., and Donna R. Sheridan. *How to Write and Publish Articles in Nursing.* 2nd ed. New York: Springer Publishing, 1997.

Physics

American Institute of Physics. *AIP Style Manual.* 4th ed. New York: American Institute of Physics, 1990.

Political Science

Stoffle, Carla J., Simon Karter, and Samuel Pernacciaro. *Materials and Methods for Political Science Research.* New York: Neal-Schuman, 1979.

Psychology

American Psychological Association. *Publication Manual of the American Psychological Association.* 4th ed. Washington, DC: APA, 1994. For a summary of APA-style documentation, see the second appendix.

Science, General

See also "Technical Writing."

Barrass, Robert. *Scientists Must Write: A Guide to Better Writing for Scientists, Engineers and Students.* New York: Chapman and Hall, 1978.

Day, Robert A. *How to Write and Publish a Scientific Paper.* 4th ed. Phoenix: Oryx Press, 1994.

Social Science, General

Mullins, Carolyn J. *A Guide to Writing and Publishing in the Social and Behavioral Sciences.* Melbourne, FL: R. E. Krieger, 1983 (reprint of 1977 ed.).

Social Work

National Association of Social Workers. *Writing for the NASW: Information for Authors about NASW Publications.* Annapolis Junction, MD: NASW, 1994.

Sociology

Gruber, James, Judith Pryor, and Patricia Beige. *Materials and Methods for Sociology Research.* New York: Neal-Schuman, 1980.

Strenski, Judith, et al. *A Guide to Writing Sociology Papers.* New York: St. Martin's Press, 1986.

Technical Writing

Bell, Paula. *High Tech Writing: How to Write for the Electronics Industry.* New York: John Wiley, 1985.

Brusaw, Charles T., et al. *The Concise Handbook for Technical Writing.* New York: St. Martin's Press, 1996.

Sides, Charles H. *How to Write and Present Technical Information.* Phoenix: Oryx Press, 1991.

General Guides

Allen, George R. *The Graduate Students' Guide to Theses and Dissertations: A Practical Manual for Writing and Research.* San Francisco: Jossey-Bass, 1973.

Chicago Guide to Electronic Manuscripts for Authors and Publishers. Chicago: University of Chicago Press, 1987.

Rodda Quaratello, Arlene. *The College Student's Research Companion.* New York: Neal-Schuman, 1996.

Index

Free verse, 458
Freewriting
  in essay exams, 482
  invention and, 71–74, 78, 85
  on literature, 463
  organization and, 97
  research and, 332
Funnel paragraphs, 241, 242
Fused sentences, 515
Future tense, 495

Gazetteers, 339
Gender
  of pronouns, 490, 491
  sexist language, 298–300, 511
Generalizations, 86, 137, 293
  hasty, 9, 32
  in opening paragraph, 241
  qualifying, 7–8
General words, 291–93
Geography, style manuals for, 574
Geology, style manuals for, 574
Gerunds, 492, 501
Glossary of usage, 546–62
Gopher (Internet search service),
  351
Government documents, 347
  citing, 388
  on Internet, 349, 566
Grammar, 106, 290, 367, 489–504
  in paragraphs, 219
  parts of speech, 489–500
  in sentences, 252, 255, 265
  sexist, 300
Guide to Reference Books, 339

Hasty generalizations, 9, 32
Helping verbs, 494
High informal style, 321–23
History, style manuals for, 574–75
Home pages, 391
Humor, 419
Hyperlinks, 351
Hyphens, 543–44
Hypothesis, 28, 137

Ideas, 88, 106
  coherence of, 212, 219
  documentation of, 379
  generating, 69–81

grouping, 213–14
main, 182, 216, 219–20, 234, 257,
  264
movement between, 217–18
organizing, 93, 97
subordinate, 259, 260
supporting, 95, 104, 429
Idiom, 290
Illustration, 210
  organization and, 226, 235–36, 239,
    240
  in paragraph development, 189,
    190, 195–97
Imagery, 13, 315, 455
  in literature, 446, 447, 466
  in opening sentence, 243
Imperative mood, 496
Impersonal writing, 280
In-class essays. *See* Essay examinations, in-class
Indefinite articles, 497
Indefinite pronouns, 491, 508–09,
  510–11
Indentation of quotations, 366–67
Independent clauses, 254–60, 273,
  501–03, 515
  punctuation of, 529
  sentence fragments and, 319
Indexes
  on CD-ROM, 342, 343
  periodical, 341, 342–44
Indicative mood, 496
Indirect language, 281–83
Indirect objects, 252
Indirect sources, 399–400, 418
Induction, 25–30
Inferences
  in argument, 21–24, 25, 26, 31,
    152
  and logical fallacies, 32, 260
Infinitive phrases, 501
Infinitives, split, 561
Infinitive (verb form), 494
Informal outlines, 95
Information services, 390
Informed speculation, 462–63, 474
Infoseek (search engine), 351
Infotrac (database), 341
Intensive pronouns, 490
Interactive resources, 350

A GUIDE TO THE HANDBOOK OF GRAMMAR, PUNCTUATION, MECHANICS, AND USAGE